Corporate Governance

Corporate Governance

SIXTH EDITION

Christine A. Mallin

OXFORD
UNIVERSITY PRESS

UNIVERSITY PRESS

Great Clarendon Street, Oxford, OX2 6DP,
United Kingdom

Oxford University Press is a department of the University of Oxford.
It furthers the University's objective of excellence in research, scholarship,
and education by publishing worldwide. Oxford is a registered trade mark of
Oxford University Press in the UK and in certain other countries

Published in the United States of America by Oxford University Press
198 Madison Avenue, New York, NY 10016, United States of America

British Library Cataloguing in Publication Data

Data available

Library of Congress Control Number: 2018956933

ISBN 978-0-19-880676-9

Printed in Great Britain by
Bell & Bain Ltd., Glasgow

To: Mum and Dad

Preface

Corporate governance is an area that has grown rapidly over recent decades. The global financial crisis, corporate scandals and collapses, and public concern over the apparent lack of effective boards and perceived excessive executive remuneration packages have all contributed to an explosion of interest in this area. The corporate and investment sectors, as well as public, voluntary, and non-profit organizations, are all placing much more emphasis on good governance. More and more universities, both in the UK and internationally, are offering corporate governance courses on undergraduate or postgraduate degree programmes. Some universities have dedicated taught masters in corporate governance and/or PhD students specializing in this as their area of research.

Corporate governance is now an integral part of everyday business life and this book provides insights into its importance not just in the UK, but also globally, including the USA, Europe, Asia, South Africa, Latin America, Egypt, India, and Australia. The book is designed to provide an understanding of the development of corporate governance over the past 30 years and to illustrate the importance of corporate governance to the firm, to directors, shareholders, and other stakeholders, and to the wider business community. It also seeks to shed light on why there are continuing incidences of corporate scandals, to what extent these are a corporate governance failure, and in which ways corporate governance—and the behaviour of those involved in ensuring good governance and an ethical culture in their business—may be improved in the future.

At the time of writing, the UK is on course with Brexit and plans to exit the European Union in 2019. The UK has a good reputation for its sound corporate governance framework and as can be seen in this book, the UK and the EU's corporate governance and company law are closely related. It will be essential going forward for the UK to maintain its reputation for transparency, accountability, and integrity in business and to continue to ensure that its corporate governance framework is fit for purpose in a changing world.

CAM
July 2018

Acknowledgements

I would like to thank everyone who has encouraged and supported me in writing this book.

First, thanks go to those who have encouraged me to research and write about corporate governance. In the early 1990s, Sir Adrian Cadbury inspired me to undertake research in the field of corporate governance and was always very supportive. Other leading figures who have influenced me with their contributions to the development of corporate governance include Robert (Bob) A.G. Monks, Nell Minow, Jonathan Charkham, Steve Davis, and Professor Bob Tricker, to name but a few.

Thank you to everyone at Oxford University Press who has contributed to the publication of this book. Thanks also go to the anonymous reviewers who constructively reviewed earlier drafts of the book and gave many helpful comments.

A heartfelt thanks to family and friends who have encouraged me to write this book, and have always been there for me, especially to: Paul; Rita, Bernard, and Christopher; Pam and Tom; Liz; Alice, Yu Loon, and Thorsten; Ioana, Costin, and Mara; and Jane. Also a special thank you to Ben. Finally, to Merlin and Harry ('the two magicians') for their patience, devotion, and sense of fun at all times.

Contents

How to use this book

 Learning objectives

- To understand the various main theories that underlie th corporate governance
- To be aware of the impact of the form of legal system, ca ownership structure on the development of corporate g

Learning Objectives

Introducing you to every chapter, learning objectives outline the main concepts and themes covered in each chapter to clearly identify what you can expect to learn. They can also be used to review your learning and effectively plan your revision.

Example: Cadbury Plc, UK

This is an example of a family firm that grew over time, developed an c became an international business.

Today, Cadbury is a household name in homes across the world. It the nineteenth century when John Cadbury decided to establish a b and marketing of cocoa. His two sons joined the firm in 1861 and, ov joined, and subsequently the firm became a private limited liability c A board of directors was formed consisting of members of the famil

Examples and Mini Case Studies

Topical, diverse examples and cases illustrate the theories and concepts discussed in the chapter with events at real-life organizations, prompting you to analyse how organizations actually apply these ideas in practice.

Questions

The discussion questions to follow cover the key learning points the additional reference material will enhance the depth of stud of these areas.

1. Critically discuss the main theories that have influenced th governance.
2. Do you think that different theories are more appropriate f

Questions

Check your progress and test your knowledge with these end-of-chapter questions, which cover the key learning points of each chapter.

Useful websites

www.accaglobal.com The website of the Association of Chart information about corporate governance and their related a
www.bankofengland.co.uk The website of the Prudential Reg a part of the Bank of England and responsible for the pruder banks, building societies, credit unions, insurers, and major i

Useful Websites

Advance your learning and further develop your understanding with relevant and recommended websites that can assist your research and revision.

Financial Times Clippings

Further real-life, topical examples of corporate governance reported in the *FT* demonstrate how frequently the subject permeates our daily news and highlight the most recent and significant governance issues from the last couple of years.

Rothschild's chairman bank's dynastic reins t

Change coincides with effort to help ride out lean periods in European M&A market

Hannah Murphy

Financial Times, 27 February 2018

operations a
sizeable acqu
bank.
  The elder N
born in New

End-of-Part Case Studies

Longer, integrative case studies pull together ideas from across different chapters to better contextualize how businesses navigate the range of issues in corporate governance.

Part Two case study   Institutional investor

*This case study illustrates some of the complex issues of a country tran
how, when an influential group of institutional investors work togethe
of their investee companies which are in a country where there are hu
instability, and unacceptable risks. This action was part of the SRI rem
Finally it summarizes recent developments relating to corporate gove
  The political instability and human rights abuses make Myanmar*

How to use the online resources

Supporting content for both students and registered lecturers of the book is available in the online resources. Students can test themselves with fill-in-the-blank questions or explore the subject further with web links to relevant content. Lecturers can download PowerPoint slides and access additional case studies for use in their teaching.

There is also a link to the **Corporate Governance blog**, regularly updated by Christine Mallin and Bob Tricker, offering comment on current events in the world of business, economics, and finance, from the perspective of corporate governance.
Visit www.oup.com/uk/mallin6e/ to find out more.

List of examples and case studies

List of figures and tables

Figures

Tables

List of abbreviations

ABI	Association of British Insurers
ACGA	Asian Corporate Governance Association
AFG	L'Association Française de la Gestion Financière
AFL-CIO	The American Federation of Labor and Congress of Industrial Organizations
AITC	Association of Investment Trust Companies
APEC	Asia-Pacific Economic Co-operation
ASIC	Australian Securities and Investments Commission
ASX	Australian Stock Exchange
BEIS	Department for Business, Energy & Industrial Strategy
BIS	Department for Business, Innovation & Skills
BVCA	British Private Equity and Venture Capital Association
CACG	Commonwealth Association for Corporate Governance
CalPERS	California Public Employees' Retirement System
CEO	Chief executive officer
CEPS	Centre for European Policy Studies
CFO	Chief financial officer
CLERP	Corporate Law Economic Reform Program
CLR	Company Law Review
CR	Corporate responsibility
CSR	Corporate social responsibility
CSRC	China Securities Regulatory Commission
Defra	Department for Environment, Food and Rural Affairs
DVCA	Danish Venture Capital and Private Equity Association
ecoDa	European Confederation of Directors' Associations
EFAMA	European Fund and Asset Management Association
EIRIS	Ethical Investment Research Service
FESE	Federation of European Securities Exchanges
FRC	Financial Reporting Council
FSA	Financial Services Authority
FTSE	Financial Times Stock Exchange
ICGN	International Corporate Governance Network
IIC	Institutional Investor Committee
ILO	International Labour Organization

IMA	Investment Management Association
IMF	International Monetary Fund
IoD	Institute of Directors
ISC	Institutional Shareholders' Committee
IWG	International Working Group of Sovereign Wealth Funds
KPI	Key performance indicator
MOF	Ministry of Finance
NAPF	National Association of Pension Funds
NCVO	National Council for Voluntary Organisations
NEST	National Employment Savings Trust
NGO	Non-governmental organization
NHS	National Health Service
OECD	Organisation for Economic Co-operation and Development
OPSI	Office of Public Sector Information
PBOC	People's Bank of China
PIRC	Pensions Investment Research Consultants
PLSA	Pensions and Lifetime Savings Association
PSPD	People's Solidarity for Participatory Democracy
QCA	Quoted Companies Alliance
RREV	Research recommendations electronic voting
SE	Societas Europaea
SETC	State Economic and Trade Commission
SID	Senior independent director
SRI	Socially responsible investment
SVWG	Shareholder Voting Working Group
SWF	Sovereign wealth fund
UKSIF	UK Sustainable Investment and Finance Association
UN	United Nations
UNPRI	United Nations Principles of Responsible Investment

Glossary

Agency theory One party (the principal) delegates work to another party (the agent). In a corporate scenario, the principal is the shareholder and the agent the directors/managers. Agency theory relates to the costs involved in this principal–agent relationship, including the costs of aligning the two sets of interests.

Audit The examination by an independent external auditor to determine whether the annual report and accounts have been appropriately prepared and give a true and fair view.

Audit committee A subcommittee of the board that is generally comprised of independent non-executive directors. It is the role of the audit committee to review the scope and outcome of the audit, and to try to ensure that the objectivity of the auditors is maintained.

Auditor rotation The audit firm is changed after a number of years in order to help ensure that the independence of the external auditor is retained. There are disparate views on the effectiveness of auditor rotation.

Bank-oriented system Banks play a key role in the funding of some companies and so may be able to exercise some control via the board structure, depending on the governance system.

Board diversity Gender, ethnicity, and other characteristics considered to make the board more diverse.

Board evaluation Boards should be evaluated annually to determine whether they have met the objectives set. The board as a whole, the board subcommittees, and individual directors should each be assessed.

Board subcommittees The board of directors may delegate various duties in specific areas to specialized committees, such as the audit committee, remuneration committee, and nomination committee.

Chair Responsible for the running of the board and chairing board meetings.

Chief executive officer Responsible for the running of the company.

Civil law Tends to be prescriptive and based on specific rules. Generally gives less protection to minority shareholders.

Co-determination The right of employees to be kept informed of the company's activities and to participate in decisions that may affect the workers.

Common law Based on legal principles supplemented by case law. Generally gives better protection to minority shareholders.

Comply or explain A company should comply with the appropriate corporate governance code but, if it cannot comply with any particular aspect of it, then it should explain why it is unable to do so.

Controlling shareholders Those who have control of the company, although this may be indirectly through their holdings in other entities, and not directly.

Corporate social responsibility Voluntary actions that a company may take in relation to the management of social, environmental, and ethical issues.

Directors' remuneration Can encompass various elements, including base salary, bonus, stock options, stock grants, pension, and other benefits.

Directors' share options Directors may be given the right to purchase shares at a specified price over a specified time period.

Dual board A dual board system consists of a supervisory board and an executive board of management.

Fiduciary duty This is an obligation to act in the best interests of another party, for example, directors have a fiduciary duty to act in the best interests of the shareholders.

Hard law Legally binding pronouncements such as laws, regulations, and directives.

Inclusive approach The company considers the interests of all of its stakeholders.

Independent directors who have no relationships with the business, or its directors and management, or other circumstances, which could affect their judgement.

Information asymmetries Different parties may have access to different levels of information, which may mean that some have a more complete or more accurate picture than others.

Insider system Ownership of shares is concentrated in individuals or a group of individuals, such as families or holding companies.

Institutional investors Generally large investors, such as pension funds, insurance companies, and mutual funds.

Internal controls Policies, procedures, and other measures in an organization that are designed to ensure that the assets are safeguarded, that systems operate as intended, that information can be produced in a timely and accurate manner, and that the business operates effectively and efficiently.

Market-oriented system The influence of banks does not tend to be prevalent and does not impact on the company's board structure.

Minority rights The rights of shareholders who own smaller stakes in a company. They should have the same rights as larger shareholders but often this is not the case.

Minority shareholders who have smaller holdings of shares.

Nominated advisor A firm or company that acts as an advisor to a company coming to/on the Alternative Investment Market.

Nomination committee A subcommittee of the board and should generally comprise independent non-executive directors. Its role is to make recommendations to the board on all new board appointments.

Non-executive director These are not full-time employees of the company (unlike most executive directors). As far as possible they should be independent and capable of exercising independent judgement in board decision-making.

Outsider system There is dispersed ownership of shares and hence individuals, or groups of individuals, do not tend to have direct control.

Pay ratio The ratio of the pay of the company's CEO to the pay of the average worker.

Private equity A private equity fund is broadly defined as one that invests in equity which is not traded publicly on a stock exchange.

Proxy vote The casting of shareholders' votes by shareholders, often by mail, fax, or electronic means.

Remuneration committee A subcommittee of the board and should generally comprise independent non-executive directors. Its role is to make recommendations to the board on executive directors' remuneration.

Risk assessment An assessment of the overall risk that a company may be exposed to. Overall risk can include many different types of risk, including financial risk, operating risk, and reputation risk.

Say on pay Shareholder vote on the remuneration packages of executive directors, may be binding or non-binding on the company.

Shareholder value The value of the firm after deducting current and future claims.

Socially responsible investment Involves considering the ethical, social, and environmental performance of companies selected for investment as well as their financial performance.

Soft law Best practice or self-regulation pronouncements such as codes, principles, and guidelines.

Sovereign wealth fund A fund, often very large and influential, which is owned by a government.

Stakeholder theory This theory takes into account the views of a wider stakeholder group and not just the shareholders.

Stakeholders Any individual or group on which the activities of the company have an impact, including the employees, customers, and local community.

Supervisory board In a dual board system the supervisory board oversees the direction of the business, whilst the management board is responsible for the running of the business.

Transaction cost economics Views the firm itself as a governance structure, which in turn can help align the interests of directors and shareholders.

Unitary board A unitary board of directors is characterized by one single board comprising of both executive and non-executive directors.

Introduction

Businesses around the world need to be able to attract funding from investors in order to expand and grow. Before investors decide to invest their funds in a particular business, they will want to be as sure as they can be that the business is financially sound and will continue to be so in the foreseeable future. Investors therefore need to have confidence that the business is being well managed and will continue to be profitable.

In order to have this assurance, investors look to the published annual report and accounts of the business, and to other information releases that the company might make. They expect that the annual report and accounts will represent a true picture of the company's present position; they are, after all, subject to an annual audit whereby an independent external auditor examines the business's records and transactions, and certifies that the annual report and accounts have been prepared in accordance with accepted accounting standards and give a 'true and fair view' of the business's activities. However, although the annual report may give a reasonably accurate picture of the business's activities and financial position at that point in time, there are many facets of the business that are not effectively reflected in it.

There have been a number of high-profile corporate collapses that have arisen despite the fact that the annual report and accounts seemed fine. These corporate collapses have had an adverse effect on many people: shareholders who have seen their financial investment reduced to nothing; employees who have lost their jobs and, in many cases, the security of their company pension, which has also evaporated overnight; suppliers of goods or services to the failed companies; and the economic impact on the local and international communities in which the failed companies operated. In essence, corporate collapses affect us all. Why have such collapses occurred? What might be done to prevent such collapses happening again? How can investor confidence be restored?

The answers to these questions are all linked to corporate governance. Companies with a sound corporate governance structure should have a balanced board comprised of independent and non-independent directors with appropriate skills and knowledge to contribute to the ongoing success of the company and the confidence to question matters they feel may not be in the best interests of the company. The board should be diversified in terms of gender, ethnicity, age, education, experience to help ensure diversity of thought. The roles of CEO and Chair are generally perceived as being more appropriately vested in two individuals rather than in one individual who may then wield too much power in the company. Board subcommittees, including audit and remuneration committees, should be established and comprised of appropriately qualified individuals. There should be robust internal controls in place and an appropriate risk management structure which considers all aspects of risk, financial and non-financial, to which the business may be exposed. However a lack of effective corporate governance has meant that high profile collapses could occur; good corporate governance can help prevent such collapses happening again and restore investor confidence.

To illustrate why corporate failures might occur, despite the companies seeming healthy, it is helpful to review a few examples from over the years, each of which has sent shock waves through stock markets around the world.

Barings Bank

The downfall in 1995 of one of England's oldest established banks was brought about by the actions of one man, Nick Leeson, whose actions have been immortalized in the film *Rogue Trader*. Nick Leeson was a clever, if unconventional, trader with a gift for sensing the way that stock market prices would move in the Far Eastern markets. In 1993 he was based in Singapore and made more than £10 million, about 10 per cent of Barings' total profit that year. He was highly thought of at that time.

However, his run of good luck was not to last and, when a severe earthquake in Japan affected the stock market adversely, he incurred huge losses of Barings' money. He requested more funds from Barings' head office in London, which were sent to him, but unfortunately he suffered further losses. The losses were so great (£850 million) that Barings Bank collapsed and was eventually bought for £1 by ING, the Dutch banking and insurance group.

Barings Bank has been criticized for its lack of effective internal controls at that time, which left Nick Leeson able to cover up the losses that he was making for quite a number of months. The case also illustrates the importance of having effective supervision, by experienced staff with a good understanding of the processes and procedures, of staff who are able to expose the company to such financial disaster. The collapse of Barings Bank sent ripples through financial markets across the world as the importance of effective internal controls and appropriate monitoring was reinforced.

Enron

Enron was ranked in the USA's Fortune top ten list of companies, based on its turnover in 2000. Its published accounts for the year ending 31 December 2000 showed a seemingly healthy profit of US$979 million and there was nothing obvious to alert shareholders to the impending disaster that was going to unfold over the next year or so, making Enron the largest bankruptcy in US history.

Enron's difficulties related to its activities in the energy market and the setting up of a series of 'special purpose entities' (SPEs). Enron used the SPEs to conceal large losses from the market by giving the appearance that key exposures were hedged (covered) by third parties. However, the SPEs were really nothing more than an extension of Enron itself and so Enron's risks were not covered. Some of the SPEs were used to transfer funds to some of Enron's directors. In October 2001 Enron declared a non-recurring loss of US$1 billion and also had to disclose a US$1.2 billion write-off against shareholders' funds. Later in October Enron disclosed another accounting problem, which reduced its value by over US$0.5 million. It looked as though a takeover might be on the cards from a rival, Dynegy, but in November, announcements by Enron of further debts led to the takeover bid falling through. In December 2001 Enron filed for bankruptcy.

In retrospect, it seems that the directors were not questioned closely enough about the use of the SPEs and their accounting treatment. What has become clear is that there was some concern amongst Enron's auditors (Andersen) about the SPEs and Enron's activities. Unfortunately, Andersen failed to question the directors hard enough and Andersen's own fate was sealed when some of its employees shredded paperwork relating to Enron, thus obliterating vital evidence and contributing to the demise of Andersen, which has itself been taken over by various rivals.

Lawsuits were brought against the directors of Enron and whilst it was notable that some directors were able to settle the lawsuits by paying hugely significant sums of money personally, others received hefty jail sentences. In 2006 Jeffrey Skilling, former Enron Chief Executive, was found guilty of fraud and conspiracy and sentenced to more than 24 years in prison. In April 2012 the Supreme Court rejected his appeal, although his sentence may be shortened. Kenneth Lay, also a former Chairman and Chief Executive of Enron, was similarly found guilty of fraud and conspiracy although he died in 2006, no doubt taking to the grave many of the details of what went on at Enron.

Interestingly, one of the employees at Enron, Sherron Watkins, had made her concerns known to Andrew Fastow, the Chief Finance Officer, and to the firm's auditors, Arthur Andersen, about some of the accounting transactions taking place at Enron as early as 1996. However, no notice was apparently taken of her concerns and she moved to work in a different area of the company. In 2001 she was again back in the finance department and became aware that an extensive fraud was taking place with SPEs being used as vehicles to hide Enron's growing losses. She then expressed her concerns more openly and became the whistle-blower to one of the most infamous corporate scandals of all time.

The Enron case highlights the overriding need for integrity in business: for the directors to act with integrity and honesty, and for the external audit firm to be able to ask searching questions of the directors without holding back for fear of offending a lucrative client. This latter situation is exacerbated when auditors receive large fees for non-audit services that may well exceed the audit fee itself, thus endangering the independence of the auditors. Enron also highlights the need for independent non-executive directors who are experienced enough to be able to ask searching questions in board and committee meetings to try to ensure that the business is operated appropriately.

Parmalat

Parmalat, an Italian company specializing in long-life milk, was founded by Calisto Tanzi. It seemed to be a marvellous success story although, as it expanded by acquiring more companies, its debt increased and, in late 2003, Parmalat had difficulty making a bond payment despite the fact that it was supposed to have a large cash reserve. After various investigations had been carried out, it transpired that the large cash reserves were non-existent and Parmalat went into administration. With debts estimated at £10 billion, Parmalat has also earned itself the name of 'Europe's Enron'.

Calisto Tanzi was a central figure in one of Europe's largest fraud trials which started during 2005. He was accused of providing false accounting information and misleading the Italian stock-market regulator. In December 2008 after a trial lasting more than three years, he was found guilty on a number of counts, including falsifying accounts, and misleading investors and regulators. He was given a ten-year sentence.

Satyam

Satyam Computer Services was India's fourth largest information technology group by revenue. In early 2009 its Chairman, B. Ramalinga Raju, wrote to the board and confessed to having manipulated many of the figures in the company's annual financial statements over a number of years, resulting in overstated profits and non-existent assets. The case has been called 'India's Enron' and has undermined confidence in Indian companies, with the Bombay Stock Exchange suffering a significant fall in share prices. The Securities and Exchange Board of India (SEBI) moved quickly to make it mandatory for controlling shareholders to declare whether they have pledged any shares to lenders as this was one of the contributory factors in this case. Satyam was sold in 2009 to Tech Mahindra and was later renamed Mahindra Satyam. In March 2012 Tech Mahindra announced plans to combine with Mahindra Satyam which were approved in 2013; the combined group is known as Tech Mahindra. The combined group still faced legal charges brought by shareholders in relation to the Satyam scandal. In 2015, B. Ramalinga Raju, former Chairman of Satyam Computer Services, was jailed for seven years and nine others were also found guilty of corporate fraud.

Securency

Securency, a Reserve Bank of Australia (RBA) subsidiary which produces and supplies polymer banknotes, has been the subject of allegations of bribery and corruption. The allegations centred on Securency's payment of commissions to foreign middlemen, who it is believed would then attempt to bribe central banking officials in countries throughout Asia, Latin America, and Africa to replace their paper notes with Securency's polymer banknotes. The allegations were made by a Securency insider who witnessed much of this behaviour first-hand. KPMG Forensics prepared an audit report that showed impropriety on the part of Securency's officials, and in April 2012 the RBA fired two top executives of Securency, the former Managing Director and the former Director of Commercial Services.

In 2016, David Ellery, Securency's financial controller and company secretary until 2010, admitted in court that he had lied a few times to cover up alleged corrupt activities at Securency and he was given a suspended sentence on one count of false accounting, conditional on his co-operation with prosecutors and giving evidence in other trials. In 2016, he gave evidence against Peter Chapman, Securency's former African business development director, who he alleged had given bribes to officials in Nigeria. Although the Judge found Peter Chapman guilty, the sentence he gave was mitigated because of the role he felt that Securency's management had played putting pressure on Chapman to achieve sales and also that they had been aware of the bribes that were being paid. The Judge's sentence of 30 months meant that Chapman was effectively a free man after his trial as he had already served time in Brazil's notorious Ary Franco prison whilst awaiting extradition to the UK and then in prison in the UK awaiting his trial.

China Forestry

China Forestry was a company engaged in the management of forests, and the harvesting and sales of timber logs. In 2008 and 2009 it had attracted investments from private equity firms including the USA's Carlyle Group and Switzerland-based Partners Group. Subsequently, China Forestry's auditors informed the board of irregularities in the books which led to a suspension in the trading of the company's shares. It transpired that China Forestry's former management team provided the auditor with false bank statements, as well as inconsistent insurance policy documentation and falsified logging permits. Most of the group's sales from 2010 were conducted in cash and Mr Li Han Chun, the former Chief Executive Officer, kept more than one set of books, meaning that movements in cash could be concealed from the board. China Forestry reported a loss for 2010 of 2.71 billion yuan after drastically lowering the value of its plantation holdings, which are the company's chief asset.

Mr Li Han Chun was arrested by Chinese authorities on allegations that he embezzled 30 million yuan from the company, and other senior staff including the Chief Financial Officer left the company. China Forestry subsequently proposed a number of changes, including improved centralized financial reporting and new management to oversee it. However its shares have been suspended since January 2011 and the company is in liquidation and in the delisting process after possible accounting irregularities were found by the company's auditors.

In 2017, the Hong Kong Securities and Futures Commission (SFC) sought unspecified damages for market misconduct over the IPO prospectus of China Forestry which was filed in November 2009, as well as the 2009 annual report, and annual results, and the results for the first six months of 2010. The SFC also sued China Forestry itself, together with the company's two co-founders Li Kwok Cheong and Li Han Chun, and KPMG, which was China Forestry's auditor.

Olympus Corporation

Olympus is a long-established Japanese manufacturer of optics and reprography products. In April 2011 Michael Woodford became its President and CEO, replacing Tsuyoshi Kikukawa, who became Chairman. Woodford became suspicious about various transactions that had taken place, including in relation to the acquisition of UK medical equipment maker Gyrus, and confronted the board about them. He was removed from office after questioning the transactions. He subsequently passed on information to the British Serious Fraud Office and requested police protection. It transpired that substantial fees were paid to middlemen in merger and acquisition transactions. It also seemed that some of the assets of the business were overvalued in the accounts. Later in 2011 the company admitted that the money had been used to cover up losses on investments dating back to the 1990s and that the company's accounting practices had not been appropriate.

In February 2012 a number of Olympus executives were arrested, including the ex-President, Tsuyoshi Kikukawa, the auditor, Hideo Yamada, and the Executive Vice-President, Hisashi Mori, together with the former bankers, Akio Nakagawa and Nobumasa Yokoo and two others, suspected of having helped the board to hide significant losses. Three former executives of Olympus have been given suspended jail terms for their roles in the accounting scandal—in 2013, Mr Kikukawa and Mr Yamada were given three-year sentences and Mr Mori a two-and-a-half-year sentence. Olympus was ordered to pay 700 million yen ($7 million; £4.6 million) in fines for its role. Subsequently, in 2017, six executives, including Tsuyoshi Kikukawa, were ordered to pay US$529 million in damages.

The Olympus scandal shocked Japan and is seen as something of a litmus test of corporate governance in the country, in the sense of whether it will lead to improved corporate governance practices—for example, in the way that new directors are nominated to try to ensure independence—or whether it will stay as a reflection of the old ways where companies such as Olympus retain a high level of cross-holdings with their financial institutions.

Petrobras

Petrobras is a state-controlled, publicly traded Brazilian company which operates in the oil, gas, and energy sector. The company has a near monopoly over Brazil's deepwater oil reserves and in 2015 was implicated in a massive multi-million dollar corruption scandal. Senior executives of Petrobras and top politicians are alleged to have colluded and taken bribes from engineering and construction companies with which Petrobras contracted. In February 2015, the CEO, Maria das Gracas Silva Foster, and five other executives resigned, whilst in March 2015 Brazil's Supreme Court named some 54 individuals, including top politicians, who are to be investigated in connection with the scandal.

The damage to Petrobras' finances and reputation is immense. Whilst the true extent of financial damage is as yet unknown, estimates of $10 billion have been made of the amount stolen from Petrobras, not to mention the subsequent damage caused by the drop in its share price.

A number of large institutional investors have decided to take their own legal action against Petrobras separate to a class action lawsuit that has been brought against the company. It is possible that investors may achieve more favourable settlement terms by pursuing their own individual claims as opposed to joining a class action.

The President of Brazil, Dilma Rousseff, was Chairman of Petrobras until she took up her government office in 2010. She has denied any knowledge of the corruption practices at Petrobras but she was impeached by the Senate in 2016 and thrown out of office. Also in 2016, Marcelo Odebrecht, former CEO of Petrobras, was jailed for 19 years for his part in the corruption scandal. In July 2017, the former President of Brazil, Luiz Inacio Lula da Silva, was sentenced to nearly 10 years in jail for his part in the corruption scandal at Petrobras. His solicitors lodged an appeal which was heard in January 2018 but was unsuccessful with the Brazilian appeals court unanimously upholding the original court decision.

The Petrobras scandal has shocked Brazil and sent ripples across the world given the number of individuals involved with the scandal and their level of public office. It is possible that more high profile convictions will follow in the future.

Steinhoff

Steinhoff is a global retailer in household goods and general merchandise operating in over 30 countries. It has expanded from its South African base through a series of acquisitions and now generates around 50 per cent of its sales in Europe and another 20 per cent in the US and Australia. It has a dual listing, being listed on the Frankfurt Stock Exchange as well as the Johannesburg Stock Exchange.

In December 2017 Steinhoff disclosed accounting irregularities and suspended the release of its 2017 financial results leading to a substantial drop in its share price. This in turn has led to disquiet and concern amongst banks who had lent around US$1.9 billion to Steinhoff's then Chairman, Christo Wiese, with the loans secured against his shares in Steinhoff. With the drop in share price, the shares are now worth a lot less than the money borrowed. Since the announcement of the accounting irregularity, Christo Wiese has resigned from the company; its CEO, Markus Jooste, has also resigned and Steinhoff's Moody's rating has been downgraded.

Investigations are taking place in both Germany (where Steinhoff has a Frankfurt listing) to determine whether Steinhoff inflated its asset and revenue values, and in South Africa where South Africa's state pension fund stands to make substantial losses as it held nearly 10 per cent of Steinhoff's shares. Deloitte has also come under mounting pressure as the long-term auditor of Steinhoff.

Carillion

Carillion Plc is a British multinational facilities management and construction services company. Its facilities management services include areas such as hospital maintenance and cleaning services, engineering design, and project management services. Its construction activities cover a wide range of sectors including healthcare such as new hospitals, education, central and local government, defence, commercial, and many more. Whilst most of Carillion's business is in the UK, it operates in other parts of the world including the Middle East and Canada.

Carillion issued profits warnings in 2017 and £845 million of contract write downs were also revealed. Nonetheless it continued to pay dividends to its shareholders at a time when its profits and cash flow were declining and debts increasing. It carried on winning government contracts during 2017 though it seems these contracts may have been mis-priced and contributed to Carillion's financial woes. Carillion's directors have been criticized for the perceived generous pay packages, for example, just a year before Carillion went into liquidation, Mr Howson, the CEO, received a £1.5 million pay package which included a £245,000 bonus and a £346,000 share-based award. Such sums will no doubt become a focus of attention as the company's problems become more apparent.

In early January, Carillion sought financial help from the UK government in the form of £25 million forward funding but it was not forthcoming. A short time later, Carillion announced it was going into liquidation. The High Court appointed the Official Receiver as liquidator of Carillion Plc and its group companies. Special Managers who act as agents of the Official Receiver, without personal liability, were appointed by the High Court to help manage the affairs, business, and property of Carillion Plc and 16 group companies, in accordance with the powers and duties contained in the order appointing them. The Work and Pensions and Business, Energy and Industrial Strategy (BEIS) Committees launched a joint inquiry in January 2018 into the collapse of Carillion.

In the meantime the UK government has been required to provide funding for Carillion's public sector work which continues despite the company's entry into compulsory liquidation. The conduct of Carillion's directors will be investigated to determine what role they may have played in the company's demise. KPMG, Carillion's external auditor, is also under the spotlight and is the subject of an investigation by the Financial Reporting Council (FRC) to consider several aspects of its audit work at Carillion.

Several stakeholder groups are deeply affected by the collapse of Carillion including its employees both present and past (the pension scheme is also badly affected), its subcontractors including smaller firms which may not be able to survive if they are not paid for work already done for Carillion, its other creditors, and those who use the buildings it constructs such as people waiting for treatment in new hospitals whose completion will be delayed.

Shortcomings in companies' corporate governance

These examples of high-profile corporate collapses and scandals in the UK, USA, Europe, Australia, China, Japan, India, Brazil, and South Africa have had, and continue to have, international implications, and would seem to illustrate a number of shortcomings in the way that the companies were run and managed:

- Barings appears to highlight the lack of effective internal controls and the folly of trusting one employee without adequate supervision and understanding of his activities.

- Enron appears to highlight a basic need to ensure, as far as possible, that directors are people of integrity and act honestly; that external auditors must be able to ask searching questions unfettered by the need to consider the potential loss of large audit/accounting fees; and that independent directors on boards and committees who question intelligently and insightfully can make a significant contribution.

- Parmalat appears to highlight some of the weaknesses that may exist in family-owned firms where members of the family take a dominant role across the board structure as a whole. In Parmalat's case, the board lacked independence as, of the 13 directors, only three were independent. This had a knock-on effect on the composition of the various board committees where independent directors were a minority rather than a majority. There was also a lack of timely disclosure of information.

- Satyam Computer Services appears to highlight the risks associated with a powerful chairman who was able to falsify accounts over a period of time, seemingly without raising the suspicions of the auditors or anyone in the company. It also highlights the effects of a lack of appropriate disclosure requirements so that controlling shareholders did not need to disclose information that could have an adverse effect on minority shareholders.

- Securency appears to highlight a lack of ethical behaviour by some of the key directors. Given the recent tighter controls on bribery and corruption, it is particularly likely that firms that make payments as bribes to try to gain business will be brought to account in the current global regulatory environment. Such firms risk incurring both financial losses and reputational damage, and therefore directors should be instilling an ethical culture, and also facilitating whistle-blowing.

- China Forestry appears to highlight the risks associated with dishonest individuals who are in a position to manipulate the accounting figures and provide inaccurate paperwork to apparently back these up. This case serves to illustrate the importance of appropriate internal controls and segregation of duties in the handling of, and accounting for, the company's transactions.

- Olympus appears to highlight the risks associated with collusion between key executives, the auditor, and bankers. A lack of independent directors and a negative attitude towards whistle-blowing served to compound the problems that arose at Olympus.

- Petrobras appears to highlight what can happen when corrupt executives and politicians collude with engineering and contracting firms. It seems to be the case that Petrobras' anti-corruption policies and internal controls were not effective.

- Steinhoff appears to highlight the need to ensure that directors act ethically and that they do not apparently engage in accounting irregularities to make the performance of the company look better than it is. It also seems to highlight that auditors need to be aware that such instances may occur and that they should be alert to them.

- Carillion appears to highlight that directors need to be aware of the strategic implications of potentially mis-pricing contracts, the impact on cash flow, and the dangers of higher debt levels. Also the perceived benefits of being a consistent dividend payer need to be weighed against the sources of finance used to pay those dividends and the legality of the dividend payment assured. It also seems to highlight that auditors should be alert to clients' potential financial difficulties.

The role of corporate governance

This brings us back to our original questions about corporate failures such as those mentioned earlier. Why have such collapses occurred? What might be done to prevent such collapses happening again? How can investor confidence be restored? The answers to these questions are all linked to corporate governance.

Corporate governance is an area that has grown very rapidly in the last two decades, particularly since the collapse of Enron in 2001 and the subsequent financial problems of other companies in various countries. As already mentioned, emerging financial scandals will continue to ensure that there is a sharp focus on corporate governance issues, especially relating to transparency and disclosure, control and accountability, and to the most appropriate form of board structure that may be capable of preventing such scandals occurring in future. Not surprisingly, there has been a significant interest shown by governments in trying to ensure that such collapses do not happen again because these lead to a lack of confidence in financial markets. In order to realize why corporate governance has become so important, it is essential to have an understanding of what corporate governance actually is and how it may improve corporate accountability.

A fairly narrow definition of corporate governance is given by Shleifer and Vishny (1997): 'Corporate governance deals with the ways in which suppliers of finance to corporations assure themselves of getting a return on their investment.' A broader definition is provided by the Organisation for Economic Co-operation and Development (OECD) (1999), which describes corporate governance as: 'a set of relationships between a company's board, its shareholders and other stakeholders. It also provides the structure through which the objectives of the company are set, and the means of attaining those objectives, and monitoring performance, are determined.' Similarly, Sir Adrian Cadbury (1999) said: 'Corporate governance is concerned with holding the balance between economic and social goals and between individual and communal goals ... the aim is to align as nearly as possible the interests of individuals, corporations and society.' These definitions serve to illustrate that corporate governance is concerned with both the shareholders and the internal aspects of the company, such as internal control, and the external aspects, such as an organization's relationship with its shareholders and other stakeholders. Corporate governance is also seen as an essential mechanism helping the company to attain its corporate objectives and monitoring performance is a key element in achieving these objectives.

It can be seen that corporate governance is important for a number of reasons, and is fundamental to well-managed companies and to ensuring that they operate at optimum efficiency. Some of the important features of corporate governance are as follows:

- It helps to ensure that an adequate and appropriate system of controls operates within a company and hence assets may be safeguarded.
- It prevents any single individual having too powerful an influence.
- It is concerned with the relationship between a company's management, the board of directors, shareholders, and other stakeholders.
- It aims to ensure that the company is managed in the best interests of the shareholders and the other stakeholders.
- It tries to encourage both transparency and accountability, which investors are increasingly looking for in both corporate management and corporate performance.

The first feature refers to the internal control system of a company whereby there are appropriate and adequate controls to ensure that transactions are properly recorded and that assets cannot be misappropriated. Each year a company has an annual audit and a key part of the auditor's job is to assess whether the internal controls in a business are operating properly. Of course, the auditor has to exercise a certain degree of judgement regarding the assurances given by the directors, the directors being ultimately responsible for the implementation of an appropriate internal control system in the company. The directors are also responsible for ensuring that there are risk assessment procedures in place to identify the risks that companies face in today's business environment, including, for example, exposures to movements in foreign exchange and risks associated with business competition.

As well as being fundamental to investor confidence, good corporate governance is essential to attracting new investment, particularly for developing countries where good corporate governance is often seen as a means of attracting foreign direct investment at more favourable rates. As the emphasis on corporate governance has grown during the last decade, we have seen a sea change in many countries around the world. Developed and developing countries alike have introduced corporate governance codes by which companies are expected to abide. The codes emphasize the importance of transparency, accountability, internal controls, board composition and structure, independent directors, and performance-related executive pay. There is much emphasis on the rights of shareholders and an expectation that shareholders, especially institutional investors, will take a more proactive role in the companies in which they own shares and actually start to act more as owners rather than playing a passive shareholder role. Corporate governance is an exciting area, fast developing to accommodate the needs of a changing business environment where investor expectations are higher than ever before; the cost to companies that ignore the benefits of good corporate governance can be high and, ultimately, can mean the collapse of the company.

The global financial crisis—which started in 2006, rippled into 2007, exploded in 2008, and from which the aftershock is still being felt and no doubt will be for years to come—led to statements about corporate governance in times of financial crisis and the lessons that can be learned. The International Corporate Governance Network (ICGN) issued a Statement on the Global Financial Crisis in November 2008, and stated: 'corporate governance failings were not the only cause but they were significant, above all because boards failed to understand and manage risk and tolerated perverse incentives. Enhanced governance structures should therefore be integral to an overall solution aimed at restoring confidence to markets and protecting us from future crises.' The ICGN describe the crisis as a 'collective problem with many and varied causes' and the statement is therefore aimed at all concerned, 'including financial institutions and their boards, regulatory and policy makers and, of course, shareholders themselves'. The statement advocates strengthening shareholder rights; strengthening boards; fair and transparent markets; accounting standards (set without political interference); remuneration (having a 'say on pay'; encouraging boards to ensure that their policies do not foster excessive risk-raking; incentives aligned with medium- and long-term strategy and no payments for failure); and credit-rating agencies (there should be more competition in this market). A second statement by the ICGN in March 2009 reiterates the ICGN's view about 'the role that corporate governance can and should play in restoring trust in global capital markets'.

Similarly, the OECD issued a report in February 2009 entitled *Corporate Governance Lessons from the Financial Crisis*. The report states that 'the financial crisis can be to an important extent attributed to failures and weaknesses in corporate governance arrangements. When they were put to a test, corporate governance routines did not serve their purpose to safeguard against excessive risk taking in a number of financial services companies.' The report highlights failures in risk management systems; lack of information about risk exposures reaching the board; lack of monitoring by boards of risk management; lack of disclosure relating to risks and their management; inadequate accounting standards and regulatory requirements in some areas; and remuneration systems not being related to the strategy and longer term interests of the company. The report concludes that the adequacy of the OECD corporate governance principles will be re-examined to determine whether additional guidance and/or clarification are needed. The OECD circulated the *Principles of Corporate Governance—Draft for Public Comment November 2014* and following the consultation the *G20/OECD Principles of Corporate Governance 2015* were issued.

Clarke (2010) highlights that 'the prolonged systemic crisis in international financial markets commencing in 2007 was also a crisis in corporate governance and regulation. The apparent ascendency of Anglo-American markets and governance institutions was profoundly questioned by the scale and contagion of the global financial crisis.' Clarke's words will resonate with many who wonder what went wrong with corporate governance; how could we have had so many developments over the years in terms of regulation, self-regulation, codes of best practice, guidelines and so on, and yet still have suffered financial scandal and collapse on such a scale? Part of the answer lies in the fact that at the root of so many problems has been a lack of ethical behaviour, a lack of consideration for others who would be affected by these actions, and a consummate greed for money, power, or both. Ultimately, it is individual integrity, and then the board as a collective of individuals acting with integrity that will help shape ethical corporate behaviour in the future. The culture within a company is therefore of fundamental importance as there has to be an environment in which it is both possible and encouraged for individuals to behave ethically. The corporate culture has to support and nurture the best in people and discourage the worst; in this way ethical behaviour will be given substance in action and not just take the form of a code of ethics. A corporate culture which is supportive of integrity in behaviour will also reduce the risk of corruption, power-seeking, and greed and hence help avoid the type of corporate governance scandals discussed earlier.

Nonetheless, the International Finance Corporation (IFC) (2010) points out that the global financial crisis also demonstrated the crucial importance of corporate governance and a strong board of directors to aid companies in managing the impact of unexpected events and that good corporate governance makes companies more resilient to unforeseen changes in the environment in which they operate.

About the book

This text seeks to chart the development of corporate governance over the last two decades and to illustrate the importance of corporate governance to the company itself, to directors, shareholders and other stakeholders, and to the wider business community. The text is structured in four major parts. Part One contains two chapters that chart the development of corporate governance and look at the various theoretical aspects, including the frameworks within which corporate governance might be developed, and the development of corporate governance codes in various countries. A section on the governance of non-governmental organizations (NGOs), the public sector, non-profit organizations, and charities is included to reflect the increased interest in governance in these organizations.

Part Two contains four chapters, the first of which, Chapter 4, looks at the role of shareholders and stakeholders, identifies the various stakeholder groups, and discusses their role in companies and in corporate governance. The text recognizes that corporate ownership across the world varies and that the family-owned firm is the dominant form of business in many countries: Chapter 5 is devoted solely to family-owned firms and their governance. Chapter 6 looks at the role of institutional investors in corporate governance; institutional investors are the predominant type of owner in the UK and the USA. Also in Chapter 6 there is a discussion of the roles of private equity investors and sovereign wealth funds. Chapter 7 is devoted to socially responsible investment, or ethical investment, because it is an area that is attracting increasing interest in many countries and in which institutional investors in particular are taking much more of an interest.

Part Three concentrates on various aspects of directors and board structure: Chapter 8 examines the role of directors, their duties, their responsibilities, and looks at the important areas of boards and board subcommittees. Non-executive directors (outsiders), emphasized in many of the corporate governance codes as being a key element of good corporate governance, are discussed in detail. Board diversity is also discussed in some depth in the light of the growing emphasis on this area. Chapter 9 looks at directors' performance and remuneration. It reviews the background to the debate on directors' remuneration and looks at the ways in which directors' performance and remuneration may be effectively linked. The 'say on pay' is examined as a mechanism through which investors can express their views on executive remuneration.

The text is designed to appeal to a global audience and Part Four is devoted to corporate governance development in various continents around the world: Chapter 10 looks at corporate governance in mainland Europe, incorporating Continental European countries; Chapter 11, corporate governance in the Central and Eastern European countries; Chapter 12, corporate governance in South East Asia; Chapter 13, corporate governance in a number of other countries, including South Africa, Egypt, India, and Brazil. Chapter 14 provides some concluding comments on these developments in corporate governance, the evolution of the various shareholder and stakeholder groups, and the potential future developments in corporate governance.

At the start of each chapter, there are learning objectives that identify the key objectives of the chapter, and at the end of each chapter, there is a useful summary of the key points raised. There are short discussion questions and mini case studies to illustrate the key issues raised in various chapters, and references to appropriate publications and websites for each chapter.

An important feature of the book is the accompanying online resources (ARC), which contains additional useful material such as student learning tools incorporating questions and web links, and lecturers' material, including PowerPoint slides, additional examples, and mini case studies. A further resource is the book's corporate governance blog at http://corporate-governanceoup.wordpress.com where topical postings are made on a regular basis.

References

Cadbury, Sir Adrian (1999), *Corporate Governance Overview*, World Bank Report, Washington DC.

Clarke, T. (2010), 'Recurring Crises in Anglo-American Corporate Governance', *Contributions to Political Economy*, Vol. 29, Issue 1, pp. 9–32.

International Corporate Governance Network (2008), *Statement on the Global Financial Crisis*, ICGN, London.

International Corporate Governance Network (2009), *Second Statement on the Global Financial Crisis*, ICGN, London.

International Finance Corporation (2010), *Navigating Through Crises: A Handbook for Boards*, IFC, Washington DC.

Organisation for Economic Co-operation and Development (1999), *Principles of Corporate Governance*, OECD, Paris.

Organisation for Economic Co-operation and Development (2009), *Corporate Governance Lessons from the Financial Crisis*, OECD, Paris.

Organisation for Economic Co-operation and Development (2015), G20/OECD *Principles of Corporate Governance*, OECD, Paris.

Shleifer, A. and Vishny, R. (1997), 'A Survey of Corporate Governance', *Journal of Finance*, Vol. LII, No. 2, pp. 737–83.

 Develop your understanding of this chapter and explore the subject further using our online resources at **www.oup.com/uk/mallin6e/**

Part 1

Developments in corporate governance

2

Theoretical aspects of corporate governance

 Learning objectives

- To understand the various main theories that underlie the development of corporate governance
- To be aware of the impact of the form of legal system, capital market, and ownership structure on the development of corporate governance

Introduction

Corporate governance has only relatively recently come to prominence in the business world; the term 'corporate governance' and its everyday usage in the financial press is a new phenomenon of the last 20 years or so. However, the theories underlying the development of corporate governance, and the areas it encompasses, date from much earlier and are drawn from a variety of disciplines including finance, economics, accounting, law, management, and organizational behaviour.

It must be remembered that the development of corporate governance is a global occurrence and, as such, is a complex area, including legal, cultural, ownership, and other structural differences. Therefore some theories may be more appropriate and relevant to some countries than others, or more relevant at different times depending on what stage an individual country, or group of countries, is at. The stage of development may refer to the evolution of the economy, corporate structure, or ownership groups, all of which affect how corporate governance will develop and be accommodated within its own country setting. An aspect of particular importance is whether the company itself operates within a shareholder framework, focusing primarily on the maintenance or enhancement of shareholder value as its main objective, or whether it takes a broader stakeholder approach, emphasizing the interests of diverse groups, such as employees, providers of credit, suppliers, customers, and the local community.

Theories associated with the development of corporate governance

Given that many disciplines have influenced the development of corporate governance, the theories that have fed into it are quite varied. Table 2.1 gives a summary of some of the theories that may be associated with the development of corporate governance.

Table 2.1 Summary of theories affecting corporate governance development

Theory name	Summary
Agency	Agency theory identifies the agency relationship where one party (the principal) delegates work to another party (the agent). In the context of a corporation, the owners are the principal and the directors are the agent.
Transaction cost economics	Transaction cost economics views the firm itself as a governance structure. The choice of an appropriate governance structure can help align the interests of directors and shareholders.
Stakeholder	Stakeholder theory takes account of a wider group of constituents rather than focusing on shareholders. Where there is an emphasis on stakeholders, the governance structure of the company may provide for some direct representation of the stakeholder groups.
Stewardship	Directors are regarded as the stewards of the company's assets and will be predisposed to act in the best interests of the shareholders.
Class hegemony	Directors view themselves as an elite at the top of the company and will recruit/promote to new director appointments taking into account how well new appointments might fit into that elite.
Managerial hegemony	Management of a company, with its knowledge of day-to-day operations, may effectively dominate the directors and hence weaken the influence of the directors.
Path dependence	Path dependence may be structure driven and rule driven; corporate structures depend on the structures with which an economy started.
Resource dependence	Directors are able to connect the company to the resources needed to achieve corporate objectives.
Institutional	The institutional environment influences societal beliefs and practices that impact on various 'actors' within society.
Political	Political theory has a significant influence on different ownership and governance structures.
Network governance	A structure of network governance allows for superior risk management.

The main theories that have affected the development of corporate governance are now discussed in more detail. For a comprehensive exposition of theories underlying the development of corporate governance, Clarke (2004) is well worth reading. Coffee (2006) also adds new dimensions with his seminal book on gatekeepers whom he defines as 'the professional agents of the board and the shareholders, who inform and advise them: auditors, attorneys, securities analysts, credit-rating agencies and investment bankers'. He states that 'only if the board's agents properly advise and warn it, can the board function properly'.

Agency theory

A significant body of work has built up in this area within the context of the principal–agent framework. The work of Jensen and Meckling (1976) in particular, and of Fama and

Jensen (1983), is important. Agency theory identifies the agency relationship where one party (the principal) delegates work to another party (the agent). The agency relationship can have a number of disadvantages relating to the opportunism or self-interest of the agent: for example, the agent may not act in the best interests of the principal, or the agent may act only partially in the best interests of the principal. There can be a number of dimensions to this, including, for example, the agent misusing his/her power for pecuniary or other advantage, and the agent not taking appropriate risks in pursuance of the principal's interests because he/she (the agent) views those risks as not being appropriate (he/she and the principal may have different attitudes to risk). There is also the problem of information asymmetry whereby the principal and the agent have access to different levels of information; in practice, this means that the principal is at a disadvantage because the agent will have more information.

In the context of corporations and issues of corporate control, agency theory views corporate governance mechanisms, especially the board of directors, as being an essential monitoring device to try to ensure that any problems that may be brought about by the principal–agent relationship are minimized. Blair (1996) states:

> Managers are supposed to be the 'agents' of a corporation's 'owners', but managers must be monitored and institutional arrangements must provide some checks and balances to make sure they do not abuse their power. The costs resulting from managers misusing their position, as well as the costs of monitoring and disciplining them to try to prevent abuse, have been called 'agency costs'.

Much of agency theory as related to corporations is set in the context of the separation of ownership and control as described in the work of Berle and Means (1932). In this context, the agents are the managers and the principals are the shareholders, and this is the most commonly cited agency relationship in the corporate governance context. However, it is useful to be aware that the agency relationship can also cover various other relationships, including those of company and creditor, and of employer and employee.

Separation of ownership and control

The potential problems of the separation of ownership and control were identified in the eighteenth century by Smith (1838): 'the directors of such companies [joint stock companies] however being the managers rather of other people's money than of their own, it cannot well be expected that they should watch over it with the same anxious vigilance [as if it were their own]'. Almost a century later, the work of Berle and Means (1932) is often cited as providing one of the fundamental explanations of investor and corporate relationships. Berle and Means' work highlighted that, as countries industrialized and developed their markets, the ownership and control of corporations became separated. This was particularly the case in the USA and the UK where the legal systems have fostered good protection of minority shareholders and hence there has been encouragement for more diversified shareholder bases.

However, in many countries, especially where there is a code of civil law as opposed to common law, the protection of minority shareholders is not effective and so there has been less impetus for a broad shareholder base. The common law system builds on England's medieval laws whilst the civil law system is based on Roman law. A succinct comparison of the two legal systems is provided by Wessel (2001), who states that 'common-law countries— including the US and other former British colonies—rely on independent judges and juries and legal principles supplemented by precedent-setting case law, which results in greater flexibility', whilst 'in civil-law countries—which include much of Latin America—judges often are life-long civil servants who administer legal codes packed with specific rules, which hobbles them in their ability to cope with change'. In countries with a civil law system, there is therefore more codification but weaker protection of rights, hence there is less encouragement to invest.

In other words, the relationship between ownership and control outlined by Berle and Means is largely applicable to the USA and the UK but not to many other countries. This was highlighted by La Porta et al. (1999) who found that the most common form of ownership around the globe is the family firm or controlling shareholders, rather than a broad shareholder base (family firms and their corporate governance implications are discussed in more detail in Chapter 5).

However, the influence of Berle and Means' work cannot be underestimated: it has coloured thinking about the way companies are owned, managed, and controlled for over 70 years, and represents the reality in many US and UK companies. Monks (2001) states: 'The tendency during this period [the twentieth century] has been the dilution of the controlling blocks of shares to the present situation of institutional and widely dispersed ownership— ownership without power.'

In the last few years, there has been increasing pressure on shareholders, and particularly on institutional shareholders who own shares on behalf of the 'man in the street', to act more as owners and not just as holders of shares. The drive for more effective shareholders, who act as owners, has come about because there have been numerous instances of corporate excesses and abuses, such as perceived overpayment of directors for poor performance, corporate collapses, and scandals, which have resulted in corporate pension funds being wiped out, and shareholders losing their investment. The call for improved transparency and disclosure, embodied in corporate governance codes and in International Accounting Standards (IASs), should improve the information asymmetry situation so that investors are better informed about the company's activities and strategies.

Once shareholders do begin to act like owners again, then they will be able to exercise a more direct influence on companies and their boards, so that boards will be more accountable for their actions and, in that sense, the power of ownership will be returned to the owners (the shareholders). Useem (1996) highlights, however, that institutional investors will ultimately become accountable to 'the millions of ultimate owners ... who may come to question the policies of the new powers that be. Then the questions may expand from whether the professional money managers are achieving maximum private return to whether they are fostering maximum public good. Their demands for downsizing and single-minded focus on shareholder benefits—whatever the costs—may come to constitute a new target of ownership challenge.'

Transaction cost economics (TCE)

TCE, as expounded by the work o[f Williamson (1975, 1984), is often viewed as closely rel]ated to agency theory. TCE views the f[irm as... whereas agency theory v]iews the firm as a nexus of contracts. E[ssentially... connected grou]p or series of contracts amongst the v[arious players, arising because it is seemingly impossib]le to have a contract that perfectly alig[ns the interests of principal and agent in a corporate co]ntrol situation.

In the earlier discussion of ag[ency... the separation of owne]rship and control of a firm was emph[asized. As firms... driven b]y the desire to achieve economies of [scale, by technological advances, or by the fact that na]tural monopolies have evolved, they [have increasing needs for capital, which has ne]eded to be raised from the capital mar[kets and a wider shareholder base has been established]. The problems of the separation of ow[nership and control, and the resultant corporate govern]ance issues have thus arisen. Coase (1[937) examines the rationale for firms' existence in the co]ntext of a framework of the efficiencie[s of internal, as opposed to external, contracting. He sta]tes:

> the operation of a market cos[ts something and by forming an organisation and allow]ing some authority (an 'entreprene[ur') to direct the resources, certain marketing costs are sav]ed. The entrepreneur has to carry out his function at less cost, taking into account the fact that he may get factors of production at a lower price than the market transactions which he supersedes.

In other words, there are certain economic benefits to the firm itself to undertake transactions internally rather than externally. In its turn, a firm becomes larger the more transactions it undertakes and will expand up to the point where it becomes cheaper or more efficient for the transaction to be undertaken externally. Coase therefore posits that firms may become less efficient the larger they become; equally, he states that 'all changes which improve managerial technique will tend to increase the size of the firm'.

Williamson (1984) builds on the earlier work of Coase, and provides a justification for the growth of large firms and conglomerates, which essentially provide their own internal capital market. He states that the costs of any misaligned actions may be reduced by 'judicious choice of governance structure rather than merely realigning incentives and pricing them out'.

Hart (1995) states that there are a number of costs to writing a contract between principal and agent, which include the cost of thinking about and providing for all the different eventualities that may occur during the course of the contract, the cost of negotiating with others, and the costs of writing the contract in an appropriate way so that it is, for example, legally enforceable. These costs tend to mean that contracts are apt to be incomplete in some way and so contracts will tend to be revisited as and when any omissions or required changes come to light. Hart indicates that, 'in a world of incomplete contracts (where agency problems are also present), governance structure does have a role. Governance structure can be seen as a mechanism for making decisions that have not been specified in the initial contract.'

Stiles and Taylor (2001) point out that 'both theories [TCE and agency] are concerned with managerial discretion, and both assume that managers are given to opportunism (self-interest

[Handwritten annotation: Introduced by Ronald Coase (1932)]

seeking) and moral hazard, and that managers operate under bounded rationality ... [and] both agency theory and TCE regard the board of directors as an instrument of control'. In this context, 'bounded rationality' means that managers will tend to satisfice rather than maximize profit (this, of course, not being in the best interests of shareholders).

Stakeholder theory

In juxtaposition to agency theory is stakeholder theory. Stakeholder theory takes account of a wider group of constituents rather than focusing on shareholders. A consequence of focusing on shareholders is that the maintenance or enhancement of shareholder value is paramount, whereas when a wider stakeholder group—such as employees, providers of credit, customers, suppliers, government, and the local community—is taken into account, the overriding focus on shareholder value becomes less self-evident. Nonetheless, many companies do strive to maximize shareholder value whilst at the same time trying to take into account the interests of the wider stakeholder group. One rationale for effectively privileging shareholders over other stakeholders is that they are the recipients of the residual free cash flow (being the profits remaining once other stakeholders, such as loan creditors, have been paid). This means that the shareholders have a vested interest in trying to ensure that resources are used to maximum effect, which in turn should be to the benefit of society as a whole.

Shareholders and stakeholders may favour different corporate governance structures and also monitoring mechanisms. We can, for example, see differences in the corporate governance structures and monitoring mechanisms of the so-called Anglo-American model, with its emphasis on shareholder value and a board comprised totally of executive and non-executive directors elected by shareholders, compared to the German model, whereby certain stakeholder groups, such as employees, have a right enshrined in law for their representatives to sit on the supervisory board alongside the directors. Chapter 4 is devoted to shareholders and stakeholders, and discusses various aspects in more detail.

An interesting development is that put forward by Jensen (2001), who states that traditional stakeholder theory argues that the managers of a firm should take account of the interests of all stakeholders in a firm but, because the theorists refuse to say how the trade-offs against the interests of each of these stakeholder groups might be made, there are no defined measurable objectives and this leaves managers unaccountable for their actions. Jensen therefore advocates enlightened value maximization, which he says is identical to enlightened stakeholder theory: 'Enlightened value maximization utilizes much of the structure of stakeholder theory but accepts maximization of the long-run value of the firm as the criterion for making the requisite trade-offs among its stakeholders ... and therefore solves the problems that arise from multiple objectives that accompany traditional stakeholder theory.'

Stewardship theory

Stewardship theory draws on the assumptions underlying agency theory and TCE. The work of Donaldson and Davis (1991) cautioned against accepting agency theory as a given and introduced an alternative approach to corporate governance: stewardship theory.

The thrust of Donaldson and Davis' paper was that agency theory

> emphasizes the control of managerial 'opportunism' by having a board chair independent of the CEO and using incentives to bind CEO interests to those of shareholders. Stewardship theory stresses the beneficial consequences on shareholder returns of facilitative authority structures which unify command by having roles of CEO and chair held by the same person ... The safeguarding of returns to shareholders may be along the track, not of placing management under greater control by owners, but of empowering managers to take autonomous executive action.

Other theoretical perspectives

Managerial hegemony and class hegemony theories highlight the potential for a gap between what boards are expected to do and what they actually do in practice. Mace (1971) points out that managers may circumvent control away from the board by various means, including information asymmetry and elite networks. Huse (2007) made a significant contribution to the thinking on how research into boards and board behaviour might be carried out by applying lessons from the behavioural theory of the firm.

Resource dependence theory views the board of directors as 'the lynch pin between a company and the resources it needs to achieve its objectives' (Tricker, 2009, 2012).

Path dependence theory identifies two sources of path dependence: structure driven and rule driven, pointing out that corporate structures depend on the structures with which the economy started: 'Initial ownership structures can affect both the identity of the rules that would be efficient and the interest group politics that can determine which rules would actually be chosen' (Bebchuk and Roe, 1999).

Institutional theory looks at the institutional environment, its influence on societal beliefs and practices which impact on various 'actors' within society (Scott, 1987).

Political theory is identified as having a deep influence on different ownership and governance structures (Roe, 2003).

Network governance, building on the work of Jones et al. (1997), Turnbull advocated the adoption of network governance as a logical way to extend the science of cybernetics to organizations. Pirson and Turnbull (2011) argue that companies should have a structure of network governance and suggest 'increasing board level information processing and decision-making capabilities by including multiple boards for different stakeholders to create a division of power and labor' which would allow superior risk management. Turnbull (2012) shows 'how an ecological form of network governance could reduce the size, scope, cost and intrusiveness of government and their regulators while improving economic efficiency, resiliency and enriching democracy with widespread citizen stakeholder engagement'.

Whilst Table 2.1 gives a summary of a range of theories that may be associated with the development of corporate governance, Figure 2.1 illustrates the main theories that have traditionally been seen as the key influences on the development of corporate governance: agency theory, transaction cost economics, stakeholder theory, and stewardship theory.

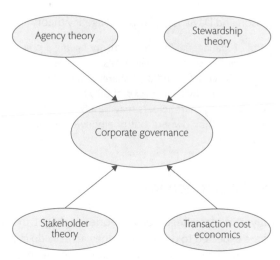

Figure 2.1 Main theories influencing the development of corporate governance

The theories in context

The approach taken in this book is to assume a public corporation business form (that is, a publicly quoted company), unless specifically stated otherwise. Therefore, the theories discussed earlier should be viewed in the light of this type of business form. In the UK this type of business form generally has a dispersed shareholder base, although there is a concentration of shareholdings amongst the institutional investors, such as the pension funds and insurance companies. Agency theory, together with the work of Berle and Means, seems particularly relevant in this context.

The theories that have affected the development of corporate governance should also be viewed in conjunction with the legal system and capital market development, as well as the ownership structure. For example, countries like the UK and the USA have a common law system that tends to provide good protection of shareholder rights, whilst civil law countries, such as France, tend to have less effective legal protection for shareholder rights, and more emphasis may be given to the rights of certain stakeholder groups.

However, it is clear that companies cannot operate in isolation without thought of the effect of their actions on the various stakeholder groups. To this end, companies need to be able to attract and retain equity investment, and be accountable to their shareholders, whilst at the same time giving real consideration to the interests of their wider stakeholder constituencies.

A recent focus of research has been the influence of culture on corporate governance. Guiso et al. (2013) study whether

on average a culture of integrity adds value and whether on average this culture is weaker among publicly traded companies. We find both these statements to be true. Integrity is positively correlated with financial performance and attractiveness of job offerings, while it is negatively correlated with the degree of unionization ... we also find that publicly traded companies are less able to sustain a high level of integrity. With few notable exceptions, the finance literature has ignored the role corporate culture can play. ... this paper shows that a company's financial choices have consequences on the corporate culture too, an aspect which is generally ignored in the finance literature.

Licht (2014) states that:

understanding the role of culture in corporate governance has become a subject of growing importance. Today, no institutional analysis of corporate governance systems would be complete without considering the cultural environment in which such systems are embedded. This paper provides an overview of different accounts on how culture interacts with the law—especially corporate law—to shape corporate governance and on how this may help explain diversity and persistence in corporate governance.

By surveying the literature 'on culture, law, and corporate governance with a view to establishing the importance of considering both formal (legal) and informal (cultural) institutions in the analysis of corporate governance systems', Licht has made an invaluable contribution to this important but under-researched area.

Hooghiemstra et al. (2015) examine the association between national culture and the amount of information that listed companies disclose on internal controls in their annual reports. Using data on 1,559 firms from 29 countries for the period 2005–2007, they find that 'national culture directly affects such disclosures [and] that national culture also indirectly affects disclosures via the level of investor protection in a country'.

The UK's Financial Reporting Council (2015) has also emphasized the importance of culture:

the issue of establishing high standards of behaviour in terms of culture, values and ethics in the boardroom, and how these behaviours are transmitted and taken up throughout companies. The development and promotion of such behaviours is a wider issue than amending or introducing new Code provisions. During 2015 the FRC will assess how effective boards are at establishing company culture and practices and embedding good corporate behaviour, and will consider whether there is a need for promoting best practice.

Following on from this, the FRC further recognized the importance of corporate culture with the publication of *Corporate Culture and the Role of Boards* in 2016. The report defined corporate culture as 'a combination of the values, attitudes and behaviours manifested by a company in its operations and relations with its stakeholders'. This report is discussed further in Chapter 3. The FRC also welcomed the recommendations in November 2017 of the UK government's independent advisory group's report *Growing a Culture of Social Impact Investing in the UK*.

Convergence

There are a number of views as to where corporate governance systems are converging or are likely to converge. Roe (2003) states: 'That corporate governance structures around the world have differed is hardly contested. The very fact that many people talk today, at the beginning of the twenty-first century, about corporate convergence due to globalization tells us that people believe that corporate structures have sharply varied.' He goes on to discuss the influence of political forces that may impact in different ways, at different times, and in different countries, and he states: 'a democratic polity does not easily accept powerful pro-shareholder institutions.' He illustrates this with the example of the USA where traditionally there have been limits on the power of pro-shareholder institutions, for example, not encouraging hostile takeovers; whilst in Europe, employees have comparatively good job protection. He sums up: 'If one fails to understand these political impulses, one cannot fully understand the world's, or any single nation's, corporate governance institutions.'

Aguilera and Jackson (2003) highlight that 'institutional change tends to occur in a slow, piecemeal fashion, rather than as a big bang. Where international pressures may lead to similar changes in one institutional domain, these effects may be mediated by the wider configuration of national institutions. This explains why internationalization has not led to quick convergence on national corporate governance models.'

Branson (2004) and Guillén (2004) argue against convergence occurring on economic, legal, and cultural grounds. For example, the family-owned firm is the dominant form of business around the globe and not the publicly owned corporation on which US and UK corporate governance is premised, hence we can see that one size is unlikely to fit all and that there will likely continue to be some divergence. There does, however, seem to be convergence on the core aspects of corporate governance, such as transparency, disclosure, and the important contribution that independent non-executive directors can make.

Rasheed and Yoshikawa (2012), in their book, analyse how cross-listing, the adoption of governance codes, and the spread of multinationals have facilitated the process of convergence. They conclude that corporate governance is moving 'towards hybridization with selective adoption and careful adaptation of governance practices by individual countries'.

Cuomo et al. (2016) reviewed previous country-level and firm-level studies on corporate governance codes up to 2014 in order to highlight recent trends and indicate future avenues of research. They found that:

> research on codes increases over time consistently with the diffusion and the relevance of the empirical phenomenon. Despite previous studies substantially enriching our knowledge of the antecedents and consequences of governance codes, our study shows there are still several opportunities to make significant contributions in this area ... Agency theory is the dominant theoretical framework, although other theoretical perspectives (especially the institutional one) are increasingly adopted.

They recommend that legislators and policymakers should continue to develop and update the recommendations of national governance codes so that they may address the potential failures of corporate governance mechanisms currently in place.

Schiehll and Martins (2016) reviewed cross-national governance research, surveying 192 cross-national comparative studies published in 23 scholarly journals in the fields of accounting, economics, finance, and management for the period 2003–2014. They find that:

> cross-national governance research has been guided mainly by an economic perspective focusing on international differences in the effectiveness of specific governance mechanisms. Few comparative studies have integrated an institutional perspective or examined the external forces that drive the diffusion and use of specific governance mechanisms. Such integrative framework would improve the understanding of cross-national differences in the salient dimensions of country-level governance factors and how they mediate the effectiveness of firm-level governance mechanisms.

They conclude that 'firm- and country-level governance mechanisms have been interacted and combined, either to address various agency problems or to compensate for a weak national environment. This calls for regulators and investors to consider national governance factors when assessing firm-level governance practices.'

Conclusions

Corporate governance is a relatively new area and its development has been affected by theories from a number of disciplines, including finance, economics, accounting, law, management, and organizational behaviour. The main theory that has affected its development, and that provides a theoretical framework within which it most naturally seems to rest, is agency theory. However, stakeholder theory is coming more into play as companies increasingly become aware that they cannot operate in isolation and that, as well as considering their shareholders, they need also to have regard to a wider stakeholder constituency. Nonetheless it is fair to say that corporate governance is still seeking its theoretical foundations and, as Tricker (2009) states, 'corporate governance, as yet, does not have a single widely accepted theoretical base nor a commonly accepted paradigm ... the subject lacks a conceptual framework that adequately reflects the reality of corporate governance'.

Future developments in the theory of corporate governance need to take account of a multitude of parts that make up the whole labyrinth of corporate governance: different business forms, different legal and cultural characteristics, and, of course, different 'actors' (directors, shareholders, and various stakeholders). The interaction of these different actors, and the effects both from, and on, the environment in which they operate, means that corporate governance is of its nature a complex and evolving system. A focus on culture and its impact on the development of corporate governance theory and practice is gaining prominence. An appropriate corporate culture will help ensure integrity within the company and should limit dysfunctional and dishonest behaviour which is detrimental to the company, its shareholders and other stakeholders, and the environment in which it operates.

Summary

- Corporate governance is a relatively new area and its development has been affected by theories from a number of disciplines, including finance, economics, accounting, law, management, and organizational behaviour.

- Agency theory has probably affected the development of the corporate governance framework the most. It identifies the agency relationship where one party (the principal) delegates work to another party (the agent). In the context of a corporation, the owners are the principal and the directors are the agent.

- Stakeholder theory takes account of a wider group of constituents rather than focusing on shareholders. Where there is an emphasis on stakeholders, then the governance structure of the company may provide for some direct representation of the stakeholder groups.

- The development of corporate governance is a global occurrence and, as such, is a complex area, including legal, cultural, ownership, and other structural differences. Therefore some theories may be more appropriate and relevant to some countries than others. There is a growing recognition that a corporate culture which embodies and encourages ethical behaviour and integrity is essential to ensure robust corporate governance.

Questions

The discussion questions to follow cover the key learning points of this chapter. Reading of some of the additional reference material will enhance the depth of students' knowledge and understanding of these areas.

1. Critically discuss the main theories that have influenced the development of corporate governance.

2. Do you think that different theories are more appropriate to different types of ownership structure?

3. What are the main problems that may arise in a principal–agent relationship and how might these be dealt with?

4. What links might there be between a country's legal system and capital market developments, and the impact of the theories underlying corporate governance?

5. Critically discuss the potential impact of the global financial crisis on the likelihood of convergence of corporate governance systems.

6. Critically discuss the role of corporate culture in helping ensure an ethical corporate environment and how it may encourage directors and other employees to act with integrity.

References

Aguilera, R. and Jackson, G. (2003), 'The Cross-National Diversity of Corporate Governance: Dimensions and Determinants', *Academy of Management Review*, Vol. 28, No. 3, pp. 447–65.

Bebchuk, L.A. and Roe, M.J. (1999), 'A Theory of Path Dependence in Corporate Ownership and Governance', *Stanford Law Review*, Vol. 52, No. 1, pp. 127–70.

Berle, A.A. and Means, G.C. (1932), *The Modern Corporation and Private Property*, Macmillan, New York.

Blair, M. (1996), *Ownership and Control: Rethinking Corporate Governance for the Twenty-first Century*, Brookings Institution, Washington.

Branson, D.M. (2004), 'The Very Uncertain Prospects of "Global" Convergence in Corporate Governance', in T. Clarke (ed.), *Theories of Corporate Governance*, Routledge, London.

Clarke, T. (2004), *Theories of Corporate Governance*, Routledge, London.

Coase, R.H. (1937), 'The Nature of the Firm', *Economica*, Vol. IV, pp. 13–16.

Coffee, J.C. (2006), *Gatekeepers, the Professions and Corporate Governance*, Oxford University Press, Oxford.

Cuomo F., Mallin C., and Zattoni A. (2016), 'Corporate Governance Codes: A Review and Research Agenda', *Corporate Governance: An International Review*, Vol. 24, Issue 3, May 2016, pp. 222–41.

Donaldson, L. and Davis, J.H. (1991), 'Stewardship Theory or Agency Theory: CEO Governance and Shareholder Returns', *Australian Journal of Management*, Vol. 16, No. 1, pp. 49–64.

Fama, E.F. and Jensen, M. (1983), 'Separation of Ownership and Control', *Journal of Law and Economics*, Vol. 26, No. 2, pp. 175–91.

Financial Reporting Council (2015), *Developments in Corporate Governance and Stewardship 2014*, FRC, London.

Financial Reporting Council (2016), *Corporate Culture and the Role of Boards*, FRC, London.

Guillén, M.F. (2004), 'Corporate Governance and Globalization: Is There Convergence Across Countries' in T. Clarke (ed.), *Theories of Corporate Governance*, Routledge, London.

Guiso, L., Sapienza, P., and Zingales, L. (2013), 'The Value of Corporate Culture', Chicago Booth Research Paper No. 13–80; Fama-Miller Working Paper. Available at SSRN: http://ssrn.com/abstract=2353486 or http://dx.doi.org/10.2139/ssrn.2353486.

Hart, O. (1995), 'Corporate Governance: Some Theory and Implications', *The Economic Journal*, Vol. 105, No. 430 (May), pp. 678–89.

Hooghiemstra, R., Hermes N., and Emanuels J. (2015), 'National Culture and Internal Control Disclosures: A Cross-Country Analysis', *Corporate Governance: An International Review*, Vol. 24, Issue 4, July 2015, pp. 357–377.

Huse, M. (2007), *Boards, Governance and Value Creation: The Human Side of Corporate Governance*, Cambridge University Press, Cambridge.

Jensen, M. (2001), 'Value Maximization, Stakeholder Theory, and the Corporate Objective Function', *Journal of Applied Corporate Finance*, Vol. 14, No. 3, pp. 7–21.

Jensen, M. and Meckling, W. (1976), 'Theory of the Firm: Managerial Behaviour, Agency Costs and Ownership Structure', *Journal of Financial Economics* Vol. 3, No. 4, pp. 305–60.

Jones, C., Hesterly, W.S., and Borgatti, S.P. (1997), 'A General Theory of Network Governance: Exchange Conditions and Social Mechanisms', *Academy of Management Review*, Vol. 22, No. 4, pp. 911–45.

La Porta, R., Lopez-de-Silanes, F., Shleifer, A., and Vishny, R. (1999), 'Corporate Ownership Around the World', *Journal of Finance*, Vol. 54, No. 2, pp. 471–517.

Licht, A.N. (2014), 'Culture and Law in Corporate Governance', European Corporate Governance Institute (ECGI)–Law Working Paper No. 247/2014. Available at SSRN: http://ssrn.com/abstract=2405538 or http://dx.doi.org/10.2139/ssrn.2405538.

Mace, M. (1971), *Directors: Myth and Reality*, Harvard University Press, Cambridge, MA.

Monks, R.A.G. (2001), *The New Global Investors*, Capstone Publishing, Oxford.

Pirson, M. and Turnbull, S. (2011), 'Corporate Governance, Risk Management, and the Financial Crisis: An Information Processing View', *Corporate Governance: An International Review*, Vol. 19, Issue 5, pp. 459–70.

Rasheed, A. and Yoshikawa, T. (eds) (2012), *The Convergence of Corporate Governance: Promise and Prospects*, Palgrave Macmillan, Basingstoke.

Roe, M.R. (2003), *Political Determinants of Corporate Governance*, Oxford University Press, Oxford.

Schiehll, E. and Martins, H.C. (2016), 'Cross-National Governance Research: A Systematic Review and Assessment', *Corporate Governance: An International Review*, Vol. 24, Issue 3, May 2016, pp. 181–99.

Scott, W.R. (1987), 'The Adolescence of Institutional Theory', *Administrative Science Quarterly*, Vol. 32, No. 4, pp. 493–511.

Smith, A. (1838), *The Wealth of Nations*, Ward Lock, London.

Stiles, P. and Taylor, B. (2001), *Boards at Work: How Directors View Their Roles and Responsibilities*, Oxford University Press, Oxford.

Tricker, B. (2009, 2012), *Corporate Governance: Principles, Policies and Practices*, Oxford University Press, Oxford.

Turnbull, S. (2012), 'A Sustainable Future for Corporate Governance Theory and Practice' in S. Boubaker, B.D. Nguyen, and D.K. Nguyen (eds), *Corporate Governance: Recent Developments and New Trends*, Springer, Berlin.

UK Government (2017), *Growing a Culture of Social Impact Investing in the UK*, London.

Useem, M. (1996), *Investor Capitalism: How Money Managers Are Changing the Face of Corporate America*, Basic Books, New York.

Wessel, D. (2001), 'Capital: The Legal DNA of Good Economies', *Wall Street Journal*, 6 September 2001.

Williamson, O.E. (1975), *Markets and Hierarchies*, Free Press, New York.

Williamson, O.E. (1984), 'Corporate Governance', *Yale Law Journal*, Vol. 93, No. 7, pp. 1197–229.

Develop your understanding of this chapter and explore the subject further using our online resources at **www.oup.com/uk/mallin6e/**

 **3**

Development of corporate governance codes

 Learning objectives

- To understand the key factors affecting the development of corporate governance codes
- To be aware of the main developments in corporate governance codes
- To have an awareness of the corporate governance codes that have been most influential globally
- To critically assess the characteristics of corporate governance codes and the mode of operation

The growth in corporate governance codes

During the last two decades, each year has seen the introduction, or revision, of a corporate governance code in a number of countries. These countries have encompassed a variety of legal backgrounds (for example, common law in the UK, civil law in France); cultural and political contexts (for example, democracy in Australia, communism in China); business forms (for example, public corporations compared to family-owned firms); and share ownership (institutional investor-dominated in the UK and USA, state ownership in China). However, in each of the countries, the introduction of corporate governance codes has generally been motivated by a desire for more transparency and accountability, and a desire to increase investor confidence (of both potential and existing investors) in the stock market as a whole. The development of the codes has often been driven by a financial scandal, corporate collapse, or similar crisis.

The corporate governance codes and guidelines have been issued by a variety of bodies ranging from committees (appointed by government departments and usually including prominent respected figures from business and industry, representatives from the investment community, representatives from professional bodies, and academics), through to stock exchange bodies, various investor representative groups, and professional bodies, such as those representing directors or company secretaries.

As regards compliance with the various codes, compliance is generally on a voluntary disclosure basis, whilst some codes (such as the UK Corporate Governance Code (2018)) are on a 'comply or explain basis': that is, either a company has to comply fully with the code and state that it has done so, or it explains why it has not.

In this chapter, the development of corporate governance in the UK is covered in some detail, particularly in relation to the Cadbury Report (1992), which has influenced the development of many corporate governance codes globally. Similarly, the Organisation for Economic Co-operation and Development (OECD) Principles are reviewed in detail as these have also formed the cornerstone of many corporate governance codes. The impact of various other international organizations on corporate governance developments, including the World Bank, Global Corporate Governance Forum (GCGF), International Corporate Governance Network (ICGN), and Commonwealth Association for Corporate Governance (CACG), are discussed. Recent developments in the EU, which have implications both for existing and potential member countries' corporate governance, are covered. There is also a brief overview of the Basle Committee recommendations for corporate governance in banking organizations.

Corporate collapses in the USA have had a significant impact on confidence in financial markets across the world and corporate governance developments in the USA are discussed in some detail.

In addition, a section on the governance of non-governmental organizations (NGOs), the public sector, non-profit organizations, and charities is included, as there is an increased focus on the governance of these organizations. The adoption of good governance should enable them to spend public money wisely and to strengthen their position.

The impact of the global financial crisis has had ramifications for corporate governance internationally, as countries seek to restore confidence in their financial markets and, in particular, in banks and other financial institutions.

Corporate governance in the UK

The UK has a well-developed market with a diverse shareholder base, including institutional investors, financial institutions, and individuals. The UK illustrates well the problems that may be associated with the separation of the ownership and control of corporations, and hence has many of the associated agency problems discussed in Chapter 2. These agency problems, including misuse of corporate assets by directors and a lack of effective control over, and accountability of, directors' actions, contributed to a number of financial scandals in the UK.

As in other countries, the development of corporate governance in the UK was initially driven by corporate collapses and financial scandals. The UK's Combined Code (1998) embodied the findings of a trilogy of reports: the Cadbury Report (1992), the Greenbury Report (1995), and the Hampel Report (1998). Brief mention is made of each of these three at this point to set the context, whilst a detailed review of the Cadbury Report (1992) is given subsequently in this chapter because it has influenced the development of many codes across the world. Reference is made to relevant sections of various codes in appropriate subsequent chapters.

Figure 3.1 illustrates the development of corporate governance in the UK. The centre oval represents the UK Corporate Governance Code, and the UK Stewardship Code, both published in 2010 by the Financial Reporting Council (FRC). Both Codes are regularly updated to ensure they stay relevant—the most recent UK Corporate Governance Code was published in July 2018 whilst the most recent UK Stewardship Code was published in September 2012 (a revision of the Stewardship Code is planned later in 2018). In the meantime, in 2016 the FRC introduced tiering of Stewardship Code signatories to distinguish between signatories who report well and demonstrate their commitment to stewardship, and those where reporting improvements are necessary. Around the centre oval, we can see the various influences since 1998

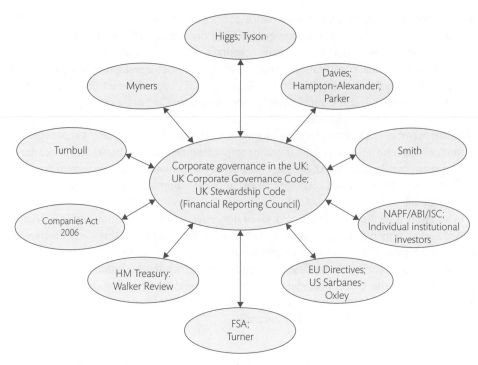

Figure 3.1 Development of corporate governance in the UK

(the original Combined Code, published in 1998, encompassed the Cadbury, Greenbury, and Hampel reports' recommendations). These influences can be split into four broad areas. First, there are reports that have looked at specific areas of corporate governance:

- the Turnbull Report on internal controls;
- the Myners Report on institutional investment;
- the Higgs Review of the role and effectiveness of non-executive directors;
- the Tyson Report on the recruitment and development of non-executive directors;
- the Smith Review of audit committees;
- the Davies Report and the Hampton-Alexander Report on board diversity (focusing on gender) and the Parker Review on board diversity (focusing on ethnicity).

Secondly, there has been the influence of institutional investors and their representative groups. Thirdly, influences affecting the regulatory framework within which corporate governance in the UK operates have included the UK company law review, the Walker Review for HM Treasury, the Financial Services Authority Review, and the Green Paper Consultation on Corporate Governance Reform. Fourthly, there have been what might be termed 'external influences' such as the EU review of company law, the EU Action Plan on European Company Law and Corporate Governance, the EU Corporate Governance Framework, the EU Shareholder Rights Directive, and the US Sarbanes–Oxley Act. Each of these is now discussed in turn.

Corporate governance codes and guidance in the UK

Cadbury Report (1992)

Following various financial scandals and collapses (Coloroll and Polly Peck, to name but two) and a perceived general lack of confidence in the financial reporting of many UK companies, the FRC, the London Stock Exchange, and the accountancy profession established the Committee on the Financial Aspects of Corporate Governance in May 1991. After the Committee was set up, the scandals at Bank of Credit and Commerce International (BCCI) and Maxwell (which respectively involved maintaining secret files for fraudulent purposes and using secret loans to try to disguise financial collapse) occurred, and as a result, the Committee interpreted its remit more widely and looked beyond the financial aspects to corporate governance as a whole. The Committee was chaired by Sir Adrian Cadbury and, when the Committee reported in December 1992, the report became widely known as 'the Cadbury Report'.

The recommendations covered: the operation of the main board; the establishment, composition, and operation of key board committees; the importance of, and contribution that can be made by, non-executive directors; and the reporting and control mechanisms of a business. The Cadbury Report recommended a Code of Best Practice with which the boards of all listed companies registered in the UK should comply, and utilized a 'comply or explain' mechanism. This mechanism means that a company should comply with the code but, if it cannot comply with any particular aspect of it, then it should explain why it is unable to do so. This disclosure gives investors detailed information about any instances of non-compliance and enables them to decide whether the company's non-compliance is justified.

Greenbury Report (1995)

The Greenbury Committee was set up in response to concerns about both the size of directors' remuneration packages, and their inconsistent and incomplete disclosure in companies' annual reports. It made, in 1995, comprehensive recommendations regarding disclosure of directors' remuneration packages. Central to the Greenbury Report recommendations were strengthening accountability and enhancing the performance of directors. These two aims were to be achieved by (i) the presence of a remuneration committee comprised of independent non-executive directors who would report fully to the shareholders each year about the company's executive remuneration policy, including full disclosure of the elements in the remuneration of individual directors; and (ii) the adoption of performance measures linking rewards to the performance of both the company and individual directors, so that the interests of directors and shareholders were more closely aligned.

Since that time (1995), disclosure of directors' remuneration has become quite prolific in UK company accounts. The main elements of directors' remuneration are considered further in Chapter 9.

Hampel Report (1998)

The Hampel Committee was set up in 1995 to review the implementation of the Cadbury and Greenbury Committee recommendations. The Hampel Committee reported in 1998 and endorsed the 'overwhelming majority of the findings of the two earlier committees'. There has been much discussion about the extent to which a company should consider the interests of various stakeholders, such as employees, customers, suppliers, providers of credit, the local community, etc., as well as the interests of its shareholders. The Hampel Report stated that 'the directors as a board are responsible *for relations with* stakeholders; but they are accountable *to* the shareholders' [emphasis in original]. However, the report does also state that 'directors can meet their legal duties to shareholders, and can pursue the objective of long-term shareholder value successfully, only by developing and sustaining these stakeholder relationships'.

Combined Code (1998)

The Combined Code drew together the recommendations of the Cadbury, Greenbury, and Hampel reports. It has two sections, one aimed at companies and another aimed at institutional investors. The Combined Code operates on the 'comply or explain' basis mentioned earlier. In relation to the internal controls of the business, the Turnbull Report issued in 1999 gave directors guidance on the implementation of the internal control requirements of the Combined Code.

Turnbull (1999)

The Turnbull Report confirms that it is the responsibility of the board of directors to ensure that the company has a sound system of internal control, and that the controls are working as they should. The board should assess the effectiveness of internal controls and report on them in the annual report. Of course, a company is subject to new risks both from the outside environment and as a result of decisions that the board makes about corporate strategy and objectives. In the managing of risk, boards will need to take into account the existing internal control system in the company and also whether any changes are required to ensure that new risks are adequately and effectively managed.

Myners (2001, 2008)

The Myners Report on Institutional Investment, issued in 2001 by HM Treasury, concentrated more on the trusteeship aspects of institutional investors and the legal requirements for trustees, with the aim of raising the standards and promoting greater shareholder activism. For example, the Myners Report expects that institutional investors should be more proactive, especially in the stance they take with underperforming companies. Some institutional investors have already shown more of a willingness to engage actively with companies to try to ensure that shareholder value is not lost by underperforming companies.

Subsequently, HM Treasury published Updating the Myners Principles: A Response to Consultation in 2008. There are six principles identified: effective decision-making; clear objectives; risk and liabilities; performance assessment; responsible ownership; transparency and reporting. The report emphasized greater industry ownership of the principles and places the onus on trustees to report on their own practices.

Higgs (2003)

The Higgs Review, chaired by Derek Higgs, reported in January 2003 on the role and effectiveness of non-executive directors. Higgs offered support for the Combined Code whilst making some additional recommendations which helped inform the Combined Code (2003). Good practice suggestions from the Higgs Report were published in 2006.

Following a recommendation in the Higgs Review, a group led by Professor Laura Tyson looked at how companies might utilize broader pools of talent with varied skills and experience, and different perspectives to enhance board effectiveness. The Tyson Report was published in 2003.

Smith (2003)

The Smith Review of audit committees, a group appointed by the FRC, reported in January 2003. The review made clear the important role of the audit committee: 'While all directors have a duty to act in the interests of the company, the audit committee has a particular role, acting independently from the executive, to ensure that the interests of shareholders are properly protected in relation to financial reporting and internal control' (para. 1.5). The review defined the audit committee's role in terms of a high-level overview; it needs to satisfy itself that there is an appropriate system of controls in place but it does not undertake the monitoring itself.

Combined Code (2003)

The revised Combined Code, published in July 2003, incorporated the substance of the Higgs and Smith reviews. However, rather than stating that no one non-executive director should sit on all three board committees, the Combined Code stated that 'undue reliance' should not be placed on particular individuals. The Combined Code also clarified the roles of the chairman and the senior independent director (SID), emphasizing the chairman's role in providing leadership to the non-executive directors and in communicating shareholders' views to the board; it also provided for a 'formal and rigorous annual evaluation' of the board's, the committees', and the individual directors' performance. At least half the board in larger listed companies were to be independent non-executive directors.

Revised Turnbull Guidance (2005)

In 2005 revised guidance on the Turnbull Report (1999) was published. There were few substantive changes but boards were encouraged to review their application of the Guidance on a continuing basis and to look on the internal control statement as an opportunity to communicate to their shareholders how they manage risk and internal control. They should notify shareholders, in the annual report, of how any 'significant failings or weaknesses' in the effectiveness of the internal control system have been dealt with.

Combined Code (2006)

An updated version of the Combined Code was issued in June 2006. There were three main changes made:

- to allow the company chairman to serve on (but not to chair) the remuneration committee where he is considered independent on appointment as chairman;
- to provide a 'vote withheld' option on proxy appointment forms to enable a shareholder to indicate that they wish to withhold their vote;
- to recommend that companies publish on their website the details of proxies lodged at general meetings where votes were taken on a show of hands.

Combined Code (2008)

The findings of the FRC Review of the Impact of the Combined Code were published in December 2007. The overall findings indicated that the Combined Code (2006) had general support and that the FRC would concentrate on improving the practical application of the Combined Code.

In June 2008, the FRC published a new edition of the Combined Code which introduced two changes. These changes were (i) to remove the restriction on an individual chairing more than one FTSE 100 company; and (ii) for listed companies outside the FTSE 350, to allow the company chairman to sit on the audit committee where he or she was considered independent on appointment.

The Combined Code (2008) took effect at the same time as new FSA Rules implementing EU requirements relating to corporate governance statements and audit committees.

Revised Smith Guidance (2008)

A new edition of the Guidance was issued in October 2008. The main changes to the Guidance as detailed on the FRC website are:

> audit committees are encouraged to consider the need to include the risk of the withdrawal of their auditor from the market in their risk evaluation and planning; companies are encouraged to include in the audit committee's report information on the appointment, reappointment or removal of the auditor, including supporting information on tendering frequency, the tenure of the incumbent auditor and any contractual obligations that acted to restrict the committee's choice of auditor; a small number of detailed changes have been made to the section dealing with the independence of the auditor, to bring the guidance in line with the Auditing Practices Board's [APB's] Ethical Standards [for Auditors (2004, revised 2008)] for auditors, which have been issued since the guidance was first published in 2003; and an appendix has been added containing guidance on the factors to be considered if a group is contemplating employing firms from more than one network to undertake the audit.

Walker Review (2009)

Following on from the financial crisis, an independent review of the governance of banks and other financial institutions was carried out by Sir David Walker. The Walker Review published its final recommendations in November 2009. The 39 recommendations comprised:

- five relating to board size, composition, and qualification (including improvements to director training and induction);

- eight relating to the functioning of the board and evaluation of performance (including several recommendations relating to the role of the Chair);

- nine relating to the role of institutional shareholders' communication and engagement (emphasizing the development and regulatory sponsorship of a Stewardship Code);

- five relating to the governance of risk (emphasizing the role of the risk committee);

- twelve relating to remuneration (including the role of the board remuneration committee; disclosure of executive remuneration; and the Code of Conduct for executive remuneration consultants written by the Remuneration Consultants Group (RCG)).

Some of the recommendations were to be taken forward by the FRC through amendments to the Combined Code, whilst others were to be taken forward by the FSA.

UK Corporate Governance Code (2010)

Following consultation, an updated corporate governance code for UK companies, incorporating some of the Walker recommendations, was issued in May 2010. Formerly known as 'the Combined Code', the newly issued UK Corporate Governance Code (hereafter 'the Code') retained the 'comply or explain' approach.

The FRC identified six main changes which were as follows. First, to improve risk management, the company's business model should be explained and the board should be responsible for the nature and extent of significant risks it is willing to take. Secondly, performance-related pay should be aligned to the long-term interests of the company and to its risk policy and systems. Thirdly, all directors of FTSE 350 companies should be put forward for re-election every year as a way of increasing their accountability. Fourthly, new principles on the leadership of the chairman, the responsibility of the non-executive directors to provide constructive challenge, and the time commitment expected of all directors will help to encourage appropriate debate in the boardroom. Fifthly, new principles on the composition and selection of the board, including the need to appoint members on merit, against objective criteria, and with due regard for the benefits of diversity, including gender diversity should encourage boards to be well balanced and avoid 'group think'. And finally, the chairman should hold regular development reviews with each director and FTSE 350 companies should have externally facilitated board effectiveness reviews at least every three years. These latter measures should help enhance the board's performance and awareness of its strengths and weaknesses.

Guidance Notes on Implementation of the UK Corporate Governance Code

The FRC has published a series of guidance notes to assist companies in applying the principles of the Code.

In 2010 the FRC published the *Guidance on Board Effectiveness*, which relates primarily to Sections A and B of the Code on the leadership and effectiveness of the board. The Guidance was developed by the Institute of Chartered Secretaries and Administrators (ICSA) on the FRC's behalf, and replaces 'Suggestions for Good Practice from the Higgs Report' (known as 'the Higgs Guidance'), which has been withdrawn.

In addition, three guidance notes have been issued in relation to Section C of the Code. Guidance on the requirement in Section C.1.3 of the Code to report on whether the business is a going concern, and other related regulatory requirements is given in *Going Concern and Liquidity Risk: Guidance for Directors of UK Companies*. Meanwhile *Internal Control: Revised Guidance for Directors* (known as 'the Turnbull Guidance') provides guidance to companies on how to apply the section of the Code dealing with risk management and internal control (Section C.2); and *Guidance on Audit Committees* (formerly known as 'the Smith Guidance'), provides guidance on Section C.3 of the Code, which deals with the audit committee and the engagement of the external auditor.

Stewardship Code (2010)

When the Code was first published, it included in Schedule C some engagement principles for institutional investors. However, Schedule C has now been deleted as it has been superseded by the UK Stewardship Code (hereafter 'the Stewardship Code'). The Stewardship Code is seen as complementary to the Code and 'aims to enhance the quality of engagement between institutional investors and companies to help improve long-term returns to shareholders and the efficient exercise of governance responsibilities'. The Stewardship Code builds largely on the ISC's work on the responsibilities of institutional shareholders (discussed in detail in Chapter 6) by essentially setting out the best practice engagement, including dialogue and voting of shares, for institutional investors in their investee companies. This should help build a much stronger link between the investment process and corporate governance. The Stewardship Code is to be applied on a 'comply or explain' basis.

Davies Report (2011, 2012–15)

Concerned by the lack of progress with the representation of women on UK boards, the UK's Coalition government invited Lord Davies to review the situation, to identify the barriers that were preventing more women from reaching the boardroom, and to make recommendations as to how this situation might be redressed. Lord Davies' report, *Women on Boards*, was published in February 2011 and reviewed the current situation on UK boards (FTSE 350) and considered the business case for having gender-diverse boards.

A number of recommendations were made including that the chairmen of FTSE 350 companies should state the percentage of women that they aim to have on their boards in 2013 and 2015, and that FTSE 100 companies should aim for a minimum 25 per cent women in the boardroom by 2015 although many might achieve a higher figure. Quoted companies should disclose annually the proportion of women on the board, women in senior executive positions, and female employees in the organizations as a whole. Furthermore, Lord Davies recommended that the FRC amend the Code to require listed companies to establish a policy on boardroom diversity, including measurable objectives for implementing the policy, and disclose a summary of the policy and the progress made towards achieving the objectives each year. It was also recommended that executive search firms should draw up a voluntary code of conduct addressing gender diversity and best practice covering the relevant search criteria and processes in relation to FTSE 350 board appointments.

Early in 2012 the first annual review was published which indicated that over the year since the original report was published, the biggest ever reported increase in the percentage of women on boards was evidenced. Subsequent annual reports were issued in 2013, 2014, and then in 2015. The final report, published in October 2015, showed that there are more women on FTSE 350 boards than ever before, with representation of women having more than doubled since 2011 and the target of 25 per cent having been exceeded on FTSE 100 boards which have 26.1 per cent of women whilst for FTSE 250 boards it stood at 19.6 per cent.

UK Corporate Governance Code (2012)

In May 2011 the FRC began consulting on possible amendments to the Code that would require companies to publish their policy on boardroom diversity and report against it annually, as recommended by Lord Davies in his *Women on Boards* report published in February 2011, and to consider the board's diversity, amongst other factors, when assessing its effectiveness. In 2012 the Financial Reporting Council (FRC) announced limited changes to the UK Corporate Governance Code and Stewardship Code intended to increase accountability and engagement through the investment chain. Changes to the UK Corporate Governance Code, as reported by the FRC (2012) included:

- FTSE 350 companies to put the external audit contract out to tender at least every ten years with the aim of ensuring a high quality and effective audit, whether from the incumbent auditor or from a different firm;
- Audit committees to provide to shareholders information on how they have carried out their responsibilities, including how they have assessed the effectiveness of the external audit process;
- Boards to confirm that the annual report and accounts taken as a whole are fair, balanced, and understandable, to ensure that the narrative sections of the report are consistent with the financial statements and accurately reflect the company's performance;
- Companies to explain, and report on progress with, their policies on boardroom diversity;
- Companies to provide fuller explanations to shareholders as to why they choose not to follow a provision of the Code.

Stewardship Code (2012)

As discussed above, in 2012 the Financial Reporting Council (FRC) announced limited changes to both the UK Corporate Governance Code and the UK Stewardship Code. The changes to the Stewardship Code were as follows:

- Clarification of the respective responsibilities of asset managers and asset owners for stewardship, and for stewardship activities that they have chosen to outsource;

- Investors to explain more clearly how they manage conflicts of interest, the circumstances in which they will take part in collective engagement, and the use they make of proxy voting agencies;

- Asset managers encouraged to have the processes that support their stewardship activities independently verified, to provide greater assurance to their clients.

Guidance on the Strategic Report (2014)

In 2014 the FRC published *Guidance on the Strategic Report* which replaced the Accounting Standards Board's *Reporting Statement: Operating and Financial Review*. The FRC views the objective of the strategic report as being to provide information for shareholders that will enable them to assess how the directors have performed their duty to promote the success of the company (section 172 of the Companies Act 2006).

The content elements for the strategic report set out in the Guidance are derived from the Companies Act 2006, and include a description of the entity's strategy, objectives, and business model. In addition, the strategic report should include an explanation of the main trends and factors affecting the entity; a description of its principal risks and uncertainties; an analysis of the development and performance of the business; and an analysis using key performance indicators. Disclosures about the environment, employees, social, community, and human rights issues are required when material. There is also a requirement to include disclosures on gender diversity.

UK Corporate Governance Code (2014)

In 2014 the UK Corporate Governance Code was again updated. The FRC stated that it

> has focussed on the provision by companies of information about the risks which affect longer term viability. In doing so the information needs of investors have been balanced against setting appropriate reporting requirements. Companies will now need to present information to give a clearer and broader view of solvency, liquidity, risk management, and viability. For their part, investors will need to assess these statements thoroughly and engage accordingly. In addition, boards of listed companies will need to ensure that executive remuneration is aligned to the long-term success of the company and demonstrate this more clearly to shareholders.

The 2014 revisions covered a number of areas of the Code. The changes relating to risk management included the following:

- Companies should state whether they consider it appropriate to adopt the going concern basis of accounting and identify any material uncertainties to their ability to continue to do so;

- Companies should robustly assess their principal risks and explain how they are being managed or mitigated;

- Companies should state whether they believe they will be able to continue in operation and meet their liabilities taking account of their current position and principal risks, and specify the period covered by this statement and why they consider it appropriate. It is expected that the period assessed will be significantly longer than 12 months;
- Companies should monitor their risk management and internal control systems and, at least annually, carry out a review of their effectiveness, and report on that review in the annual report.

In relation to the part of the Code relating to remuneration, changes included that the design of remuneration is to promote the long-term success of the company; and to recommend that provisions are put in place to recover and/or withhold remuneration when appropriate. In relation to voting, the updated Code introduces a requirement, under provision E.2.2, in relation to companies explaining, when publishing meeting results, how they intend to engage with shareholders when a significant percentage of them have voted against any resolution. This is a situation which may well arise in relation to executive remuneration though it could arise in relation to other areas of the business as well.

Guidance on Audit Committees (2016)

The FRC's Guidance on Audit Committees (2016) updated the earlier version published in 2012 (which was based on the revised Smith Guidance 2008). The Guidance—which looks at the establishment and effectiveness of the audit committee, summarizes the audit committee's roles and responsibilities, and provides an overview of communications with shareholders—aims to assist company boards in making suitable arrangements for their audit committees and to help audit committee members to carry out their role.

UK Corporate Governance Code (2016)

The amendments introduced in the 2016 update of the Code were minimal and driven by changes required from the implementation of the European Union's Audit Regulation (2014/56/EU) and Regulation (537/2014). The minor changes related to section C.3 which covers the audit committee and auditors:

- The audit committee as a whole will need competence relevant to the sector in which the company operates.
- The FTSE 350 audit tendering provision has been removed as this is superseded by the EU and the Competition and Markets Authority (CMA) requirements for mandatory tendering and rotation of the audit firm.
- The audit committee report within the annual report is now required to provide advance notice of any plans to retender the external audit.

It is important that companies view the changes alongside the revised Guidance on Audit Committees (2016) which was discussed earlier.

Green Paper on Corporate Governance Reform (2016)

The Department for Business, Energy & Industrial Strategy (BEIS) *Green Paper on Corporate Governance Reform* was issued for consultation in November 2016. It considered three specific areas of corporate governance which might be built on to enhance the UK's current corporate governance framework. These areas were: executive pay; strengthening the employee, customer, and supplier voice; and corporate governance in the UK's largest privately held businesses.

The consultation closed on 17 February 2017. Subsequently the BEIS issued its report which detailed its recommendations and conclusions based on the consultation of the Green Paper and in August 2017 published *Corporate Governance Reform, the government response to the green paper consultation*. The Executive Summary detailed nine headline proposals for reform across the three specific aspects of corporate governance on which the consultation focused. It also took into account the need for effective enforcement of the corporate governance framework.

Of particular note were that all listed companies will have to reveal the pay ratio between bosses and workers (i.e. the CEO and the average UK employee); all listed companies with significant shareholder opposition to executive pay packages will have their names published on a new public register; and new measures will seek to ensure employee voice is heard in the boardroom.

Hampton-Alexander Review (2017)

The Hampton-Alexander Review (the Review) was an independent, business-led review supported by the government which builds on the success of the Davies Reports. In 2017 it published its report *Improving Gender Balance in FTSE Leadership* and made recommendations aimed at increasing the number of women in leadership positions of FTSE 350 companies. The recommendations called for action from all stakeholders and included a target of 33 per cent women on FTSE 350 boards and 33 per cent women in FTSE 100 leadership teams by 2020 (where leadership teams are comprised of members of the Executive Committee and those senior leaders who are direct reports to Executive Committee members). The Review recommended that there should be more women appointed as Chairs, Senior Independent Directors (SIDs), and executive directors. Overall the Review suggested that all stakeholders, including the government and institutional investors, should evaluate disclosures and progress on gender balance.

Parker Review (2017)

The Parker Review Committee, led by Sir John Parker, published its Final Report, *A Report into Ethnic Diversity of UK Boards: 'Beyond One by '21'* in 2017. Starting from the premise that UK boardrooms, including those of leading public companies, do not reflect the UK's ethnic diversity nor the stakeholders that companies engage with (customers, employees, etc.), the Parker Report states that 'ethnic minority representation in the Boardrooms across the FTSE 100 is disproportionately low, especially when looking at the number of UK citizen directors of colour'. The key recommendations are: (i) increasing the ethnic diversity of UK boards;

(ii) developing candidates for the pipeline and planning for succession; and (iii) enhancing transparency and disclosure.

Guidance on the Strategic Report (2018)

In August 2017, the FRC published a consultation with proposals to amend the *Guidance on the Strategic Report*. The proposed amendments reflect the legislative changes arising from the UK implementation of the EU Directive on disclosure of non-financial and diversity information and strengthen the link between the purpose of the strategic report and the director's duty under section 172 of the Companies Act 2006 (i.e. the duty to promote the success of the company). The updated Guidance was published in July 2018.

Guidance on Board Effectiveness (2018)

In July 2018, the FRC published the updated *Guidance on Board Effectiveness (2018)* (the Guidance) aimed at stimulating boards to think about the way in which they carry out their role and how they can improve their effectiveness. The Guidance has five sections relating to board leadership and company purpose; division of responsibilities; composition, succession, and evaluation; audit, risk, and internal control; and remuneration.

In relation to the UK Corporate Governance Code (2018), the Guidance states:

> The Code places considerable emphasis on decision-making and outcomes. It promotes a more inclusive approach to stakeholder engagement and encourages boards to reflect on the way in which decisions are taken and how that might affect the quality of those decisions. By encouraging a broader focus and a willingness to listen to different voices and influences, the Code, supplemented by the Guidance, supports openness and accountability in delivering the long-term sustainable success of the company.

UK Corporate Governance Code (2018)

In December 2017 the FRC issued for consultation *Proposed Revisions to the UK Corporate Governance Code*. Along with responding to the recommendations made in the government's response to the Green Paper Consultation on Corporate Governance Reform (August 2017), the FRC has also took into account issues raised by the House of Commons' *Business, Energy and Industrial Strategy Committee's Report on Corporate Governance*, published in April 2017.

In July 2018 the UK Corporate Governance Code (2018) was issued. It is more focused than previous versions and builds on the findings from the FRC's *Culture Report (2016)* (see later) and as such it places more emphasis on the importance and value of corporate culture in building trust in the business and facilitating engagement in a meaningful way with the company's stakeholders and with wider society. The revised Code states that 'a company's culture should promote integrity and openness, value diversity and be responsive to the views of shareholders and wider stakeholders'.

The revised Code has five sections relating to board leadership and company purpose; division of responsibilities; composition, succession and evaluation; audit, risk and internal control; and remuneration. Each of these sections contains a number of Principles and 'offers flexibility through the application of the Principles and through "comply or explain" provisions and supporting guidance'.

The revised Code is also supported by the *Guidance on Board Effectiveness*. Furthermore the board of directors should also take into account additional guidance, such as the *Guidance on Audit Committees* and the *Guidance on Risk Management, Internal Control and Related Financial and Business Reporting*.

Individual sections of the revised Code are discussed in relevant later chapters of this book. A helpful summary of the revised UK Corporate Governance Code (2018) highlights is available at: https://www.frc.org.uk/getattachment/524d4f4b-62df-4c76-926a-66e223ca0893/2018-UK-Corporate-Governance-Code-highlights.pdf.

Alongside the consultation on the proposed changes to the UK Corporate Governance Code, the FRC included an initial high-level consultation on the future direction of the UK Stewardship Code. Their aim being to formally consult on changes to the UK Stewardship Code in 2018. The rationale for the consultation of both Codes is that the FRC believes that 'to achieve real change in corporate governance, and long-term success and sustainability for companies, it is important that investors play their part, which is why we are seeking views alongside the formal consultation on the revised Code'.

Corporate governance code for large privately owned companies

A Coalition Group of which the FRC is the secretariat was established in response to the Green Paper Consultation on Corporate Governance Reform. The Coalition Group comprises the FRC and senior representatives from the Institute of Directors, the Confederation of British Industry, the Institute for Family Business, the British Private Equity & Venture Capital Association, the Institute of Business Ethics, the Investment Association, the Climate Disclosure Standards Board, ICSA: the Governance Institute, and the Trades Union Congress to develop and deliver the corporate governance principles for large privately owned companies. It was announced in January 2018 that James Wates, Chairman of the Wates Group, would chair the Coalition Group. Stephen Haddrill, Chief Executive of the FRC, said: 'Large private companies are integral to the UK economy as significant employers and supporters of communities and families. It is right we develop a set of corporate governance principles to enhance confidence that they act in the public interest.'

In June 2018 *The Wates Corporate Governance Principles for Large Private Companies 2018* were issued for consultation. There are six principles relating to purpose; composition; responsibilities; opportunity and risk; remuneration; and stakeholders. An 'apply and explain' approach is envisaged so that 'using an apply and explain approach, large private companies are expected to provide a supporting statement for each principle that gives an understanding of how their corporate governance processes operate and achieve the desired outcomes'. The final version is planned for December 2018.

Compliance with the Wates Principles will satisfy the new regulatory reporting requirements proposed by the Companies (Miscellaneous Reporting) Regulations (2018)—which are presently subject to parliamentary approval—and will require all companies that do not have an existing corporate governance reporting requirement and which have more than 2,000 employees and/or a turnover of more than £200 million and a balance sheet of more than £2 billion, to include a statement in their directors' report and on their website about their corporate governance arrangements for financial years starting on or after 1 January 2019.

Risk management

Risk management is a key part of the board of directors' role and responsibilities. In 2014, the FRC published *Guidance on Risk Management, Internal Control and Related Financial and Business Reporting*. Referring to the FRC's *Boards and Risk* (2011) and the 2012 Sharman Inquiry into going concern and liquidity risk, the FRC (2014) states:

> Taken together, the conclusions of the two reports can be summarised as:
>
> - the board must determine its willingness to take on risk, and the desired culture within the company;
> - risk management and internal control should be incorporated within the company's normal management and governance processes, not treated as a separate compliance exercise;
> - the board must make a robust assessment of the principal risks to the company's business model and ability to deliver its strategy, including solvency and liquidity risks. In making that assessment the board should consider the likelihood and impact of these risks materialising in the short and longer term;
> - once those risks have been identified, the board should agree how they will be managed and mitigated, and keep the company's risk profile under review. It should satisfy itself that management's systems include appropriate controls, and that it has adequate sources of assurance;
> - the assessment and management of the principal risks, and monitoring and review of the associated systems, should be carried out as an on-going process, not seen as an annual one-off exercise; and
> - this process should inform a number of different disclosures in the annual report: the description of the principal risks and uncertainties facing the company; the disclosures on the going concern basis of accounting and material uncertainties thereto; and the report on the review of the risk management and internal control systems.

The FRC *Guidance on Risk Management, Internal Control and Related Financial and Business Reporting (2014)* amalgamated the guidance from the Turnbull Report (2005) (internal control) and *Going Concern* (2009) guidance notes, revised to reflect the finalized requirements of the 2014 Code. The changes made to the UK Corporate Governance Code 2014 in relation to risk management are detailed in the relevant section earlier in the chapter.

It is, however, worth highlighting that the FRC (2015) recognizes the link between sound corporate governance, risk management, and culture:

> No governance framework can eliminate risk and nor should it seek to do so. The difficult question of what represents an acceptable level of corporate failure will always be with us, but this does not mean that we should be complacent. We should continue to seek new ways to prevent and deal with poor governance practice. It is for this reason that we introduced references—in the preface to the [UK Corporate Governance] Code and in the associated risk guidance—to the issue of establishing high standards of behaviour in terms of culture, values and ethics in the boardroom, and how these behaviours are transmitted and taken up throughout companies.

Corporate culture

The importance of corporate culture was further recognized by the FRC with the publication of *Corporate Culture and the Role of Boards* in 2016. The report explains how discussions were held with chairmen, chief executives, investors and a broad range of stakeholders and professional organizations about corporate culture which in this context can be defined as 'a combination of the values, attitudes and behaviours manifested by a company in its operations and relations with its stakeholders.' Resulting from these discussions, the report identifies a number of key observations about corporate culture:

- Recognize the value of culture
- Demonstrate leadership i.e. leaders, and especially the CEO, must embody the desired culture, embedding this at all levels and in every aspect of the business.
- Be open and accountable
- Embed and integrate
- Align values and incentives
- Assess, measure, and engage
- Exercise stewardship i.e., effective stewardship should include engagement about culture and encourage better reporting. Investors should challenge themselves about the behaviours they are encouraging in companies and to reflect on their own culture.

The FRC also welcomed the recommendations in November 2017 of the UK government's independent advisory group's report *Growing a Culture of Social Impact Investing in the UK*. This report is discussed in more detail in Chapter 7.

'Comply or Explain'

As mentioned earlier, the Code operates on a 'comply or explain' basis. In February 2012, the FRC reported on discussions it arranged between companies and investors with the aim of comparing notes between these two groups on their perceptions of the 'explain' part of 'comply or explain'. The report found that the two groups believed that a great strength of the Code was that the principles were expressed in general, rather than very specific, terms which allowed some latitude in their implementation. Therefore, companies could still comply with the Code, even if they deviated from one or more of its provisions, by making a full explanation of why they had not complied with a particular aspect. The report concluded that 'used properly, the Code-based "comply or explain" approach can deliver greater transparency and confidence than formal regulation which is purely a matter of compliance'. The discussions were also timely in the context of some scepticism in the EU about the effectiveness of the 'comply or explain' approach and whether it is taken seriously by investors and companies. Such discussions could result in a more prescriptive and inherently less flexible approach giving more power to regulators and less to shareholders. Hence it was helpful to be able to demonstrate the strengths of the 'comply or explain' approach. The EU discussion about the quality of financial reporting and 'comply or explain' is discussed in detail later in this chapter.

It should be noted that in the UK Corporate Governance Code (2016), the FRC referred to the 'comply or explain' approach as 'the trademark of corporate governance in the UK.

It has been in operation since the Code's beginnings and is the foundation of its flexibility. It is strongly supported by both companies and shareholders and has been widely admired and imitated internationally.' Subsequently in the *Proposed Revisions to the UK Corporate Governance Code* (2017), the FRC pointed out that 'the strengths of the UK's approach—the unitary board, strong shareholder rights, the role of stewardship and flexibility through "comply or explain" in relation to the Provisions—are all still valuable today and have, therefore, been preserved'. This is reflected in the UK Corporate Governance Code (2018) which refers to the flexibility of the Code through 'comply or explain' rather than a set of rigid rules.

Influence of institutional investors and their representative groups

Institutional investors and their representative groups

Large institutional investors—mainly insurance companies and pension funds—usually belong to one of two representative bodies that act as a professional group 'voice' for their views: the Association of British Insurers (ABI) and the National Association of Pension Funds (NAPF). Both the ABI and the NAPF have best practice corporate governance guidelines that encompass the recommendations of the UK Corporate Governance Code. They monitor the corporate governance activities of companies and provide advice to members. In the Autumn of 2015, the NAPF announced that it would become the Pensions and Lifetime Savings Association (PLSA). The rebrand was to help reflect the NAPF's strategy for the future as by 2020 it wants to encompass all of the workplace pensions sector as well as aspects including lifetime savings and supporting savers in reaching a better retirement income.

Some large institutional investors are very active in their own right in terms of their corporate governance activities. Hermes is a case in point, and it published the *Hermes Responsible Ownership Principles (2013)*, which detail how it perceives its relationship with the companies in which it invests (investee companies), what its expectations are of investee companies, and what investee companies can expect from Hermes. It has also published *Stewardship* (2017) and *Corporate Governance Principles, United Kingdom* (2018).

Whilst the role and influence of institutional investors are covered in detail in Chapter 6, mention should be made here of the work of the ISC, whose *Code on the Responsibilities of Institutional Investors* formed the basis for the UK Stewardship Code (2010, updated 2012). The ISC was renamed in the summer of 2011, as the Institutional Investor Committee (IIC) whose members are the NAPF, the ABI, and the Investment Management Association (IMA). In 2014, the IMA merged with the Investment Affairs Division of the Association of British Insurers to create The Investment Association (IA). The Investment Association covers the entire range of investment issues on behalf of investment managers and clients, whether they are domestic or international individuals, discretionary managers, life companies, pension funds, family offices, or sovereign wealth funds. Following the merger, the NAPF and the IMA agreed to dissolve the ISC. However, where there is a shared agenda, the IMA and the NAPF will continue to work together.

In 2014, the Investor Forum was launched by industry practitioners with the core objective of creating long-term value. Positioning stewardship at the heart of investment decision-making by facilitating dialogue, creating long-term solutions, and enhancing value is central to this objective. Full membership of the Forum is open to any institutional investor in a UK-listed company, irrespective of where that investor is located, including both asset managers and asset owners. As at 31 December 2017, the Forum had 35 full Members.

The role of institutional investors is discussed in detail in Chapter 6.

Influences on the regulatory framework

Companies Act 2006

In the UK the corporate law had been in need of a thorough review for some years and the Modern Company Law Review culminated in July 2002 in the publication of outline proposals for extensive modernization of company law, including various aspects of corporate governance. These proposals included: statutory codification of directors' common law duties; enhanced company reporting and audit requirements, including a requirement that economically significant companies produce an annual Operating and Financial Review (OFR); disclosure on corporate websites of information relating to the annual report and accounts; and disclosure relating to voting.

The government published the Company Law Reform Bill in November 2005, and the Companies Act 2006 was enacted in late 2006. The Act updates previous Companies Acts legislation, but does not completely replace them, and it contains some significant new provisions that will impact on various constituents, including directors, shareholders, auditors, and company secretaries. The Act draws on the findings of the Company Law Review proposals.

The main features of the Companies Act 2006 are as follows:

- Directors' duties are codified.
- Companies can make greater use of electronic communications for communicating with shareholders.
- Directors can file service addresses on public record rather than their private home addresses.
- Shareholders can agree limitations on directors' liability.
- There are simpler model Articles of Association for private companies, to reflect the way in which small companies operate.
- Private companies are not required to have a company secretary.
- Private companies do not need to hold an annual general meeting unless they agree to do so.
- The requirement for an OFR has not been reinstated, rather companies are encouraged to produce a high quality business review.

- Nominee shareholders can elect to receive information in hard copy form or electronically if they wish to do so.
- Shareholders will receive more timely information.
- Enhanced proxy rights will make it easier for shareholders to appoint others to attend and vote at general meetings.
- Shareholders of quoted companies may have a shareholder proposal (resolution) circulated at the company's expense if received by the financial year end.
- Whilst there has been significant encouragement over a number of years to encourage institutional investors to disclose how they use their votes, the Act provides a power that could be used to require institutional investors to disclose how they have voted.

Overall there seems to be an increasing burden for quoted companies, whilst on the other hand the burden seems to have been reduced for private companies. In terms of the rights of shareholders, these are enhanced in a number of ways, including greater use of electronic communications, more information, enhanced proxy rights, and provision regarding the circulation of shareholder proposals at the company's expense. Equally, there is a corresponding emphasis on shareholders' responsibilities with encouragement for institutional shareholders to be more active and to disclose how they have voted.

Financial Services Authority (FSA)

In September 2002, the FSA launched a review of the listing regime with the main aim being to assess the existing rules and identify which should be retained and which changed. The areas covered by the review were: corporate governance; continuing obligations (encompassing corporate communication, and shareholders' rights and obligations); financial information; and the sponsor regime.

The FSA Review took place against the background of potentially significant changes in both the EU and UK regulatory environments, and although some changes were made, there was much continuity in the proposals introduced in 2005.

Following the global banking crisis, Lord Adair Turner, Chairman of the FSA, was asked by the Chancellor of the Exchequer to carry out a review and make recommendations for reforming UK and international approaches to the way banks are regulated. The Turner Review was published in the spring of 2009. Issues highlighted include remuneration policies designed to avoid incentives for undue risk-taking; whether changes in governance structure are needed to increase the independence of risk management functions; and consideration of the skill and time commitment required for non-executive directors of large complex banks to effectively perform their role.

In 2010 the UK government decided that it would be appropriate for the FSA to undergo some internal restructuring. The FSA streamlined its operations in the wake of the financial crisis so that it could perform more effective regulation of banks and the financial markets. The changes included combining the retail and wholesale supervision units into a single division and creating standalone risk and international units.

In 2013 the FSA became two separate regulatory authorities: the Financial Conduct Authority (FCA) and the Prudential Regulation Authority (PRA). These are discussed in turn below.

The Financial Conduct Authority (FCA)

The FCA regulates the financial services industry in the UK. Their aim is to protect consumers, ensure the industry remains stable, and promote healthy competition between financial services providers. The FCA Board keeps a close watch on how the business is operating and holds the FCA accountable for the way it works. It is made up of executive and non-executive members.

The Board has several committees to which it delegates certain functions/powers, which are: Audit Committee, Risk Committee, Remuneration Committee, Oversight Committee, Regulatory Decisions Committee, and Nominations Committee.

The Executive Committee (ExCo) is the highest ranking executive decision-making body of the FCA, and discusses issues across all areas of the organization. It oversees the strategy, direction, and activity of the FCA in general, including delivery of the FCA's annual Business Plan. It is responsible for monitoring the direction and performance of the organization within the strategic framework set by the Board. Sub-committees of ExCo include the Executive Regulatory Issues Committee, the Policy Steering Committee, the Executive Operations Committee, and the Executive Diversity Committee.

The Prudential Regulation Authority (PRA)

The Prudential Regulation Authority (PRA) is a part of the Bank of England and responsible for the prudential regulation and supervision of banks, building societies, credit unions, insurers, and major investment firms. It sets standards and supervises financial institutions at the level of the individual firm. Prudential regulation rules require financial firms to hold sufficient capital and have adequate risk controls in place. Close supervision of firms ensures that the PRA has a comprehensive overview of their activities so that they can step in if they are not being run in a safe and sound way or, in the case of insurers, if they are not protecting policyholders adequately.

The Prudential Regulation Committee (PRC) makes the PRA's most important decisions. It is made up of 12 people and is chaired by the Governor of the Bank of England whilst four other members are Bank of England Deputy Governors. The majority of PRC members come from outside the Bank of England. One is the Chief Executive of the Financial Conduct Authority, and six other external committee members are selected for their experience and expertise in financial services.

Financial Reporting Council (FRC)

The FRC used to have six operating bodies: the Accounting Standards Board (ASB), the APB, the Board for Actuarial Standards (BAS), the Professional Oversight Board, the Financial Reporting Review Panel (FRRP), and the Accountancy and Actuarial Discipline Board (AADB).

The importance placed on corporate governance was evidenced by the fact that, in March 2004, the FRC set up a new committee to lead its work on corporate governance.

Overall, the FRC is responsible for promoting high standards of corporate governance. It aims to do so by:

- maintaining an effective UK Corporate Governance Code and promoting its widespread application;
- ensuring that related guidance, such as that on internal control, is current and relevant;
- influencing EU and global corporate governance developments;
- helping to promote boardroom professionalism and diversity;
- encouraging constructive interaction between company boards and institutional shareholders.

The FRC has carried out several consultative reviews of the Combined Code which led to the amended Combined Code in 2006 and 2008; whilst the review in 2009 culminated in the issue of the UK Corporate Governance Code in 2010. Subsequent reviews took place in 2011, 2012, and 2014. The frequency of the reviews is both an indicator of the FRC's responsibility for corporate governance of UK companies, which involves leading public debate in the area, and its response to the global financial crisis, which has, in turn, affected confidence in aspects of corporate governance.

In recent years, the structure of the FRC has been reformed. The Board is supported by three governance committees: Audit Committee, Nominations Committee, and Remuneration Committee, and by two business committees: Codes & Standards Committee and Conduct Committee. In turn the Codes & Standards Committee is supported by three Councils which advise on Corporate Reporting, Audit & Assurance, and Actuarial matters. The Corporate Reporting Review Committee, the Audit Quality Review Committee, and the Case Management Committee support the Conduct Committee and have specific responsibilities as set out in the FRC's monitoring, review, and disciplinary procedures. In addition, the Financial Reporting Review Panel and the disciplinary Tribunal Panel are maintained pursuant to the Conduct Committee Operating procedures and the FRC's Disciplinary Schemes.

'External' influences

The report of the EU High-Level Group of Company Law Experts had implications for company law across Europe, including the UK, and, together with other pronouncements such as the *High-Level Group on Financial Supervision in the EU* (2009), the *Green Paper on Corporate Governance in Europe* (2011), the EU Action Plan on European Company Law and Corporate Governance, and the EU Shareholder Rights Directive (2014) will be discussed in more detail later in the context of an international development. The impact of legislation in the USA, including the Sarbanes-Oxley Act (2002), has also made its influence felt in the UK, and is also discussed in detail later.

Influential corporate governance codes

Corporate governance codes and guidelines for various countries around the world will be looked at in more detail in some of the later chapters, whilst in this chapter codes and guidelines that have had a fundamental influence on the development of corporate governance more generally will be examined. It is always slightly contentious to try to state which corporate governance codes have had the most influence on the development of corporate governance codes in other countries, but the following codes and principles have undoubtedly had a key impact on the development of corporate governance globally.

Cadbury Report (1992)

The Cadbury Report recommended a Code of Best Practice with which the boards of all listed companies registered in the UK should comply, and utilized a 'comply or explain' mechanism. Whilst the Code of Best Practice is aimed at the directors of listed companies registered in the UK, the Committee also exhorted other companies to try to meet its requirements. The main recommendations of the Code are shown in Box 3.1.

The recommendations—covering the operation of the main board, the establishment, composition, and operation of key board committees; the importance of, and contribution that can be made by, non-executive directors; and the reporting and control mechanisms of a business—had a fundamental impact on the development of corporate governance not just in the UK, but on the content of codes across the world, amongst countries as diverse as India and Russia.

Today the recommendations of the Cadbury Report and subsequent UK reports on corporate governance are embodied in the UK Corporate Governance Code. Various sections of the Code are referred to in appropriate chapters and the full text of the latest UK Corporate Governance Code (2018) is available for download from the FRC website at: https://www.frc.org.uk/getattachment/88bd8c45-50ea-4841-95b0-d2f4f48069a2/2018-UK-Corporate-Governance-Code-FINAL.PDF

Box 3.1   The Code of Best Practice

1. The Board of Directors
    1.1 The board should meet regularly, retain full and effective control over the company, and monitor the executive management.
    1.2 There should be a clearly accepted division of responsibilities at the head of a company, which will ensure a balance of power and authority, such that no one individual has unfettered powers of decision. Where the chairman is also the chief executive, it is essential that there should be a strong and independent element on the board, with a recognized senior member.
    1.3 The board should include non-executive directors of sufficient calibre and number for their views to carry significant weight in the board's decisions.
    1.4 The board should have a formal schedule of matters specifically reserved to it for decision to ensure that the direction and control of the company is firmly in its hands.
    1.5 There should be an agreed procedure for directors in the furtherance of their duties to take independent professional advice if necessary, at the company's expense.
    1.6 All directors should have access to the advice and services of the company secretary, who is responsible to the board for ensuring that board procedures are followed and that applicable rules and regulations are complied with. Any question of the removal of the company secretary should be a matter for the board as a whole.

2. Non-executive Directors

2.1 Non-executive directors should bring an independent judgement to bear on issues of strategy, performance, resources, including key appointments, and standards of conduct.

2.2 The majority should be independent of management and free from any business or other relationship which could materially interfere with the exercise of their independent judgement, apart from their fees and shareholding. Their fees should reflect the time which they commit to the company.

2.3 Non-executive directors should be appointed for specified terms and reappointment should not be automatic.

2.4 Non-executive directors should be selected through a formal process and both this process and their appointment should be a matter for the board as a whole.

3. Executive Directors

3.1 Directors' service contracts should not exceed three years without shareholders' approval.

3.2 There should be full and clear disclosure of directors' total emoluments and those of the chairman and highest paid UK director, including pension contributions and stock options. Separate figures should be given for salary and performance-related elements and the basis on which performance is measured should be explained.

3.3 Executive directors' pay should be subject to the recommendations of a remuneration committee made up wholly or mainly of non-executive directors.

4. Reporting and Controls

4.1 It is the board's duty to present a balanced and understandable assessment of the company's position.

4.2 The board should ensure that an objective and professional relationship is maintained with the auditors.

4.3 The board should establish an audit committee of at least three non-executive directors with written terms of reference which deal clearly with its authority and duties.

4.4 The directors should explain their responsibility for preparing the accounts next to a statement by the auditors about their reporting responsibilities.

4.5 The directors should report on the effectiveness of the company's system of internal control.

4.6 The directors should report that the business is a going concern, with supporting assumptions or qualifications as necessary.

Source: Cadbury Code (1992).

OECD *Principles of Corporate Governance* (1999) as revised (2004 and 2015)

The OECD published its *Principles of Corporate Governance* in 1999, following a request from the OECD Council to develop corporate governance standards and guidelines. Prior to producing the Principles, the OECD consulted the national governments of member states, the private sector, and various international organizations, including the World Bank.

The OECD Principles focus on publicly traded companies but, as in the Cadbury Report, there is an encouragement for other business forms, such as privately held or state-owned enterprises, to utilize the Principles to improve corporate governance.

The OECD recognizes that 'one size does not fit all', that is, that there is no single model of corporate governance that is applicable to all countries. However, the Principles represent certain common characteristics that are fundamental to good corporate governance. The OECD Principles were reviewed and revised in 2004.

The OECD Principles are non-binding but, nonetheless, their value as key elements of good corporate governance has been recognized and they have been incorporated into codes in many different countries. For example, the Committee on Corporate Governance in Greece produced its *Principles on Corporate Governance in Greece* in 1999, which reflected the OECD Principles, whilst the China Securities Regulatory Commission published its *Code of Corporate Governance for Listed Companies in China* in 2001, which also drew substantially on the OECD Principles.

In 2006 the OECD published its *Methodology for Assessing Implementation of the OECD Principles of Corporate Governance*. This was followed in 2008 by the publication *Using the OECD Principles of Corporate Governance: A Boardroom Perspective* which gives guidance on how the Principles have been put into practice in different companies using real life examples.

In 2009 the OECD launched an action plan to address weaknesses in corporate govern-ance related to the financial crisis with the aim of developing a set of recommendations for improving board practices, risk management, governance of the remuneration process, and the exercise of shareholder rights. In 2010 *Corporate Governance and the Financial Crisis: Con-clusions and Emerging Good Practices to Enhance Implementation of the Principles* was pub-lished. The OECD's Corporate Governance Committee noted that the ability of the board to effectively oversee executive remuneration—including both the amount and also the way in which remuneration is aligned with the company's longer term interests—appears to be a key challenge in practice and remains one of the central elements of the corporate govern-ance debate in a number of countries. The OECD underlines the importance of boards being able to treat remuneration and risk alignment as an iterative process, recognizing the links between the two, and disclosing in a remuneration report the specific mechanisms that link compensation to the longer term interests of the company. The capacity of a firm's govern-ance structure to produce such a balanced incentive system is critical and therefore ways to enhance governance structures have received more emphasis recently including the role of independent non-executive directors and the 'say on pay', whereby shareholders may have either a binding or non-binding vote on executive pay.

Subsequently, in 2011 the OECD published *Board Practices, Incentives and Governing Risks* in which it looked at how effectively boards manage to align executive and board remu-neration with the longer term interests of their companies as this was one of the key failures highlighted by the financial crisis. The OECD highlights that 'aligning incentives seems to be far more problematic in companies and jurisdictions with a dispersed shareholding structure since, where dominant or controlling shareholders exist, they seem to act as a moderating force on remuneration outcomes'.

The OECD circulated the *G20/OECD Principles of Corporate Governance—Draft for Public Comment November 2014* for consultation. All G20 countries were invited to participate in the review on equal terms with the OECD member countries. Experts from key international institutions such as the World Bank Group also participated in the review as did a variety of stakeholders via an open online public consultation. Following the consultation, the *G20/ OECD Principles of Corporate Governance* was published in 2015.

The revised Principles are shown in Box 3.2.

The *G20/OECD Principles of Corporate Governance* recognize that 'good corporate governance is not an end in itself. It is a means to create market confidence and business integrity, which in turn is essential for companies that need access to equity capital for long term investment'. As with the earlier versions of the Principles, there is a recognition that whilst larger companies may be the main focus of corporate governance, policymakers may decide to raise awareness of good corporate governance for all companies, including smaller and unlisted companies.

The Principles provide a benchmark for individual countries around the world. Furthermore they are utilized by key organizations such as the Financial Stability Board (FSB) which was established in April 2009 as the successor to the Financial Stability Forum (FSF)

Box 3.2   G20/OECD *Principles of Corporate Governance* (2015)

Principle	Narrative
I. Ensuring the basis for an effective corporate governance framework	The corporate governance framework should promote transparent and fair markets, and the efficient allocation of resources. It should be consistent with the rule of law and support effective supervision and enforcement.
II. The rights and equitable treatment of shareholders and key ownership functions	The corporate governance framework should protect and facilitate the exercise of shareholders' rights and ensure the equitable treatment of all shareholders, including minority and foreign shareholders. All shareholders should have the opportunity to obtain effective redress for violation of their rights.
III. Institutional investors, stock markets and other intermediaries	The corporate governance framework should provide sound incentives throughout the investment chain and provide for stock markets to function in a way that contributes to good corporate governance.
IV. The role of stakeholders in corporate governance	The corporate governance framework should recognize the rights of stakeholders established by law or through mutual agreements and encourage active co-operation between corporations and stakeholders in creating wealth, jobs, and the sustainability of financially sound enterprises.
V. Disclosure and transparency	The corporate governance framework should ensure that timely and accurate disclosure is made on all material matters regarding the corporation, including the financial situation, performance, ownership, and governance of the company.
VI. The responsibilities of the board	The corporate governance framework should ensure the strategic guidance of the company, the effective monitoring of management by the board, and the board's accountability to the company and the shareholders.

Source: G20/OECD Principles of Corporate Governance (OECD, 2015)

and monitors and assesses vulnerabilities affecting the global financial system and proposes actions needed to address them. In addition, it monitors and advises on market and systemic developments, and their implications for regulatory policy. The Principles are one of the FSB's Key Standards for Sound Financial Systems and also provide the basis for assessment of the corporate governance component of the Reports on the Observance of Standards and Codes of the World Bank.

World Bank

In the World Bank corporate governance is part of the Financial Market Integrity (FMI) group's remit. The corporate governance group within FMI focuses on improving corporate governance in emerging market countries. In carrying out its corporate governance remit, the World Bank states that the corporate governance group

has four focus areas:

(i)   developing the legal and regulatory foundation for corporate governance of listed and unlisted companies;

(ii) improving the governance of banking institutions, in particular state-owned banks (development and commercial banks);

(iii) improving the governance of micro-finance institutions and financial cooperatives; and

(iv) strengthening the capacity of regulators and supervisors to implement and enforce reforms.

The group works closely with the Corporate Governance Group of the International Monetary Fund (IMF) and conducts corporate governance country assessments under the Report on the Observance of Standards and Codes (ROSC) initiative which was launched in 1999. The ROSC initiative is aimed at promoting greater financial stability, both domestically and internationally, through the development, dissemination, adoption, and implementation of international standards and codes.

In this context, the World Bank assists its member countries in strengthening their corporate governance frameworks. The World Bank states that the goal of the ROSC initiative is to strengthen corporate governance policies and practices of listed companies in emerging markets.

The ROSC assessment:

● Reviews the country's legal and regulatory framework as well as the practices and compliance of its listed firms;

● Assesses the framework and practices relative to an internationally accepted benchmark as per the OECD Principles of Corporate Governance;

● Provides policy recommendations for strengthening corporate governance in terms of board practice, control and audit structures, transparency and disclosure, and protection of shareholder rights—prioritized according to high, medium, and lower priority;

● Offers a country action plan which sets out key steps, responsibilities, and timelines, and which provides annex model corporate governance policies from other emerging and developing markets.

Global Corporate Governance Forum (GCGF)

The GCGF is at the heart of corporate governance co-operation between the OECD and the World Bank. It is, as its name suggests, an international initiative aimed at bringing together leading groups in governance, including banks, organizations, country groupings, the private sector, and professional standard-setting bodies. The GCGF's mandate is 'to promote the private sector as an engine of growth, reduce the vulnerability of developing and emerging markets to financial crisis, and provide incentives for corporations to invest and perform efficiently in a transparent, sustainable, and socially responsible manner'.

International Corporate Governance Network (ICGN)

The ICGN was founded in 1995. Its membership encompasses major institutional investors, investor representative groups, companies, financial intermediaries, academics, and others with an interest in the development of global corporate governance practices. Its objective is to facilitate international dialogue on corporate governance issues.

In 1999 the ICGN issued its *Statement on Global Corporate Governance Principles*, which comprised three main areas. First is a statement on the OECD Principles, which the ICGN views as 'a remarkable convergence on corporate governance common ground among diverse interests, practices, and cultures', and which it sees as the minimum acceptable standard for companies and investors around the world. Secondly, the ICGN statement discusses its approach to the OECD Principles, a 'working kit' statement of corporate governance criteria that encompasses ten areas: the corporate objective, communications and reporting, voting rights, corporate boards, corporate remuneration policies, strategic focus, operating performance, shareholder returns, corporate citizenship, and corporate governance implementation. Thirdly, the ICGN statement amplifies the OECD Principles, emphasizing or interpreting each principle as appropriate. For example, in relation to 'The Rights of Shareholders', the ICGN amplification includes the statement that 'major strategic modifications to the core business(es) of a corporation should not be made without prior shareholder approval of the proposed modification'.

Following the revision of the OECD Principles (2004), the ICGN reviewed its global corporate governance principles and published revised principles in 2005 (ICGN, 2005). Again building on the OECD Principles, the ICGN revised principles also identify some additional principles of particular concern to the ICGN and its members. The ICGN Principles cover eight areas: corporate objective, shareholder returns; disclosure and transparency; audit; shareholders' ownership, responsibilities, and voting rights and remedies; corporate boards; corporate remuneration policies; corporate citizenship, stakeholder relations, and the ethical conduct of business; and corporate governance implementation.

Further revisions followed in 2009 and 2014 with the latest revision of the ICGN *Global Governance Principles* being in 2017. There are eight principles covering: board role and responsibilities; leadership and independence; composition and appointment; corporate culture; risk oversight; remuneration; reporting and audit; and shareholder rights. The ICGN states that the *Global Governance Principles* should be read alongside the ICGN *Global Stewardship Principles (2015)* which set out best practices in relation to investor governance and stewardship obligations, policies, and processes. There are seven global stewardship principles: internal governance: foundations of effective stewardship; developing and implementing stewardship policies; monitoring and assessing investee companies; engaging companies and investor collaboration; exercising voting rights; promoting long-term value creation and integration of environmental, social, and governance (ESG) factors; enhancing transparency, disclosure, and reporting. Together these two documents promote ICGN's long-held stance that 'both companies and investors share a mutual responsibility to preserve and enhance long-term corporate value, and thereby contribute to sustainable capital markets and societal prosperity'.

Commonwealth Association for Corporate Governance (CACG)

The CACG has produced some useful guidelines and principles of guidelines. The guidelines cover 15 principles detailing the board's role and responsibilities. These cover areas such as leadership, board appointments, strategy and values, company performance, compliance, communication, accountability to shareholders, relationships with stakeholders, balance of power, internal procedures, board performance assessment, management appointments and development, technology, risk management, and an annual review of future solvency.

EU and corporate governance

The EU High-Level Group of Company Law Experts, comprised of a group of lawyers, was established in late 2001 by the EU to provide independent advice for modernizing company law in Europe. The group was headed by Jaap Winter, hence the report produced by the group is sometimes referred to as 'the Winter Report' (2002). In relation to corporate governance issues, the group made the following recommendations for listed companies:

- EU law should require companies to publish an annual corporate governance statement in their accounts and on their websites. Companies would need to state their compliance with their national corporate governance code, on a 'comply or explain' basis.
- The nomination and remuneration of directors, and the audit of accounts, should be decided upon by non-executive or supervisory directors, the majority of whom are independent.
- Companies should disclose in their annual corporate governance statement who their independent directors are, why they are independent, what their qualifications are to serve on the board, and their other directorships.
- The remuneration of individual directors should be disclosed in detail.
- Share option schemes would require the prior approval of the shareholders.
- In relation to (annual) general meetings, companies should be required to publish all relevant material on their website, and should offer facilities for electronic voting.
- Companies should inform shareholders of the procedure for asking questions at general meetings, and also of the process for submitting shareholder resolutions (proposals).

Frits Bolkestein, the European Commissioner for Internal Market and Services, promised an action plan to take forward the recommendations of the group, with the aim of providing a comprehensive, dynamic, and flexible framework for corporate governance in Europe. There are clear implications for all members of the EU. As far as the UK is concerned, the group's recommendations are generally similar to those of the UK Company Law Review (now embodied in the Companies Act 2006) and do not pose any problems.

In 2006 the European Commission organized a public hearing on future priorities for the Action Plan on 'Modernizing Company Law and Enhancing Corporate Governance in the EU'. These priorities included shareholders' rights and obligations, internal control, and the modernization and simplification of European company law. Also in 2006 amendments to the fourth and seventh Company Law Directives were issued with the aim of enhancing confidence in financial statements and annual reports. These amendments prescribe that, inter alia, listed companies must now publish a separate corporate governance statement in the annual report, and board members are to take collective responsibility for the annual report and accounts. The Directive on statutory audit of annual and consolidated accounts clarifies the duties of auditors; a key provision requires listed companies to have audit committees with at least one member of the audit committee being independent and competent in accounting/auditing.

In June 2007 the Commission published an external study on proportionality between capital and control in EU listed companies. Proportionality is the relationship between capital and control ('one share, one vote'). The study, carried out by Institutional Shareholder Services Europe (ISS Europe), the European Corporate Governance Institute (ECGI), and the law firm Shearman & Sterling LLP, found that:

> on the basis of the academic research available, there is no conclusive evidence of a causal link between deviations from the proportionality principle and either the economic performance of listed companies or their governance. However, there is some evidence that investors perceive these mechanisms negatively and consider more transparency would be helpful in making investment decisions.

In 2007 the Directive on the exercise of shareholder rights was issued. This Directive recommended that shareholders have timely access to information, and that there should be the facility to vote at a distance, that is, without having to be physically present at the meeting to vote. The practice of share-blocking, which required shareholders to deposit shares at a specified institution for a period of time around the company's annual general meeting, which then meant that the shares could not be traded during that time, is abolished. These changes all facilitate the shareholders' ability to exercise their votes and enhance cross-border voting practices.

Following on from the global financial crisis, the High-Level Group on Financial Supervision in the EU, chaired by Jacques de Larosière, published its report in February 2009. It highlighted failures in corporate governance as one of the most important failures of the crisis, and made recommendations regarding compensation incentives and internal risk management. Importantly, the report advocated the creation of a European Systemic Risk Council (ESRC). The ESRC was subsequently established in December 2010 and is responsible for the macro-prudential oversight of the financial system within the EU to help prevent and mitigate systemic risks to financial stability.

In 2011 the EU issued the *Green Paper on the EU Corporate Governance Framework* which launched a public consultation on possible ways forward to improve existing corporate governance mechanisms. The Green Paper contained three chapters: boards, shareholders, and the 'comply or explain' principle. The objective of the Green Paper was to have a broad debate on the issues raised.

In late 2012, the EU issued a draft Directive on the gender balance of non-executive directors of listed companies; whilst in December 2012, the EU published an Action Plan on European Company Law and Corporate Governance which detailed a number of legislative and other initiatives on company law and corporate governance which the EU planned to start in 2013 and 2014. These included, inter alia, proposals to improve the quality of corporate governance reporting; to give shareholders more oversight of directors' remuneration; and to require institutional investors to disclose their voting and engagement policies. The EU Commission's recommendation on the quality of corporate governance reporting ('comply or explain' principle) aims to improve the quality of corporate governance statements and especially the quality of explanations where companies have not complied with code recommendations. In such cases, companies should clearly state why they have not complied with a particular principle, why they have departed from it, and how they reached the decision to depart from the principle. If they have taken any mitigating measures against their non-compliance with a particular principle, they should also mention this.

An EU Directive on Disclosure of Non-Financial and Diversity Information issued in 2014 states that large companies have to publish reports on the policies they implement in relation to environmental protection; social responsibility and treatment of employees; respect for human rights; anti-corruption and bribery; and diversity on company boards (in terms of age, gender, educational, and professional background).

In March 2017 the European Parliament voted on the revised EU Shareholders' Rights Directive. The Directive should enter into force two years after its publication in the Official Journal. The Directive covers many aspects of investor and company relations and interaction including stronger shareholders' rights and facilitation of cross-border voting; long-term engagement of institutional investors and asset managers; more transparency of proxy advisors; a 'say on pay' for shareholders; and some stricter aspects for related party transactions.

Following Brexit, in November 2017 the EU issued a notice to stakeholders regarding the withdrawal of the UK from the EU and the EU rules on company law which highlighted areas of EU company law which will no longer apply to the UK after its withdrawal from the EU, for example, UK incorporated companies will be classed as third country companies.

Basle Committee

The Basle Committee (1999) guidelines related to enhancing corporate governance in banking organizations. The guidelines have been influential in the development of corporate governance practices in banks across the world. Sound governance can be practised regardless of the form of a banking organization. The Basle Committee issued updated guidance, *Enhancing Corporate Governance for Banking Organisations* (2006). However, following on from various corporate governance failures and lapses that came to light in subsequent years, the Committee revisited the 2006 guidance. Taking into account the lessons learned during the financial crisis, the Committee reviewed and revised the Principles and reaffirmed their continued relevance and the critical importance of their adoption by banks and supervisors. The Committee issued its *Principles for Enhancing Corporate Governance* (2010) and identified some key areas—board practices; senior management; risk management and internal controls; compensation; complex or opaque corporate structures; and disclosure and transparency—which it believed should be the areas of greatest focus and listed 14 Principles in relation to these.

In 2015, the Committee issued a revised set of principles *Corporate Governance Principles for Banks*. There are 13 principles covering: board's overall responsibilities; board qualifications and composition; board's own structure and practices; senior management; governance of group structures; risk management function; risk identification, monitoring, and controlling; risk communication; compliance; internal audit; compensation; disclosure and transparency; and the role of supervisors. The revised guidance 'emphasises the critical importance of effective corporate governance for the safe and sound functioning of banks. It stresses the importance of risk governance as part of a bank's overall corporate governance framework and promotes the value of strong boards and board committees together with effective control functions.'

US corporate governance

Like the UK, the USA has a well-developed market with a diverse shareholder base, including institutional investors, financial institutions, and individuals. It also has many of the agency problems associated with the separation of corporate ownership from corporate control.

In the USA there have been various state and federal developments over a number of years, although the passage of Sarbanes–Oxley (2002), the New York Stock Exchange (NYSE) Corporate Governance Rules (2003), and subsequent developments signalled more national developments in corporate governance. Some idiosyncratic features of the USA include: the Delaware General Corporation Law, which essentially gives companies incorporated in Delaware certain advantages; and the Employee Retirement Income Security Act 1974 (ERISA), which mandates private pension funds to vote their shares. Each of these is now dealt with in more detail.

Delaware corporate law

Over the years Delaware has built up a body of corporate case law that has become the norm in corporate America. The Delaware approach has been seen as 'company friendly' and indeed the majority of US companies listed on the NYSE are registered in Delaware in order to be able to take advantage of the more flexible non-prescriptive approach. The emphasis is on giving boards of directors the authority to pursue corporate strategy and objectives whilst at the same time operating within the concept of fiduciary duty (usually this would mean acting in the best interests of the shareholders, who are the ultimate beneficiaries of the company). In addition, there are certain statutory requirements that need to be abided by, such as protection of minority interests. However, on balance, the Delaware law is less procedural than other state law in the USA and hence Delaware is an attractive state in which to register a company.

Employee Retirement Income Security Act 1974 (ERISA)

ERISA established federal statutory duties of loyalty and prudence for trustees and managers of private pension funds. ERISA has been interpreted as effectively mandating private pension funds to vote their shares, and this includes not just shares held in the USA (domestic shares), but shares held overseas too. It is recommended that a cost–benefit analysis be carried out before purchasing overseas shareholdings to ensure that it will be viable (cost-effective) to vote the overseas shares. Whilst public pension funds are not covered by ERISA, as private pension funds are mandated to vote, there is an expectation that public pension funds will also vote, and this has been the case in practice.

Sarbanes-Oxley Act 2002

Following directly from the financial scandals of Enron, Worldcom, and Global Crossing, in which it was perceived that the close relationship between companies and their external auditors was largely to blame, the US Congress agreed reforms together with changes to the NYSE Listing Rules that have had a significant impact not just in the USA but around the world. The changes are embodied in the Accounting Industry Reform Act 2002, widely known as the 'Sarbanes-Oxley Act'.

Initially, one of the most publicized aspects of the Sarbanes-Oxley Act was the require-ment for chief executive officers (CEOs) and chief finance officers to certify that quarterly and annual reports filed on forms 10-Q, 10-K, and 20-F are fully compliant with applicable securities laws and present a fair picture of the financial situation of the company. The penal-ties for making this certification when aware that the information does not comply with the requirements are severe: up to US$1 million fine or imprisonment of up to ten years, or both.

The Sarbanes-Oxley Act seeks to strengthen (external) auditor independence and also to strengthen the company's audit committee. The Act establishes a new regulatory body for auditors of US-listed firms—the Public Company Accounting Oversight Board (PCAOB)—with which all auditors of US-listed companies have to register, including non-US audit firms. Correspondingly, the Securities Exchange Commission (SEC) has issued separate rules that encompass the prohibition of some non-audit services to audit clients, mandatory rotation of audit partners, and auditors' reports on the effectiveness of internal controls.

The Sarbanes-Oxley Act provides for far-reaching reform and has caused much disquiet outside the USA because the Act applies equally to US and non-US firms with a US listing. However, some of the provisions of the Sarbanes-Oxley Act are in direct conflict with provi-sions in the law/practice of other countries. In reality, this has led to some companies delisting from the NYSE and has deterred other non-US firms from applying to be listed on the NYSE.

Commission on Public Trust and Private Enterprise 2003

The Commission on Public Trust and Private Enterprise was formed by the Conference Board, an influential US-based non-profit-making organization, to look at the circumstances that gave rise to corporate scandals, which resulted in a loss of confidence in the US markets. The Commission's work focused on three main areas: executive compensation, corporate governance, and auditing and accounting. The Commission issued its report on executive compensation in 2002 and this is covered in Chapter 9; the second report, being on corporate governance, and auditing and accounting, was issued in early 2003.

The Commission listed nine principles relating to corporate governance, which cover the following areas:

- relationship of the board and management;
- fulfilling the board's responsibilities;
- director qualifications;
- role of the nominating/governance committee;
- board evaluation;
- ethics oversight;
- hiring special investigative counsel;
- shareowner involvement;
- long-term share ownership.

In relation to the board, the Commission recommends that careful thought should be given to separating the roles of chairman and CEO. This is an interesting development because the roles of chairman and CEO have traditionally tended to be combined in US companies. By splitting these roles, as in the UK, the US corporations would achieve the separation of the running of the board of directors (chairman) from the executive running of the business (chief executive).

In relation to audit and accounting, the Commission states seven principles:

- Principle 1—the enhanced role of the audit committee.
- Principle 2—audit committee education.
- Principle 3—improving internal controls and internal auditing.
- Principle 4—auditor rotation.
- Principle 5—professional advisors for the audit committee.
- Principle 6—services performed by accounting firms.
- Principle 7—the business model of accounting firms.

The Commission views the seven principles as strengthening the reforms begun by the Sarbanes-Oxley Act and the NYSE, and hopes that they will help to restore public confidence in audit firms, audited financial statements, and hence in the market generally.

NYSE Corporate Governance Rules (2003)

In November 2003 the Securities and Exchange Commission approved new rules on corporate governance proposed and adopted by the NYSE and the Nasdaq Stock Market. The rules include that the majority of directors are independent and give detailed guidance on who would be classed as independent; and that a nominating/corporate governance committee, a compensation committee, and an audit committee should each be established and be comprised entirely of independent directors. The new rules mean a significant strengthening of corporate governance standards for listed companies and are designed to enable the directors, officers, and employees to operate more effectively. The new rules should also enable shareholders to monitor the companies better in terms of their performance, and hopefully to reduce the incidences of corporate scandals or collapses.

NACD Key Agreed Principles to Strengthen Corporate Governance for US Publicly Traded Companies (2008)

The National Association of Corporate Directors issued its *Key Agreed Principles to Strengthen Corporate Governance for US Publicly Traded Companies (2008)* with the aim of encouraging thoughtful governance rather than a 'tick box' approach. The Principles are as follows:

- Principle 1—board responsibility for governance.
- Principle 2—corporate governance transparency.
- Principle 3—director competency and commitment.
- Principle 4—board accountability and objectivity.
- Principle 5—independent board leadership.
- Principle 6—integrity, ethics, and responsibility.
- Principle 7—attention to information, agenda, and strategy.
- Principle 8—protection against board entrenchment.
- Principle 9—shareholder input in director selection.
- Principle 10—shareholder communications.

Dodd-Frank Wall Street Reform and Consumer Protection Act (2010)

In July 2010 the USA passed the Dodd-Frank Wall Street Reform and Consumer Protection Act that amended US requirements relating to executive compensation practices in a number of respects. From mid-2011 the SEC required listed companies compensation committee members to be independent directors. There are new 'say on pay' provisions such that the Act requires that, at least once every three years, there is a shareholder advisory vote to approve the company's executive compensation, as well as to approve 'golden parachute' compensation arrangements. Whilst the 'say on pay' takes place at least once every three years, it may occur every year.

In 2015 the SEC adopted amendments to Section 953(b) of the Dodd-Frank Wall Street Reform and Consumer Protection Act, and Item 402(u) of Regulation S-K, on pay ratio disclosure such that companies must provide details of the relationship of the annual total compensation of their employees and the annual total compensation of their CEO, i.e. the ratio of the CEO pay to the median of the annual total compensation of all employees. This applies to companies for their first fiscal year beginning on or after 1 January 2017.

New York Stock Exchange (NYSE) Commission on Corporate Governance (2010)

The NYSE Commission on Corporate Governance was established in 2009 to examine core governance principles that could achieve broad consensus from amongst various market participants. The Commission reported in September 2010 with ten principles covering the board's fundamental objective; the responsibility for creating an environment in which a culture of performance with integrity can flourish; the right and responsibilities of shareholders to vote their shares; the integration of good corporate governance with the company's business strategy and objectives; a preference for market-based solutions once the 'basic tenets' of corporate governance have been established by law and agency rule-making; transparency, disclosure, and communication via dialogue and engagement; independence and objectivity are needed for board members but also a mix of expertise, diversity, and knowledge on the board; proxy advisory firms should have appropriate standards of transparency and accountability; the SEC should work with the NYSE and other exchanges to reduce the burden of proxy voting and also encourage more participation by individual investors in the proxy voting process; and finally the SEC and/or the NYSE should take into account a wide range of views when considering the impact of major corporate governance reforms on corporate performance in the last 10 years. Likewise the impact of such reforms on the promotion of sustainable, long-term corporate growth and sustained profitability should be considered periodically.

Investor Stewardship Group (ISG) Corporate Governance Principles for Listed Companies (2017)

The Investor Stewardship Group (ISG) is a collective of some of the largest US-based institutional investors and global asset managers, along with several of their international counterparts. The ISG was formed to bring all types of investors together to establish a framework of basic standards of investment stewardship and corporate governance for US institutional investor and boardroom conduct. The framework is not intended to replace or supersede any existing federal or state law and regulation, or any listing rules that apply to a company or an institutional investor.

The corporate governance framework articulates six principles that the ISG believes are fundamental to good corporate governance at US-listed companies. They are designed to establish a foundational set of investor expectations about corporate governance practices in US publicly listed companies. There are six principles detailed in the *Corporate Governance Principles for Listed Companies* (2017) as follows:

Principle 1: Boards are accountable to shareholders.

Principle 2: Shareholders should be entitled to voting rights in proportion to their economic interest.

Principle 3: Boards should be responsive to shareholders and be proactive in order to understand their perspectives.

Principle 4: Boards should have a strong, independent leadership structure.

Principle 5: Boards should adopt structures and practices that enhance their effectiveness.

Principle 6: Boards should develop management incentive structures that are aligned with the long-term strategy of the company.

The ISG encourages company directors to apply the corporate governance principles at the companies on whose boards they serve.

Investor Stewardship Group (ISG) Stewardship Framework for Institutional Investors (2017)

The stewardship framework seeks to articulate a set of fundamental stewardship responsibilities for institutional investors who should implement the stewardship principles in a manner they deem appropriate. The ISG encourages institutional investors to be transparent in their proxy voting and engagement guidelines and to align them with the stewardship principles.

There are six principles which form the *Stewardship Framework for Institutional Investors (2017)* as follows:

Principle A: Institutional investors are accountable to those whose money they invest.

Principle B: Institutional investors should demonstrate how they evaluate corporate governance factors with respect to the companies in which they invest.

Principle C: Institutional investors should disclose, in general terms, how they manage potential conflicts of interest that may arise in their proxy voting and engagement activities.

Principle D: Institutional investors are responsible for proxy voting decisions and should monitor the relevant activities and policies of third parties that advise them on those decisions.

Principle E: Institutional investors should address and attempt to resolve differences with companies in a constructive and pragmatic manner.

Principle F: Institutional investors should work together, where appropriate, to encourage the adoption and implementation of the Corporate Governance and Stewardship principles.

Non-Governmental Organizations (NGOs), public sector, non-profit organizations, and charities

As mentioned earlier there is an increased focus on the governance of NGOs, the public sector, non-profit organizations, and charities. Such organizations may play a key role in providing social services, the provision of healthcare and education, as well as raising funds for a variety of charitable causes.

In 2005 the Independent Commission for Good Governance in Public Services, chaired by Sir Alan Langlands, produced the *Good Governance Standard for Public Services*. The Standard presents six principles of good governance that are common to all public service organizations and are intended to help all those with an interest in public governance to assess good governance practice. It is intended for use by all organizations and partnerships that work for the public, using public money.

The National Council for Voluntary Organisations (NCVO) is a registered charity and is the largest umbrella body for the voluntary and community sector in England. In June 2005 it published *Good Governance: A Code for the Voluntary and Community Sector*. In October 2010, the NCVO published the second edition of the Code. The Code is based on an 'apply or explain' approach; the NCVO anticipate that the 'apply or explain' principle will be adopted. If one good governance characteristic appears not to be valid in a particular setting, then an alternative may be sought, but organizations should be pre-pared to give reasons for that decision. The six principles of good governance have been designed to be valid for the entire voluntary and community sector. The Code states that an effective board will provide good governance and leadership by understanding their role, ensuring delivery of organizational purpose, working effectively both as individuals and as a team, exercising effective control, behaving with integrity, and being open and accountable.

The Charity Commission for England and Wales is established by law as the regulator and registrar of charities in England and Wales. Their aim is to provide the best possible regula-tion of these charities in order to increase charities' efficiency and effectiveness and public confidence and trust in them. In 2017 the Charity Governance Code Steering Group (CGCSG) published two corporate governance codes, being the *Charity Governance Code for Larger Charities* (2017) and the *Charity Governance Code for Smaller Charities* (2017). The CGCSG is a cross-sector collaboration with an independent chair; the Charity Commission is an observer on the group. The seven Code principles relate to organizational purpose; leadership; integ-rity; decision-making, risk, and control; board effectiveness; diversity; and openness and accountability. The CGCSG recommends that charities with a typical income of over £1 mil-lion a year, and whose accounts are externally audited, use the larger version and charities below this threshold use the smaller version. The Code uses an 'apply or explain' approach and is not a legal or regulatory requirement for charities. Whilst this Code is intended for use by charities, much of it will also apply to other not-for-profit organizations that deliver a public or community benefit and those with a social purpose. Some charities work in areas, such as housing and sport, which have their own sector-specific governance codes which may then take precedence over this Code.

In the UK the National Health Service (NHS) is comprised of various types of trust, includ-ing, inter alia, acute trusts (hospitals) and primary care trusts. For these trusts, non-exec-utive director appointments are made by the Appointments Commission. However, there are also foundation trusts which have more independence. These are regulated by Monitor which is the independent regulator of NHS foundation trusts. It is independent of central government, is directly accountable to Parliament, and was established in January 2004 to authorize and regulate NHS foundation trusts. Monitor has developed a non-executive director development programme to help ensure that non-executive directors are aware of their role and duties in this area and have a good understanding of the health sector. The *NHS Foundation Trust Code of Governance (2014)* provides guidance for NHS foundation trusts to help ensure that trust boards are founded on, and supported by, strong govern-ance structures. The Code draws on the principles of the UK Corporate Governance Code. NHS Direct has adopted the 'Codes of Conduct and Accountability' from the Department of Health, and all members of the board are required to act in accordance with the Codes. In addition, the board of directors have adopted the public service values detailed within the Nolan Report.

Whilst the codes and guidelines on NGOs, the public sector, non-profit organizations, and charities discussed earlier relate to the UK, there are similar developments in many countries around the world, all seeking to ensure that these types of organizations in their country are governed to best effect, to ensure appropriate use of funds, effective management, and to help maintain confidence in them.

Conclusions

Corporate governance is very much an evolving area. In recent years its development has been driven by the need to restore investor confidence in capital markets. Investors and governments alike have been proactive in seeking reforms that will ensure that corporate boards are more accountable, that qualified independent non-executive (outside) directors can play a key role, that audit committees are able to operate effectively, and that external audit firms are able to perform their audits properly and appropriately. These measures will also help ensure that the rights of shareholders are protected.

However, the recent global financial crisis has highlighted that, despite all the developments in corporate governance codes across the world, there are still evident deficiencies. For example, powerful individuals are still able to exercise too much power without appropriate restraint; boards of directors have not taken adequate account of the risks their business may be subject to; independent non-executive directors may not have had the skills and experience to question effectively the use of complex instruments, which subsequently became 'toxic assets'; executive directors' compensation has seemingly often not been linked to appropriate performance measures; and generous remuneration packages and hefty pension pots have caused concern amongst government, investors, and the public alike.

Many of the codes operate using a 'comply or explain' basis and, as we have seen, this means either that a company has to comply fully with the code and state that it has done so, or that it explains why it has not complied fully. Investors will therefore be able to determine to what extent a company has or has not complied, and to assess the company's stated reasons for non-compliance. Investor pressure would tend to be the most immediate response to non-compliance, and such instances may lead investors—particularly those who can exert significant influence on the company, for example, because of the size of their shareholding—to seek further information/assurance from the directors. There has been some discussion about whether 'apply or explain' might be a more appropriate wording than 'comply or explain' as it may be that some companies comply only with those principles which they consider cost-effective, or which they wish to comply with, and then they explain why they don't comply with the other principles. It is fair to say that 'apply or explain' carries with it more of an expectation that companies will apply the principles and therefore that the incidences of 'explain' will be fewer.

We have seen the influence of the Cadbury Code and the OECD Principles on the development of corporate governance codes in many countries. We have discussed the roles of several international bodies—such as the World Bank, the GCGF, the ICGN, and the CACG—in the development of corporate governance globally. The report of the EU High-Level Group of Company Law Experts and the subsequent corporate governance reforms have had implications for company law and corporate governance across Europe. The EU Action Plan on European Company Law and Corporate Governance has a continuing impact on corporate governance in the EU. The impact of legislation in the USA, the Sarbanes-Oxley Act, and further developments in US corporate governance, especially in the light of the meltdown in the financial markets, has been highlighted. The growth and importance of governance for NGOs, the public sector, non-profit organizations, and charities have also been discussed.

Whilst one can argue that a single model of corporate governance is not suitable for all countries—and certainly the stage of development of the country, its cultural traditions, legal structure, and ownership structure make it unlikely that one model would be appropriate for all countries at any given time—we have seen that there are common core principles that have been influential in the setting of codes across the globe. Whilst there should be flexibility in individual countries, it would seem that there is also a recognition of the key elements of good corporate governance in an international dimension. The latest global financial crisis led to calls for action to be taken on a global basis, encouraging countries to co-operate and work together more to try to restore confidence in shattered markets.

There seems to be more emphasis being placed on the appropriate management of risk and also on corporate culture. A corporate culture which advocates and actively promotes ethics and integrity is also one which will nurture robust corporate governance and enable effective risk management. This can only be to the benefit of shareholders and other stakeholders.

Summary

- The development of corporate governance has been driven, to a large extent, by the desire for more transparency and accountability to help restore investor confidence in the world's stock markets after the damage caused by financial scandals and corporate collapses.

- The Cadbury Code and the OECD Principles, in particular, have each played a major role in the development of corporate governance codes around the world.

- The Cadbury Code's main recommendations include the establishment of key board committees (audit and remuneration), with a nomination committee suggested as an appropriate way to ensure a transparent appointments process; the appointment of at least three independent non-executive (outside) directors; and the separation of roles of chairman and CEO.

- The Cadbury Code utilizes a best practice 'comply or explain' approach in contrast to a mandatory or legislative approach.

- The G20/OECD Principles (2015) encompass six main areas: ensuring the basis for an effective corporate governance framework; the rights and equitable treatment of shareholders and key ownership functions; institutional investors, stock markets, and other intermediaries; the role of stakeholders in corporate governance; disclosure and transparency; and the responsibilities of the board.

- Following a few years after the publication of the Cadbury Report, the Greenbury Report on disclosure of directors' remuneration, and the Hampel Report, which reviewed the implementation of the Cadbury and Greenbury recommendations, were published. In 2003 the Combined Code was revised to take into account the Higgs and Smith Reviews. The Combined Code was further revised in 2006, 2008, and 2009, culminating in the UK Corporate Governance Code (2010); the UK Stewardship Code was also issued in 2010. The UK Corporate Governance Code has been revised several times, most recently in 2018. The UK Stewardship Code was revised in 2012 with a revised version expected later in 2018. UK companies law has also been through a major update with the enactment of the Companies Act 2006.

- The Davies Reports have had a significant influence on increasing board gender diversity in UK companies. The subsequent Hampton-Alexander Review (2017) also focuses on gender diversity whilst the Parker Review (2017) focuses on ethnic diversity on boards.

- A number of influential organizations have issued corporate governance guidelines/ statements or have been instrumental in the implementation of better corporate governance globally. These organizations include the World Bank, the GCGF, the CACG, and the ICGN.

- The EU High-Level Group of Company Law Experts reported in 2002, making various corporate governance recommendations for listed companies. The *Green Paper on the EU Corporate Governance Framework* discusses boards, shareholders, and the 'comply or explain' principle. The EU Action Plan on European Company Law and Corporate Governance seeks to improve the quality of corporate governance reporting; to give shareholders more oversight of directors' remuneration; and to require institutional investors to disclose their voting and engagement policies.

- The USA has a number of interesting features, including the Delaware General Corporation Law, which gives companies incorporated in Delaware certain advantages, and ERISA, which mandates private pension funds to vote their shares.

- The US Sarbanes-Oxley Act is far reaching, encompassing not only US firms but non-US firms with a US listing. The Act seeks to strengthen auditor independence and also establishes a new regulatory body for auditors for US-listed firms—the Public Company Accounting Oversight Board—with which all auditors of US-listed companies, including non-US audit firms, have to register.

- The US issued the Dodd-Frank Wall Street Reform and Consumer Protection Act (2010) which introduced the 'say on pay' and other remuneration-related provisions more widely. The NYSE Commission on Corporate Governance (2010) introduced further corporate governance principles.

- There is an increased focus on the governance of NGOs, the public sector, non-profit organizations, and charities reflecting the fact that these organizations need to be seen to have effective boards and to utilize public funds in an appropriate way.

Questions

The discussion questions to follow cover the key learning points of this chapter. Reading of some of the additional reference material will enhance the depth of the students' knowledge and understanding of these areas.

1. What have been the main influences on the development of corporate governance codes and guidelines? What might be the shortcomings in the implementation of corporate governance codes and guidelines?

2. Critically discuss whether it would be desirable to have one model of corporate governance applicable to all countries.

3. What are the advantages and disadvantages of a 'comply or explain' model of corporate governance? How does this compare to a mandatory model?

4. In what ways might the *G20/OECD Principles of Corporate Governance* help improve shareholders' rights?

5. In what ways might the legal and cultural context of a country impact on the development of the corporate governance model in a given country?

6. Why is good governance important in NGOs, the public sector, non-profit organizations, and charities? How might it best be achieved?

References

Auditing Practices Board (2004), *Ethical Standards for Auditors*, FRC, London.

Auditing Practices Board (2008), *Revised Ethical Standards for Auditors*, FRC, London.

Basle Committee on Banking Supervision (1999), *Enhancing Corporate Governance for Banking Organisations*, Bank for International Settlements, Basle.

Basle Committee on Banking Supervision (2006), *Enhancing Corporate Governance for Banking Organisations*, Bank for International Settlements, Basle.

Basle Committee on Banking Supervision (2010), *Principles for Enhancing Corporate Governance*, Bank for International Settlements, Basle.

Basle Committee on Banking Supervision (2015), *Corporate Governance Principles for Banks*, Bank for International Settlements, Basle.

Cadbury, Sir Adrian (1992), Report of the Committee on the Financial Aspects of Corporate Governance, Gee & Co. Ltd, London.

Capital Market Commission, Athens (1999), *Principles on Corporate Governance in Greece: Recommendations for its Competitive Transformation*, Capital Market Commission, Athens.

Charity Governance Code Steering Group (2017a), *Charity Governance Code for Larger Charities* (2017), London, UK.

Charity Governance Code Steering Group (2017b), *Charity Governance Code for Smaller Charities* (2017), London, UK.

China Securities Regulatory Commission (2001), *Code of Corporate Governance for Listed Companies in China*, China Securities Regulatory Commission, State Economic Trade Commission, Beijing.

Combined Code (1998), *Combined Code, Principles of Corporate Governance*, Gee & Co. Ltd, London.

Combined Code (2003), *The Combined Code on Corporate Governance*, FRC, London.

Combined Code (2006), *The Combined Code on Corporate Governance*, FRC, London.

Combined Code (2008), *The Combined Code on Corporate Governance*, FRC, London.

Companies (Miscellaneous Reporting) Regulations (2018), UK Statutory Instrument, London.

Conference Board (2003), *Commission on Public Trust and Private Enterprise Findings and Recommendations Part 2: Corporate Governance and Part 3: Audit and Accounting*, Conference Board, New York.

Davies E.M. (2011), *Women on Boards*, BIS, London.

Davies E.M. (2012), *Women on Boards, One Year On*, BIS, London.

Davies E.M. (2015), *Women on Boards, Five Year Summary*, BIS, London.

de Larosière, J. (2009), *High-Level Group on Financial Supervision in the EU*, EU, Brussels.

Department for Business, Energy & Industrial Strategy (BEIS) (2016), *Green Paper on Corporate Governance*, UK Government, London.

Department for Business, Energy & Industrial Strategy (BEIS) (2017), *Corporate Governance Reform: The Government response to the green paper consultation*, UK Government, London.

Dodd-Frank Wall Street Reform and Consumer Protection Act (2010), US Congress, Washington DC.

Employee Retirement Income Security Act (1974), Department of Labor, Washington DC.

European Union (2011), *Green Paper, The EU Corporate Governance Framework*, European Commission, Brussels.

European Union (2012), *Action Plan: European Company Law and Corporate Governance—a modern legal framework for more engaged shareholders and sustainable companies*, European Commission, Brussels.

European Union (2014a), *Shareholder Rights Directive*, European Commission, Brussels.

European Union (2014b), Directive on Disclosure of Non-Financial and Diversity Information, European Commission, Brussels.

Financial Reporting Council (2007), *Review of the Impact of the Combined Code*, FRC, London.

Financial Reporting Council (2009), *Going Concern and Liquidity Risk: Guidance for Directors of UK Companies*, FRC, London

Financial Reporting Council (2010a), *Guidance on Board Effectiveness*, FRC, London.

Financial Reporting Council (2010b), *UK Corporate Governance Code*, FRC, London.

Financial Reporting Council (2010c), *UK Stewardship Code*, FRC, London.

Financial Reporting Council (2011a), *Developments in Corporate Governance 2011: The impact and implementation of the UK Corporate Governance and Stewardship Codes*, FRC, London.

Financial Reporting Council (2011b), *Boards and Risk. A Summary of Discussions with Boards, Investors and Advisers*, September 2011, FRC, London.

Financial Reporting Council (2012a), *What Constitutes An Explanation Under 'Comply or Explain'? Report of Discussions Between Companies and Investors*, FRC, London.

Financial Reporting Council (2012b), *UK Corporate Governance Code*, FRC, London.

Financial Reporting Council (2012c), *UK Stewardship Code*, FRC, London.

Financial Reporting Council (2014a), *UK Corporate Governance Code*, FRC, London.

Financial Reporting Council (2014b), *Guidance on Risk Management, Internal Control and Related Financial and Business Reporting*, September 2014, FRC, London.

Financial Reporting Council (2014c), *Guidance on the Strategic Report*, FRC, London.

Financial Reporting Council (2015), *Developments in Corporate Governance and Stewardship 2014*, FRC, London.

Financial Reporting Council (2016a), *Corporate Culture and the Role of Boards*, FRC, London.

Financial Reporting Council (2016b), *Developments in Corporate Governance and Stewardship 2015*, FRC, London.

Financial Reporting Council (2016c), *Guidance on Audit Committees*, FRC, London.

Financial Reporting Council (2017a), *Developments in Corporate Governance and Stewardship 2016*, FRC, London.

Financial Reporting Council (2017b), *Proposed Revisions to the UK Corporate Governance Code 2017*, FRC, London.

Financial Reporting Council (2018a) *Guidance on Board Effectiveness*, FRC, London.

Financial Reporting Council (2018b) *The UK Corporate Governance Code (2018)*, FRC, London.

Financial Reporting Council (2018c) *The Wates Corporate Governance Principles for Large Private Companies 2018*, FRC, London.

Greenbury, Sir Richard (1995), *Directors' Remuneration*, Gee & Co. Ltd, London.

Hampel, Sir Ronnie (1998), *Committee on Corporate Governance: Final Report*, Gee & Co. Ltd, London.

Hampton-Alexander Review (2017), *Improving Gender Balance in FTSE Leadership*, FTSE Women Leaders, sponsored by KPMG, London.

Hermes (2013), *Responsible Ownership Principles*, Hermes, London.

Hermes (2017), *Stewardship*, Hermes, London.

Hermes (2018), *Corporate Governance Principles, United Kingdom*, Hermes, London.

HM Treasury (2008), *Updating the Myners Principles: A Response to Consultation*, Her Majesty's Treasury, London.

Higgs, D. (2003), *Review of the Role and Effectiveness of Non-Executive Directors*, Department of Trade and Industry, London.

International Corporate Governance Network (1999), *Statement on Global Corporate Governance Principles*, ICGN, London.

International Corporate Governance Network (2005), *Statement on Global Corporate Governance Principles*, ICGN, London.

International Corporate Governance Network (2009), *ICGN Global Corporate Governance Principles (Revised) 2009*, ICGN, London.

International Corporate Governance Network (2014), *ICGN Global Governance Principles*, ICGN, London.

International Corporate Governance Network (2015), *Global Stewardship Principles*, ICGN, London.

International Corporate Governance Network (2017), *ICGN Global Governance Principles*, ICGN, London.

Investor Stewardship Group (2017a), *Corporate Governance Principles for Listed Companies (2017)*.

Investor Stewardship Group (2017b), *Stewardship Framework for Institutional Investors (2017)*.

ISS, ECGI, and Shearman & Sterling (2007), *Report on the Proportionality Principle in the European Union*, EU, Brussels.

Langlands, Sir A. (2005), *Good Governance Standard for Public Services*, The Independent Commission for Good Governance in Public Services, Office for Public Management and the Chartered Institute of Public Finance and Accountancy in partnership with the Joseph Rowntree Foundation, London.

Monitor (2014), *NHS Foundation Trust Code of Governance*, UK Government, London.

Myners Report (2001), *Myners Report on Institutional Investment*, HM Treasury, London.

National Association of Corporate Directors (NACD) (2008), *Key Agreed Principles to Strengthen Corporate Governance for U.S. Publicly Traded Companies*, NACD, Washington DC.

National Association of Pension Funds (2007), *Institutional Investment in the UK: Six Years On*, NAPF, London.

National Council for Voluntary Organisations (2005), *Good Governance: A Code for the Voluntary and Community Sector*, published by NCVO on behalf of the *National Hub of Expertise in Governance*, London.

National Council for Voluntary Organisations (2010), *Good Governance: A Code for the Voluntary and Community Sector*, published by NCVO on behalf of the National Hub of Expertise in Governance, London.

New York Stock Exchange (2003), *Final NYSE Corporate Governance Rules*, NYSE, New York.

New York Stock Exchange (2010), *Report of the New York Stock Exchange Commission on Corporate Governance*, New York.

Organisation for Economic Co-operation and Development (1999), *Principles of Corporate Governance*, OECD, Paris.

Organisation for Economic Co-operation and Development (2004), *Principles of Corporate Governance*, OECD, Paris.

Organisation for Economic Co-operation and Development (2006), *Methodology for Assessing Implementation of the OECD Principles of Corporate Governance*, OECD, Paris.

Organisation for Economic Co-operation and Development (2008), *Using the OECD Principles of Corporate Governance: A Boardroom Perspective*, OECD, Paris.

Organisation for Economic Co-operation and Development (2010), *Corporate Governance and the Financial Crisis: Conclusions and Emerging Good Practices to Enhance Implementation of the Principles*, OECD, Paris.

Organisation for Economic Co-operation and Development (2011), *Board Practices, Incentives and Governing Risks*, OECD, Paris.

Organisation for Economic Co-operation and Development (2014), *Principles of Corporate Governance–Draft for Public Comment November 2014*, OECD, Paris.

Organisation for Economic Co-operation and Development (2015), *G20/OECD Principles of Corporate Governance*, OECD, Paris.

Parker Review (2017), *A Report into Ethnic Diversity of UK Boards: 'Beyond One by '21'*, sponsored by EY and Linklaters, London.

Sarbanes–Oxley Act (2002), US Legislature.

Smith, Sir Robert (2003), *Audit Committees Combined Code Guidance*, FRC, London.

Smith, Sir Robert (2008), *Guidance on Audit Committees*, FRC, London.

Turnbull, N. (1999), *Internal Control: Guidance for Directors on the Combined Code*, Institute of Chartered Accountants in England and Wales, London.

Turnbull, N. (2005), *Internal Control: Revised Guidance for Directors on the Combined Code*, FRC, London.

Turner, A. (2009), *The Turner Review–A Regulatory Response to the Global Banking Crisis*, Financial Services Authority, London.

Tyson, L. (2003), *The Tyson Report on the Recruitment and Development of Non-Executive Directors*, London Business School, London.

UK Government (2017), *Growing a Culture of Social Impact Investing in the UK*, London.

Walker, D. (2009), *A Review of Corporate Governance in UK Banks and Other Financial Industry Entities, Final Recommendations*, HM Treasury, London.

Winter, J. (2002), *Report of the High-Level Group of Company Law Experts on a Modern Regulatory Framework for Company Law in Europe*, European Commission, Brussels.

Useful websites

www.accaglobal.com The website of the Association of Chartered Certified Accountants gives information about corporate governance and their related activities.

www.bankofengland.co.uk The website of the Prudential Regulation Authority (PRA) which is a part of the Bank of England and responsible for the prudential regulation and supervision of banks, building societies, credit unions, insurers, and major investment firms.

www.bis.gov.uk The website of the Department for Business, Innovation & Skills (created in June 2009 from the merger of the Department for Business, Enterprise and Regulatory Reform and the Department for Innovation, Universities and Skills) contains information about the Department's activities.

www.bis.org The website of the Bank for International Settlements contains information about central banks and other agencies and has the full text of the Basle Committee corporate governance recommendations.

www.gov.uk/government/organisations/charity-commission The website of the Charity Commission for England and Wales.

www.conference-board.org The Conference Board website gives details of their corporate governance activities and publications.

www.ecgi.global The European Corporate Governance Institute website has details of global corporate governance developments. Corporate governance codes for countries around the world are listed and in most cases can be downloaded.

www.fca.org.uk The website of the Financial Conduct Authority (FCA) which regulates the financial services industry in the UK.

www.frc.org.uk The Financial Reporting Council's website contains details of its activities and those of its operating bodies.

www.fsa.gov.uk The Financial Services Authority (FSA) has now become two separate regulatory authorities, the PRA and the FCA. The FSA website is no longer updated but retains links to documents such as The Turner Review.

www.hm-treasury.gov.uk The website of Her Majesty's Treasury.

www.icaew.com The website of the Institute of Chartered Accountants in England and Wales provides updates on corporate governance issues.

www.icgn.org This website contains information about corporate governance developments and guidelines issued by the International Corporate Governance Network.

www.icsa.org.uk This website of the Institute of Chartered Secretaries and Administrators contains useful information about various aspects of corporate governance.

www.improvement.nhs.uk NHS Improvement is responsible for overseeing foundation trusts and NHS trusts, as well as independent providers that provide NHS-funded care. The activities of Monitor are now part of NHS Improvement.

www.legislation.gov.uk This website brings together the legislative content previously held on the OPSI website and revised legislation from the Statute Law Database to provide a single legislation service.

www.ncvo-vol.org.uk The website of the National Council for Voluntary Organisations.

www.oecd.org The OECD website contains useful information relating to corporate governance for both member and non-member states.

www.plsa.co.uk The Pensions and Lifetime Savings Association (PLSA) website contains useful information relating to various aspects of pensions and lifetime savings for pension professionals and individuals. Formerly the National Association of Pension Funds (NAPF).

www.theinvestmentassociation.org The Investment Association is the trade body that represents UK investment managers.

www.ukgi.org.uk UK Government Investments (UKGI) is the government's centre of excellence in corporate finance and corporate governance.

www.worldbank.org The World Bank website has information about various corporate governance developments.

Develop your understanding of this chapter and explore the subject further using our online resources at www.oup.com/uk/mallin6e/

 FT Clippings

FT: For and not-for-profit face similar tasks

By Stefan Stern

Financial Times, 28 May 2015, Executive Appointments Supplement, Page 3.

Private sector companies succeed when they give us what we want, at the right price. Not-for-profit organizations, charities or the public sector, are there to give us what they think we need. It is a fundamental difference.

Both for-profit and not-for-profit organizations require governance and many public sector institutions and charities are led by formally constituted boards. Does it follow that, because the underlying purpose of these organizations is so different, an alternative approach to governance is also required? Should these boards be assessed according to separate and distinct criteria?

A consultancy called Socia has been looking at these questions and has come up with what is perhaps a slightly surprising answer. Of course, the public sector recognizes the need to be businesslike and efficient. With the constraints on resources these days, there is no other choice.

But some in the public sector may also think that governance approaches from the private sector will have little relevance for them. In the worst case, assessing the performance of public sector boards with the values and attitudes of private ones might constitute a 'category error'. The private sector should perhaps mind its own business.

Socia recently surveyed 100 board members and then brought a selection of

public and private sector directors together to discuss its findings. It turns out that all boards worry about many similar things.

As Alex Cameron, a director of Socia, wrote in last month's Governance magazine: 'While boards in the charity and public sector will have a different mission to a PLC board when it comes to their own operation—the setting of priorities, the way they make decisions, getting access to the right skills and, critically, how they view their own performance improvement—there are far more similarities than differences.'

Far from shying away from using governance codes designed to monitor the performance of for-profit businesses, such as the UK's combined code from the Financial Reporting Council, not-for-profit organizations could benefit from deploying them.

However, as David Archer, another Socia director, points out, some charities and public sector bodies prefer the idea of submitting to an external inspection or a test that has to be passed rather adopting the FRC's 'comply or explain' mechanism.

Today, the public and charitable sectors are big business. In the UK, for example, the health sector now has more than 140 'Foundation Trust' hospitals, with a total annual income of £41bn. These organizations have to be led well; the consequence of failure is far reaching.

The two tribes are more alike than either side realizes and they have much to learn from each other.

Part 2

Owners and stakeholders

4

Shareholders and stakeholders

 Learning objectives

- To understand the difference between shareholders and stakeholders

- To be aware of the various different stakeholder groups

- To have an overview of the way that shareholders and stakeholders are provided for in various corporate governance codes and guidelines

- To understand the roles that shareholders and stakeholders can play in companies and the development of corporate governance

Shareholders and stakeholders

The term 'stakeholder' can encompass a wide range of interests: it refers to any individual or group on which the activities of the company have an impact. Shareholders can be viewed as a stakeholder group but, for the purposes of this discussion, we will view shareholders as being distinct from other stakeholder groups. Why? First, shareholders invest their money to provide risk capital for the company and, secondly, in many legal jurisdictions, shareholders' rights are enshrined in law whereas those of the wider group of stakeholders are not. Of course, this varies from jurisdiction to jurisdiction, with creditors' rights strongly protected in some countries, and employees' rights strongly protected in others.

As highlighted in Chapter 2 in the discussion of stakeholder theory, one rationale for effectively privileging shareholders over other stakeholders is that they are the recipients of the residual free cash flow (being the profits remaining once other stakeholders, such as loan creditors, have been paid). This means that the shareholders have a vested interest in trying to ensure that resources are used to maximum effect, which in turn should be to the benefit of society as a whole.

The simplest definition of a shareholder seems straightforward enough: an individual, institution, firm, or other entity that owns shares in a company. Of course, the reality of the situation can be much more complicated with beneficial owners and cross-holdings making the chain of ownership complex. Shareholders' rights are generally protected by law, although the extent and effectiveness of this protection varies from country to country. However, the definition of a stakeholder is much less clear and along with this lack of clarity comes an opaqueness regarding the role of stakeholders and the protection of their rights.

There are various stakeholder groups that may have an interest in a company's performance and activities. Stakeholders include: employees, suppliers, customers, banks, and

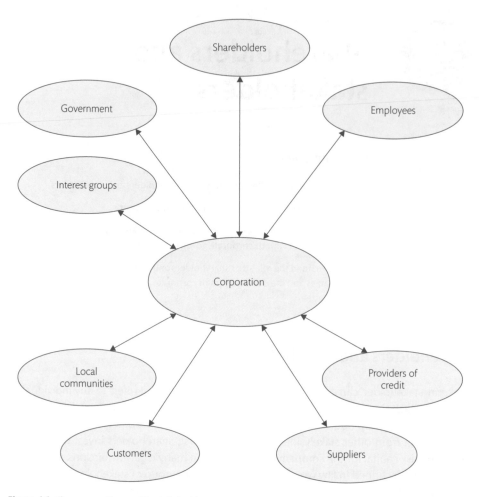

Figure 4.1 The corporation and its stakeholders

other creditors; the government; various 'interest' groups, for example, environmental groups; indeed anyone on whom the activities of the company may have an impact. Figure 4.1 illustrates the various main groups whose interests the company may need to take into account.

Stakeholder groups

There are various stakeholder groups: some directly related to the company, such as employees, providers of credit, suppliers and customers; others more indirectly related to the company, such as the local communities of the towns or cities in which it operates; environmental groups; and the government. Looking at each of these in turn, we can clarify the interest that each group might have as a stakeholder.

Employees

The employees of a company have an interest in the company because it provides their livelihood in the present day and, at some future point, employees will often also be in receipt of a pension provided by the company's pension scheme. In terms of present-day employment, employees will be concerned with their pay and working conditions, and how the company's strategy will impact on these. Of course, the long-term growth and prosperity of the company is important for the longer term view of the employees, particularly as concerns pension benefits in the future.

Most companies include, in their annual report and accounts, a statement or report to the employees stating in what ways they are looking after the employees' interests. The report will usually mention training programmes, working conditions, and equal opportunities. Many companies have employee share schemes that give the employees the opportunity to own shares in the company, and feel more of a part of it; the theory being that the better the company performs (through employees' efforts, etc.), the more the employees themselves will benefit as their shares increase in price.

Companies need also to consider and work with the employees' trade unions, recognizing that a good relationship with the unions is desirable. The trade unions may, amongst other things, act as a conduit for company employee information dissemination, or be helpful when trying to ascertain the employees' views. Increasingly, trade unions are exerting their influence, via the pension funds, pressing for change by use of their voting rights.

Companies need also to consider and comply with employee legislation, whether related to equal opportunities, health and safety at work, or any other aspect. Companies should also have in place appropriate whistle-blowing procedures for helping to ensure that if employees feel that there is inappropriate behaviour in the company, they can 'blow the whistle' on these activities whilst minimizing the risk of adverse consequences for themselves as a result of this action.

The EU Commission places a particular emphasis on the role of employees as a stakeholder. In its 2012 *Action Plan: European company law and corporate governance—a modern legal framework for more engaged shareholders and sustainable companies*, it includes a section on employee share ownership which is seen as beneficial both for the employees and the companies concerned. This is discussed in more detail in the relevant section later in this chapter.

Providers of credit

Providers of credit include banks and other financial institutions. Providers of credit want to be confident that the companies to which they lend are going to be able to repay their debts. They will seek assurance from the annual report and accounts, and from various management accounts and forecasts that companies produce. It is in the company's best interests to maintain the confidence of providers of finance to ensure that no calls are made for repayment of funds, that they are willing to lend to the company in the future, and that the company is able to borrow at the best possible rate.

Suppliers

Suppliers have an interest in the companies that they supply on two grounds. First, having supplied the company with goods or services, they want to be sure that they will be paid for these and in a timely fashion. Secondly, they will be interested in the continuance of the company because they will wish to have a sustainable outlet for their goods and services.

Sometimes, suppliers will be supplying specialized equipment or services and, if the company it supplies has financial difficulties, then this can have a severe impact on the supplier as well. Of course, on an ongoing basis, suppliers of goods and services will also like to be paid on time because otherwise they will have problems with their own cash flow and meeting their own costs, such as labour and materials, incurred in supplying the company in the first place. So, ideally, the companies supplied will treat their suppliers with understanding and ensure that they settle their debts on time. In practice, many large companies will make their suppliers wait for payment, occasionally for such a length of time that the supplier either ends up with severe financial difficulties or refuses to supply the company in future.

Customers

A company's customers will want to try to make sure that they can buy the same product time and again from the company. The company itself will presumably be building up its customer loyalty through various marketing exercises, and customers themselves will get used to a familiar product that they will want to buy in the future. Sometimes, a product bought from one company will become part of a product made by the customer, and again it will be important for the customer to be assured that they can continue to buy and incorporate that product into their own production.

Increasingly, customers are also more aware of social, environmental, and ethical aspects of corporate behaviour and will try to ensure that the company supplying them is acting in a corporately socially responsible manner.

Local communities

Local communities have a number of interests in the companies that operate in their region. First, the companies will be employing large numbers of local people and it will be in the interest of sustained employment levels that companies in the locality operate in an efficient way. Should the company's fortunes start to decline, then unemployment might rise and may lead to part of the workforce moving away from the area to seek jobs elsewhere. This, in turn, would have an effect on local schools, as the number of pupils declined, and the housing market would be hit too, as demand for housing in the area declined. However, local communities will also be concerned that companies in the area act in an environmentally friendly way because the last thing they want is pollution in local rivers, in the soil, or in the atmosphere more generally. It is therefore in the local community's interest that companies in their locality continue to thrive, but do so in a way that takes account of local and national concerns.

Environmental groups

Environmental groups will seek to ensure that companies operate to both national and international environmental standards such as the *Ceres Principles* and the *Global Reporting Initiative Sustainability Guidelines* (these are discussed in more detail in Chapter 7). Increasingly, environmental issues are viewed as part of the mainstream rather than being at the periphery as a 'wish list'. The recognition that an environmentally responsible company should also, in the longer term, be as profitable, if not more so, as one that does not act in an environmentally responsible way is in many ways self-evident. An environmentally responsible company will not subject its workers to potentially hazardous processes without adequate protection (which unfortunately does still happen despite the best endeavours of health and safety regulations); will not pollute the environment; and will, where possible, use recyclable materials or engage in a recycling process. Ultimately, all of these things will benefit society at large and the company itself.

Government

The government has an interest in companies for several diverse reasons. First, as with the local and environmental groups—although not always with such commitment—it will try to make sure that companies act in a socially responsible way, taking account of social, ethical, and environmental considerations. Secondly, it will analyse corporate trends for purposes such as employment levels, monetary policy, and market supply and demand of goods and services. Lastly, but not least, it will be looking at various aspects to do with fiscal policy, such as capital allowances, incentives for investing in various industries or various parts of the country, and, of course, the taxation raised from companies.

Guidance on shareholders' and stakeholders' interests

There are a variety of codes, principles, and guidelines that include a discussion of the role of shareholders' and stakeholders' interests in a company and how the corporate governance system might accommodate these interests. Corporate governance codes, principles, and guidelines are generally examples of 'soft law' and tend to indicate best practice, usually on a self-regulation basis, whilst laws, regulations, and directives, for example, are termed 'hard law' and are legally binding. This section looks at some of the most influential of these publications starting with some examples of soft law codes and guidance in the UK followed by a hard law example, the UK Companies Act (2006). Then some examples of international codes and guidance are considered.

UK guidance

Hampel (1998)

The Hampel Committee was established in the UK in 1995 following the recommendations of the Cadbury (1992) and Greenbury (1995) committees that a new committee should review the implementation of their findings. Whilst recognizing that 'good governance ensures that constituencies (stakeholders) with a relevant interest in the company's business are fully taken into account', the Hampel Report (1998) stated quite clearly that the objective of all listed companies is the 'preservation and the greatest practicable enhancement over time of their shareholders' investment'.

The report took the view that whilst management should develop appropriate relation-ships with its various stakeholder groups, it should have regard to the overall objective of the company: to preserve and enhance shareholder value over time. The report also highlighted the practical point that 'directors as a board are responsible *for relations with* stakeholders; but they are accountable *to* shareholders' [emphasis in original]. This is a fundamental point because, if it were not so, then it would be very difficult to identify exactly to which stake-holder groups directors might be responsible and the extent of their responsibilities.

The UK Corporate Governance Code (2018)

The FRC (2018a) issued the UK Corporate Governance Code 2018 which emphasizes the importance of positive relationships between companies, shareholders and stakeholders. The FRC (2018b) identifies the highlights of the revised UK Corporate Governance Code 2018. In relation to stakeholders, some of the highlights relate to the workforce, for exam-ple, 'board responsibility for workforce policies and practices which reinforce a healthy culture' and 'engaging with the workforce through one, or a combination, of a director appointed from the workforce, a formal workforce advisory panel and a designated non-executive director, or other arrangements which meet the circumstances of the company and the workforce.'

Overall the UK Corporate Governance Code (2018) emphasizes relationships with a wider range of stakeholders, the importance of corporate culture, a focus on board diversity, and remuneration aspects (the latter two areas are discussed further in Chapters 8 and 9).

The Royal Society of Arts (RSA) and Tomorrow's Company

The RSA in the UK is a multidisciplinary independent body that has commissioned reports in various areas, including one called the *Tomorrow's Company Report* (2005), which was led by Mark Goyder. The report advocated an inclusive approach for business in its relationship with various stakeholder groups. The inclusive approach recognizes that there is an interdepend-ence between the employees, investors, customers, and suppliers, which increasingly means that the business needs to take a long-term view rather than having the short-term focus on increasing shareholder value that many businesses are perceived as having.

There was significant demand from businesses involved in the RSA Inquiry for an organiza-tion to carry forward its work and Tomorrow's Company is now well established as 'a not-for-profit research and agenda-setting organisation committed to creating a future for business which makes equal sense to staff, shareholders and society'. The organization has expanded its horizons and joined with other business and non-governmental organization (NGO) lead-ers around the globe to publish *Tomorrow's Global Company: Challenges and Choices* (2007), which advocates that companies should work with governments, NGOs, and others to cre-ate stronger frameworks of law and regulation for the world's markets. The report argues that 'stronger frameworks are needed to enable companies to create wealth and shareholder value at the same time as delivering practical solutions to global issues such as climate change, persistent poverty and human rights abuses'.

In 2008 the RSA published *Tomorrow's Investor*, by Rowland Manthorpe, which highlighted 'the looming pensions crisis, exacerbated by the financial crisis, is one of the most pressing problems society faces. The issues are well known: a population in which not enough people are saving; where saving is declining; where investors are being let down by their representatives.' The report also looks at ways in which transparency and accountability might be improved, and investor engagement made more effective. It argues that pension funds should 'take more advantage of the resources at their disposal by utilising new methods of social engagement'.

In December 2010 *Tomorrow's Investor: Building the Consensus for a People's Pension in Britain* by David Pitt-Watson was published by RSA Projects. The report finds that the system of occupational and private pensions in the UK is not fit for purpose. It details how the UK has ended up in such a poor position, and the key questions that pension policymakers now need to address to help build an effective pensions architecture.

In recent years, Tomorrow's Company has published reports on various aspects of corporate governance and stewardship including *Governing Culture: Risk and Opportunity?* (2016), *NEDS—Monitors to Partners* (2017) and *Better Stewardship—An Agenda for Concerted Action* (2018). In the Executive Summary of the latter publication, there is a succinct discussion of the disconnect that exists in society today and how this might be resolved:

> There is a troubling disconnect between our system of wealth creation, and the society which it serves. The symptoms include public anger about corporate failure and excessive executive pay; the continuing impacts on living standards from the global financial crisis; low investment; poor returns for savers, pressure on pensions, and high levels of debt, especially for graduates. Public trust in the whole system—including governments, universities and the media, not just business and investment—is low. Too often the attempt to tackle these problems deals only with individual symptoms. Effective solutions will only flow from a better diagnosis of the underlying problem, and combined actions by all involved.

> The wellbeing of savers and investors can only be promoted if the underlying performance of investee companies is improved. Competition between asset managers on relative performance is ultimately a zero sum game. This is where stewardship comes in. Stewardship means the responsible management of inherited resources so that they are passed on in better condition. Stewardship is the golden thread that can connect, and guide the actions of, all those who play their part in the flow of money from the savings of citizens through wealth creation and back to those citizens.

Hermes Principles (2002, 2006, 2010)

Hermes is one of the largest institutional investors in the UK with several million people depending on Hermes' investments to generate their retirement income. Hermes has long been one of the most active institutional investors in corporate governance and, in 2002, it published *The Hermes Principles*. In introducing the Principles, Hermes state:

> Hermes' overriding requirement is that companies be run in the long-term interest of shareholders. Companies adhering to this principle will not only benefit their shareholders, but also we would argue, the wider economy in which the company and its shareholders participate. We believe a company run in the long-term interest of shareholders will need to manage effectively relationships with its employees, suppliers and customers, to behave ethically and have regard for the environment and society as a whole.

In 2006 Hermes introduced its *Hermes Corporate Governance Principles*, which form the basis of its engagement with the companies in which it, or its clients, invest. These Principles have two parts: the Global Principles and the Regional Principles. The former are based on the *International Corporate Governance Network's Global Corporate Governance Principles*, whilst the latter explain which corporate governance codes or guidance, produced by local market participants or regulators, are supported by Hermes. In 2010 Hermes published *The Hermes Responsible Ownership Principles*, updated in 2013, detailing what they expect of listed companies and what listed companies can expect from them. By 2018, Hermes had published regional corporate governance principles for 19 countries. Whilst the same core corporate governance aspects frequently appear, for some countries there are sections discussing, for example, bribery and corruption.

Pensions and Lifetime Savings Association (PLSA)

In 2015, the Pensions and Lifetime Savings Association (PLSA) published a stewardship 'toolkit' for pension funds, providing advice on the type of information their members should request from the companies they invest in about their workforces and corporate cultures. The toolkit builds on the themes covered by their discussion paper *Where's the Workforce in Corporate Reporting?*, which highlighted how the extent to which companies invest in training, developing and motivating their workers, and ensuring they feel empowered and fairly treated at work, is critical to its long-term success.

In November 2015 they wrote to the Chair of every FTSE 350 company asking them to share fuller information with investors about the culture and working practices of their workforce. The letter included a copy of their recent stewardship toolkit for PLSA members, outlining the type of information that pension funds should request from the companies they invest in about their workforce.

Information about the workforces they are invested in is critical to PLSA members as investors. However, the PLSA state that:

> most annual reports currently fail to fully relate the role played by a company's workers in achieving past or future performance. The annual report, specifically the strategic report intended to explain the company's business model and key risks facing the organisation, was generally recognised as being the most appropriate format for communicating issue about the workforce. Throughout our discussions with stakeholders, a preference was expressed for narrative reporting that links the company's approach to its workers to its underlying purpose and strategy, over 'boilerplate' box ticking against a long list of prescribed metrics. At the same time, however, it was generally agreed that it would be impossible to communicate this narrative in a meaningful way without the use of certain consistently reported, concrete, comparable data. These metrics should provide evidence in support of the narrative, while the narrative should contextualise the data. In particular, we recommend that our members encourage investee companies to report against the following metrics as standard, at group level and across relevant markets, businesses and levels of the company hierarchy:

- Gender diversity
- Employment type—for example, full-time, part-time or agency workers
- Staff turnover

- Accidents, injuries and workplace illnesses
- Investment in training and development
- Pay ratios between the highest paid and median and lowest quartile workers across the company
- Employee engagement score

Together these measures serve as useful proxies for investors wanting to measure the corporate cultures in effect within an investee company, and the four key themes of composition; stability; skills and capabilities; and employee engagement identified in our previous discussion paper—who is working for the company they invest in; how secure this employment model is; how different people in the company are treated; and thus how motivated and committed to corporate goals they might be.

Companies Act (2006)

The UK Companies Act (2006) was published in November 2006. There are several significant provisions in relation to shareholders and stakeholders that it is appropriate to mention in this chapter.

First, in relation to directors' duties, the Companies Act (2006) draws on the concept of 'enlightened shareholder value'. In the Department of Trade and Industry consultative *Company Law Reform* (2005) document which preceded the Companies Act (2006), in relation to directors' duties, it said:

> The statement of duties will be drafted in a way which reflects modern business needs and wider expectations of responsible business behaviour. The CLR [Company Law Review] proposed that the basic goal for directors should be the success of the company for the benefit of its members as a whole; but that, to reach this goal, directors would need to take a properly balanced view of the implications of decisions over time and foster effective relationships with employees, customers and suppliers, and in the community more widely. The Government strongly agrees that this approach, which the CLR called 'enlightened shareholder value', is most likely to drive long-term company performance and maximise overall competitiveness and wealth and welfare for all. It will therefore be reflected in the statement of directors' duties.

In the Companies Act (2006), it is made clear that a director's duty is to

> act in the way he considers, in good faith, would be most likely to promote the success of the company for the benefit of its members as a whole and, in doing so have regard (amongst other matters) to:
>
> a. the likely consequences of any decision in the long term,
>
> b. the interests of the company's employees,
>
> c. the need to foster the company's business relationships with suppliers, customers and others,
>
> d. the impact of the company's operations on the community and the environment,
>
> e. the desirability of the company maintaining a reputation for high standards of business conduct, and
>
> f. the need to act fairly as between members of the company. (Part 10, Chapter 2, section 172)

Clearly, there is a significant emphasis being given here for directors to have regard to wider stakeholder interests as well as to the shareholders. Unless the company is classified as a small company, the Directors' Report must contain a business review that would comply with the aforementioned EU Accounts Modernization Directive as well as the Companies Act 2006. The Companies Act states that the business review must contain a fair review of the company's business, and a description of the principal risks and uncertainties facing the company.

> The business review must, to the extent necessary for an understanding of the development, performance or position of the company's business, include:
>
> a. the main trends and factors likely to affect the future development, performance and position of the company's business; and
>
> b. information about—
>
>   i.   environmental matters (including the impact of the company's business on the environment),
>
>   ii. the company's employees, and
>
>   iii. social and community issues, including information about any policies of the company in relation to those matters and the effectiveness of those policies;
>
> The review must, to the extent necessary for an understanding of the development, performance or position of the company's business, include—
>
> a. analysis using financial key performance indicators, and
>
> b. where appropriate, analysis using other key performance indicators, including information relating to environmental matters and employee matters.
>
> 'Key performance indicators' means factors by reference to which the development, performance or position of the company's business can be measured effectively. (Part 15, Chapter 5, section 417)

In January 2006 the Department for Environment, Food, and Rural Affairs (Defra) issued voluntary guidance on environmental key performance indicators (KPIs) that companies might include in their disclosures about environmental reporting. The KPIs might also provide appropriate information for the business review.

International guidance

Organisation for Economic Co-operation and Development (OECD)

There are two main OECD publications that give some thought to this area. First, there is the OECD (1998) report on *Corporate Governance: Improving Competitiveness and Access to Capital in Global Markets* by the Business Sector Advisory Group on Corporate Governance. This report recognizes that the companies' central mission is long-term enhancement of shareholder value, but that companies operate in the larger society, and that there may be different societal pressures and expectations that may impact on the financial objective to some extent, so that non-financial objectives may need to be addressed as well.

The OECD *Principles of Corporate Governance* (1999), revised in 2004, include, as one of the principles, the role of stakeholders in corporate governance. The Principles (2004) state that 'the corporate governance framework should recognize the rights of stakeholders established by law or through mutual agreements and encourage active co-operation between corporations and stakeholders in creating wealth, jobs, and the sustainability of financially sound enterprises'. This really highlights two aspects: first, that the rights of stakeholders will depend to a large extent on the legal provision for stakeholders in any given country (one would expect that stakeholders would have a right of redress for any violation of their rights); secondly, that stakeholders do have a role to play in the long-term future of businesses, that the corporate governance framework should 'permit performance-enhancing mechanisms for stakeholder participation', and that stakeholders should have access to relevant information in order to participate effectively. The OECD circulated the *Principles of Corporate Governance—Draft for Public Comment November 2014* with consultation responses received by early 2015. Following the consultation, the *G20/OECD Principles of Corporate Governance* were published in 2015.

The OECD publication *Using the OECD Principles of Corporate Governance: A Boardroom Perspective* (2008) detailed real-life examples of the ways in which the Principles (2004) have been put into action in the boardroom by business leaders. In the context of stakeholders—which, as we have discussed, encompass many different groups—one example in relation to employees is that site visits by the board and direct communication with employees are beneficial; whilst another example, this time in the context of social responsibility and philanthropy, is that the board should consult with shareholders, employees, and other appropriate stakeholders regarding their philanthropic agenda.

King Report (1994, 2002, 2009, 2016)

The King Report (2002) is a comprehensive document that provides guidelines for corporate governance in South Africa. It builds on the earlier King Report published in 1994, which stated that there should be an integrated approach to corporate governance and took into account the interests of various stakeholder groups. King (2002) states that the inclusive approach is fundamental to the operation of business in South Africa. The company should define its purpose, decide on the values by which the company's day-to-day activities will be carried on, and identify its stakeholders; all of these aspects should be taken into account when the company develops its strategies for achieving corporate objectives. The King Report was updated in 2009. The King Report (2002, 2009) is covered in more detail in Chapter 13 but it is mentioned here as a good example of a code that emphasizes the inclusive approach and the importance of considering the interests of stakeholders.

The latest version of the King Report was published in 2016. The introduction to the report states 'New global realities are testing the leadership of organisations on issues as diverse as inequality, globalised trade, social tensions, climate change, population growth, ecological overshoot, geopolitical tensions, radical transparency and rapid technological and scientific advancement. The United Nations Sustainable Development Goals, which were agreed by all governments in 2015, the Africa 2063 Agenda and the (South African) National Development Plan 2030 (NDP) have a common theme of value creation that is accomplished in a sustainable manner. This is a fundamental concept of King IV.' Furthermore in relation to stakeholder management, the report states:

In order to know and understand the legitimate and reasonable needs, interests and expectations of an organisation's major stakeholders, management needs an ongoing relationship with those stakeholders. Some organisations have appointed a corporate stakeholder relationship officer whose sole task is to communicate with stakeholders and inform management of their legitimate and reasonable needs, interests and expectations. This officer will also inform stakeholders what the organisation expects of them. Understanding stakeholders' expectations will greatly assist the executive to develop better strategy. Stakeholder relationships should be a recurring item on the governing body's agenda so that the board can be kept apprised of the current state of the relationships between the organisation and its stakeholders.

EU Accounts Modernization Directive

The EU Accounts Modernization Directive was intended to produce more comparability across the financial reporting of its Member States. By its provisions, companies in various countries in the EU are subject to common standards of both the level of disclosure and content of disclosures. The Directive applied to all medium and large EU companies and, effective from 1 April 2005, the Directive required additional material to be included in the Director's Report to provide an enhanced review of a company's business. The Directive states that:

> the review must, to the extent necessary for an understanding of the development, performance or position of the business of the company, include:
>
> a. analysis using financial key performance indicators, and
>
> b. where appropriate, analysis using other key performance indicators, including information relating to environmental matters and employee matters.

EU: A Renewed EU Strategy 2011–14 for Corporate Social Responsibility

In 2011, the EU Commission published its *A Renewed EU Strategy 2011–14 for Corporate Social Responsibility*. In that document, the multidimensional nature of CSR was discussed:

> According to these principles and guidelines, CSR at least covers human rights, labour and employment practices (such as training, diversity, gender equality and employee health and well-being), environmental issues (such as biodiversity, climate change, resource efficiency, life-cycle assessment and pollution prevention), and combating bribery and corruption. Community involvement and development, the integration of disabled persons, and consumer interests, including privacy, are also part of the CSR agenda. The promotion of social and environmental responsibility through the supply-chain, and the disclosure of non-financial information, are recognised as important cross-cutting issues.

EU: Next Steps for a Sustainable European Future: European action for sustainability (2016)

Following on from various landmark international agreements in 2015, including the adoption of the UN 2030 Agenda and Sustainable Development Goals and the Paris Climate Agreement, the EU set itself ambitious climate, environmental, and sustainability targets, through its 2030 Energy and Climate framework, the Energy Union, and its Circular Economy Action

Plan. In November 2016, the EU Commission issued *Next Steps for a Sustainable European Future: European action for sustainability*. In this publication, the EU states:

> Sustainable development has since long been at the heart of the European project. The EU Treaties give recognition to its economic, social and environmental dimensions which should be addressed together … Sustainable development requires a holistic and cross-sector policy approach to ensure that economic, social and environmental challenges are addressed together. Hence, ultimately sustainable development is an issue of governance and requires the right instruments to ensure policy coherence, across thematic areas as well as between the EU's external action and its other policies.

Subsequently, the EU Commission established the independent High-Level Expert Group on Sustainable Finance (HLEG) in December 2016.

EU: Final Report of the High-Level Expert Group on Sustainable Finance (2018)

In 2018 the EU Commission *Final Report of the High-Level Expert Group on Sustainable Finance* was issued. The Report sets out strategic recommendations for a financial system that supports sustainable investments and provides a roadmap which means that the EU Commission can now finalize its strategy on sustainable finance. The EU Commission states:

> Delivering an EU strategy on sustainable finance is a priority action of the Commission's Capital Markets Union (CMU) Action Plan, as well as one of the key steps towards implementing the historic Paris Agreement and the EU's Agenda for sustainable development. To achieve the EU's 2030 targets agreed in Paris, including a 40% cut in greenhouse gas emissions, we need around €180 billion of additional investments a year. The financial sector has a key role to play in reaching those goals, as large amounts of private capital could be mobilised towards such sustainable investments. The Commission is determined to lead the global work in this area and help sustainability-conscious investors to choose suitable projects and companies.

The HLEG Report (2018) *Financing a Sustainable European Economy* key recommendations are:

1. Establish and maintain a common sustainability taxonomy at the EU level
2. Clarify investor duties to better embrace long-term horizon and sustainability preferences
3. Upgrade disclosure rules to make sustainability risks fully transparent, starting with climate change
4. Key elements of a retail strategy on sustainable finance: investment advice, ecolabel and SRI minimum standards
5. Develop and implement official European sustainability standards and labels, starting with green bonds
6. Establish 'Sustainable Infrastructure Europe'
7. Governance and Leadership
8. Include sustainability in the supervisory mandate of the ESAs and extend the horizon of risk monitoring

The Report also makes eight recommendations which are described as 'cross-cutting recommendations'; eight recommendations relating to financial institutions and sectoral recommendations; and four relating to social and broader environmental sustainability recommendations.

The Report will form the basis of the Commission's comprehensive Action Plan on sustainable finance which will be put forward during 2018.

EU: Action Plan: European company law and corporate governance

In 2012, the EU Commission published its *Action Plan: European company law and corporate governance—a modern legal framework for more engaged shareholders and sustainable companies*. It states that 'a modern and efficient company law and corporate governance framework for European undertakings, investors and employees must be adapted to the needs of today's society and to the changing economic environment'.

The EU Action Plan, Section 3.5 relates to employee share ownership. The EU Commission:

> believes that employees' interest in the sustainability of their company is an element that ought to be considered in the design of any well-functioning governance framework. Employees' involvement in the affairs of a company may take the form of information, consultation and participation in the board. But it can also relate to forms of financial involvement, particularly to employees becoming shareholders. Employee share ownership schemes already have a successful tradition and track record in many Member States. Research conducted in preparation for the 2011 Green Paper and responses to it indicate that employee share ownership schemes could play an important role in increasing the proportion of long-term oriented shareholders. Since there are many angles to this issue (for instance taxation, social security and labour law) the Commission finds it important to analyse this subject in more detail, in particular as regards its internal market dimension. In the light of this analysis, it will identify which initiatives may be appropriate to encourage the development of trans-national employee share ownership schemes in Europe.

The next stage was for the EU Commission to 'identify and investigate potential obstacles to transnational employee share ownership schemes, and [it] will subsequently take appropriate action to encourage employee share ownership throughout Europe'. In relation to this, a study entitled *The Promotion of Employee Ownership and Participation* was commissioned by the EU (2014). The study gives an overview of employee financial participation, especially employee share ownership, across the EU-28 and highlights the growth of employee financial participation and its positive impact on employment and productivity. The study makes a number of recommendations including the establishment of a Virtual Centre for employee financial participation, the development of a code of conduct for the mid-term and, for the long term, an optional Common European regime on Employee Financial Participation.

Roles of shareholders and stakeholders

In reality, the involvement of shareholders and stakeholders will depend on national laws and customs, and also the individual company's approach. However, even in countries where companies traditionally have not been profit-oriented (such as state-owned enterprises) as those countries now seek to develop their capital markets and raise external finance, the shareholders' interests will likely tend to rise to the top of the corporate agenda. However, it is of fundamental importance that stakeholders' interests cannot, and should not, be ignored.

As can be seen from the codes/principles discussed earlier, whilst recognizing that companies need to take into account the views of stakeholders, in the UK, the prima facie purpose of a company is the maintenance or enhancement of long-term shareholder value. In the UK neither the legal nor the corporate governance systems make any provision for employee representation on the board, nor for representation of other stakeholder groups such as providers of finance, and there has been consistent opposition to representation of stakeholder groups on corporate boards. However, the UK has employee share schemes so employees can be involved in that way, although, of course, they do not have the same type of input as if they were represented on the board.

In the UK and the USA the emphasis is on the relationship between the shareholders (owners) and the directors (managers). In contrast, the German and French corporate governance systems, which view companies as more of a partnership between capital and labour, provide for employee representation at board level, whilst banks (providers of finance) may also be represented on the supervisory board. However, it is interesting to note that one downside of employee representation on the board is that decisions, which may be in the best interests of the company as a whole but not of the workforce, may not get made, so may lead to suboptimal decision-making. Whilst the German and French corporate governance systems are dealt with in detail in Chapter 10, it is useful at this point to highlight the different approach to stakeholders and the impact that this may have on the company.

Another important point is that if the directors of a company were held to be responsible to shareholders and the various stakeholder groups alike, then what would be the corporate objective? How could the board function effectively if there were a multiplicity of different objectives, no one of which took priority over the others? At present in many countries, the enhancement of shareholder wealth is the overriding criterion, but if it were not, what would be? This could actually lead to quite a dangerous situation where directors and managers were not really accountable.

Given that all companies operate within a wider society, the interests of shareholders and stakeholders are often intertwined. Also, the distinction between shareholders and stakeholders is often not clear-cut. For example, Charkham and Simpson (1999) point out that, in the UK, shareholders are often drawn from other stakeholder groups: 'Pension funds are the largest group of shareholders, yet their assets are drawn from the savings of half the workforce and invested to provide retirement income when this group becomes pensioners.' Similar statements can be made about the insurance companies, and also about individual shareholders who may also be customers of the companies in which they invest, for example, utilities.

Significantly, Goergen et al. (2010a) point out that 'understandings of corporate governance that are concerned only with the rights of owners and shareholders and the relationship between them and the management of the business are inevitably limited. Organizations are complex bodies and have many other parties involved, including regulators, customers, suppliers, and local citizens.' Goergen et al. (2010b) point out that 'in the UK it is still controversial to regard stakeholders as "actors" within the landscape of corporate governance' but that 'shareholders, employees, stakeholders and gatekeepers are all part of the complex social ecosystem surrounding the corporation'. They advocate using the principles of complexity theory to analyse the complex behaviour between the multiple stakeholders within the corporate governance social ecosystem.

Harper Ho (2010) urges 'a vision of the corporation and its purpose that transcends the shareholder-stakeholder divide'. Under this 'enlightened shareholder value' approach, attention is given to corporate stakeholders, including the environment, employees, and local communities, as these groups are now being seen as critical to generating long-term shareholder wealth and to effective risk management.

Lan and Heracleous (2010), in an innovative proposal drawing from legal theory, redefine agency theory along three key dimensions, 'redefining the principal from shareholders to the corporation, redefining the status of the board from shareholders' agents to autonomous fiduciaries, and redefining the role of the board from monitors to mediating hierarchs'. Furthermore, they state that 'our redefined agency theory may be seen as more applicable and palatable to countries other than those in the Anglo-Saxon world, such as China, Germany, Japan, and Russia, that are more stakeholder oriented and where shareholders are not always treated as primary. Even so, as we have shown, the legal systems in the Anglo-Saxon world also support this approach.'

Subsequently, Claessens and Ueda (2014) consider

the important, growth-enhancing roles of bank branch deregulation and employment protection, using concurrent institutional changes in both financial and labor markets in the U.S. over the period 1972 to 1993. Our results also speak to a broader corporate governance debate in countries other than the U.S. In particular, basic labor standards likely create a better alignment of bargaining powers among workers, creditors, and shareholders, and should thus be especially important for emerging markets, also given the typical dominance of banks in financial intermediation. We surmise though that the relationship between employment protection and economic outcomes may be nonlinear. This is because the stakeholders' view, prevalent in developed countries other than the U.S., such as continental Europe and Japan, where both banks and labor play a large role in firm monitoring and governance, appears to be associated with many negative outcomes according to the labor literature. As such, it may be that basic employment protection or 'labor standards' as adopted in the U.S. may be beneficial, while the broader labor protection as practiced in continental Europe may not. This is not more than a conjecture, however, and as such, we see a fruitful research area to find out the circumstances under which stakeholder governance pays off.

Finally, Mehrotra and Morck (2017) state that

'other stakeholders—entrepreneurial founders or CEOs, employees, customers, suppliers, communities or governments, having made firm-specific investments, may exert stronger claims than atomistic public shareholders have to shares of their firms' quasirents. Consistent with this, their contractual claims are often augmented by residual claims and liabilities. Still, shareholder value maximization constitutes something of a bright line; whereas stakeholder welfare maximization is an ill-defined charge to assign boards that gives self-interested insiders broader scope for private benefits extraction. The common law concept of 'the interests of the corporation' captures this ambiguity.

Conclusions

Companies operate in a wider society not within a defined corporate vacuum. Therefore, companies should take account of the views of various stakeholders in addition to those of shareholders. Whilst the corporate objective is generally to maintain or enhance shareholder value, the impact of the company's activities on its other stakeholders must be taken into account when deciding the strategy to be developed for achieving the corporate objective.

By taking account of the views and interests of its stakeholders, the company should be able to achieve its objectives with integrity and help to achieve sustainability of its long-term operations. The employee as a stakeholder has a particular emphasis as can be seen from EU Commission pronouncements on this aspect. Globally the sustainability of resources and the adoption of an ethical culture in companies are gaining more credence.

Summary

- Shareholders are the providers of capital. Often, the corporate objective is expressed in terms of maximizing shareholder value.

- Stakeholders include employees, providers of credit, customers, suppliers, local communities, government, environmental and social groups; in fact, any group on which the company's activities may have an impact.

- Most corporate governance codes and guidelines tend to perceive the prima facie objective of the company as the maximization of shareholder wealth. However, there is also the understanding that the achievement of this objective should have regard to the interests of various stakeholder groups.

- Stakeholders can make their views known to the company and, in some countries, may have representation on the company's decision-making bodies (such as the supervisory board in Germany). However, in the UK and many other countries, it is the shareholders who can hold the board of directors accountable for their actions.

Questions

The discussion questions to follow cover the key learning points of this chapter. Reading of some of the additional reference material will enhance the depth of the students' knowledge and understanding of these areas.

1. What stakeholder groups might directors of a company have to take into consideration, and how might the stakeholders' interests impact on the company?

2. In what ways might stakeholders' interests conflict with each other?

3. What role do you believe stakeholders should play in corporate governance, and are there particular roles for employees to play?

4. Corporate governance supports investment as a powerful driver of growth. Critically discuss in the context of shareholder–stakeholder relationships.

5. 'A company's long-term success is dependent on its stakeholders, therefore it can no more fail to take stakeholders' interests into consideration than it can those of its shareholders.' Critically discuss this statement.

6. What corporate governance mechanisms might help with representing the views of stakeholders?

References

Cadbury, Sir Adrian (1992), *Report of the Committee on the Financial Aspects of Corporate Governance*, Gee & Co. Ltd, London.

Charkham, J. and Simpson, A. (1999), *Fair Shares: The Future of Shareholder Power and Responsibility*, Oxford University Press, Oxford.

Claessens, S. and Ueda, K. (2014), *Stakeholder Corporate Governance: The Combined Effects of Bank Competition and Employment Protection* (31 May 2014). Available at SSRN: http://ssrn.com/abstract=2444152 or http://dx.doi.org/10.2139/ssrn.2444152.

Companies Act (2006), Her Majesty's Stationery Office, London.

Department for Environment, Food, and Rural Affairs (Defra) (2006), *Environmental Key Performance Indicators, Reporting Guidelines for UK Business*, Defra/Trucost, London.

EU Commission (2011), *A Renewed EU Strategy 2011-14 for Corporate Social Responsibility*, EU Commission, Brussels.

EU Commission (2012), *Action Plan: European company law and corporate governance—a modern legal framework for more engaged shareholders and sustainable companies*, EU Commission, Brussels.

EU Commission (2014), *The Promotion of Employee Ownership and Participation—28.10.2014*, Inter-University Centre for European Commission's DG MARKT (Contract MARKT/2013/0191F2/ST/OP).

EU Commission (2016), *Next Steps for a Sustainable European Future: European action for sustainability*, EU Commission, Brussels.

EU Commission (2018), *Final Report of the High-Level Expert Group on Sustainable Finance*, EU Commission, Brussels.

Financial Reporting Council (2018a) *The UK Corporate Governance Code 2018*, FRC, London.

Financial Reporting Council (2018b) *Revised UK Corporate Governance Code 2018 Highlights*, FRC, London.

Goergen M., Brewster C., and Wood, G. (2010a), 'Corporate Governance: Nonequity Stakeholders' in H. Kent Baker and R. Anderson (eds), *Corporate Governance: A Synthesis of Theory, Research and Practice*, The Robert W. Kolb Series in Finance, John Wiley & Sons Inc., New Jersey.

Goergen M., Mallin C., Mitleton-Kelly E., Al-Hawamdeh A., and Chui H-Y. (2010b), *Corporate Governance and Complexity Theory*, Edward Elgar Publishing Ltd, Cheltenham.

Greenbury, Sir Richard (1995), *Directors' Remuneration*, Gee & Co. Ltd, London.

Hampel, Sir Ronnie (1998), *Committee on Corporate Governance: Final Report*, Gee & Co. Ltd, London.

Harper Ho, V.E. (2010), ' "Enlightened Shareholder Value": Corporate Governance Beyond the Shareholder-Stakeholder Divide', *Journal of Corporation Law*, Vol. 36, No. 1, pp. 59–112.

Hermes (2002), *The Hermes Principles*, Hermes Pensions Management Ltd, London.

Hermes (2006), *Hermes Corporate Governance Principles*, Hermes Pensions Management Ltd, London.

Hermes (2010), *The Hermes Responsible Ownership Principles*, Hermes Pensions Management Ltd, London.

King, M. (1994), *King Report on Corporate Governance for South Africa—1994*, King Committee on Corporate Governance, Institute of Directors in Southern Africa, Parktown, South Africa.

King, M. (2002), *King Report on Corporate Governance for South Africa—2002*, King Committee on Corporate Governance, Institute of Directors in Southern Africa, Parktown, South Africa.

King, M. (2009), *King Code of Governance for South Africa 2009*, King Committee on Corporate Governance, Institute of Directors in Southern Africa, Parktown, South Africa.

King, M. (2016), *King IV—Report on Corporate Governance for South Africa 2016*, King Committee on Corporate Governance, Institute of Directors in Southern Africa, Parktown, South Africa.

Lan, L.L. and Heracleous, L. (2010), 'Rethinking Agency Theory: The View from Law', *Academy of Management Review*, Vol. 35, No. 2, pp. 294–314.

Manthorpe, R. (2008), *Tomorrow's Investor* (2008), RSA, London.

Mehrotra V. and Morck, R. (2017), *Governance and Stakeholders* (1 May 2017). European Corporate Governance Institute (ECGI) – Finance Working Paper No. 507/2017. Available at SSRN: https://ssrn.com/abstract=2971943.

Organisation for Economic Co-operation and Development (1998), *Corporate Governance: Improving Competitiveness and Access to Capital in Global Markets*, A report to the OECD by the Business Sector Advisory Group on Corporate Governance, OECD, Paris.

Organisation for Economic Co-operation and Development (1999), *Principles of Corporate Governance*, OECD, Paris.

Organisation for Economic Co-operation and Development (2004), *Principles of Corporate Governance*, OECD, Paris.

Organisation for Economic Co-operation and Development (2008), *Using the OECD Principles of Corporate Governance: A Boardroom Perspective*, OECD, Paris.

Organisation for Economic Co-operation and Development (2015), G20/OECD *Principles of Corporate Governance*, OECD, Paris.

Pensions and Lifetime Savings Association (2015), *Where's the Workforce in Corporate Reporting?*, PLSA, London.

Pitt-Watson, D. (2010), *Tomorrow's Investor: Building the Consensus for a People's Pension in Britain*, RSA, London.

Tomorrow's Company Report (2005), RSA, London.

Tomorrow's Company (2007), *Tomorrow's Global Company: Challenges and Choices*, Tomorrow's Company, London.

Tomorrow's Company (2016), *Governing Culture: Risk and Opportunity?* Tomorrow's Company, London.

Tomorrow's Company (2017), *NEDS—Monitors to Partners*, Tomorrow's Company, London.

Tomorrow's Company (2018), *Better Stewardship—An Agenda for Concerted Action*, Tomorrow's Company, London.

Useful websites

www.bis.gov.uk The website of the Department for Business, Innovation & Skills (created in June 2009 from the merger of the Department for Business, Enterprise and Regulatory Reform, and the Department for Innovation, Universities and Skills) contains information about the Department's activities.

www.bsr.org This is the website of Business for Social Responsibility, a global non-profit organization that promotes corporate success in ways that respect ethical values, people, communities, and the environment.

www.gov.uk/government/organisations/department-for-environment-food-rural-affairs The website of the Department for Environment, Food and Rural Affairs, which contains various publications relating to the environment, sustainability, and related matters.

https://ec.europa.eu/info/business-economy-euro/doing-business-eu/company-law-and-corporate-governance_en The website of the EU Commission dealing with the modernization of company law and the enhancement of corporate governance.

www.legislation.gov.uk This website brings together the legislative content previously held on the OPSI website and revised legislation from the Statute Law Database to provide a single legislation service.

www.parliament.uk The website of the UK Parliament covers parliamentary debates in the House of Commons and House of Lords and has a wide range of publications.

www.plsa.co.uk The Pensions and Lifetime Savings Association (PLSA) website contains useful information relating to various aspects of pensions and lifetime savings for pension professionals and individuals. Formerly the National Association of Pension Funds (NAPF).

www.thersa.org The website of the Royal Society of Arts, a charity that encourages the development of a principled, prosperous society.

www.tomorrowscompany.com The website of Tomorrow's Company contains various publications produced to help achieve Tomorrow's Company's objectives.

 Develop your understanding of this chapter and explore the subject further using our online resources at www.oup.com/uk/mallin6e/

 FT Clippings

Some stakeholders seem more equal than others

By David Pitt-Watson

Financial Times, 29 January 2017

It is not often that august bodies representing company directors, workers, international investors, and company secretaries agree on anything. Rarer still when they reach agreement on a topic as contentious as corporate governance.

So the letter that the Institute of Directors, the Trades Union Congress, the International Corporate Governance Network and the Institute for Company Secretaries jointly wrote and delivered last week to Theresa May, the UK prime minister, is worth noting.

The letter makes one particular request. It asks that the government, which is in the process of reviewing corporate governance practices in the UK, finds a way to police legal obligations that everyone agrees are good ones, but which can be breached with impunity.

The duties of the boards of directors who run British companies are well defined. They are to promote the success of the company for the benefit of all shareholders, and in so doing to have regard for the interests of workers, consumers and other stakeholders.

That is what Section 172 of the Companies Act, main piece of legislation governing company law, requires. It would seem to many that directors of Sports Direct, the UK retailer accused of employment abuses, and BHS, the retailer that collapsed last year and jeopardised its pension fund in the process, breached some of those duties. But there was no one to hold them to account.

There are of course many aspects of corporate governance. Remuneration and private companies were two on which the signatories commented. But this proposal simply asks that those who are protected by law can ask that the law be respected.

Such a proposal is complementary to the role of investors in shareholder stewardship.

Such stewardship is an important part of our governance system. If it is done well it will help prevent bad practice. But it is not the job of any investor to police the law. And for small investors it is impossible.

That is why the UK Shareholders Association, which represents small investors, told the parliamentary committee investigating corporate governance that 'at the moment it appears that companies can ignore [the law] when it suits them, provided it does not upset the major institutional shareholders'.

Study after study suggests that companies who pay attention to their stakeholders end up being more successful financially.

Those companies that breach obligations hit the headlines, and bring the system into disrepute. It is no use telling those who have suffered that they shouldn't worry because most businesses behave well. They need to have someone to complain to, who is free of conflicts and who can set things straight.

This does not mean that people need to go to court. In other fields, such as broadcasting standards, there is a simple mechanism where people can complain. No one goes to jail, but if a broadcaster knowingly and repeatedly breaches required standards, they cannot expect their licence to be renewed.

It is in no one's interest if, when our carefully crafted laws are breached, you cannot make a complaint and the abused can find no remedy.

It should have particular resonance for Mrs May, who, in her first speech as prime minister, told us that she would be on the side of working families, workers, consumers, stakeholders, and—through their pensions—investors in our capitalist system.

She said her government would 'do everything we can to give you more control over your lives. When we take the big calls, we'll think not of the powerful, but you.'

Here is an opportunity, with broad industry support, to do just that.

Family-owned firms

 Learning objectives

- To be aware of the predominance of family-owned firms in many countries around the world

- To understand the evolution of governance structures in family-owned firms

- To realize the benefits that good corporate governance may bring to family-owned firms

- To understand the problems that may be faced by family-owned firms in implementing good corporate governance

Introduction

The dominant form of business around the world is the family-owned business. In many instances, the family-owned business takes the form of a small family business whilst in other cases, it is a large business interest employing hundreds, or even thousands, of staff. The family-owned business can encompass sole traders, partnerships, private companies, and public companies. In fact, family ownership is prevalent not only amongst privately held firms but also in publicly traded firms in many countries across the globe. However, whatever the size of the business, it can benefit from having a good governance structure. Firms with effective governance structures will tend to have a more focused view of the business, be willing to take into account, and benefit from, the views of 'outsiders' (that is, non-family members), and be in a better position to evolve and grow into the future.

Ownership structures around the world

La Porta et al. (1999) studied the ownership structure in a number of countries and found that the family-owned firm is quite common. Analysing a sample of large firms in 27 countries, La Porta et al. used as one of their criteria a 10 per cent chain definition of control. This means that they analysed the shareholdings to see if there were 'chains' of ownership: for example, if company B held shares in company C, who then held company B's shares. On this 10 per cent chain definition of control, only 24 per cent of the large companies are widely held, compared to 35 per cent that are family controlled, and 20 per cent state controlled. Overall, they show that:

1) Controlling shareholders often have control rights in excess of their cash flow rights.
2) This is true of families, who are so often the controlling shareholders. 3) Controlling

families participate in the management of the firms they own. 4) Banks do not exercise much control over firms as shareholders … 5) Other large shareholders are usually not there to monitor the controlling shareholders. Family control of firms appears to be common, significant, and typically unchallenged by other equity holders.

La Porta et al.'s paper made an important contribution to our understanding of the prevalence of family-owned/controlled firms in many countries across the world.

A key influence on the type of ownership and control structure is the legal system. Traditionally, common law legal systems, such as in the UK and USA, have better protection of minority shareholders' rights than do civil law systems, such as those of France, Germany, and Russia. Often, if the legal environment does not have good protection of shareholders' rights, then this discourages a diverse shareholder base whilst being more conducive to family-owned firms where a relatively small group of individuals can retain ownership, power, and control. For example, in the UK and USA, where the rights of minority shareholders are well protected by the legal system, there are many more companies with diversified shareholder bases, and family-controlled businesses are much less common.

However, research by Franks et al. (2005a) highlighted that, in the UK in the first half of the twentieth century, there was an absence of minority investor protection as we know it today, and yet there still occurred a move from family ownership to a more dispersed share ownership. This was attributable to the issuance of shares through acquisitions and mergers, although families tried to retain control of the board by holding a majority of the seats. Franks et al. (2005b) state:

> the rise of hostile takeovers and institutional shareholders made it increasingly difficult for families to maintain control without challenge. Potential targets attempted to protect themselves through dual class shares and strategic share blocks but these were dismantled in response to opposition by institutional shareholders and the London Stock Exchange (LSE). The result was a regulated market in corporate control and a capital market that looked very different from its European counterparts. Thus, while acquisitions facilitated the growth of family controlled firms in the first half of the century, they also diluted their ownership and ultimately their control in the second half.

In many countries, including European countries such as France, many Asian countries, and South American countries, the legal protection of minority shareholders is today still either non-existent or ineffective, and so families often retain control in companies because non-family investors will not find the businesses an attractive investment when their rights are not protected.

However, many countries are recognizing that, as the business grows and needs external finance to pursue its expansion, then non-family investors will only be attracted to the business if there is protection of their rights, both in the context of the country's legal framework and also in the corporate governance of the individual companies in which they invest. This is leading to increasing pressure both for legal reforms to protect shareholders' rights and for corporate governance reforms within the individual companies. However, balanced against the pressures for reform are the often very powerful voices of family shareholders with controlling interests, who may not wish to see reform to give better protection to minority interests because this would effectively dilute their control.

Family-owned firms and governance

When a family-owned business is relatively small, the family members themselves will be able to manage and direct it. One advantage of a family-owned firm is that there should be less chance of the type of agency problems discussed in Chapter 2. This is because, rather than being split, ownership and control are still one and the same, and so the problems of information asymmetry and opportunistic behaviour should (in theory, at least) be lessened. As a result of this overlap of ownership and control, one would hope for higher levels of trust and hence less monitoring of management activity should be necessary. However, problems may still occur and especially in terms of potential for minority shareholder oppression, which may be more acute in family-owned firms. Morck and Yeung (2003) point out some of the potential agency costs in family-owned firms:

> In family business group firms, the concern is that managers may act for the controlling family, but not for shareholders in general. These agency issues are: the use of pyramidal groups to separate ownership from control, the entrenchment of controlling families, and non-arm's-length transactions (aka 'tunnelling') between related companies that are detrimental to public investors.

In some countries remedies such as formal shareholder agreements, in which the nature of each shareholder's participation in the company is recorded, may be utilized as a mechanism to help resolve the potential oppression of minorities. Furthermore, the European Commission's Shareholder Rights Directive, adopted in 2007, is designed to help strengthen the role of shareholders by ensuring that they have relevant information in a timely manner and are able to vote in an informed way. Although the Directive is aimed at listed companies, and so likely primarily to affect institutional investors, Member States are free to extend to non-listed companies some or all of the provisions of the proposed Directive.

Another advantage of family-owned firms may be their ability to be less driven by the short-term demands of the market. Of course, they still ultimately need to be able to make a profit, but they may have more flexibility as to when and how they do so.

However, even when a family business is still relatively small, there may be tensions and divisions within the family as different members may wish to take different courses of action that will affect the day-to-day way the business operates and its longer term development. In the same way, as different generations of a family will have diverse views on various aspects of life, so they will in the business context as well. Similarly, as siblings may argue about various things, so are they likely to differ in their views of who should hold power within the business and how the business should develop. Even in the early stages of a family firm, it is wise to have some sort of forum where the views of family members regarding the business and its development can be expressed. One such mechanism is the family meeting or assembly, where family members can meet, often on a formal pre-arranged basis, to express their views. As time goes by and the family expands by marriage and new generations, then the establishment of a family council may be advisable. Neubauer and Lank (1998) suggest that a family council may be advisable once there are more than 30 to 40 family members.

When a business is at the stage where family relationships are impeding its efficient operation and development, or even if family members just realize that they are no longer

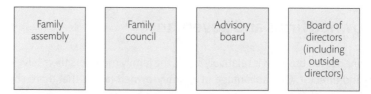

Figure 5.1 Possible stages in a family firm's governance

managing the business as effectively as they might, then it is definitely time to develop a more formal governance structure. There may be an intermediate stage where the family is advised by an advisory board, although this would not provide the same benefits to the family firm as a defined board structure with independent non-executive directors. Figure 5.1 illustrates the possible stages in a family firm's governance development.

Cadbury (2000) states that establishing a board of directors in a family firm is a means of progressing from an organization based on family relationships to one that is based primarily on business relationships. The structure of a family firm in its formative years is likely to be informal and to owe more to past history than to present needs. Once the firm has moved beyond the stage where authority is vested in the founders, it becomes necessary to clarify responsibilities and the process for taking decisions.

The advantages of a formal governance structure are several. First of all, there is a defined structure with defined channels for decision-making and clear lines of responsibility. Secondly, the board can tackle areas that may be sensitive from a family viewpoint but which nonetheless need to be dealt with: succession planning is a case in point, i.e. deciding who would be best to fill key roles in the business should the existing incumbents move on, retire, or die. Succession planning is important too in the context of raising external equity because, once a family business starts to seek external equity investment, then shareholders will usually want to know that succession planning is in place. The third advantage of a formal governance structure is also one in which external shareholders would take a keen interest: the appointment of non-executive directors. It may be that the family firm, depending on its size, appoints just one, or maybe two, non-executive directors. The key point about the non-executive director appointments is that the persons appointed should be independent; it is this trait that will make their contribution to the family firm a significant one. Of course, the independent non-executive directors should be appointed on the basis of the knowledge and experience that they bring to the family firm: their business experience, or a particular knowledge or functional specialism of relevance to the firm, which will enable them to 'add value' and contribute to the strategic development of the family firm.

Cadbury (2000) sums up the three requisites for family firms to manage successfully the impacts of growth: 'They need to be able to recruit and retain the very best people for the business, they need to be able to develop a culture of trust and transparency, and they need to define logical and efficient organisational structures.' A good governance system will help family firms to achieve these requisites.

In the context of succession planning, Bennedsen et al. (2007), in a study of family firms in Denmark, report that their empirical results demonstrate that professional, non-family chief executive officers (CEOs) provide extremely valuable services to the organizations they head.

On the other hand, they report that family CEO underperformance is particularly large in fast-growing industries, industries with a highly skilled labour force, and relatively large firms.

In a study of family firms in Belgium, Bammens and Voordeckers (2009), find that 'contrary to traditional agency wisdom, family firm boards devote substantial attention to controlling the management team ... those family firms that employ trust and control in a complementary manner will be most effective'. Bammens et al. (2011) provide an interesting discussion on boards of directors in family businesses and the literature relating thereto.

Bennedsen et al. (2010) make the point that 'family firms are unique because the governance of these firms is determined by the governance of the family behind the family firm'. The International Finance Corporation (IFC) (2011) point out that:

family members' duty is not only limited to the governance of their company, they are also responsible for the governance of the family and its relationship with the business. Setting up a solid family governance system early in the lifecycle of the family will help anticipate and resolve potential conflicts among family members about issues. This will make it possible for family members to concentrate on other key issues such as growing the business.

Furthermore, Franks et al. (2011) find that:

family firms evolve into widely held companies as they age only in countries with strong investor protection, well-developed financial markets and active markets for corporate control. In countries with weak investor protection, less developed financial markets and inactive markets for corporate control, family control is very persistent over time. This happens for both private and public firms.

Arcot and Brunoy (2012), in a study of both compliance with the UK Corporate Governance Code and explanations given for non-compliance by FTSE 350 non-financial companies between 1998 and 2004, find that:

family firms are more likely to deviate from standards of best practice in corporate governance. However, lesser governance standards in family firms are not associated with lower performance because the family shareholder is the monitor in-place. In contrast, governance practices and disclosures matter in widely-held firms because they alleviate the conflicts between managers and dispersed shareholders. More broadly, our results show that family ownership and board governance practices are substitute governance mechanisms.

Using a large firm-level data set of 2,949 publicly listed family-controlled firms (FCFs) across 27 European countries, van Essen et al. (2015) find that FCFs financially outperform non-FCFs during the financial crisis (2007–2009) but show no significant differences during the stable growth period between 2004 and 2006. They evaluate two employee outcomes being downsizing and wage decreases, and find that FCFs are less likely to downsize their workforce or cut wages in both pre-crisis and crisis conditions.

Another study which focuses on family firms and the financial crisis is that of Minichilli et al. (2016). Using a data set comprising all Italian industrial family and non-family publicly listed companies over the period 2002–2012, they 'observe a significantly and consistently better performance of family-controlled firms during the financial and economic crisis. Then, focusing on family firms only, we find that mixed configurations (family CEOs with relatively lower family ownership concentration) produce better performance in the face of an external hazard.'

Pindado and Requejo (2015) provide a comprehensive review of 350 empirical research articles relating to family firms, business performance, and corporate governance. Their insightful review provides an in-depth analysis of the family business governance system and 'highlights the need to contemplate the multiple relations that exist among the various governance dimensions of family firms to explain their unique performance ... [moreover] the review highlights the need for interdisciplinary collaboration to advance family business research and thus to consolidate it as a distinctive academic field.'

Smaller quoted companies

In the UK many firms with family control will be smaller quoted companies, either on the main market or on the UK's Alternative Investment Market (AIM), which can be seen as a way for smaller firms to obtain market recognition and access to external sources of finance, often before moving on to the main market.

The UK Corporate Governance Code 2010 forms part of the UK Listing Authority's Rules and is applicable to all UK-listed companies. This means that there should be no distinction between the governance standards expected of larger and smaller companies. The UK Corporate Governance Code encourages smaller companies to adopt the Code's approach. However, in relation to smaller companies (those outside the FTSE 350), it states that they should have at least two independent non-executive directors (rather than half the board being independent non-executive directors, which is the requirement for larger companies); and also for listed companies outside the FTSE 350, it allows the company chairman to sit on, but not chair, the audit committee where he/she was considered independent on appointment.

The Quoted Companies Alliance (QCA), formerly the City Group for Smaller Companies (CISCO), is an association representing the interests of smaller companies and their advisors. The QCA fully embraces the principles of corporate governance contained in the UK Corporate Governance Code and advocates that these principles should be adopted by all public quoted companies in so far as it is practicable for their size. Over the years, the QCA has published guidance on corporate governance as follows: the QCA *Guidance for Smaller Companies* (2001), updated in 2004, urged smaller companies to comply with the Combined Code as far as they were able, but where they were unable to comply fully, then they should explain why they were unable to comply. The QCA Corporate Governance Committee (2005, updated in 2007) published a corporate governance guide for AIM companies to help smaller companies seeking to develop their governance, or to meet the expectations of institutional investors. The 2007 QCA Guidelines were superseded by a new publication, *Corporate Governance Guidelines for Smaller Quoted Companies* (the QCA Guidelines) published in September 2010. The QCA Guidelines took into account the UK Corporate Governance Code 2010.

The underlying theme behind the QCA Guidelines (2010) is that trust and transparency between an AIM company's board and its shareholders will reduce the need for more regulation. The QCA Guidelines promulgate four key elements to effective corporate governance: the chairman's responsibility for corporate governance, the board acting together as a team, the adoption of best practice corporate governance processes, and non-executive directors being truly independent. The independence of a board member should be defined according to the individual's approach to the role and his/her ability to behave independently and appropriately, rather than an absence of connections.

The QCA updated the Guidelines again with the *Corporate Governance Code for Small and Mid-Size Quoted Companies 2013*. The QCA states that its 2013 Code adopts key elements of the UK Corporate Governance Code [2012], current policy initiatives, and other relevant guidance and then applies these to the needs and particular circumstances of small and mid-size quoted companies on a public market. It focuses on 12 principles and a set of minimum disclosures.

The QCA published *Remuneration Committee Guide For Small and Mid-Size Quoted Companies (2016)* which covers the operational aspects of the committee, the roles and responsibilities of those on the committee, and those that work with the committee; Directors' remuneration reporting regulations; factors to consider in setting remuneration policy; communicating with shareholders; and the remuneration report.

The QCA together with UHY Hacker Young published a *Corporate Governance Behaviour Review* in 2017. They benchmarked corporate governance disclosures made by 100 small and mid-size quoted companies against the minimum disclosures of the QCA Corporate Governance Code. The results were then examined by a group of institutional investors at a discussion roundtable after which five recommendations were made to help companies improve their corporate governance disclosures. These recommendations were: to show clear links between strategy and corporate governance; avoid boilerplate disclosures; show how board performance is evaluated and what action is then taken; provide a single total remuneration figure for each director in the remuneration report; and board roles to be adequately described and illustrate an appropriate balance of skills and experience.

There has been relatively little research into aspects of corporate governance in small companies, with a few exceptions being Collier (1997) on audit committees in smaller listed companies, and Mallin and Ow-Yong (1998a, 1998b) on corporate governance in AIM companies and corporate governance in small companies on the main market. Mallin and Ow-Yong (2008) carried out a further study of corporate governance in AIM companies and highlighted a concern that 'with the rapid expansion of AIM and the increasing number of overseas companies, from countries whose culture of good governance may be weaker than that of the UK, a damaging financial scandal or collapse is only a matter of time'. They recommended that:

> the role of the NOMAD [nominated advisor] be re-examined; the admission of overseas companies to AIM should be more closely scrutinized; small boards which may not be able to institute all the features of 'good' corporate governance should consider increasing the number of directors on their board, subject to resource constraints; and the regulatory authorities should monitor more closely the governance of AIM companies which have yet to start trading.

Mendoza (2008) analysed how AIM's regulatory regime has contributed to the success of low-cost listing stock exchanges. However, he argued that NOMADs as AIM's regulators may be questioned on the grounds that these entities are paid by the firms they counsel. On the other hand, he argues that it is in the NOMADs' interest to avoid any damage to their reputation which might then impact on their future business. He draws a number of conclusions about the future continued success of AIM, including that the LSE should remain vigilant in overseeing the NOMADs and their client firms.

Mallin and Ow-Yong (2011a) highlighted potential shortcomings of AIM which might have ethical and governance implications but felt that, in general, the 'lighter touch' on corporate governance for AIM companies seems to be working quite well, with directors' own sense of best practice and investor expectation usually helping to ensure that appropriate governance practices are adopted. However, they conclude that 'potential ethical issues, whether relating to corporate governance shortcomings or due diligence pre or post listing, can largely be overcome by the more rigorous processes and reviews established recently by the LSE, and especially the monitoring mechanism of regular reviews of NOMADs'.

Another strand of the literature concentrates on firm-level characteristics that may serve to differentiate large and small firms. Larger firms tend to be more complex, whereas smaller firms adopt simpler systems and structures; smaller firms tend to have more concentrated leadership, whilst in a larger firm control may be more diffuse, or more subject to question by a larger board (Fama and Jensen 1983; Begley and Boyd 1987). In terms of the impact on corporate governance structures, it can be expected that, in general, small and medium-sized firms will have simpler corporate governance structures than large firms—this may include: combining various of the key committees (audit, remuneration, nomination); a smaller number of non-executive directors (NEDs); a combined chair/CEO; and longer contractual terms for directors due to the more difficult labour market for director appointments into small and medium-sized companies.

Mallin and Ow-Yong (2011b) examine the relationship between company and ownership characteristics and the disclosure level of compliance with QCA recommendations on corporate governance in AIM companies. They find that compliance increases with company size, board size, the proportion of independent non-executive directors, the presence of turnover revenue, and being formerly listed on the Main Market. They find no evidence that ownership structure or the type of NOMAD is related to disclosure of compliance with QCA Guidelines.

The role and importance of NEDs was emphasized in the Cadbury Report (1992) and in the Code of Best Practice it is stated that NEDs 'should bring an independent judgement to bear on issues of strategy, performance, resources, including key appointments, and standards of conduct' (para. 2.1). Similarly, the Hampel Report (1998) stated: 'Some smaller companies have claimed that they cannot find a sufficient number of independent non-executive directors of suitable calibre. This is a real difficulty, but the need for a robust independent voice on the board is as strong in smaller companies as in large ones' (para. 3.10). The importance of the NED selection process is also emphasized: they 'should be selected through a formal process and both this process and their appointment should be a matter for the board as a whole' (para. 2.4).

From Table 5.1, it can be seen that the areas where potential difficulties are most likely to arise tend to be those relating to the appointment of directors, particularly non-executive directors, which has implications for board structure. These differences arise partly because of the difficulties of attracting and retaining suitable non-executive directors in small companies.

Table 5.1 Areas of the UK Corporate Governance Code that may prove difficult for smaller companies

UK Corporate Governance Code recommendations	Potential difficulty
Minimum two independent NEDs	Recruiting and remunerating independent NEDs
Split roles of chair/CEO	May not be enough directors to split the roles
Audit committee comprised of two NEDs	Audit committee may include executive directors
NEDs should be appointed for specific terms	NEDs often appointed for longer term

Mallin and Ow-Yong (1998b) found that the most important attribute for small businesses when recruiting non-executive directors was their business skills and experience. Overall, the inference could be made that the ability to 'add value' to the business is the most important factor influencing NED appointments, which is in line with a study by Collier (1997). Similarly, the Hampel Committee (1998) stated: 'particularly in smaller companies, non-executive directors may contribute valuable expertise not otherwise available to management' (para. 3.8). However, many small companies do not have a nomination committee, and therefore non-executive director appointments are often made by the whole board. Interestingly, Mallin and Ow-Yong (2008) found that the factor that was considered to be most influential when making non-executive director appointments was considered to be 'objectivity and integrity' followed by 'relevant business skills and experience'. This perhaps highlights the impact of various corporate scandals and collapses in bringing to the fore the importance of these characteristics of objectivity and integrity.

In terms of the adoption of board committees, small companies tend to have adopted audit and remuneration committees fairly widely but not nomination committees. In some smaller companies, the committees may carry out combined roles where, for example, the remuneration and nomination committees are combined into one; often the board as a whole will carry out the function of the nomination committee rather than trying to establish a separate committee from a small pool of non-executive directors.

A word of caution should be sounded though in relation to quoted companies where there is still a large block of family ownership (or indeed any other form of controlling shareholder). Charkham and Simpson (1999) point out:

> The controlling shareholders' role as guardians is potentially compromised by their interest as managers. Caution is needed. The boards may be superb and they may therefore be fortunate enough to participate in a wonderful success, but such businesses can decline at an alarming rate so that the option of escape through what is frequently an illiquid market anyway may be unattractive.

The points made are twofold: first, that despite a good governance structure on paper, in practice, controlling shareholders may effectively be able to disenfranchise the minority shareholders; secondly, that in a family-owned business, or other business with a controlling shareholder, the option to sell one's shares may not be either attractive or viable at a given point in time.

Unlisted companies

European Confederation of Directors' Associations (ecoDa) Corporate Governance Guidance and Principles for Unlisted Companies in Europe 2010

In 2010 ecoDa issued the *Corporate Governance Guidance and Principles for Unlisted Companies in Europe*. The financial crisis highlighted the importance of good corporate governance including for unlisted enterprises many of which

> are owned and controlled by single individuals or coalitions of company insiders (e.g. a family). In many cases, owners continue to play a significant direct role in management. Good governance in this context is not a question of protecting the interests of absentee shareholders. Rather, it is concerned with establishing a framework of company processes and attitudes that add value to the business and help ensure its long-term continuity and success.

The ecoDa Principles follow a phased approach with phase 1 principles, which represent a core framework of basic governance principles, applying to all unlisted companies, whatever their size; whilst phase 2 principles are those that are relevant to larger or more complex unlisted companies, or those with significant external funding. EcoDa highlights that the most important of the phase 2 principles is appointing independent directors to the board as 'it normally signals an irreversible step towards good governance and is likely to exert an immediate effect over the culture of boardroom behaviour'.

Phase 1 principles: Corporate governance principles applicable to all unlisted companies

- Principle 1—Shareholders should establish an appropriate constitutional and governance framework for the company.
- Principle 2—Every company should strive to establish an effective board, which is collectively responsible for the long-term success of the company, including the definition of the corporate strategy. However, an interim step on the road to an effective (and independent) board may be the creation of an advisory board.
- Principle 3—The size and composition of the board should reflect the scale and complexity of the company's activities.
- Principle 4—The board should meet sufficiently regularly to discharge its duties, and be supplied in a timely manner with appropriate information.
- Principle 5—Levels of remuneration should be sufficient to attract, retain, and motivate executives and non-executives of the quality required to run the company successfully.
- Principle 6—The board is responsible for risk oversight and should maintain a sound system of internal control to safeguard shareholders' investment and the company's assets.
- Principle 7—There should be a dialogue between the board and the shareholders based on the mutual understanding of objectives. The board as a whole has responsibility for ensuring that a satisfactory dialogue with shareholders takes place. The board should not forget that all shareholders have to be treated equally.
- Principle 8—All directors should receive induction on joining the board and should regularly update and refresh their skills and knowledge.
- Principle 9—Family-controlled companies should establish family governance mechanisms that promote coordination and mutual understanding amongst family members, as well as organize the relationship between family governance and corporate governance.

Phase 2 principles: Corporate governance principles applicable to large and/or more complex unlisted companies

- Principle 10—There should be a clear division of responsibilities at the head of the company between the running of the board and the running of the company's business. No one individual should have unfettered powers of decision.
- Principle 11—Board structures vary according to national regulatory requirements and business norms. However, all boards should contain directors with a sufficient mix of competencies and experiences. No single person (or small group of individuals) should dominate the board's decision-making.
- Principle 12—The board should establish appropriate board committees in order to allow a more effective discharge of its duties.
- Principle 13—The board should undertake a periodic appraisal of its own performance and that of each individual director.
- Principle 14—The board should present a balanced and understandable assessment of the company's position and prospects for external stakeholders, and establish a suitable programme of stakeholder engagement.

EcoDa states that 'the implementation of phase 2 principles is likely to increase the formality of governance arrangements. However, this is invariably a necessary step in larger or more complex enterprises in order to provide the necessary reassurance to owners or external creditors regarding the longer-term sustainability of the enterprise.'

Overall, the Principles provide a governance road map for family owners or founder-entrepreneurs as they look ahead to the life cycle of the business.

Corporate Governance Guidance and Principles for Unlisted Companies in the UK 2010

The *Corporate Governance Guidance and Principles for Unlisted Companies in the UK 2010* published by the UK Institute of Directors is based on the ecoDa guidance discussed in detail above and so the principles will not be outlined again here.

The rationale for this guidance in the UK is that the vast majority of the UK's 2.6 million registered companies are small or medium-sized enterprises or start-up companies which remain under the ownership and control of the founder or founding family. The Institute of Directors

is convinced that appropriate corporate governance practices can contribute to the success of UK companies of all types and sizes, including those that are unlisted or privately held ... Unlisted companies—such as founder and family-owned businesses—can utilize this stepwise framework to ensure their long-term sustainability, to bring external parties to their boards, to attract funds, and to solve issues between shareholders and other stakeholders.

Corporate Governance Code for Large Privately-Owned Companies

A Coalition Group of which the FRC is secretariat was established in response to the Green Paper Consultation on Corporate Governance Reform to develop and deliver the corporate governance principles for large privately owned companies. The Group is chaired by James Wates and in June 2018 *The Wates Corporate Governance Principles for Large Private Companies 2018* were issued for consultation. This has been discussed in more detail in Chapter 3.

Conclusions

In many countries, family-owned firms are prevalent. Corporate governance is of relevance to family-owned firms, which can encompass a number of business forms, including private and publicly quoted companies, for a number of reasons. Corporate governance structures can help the company to develop successfully; they can provide the means for defined lines of decision-making and accountability, enable the family firm to benefit from the contribution of independent non-executive directors, and help ensure a more transparent and fair approach to the way the business is organized and managed. Family-owned firms may face difficulties in initially finding appropriate independent non-executive directors, but the benefits that such directors can bring are worth the time and financial investment that the family-owned firm will need to make.

Summary

- Family ownership of firms is the prevalent form of ownership in many countries around the globe.

- The legal system of a country tends to influence the type of ownership that develops, so that in common law countries with good protection for minority shareholders' rights, the shareholder base is more diverse, whereas in civil law countries with poor protection for minority shareholders' rights, there tends to be more family ownership and control.

- The governance structure of a family firm may develop in various stages, such as starting with a family assembly, then a family council, advisory board, and, finally, a defined board structure with independent non-executive directors.

- The advantages to the family firm of a sound governance structure are that it can provide a mechanism for defined lines of decision-making and accountability, enable the family firm to benefit from the contribution of independent non-executive directors, and help ensure a more transparent and fair approach to the way the business is organized and managed.

- The ecoDa *Corporate Governance Guidance and Principles for Unlisted Companies in Europe 2010* provides a phased framework of corporate governance guidance for unlisted companies.

- The UK is preparing a *Corporate Governance Code for Large Privately-Owned Companies* to help enhance confidence through greater transparency; build a strong corporate culture and integrity; ensure consideration of employees and the wider stakeholder group; and maintain investor, creditor, and lender confidence.

Example: Cadbury Plc, UK

This is an example of a family firm that grew over time, developed an appropriate governance structure, and became an international business.

Today, Cadbury is a household name in homes across the world. It was founded in the first part of the nineteenth century when John Cadbury decided to establish a business based on the manufacture and marketing of cocoa. His two sons joined the firm in 1861 and, over the years, more family members joined, and subsequently the firm became a private limited liability company, Cadbury Brothers Ltd. A board of directors was formed consisting of members of the family.

Non-family directors were first appointed to the firm in 1943, and in 1962, the firm became a publicly quoted company with the family members still being the majority on the board and holding a controlling interest (50 per cent plus) in the shares. Cadbury merged with Schweppes in the late 1960s, and over the next 40 years, Cadbury Schweppes developed a diverse shareholder base and a board of directors appointed from the wider business community. The direct family involvement, via either large shareholdings or board membership, therefore declined over the years. In the spring of 2007, Cadbury Schweppes revealed plans to split its business into two separate entities: one focusing on its main chocolate and confectionery market; the other on its US drinks business. The demerger took effect in May 2008 so that Cadbury Schweppes Plc became Cadbury Plc (focusing on the former market) and Dr Pepper Snapple Group Inc. (focusing on the US drinks business).

In 2009 Kraft launched a hostile takeover bid for Cadbury. Cadbury decided to fight to retain its independence but the firm's shareholders eventually accepted Kraft's hostile takeover and accepted a bid of £11.5 billion in January 2010.

Kraft's purchase was hugely controversial given that Cadbury is viewed as a great British institution. Unfortunately, once the sale went through, Kraft closed Cadbury's Somerdale factory near Bristol, with a loss of 400 jobs. In 2011 Kraft announced that another 200 jobs were being cut through voluntary redundancies and redeployment, though it has also announced a £50 million investment in the business. In 2012 a twist to the tale was that the great-granddaughter of the founder of Cadbury decided to set up her own chocolate business. From October 2012, Kraft Foods split into two companies with the confectionery business of Kraft becoming Mondelez International, of which Cadbury is a subsidiary. As a result of declining margins in its businesses, in 2014 Mondelez undertook a cost-cutting programme and in 2015 Mondelez began closing Cadbury factories in several countries including Ireland, Canada, the United States, and New Zealand and moving production to countries with lower production costs such as China, India, and Brazil. Whilst shareholders generally approved of these plans, the closures resulted in upset at the job losses and the loss of the connection with such a well-established name as Cadbury.

Example: CK Hutchison, Hong Kong

This is an example of an international company where there is controlling ownership by a family via a pyramid shareholding.

CK Hutchison has its origins in Hutchison Whampoa which was a multinational conglomerate with six core businesses, including ports and related services, property and hotels, telecommunications, retail and manufacturing, energy, and infrastructure. Hutchison Whampoa ranked as one of the most valuable companies in Hong Kong and a large proportion of it was controlled by Cheung Kong Holdings in which the Li Ka Shing family had a significant interest, which meant that the family had significant influence over both companies, one through direct ownership, the other via an indirect, or pyramid, shareholding.

(continued)

Hutchison Whampoa had, for many years, been the recipient of various awards and accolades. Whilst having a controlling family interest, Hutchison Whampoa was committed to good corporate governance and to its wider shareholder base. In the last ten years, its accolades have been many and included the following: in 2008 it was recognized by Corporate Governance Asia as one of 'The Best of Asia', that is one of 'Asia's Best Companies for Corporate Governance'; in 2011, its awards included: Asiamoney 'Best Managed Company Awards: Hong Kong—Large-cap Corporate of the Year in Hong Kong'; and Corporate Governance Asia 'Asia's Best CFO (Mr Frank Sixt)', 'Asia's Best CSR', and 'Best Investor Relations by Hong Kong Company'; whilst in 2015, it was awarded the FinanceAsia 'Asia's Best Conglomerate' award, IFR Asia 'Asia's Investment-Grade Bond of the Year', and The Hong Kong Council of Social Service '10 Years Plus Caring Company Logo'.

It was also in early 2015 that momentous changes to Hutchison Whampoa's structure were announced as Li Ka Shing, together with his son and heir, Victor Li, announced a plan to split the two main companies, Hutchison Whampoa and Cheung Kong, into a ports-to-pharmacies conglomerate and a property group. The plan was well received by the stock market as it was seen as an appropriate reorganization which secured a clean split between the conglomerate side of the business and the property business. It would also help unlock value from the cross-shareholding structure. The two companies were later merged as CK Hutchison which is among the largest companies listed on the main board of The Hong Kong Stock Exchange. CK Hutchison has five core businesses—ports and related services, retail, infrastructure, energy, and telecommunications.

On CK Hutchison's website, they state: 'The multicultural mix of our executives and staff reflects the diversity and reach of our operations. CK Hutchison is dedicated to upholding the highest standards of corporate governance, transparency and accountability.' The company has a 16-page Corporate Governance Report which contains details of the board of directors including directors' gender, ethnicity, and age group. There is also a separate 14-page Environmental, Social and Governance Report. CK Hutchison continues to receive many awards for its corporate governance, investor relations, and corporate social responsibility as well as for aspects of stakeholder relations; for example, in 2017, in the 8th Asia's Best Employer Brand Awards—'Asia's Best Employer Brand'; and the Hong Kong Council of Social Service '10 Years Plus Caring Company Logo'.

 ## Mini case study   Fiat (now FCA), Italy

This is a good example of a firm where the founding family still has significant influence through a complex shareholding structure. It also illustrates several international aspects including FCA listing on the NYSE as a foreign private issuer whilst following the Dutch Corporate Governance Code as FCA is incorporated in The Netherlands.

Fabbrica Italiana Automobili Torino, better known as Fiat, was founded in 1899 by a group of investors including Giovanni Agnelli. Fiat automobiles were immediately popular not just in Italy but internationally too. Fiat expanded rapidly in the 1950s and, in 1966, the founder's grandson, also Giovanni Agnelli, became the company's Chairman. As well as cars, Fiat's business empire included commercial vehicles, agricultural, and construction equipment, insurance, aviation, the press, electric power, and natural gas distribution. In past years, it has achieved enormous financial success.

More than 90 per cent of Italian-registered companies are family owned, with many companies being run by Italian families who wield great power. Traditionally, control has been achieved, often

(continued)

with the minimum of capital outlay, through a complex structure involving a series of holding companies. In the case of Fiat, control by the Agnelli family is via pyramids (indirect holdings) and voting trusts, particularly Ifi (a financial holding company) in which the Agnelli family has control of all the votes.

By 2002 Fiat had significant financial problems with losses of US$1.2 billion in that year. General Motors, which had acquired a 20 per cent shareholding in Fiat at a cost of US$2.4 billion, was asked to invest further in Fiat but was reluctant to do so. In 2003 the group restructured its core business area by again focusing manufacturing and service activities on the traditional motor vehicle sector.

In 2003 Umberto Agnelli died, and in 2004, Luca Cordero di Montezemolo was nominated as Chairman. Also in 2004 Sergio Marchionne was appointed as Chief Executive of Fiat and this marked a turning point in the company's fortunes. An astute and experienced businessman, Mr Marchionne oversaw changes to various areas of the Fiat business. At the beginning of 2005 Fiat announced the creation of Fiat Powertrain Technologies, a new industrial unit designed to integrate the groups' innovation capabilities and expertise in engines and transmissions. In February 2005 the boards of directors of Fiat and General Motors met to approve a contract to terminate the master agreement and related joint ventures between the two companies. The Chairman of Fiat, Luca Cordero di Montezemolo, said:

> We are delighted to have been able to conclude this agreement with General Motors. While highly beneficial to both Fiat and GM since 2000, the arrangements had become too confining for the development of Fiat Auto in today's market environment. We now have all the necessary freedom to develop strategic growth alternatives for Fiat Auto, while retaining a base on which to build a much more constructive relationship with GM in the future.

There were also important changes to Fiat's corporate governance structure in June 2005, with Fiat extending its board of directors to 15 members, so that the board comprised a majority of independent non-executive directors. At the same time, Fiat strengthened its independence requirements for directors. In its press release, it stated:

> After a thorough review of current international practice on this issue, the Company has adopted a set of criteria which are designed to ensure that the independence qualification is held to the highest possible standard. As an example, directors who have served on the Board for more than nine years, even though not consecutively, are deemed not to be independent. Furthermore, board members who are executive directors of other companies on whose board[s] sit executive board members of Fiat are also deemed not to be independent.

In January 2006 Fiat announced another significant strategic change with the signing of an agreement to co-operate on dealer networks with Tata Motors Ltd, which meant that Fiat cars could be distributed via the Tata network in India. Late in January 2006 Fiat announced that it had seen its first positive quarterly trading profit after 17 successive quarters of losses.

With the revision of Italian corporate governance provisions, the Fiat Group adopted and abides by the Corporate Governance Code of Italian Listed Companies issued in March 2006. Fiat provides information regarding how it meets the individual principles and criteria of the Corporate Governance Code by providing a reprise of the individual principles and criteria, and then summarizing how each of these is implemented at Fiat.

2006 saw the strengthening of Fiat's presence in Europe and the gaining of access into markets, including China, India, and Russia. In 2007 Sergio Marchionne announced the 2007–10 plan geared towards growth. In 2009 he unveiled his plan to put Fiat at the heart of the car-making industry globally by forging an alliance with the giant troubled US car manufacturers Chrysler and General Motors (Opel, the European arm). In June 2009 Fiat and Chrysler announced that they had finalized

(continued)

a global strategic partnership to begin immediately. The ultimate success of the alliance will depend on many factors and will likely have implications for the workforces in the various countries affected, including Germany and the UK.

In December 2011 Fiat made a groundbreaking deal with the Italian trade unions, which gives it more flexibility in labour contracts in exchange for a rise in wages. By early 2012 Fiat and Chrysler together were selling more than four million cars.

In October 2014, the merger of Fiat S.p.A. with and into Fiat Investments N.V. took place at which time Fiat Investments N.V. was renamed Fiat Chrysler Automobiles N.V. (or FCA NV). FCA NV's official headquarters were moved to London and the combined company was incorporated in the Netherlands. Marchionne also listed new FCA stock on the New York Stock Exchange. FCA is headed by Sergio Marchionne (CEO) and John Elkann, the great-great-grandson of Fiat founder Giovanni Agnelli, is the Chairman.

In FCA's annual report for the year ended 31 December 2016, the firm's major shareholders are identified and of particular note is the following:

> Exor N.V. is the largest shareholder of FCA through its 29.41 percent shareholding interest in our issued common shares (as of February 27, 2017). On December 16, 2016, Exor N.V. received 73,606,222 of FCA common shares in connection with the mandatory conversion of the mandatory convertible securities due 2016. As a result of the loyalty voting mechanism, Exor N.V.'s voting power is 42.60 percent. Consequently, Exor N.V. could strongly influence all matters submitted to a vote of FCA shareholders, including approval of annual dividends, election and removal of directors and approval of extraordinary business combinations. Exor N.V. is controlled by Giovanni Agnelli BV ('GA'), which holds 52.99 percent of its share capital. GA is a private limited liability company under Dutch law with its capital divided in shares and currently held by members of the Agnelli and Nasi families, descendants of Giovanni Agnelli, founder of Fiat. Its present principal business activity is to purchase, administer and dispose of equity interests in public and private entities and, in particular, to ensure the cohesion and continuity of the administration of its controlling equity interests. The directors of GA are John Elkann, Tiberto Brandolini d'Adda, Alessandro Nasi, Andrea Agnelli, Eduardo Teodorani-Fabbri, Luca Ferrero de Gubernatis Ventimiglia, Jeroen Preller and Florence Hinnen.

The report also explains that:

> the purpose of the loyalty voting structure is to grant long-term shareholders an extra voting right by means of granting a special voting share (shareholders holding special voting shares are entitled to exercise one vote for each special voting share held and one vote for each common share held), without entitling such shareholders to any economic rights, other than those pertaining to the common shares.

In general such arrangements are sometimes known as control enhancing mechanisms (CEMs) and include pyramid structures, shareholders' agreements, cross-shareholdings, multiple voting rights, golden shares, and ownership ceilings.

In the Corporate Governance section of the annual report, the corporate governance rules governing FCA are discussed:

> The Company qualifies as a foreign private issuer under the New York Stock Exchange ('NYSE') listing standards and its common shares are listed on the NYSE and on the Mercato Telematico Azionario managed by Borsa Italiana S.p.A. ('MTA'). In accordance with the NYSE Listed Company Manual, the Company is permitted to follow home country practice with regard to certain corporate governance standards. The Company has adopted, except as discussed below,

(continued)

the best practice provisions of the Dutch corporate governance code issued by the Dutch Corporate Governance Code Committee.

One of the exceptions referred to relates to the fact that the Dutch Corporate Governance Code provisions primarily refer to companies with a two-tier board structure (consisting of a management board and a separate supervisory board), while the Company has implemented a one-tier board. FCA's Corporate Governance section states that the best practices reflected in the Dutch Corporate Governance Code for supervisory board members apply by analogy to non-executive directors.

In terms of overall board structure, there is a unitary (one-tier board) consisting of a total of 11 executive and non-executive directors (seven directors qualified as independent, representing a majority). The board of directors has appointed Mr Ronald L. Thompson as Senior Non-Executive Director. During 2016, there were six meetings of the board of directors with an average attendance at those meetings of 97 percent.

There are three board committees: an Audit committee (10 meetings held with an average 100 per cent attendance), a Compensation Committee (two meetings held with an average attendance of 100 per cent) and a Governance and Sustainability Committee (one meeting held with 100 per cent attendance).

Going forward potential avenues which may be open to FCA include partnerships, mergers, or selling off certain brands in the increasingly competitive automobile market.

Mini case study questions

1. Consider the development of FCA as a firm with influential family ownership. How does this compare to other firms with family ownership?

2. What features of a robust corporate governance structure does FCA have?

3. Consider the more idiosyncratic features of FCA's corporate governance. To what extent might minority interests be affected?

Questions

The discussion questions to follow cover the key learning points of this chapter. Reading of some of the additional reference material will enhance the depth of the students' knowledge and understanding of these areas.

1. What are the key factors affecting the ownership structure of businesses in different countries, and how might these impact on the development of a business?

2. What are the advantages and disadvantages of a family-owned firm?

3. How might the corporate governance structure in a family firm develop?

4. Critically discuss the value of a board, including the contribution to the family firm that may be made by independent non-executive directors.

5. 'The need for a professional business approach is arguably even greater in a family than in a non-family firm' (Sir Adrian Cadbury, 2000). Critically discuss this statement.

6. What evidence is there to indicate that family firms may be more resilient in times of financial crisis and better able to absorb exogenous shocks?

References

Arcot, S., and Brunoy, V. (2012), 'Do Standard Corporate Governance Practices Matter in Family Firms?' Financial Markets Group Discussion Paper 710, LSE, London.

Bammens, Y. and Voordeckers, W. (2009), 'The Board's Control Tasks in Family Firms' in M. Huse (ed.), *The Value Creating Board*, Routledge, London.

Bammens, Y., Voordeckers, W., and Van Gils, A. (2011), 'Boards of Directors in Family Businesses: A Literature Review and Research Agenda', *International Journal of Management Reviews*, Vol. 13, Issue 2, pp. 134–52.

Begley, T.M. and Boyd, D.P. (1987), 'Psychological Characteristics Associated with Performance in Entrepreneurial Firms and Smaller Businesses', *Journal of Business Venturing*, Vol. 2, No. 1, pp. 79–93.

Bennedsen, M., Nielsen, K.M., Perez-Gonzalez, F., and Wolfenzon, D. (2007), 'Inside the Family Firm: The Role of Families in Succession Decisions and Performance', *Quarterly Journal of Economics*, Vol. 122, No. 2, pp. 647–91.

Bennedsen, M., Pérez-González F., and Wolfenzon, D. (2010), 'The Governance of Family Firms' in H. Kent Baker and R. Anderson (eds), *Corporate Governance, A Synthesis of Theory, Research and Practice*, The Robert W. Kolb Series in Finance, John Wiley & Sons Inc., New Jersey.

Cadbury, Sir Adrian (1992), *Report of the Committee on the Financial Aspects of Corporate Governance*, Gee & Co. Ltd, London.

Cadbury, Sir Adrian (2000), *Family Firms and their Governance: Creating Tomorrow's Company from Today's*, Egon Zehnder International, London.

Charkham, J. and Simpson, A. (1999), *Fair Shares: The Future of Shareholder Power and Responsibility*, Oxford University Press, Oxford.

Collier, P. (1997), 'Audit Committees in Smaller Listed Companies' in K. Keasey and M. Wright (eds), *Corporate Governance: Responsibilities, Risks and Remuneration*, John Wiley & Sons, London.

ecoDa (2010), *ecoDa Corporate Governance Guidance and Principles for Unlisted Companies in Europe*, ecoDa, Brussels.

Fama, E.F. and Jensen, M.C. (1983), 'Separation of Ownership and Control', *Journal of Law and Economics*, Vol. 26, No. 2, pp. 301–25.

Financial Reporting Council (2018) *The Wates Corporate Governance Principles for Large Private Companies 2018*, FRC, London.

Franks, J.R., Mayer, C., and Rossi, S. (2005a), 'Ownership: Evolution and Regulation', ECGI–Finance Working Paper No. 09/2003.

Franks, J.R., Mayer, C., and Rossi, S. (2005b), 'Spending Less Time with the Family: The Decline of Family Ownership in the UK', in R.K. Morck (ed.), *A History of Corporate Governance around the World: Family Business Groups to Professional Managers*, University of Chicago Press, Chicago.

Franks, J. R., Mayer, C., Volpin, P. F., and Wagner, H. F. (2011), 'The Life Cycle of Family Ownership: International Evidence' (2 September 2011). Paris, December 2011 Finance Meeting EUROFIDAI–AFFI. Available at SSRN: http://ssrn.com/abstract = 1102475 or http://dx.doi.org/10.2139/ssrn.1102475.

Hampel, Sir Ronnie (1998), *Committee on Corporate Governance: Final Report*, Gee & Co. Ltd, London.

Institute of Directors (2010), *Corporate Governance Guidance and Principles for Unlisted Companies in the UK*, Institute of Directors, London.

International Finance Corporation (2011), *IFC Family Business Governance Handbook*, IFC, Washington DC.

La Porta, R., Lopez-de-Silanes, F., Shleifer, A., and Vishny, R. (1999), 'Corporate Ownership Around the World', *Journal of Finance*, Vol. 54, No. 2, pp. 471–517.

Mallin, C.A. and Ow-Yong, K. (1998a), 'Corporate Governance in Small Companies: the Alternative Investment Market', *Corporate Governance: An International Review*, September 1998.

Mallin, C.A. and Ow-Yong, K. (1998b), *Corporate Governance in Small Companies on the Main Market*, ICAEW Research Board, ICAEW, London.

Mallin, C.A. and Ow-Yong, K. (2008), *Corporate Governance in Alternative Investment Market (AIM) Companies*, Institute of Chartered Accountants of Scotland, Edinburgh.

Mallin, C.A. and Ow-Yong, K. (2011a), 'The UK Alternative Investment Market-Ethical Dimensions' *Journal of Business Ethics*, Vol. 95, Issue 2, pp. 223–39.

Mallin, C.A. and Ow-Yong, K. (2011b), 'Factors Influencing Corporate Governance Disclosures in Alternative Investment Market (AIM) Companies', *European Journal of Finance*, Vol. 18, No, 16, pp. 515–33.

Mendoza, J.M. (2008), 'Securities Regulation in Low-Tier Listing Venues: The Rise of the Alternative Investment Market', *Fordham Journal of Corporate & Financial Law*, Vol. XIII, pp. 257–328.

Minichilli A., Brogi M., and Calabrò, A. (2016), 'Weathering the Storm: Family Ownership, Governance, and Performance Through the Financial and Economic Crisis', *Corporate Governance: An International Review*, Vol. 24, Issue 6, November 2016, pp. 552–68.

Morck, R. and Yeung, B. (2003), 'Agency Problems in Large Family Business Groups', *Entrepreneurship: Theory and Practice*, Summer, Vol. 27, No. 4, pp. 401–16.

Neubauer, F. and Lank, A.G. (1998), *The Family Business: Its Governance for Sustainability*, Macmillan, Basingstoke.

Pindado J., and Requejo I. (2015), 'Family Business Performance from a Governance Perspective: A Review of Empirical Research', *International Journal of Management Reviews*, Vol. 17, Issue 3, July 2015, pp. 279–311.

Quoted Companies Alliance (2001), *Guidance for Smaller Companies*, QCA, London.

Quoted Companies Alliance (2005), *Corporate Governance Guidelines for AIM Companies*, QCA, London.

Quoted Companies Alliance (2007), *Corporate Governance Guidelines for AIM Companies*, QCA, London.

Quoted Companies Alliance (2010), *Corporate Governance Guidelines for Smaller Quoted Companies*, QCA, London.

Quoted Companies Alliance (2013), *Corporate Governance Code for Small and Mid-Size Quoted Companies*, QCA, London.

Quoted Companies Alliance (2016), *Remuneration Committee Guide For Small and Mid-Size Quoted Companies (2016)*, QCA, London.

QCA and UHY Hacker Young (2017), *Corporate Governance Behaviour Review*, QCA, London.

van Essen M., Strike V.M., Carney M., and Sapp S. (2015), 'The Resilient Family Firm: Stakeholder Outcomes and Institutional Effects', *Corporate Governance: An International Review*, Vol. 23, Issue 3, May 2015, pp. 167–83.

Useful websites

http://rru.worldbank.org The website of the Rapid Response Unit of the World Bank has matters of interest to a range of companies and countries.

www.ecgi.global The website of the European Corporate Governance Institute has details of recent research into family-owned firms and their governance.

www.ecoda.org The website of The European Confederation of Directors' Associations where information can be found about their activities relating to representing the views of company directors from EU Member States to corporate governance policymakers at EU level.

www.fbn-i.org The Family Business Network website has items of interest to family businesses.

www.financeasia.com The website of FinanceAsia has information relating to various matters, including corporate governance, of particular interest to firms and investors in Asia.

www.ifb.org.uk The website of the Institute for Family Business, with an emphasis on the UK, has items of interest to family businesses.

www.iod.com The website of the Institute of Directors where information can be found about its activities in support of business including corporate governance.

www.theqca.com The website of the Quoted Companies Alliance has items of particular interest to companies outside the UK's FTSE 350.

 Develop your understanding of this chapter and explore the subject further using our online resources at **www.oup.com/uk/mallin6e/**

FT Clippings

Digital endurance runner picks up pace with Penguin deal

Corporate person in the news: Thomas Rabe, Chief Executive, Bertelsmann

Guy Chazan

Financial Times, 16 July 2017

For years, Thomas Rabe has cultivated an air of a digital pioneer, proudly boasting of his big bets on elearning, advertising technology and multichannel networks.

A wiry, teetotal 51-year-old, who runs, rows or cycles about 100km a week, the chief executive has steered his company, Bertelsmann, towards a bright future of fast growth, dynamic markets and cutting–edge online services.

So there were more than a few eyebrows raised this week when he unveiled Bertelsmann's latest big investment, in Penguin Random House, a traditional ink-on-paper publisher. The German group, which already owns 53 per cent of PRH, will pay $780m to buy an additional 22 per cent from its partner Pearson.

The deal cements Bertelsmann's status as the dominant force in global publishing, but seems somewhat at odds with its digital-first strategy. Mr Rabe sees no contradiction. Bertelsmann, he said, must maintain a balance between high-growth investments and stable, cash-generative businesses like PRH. 'Its margins are high, [and it] contributes to the cash flows Bertelsmann needs to invest in new business with higher growth potential than book publishing,' he said.

But there is no disguising the fact that the PRH deal was not part of Mr Rabe's master plan. Bertelsmann was blindsided this year when Pearson announced it was selling out, and had already committed capital to its other divisions. Renowned for its prudence, it suddenly had to work out how to fund a major acquisition it never wanted to make, without more debt.

Mr Rabe has wrestled with that tension ever since becoming chief executive in 2012. On the one hand, he is committed to growth—Bertelsmann is targeting revenues of €20bn in three to five years, up from €17bn last year. But achieving that is hard: the company, founded in 1835 as a publisher of hymn books, is privately owned and obsessed with preserving its prized Baaa1 credit rating. Bold, transformative M&A is hard. 'It's a real balancing act for him,' says one analyst who covers Bertelsmann.

Prudence is not a word one would associate with the younger Rabe. Thirty years ago he was a punk rocker with green hair, playing bass in a band called the White Lies. But that was an interlude in an otherwise orthodox trajectory. Born in Luxemburg, he grew up in Brussels, where his father worked as an EU civil servant. Having earned a doctorate in economics and an MBA at Cologne University, he did a stint at the European Commission before switching in 1993 to Treuhand, the agency that sold assets held by the former East Germany.

The late 1990s saw him at Clearstream, Deutsche Börse's settlement business and in 2000, he became chief financial officer at RTL group, the Bertlesmann-owned broadcaster. Six years later, he moved to the mother company, first as CFO, and later as chief executive.

In that role, he merged Bertelsmann's book division Random House with Penguin to create the world's largest publisher by sales, and took full control of BMG, the world's fourth biggest owner of music rights.

But the company still faces pressures. RTL is challenged by online video and disrupters such as Netflix, PRH by Amazon and self-publishing, and the magazine business Gruner + Jahr by the decline in print advertising revenue and falling circulation.

Mr Rabe has responded by diversifying Bertelsmann out of Europe, investing in digital start-ups in China, India and Brazil and branching into online education in the US.

The bright digital-first future is still far off. But Mr Rabe, an endurance runner, relishes a long and winding road.

Rothschild's chairman to hand bank's dynastic reins to son

Change coincides with effort to help ride out lean periods in European M&A market

Hannah Murphy

Financial Times, 27 February 2018

David de Rothschild is stepping aside as chairman of Rothschild this summer to pass the reins to his son Alexandre in a long-awaited changing of the guard at the Franco-British investment bank.

The younger Mr de Rothschild has long been groomed to succeed his father as the seventh generation of the banking dynasty that was founded 200 years ago. Currently executive deputy chairman, he first joined the bank in 2008 after stints in both investment banking and private equity at Bank of America and Bear Stearns.

The dynastic handover, expected to take place in June, comes amid a push by the investment bank to diversify from its core French and British advisory business to help it ride out less buoyant periods in Europe's mergers and acquisitions market.

Since joining the bank, Mr de Rothschild, 37, has set up and helped oversee the private equity business. The group has also been increasingly investing in its small US operations and last year completed its first sizeable acquisition to expand its private bank.

The elder Mr de Rothschild, who was born in New York, oversaw the merger of the then-separate French and UK banks in 2012 in a combination designed to unify two branches of the Rothschild family and bolster the balance sheet. Before that, the 75-year-old had been running the UK part of the bank after Evelyn de Rothschild, his cousin, retired in 2004.

The overhaul of the corporate structure was an opportunity for Mr de Rothschild to put in motion a succession plan by bringing his third child and only son to the supervisory board. It also allowed the family to tighten control over the group by buying out minority shareholders.

Still, his tenure has occasionally been dogged by family infighting among offshoots of the financial dynasty that sit outside the unified group.

Today, the family has 58 per cent of voting rights and owns a 49 per cent stake in the company. Just over 26 per cent of the group's shares are listed on Paris' Euronext exchange.

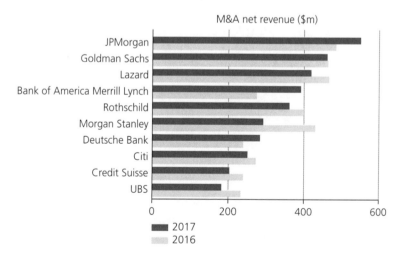

Figure 5.2 Top banks for European deal making

Source: Dealogic. Used under licence from the *Financial Times*. All rights reserved.

Rothschild's latest half-year results, published in November, showed revenue from its global advisory business, which accounts for about three-fifths of revenues, fell 8 per cent to €492m. By contrast, its private wealth and asset management and merchant banking divisions each posted growth of more than 30 per cent in the six months to September. Overall, revenues rose 6 per cent year on year to €852m and pre-tax profit increased 10 per cent to €206m.

Despite the dip in advisory revenue, the bank remained steady in fifth position by EU M&A revenue in 2017 as with the previous year, taking a 6 per cent share of the market, according to Dealogic.

Rothschild's shares, which were hit dramatically in the wake of the financial crisis, have gained more than 15 per cent since the beginning of 2017.

The bank boasts Emmanuel Macron, the French president, as a former employee. Mr Macron became known as the 'Mozart of finance' for his role at Rothschild in advising Nestlé on its $12bn acquisition of a Pfizer unit in 2012.

The company declined to comment on the handover.

6

The role of institutional investors in corporate governance

◎ Learning objectives

- To appreciate who institutional investors are

- To understand the growing influence of institutional investors and why they are increasingly interested in corporate governance

- To realize the importance of institutional investors' relationships with their investee companies and the role of stewardship

- To be aware of the 'tools of governance' that institutional investors have available to them

- To be able to assess the potential impact of 'good' corporate governance on corporate performance

Introduction

The potential influence of large shareholders was identified back in the 1930s when Berle and Means (1932) highlighted the separation of the owners (shareholders) from the control of the business, 'control' being in the hands of the directors. This separation of ownership and control leads to the problems associated with agency theory, so that the managers of the business may not act in the best interests of the owners. Throughout the twentieth century, the pattern of ownership continued to change and, in the USA and UK in particular, individual share ownership has declined and institutional share ownership has increased. Over 80 years later, institutional investors own large portions of equity in many companies across the world, and the key role played by institutional investors in corporate governance cannot be under-estimated. With the internationalization of cross-border portfolios, and the financial crises that have occurred in many parts of the world, it is perhaps not surprising that institutional investors increasingly look more carefully at the corporate governance of companies. After all, corporate governance goes hand in hand with increased transparency and accountability. In this chapter, the rise of the institutional investors and their role in corporate governance are examined.

Growth of institutional share ownership

In the UK overall the level of share ownership by individuals has decreased over the last 50 years, whilst ownership by institutional investors has increased. These institutional investors have traditionally comprised mainly pension funds and insurance companies, although newer types of investor, including hedge funds (included in the 'Other financial institutions' category below) are now gaining more foothold. The nature of the changing composition of the UK shareholder base is summarized in Table 6.1.

In 1963 individual investors owned 54 per cent of shares in the UK. The proportion of shares owned by this group fell steadily until, by 1989, it had dropped to just under 21 per cent. Since 1989 there have been a few factors that should have encouraged individual share ownership. First, there were the large privatization issues that occurred in the UK in the early 1990s, and then the demutualization of some of the large building societies. However, by 2016, the percentage had dropped to 12.3 per cent.

In contrast to the individual investors' level of share ownership, the ownership of shares by the insurance companies and the pension funds increased dramatically over the same period to 13.4 per cent and 12.8 per cent respectively in 2008. However, the latest ONS (2017) survey of share ownership, which gives statistics as at the end of December 2016, shows that the relative percentages owned by these two groups have fallen to their lowest level since the share ownership survey began in 1963, with 4.9 per cent and 3.0 per cent for insurance companies and pension funds respectively. This might reflect insurance companies switching from UK equities to alternative investments, whilst pension fund managers have broadened their portfolios attempting to obtain higher returns and to spread risk. However, it is important to note that the ONS changed their methodology for their 2012 survey—for example, by updating the sector analysis for pooled nominee accounts—and this had a large impact on the results, and they caution that this should be taken into account when making comparisons with earlier years. There were also some changes in the 2016 survey but the methodology used for it was broadly the same as for the 2014 survey. Nonetheless, insurance companies

Table 6.1 Summary of main categories of share ownership in the UK 1963–2016

Type of investor	1963	2016
	%	%
Individuals	54	12.3
Insurance companies	10	4.9
Pension funds	6	3.0
Unit trusts	1	9.5
Other financial institutions	11.3	8.1
Overseas	7	53.9

Source: Ownership of UK quoted shares, 2016, Office for National Statistics (ONS), 2017.
(Other categories owning shares include banks, investment trusts, public sector, private non-financial companies, and charities.)

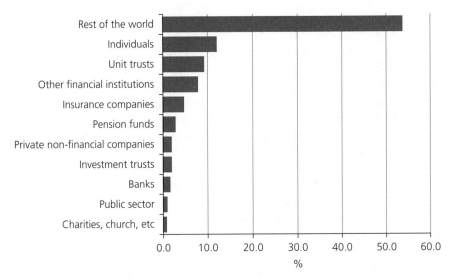

Figure 6.1 Beneficial ownership of quoted shares in UK-domiciled companies at 31 December 2016
Source: Ownership of UK quoted shares, 2016, Office for National Statistics (ONS), 2017

and pension funds retain their influence as key institutional investors in the corporate governance of their investee companies. There has also been a notable increase in the overseas level of ownership—this is particularly noteworthy because it has increased from 7 per cent in 1963 to 53.9 per cent in 2016. Many of the overseas holdings are US investors (48.1 per cent), with the other large holdings being European (25.7 per cent), and Asian (15.5 per cent). The ONS additional analysis of the overseas ownership in the 2016 survey shows that of the overseas investment made in the UK, 63.8 per cent is in unit trusts, 51.6 per cent is in other financial institutions, and 26.8 per cent is in pension funds. The US institutional investors tend to be much more proactive in corporate governance and over the years this stance has influenced the behaviour of both UK institutional investors and UK companies. The extent of institutional share ownership can be seen quite clearly in Figure 6.1, which shows the beneficial ownership of quoted shares in UK-domiciled companies at the end of 2016. Similarly, the influence of overseas investors on corporate UK is shown by their level of equity ownership.

Influence of institutional investors

Given the size of their shareholdings, the power of the institutional investors cannot be doubted. In his seminal work, Hirschman (1970) identified the exercise of institutional power within an 'exit and voice' framework, arguing that 'dissatisfaction [may be expressed] directly to management' (the *voice* option) or by selling the shareholding (the *exit* option). The latter choice is not viable for many institutional investors given the size of their holdings or a policy of holding a balanced portfolio.

The Cadbury Committee (1992) viewed institutional investors as having a special responsibility to try to ensure that its recommendations were adopted by companies, stating that 'we look to the institutions in particular ... to use their influence as owners to ensure that the companies in which they have invested comply with the Code'. A similar view was expressed in the Greenbury Report (1995), as one of the main action points is 'the investor institutions should use their power and influence to ensure the implementation of best practice as set out in the Code'. Similarly, in the Hampel Report (1998), it states: 'it is clear ... that a discussion of the role of shareholders in corporate governance will mainly concern the institutions'. Therefore, three influential committees, which have reported on corporate governance in the UK, have clearly emphasized the role of institutional investors. The institutional investors' potential to exert significant influence on companies has clear implications for corporate governance, especially in terms of the standards of corporate governance and issues concerned with enforcement. Until the revision of the Combined Code in 2010, the Combined Code included principles of good governance relating to institutional shareholders. However, when the Combined Code was revised and renamed the UK Corporate Governance Code in 2010, the section on institutional shareholders was removed and a new UK Stewardship Code was introduced (discussed later).

In 2002 Hermes, a large and influential institutional investor based in the UK, issued *The Hermes Principles*. The first principle was that 'companies should seek an honest, open and ongoing dialogue with shareholders'. This clearly reflects Hermes' intention to have a dialogue with its investee companies. Similarly, in *The Hermes Corporate Governance Principles* (2006), global principle 3, relating to the board of directors, states that 'the board is responsible for facilitating a satisfactory dialogue with the shareholders'. In 2010 Hermes published *The Hermes Responsible Ownership Principles*, updated in 2013, detailing what they expect of listed companies and what listed companies can expect from them. Hermes' expectations of listed companies encompass 12 principles relating to transparency and communication; corporate culture; strategy; financial disciplines and structure, and risk management; stakeholders, environmental, and social issues; and governance. In turn, listed companies can expect five core principles of stewardship and engagement that Hermes feels responsible shareholders ought to observe. These are a clearly communicated set of expectations on investor communications, corporate culture, operations, strategy, financial disciplines and structure, sustainability and governance; a consistent approach; a thorough understanding of markets and companies around the world; a long-term perspective when exercising ownership rights; and a constructive, confidential dialogue with boards and senior management. In addition Hermes has published *Regional Corporate Governance Principles* for 18 different countries, including *Corporate Governance Principles, United Kingdom* (2018), as well as *Stewardship* (2017) and various other publications covering, for example, Engagement Objectives and Plan.

The perception of the key role to be played by institutional investors is not purely a UK phenomenon. Useem (1996) detailed the rise of 'investor capitalism' in the USA and described how the concentration of shares, and hence power, into a relatively small number of hands, has enabled institutional investors to challenge management directly on issues of concern. Monks (2001) identified 'global investors' as being:

> the public and private pension funds of the US, UK, Netherlands, Canada, Australia and Japan. Through extrapolating the specific holding of a number of the largest pension schemes, we conclude that the level of ownership in virtually all publicly quoted companies in the world is large enough to permit the effective involvement of owners in the governance of those corporations.

Similarly, in the context of the Australian market, Bosch (1993) stated that 'institutional shareholders because of their increasing influence, by virtue of their size, should take an active interest in the governance of the Company and develop their own principles of good practice'.

This emphasis is to be expected from countries such as the USA, UK, and Australia, which all have a significant concentration of share ownership in the hands of institutional investors. However, the Centre for European Policy Studies (CEPS) 1995 report stated that 'in any attempt to understand the control of corporations, the role of insurance companies, pension funds, and other institutional investors, and other actors, such as employees or banks, has to be taken into account to different extents in European countries'. The report goes on to state:

> International diversification and increasing cross-border activity of institutional investors will accelerate this process. American and British pension funds, in particular, which represent about 72 per cent of total pension fund assets in the western world, can be instrumental in changing corporate governance standards as a result of the active stance towards investment that is required by local laws and codes.

The aspect of foreign share ownership should not be underestimated, as these 'new' investors in Europe will tend to be institutional investors from the USA, the UK, and other countries. The large proportion of institutional share ownership in both the USA (where around 55 per cent of US equities are owned by institutional investors and 80 per cent of all share trades are made by institutional investors) and the UK (where institutional ownership is around 65–80 per cent) means that the voice of the institutional investor cannot go unheard. The Federation of European Securities Exchanges (FESE) (2008) also highlighted the trend towards higher ownership by foreign investors in the listed shares of European exchanges.

Mallin and Melis (2012) highlight that shareholders are the providers of risk capital and therefore they need to be able to protect their investment by ensuring that a competent board is in place to manage the company and to ensure that effective strategies are in place for the company's overall corporate performance and long-term sustainability. Well governed companies which consider all the risks of the business, both financial and non-financial, are perceived as less likely to operate in a way that reduces the value of shareholders' investments and hence impacts negatively on other stakeholders. McCahery et al. (2016) find that corporate governance is of importance to institutional shareholders in their investment decisions and a number of them are willing to engage in shareholder activism. Over the last five years or so there has been increasing pressure from government, ultimate beneficiaries, and various stakeholders on institutional investors to engage with their investee companies.

Some institutional investors may be reluctant to engage with investee companies because of, for example, the monetary costs of monitoring and engagement; on the other hand, some activist investors, such as hedge funds, may be willing to engage more fully. Gilson and Gordon (2013) posit that 'shareholder activists should be seen as playing a specialized capital market role of setting up intervention proposals for resolution by institutional investors. The effect is to potentiate institutional investor voice, to increase the value of the vote, and thereby to reduce the agency costs we have identified.'

Stewardship

The concept of 'stewardship' has also come to the fore, as we shall see in the discussion of the ISC recommendations on the responsibilities of institutional investors, and subsequent development of the Stewardship Code in 2010—discussed in detail later. However, it is useful at this point to consider what is meant by 'stewardship'. Tomorrow's Company (2009) has contributed significantly to the stewardship debate and declares that 'stewards are people who look after the resources entrusted to them ... stewardship is the process through which shareholders, directors, and others seek to influence companies in the direction of long-term, sustainable performance that derives from contributing to human progress and the well-being of the environment and society'. Moreover 'the main resources with which institutional shareholders are entrusted are their client's funds ... once the institution uses a client's fund to buy shares in a company this reinforces the shareholder's interest in the stewardship of that company' (Tomorrow's Company, 2009). Recently Tomorrow's Company published *Better Stewardship—An Agenda for Concerted Action (2018)* where they point out that:

> overall quality of investor stewardship has improved since the introduction of the Stewardship Code in 2010 but a 'critical mass' of stewardship investors has not yet materialised ... Stewardship needs to be central to the terms of reference of the Financial Conduct Authority. The Stewardship Code should start by linking stewardship to promoting the long-term success of a company. It should apply to asset owners, asset managers, investment consultants, research analysts and all relevant service providers and advisors. It should require each investment entity to state its purpose and report against it, and report resources invested in stewardship.

Talbot (2010) states: 'shareholder stewardship requires institutional shareholders to take an active role in corporate governance and empowers them, both legally and morally, to do so. Previous conceptions of stewardship viewed directors and not shareholders as worthy stewards of the company's best interests.' Whilst FairPensions (2011), in a discussion encompassing various dimensions of fiduciary responsibility, conclude that 'there is a need to align the legal framework governing investors with the "enlightened shareholder value" ethos underpinning the duties of company directors, encouraging a responsible, long-term approach to serving beneficiaries' interests'.

Tilba and McNulty (2013), in a study of UK pension funds, find that:

> a very small number of well-resourced and internally managed pension funds exhibit engaged ownership behavior. By contrast, the vast majority of pension funds operate at a considerable distance from their investee corporations having delegated pension fund investment management to a chain of external relationships involving actuaries, investment consultants, and fund managers. These relationships are laced with divergent interests and influence dynamics, which explain why these pension funds give primary emphasis to fund investment performance and display little concern for matters of ownership and corporate governance.

This finding therefore raises doubts about placing reliance on institutional investor engagement and the stewardship role envisaged in the UK Stewardship Code.

Finally Rock (2015) points out that:

> although traditional Institutional Investors have not emerged as active 'stewards,' there has been a more modest, although still important change in institutional investor behavior: first, Institutional Investors are engaging with management in a much more active way than ever before; and, rather than always supporting management, Institutional Investors are now willing to support hedge funds and other corporate governance activists when they are convinced that doing so will increase firm value.

Development of guidance on institutional investors' responsibilities

The power of institutional investors such as those cited above clearly cannot be underestimated, and the influence that they can wield is enormous. The institutional investors may be influenced in their views by the various institutional investor representative groups in the UK. Large institutional investors, mainly insurance companies and pension funds, usually belong to one of two representative bodies that act as a professional group 'voice' for their views. These two bodies are the Association of British Insurers (ABI) and the National Association of Pension Funds (NAPF). Both the ABI and the NAPF have best practice corporate governance guidelines, which encompass the recommendations of the Combined Code. They monitor the corporate governance activities of companies and will provide advice to members. Institutional investors will generally consult ABI and/or NAPF reports on whether particular companies are complying with 'good' corporate governance practice, as well as undertaking their own research and analysis. Most large institutional investors have terms of reference that incorporate corporate governance aspects, or have issued separate corporate governance guidelines. These guidelines are generally based around the UK Corporate Governance Code recommendations, and further guidance that may have been issued by the NAPF or ABI. Companies will try to ensure that they meet these guidelines.

The Myners Report on institutional investment, issued in 2001 by HM Treasury, concentrated more on the trusteeship aspects of institutional investors and the legal requirements for trustees, with the aim of raising the standards and promoting greater shareholder activism. For example, the Myners Report expects that institutional investors should be more proactive especially in the stance they take with underperforming companies.

The Institutional Shareholders' Committee (ISC), whose members comprised the ABI, the NAPF, the Association of Investment Trust Companies (AITC), and the Investment Management Association (IMA), issued a statement on the responsibilities of institutional investors in late 2002 (the ISC was renamed in the summer of 2011, as the Institutional Investor Committee (IIC) whose members were the NAPF, the ABI, and the IMA). Several updates were made to the statement over the subsequent years and in November 2009 the ISC issued the *Code on the Responsibilities of Institutional Investors*. The Code built on the statements on institutional investors' responsibilities issued previously by the ISC. The ISC stated that 'the Code aims to enhance the quality of the dialogue of institutional investors with companies to help improve long-term returns to shareholders, reduce the risk of catastrophic outcomes due to bad strategic decisions, and help with the efficient exercise of governance responsibilities'.

In 2014, the IMA merged with the Investment Affairs Division of the Association of British Insurers to create The Investment Association (IA). The Investment Association covers the entire range of investment issues on behalf of investment managers and clients, whether they are domestic or international individuals, discretionary managers, life companies, pension funds, family offices or sovereign wealth funds. Following the merger, the NAPF and the IMA agreed to dissolve the ISC. However where there is a shared agenda, the IMA and the NAPF will continue to work together. In 2015, the NAPF was rebranded as the Pensions and Lifetime Savings Association (PLSA).

In 2015 the PLSA issued its *Corporate Governance Policy and Voting Guidelines 2015/16*. In the section covering the UK Voting Guidelines, the PLSA state:

> The voting recommendations assume that shareholders have evaluated explanations for non-compliance, taken account of a company's individual circumstances and engaged as appropriate ... Shareholders are encouraged to make systematic use of all of the powers at their disposal as necessary in order coherently to support the highest standards of corporate governance at the companies in which they invest ... Finally, shareholders should always balance the 'signalling' effect of a voting sanction against the potential for it to exacerbate the situation which they seek to remedy.

The PLSA subsequently issued *Corporate Governance Policy and Voting Guidelines 2018*. As in the earlier version there is detailed voting guidance on individual resolutions that may arise at investee companies. The Guidelines emphasize both the importance of companies engaging with their long-term investors and of investors being open to full engagement with companies. The PLSA states that it

> is always willing to facilitate active engagement between issuers and pension fund investors in order to discuss substantive matters of concern or company-specific issues. We will initiate a proactive set of engagement dialogues for our members with relevant companies on key strategic issues where we believe long-term value may be at stake.

In 2014, the Investor Forum was launched by industry practitioners with the core objective of creating long-term value. Positioning stewardship at the heart of investment decision-making by facilitating dialogue, creating long-term solutions, and enhancing value is central to this objective. In January 2018, the Investor Forum's *Review 2017* reveals how during 2017, they further developed

> two aspects of their work which are complementary to core company-specific engagement. Having originally been involved almost exclusively with companies who were already struggling with their shareholders, and where the share price had therefore usually already suffered a significant set-back, the Stewardship and Strategy Forums and the Stewardship 360 programme have allowed us to take a more proactive approach to engage with companies that are doing well, before value has been lost due to poor stewardship.

The International Corporate Governance Network (ICGN) produced a *Statement of Shareholder Responsibilities* (2007) which set out the ICGN's view of the responsibilities of institutional shareholders both in relation to their external role as owners of company equity, and also in relation to their internal governance. Both these areas are of interest to beneficiaries and other stakeholders. Ownership of equity carries important responsibilities, and the rights attached to share ownership must be exercised responsibly. Responsible ownership requires high standards of transparency, probity, and care on the part of institutions. Furthermore, the ICGN (2009) stated: 'It will help establish a role for governance and shareholders, as well as preserve shareholder rights if institutions formally commit to the principles laid out in the "ICGN Statement of Principles on Institutional Shareholder Responsibilities (2007)".' The ICGN revised the Statement of Principles on Institutional Shareholder Responsibilities in 2013 and stated that 'institutions that comply with these Principles will have both a stronger claim to the trust of their end beneficiaries and to the exercising of investor rights on their behalf. The implementation of these principles will help generate sustainable returns for beneficiaries and help secure a healthy corporate sector.'

The ICGN states that the revised *Global Governance Principles* (2017) should be read alongside the ICGN *Global Stewardship Principles* (2015) which set out best practices in relation to investor governance and stewardship obligations, policies, and processes. There are seven global stewardship principles: internal governance: foundations of effective stewardship; developing and implementing stewardship policies; monitoring and assessing investee companies; engaging companies and investor collaboration; exercising voting rights; promoting long-term value creation and integration of environmental, social and governance (ESG) factors; enhancing transparency, disclosure and reporting. Together these two documents promote ICGN's long-held stance that 'both companies and investors share a mutual responsibility to preserve and enhance long-term corporate value, and thereby contribute to sustainable capital markets and societal prosperity.'

Following on from the financial crisis, an independent review of the governance of banks and other financial institutions was carried out by Sir David Walker. The Walker Review published its final recommendations in November 2009, and nine of its 39 recommendations related to the role of institutional shareholders' communication and engagement (emphasizing the development and regulatory sponsorship of a Stewardship Code). When the UK Corporate Governance Code was issued in 2010, a Stewardship Code was produced alongside, largely based on the ISC Code discussed earlier, and the first of its kind in the world.

UK Stewardship Code 2010 (revised 2012)

The Financial Reporting Council (FRC) issued the UK Stewardship Code in June 2010, which set out the good practice on engagement with investee companies that it believes institutional shareholders should aspire to. As mentioned earlier, the UK Stewardship Code is largely based on the ISC *Code on the Responsibilities of Institutional Investors*; in fact only a few minor amendments were made to the latter before it was adopted as the UK Stewardship Code, with the FRC assuming responsibility for its oversight.

The seven principles of the UK Stewardship Code are that institutional investors should:

- Principle 1—publicly disclose their policy on how they will discharge their stewardship responsibilities.
- Principle 2—have a robust policy on managing conflicts of interest in relation to stewardship and this policy should be publicly disclosed.
- Principle 3—monitor their investee companies.

- Principle 4—establish clear guidelines on when and how they will escalate their activities as a method of protecting and enhancing shareholder value.
- Principle 5—be willing to act collectively with other investors where appropriate.
- Principle 6—have a clear policy on voting and disclosure of voting activity.
- Principle 7—report periodically on their stewardship and voting activities.

The Stewardship Code is applied on a 'comply or explain' basis. The UK Stewardship Code applies to firms who manage assets on behalf of institutional shareholders such as pension funds, insurance companies, investment trusts, and other collective vehicles. However, pension fund trustees and other owners may also monitor company performance and so the FRC encourages all institutional investors to report whether, and how, they have complied with the Stewardship Code. The FRC expects such firms to disclose on their websites how they have applied the Stewardship Code or to explain why it has not been complied with.

There has generally been a good take-up of the Stewardship Code, with over 180 asset managers, over 50 asset owners, and 14 service providers signing up to it. Whilst most of those signing up are supportive of the Stewardship Code's principles, Mallin (2012) reports that statements that organizations will not be complying with the Stewardship Code fall into two groups: (i) those not signing based on their specific investment strategy (for example, they do not invest in UK equities), and (ii) those who do not commit to codes in individual jurisdictions.

The Stewardship Code has generally been well received and has been emulated by other countries including Japan and Malaysia. Its effectiveness will be measured by the extent to which there is full engagement with investee companies, with appropriate monitoring and the use of the various tools of corporate governance.

In 2012, the revised UK Stewardship Code was issued with a few changes aimed at clarifying how stewardship responsibilities are being carried out. These changes related to clarification of the respective responsibilities of asset managers and asset owners for stewardship, and for stewardship activities that they have chosen to outsource; investors are to explain more clearly how they manage conflicts of interest, the circumstances in which they will take part in collective engagement, and the use they make of proxy voting agencies; and asset managers encouraged to have the processes that support their stewardship activities independently verified, to provide greater assurance to their clients.

ShareAction's (2015) *Asset Manager Voting Practices: In Whose Interests? Survey of 2014's AGM season* highlighted that:

> overall, there is room for improvement in the voting practices and disclosure of the majority of the UK's largest asset managers. There is a role for regulators, clients and asset managers in driving these improvements. The Financial Reporting Council (FRC) and Financial Conduct Authority (FCA) could do more to ensure that managers comply with the Stewardship Code in respect of disclosure of voting records, and make less use of their right to explain. It is clear that current regulation is not leading to the level of disclosure that is desirable in the market. We suggest that the Stewardship Code needs to be revisited in light of these failings and that some mechanism is needed to prevent managers claiming to comply with the Code when they do not.

In 2015, in its review of *Developments in Corporate Governance and Stewardship 2014*, the FRC expressed its concern about the state of commitment to the Stewardship Code. It stated: 'In 2015, the FRC will undertake greater scrutiny of adherence to the Code. If reporting improvements are not evident, the FRC will develop options to address those signatories which, on an ongoing basis, fail to respond to the concerns we raise with them.'

In 2016 the FRC assessed signatories based on the quality of their Stewardship Code statements with the aims of improving the quality of reporting against the Stewardship Code, encouraging greater transparency in the market, and maintaining the credibility of the Stewardship Code. There were three tiers designed to distinguish between signatories who report well and demonstrate their commitment to stewardship, and those where reporting improvements are necessary. The three tiers are:

- Tier 1—Signatories provide a good quality and transparent description of their approach to stewardship and explanations of an alternative approach where necessary.
- Tier 2—Signatories meet many of the reporting expectations but report less transparently on their approach to stewardship or do not provide explanations where they depart from provisions of the Code.
- Tier 3—Significant reporting improvements need to be made to ensure the approach is more transparent. Signatories have not engaged with the process of improving their statements and their statements continue to be generic and provide no, or poor, explanations where they depart from provisions of the Code.

The assessments which focused on the quality of descriptions of signatories' approach to stewardship and their explanations in accordance with the 'comply or explain' basis of the Stewardship Code, were published in November 2016 and indicated much improved reporting against the Code and greater transparency in the UK market. With nearly 300 signatories to the Code, more than 120 are in Tier 1, an increase from approximately 40 at the beginning of the exercise which represents nearly 90 per cent of assets under management of members of the Investment Association.

The FRC has indicated that asset managers who have not achieved at least Tier 2 status after six months will be removed from the list of signatories as their reporting does not demonstrate commitment to the objectives of the Code. The FRC has stated that it welcomes contact from signatories, particularly those in Tier 3, to discuss improvements to reporting.

The FRC will continue to assess the overall quality of reporting on an annual basis, consider possible revisions to the UK Stewardship Code (planned for 2018), and look at how it can better support international investors to meet the requirements of international Stewardship Codes.

Interestingly, the European Fund and Asset Management Association (EFAMA) published the *EFAMA Code for External Governance: Principles for the exercise of ownership rights in investee companies* in April 2011. There are six principles for investment management companies (IMCs) detailing how they should:

- have a documented policy available to the public on whether, and if so how, they exercise their ownership responsibilities;
- monitor their investee companies;

- establish clear guidelines on when and how they will intervene with investee companies to protect and enhance value;
- consider co-operating with other investors, where appropriate, having due regard to applicable rules on acting in concert;
- exercise their voting rights in a considered way;
- report on their exercise of ownership rights and voting activities and have a policy on external governance disclosure.

EU Shareholder Rights Directive (2014)

In December 2012, the EU published an Action Plan on European Company Law and Corporate Governance which detailed a number of legislative and other initiatives on company law and corporate governance which the EU planned to start in 2013 and 2014. One of these initiatives related to requiring institutional investors to disclose their voting and engagement policies. This has now been embodied in the EU Shareholder Rights Directive which covers many aspects of investor and company relations and interaction including institutional investors developing an engagement policy detailing how they engage with their investee companies; and voting on remuneration.

The Directive states that:

institutional investors and asset managers are important shareholders of listed companies in the Union and therefore can play an important role in the corporate governance of these companies, but also more generally with regard to the strategy and long-term performance of these companies. However, the experience of the last years has shown that institutional investors and asset managers often do not engage with companies in which they hold shares and evidence shows that capital markets exert pressure on companies to perform in the short term, which may lead to a suboptimal level of investments, for example in research and development to the detriment to long-term performance of both the companies and the investor.

In relation to the institutional investor engagement policy, this should include the integration of shareholder engagement in their investment strategy; monitoring investee companies, including on their non-financial performance; conducting dialogue with investee companies; exercising voting rights; using services provided by proxy advisors; and co-operating with other shareholders. The engagement policy should also cover how potential conflicts of interest are managed.

Institutional investors are required to publicly disclose, on an annual basis, their engagement policy, how it has been implemented, and the outcomes. Furthermore, institutional investors are required to disclose 'if and how they cast their votes in the general meetings of the companies concerned and provide an explanation for their voting behaviour. Where an asset manager casts votes on behalf of an institutional investor, the institutional investor shall make a reference as to where such voting information has been published by the asset manager.' If an engagement policy is not developed, or not disclosed, then the institutional investor should give a clear and reasoned explanation as to why they have chosen to do this.

Private equity and sovereign wealth funds (SWFs)

Two types of investor that have gained increasing influence and prominence during the last decade are private equity firms and SWFs. In each case there has been some unease about the lack of transparency associated with these types of investor. As a result, pressure has been brought to bear to encourage more disclosure and transparency by these funds. We will look first at private equity funds.

Private equity

A private equity fund is broadly defined as one that invests in equity which is not traded publicly on a stock exchange. Sometimes private equity firms acquire companies, which may be large well-known companies, and the funds for such deals often come from institutional investors. Private equity investments can be broadly divided into categories including venture capital, buy-out, acquisition of a significant portion or a majority control in a more mature company, investment in a distressed company, or investment in a company where value can be unlocked.

The Walker Working Group (Private Equity Working Group on Transparency and Disclosure) published, in November 2007, *Guidelines for Disclosure and Transparency in Private Equity*. These Guidelines are aimed at private equity firms authorized by the Financial Services Authority and by UK portfolio companies owned by private equity funds.

Walker Guidelines for Disclosure and Transparency in Private Equity

The voluntary guidelines were drawn up for the British Private Equity and Venture Capital Association (BVCA). The Guidelines place much greater onus on private equity funds to provide more details of the financial performance of companies they take over. The new rules require private equity companies to publish accounts for the larger companies they own no later than six months after financial year-ends.

Since the publication of the Guidelines, about a dozen private equity firms—including Apax Partners, Terra Firma, Permira, and Cinven—have published annual reviews, giving details of their senior managers, investors, strategies, and portfolio companies. Sir Michael Rake, Chairman of the Walker Guidelines Monitoring Group, in an interview with the *Financial Times* in August 2008 stated that 32 private equity firms and 55 portfolio companies have committed to comply with the Walker Recommendations.

The Organisation for Economic Co-operation and Development (OECD) (2008a and 2008b) also published two useful documents in relation to private equity firms. These were the *Codes and Industry Standards Covering the Behaviour of Alternative Investors*, which is a list of private sector initiatives aimed at addressing policy issues, and *The Role of Private Equity and Activist Hedge Funds in Corporate Governance—Related Policy Issues*. The latter document concludes that private equity firms and activist hedge funds often act as informed owners and are more active in monitoring the performance of companies and their management than other institutional investors. The report also concluded that any corporate governance concerns that relate to governance practices by private equity firms and activist hedge funds are best addressed within the framework of the existing OECD Principles.

Sovereign Wealth Funds (SWFs)

A sovereign wealth fund (SWF) is a fund owned by a government and these funds are often very large and influential. Table 6.2 indicates the size of the SWF market and shows how China accounts for 28 per cent, followed by the United Arab Emirates 17 per cent, Norway 13 per cent, and Saudi Arabia 10 per cent. Norway's SWF, which accounts for 13 per cent, has stakes in some 3,500+ companies but is seen as being fairly transparent and relatively unthreatening, whereas the sovereign funds of some of the Middle and Far Eastern countries are seen as being much more opaque. This can become a problem when these funds start to buy into strategic businesses, and their motivation and long-term investment strategy is unknown.

Table 6.2 SWFs market share by country

End 2017	US$bn	% share
China	2098	28
United Arab Emirates	1307	17
Norway	999	13
Saudi Arabia	718	10
Kuwait	524	7
Singapore	556	7
Qatar	320	4
Others	1059	14
Total	**7581**	**100***

*Rounded
Source: Based on SWF Institute estimates.

The Santiago Principles

The International Working Group of Sovereign Wealth Funds (IWG), with a membership of 26 countries with SWFs, was established in May 2008. The IWG met three times to identify and draft a set of generally accepted principles and practices (GAPP) that properly reflects their investment practices and objectives: the Santiago Principles.

The GAPP are underpinned by the following guiding objectives for SWFs:

● to help maintain a stable global financial system and free flow of capital and investment;

● to comply with all applicable regulatory and disclosure requirements in the countries in which they invest;

- to invest on the basis of economic and financial risk and return-related considerations; and

- to have in place a transparent and sound governance structure that provides for adequate operational controls, risk management, and accountability.

Members of the IWG 'either have implemented or intend to implement the following principles and practices, on a voluntary basis, *each of which is subject to* home country laws, regulations, requirements and obligations' [emphasis in original].

There are 24 GAPP which cover areas such as:

- the legal framework of the SWF;

- its policy and purpose;

- the requirement for clear and public disclosure of policies and of statistical data;

- a sound governance framework which establishes a clear and effective division of roles and responsibilities in order to facilitate accountability and operational independence in the management of the SWF to pursue its objectives;

- a defined accountability framework;

- the publication of an audited set of financial statements in a timely manner;

- professional and ethical standards in SWFs;

- an investment policy that is clear and consistent with the SWF's defined objectives, risk tolerance, and investment strategy;

- shareholder ownership rights that are viewed as a fundamental element of the SWF's equity investments' value;

- a framework that identifies, assesses, and manages the risks of its operations;

- a regular review of the extent to which the GAPP have been followed.

These GAPP should help ensure that there is more confidence in the activities of SWFs, which will help maintain stability in international financial markets and ensure that there is more trust in them.

Megginson and Fotak (2015) survey the literature documenting the rise of SWFs and find that more than 25 countries have launched or proposed new SWFs since January 2008 and that the most salient and controversial feature of SWFs is that they are state-owned; and that SWF funding sources arise from oil sales revenues versus excess reserves from export earnings. They summarize

the empirical literature studying how SWFs actually do allocate funds—across asset classes, geographically, and across industries. We document that most SWF equity investments in publicly traded firms involve cross-border purchases of sizeable minority stakes (median around 20%) in target firms, with a strong preference for investments in the financial sector. Next, we assess empirical studies examining the impact of SWF stock investments on target firm financial and operating performance, and find universal support for a positive announcement period stock price increase of 1–3%. This, however, is significantly lower than the 5% abnormal return documented for stock purchases by comparable privately owned financial investors in recent studies, indicating a 'sovereign wealth fund discount'.

Institutional investors' relationship with investee companies

Corporate governance may be used as a tool for extracting value for shareholders from underperforming, undervalued companies. This approach has been very successful for Lens Inc., CalPERS, Hermes, and Active Value Advisors, to name but a few. By targeting companies that are underperforming in one of the main market indices, and analysing those companies' corporate governance practices, improvements can be made that unlock the hidden value. These improvements often include replacing poorly performing directors and ensuring that the companies comply with perceived best practice in corporate governance.

Corporate governance may also be used to help restore investor confidence in markets that have experienced financial crises. We have seen this happening in the last few years in Malaysia, Japan, and India, for example. In these countries, as in a number of other countries that have similarly been affected by a lack of investor confidence, particularly overseas investor confidence, new or improved corporate governance practices have been introduced. Key features of these changes include measures to try to improve investor confidence by improving transparency and accountability in these markets.

We have seen earlier that there is increasing pressure on institutional investors to engage with their investee companies from a number of sources, including government. The EU also identified, in the Commission *Green Paper on Corporate Governance in Financial Institutions and Remuneration Policies 2010*, that 'a lack of appropriate shareholder interest in holding financial institutions' management accountable contributed to poor management accountability and may have facilitated excessive risk taking in financial institutions'. Some of the reasons cited include the cost of engagement, the difficulty of valuing the return on engagement, and the uncertainty of the outcome of engagement, including 'free rider' behaviour.

In the UK the Department for Business, Innovation & Skills commissioned Professor John Kay to assess the effect of UK equity markets on the competitiveness of UK business. The *Kay Review of UK Equity Markets and Long-Term Decision Making, Interim Report* was published in February 2012. It highlighted a number of areas based on the submissions received and on discussions with market participants. An area of concern is the issuance of quarterly or interim earnings statements by companies, as this can lead to a short-term focus by investors (and companies) rather a longer term perspective.

The OECD (2011) in its publication *The Role of Institutional Investors in Promoting Good Corporate Governance* reviewed the role of institutional investors, including their engagement with investee companies, the incentives they have to promote engagement, and the barriers to engagement. It covers 26 jurisdictions with an in-depth review of Australia, Chile, and Germany. The review demonstrates that institutional investors can play an important role in jurisdictions characterized by both dispersed and concentrated ownership. However, the report points out that 'the nature of institutional investors has evidently evolved over the years into a complex system of financial institutions and fund management companies with their own corporate governance issues and incentive structures'.

The ICGN issued the *ICGN Model Mandate Initiative* in 2012, which discusses model contract terms between asset owners and their managers. It identifies areas that are most significant in this regard: standards and high-level commitment; risk management; integration of long-term factors; stewardship activities; long-termism and alignment; and commission and counterparties. In another section on accountability and reporting it points out 'as important as setting standards within fund management contracts is how clients can effectively call their fund managers to account in respect of these mandates'. One of the ICGN Policy Priorities in 2018 is 'making successful stewardship a reality'. Stewardship codes and their development in developing and emerging economies will be a point of focus as will the internal governance of investors which the ICGN views as a fundamental aspect of effective stewardship.

In the UK, the UK Corporate Governance Code 2018, under the section on Board Leadership and Company Purpose, includes Principle D: 'In order for the company to meet its responsibilities to shareholders and stakeholders, the board should ensure effective engagement with, and encourage participation from, these parties.' In 2018, the FRC is formally consulting on changes to the UK Stewardship Code as the FRC believes that 'to achieve real change in corporate governance, and long-term success and sustainability for companies, it is important that investors play their part ...'.

From the discussion earlier, it is clear that with institutional investors under the spotlight and an emphasis on their stewardship role, we can expect to see more use being made of the tools of corporate governance.

Tools of corporate governance

(i) One-to-one meetings

The meetings between institutional investors and companies are extremely important as a means of communication between the two parties. This is one clear example of the way in which individual investors are at a disadvantage to institutional investors: corporate management will usually only arrange such meetings with large investors who are overwhelmingly institutional investors.

A company will usually arrange to meet with its largest institutional investors on a one-to-one basis during the course of the year. The meetings tend to be at the highest level and usually involve individual key members of the board in a meeting once, or maybe twice, a week. Their 'target' institutional investor audience will include large shareholders (perhaps the top 30) and brokers' analysts (perhaps the top ten), and any large investors who are underweight or selling their shares. In addition, they will tend to phone an institutional investor if they have not seen them in the last 12 to 18 months. Meetings are often followed up with phone calls by the firm to the institutional investor to ensure that everything has been discussed.

The issues that are most discussed at these meetings between firms and their large institutional investors include areas of the firm's strategy and how the firm is planning to achieve its objectives, whether objectives are being met, and the quality of the management. Institutional investors are seen as 'important for the way the business is managed', and their views may be fed back to the board in the planning process, and incorporated, as appropriate, in an annual strategy paper. They are seen as having a collective influence, with management paying most attention to the commonality of institutional investors' views in meetings over time. The firms want to ensure that institutional investors understand the business and its strategy so that the value of the business is fully recognized.

As a way of saying 'well done', Hermes sent letters to various companies stating when they found their annual report particularly informative and useful in terms of various areas, for example, directors' remuneration and risk management. In 2008 the Institute of Chartered Secretaries and Administrators (ICSA) and Hermes joined forces to launch the ICSA Hermes Awards for UK companies whose annual reports and accounts achieved best practice in governance disclosure.

In 2016, Hermes began talks with other fund managers to draw up a new contract between investors and the pension funds that employ them based on longer term performance and broader criteria than immediate financial return. The idea is to move away from the focus on short-termism and push fund managers to focus on the social, environmental, and economic consequences of investment decisions.

(ii) Voting

The right to vote that is attached to voting shares (as opposed to non-voting shares) is a basic prerogative of share ownership, and is particularly important given the division of ownership (shareholders) and control (directors) in the modern corporation. The right to vote can be seen as fundamental for some element of control by shareholders.

The institutional investors can register their views by postal voting, or, in many companies, the facility to vote electronically is now available. Most of the large institutional investors now have a policy of trying to vote on all issues that may be raised at their investee company's annual general meeting (AGM). Some may vote directly on all resolutions, others may appoint a proxy (which may be a board member). Generally, an institutional investor will try to sort out any contentious issues with management 'behind the scenes'; however, if this fails, then they may abstain from voting on a particular issue (rather than voting with incumbent management as they generally would) or they may actually vote against a resolution. In this case, they would generally inform the firm of their intention to vote against. It tends to be corporate governance issues that are the most contentious, particularly directors' remuneration and lengths of contract.

The high level of institutional share ownership in the UK has been discussed earlier. Looking back at the Cadbury Report (1992), this states: 'Given the weight of their votes, the way in which institutional investors use their power ... is of fundamental importance'. It encourages institutional investors to 'make positive use of their voting rights and disclose their policies on voting'.

A number of similar statements can be found in the guidelines issued by various institutional investor representative groups. For example, the two main groups representing institutional investors in the UK, the NAPF and the ABI, both advocate voting by institutional investors. In 1999 the ABI and NAPF issued some joint guidance on responsible voting in which they emphasized the importance of voting and advocated that voting should be done in a considered fashion rather than 'box ticking', that it could contribute to effective corporate governance, and that it could be seen as an integral part of the investment management function. So, it would seem that the main institutional investor representative groups in the UK are in agreement that votes should be exercised on a regular basis in an informed manner.

There have been a number of efforts to try to ensure that voting levels do improve. These include the NAPF *Report of the Committee of Inquiry into UK Vote Execution* (1999). The report identified various impediments to voting, a major one being the cumbersome and outdated paper-based system. As a result of this, a number of projects were established to try to find a suitable electronic voting system to make voting easier and the process more efficient. The NAPF report additionally identified a number of other areas of concern, including a 'lack of auditability or adequate confirmatory procedure in the voting system' and communication problems between the pension funds, fund managers, custodians, registrars, and companies.

The Shareholder Voting Working Group (SVWG) was established in 1999, under the chairmanship of Terry Pearson, as an industry-wide body to address the issue of improving the voting process in the UK. The SVWG has subsequently been chaired by Paul Myners and has issued several reports including in 2004 the *Review of the Impediments to Voting UK Shares* identifying areas such as the complexity of the voting system, and making recommendations on a number of areas to help improve the situation and remedy the problem of 'lost' votes. The report recommends that the voting system should be more efficient and transparent, and highlights that institutional shareholders could be doing more to try to ensure that their votes were appropriately recorded.

Voting levels by institutional investors in the UK have gradually increased in recent years as institutional investors recognized that unless voting levels increased across their investee companies, the government might make voting mandatory. Whilst the question of mandatory voting has been fairly widely discussed in the UK, there is no real consensus on this issue. However, there is undoubtedly a sense that institutional investors should have a more active involvement, especially in areas of corporate governance such as voting, and, in the course of time, if voting levels do not improve, then voting may well become mandatory. There is also a concern to try to ensure that individual shareholders who hold shares through nominees and not directly do not lose their right to vote; this is another dimension of institutional investor power and influence.

In 2018, the PLSA published its *AGM Voting Review* for 2017 which detailed levels of dissent of 20 per cent or more at UK companies during their 2017 AGMs. Their analysis of companies found that across the FTSE 350, there were 117 AGM resolutions that attracted dissent levels of over 20 per cent at 73 different companies in 2017. Significant dissent was more common across the FTSE 250 than the FTSE 100 index of Britain's biggest companies, but in both cases roughly one fifth of companies experienced significant dissent over at least one resolution at their AGM. Executive remuneration, a perennial corporate governance hot topic, was an issue that led to higher dissent levels.

A number of large institutional investors including Hermes, Aviva, Standard Life, and Baillie Gifford disclose details of their voting and other engagement activities at individual companies.

The situation in continental Europe is rather different because the shareholder structure in many European countries differs quite significantly from that in the UK: for example, large banks and corporations tend to dominate German and French companies, whilst Italian companies tend to be dominated by non-financial holding companies and families. However, the report of the CEPS working party set up to give policy directions on the future of corporate governance in Europe stated: 'Shareholders should be given the responsibility to exercise their voting rights in an informed and independent manner. This activity should also be adapted to the growing internationalization of shareholding and not be limited to national borders.' This seems to indicate that whatever the shareholding structure in a particular country, the vote is seen as being of importance, and once again informed voting is emphasized. It is also interesting to note the reference to the internationalization of shareholdings and the implication that cross-border holdings should be voted.

In 2002 the EU High-Level Group of Company Law Experts, chaired by Jaap Winter, emphasized the importance of facilitating voting by electronic and other means, and also of enabling cross-border voting. The recommendations of this group fed into the EU Communication, 'Modernizing Company Law and Enhancing Corporate Governance in the European Union— A Plan to Move Forward'. Approximately one-third of the share capital of EU listed companies in any given country is held by non-residents. Non-residents may face a number of obstacles when trying to exercise their shareholder rights, such as lack of sufficient information being received in a timely manner, share blocking, and difficulties in voting cross-border shares. In the context of shareholder rights, two main objectives were identified: (i) 'to strengthen shareholder rights and third party protection, with a proper distinction between categories of companies'; and (ii) 'to foster efficiency and competitiveness of business, with special attention to some specific cross-border issues'. In practice, this led to the issue in January 2006 of a Directive on Shareholders' Rights, which made the following proposals to enhance shareholders' rights:

- General meetings should be convened with at least one month's notice. All relevant information should be available on that date at the latest, and posted on the issuer's website. The meeting notice should contain all necessary information.

- Share blocking should be abolished and replaced by a record date, which should be set no earlier than 30 days before the meeting.

- The right to ask questions should be accessible to non-residents. The maximum shareholding thresholds to benefit from the right to table resolutions should not exceed 5 per cent, in order to open this right to a greater number of shareholders while preserving the good order of general meetings.

- Proxy voting should not be subject to excessive administrative requirements, nor should it be unduly restricted. Shareholders should have a choice of methods for distance voting.

- Voting results should be available to all shareholders and posted on the issuer's website.

The EU Directive (2007a) was formally adopted in June 2007 and had to be incorporated into Member States' laws by summer 2009 and 'will ensure in particular that shareholders have timely access to the complete information relevant to general meetings and facilitates the exercise of voting rights by proxy. Furthermore, the directive provides for the replacement of share blocking and related practices through a record date system.'

In June 2007 the European Commission (2007b) published an external study on proportionality between capital and control in EU listed companies. Proportionality is the relationship between capital and control ('one share, one vote'). The study, carried out by Institutional Shareholder Services Europe (ISS Europe), the European Corporate Governance Institute (ECGI), and the law firm Shearman & Sterling LLP, found that:

> on the basis of the academic research available, there is no conclusive evidence of a causal link between deviations from the proportionality principle and either the economic performance of listed companies or their governance. However, there is some evidence that investors perceive these mechanisms negatively and consider more transparency would be helpful in making investment decisions.

In December 2007, the OECD published a paper on the *Lack of Proportionality Between Ownership and Control: Overview and Issues for Discussion*. The paper states that 'proportionality between corporate ownership and control implies that any shareholder owns the same fraction of cash flow rights and voting rights'. In some countries there is a departure from this principle of proportionality and this may cause concern. The paper highlights that the cost of regulating proportionality would be significant and that a preferred approach is to strengthen corporate governance frameworks and, where necessary, target specific problems in some countries with regulation.

The EU Shareholder Rights Directive (2014) requires institutional investors to disclose 'if and how they cast their votes in the general meetings of the companies concerned and provide an explanation for their voting behaviour. Where an asset manager casts votes on behalf of an institutional investor, the institutional investor shall make a reference as to where such voting information has been published by the asset manager.'

Like the UK, the US stock market is dominated by institutional investors. One significant difference from the UK though is that private pension funds are mandated to vote by the Department of Labor's (DOL) regulations governing proxy voting by Employee Retirement Income Security Act (ERISA) funds. ERISA was enacted in 1974 and established federal fiduciary standards for private pension funds. The fiduciary duty is deemed to encompass voting. The DOL has, especially in more recent years, been fairly proactive in monitoring compliance with ERISA, and in offering interpretive advice on it. Early in 1994 Olena Berg, Assistant Secretary for Pension and Welfare Benefits, clarified the issue of global voting by stating that 'voting foreign proxies should be treated the same way as voting domestic proxies'. However, it was recognized that voting overseas proxies can be an expensive business and it is advised that fiduciaries look at possible difficulties of voting a particular stock *before* purchasing it and also evaluate the cost of voting the shares against the potential value to the plan of voting the shares. Combined with the dramatic growth in the level of US institutional investors' holdings of overseas equities, this pronouncement can also be expected to have a significant effect on the attitude towards voting in the overseas countries in which US institutional investors hold equities.

ERISA does not apply to public pension funds but the major public pension funds tend to vote their own shares or instruct their managers how to vote. Funds like the California Public Employees' Retirement System (CalPERS), the New York City Employees' Retirement System (NYCERS), and the State of Wisconsin Investment Board (SWIB) all have a policy of voting all their shares and funds such as CalPERS make available their voting actions on their websites.

In the Australian context, the Bosch Committee (1993) stated that institutional investors should 'take an active interest in the governance of their company' and commented that shareholders in general should make 'a sufficient analysis to vote in an informed manner on all issues raised at general meetings'. Stephen Smith, Chairman of the Parliamentary Joint Committee on Corporations and Securities, argued that 'institutional investors have a clear moral, if not legal, obligation to examine each proposal and decide how they will best exercise their voting rights'. In its 1995 guidelines, the Australian Investment Managers' Association recommended that 'voting rights are a valuable asset of the investor and should be managed with the same care and diligence as any other asset', and urges that 'institutions should support boards by positive use of their voting power unless they have good reasons for doing otherwise'.

A survey of institutional investors carried out by the ICGN in 2001 found that most institutional investors state that they try to exercise their overseas proxies but that there may be problems in trying to do so. Problems that may be encountered when trying to vote cross-border include the following:

- timing problems whereby just a couple of weeks' notice of the agenda items to be voted on at the companies' AGM may be given, making for a very tight deadline;
- information relating to agenda items being insufficient and/or in a foreign language, making detailed analysis of items very difficult in the available timescale;
- the blocking or depositing of shares, which means that shares have to be deposited with a central depository, public notary, or depositary named by the company, and so cannot be traded for a period of time before the company's AGM (usually between five and eight days);
- voting procedures or methods may be problematic in cross-border voting, for example, having physically to attend the AGM to vote rather than being able to send in votes by post or other appropriate means.

Recent developments in a number of countries, including various EU countries, have gone some way towards addressing a number of these issues.

However, the OECD (2011) identified that a key problem is that:

> domestic investors in many jurisdictions do not vote their foreign equity. This is important because foreign shareholders make up around 30 per cent of ownership in many jurisdictions. Barriers to cross-border voting that raise the costs of exercising voting rights remain, but evidence shows that there is also a lack of knowledge by institutional investors about foreign companies in their portfolios.

Whilst there remain a number of barriers to the effective exercise of voice by means of voting, it is, though, a powerful and public means of exercising voice. We are likely to see increased voting levels over time as there is both increasing pressure from institutional investors on companies to try to ensure a more efficient and effective voting system, and pressure from governments on institutional investors for more institutional investors to vote regularly. Over the last two decades there has been a slow increase in voting levels and maybe the threat of mandatory voting is receding. However, if institutional investor voting levels are not sustained, and increased over time, then the UK government may legislate so that voting becomes mandatory; but this is something that both the government and institutional investors would prefer not to happen, as it is felt that this might lead to mere 'box ticking' rather than to considered voting.

Aggarwal et al. (2015) investigate voting preferences of institutional investors using the unique setting of the securities lending market. They find that:

> investors restrict lendable supply and/or recall loaned shares prior to the proxy record date to exercise voting rights. Recall is higher for investors with greater incentives to monitor, for firms with poor performance or weak governance, and for proposals where returns to governance are likely higher. At the subsequent vote, recall is associated with less support for management and more support for shareholder proposals. Our results indicate that institutions value their vote and use the proxy process to affect corporate governance.

(iii) Shareholder proposals/resolutions

Shareholder proposals or shareholder resolutions are quite widespread in the USA, with 800–900 per annum. In the USA shareholder proposals have often been in relation to social, environmental, or ethical issues. However, it is expected that in future increasing numbers will relate to dissatisfaction with executive remuneration packages.

In contrast, in the UK a company has a duty to circulate resolutions proposed by shareholders and intended to be moved at an AGM if a certain number of members request it. The number of members necessary is: (i) members having 5 per cent of the voting power of the company, or (ii) 100 or more shareholders whose paid-up capital averages at least £100 each. The resolution may be circulated at the expense of the members making the request, unless the company resolves otherwise. Given the practical difficulties of meeting either of these two conditions, the number of shareholder proposals in the UK has tended to be low, usually fewer than ten per annum. However, it is expected that the number will increase given the dissatisfaction with executive remuneration, which seems to have already triggered an increased number of shareholder proposals.

Bauer et al. (2015) study more than 12,000 shareholder proposals that were filed to S&P 1500 companies from 1997 to 2009. They find that where proposals are filed by influential investors, they are more likely to be withdrawn than proposals filed by private investors.

ShareAction published *Warming Up: A spotlight on institutional investors' voting patterns on key US climate change resolutions in 2017*. The report

> reviews how votes were cast during the 2017 US proxy season by the largest 30 shareholders in 7 high-carbon companies on shareholder resolutions addressing climate-related risk management. In every instance, the management and boards of these companies rejected the resolution and recommended shareholders vote against them. The resolutions examined in this analysis were filed at Exxon Mobil, Devon Energy, PPL Corporation, Occidental Petroleum Corporation, Southern Company, Kinder Morgan and DTE Energy. These resolutions were broadly similar, requesting that management report to shareholders on the business impacts of climate change ... In 2017, Southern Company, Devon Energy, PPL Corporation, DTE Energy and Exxon Mobil all saw 6 or more of their largest shareholders move from either 'abstain' or 'support management' to supporting climate resolutions filed by independent shareholders in the company ... We find that major asset management firms are becoming more comfortable about expressing, on behalf of clients, their discontent with corporate management about weak disclosures on climate-related risks.

(iv) Focus lists

A number of institutional investors have established 'focus lists', whereby they target underperforming companies and include them on a list of companies that have underperformed a main index, such as Standard and Poor's. Underperforming the index would be a first point of identification; other factors would include not responding appropriately to the institutional investor's enquiries regarding underperformance, and not taking account of the institutional investor's views. After being put on the focus list, the companies receive the often unwanted attention of the institutional investors who may seek to change various directors on the board.

The California Public Employees' Retirement System (CalPERS) was one of the original proponents of a focus list. More recently firms such as NEI Investments Ethical Funds have employed the strategy of a focus list. They state:

> The centrepiece of our corporate engagement strategy is the Focus List—an annual program of targeted, in-depth dialogues on specific environmental, social and governance (ESG) topics. Focus List companies can include sector leaders capable of breakthroughs in corporate sustainability practice and disclosure, sector laggards that need to catch up with the leaders, and companies facing major sustainability challenges that are under special observation for continuing inclusion in Ethical Funds.

(v) Corporate governance rating systems

With the increasing emphasis on corporate governance across the globe, it is perhaps not surprising that a number of corporate governance rating systems have been developed. Examples of firms that have developed corporate governance rating systems are Deminor, Standard and Poor's, and Governance Metrics International (GMI). The rating systems cover several markets: for example, Deminor has tended to concentrate on European companies, whilst Standard and Poor's has used its corporate governance rating system in quite different markets, such as Russia. GMI ratings cover a range of countries, including the USA, various countries in the Asia-Pacific region, and Europe. These corporate governance rating systems should be of benefit to investors, both potential and those presently invested, and to the companies themselves.

In turn, the ratings will also be useful to governments in identifying perceived levels of corporate governance in their country compared to other countries in their region, or outside it, whose companies may be competing for limited foreign investment. In emerging market countries in particular, those companies with a corporate governance infrastructure will, *ceteris paribus*, be less subject to cronyism and its attendant effects on corporate wealth. These companies will tend to be more transparent and accountable, and hence more attractive to foreign investors.

A corporate governance rating can be a powerful indicator of the extent to which a company currently is adding, or has the potential to add in the future, shareholder value. This is because a company with good corporate governance is generally perceived as more attractive to investors than one without. Good corporate governance should, for example, indicate a board that is prepared to participate actively in dialogue with its shareholders, ensuring the effective exercise of voice (Hirschman 1970) thus enabling investors to articulate their interests.

An appropriate approach for a corporate governance rating system is first to have a rating of the corporate governance in a given country, for example:

- How transparent are accounting and reporting practices generally in the country?
- Are there existing corporate governance practices in place?
- Is there a code of best practice?
- To what extent is that code complied with?
- What sanctions are there against companies which do not comply?

Having set the scene in any given country, the individual company can then be given a corporate governance rating. With regard to the individual company, the ratings will generally be based on the company's approach to the rights of shareholders, the presence of independent non-executive (outside) directors, the effectiveness of the board, and the accountability and transparency of the company. Corporate governance rankings of companies in, for example, the banking sector can be assessed both within a country and also across countries, providing a valuable additional indicator/comparator benchmark for investors.

Overall, corporate governance rating systems should provide a useful indication of the corporate governance environment in specific countries, and in individual companies within those countries. Such systems will provide a useful benchmark for the majority of investors who identify good corporate governance with a well-run and well-managed company, and investors will increasingly take into account companies' governance profiles in investment decisions.

An interesting study by Rowley at al. (2017) analysed the impact of ratings on the adoption of governance practices. Using the leading corporate governance ranking in Canada, they

> find that rankings could have adverse effects: when firms have both poor governance ranking and poor profitability they are less likely to adopt governance practices, contrary to the ranking creators' intentions. The findings show that there is a hierarchy of firms' goals, where the goal of profitability comes ahead of other goals imposed by external agencies through ratings and rankings.

Corporate governance and corporate performance

Is there a link between corporate governance and corporate performance? Whilst there have been many studies carried out on this area, the evidence appears to be fairly mixed.

One of the earlier and much-quoted studies is that of Nesbitt (1994). Nesbitt reported positive long-term stock price returns to firms targeted by CalPERS. Nesbitt's later studies show similar findings. Subsequently, Millstein and MacAvoy (1998) studied 154 large publicly traded US corporations over a five-year period and found that corporations with active and independent boards appear to have performed much better in the 1990s than those with passive, non-independent boards. However, the work of Dalton et al. (1998) showed that board composition had virtually no effect on firm performance, and that there was no relationship between leadership structure (chief executive officer (CEO)/chairman) and firm performance. Patterson (2000), of the Conference Board, produced a comprehensive review of the literature relating to the link between corporate governance and performance, and stated that the survey did not present conclusive evidence of such a link.

Whilst the evidence seems to be quite mixed, there does appear to be a widely held perception that corporate governance can make a difference to the bottom line. The findings of a survey by McKinsey (2002) found that the majority of investors would be prepared to pay a premium to invest in a company with good corporate governance as it is the investor's perception and belief that corporate governance is important and that belief leads to the willingness to pay a premium for good corporate governance.

Some of the significant papers that have found evidence of a positive link include Gompers et al. (2003) and Deutsche Bank (2004a and 2004b). Gompers et al. (2003) examined the ways in which shareholder rights vary across firms. They constructed a 'Governance Index' to proxy for the level of shareholder rights in approximately 1,500 large firms during the 1990s. An investment strategy that bought firms in the lowest decile of the index (strongest rights) and sold firms in the highest decile of the index (weakest rights) would have earned abnormal returns of 8.5 per cent per year during the sample period. They found that firms with stronger shareholder rights had higher firm value, higher profits, higher sales growth, lower capital expenditures, and made fewer corporate acquisitions. Deutsche Bank (2004a and 2004b) explored the implications of corporate governance for portfolio management and concluded that corporate governance standards are an important component of equity risk. Its analysis also showed that for South Africa, Eastern Europe, and the Middle East, the performance differential favours those companies with stronger corporate governance.

Hermes (2005) provided a succinct summary of academic and practitioner research in this area, splitting it into three categories: opinion-based research (such as McKinsey (2002)); focus list research and performance of shareholder engagement funds (such as 'the CalP-ERS effect', on which there were various studies such as Nesbitt (1994)); and finally, governance ranking research (such as Deutsche Bank (2004)). Hermes concludes its 2005 review of the literature by stating that it recognizes that a number of the authors of the various studies cited in the review have mentioned that there is further empirical work needed on the issue of causation but that, 'nevertheless, we consider there to be sufficient evidence in support of our view that good corporate governance improves the long-term performance of companies'.

In 2007 Hermes published another summary of the research in this area, identifying the missing links. The effectiveness of engagement is highlighted by the study carried out by Becht et al. (2009) whereby the researchers were given unlimited access to Hermes' resources, including letters, memos, minutes, presentations, transcripts/recordings of telephone conversations, and client reports, documenting its work with the companies in which Hermes' UK Focus Fund invested in a period over five years (1998–2004). They reviewed all forms of public and private engagement with 41 companies. They found that when the engagement objectives led to actual outcomes, there were economically large and statistically significant positive abnormal returns around the announcement date. On the basis of their findings, they concluded that shareholder activism can produce corporate governance changes that generate significant returns for shareholders.

Lantz et al. (2010), in a study of French companies, found that institutional investors are becoming more active in their portfolio management. They point out that since 1999, Société des Bourses Françaises (SBF) 120 companies in France that do not respect the 'Code of Best Practices on Corporate Governance as set out by the AFG' are added to a widely circulated 'target list'. They examine the AFG alerts on financial performance, using a short-term event study methodology and their findings indicate a negative effect on the wealth of shareholders on the day of the alert. They conclude, therefore, that the impact depends on past performance measured by book ratios or expressed in relation to the future premium opportunity for shareholders.

Renders et al. (2010) report that, in a cross-European sample, their results 'imply that corporate-governance ratings are relevant and that in adhering to good corporate-governance practices, companies can significantly improve their performance'. Aggarwal et al. (2011) found that institutional investors influence the development of corporate governance in other countries, and especially in terms of improving investor protection in countries where it is weaker than their own. They provide evidence that:

> institutional ownership has a direct effect on corporate governance outcomes, functioning as a disciplinary mechanism in terminating poorly performing CEOs. Furthermore, increases in institutional ownership lead to increases in firm valuation, suggesting that institutional investment not only affects governance mechanisms, but also has real effects on firm value and board decisions ... we conclude that monitoring and activism by institutions travel beyond country borders and lead to better firm performance.

Agrawal and Knoeber (2012) provide an insightful overview of the literature on corporate governance and firm performance in economies with relatively dispersed stock ownership and an active market for corporate control, such as the US and the UK. They identify some remaining puzzles and unresolved issues for future research.

Meanwhile Francis et al. (2015) identify that directors from academia served on the boards of around 40 per cent of Standard & Poor's (S&P) 1,500 firms over the 1998–2011 period. Their paper investigates the effects of academic directors on corporate governance and firm performance. They find that 'companies with directors from academia are associated with higher performance and this relation is driven by professors without administrative jobs. We also find that academic directors play an important governance role through their advising and monitoring functions.'

In sum, the evidence, both academic and practitioner, points on balance towards the view that good corporate governance helps realize value and create competitive advantage; this is more of an intuitive feeling because the studies are trying to single out corporate governance variables that may affect performance and this is very difficult to do. However, shareholder activism is the key to ensuring good corporate governance and, without this, there is less accountability and transparency, and hence more opportunity for management to engage in activities that may have a negative effect on the bottom line.

Conclusions

In this chapter, the extent of institutional share ownership, and hence the growth of institutions' power and influence, has been examined. The chapter highlights the emphasis that is increasingly placed on the role of institutional investors in corporate governance in a global context. The tools of governance for institutional investors, including one-to-one meetings, voting, shareholder proposals/resolutions, the use of focus lists, and rating systems are discussed.

We have seen how, in the UK and the USA, institutional investors have become very important over the last 40 or so years as their share ownership has increased and they have become more active in their ownership role. Institutional investors tend to have a fiduciary responsibility, i.e. the responsibility to act in the best interests of a third party (generally the beneficial or ultimate owners of the shares). Until recently, this responsibility has tended to concentrate on ensuring that they invest in companies that are not only profitable but that will continue to have a growing trend of profits. Whilst this remains the case, governments and pressure groups have raised the question of how these profits are achieved. We now see institutional investors being much more concerned about the internal governance of the company, corporate culture, ethics, and the company's relationship with other stakeholder groups. The growth of institutional investor interest in socially responsible investment is the subject of Chapter 7.

Summary

- Institutional investors, such as large pension funds, insurance companies, and mutual funds, have become the largest shareholders in many countries, having significant shareholdings in the companies in which they invest.

- Sovereign wealth fund, private equity firms, and hedge funds have all come under the spotlight in relation to corporate governance issues.

- The relationship between institutional investors and their investee companies is very important. Institutional investors can have a powerful 'voice' in their investee companies.

- There is an increased emphasis on the stewardship role that should be played by institutional investors.

- The 'tools' of governance include one-to-one meetings, voting, shareholder proposals/resolutions, focus lists, and rating systems.

- The evidence as to whether 'good' corporate governance impacts on corporate performance is rather mixed but, looking at it another way, good governance can help ensure that companies do not fail. Also, a company with good corporate governance is more likely to attract external capital flows than one without.

Example: Chevron, USA

This is an example of a US company which has been the focus of institutional investor attention in recent years with various shareholder proposals on corporate governance and corporate social responsibility issues.

Chevron is one of the world's leading integrated energy companies. It explores for crude oil and natural gas; it refines, markets, and distributes transportation fuels and lubricants; manufactures and sells petrochemical products; generates power and produces geothermal energy; invests in profitable renewable energy and energy efficiency solutions; and develops the energy resources of the future, including researching advanced biofuels.

For the year ended 31 December 2016, Chevron's net oil-equivalent daily production was 2.6 million barrels per day and its sales and other operating revenue was US$110.2 billion. It had a workforce of just under 52,000 employees.

In its 2017 Proxy Statement issued in advance of the company's AGM in May 2017, Chevron stated that:

> since Chevron's last Annual Meeting, an engagement team consisting of senior executives, subject matter experts on governance, compensation, and environmental and social issues, and, when appropriate, our independent Lead Director and the Chair of our Management Compensation Committee, conducted more than 45 in-depth discussions with stockholders representing more than 36 percent of Chevron's outstanding common stock. Of those meetings, our Lead Director

(continued)

and Chairman of our Management Compensation Committee met with stockholders comprising 29 percent of our outstanding stock. In addition, our engagement team met with many of the stockholders who submitted proposals for inclusion in our Proxy Statement to discuss their concerns and areas of agreement and disagreement. Chevron gained valuable feedback during these engagements, and this feedback was shared with the Board and its relevant committees.

At Chevron's annual general meeting (AGM) in May 2017, some large pension funds such as the California Public Employees' Retirement System (CalPERS) voted for a number of shareholder proposals including proposals for a report on lobbying, a report on Transition to a Low Carbon Economy, Independent Board Chair, Environmental Expertise on Board, and Right to Call a Special Meeting. However none of these shareholder proposals achieved an overall majority vote in favour despite support from several large pension funds.

A shareholder proposal put forward by Hermes EOS (Hermes) and Wespath Investment Management (Wespath), together with multiple co-filers, requesting an annual assessment of long-term portfolio impacts of plausible climate change scenarios, including disclosure of the impacts of multiple, fluctuating demand and price scenarios on the company's reserves and resource portfolio was withdrawn from the 2017 proxy after Chevron published a report 'Managing Climate Change Risks: a perspective for investors'. Whilst not providing all of the information requested about climate change, Hermes and Wespath believed that Chevron had come some way with this report and they withdrew the shareholder proposal with the intention of pursuing further dialogue with Chevron management to address the remaining issues.

Michael Wirth took over as Chevron's new CEO/Chair in February 2018 and he looks set to face more shareholder proposals at Chevron's next AGM, relating to both corporate social responsibility issues such as its corporate responsibility in relation to oil pollution in Ecuador (inherited from its takeover of Texaco back in 2000), and also to corporate governance, e.g. its board structure where the roles of CEO and Chair would ideally be held by two separate individuals, and also board diversity in terms of expertise with the appointment of an environmental specialist to the board.

Example: ThyssenKrupp, Germany

This is an example of a German company which has become the focus of institutional investor activism as its strategy is not producing the returns some investors seek.

Today benefitting from a 200-year-old brand name, the company was originally established by two families, Thyssen and Krupp; ThyssenKrupp AG was formed in March 1999. Nearly 20 years later the company has sales of around €41.5 billion and employs over 158,000 people operating in 80 countries. Its business operations cover a range of business areas: components technology, elevator technology, industrial solutions, materials services, and steel. Nonetheless, despite the company's group divisions being reduced since 2011 and with further restructuring of the group planned when ThyssenKrupp merges its European steel operations with those of Tata Steel later in 2018, some investors are still concerned at the overall complex structure of the company's operations and would like the company to review its strategy further given their perception of its poor financial performance. A chief proponent of demands for further action to improve the company's strategy has been Cevian Capital, an international investment firm acquiring significant ownership positions in publicly listed European companies, where long-term value can be enhanced through active ownership. It seeks to realize value-enhancement potential in operations, corporate strategy/organizational structure, financial management, and corporate governance. According to

(continued)

ThyssenKrupp's Annual Report 2016/17, Cevian Capital, Stockholm and Zurich, holds 15.08 per cent of the capital stock.

For their part, in their Annual Report 2016/17, ThyssenKrupp state:

> The past fiscal year 2016/2017 was a year of major decisions. We sold the Brazilian steel mill CSA and signed a memorandum of understanding with Tata Steel on a joint venture for our European steel activities. These were two important milestones on thyssenkrupp's Strategic Way Forward towards becoming a diversified industrial group ... we not only brought the loss-making chapter of 'Steel Americas' to an end but also offered the business and its employees the key to a sustainable future. At the same time we reduced future risks for thyssenkrupp as a whole and opened important options for our European steel business.

A further strategic review of ThyssenKrupp's divisions may be undertaken later in 2018 once the joint venture with Tata Steel is completed.

 ## Mini case study   Rio Tinto Plc, UK

This is an interesting example of institutional investors trying to protect their interests when they feel that the company's proposed strategy is not in the best interests of the current shareholders. After institutional investors expressed their concerns, the board engaged in dialogue with them to discuss these concerns and explain their strategy more fully. Subsequently concerns were raised about aspects of both Rio Tinto's corporate responsibility in relation to climate change and also about its corporate governance in relation to board diversity.

Rio Tinto is a leading international mining group headquartered in the UK, combining Rio Tinto Plc, a London and New York Stock Exchange (NYSE) listed company, and Rio Tinto Limited, which is listed on the Australian Securities Exchange. The group's activities are the finding, mining, and processing of mineral resources. Its major products include aluminium, copper, diamonds, energy (coal and uranium), gold, industrial minerals (borax, titanium dioxide, salt, talc), and iron ore.

In February 2009 Rio Tinto announced a deal with Aluminium Corporation of China (Chinalco) which would create a strategic partnership through joint ventures whilst also giving Rio Tinto a cash injection from Chinalco. The cash injection would help solve some of the financial problems arising from Rio Tinto's large US$39 billion debt burden. However, the cash injection would involve the sale of stakes in prized mines and also the issue of US$7.2 billion of convertible bonds to Chinalco, together raising some US$19.5 billion.

However, investors, including Legal General Investment Management (the second largest shareholder in Rio Tinto), Scottish Widows Investment Partnership, and Aviva Investors were concerned that this proposed deal would result in a dilution of their shareholdings as they had not been offered the opportunity to participate in a rights issue. Rights issues have been a traditional way to raise funds from existing shareholders in the UK, Europe, and Australasia. Existing shareholders are offered the chance to acquire new shares, at a discount, in proportion to their existing holding. Shareholders taking up the rights will retain the same proportion of the share capital overall as they had prior to the rights issue. However, shareholders not taking up the rights issue shares will have a lower proportion of the company's share capital than they did prior to the rights issue, i.e. their stake will be diluted. To avoid any dilution that would occur when companies do not offer shares to their existing shareholders first, in some jurisdictions the concept of pre-emption rights (that is, new shares have to be offered to existing shareholders first) has long been enshrined in company law. In addition

(continued)

to the concern over the lack of opportunity to existing shareholders to partake in any new issues of shares, the institutional investors pointed out that potential conflicts of interest could arise if Chinalco had seats on the Rio Tinto board, and also held stakes in some of Rio Tinto's best assets.

Interestingly, Jim Leng, who was the Chairman Designate for Rio Tinto, resigned over the matter as he had reservations about the Chinalco deal and favoured a rights issue. However, Tom Albanese, the Chief Executive, and Paul Skinner, who was due to retire from the Chairman's post and make way for Jim Leng, both argued in favour of the Chinalco deal.

Institutional investors threatened to vote against the deal, and the board engaged in dialogue with the investors to try to convince them to approve the deal. However, many of the institutional investors still favoured a rights issue over the proposed deal. In May 2009 Chinalco walked away from the proposed deal with Rio Tinto amid the intense investor pressure, and Rio Tinto announced a rights issue. Chinalco participated in the rights issue along with other shareholders, taking up the rights offered.

In December 2010 Rio Tinto and Chinalco signed a non-binding Memorandum of Understanding (MoU) to establish a landmark exploration joint venture in China, with Chinalco holding a 51 per cent interest in the joint venture and Rio Tinto holding a 49 per cent interest.

In 2012 Rio Tinto completed an agreement with the Aluminum Corporation of China Limited (Chalco), a listed arm of Chinalco, to set up a joint venture for the development of the Simandou iron ore mine in Guinea, West Africa. According to the agreement, Rio Tinto and Chinalco will hold 53 per cent and 47 per cent stakes, respectively, in the joint venture, which translates into a 50.35 per cent and 44.65 per cent interest in the Simandou project; the remaining 5 per cent will go to the International Finance Corporation, a member of the World Bank Group.

The issue of climate change and company strategy in this regard has increasingly become a focus of investors in recent years. 'Aiming for A' is a coalition, originally convened by the Interfaith Center on Corporate Responsibility (ICCR) in 2011/12, which includes the Local Authority Pension Fund Forum (LAPFF) and the largest members of the Church Investors Group, together with Hermes Investment Management. ICCR state:

> The group is undertaking engagement with the ten largest UK-listed extractives and utilities companies, with a particular focus on the companies' CDP [Carbon Disclosure Project] performance bands. There are several reasons why UK asset owners and managers have come together to support companies in their preparations for the low-carbon transition. These range from systemic risk management and our collective fiduciary duty to engage in economic transformation, through to amplifying longer-term investor voices and involving ultimate beneficiaries. ... We believe that supportive but stretching shareholder resolutions can play a positive stewardship role in the UK and emphasise the need to balance the short- and longer-term aspects of shareholder value creation. The wider co-filing group includes institutional asset owners and fund managers from both the UK and overseas.

The shareholder resolution which was put forward at Rio Tinto's AGM in April 2016 covered five related areas: ongoing operational emissions management; asset portfolio resilience to post-2035 scenarios; low carbon energy research and development (R&D) and investment strategies; strategic key performance indicators (KPIs) and executive incentives; and public policy interventions. The group engaged with the board who also supported the resolution which was passed at Rio Tinto's 2016 AGM with a significant majority.

At Rio Tinto's AGM in 2017, there was recognition that Rio Tinto had achieved a reduction in greenhouse gas emissions of 21 per cent between 2008 and 2015, significantly exceeding the original target of 10 per cent. The target has been extended from 21 per cent to 24 per cent for the period ending 2020. However many investors felt that much more information and disclosure were required,

(continued)

for example, more disclosures on financial risk in relation to the low carbon scenarios. Also that further disclosure was needed in order to meet the then draft recommendations of the Financial Stability Board's (FSB) Taskforce on Climate-Related Financial Disclosures. Rio Tinto's Sustainability Committee includes climate change as one of its areas of focus and it will be interesting to see how the company progresses in future years with its long-term strategy to decarbonize its mining and smelting operations and the extent to which it includes climate change-related metrics in its executive remuneration performance measures.

At Rio Tinto's AGM in 2017, there was another 'hot topic' issue, that of the lack of board diversity which aroused the concern of some institutional investors. For example, Hermes decided to make a protest vote against the re-election of the Rio Tinto Chairman, Jan du Plessis, who chaired the company's nomination committee. Hermes took this action as it felt that there was a lack of women on the board and also lack of a credible plan to address this issue. Jan du Plessis had already announced his attention to leave Rio Tinto to take up the Chairman's role at BT and his replacement, Mr Simon Thompson, took over as Rio Tinto Chairman in the Spring 2018. Interestingly—in another example of institutional shareholder activism—Rio Tinto had been viewing Mick Davis, former head of the mining group Xstrata, as a possible replacement for Jan du Plessis but some of Rio Tinto's largest investors were against his appointment because of his association with high executive remuneration and aggressive deal making whilst at Xstrata, and instead supported Simon Thompson.

In 2017, Rio Tinto, its former CEO Tom Albanese and former CFO Guy Elliott, were charged with fraud by the US Securities Exchange Commission (SEC) in relation to allegedly hiding the scale of a write down of US$3 billion in relation to the purchase of a coal asset in Mozambique in 2011 as the company failed to gain permission to ship coal down river, rendering the project worthless. Both men deny any wrongdoing and Rio Tinto has said the charges are 'unwarranted'. In October 2017 the UK Financial Conduct Authority (FCA) fined Rio Tinto £27 million over the matter stating that it had breached the Disclosure and Transparency Rules but did not find evidence of fraud. As at January 2018, the SEC maintains that Rio Tinto and the two former directors must face fraud charges.

In terms of Rio Tinto's corporate governance, investors will be keen to see the right 'tone' being set at the top. The corporate culture should then reflect the importance of ethics in a company and that compliance is the appropriate way for a company to act and that bribery and corruption are not acceptable.

Mini case study questions:

1. Which 'tools of governance' were employed by the institutional investors in this case and how effective were they in relation to the various issues raised?

2. In what ways might Rio Tinto's corporate governance and corporate culture be improved?

Questions

The discussion questions to follow cover the key learning points of this chapter. Reading of some of the additional reference material will enhance the depth of the students' knowledge and understanding of these areas.

1. Why has the influence of institutional investors grown so much in recent years, and what role do you think institutional investors should play in corporate governance?

2. How do SWFs differ from 'traditional' institutional investors?

3. To what extent is the internationalization of investment portfolios responsible for institutional investors' increased interest in corporate governance?

4. What 'tools of governance' do institutional investors have at their disposal and to what extent do they have a responsibility to use such tools?

5. What evidence is there to show that 'good' corporate governance can improve corporate performance?

6. Why might institutional investors be interested in a firm's corporate culture?

References

Aggarwal, R., Erel, I., Ferreira, M., and Matos, P. (2011), 'Does Governance Travel Around the World? Evidence from Institutional Investors', *Journal of Financial Economics*, Vol. 100, No. 1, pp. 154–81.

Aggarwal, R., Saffi P.A.C., and Sturgess, J. (2015), 'The Role of Institutional Investors in Voting: Evidence from the Securities Lending Market', *Journal of Finance*, Vol. 70, Issue 5, October 2015, pp. 2309–46.

Agrawal, A. and Knoeber, C.R. (2012), 'Corporate Governance and Firm Performance' (15 March 2012) in C.R. Thomas and W.F. Shughart II (eds), *Oxford Handbook in Managerial Economics*, Oxford University Press, Oxford.

Association of British Insurers/National Association of Pension Funds (1999), *Responsible Voting—A Joint ABI-NAPF Statement*, ABI/NAPF, London.

Bauer R., Moers F., and Viehs, M. (2015), 'Who Withdraws Shareholder Proposals and Does It Matter? An Analysis of Sponsor Identity and Pay Practices', *Corporate Governance: An International Review*, Vol. 23, Issue 6, November 2015, pp. 472–88.

Becht, M., Franks, J., Mayer, C., and Rossi, S. (2009), 'Returns to Shareholder Activism—Evidence from a Clinical Study of the Hermes UK Focus Fund', *The Review of Financial Studies*, Vol. 22, Issue 8, pp. 3093–129.

Berle, A.A. and Means, G.C. (1932), *The Modern Corporation and Private Property*, Macmillan, New York.

Bosch, H. (1993), *Corporate Practices and Conduct*, Business Council of Australia, Melbourne.

Cadbury, Sir Adrian (1992), *Report of the Committee on the Financial Aspects of Corporate Governance*, Gee & Co. Ltd, London.

Centre for European Policy Studies (1995), *Corporate Governance in Europe*, Brussels.

Dalton, D.R., Daily, C.M., Ellstrand, A.E., and Johnson, J.L. (1998), 'Meta-analytic Reviews of Board Composition, Leadership Structure, and Financial Performance', *Strategic Management Journal*, Vol. 19, No. 3, pp. 269–90.

Deutsche Bank (2004a), *Global Corporate Governance Research*, 'Beyond the Numbers—Corporate Governance in the UK', February.

Deutsche Bank (2004b), *Global Corporate Governance Research*, 'Beyond the Numbers—Corporate Governance in South Africa', October.

European Commission (2007a), Directive 2007/36/EC Shareholders' Rights, EU, Brussels.

European Commission (2007b), *Report on the Proportionality Principle in the EU*, external study by ISS Europe, the ECGI, and Shearman & Sterling LLP, EU, Brussels.

European Commission (2010), *Green Paper on Corporate Governance in Financial Institutions and Remuneration Policies*, European Commission, Brussels.

European Commission (2012), *Action Plan: European Company Law and Corporate Governance—a modern legal framework for more engaged shareholders and sustainable companies*, European Commission, Brussels.

European Commission (2014), Shareholder Rights Directive, European Commission, Brussels.

European Fund and Asset Management Association (2011), *EFAMA Code for External Governance: Principles for the exercise of ownership rights in investee companies*, EFAMA, Brussels.

FairPensions (2011), *Protecting Our Best Interests, Rediscovering Fiduciary Obligation*, FairPensions, London.

Federation of European Securities Exchanges (2008), *Share Ownership Structure in Europe*, FESE Economics and Statistics Committee, Brussels.

Financial Reporting Council (2010a), *UK Corporate Governance Code*, FRC, London.

Financial Reporting Council (2010b), *UK Stewardship Code*, FRC, London.

Financial Reporting Council (2012), *UK Stewardship Code*, FRC, London.

Financial Reporting Council (2015), *Developments in Corporate Governance and Stewardship 2014*, FRC, London.

Financial Reporting Council (2018), *UK Corporate Governance Code*, FRC, London.

Francis, B., Hasan, I., and Wu, Q. (2015), 'Professors in the Boardroom and Their Impact on Corporate Governance and Firm Performance', *Financial Management*, Vol. 44, Issue 3, Fall 2015, pp. 547–81.

Gilson, R.J. and Gordon, J.N. (2013), 'The Agency Costs of Agency Capitalism: Activist Investors and the Revaluation of Governance Rights', *Columbia Law Review*, Vol. 113, Issue 4, pp. 863–927.

Gompers, P.A., Ishii, J.L., and Metrick, A. (2003), 'Corporate Governance and Equity Prices', *Quarterly Journal of Economics*, Vol. 118, No. 1, February, pp. 107–55.

Greenbury, Sir Richard (1995), *Directors' Remuneration*, Gee & Co. Ltd, London.

Hampel, Sir Ronnie (1998), *Committee on Corporate Governance: Preliminary Report*, Gee & Co. Ltd, London.

Hermes (2002), *The Hermes Principles*, Hermes, London.

Hermes (2005), *Corporate Governance and Corporate Performance*, Hermes, London.

Hermes (2006), *The Hermes Corporate Governance Principles*, Hermes, London.

Hermes (2007), *Corporate Governance and Performance—The Missing Links*, Hermes, London.

Hermes (2010), *The Hermes Responsible Ownership Principles*, Hermes, London.

Hermes (2013), *Responsible Ownership Principles*, Hermes, London.

Hermes (2017), *Stewardship*, Hermes, London.

Hermes (2018), *Corporate Governance Principles, United Kingdom*, Hermes, London.

Hirschman, A.O. (1970), *Exit, Voice, and Loyalty*, Harvard University Press, Cambridge, MA.

Institutional Shareholders' Committee (2002), *The Responsibilities of Institutional Shareholders and Agents—Statement of Principles*, ISC, London.

Institutional Shareholders' Committee (2009), *Code on the Responsibilities of Institutional Investors*, ISC, London.

International Corporate Governance Network (2007), *Statement of Principles on Institutional Shareholder Responsibilities*, ICGN, London.

International Corporate Governance Network (2009), *Second Statement on the Global Financial Crisis*, ICGN, London.

International Corporate Governance Network (2012), *ICGN Model Mandate Initiative*, ICGN, London.

International Corporate Governance Network (2013), *Statement of Principles for Institutional Investor Responsibilities*, ICGN, London.

International Corporate Governance Network (2015), *Global Stewardship Principles*, ICGN, London.

International Corporate Governance Network (2017), *ICGN Global Governance Principles*, ICGN, London.

International Working Group of Sovereign Wealth Funds (2008), *Sovereign Wealth Funds, Generally Accepted Principles and Practices—Santiago Principles*, IWG, London.

Kay, J. (2012), *The Kay Review of UK Equity Markets and Long-Term Decision Making, Interim Report, February 2012*, Department for Business, Innovation & Skills, London.

Lantz, J.-B., Montandrau, S., and Sahut, J.-M. (2010), 'Activism of Institutional Investors, Corporate Governance Alerts and Financial Performance', *International Journal of Business*, Vol. 15, No. 2, pp. 221–40.

Mallin, C.A. (2012), 'The Stewardship Code', Working Paper, Birmingham Business School.

Mallin, C.A. and Melis, A. (2012), 'Shareholder Rights, Shareholder Voting and Corporate Performance', *Journal of Management and Governance*, Vol. 16, Issue 2, pp. 171–6.

McCahery J.A., Starks, L.T., and Sautner, Z. (2016), 'Behind the Scenes: The Corporate Governance Preferences of Institutional Investors', *Journal of Finance*, Vol. 71, Issue 6, December 2016, pp. 2905–32.

McKinsey & Co. (2002), *Global Investor Opinion Survey: Key Findings*, McKinsey & Co. London.

Megginson W.L. and Fotak V. (2015), 'Rise of the Fiduciary State: A Survey of Sovereign Wealth Fund Research', *Journal of Economic Surveys*, Vol. 29, Issue 4, September 2015, pp. 733–78.

Millstein, I.M. and MacAvoy, P.W. (1998), 'The Active Board of Directors and Performance of the Large Publicly Traded Corporation', *Columbia Law Review*, Vol. 98, No. 21, pp. 1283–322.

Monks, R. (2001), *The New Global Investors*, Capstone Publishers, London.

Myners, P. (2001), *Myners Report on Institutional Investment*, HM Treasury, London.

Myners, P. (2004), *Review of the Impediments to Voting UK Shares*, SVWG, London.

National Association of Pension Funds (1999), *Report of the Committee of Inquiry into UK Vote Execution*, NAPF, London.

Nesbitt, S.L. (1994), 'Long-term Rewards from Shareholder Activism: A Study of the "CalPERS Effect"', *Journal of Applied Corporate Finance*, Vol. 6, No. 4, pp. 75–80.

Organisation for Economic Co-operation and Development (2007), *Lack of Proportionality Between Ownership and Control: Overview and Issues for Discussion*, OECD, Paris.

Organisation for Economic Co-operation and Development (2008a), *Codes and Industry Standards Covering the Behaviour of Alternative Investors*, OECD, Paris.

Organisation for Economic Co-operation and Development (2008b), *The Role of Private Equity and Activist Hedge Funds in Corporate Governance– Related Policy Issues*, OECD, Paris.

Organisation for Economic Co-operation and Development (2011), *The Role of Institutional Investors in Promoting Good Corporate Governance*, OECD, Paris.

Office for National Statistics (2017), *Ownership of UK quoted shares: 2016*, ONS, Newport.

Patterson, D.J. (2000), *The Link Between Corporate Governance and Performance, Year 2000 Update*, Conference Board, New York.

Pensions and Lifetime Savings Association (2015), *Corporate Governance Policy and Voting Guidelines 2015/16*, PLSA, London.

Pensions and Lifetime Savings Association (2018a), *AGM Voting Review 2017*, PLSA, London.

Pensions and Lifetime Savings Association (2018b), *Corporate Governance Policy and Voting Guidelines 2018*, PLSA, London.

Renders, A., Gaeremynck, A., and Sercu, P. (2010), 'Corporate-Governance Ratings and Company Performance: A Cross-European Study', *Corporate Governance: An International Review*, Vol. 18, No. 2, pp. 87–106.

Rock, E.B. (2015), 'Institutional Investors in Corporate Governance' in J.N. Gordon and W.-G. Ringe (eds), *Oxford Handbook on Corporate Law and Governance*, Oxford University Press, Oxford.

Rowley T.J., Shipilov A.V., and Greve H.R. (2017), 'Board Reform versus Profits: The Impact of Ratings on the Adoption of Governance Practices', *Strategic Management Journal*, Vol. 38, Issue 4, April 2017, pp. 815–33.

ShareAction (2015), *Asset Manager Voting Practices: In Whose Interests? Survey of 2014's AGM season*, ShareAction, London.

ShareAction (2017), *Warming Up: A spotlight on institutional investors' voting patterns on key US climate change resolutions in 2017*, ShareAction, London.

Sovereign Wealth Fund Institute (2018), *Sovereign Wealth Fund Rankings*, SWFI, Seattle.

Talbot, L. E. (2010), 'The Coming of Shareholder Stewardship: A Contextual Analysis of Current Anglo-American Perspectives on Corporate Governance', Warwick School of Law Research Paper No. 2010/22. Available at SSRN: http://ssrn.com/abstract=1676869.

The Investor Forum (2018), *Review 2017*, The Investor Forum, London.

Tilba, A. and McNulty, T. (2013), 'Engaged versus Disengaged Ownership: The Case of Pension Funds in the UK', *Corporate Governance: An International Review*, Vol. 21, No. 2, pp. 165–82.

Tomorrow's Company (2009), *Tomorrow's Owners: Stewardship of Tomorrow's Company*, Tomorrow's Company, London.

Tomorrow's Company (2018), *Better Stewardship—An Agenda for Concerted Action*, Tomorrow's Company, London.

Useem, M. (1996), *Investor Capitalism—How Money Managers Are Changing the Face of Corporate America*, BasicBooks, HarperCollins, New York.

Walker, D. (2009), *A Review of Corporate Governance in UK Banks and Other Financial Industry Entities, Final Recommendations*, HM Treasury, London.

Walker Working Group (Private Equity Working Group on Transparency and Disclosure) (2007), *Guidelines for Disclosure and Transparency in Private Equity*, Walker Working Group, London.

Useful websites

www.abi.org.uk The website of the Association of British Insurers offers topical articles on a range of corporate governance issues of particular relevance to the UK's insurance industry.

www.bis.gov.uk The Department for Business, Innovation & Skills website offers a range of information including ministerial speeches and regulatory guidance.

www.calpers.ca.gov The website of the California Public Employees' Retirement System, a large pension fund active in corporate governance matters.

https://ec.europa.eu/info/business-economy-euro/doing-business-eu/company-law-and-corporate-governance_en The website of the European Union covering company law and corporate governance aspects.

www.fese.eu The website of the Federation of European Securities Exchanges which covers its activities in promoting relations between global stock exchanges.

www.iccr.org The Interfaith Center on Corporate Responsibility (ICCR) website details its activities in the use of shareholder advocacy to press companies on environmental, social, and governance issues.

www.manifest.co.uk The website of Manifest, providing information about global proxy governance matters.

www.plsa.co.uk The Pensions and Lifetime Savings Association (PLSA) website contains useful information relating to various aspects of pensions and lifetime savings for pension professionals and individuals. Formerly the National Association of Pension Funds (NAPF).

www.swfinstitute.org The website of the Sovereign Wealth Fund Institute covering various aspects of SWFs.

www.thecityuk.com The website of The CityUK, which has information about UK financial services at home and overseas.

Develop your understanding of this chapter and explore the subject further using our online resources at **www.oup.com/uk/mallin6e/**

FT Clippings

Consumer goods make appetising target for US activists

Nestlé, P&G and Unilever all under pressure to improve performance

Scheherazade Daneshkhu and Lindsay Fortado in London, and Anna Nicolaou in New York

Financial Times, 21 July 2017

Nelson Peltz has always had a healthy appetite for food. Heinz, Cadbury, Mondelez, PepsiCo and Danone—the veteran US activist investor has agitated for change in them all.

Mr Peltz's tastes have broadened with his ambitions. This week, the 75-year-old launched a proxy battle to get a seat on the board of Procter & Gamble, the US's biggest household products company with a $226bn market value, in which Mr Peltz's Trian investment group invested $3.3bn this year.

And Mr Peltz is not alone at the table. Nestlé, the world's largest consumer goods group, discovered last month that its SFr259bn market value was no longer a defence against activist incursion. Dan Loeb, founder and chief executive of Third Point, took a $3.5bn stake in the producer of KitKat chocolate and Nespresso coffee.

Mr Loeb called for a 'greater sense of urgency' in boosting performance at the Swiss company, which he described as 'staid' and 'stuck in its old ways'.

Mr Peltz used similar language about P&G—pointing to 'excessive cost and bureaucracy' and 'a slow moving and insular culture'.

Francois-Xavier de Mallmann, chairman of investment banking at Goldman Sachs, says that activists are stepping up their activity in the consumer goods sector: 'Activists have been investing in the consumer sector for several years but there has been a sizeable increase in both the number and size of the companies they have targeted over recent months.'

Consumer goods companies can make appetising targets. Companies such as P&G and Nestlé—alongside peers that have come into the sights of activists, such as Unilever and Mondelez—are easily criticized for their sprawling empires, weighed down by excessive costs and inefficient staff protected by the size of the business and ingrained management approaches.

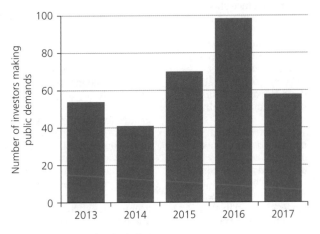

Figure 6.2 Corporate activism is on the rise in Europe

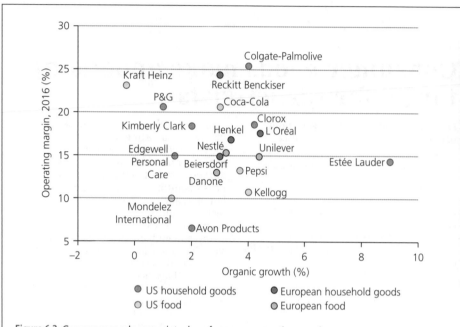

Figure 6.3 Consumer goods groups' stock performance, operating margin

But analysts say that the bulk of these companies is almost the point—within their hundreds of thousands of staff, shelves of products, and rosters of marketers lies the fat that can be trimmed.

Activists see the potential to boost profits by cutting costs and use their large, cash-dispensing balance sheets that have relatively little leverage to boost shareholder returns.

'Sales growth in consumer industries has slowed and because of this you are seeing the rise of activist investors, looking to cut costs to boost profitability,' said David Dudding, European equities fund manager at Columbia Threadneedle Investment.

Analysts say that the strongest impetus for activists is the potential to drive up profits, as demonstrated repeatedly by 3G Capital, the Brazilian-led private equity group. It has for decades been acquiring consumer companies, cutting costs and boosting profits to levels described by Peter Brabeck-Letmathe, chairman emeritus of Nestlé, as 'revolutionary'.

After 3G bought Heinz in 2013 with Warren Buffett, the ketchup maker's profit margins soared 58 per cent within two years to 28 per cent—almost twice Nestlé's 15 per cent operating profit margin. 3G and Mr Buffett's Berkshire Hathaway group went on to merge Heinz with Kraft in 2015.

This year, they stunned the consumer goods world with the $143bn takeover bid from Kraft Heinz for Unilever, which is twice the size of Kraft Heinz in revenues. The bid was quickly dropped after stiff opposition from Unilever but the bold approach has left even the biggest consumer goods companies looking vulnerable.

'The catalyst for the focus on consumer groups from activists is the increasing polarisation in the sector between those companies that have been through a 3G-style cost-cutting process and those that haven't,' said Raphaël Pitoun, chief investment officer at Seilern Investment Management. 'Companies such as Nestlé, Colgate, P&G and others haven't been through that process so activists see an opportunity to drive earnings per share growth through cost-cutting.'

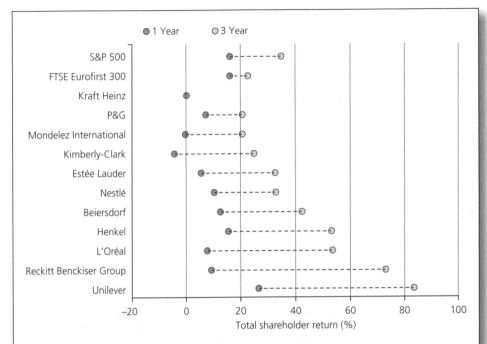

Figure 6.4 Consumer good groups' stock performance, total shareholder return

Source: Thomson Reuters Datastream. Used under licence from the *Financial Times*. All rights reserved.

Mr Peltz has highlighted P&G's weak organic growth and said its cost-cutting plans have not translated into higher operating profits and shareholder value creation. Mr Loeb's criticisms of Nestlé are similar. He has called for the company to adopt a formal margin target, something that Mark Schneider, Nestlé's new chief executive, was already considering.

Another attraction is the low levels of debt at many large consumer companies, including Nestlé, Unilever and L'Oréal, compared to other industries.

Mr Loeb has described Nestlé's net debt of 1 times earnings before interest, tax, depreciation and amortisation as 'remarkably low'. He has urged the group to double its borrowings, 'monetise' its 23 per cent stake in L'Oréal, which is valued at about $25bn, and return capital to shareholders.

Mr Schneider announced a buyback programme of up to SFr20bn a few days after Mr Loeb burst on the scene, although Nestlé said this had been planned for months.

Unilever too has been jolted into action after the failed Kraft Heinz bid. The company behind Dove soap and Ben & Jerry's ice cream has sharpened its focus on profitability, setting a target of 20 per cent operating margin by 2020, from 16 per cent last year.

Graeme Pitkethly, Unilever finance director, said on Thursday that it had made €1bn in savings in the first six months of the year out of a three-year €6bn savings programme.

The cost-cutting included reducing advertising agency fees by 17 per cent and lowering the average cost of making an ad by 14 per cent. Staff had taken 30 per cent fewer flights, and each seat cost a quarter less.

But activist investors are also flush with cash and on the hunt for returns outside the US. For investors such as Mr Loeb, Europe was once seen as an uncertain place to attempt to mount a campaign given varying laws and shareholder rights.

All that has changed given the perception of better value in many industries than in the US. David Neuhauser, founder of the small Chicago-based activist investor Livermore Partners, says his fund is increasingly looking to Europe.

'I see a lot more things to do in Europe than in the US, and a lot of that is due to valuation and opportunity and growth prospects,' said Mr Neuhauser. 'Some of the things in the US, the valuations are high and they do seem to have their defences up quicker.'

Moody's, the rating agency, said that despite experiencing outflows last year 'activists still have plenty of spending power to take on even the largest companies', although it added that they usually target smaller groups.

Chris Plath, a Moody's vice-president, expects more activist campaigns this year. 'International activism continues to gain steam. This increase reflects the relative lack of low-hanging fruit among US large-caps.'

The big question being asked by executives in the sector is whether the increased activist appetite will be healthy for the industry—stimulating faster change as it grapples with low growth and a shift in the way people buy food and household goods.

Or whether activists end up benefiting their funds more than the longer-term growth potential of the companies.

Mr Dudding said: 'We tend to be agnostic about activists' presence on shareholder registers. In the long run, consumer staples stocks do better when they reinvest cost savings in driving top line growth and shouldn't be bullied into prioritising short-term profitability over long-term brand equity.'

The ideal is when both sides win. Mr Peltz in 2013 argued that PepsiCo was plagued by a 'culture of sycophants', pushing the company to split its drinks business from its faster-growing snacks unit. Indra Nooyi, chief executive, resisted but eventually agreed to add a Trian representative to the board.

PepsiCo shares gained 50 per cent over the course of the campaign, as the company aggressively cut costs and improved margins to take the edge off Trian's pressure.

'In a slow-moving industry like consumer packaged goods, you have a good safety net so companies don't blow up. So a lot of them have been complacent,' said Ali Dibadj, analyst at Bernstein. 'It's perfect for activism because they have the room to cut massive amounts of costs.'

US activists make their mark in Europe

When Dan Loeb announced his largest ever stake in Switzerland-based Nestlé this summer, *writes Lindsay Fortado*, the move was the latest sign of the interest taken in Europe by activist shareholders from the US.

Mr Loeb has been busy this year having also acquired stakes in UniCredit, the Italian lender, and German utility Eon. He was not alone. Elsewhere, Keith Meister's Corvex Management joined with 40 North to take a 7.2 per cent stake in Clariant, the Swiss chemicals group, in the hope of scuppering its $20bn merger with US rival Huntsman.

They follow San Francisco-based ValueAct, which built a 10.8 per cent stake in Rolls-Royce beginning in 2015, and Elliott, Paul Singer's hedge fund, which has been active in Europe for decades but has been ramping up activity.

'As markets rise, people are starting to look for opportunities,' said Reade Griffith, the London-based chief investment officer of hedge fund Polygon's European event-driven strategy, which sometimes takes a behind-the-scenes activist approach.

'There is less competition for activists here and the economic cycle is just turning so the upside in company margins in Europe is significant across many sectors,' Mr Griffith said. 'Europe is around the second or third inning out of nine in its economic recovery, while the US is around the seventh or ninth inning, depending on how Trump does.'

Europe is no stranger to shareholder activism but most in the past has been conducted by local firms and often with a more 'constructivist' behind-the-scenes approach. European activists have already made inroads, however, such as Cevian Capital, Chris Hohn's TCI, and some smaller peers such as CIAM in Paris and Knight Vinke in Monaco.

But Europe may still prove a harder, and unfamiliar, place for US activists to mount campaigns.

'In Europe, whilst there are some commonalities, such as antitrust law, that cut across multiple markets, there are a lot of specificities and cultural differences that are unique to each country, so you have to have an understanding of each jurisdiction to be successful,' said Mr Griffith.

Eleazer Klein, head of the shareholder activism group at the law firm Schulte, Roth & Zabel, which represents a number of hedge funds, says that Europe is far from being under attack.

'As much as you're seeing the expansion of US activists into Europe, I don't view it as anything other than a lot of these funds are looking at companies that are underperforming, and they are funds that are not limited to companies that are wholly located in the US,' he said.

Sovereign wealth funds quadruple investment in student housing

Javier Espinoza

Financial Times, 12 February 2018

Sovereign wealth funds have quadrupled their investment in student housing in a bet on the growth of wealthier middle classes in emerging economies who want to send their children to study abroad.

Investment in student accommodation in the US and Europe has gone from less than 4 per cent a year of worldwide spending by SWFs between 2011 and 2015 to more than 15 per cent in 2016, according to the latest figures from IE Business School in Madrid.

Javier Capapé, director of the Sovereign Wealth Lab at IE Business School, said: 'SWFs are looking at ways they can invest for the next 10 to 15 years and capture trends that will affect their returns and give them a profitable business.

They expect middle-class families in places like China and India to increasingly be able to send their children to study in Europe and the US.'

Singapore's GIC wealth fund was the most active investor last year with a string of deals, including a $1.6bn student accommodation deal in the US alongside the Canada Pension Plan Investment Board (CPPIB) and property management company Scion Group, and the £700m acquisition of student halls in the UK.

SWFs have also increased their investment in commercial warehouses across Europe as ecommerce continues to grow.

Between 2011 and 2015, large institutional investors spent an average 21.5 per cent a year of real estate investment on logistics and industrial properties, IE reports. In 2016, spending in the sector accounted for 26.5 per cent. The biggest deal in the sector that year was GIC's €2.4bn purchase of P3 Logistics Park.

In the first six months of 2017, logistics accounted for 75.8 per cent of all real estate foreign direct investment thanks mainly to China Investment Corporation's €12.25bn acquisition of Logicor, a pan-European logistics company.

SWFs are looking further afield and becoming more creative about niche investments, the report said.

Since 2011, many have started looking more at 'real estate sectors that were once deemed gritty and obscure, such as industrial warehouses on the outskirts of major metropolitan areas and student residence halls in leading university towns', added the report, which was sponsored by the Spanish Institute for Foreign Trade.

Figures last year showed sovereign wealth funds investing more in the hotel sector and pursuing more private transactions, as they move away from buying 'trophy' assets such as Porsche, Tiffany and LVMH.

Socially responsible investment

⊙ Learning objectives

- To be aware of the origins of socially responsible investment

- To understand the different approaches that may be used for socially responsible (ethical) investment

- To appreciate the role of institutional investors in socially responsible investment

- To be aware of the different ethical indices that may be used to assess the performance of socially responsible funds

- To be aware of the evidence analysing the performance of socially responsible investment funds

Introduction

We have seen that corporate governance is concerned with many facets of a business and how that business is managed. The previous chapter highlighted how, over the last 40 or so years, institutional investor share ownership has increased substantially and the majority of UK equity is now owned by institutional investors. In recent years, there has been an increasing awareness of socially responsible investment (SRI) issues in the UK and in many other countries, and these have, in many cases, become an integral part of corporate governance policies, both of individual companies and of institutional investors.

SRI involves considering the ethical, social, and environmental performance of companies selected for investment as well as their financial performance. The phrase 'ethical investment' is often used interchangeably with the phrase 'socially responsible investment'.

The origins of SRI lie in various religious movements such as the Quakers and the Methodists. From the nineteenth century onwards, religious groups such as these have sought to invest their funds without compromising their principles. So, for example, the churches would avoid investing in companies involved in alcohol and gambling. This type of policy is common across many religions, including Christianity and Islam. During the course of the twentieth century there were various incidences with which religious groups sought to avoid investment contact; latterly one such incidence has been the avoidance of involvement with tobacco companies. It is worth mentioning that US church groups tend to be one of the most active in putting forward socially based shareholder proposals at companies' annual general meetings. Such shareholder proposals include areas such as trying to ensure that advertising does not encourage young people to smoke.

SRI covers a wide range of areas, including genetic engineering, the environment, employ-ment conditions, and human rights. Recent cases of companies highlighted for not being socially responsible include those that have used child labour in the manufacture of their clothes overseas and retailers selling carpets that have been made by small children who are exploited by working long hours for little, if any, pay.

SRI and corporate governance

Increasingly, institutional investors have become aware of the importance of SRI on a number of fronts: client demand, corporate citizenship, and potential economic benefits. The Organi-sation for Economic Co-operation and Development (OECD) (1998) corporate governance report stated:

> In the global economy, sensitivity to the many societies in which an individual corporation may operate can pose a challenge. Increasingly, however, investors in international capital markets expect corporations to forego certain activities—such as use of child or prison labour, bribery, support of oppressive regimes, and environmental disruption—even when those activities may not be expressly prohibited in a particular jurisdiction in which the corporation operates.

It is key to the development of SRI that the large institutional investors in both the UK and the USA have become more involved and willing to screen potential investments as appropriate. Increasingly, this approach is fuelled by client demand for SRI. A number of pension schemes in the UK, including British Coal and the Universities Superannuation Scheme, have asked their fund managers to take ethical and social issues into account in their investment strategy. A further motivation for SRI is highlighted by the OECD (1998):

> In accommodating the expectations of society, corporations must not lose sight of the pri-mary corporate objective, which is to generate long-term economic profit to enhance share-holder (or investor) value. The Advisory Group recognises that, over the long term, acting as a responsible corporate citizen is consistent with this economic objective.

The growing awareness of SRI and the involvement of the government via legislation mean that institutional investors are becoming increasingly active in this field, for example, by set-ting up special funds or screening existing and potential investments. The value of UK ethical funds has increased substantially in the last decade and is now over £15 billion. It is expected that this trend will continue given the clear indication of the growing interest in this area.

An important development in the UK was that, from 3 July 2000, pension fund trustees have had to take account of SRI in their *Statement of Investment Principles*. This change means that pension fund trustees must state 'the extent (if at all) to which social, environmental or ethical considerations are taken into account in the selection, retention, and realisation of invest-ments' (amendment to Pensions Act 1995). Therefore pension fund trustees are required to state their policy on social, environmental, and ethical issues, and if they do not have a policy in place, then this provision will also highlight that fact. A survey of pension fund trustees carried out by Gribben and Gitsham (2006) found that 'only one in ten trustees believe that companies are providing sufficient information to enable social and environmental impacts and risks to be assessed effectively'.

Boersch (2010) reported the results of a survey conducted by Allianz Global Investors and the Centre for European Economic Research (ZEW) amongst pension experts in France, Germany, Italy, the Netherlands, Switzerland, and the UK on the future of SRI in pension fund portfolios. He stated that:

> on average, most of the pension experts surveyed believe that, in the future, SRI criteria will play an increasingly important role in how pension funds make investment decisions. Environmental criteria are considered to be the most important element of the SRI concept. Respondents agreed that the growing SRI trend is being driven much less by the expectation of higher returns or lower risk as it is by public pressure.

In 2014, the Law Commission published *Fiduciary Duties of Investment Intermediaries*, recommending that the government clarify trustees' duties to consider long-term, systemic risks such as climate change and in its subsequent report *Pension Funds and Social Investment* (2017) it reinforces this view. In December 2017 the Department of Work and Pensions (DWP) issued an interim response which viewed favourably the Law Commission's proposal that 'regulatory clarity would help remind trustees that they should take account of all relevant financially material factors, whether these are "traditionally" financial or related to broader risks or opportunities, such as environmental, social and governance issues'. This is a welcome step towards requiring trust-based pension schemes to report on their approach to environmental, social, and governance (ESG) factors, ethical investment and stewardship, saying it is 'minded' to introduce the changes. The proposed reform will affect contract-based schemes as well but the FCA is responsible for these and so far has not committed on the proposed reform.

Strategies for SRI

EIRIS is a leading provider of independent research into corporate social, environmental, and ethical performance, and was established in 1983 to help investors make responsible investment decisions. EIRIS has identified three basic strategies for SRI:

- **Engagement**—identify areas for improvement in the ethical, social, and environmental policies of the companies invested in, and encourage them to make improvements.
- **Preference**—fund managers work to a list of guidelines that trustees prefer companies invested in to meet.
- **Screening**—trustees ask for investments to be limited to companies selected (screened) for their ethical behaviour. May be 'positive' or 'negative' screening.

EIRIS provides more detailed definitions for each of these strategies as follows.

Engagement

Engagement involves identifying areas for improvement in the ethical, social, and environmental policies of the companies invested in, and encouraging them to make those improvements. This can be done by:

- the investor telling the companies their policy and letting them know how it affects their decisions to invest in a company or respond to takeovers and share issues;

- the investor trying to persuade the company, via regular meetings, to improve their practices on issues such as employment practices, recycling, and pollution reduction;

- offering to help them formulate their own policy; this might be done through existing corporate governance voting policies by extending them to include ethical issues.

Preference

Fund managers work to a list of guidelines that the trustees prefer the companies they invest in to meet. They then select investments or portfolio weightings in these companies, taking into account how closely a company meets, or sets about meeting, these parameters. This approach also enables the investor to integrate ethical with financial decision-making; in cases where two companies get a similar rating against traditional financial indicators, they can be compared against the investor's ethical indicators, and the company with the better all-round performance is selected.

Screening

Trustees ask the fund manager to limit their investments to a list of companies selected (screened) for their ethical behaviour. They may be companies whose conduct is viewed positively, such as those with good employment practices or those taking active steps to reduce levels of pollution. Or they may be selected for not indulging in certain 'negative' practices or proscribed industries, for example, the armaments industry.

More recently, Eurosif (2016) in a survey of SRI covering 13 different European countries, discuss the different SRI strategies which may be used being: exclusion (e.g. weapons industry), norms-based screening (e.g. complies with UN Global Compact, ILO Convention, or OECD Guidelines, etc.), engagement and voting, ESG integration, best in class (e.g. the 'best' firm, based on SRI criteria, in a particular industry), sustainability themed (e.g. renewal energy, low carbon), and impact/community investing (e.g. to have a positive impact on sustainable developments).

Institutional investors' policies—UK

National Association of Pension Funds (NAPF)

In 1996 the National Association of Pension Funds (NAPF), in its guidance on good corporate governance, stated that:

> NAPF believes it is inconceivable that, in the long run, a company can enhance shareholder value unless it takes good care to retain and develop its customer relationships; unless it provides encouragement to its employees; unless it develops effective relationships with its suppliers so that they can see the common interest in working to lower costs; unless it pays proper attention to preserving its 'licence to operate' from the community.

The sentiments embodied in this statement have become broadly accepted, and in the context of SRI, the last point is particularly pertinent: one has to have an awareness of the impact of a business's activities on the community at large and all that that implies, including the impact on the environment, and ethical aspects.

In 2009 the NAPF issued its *Responsible Investment Guidance*; an updated Guide was issued in 2013 which defined 'responsible investing' as

> an investment approach in which investors recognise the importance of the long-term health and stability of the market as a whole; seeking to incorporate material extra-financial factors alongside other financial performance and strategic assessments within investment decisions; and utilise ownership rights and responsibilities attached to assets to protect and enhance shareholder value over the long term—primarily through voting and engagement.

In 2015, the NAPF was rebranded as the Pensions and Lifetime Savings Association (PLSA).

Pensions and Lifetime Savings Association (PLSA)

Sometimes guidance is issued on specific aspects, for example in December 2017, the PLSA published guidance for its pension fund members entitled *More Light, Less Heat: A Framework for Pension Fund Action on Climate Change*. The PLSA state: 'the climate is changing as a result of human activity—and this will have profound consequences for pension funds' investments. As such, governance bodies [such as trustee boards] must take steps to prepare for the economic ramifications of climate change.'

The framework covers four areas: governance, reporting, investment, and engagement. Let us look in turn at two of the recommendations from the governance area and two from the engagement area. From the governance area, two of the recommendations are as follows: 'Governance body members should undertake training to familiarise themselves with the economic impacts of climate change, the impact it will have on investment portfolios and how investors are responding' and 'Governance bodies should set out how they believe climate change relates to their investment strategy in their *Statement of Investment Principles* and state how they are mitigating climate change-related risk.' From the engagement area, two of the recommendations are: 'Governance bodies should review current and prospective asset managers' approach to engagement on climate-related risk and opportunity—including whether or not they can demonstrate a track record of successful engagements in this respect' and 'Pension funds should put policies in place to ensure that at company AGMs their shares are voted in support of companies and directors that take an engaged, long-term approach to the governance, strategy and reporting of climate-related risk and opportunity, and against those that do not.'

Association of British Insurers (ABI)

Recognition of the growing importance of SRI was also evidenced by the Association of British Insurers (ABI) (2001) with the publication of its *Socially Responsible Investment Guidelines*. The main focus of the Guidelines is the identification and management of risks arising from social, environmental, and ethical issues that may affect either short-term or long-term business value. The flip side of this is that appropriate management of these risks may mean opportunities to enhance value. The ABI issued its *Guidelines on Responsible Investment Disclosure* in February 2007, which updated and replaced its *Socially Responsible Investment Guidelines* (2001). The updated guidelines highlight aspects of responsibility reporting on which shareholders place particular value. This is narrative reporting, which 'sets environmental, social, and governance (ESG) risks in the context of the whole range of risks and opportunities facing the company; contains a forward looking perspective; and describes the actions of the Board in mitigating these risks'. They also state that 'investors continue to believe that, by focusing on the need to identify and manage ESG risks to the long and short-term value of the business, the Guidelines highlight an opportunity to enhance value' and 'Reporting in connection with these risks should be set firmly in the context of the full range of strategic, financial and operational risks facing the business'.

There is also an emphasis that for institutional investors, consideration of these risks and opportunities should be in the context of their overarching objective of enhancing shareholder value; it should be an integral part of the investment process, rather than a separate 'add-on' consideration.

The Guidelines give guidance to companies as to what disclosures an institutional investor might expect to see in a company's annual report. These disclosures include whether, as part of its regular risk assessment procedures, it takes account of the significance of ESG matters to the business of the company; whether ESG (as well as other) risks have been identified and systems are in place to manage such risks; and whether account is taken of ESG matters in the training of directors. With regard to the remuneration report, the remuneration committee should state whether it is able to consider corporate performance on ESG issues when setting remuneration of executive directors, and if not, why not; and also whether the remuneration committee has ensured that the incentive structure for senior management does not raise ESG risks by inadvertently motivating irresponsible behaviour.

The UK Sustainable Investment and Finance Association (UKSIF)

The UK Sustainable Investment and Finance Association (UKSIF) is an active force in promoting the adoption, and propounding the virtues, of SRI in the UK. Its members encompass a wide range of interested parties, including fund managers, organizations, companies, and individuals. In 2010 UKSIF published *Focused on the Future: Celebrating ten years of responsible investment disclosure by UK occupational pension funds*. The report highlights ten key actions to ensure the protection and enhancement of pension fund assets through responsible ownership and investment. These are:

- **Sustainability governance**—Pension fund trustees and insurance company boards will increase their skills in sustainability governance; it will become good practice to have at least one member with sustainability expertise.

- **Transparency**—Major pension funds will implement web-based disclosure of how their responsible investment strategies are implemented.

- **Leadership**—Major new pension providers, such as the UK's NEST Corporation, will sign and implement the UN-backed *Principles for Responsible Investment*, and seek to be beacons for responsible ownership and investment.

- **Public procurement**—Public sector asset owners, such as UK local government pension schemes, will be required by governments to sign and implement the UN-backed *Principles for Responsible Investment*.

- **Responsible procurement**—Pension funds will demand responsible investment as part of risk transfer negotiations (e.g. pension fund buy-outs) and for both established investment services and emerging asset classes.

- **Empowering shareholders as owners**—A forward-looking resilience and sustainability strategy will be published annually addressing opportunities, risks, and economic and social impact; companies will put this to a shareholder vote; executive pay will be linked to key sustainability achievements.

- **Responsible pension plan sponsorship**—Companies will encourage responsible investment by the occupational or personal pension funds they sponsor or provide access to; sustainability expertise will be made available as part of the employer's pension fund support.

- **Scrutiny from non-governmental organizations (NGOs)**—NGOs will build capacity and consumer support for understanding, scrutinizing, and challenging pension and insurance investment decisions.

- **Support from the professions**—Professional associations will promote responsible investment skills development and encourage debate on the social and environmental impact of investment regulation, policies, and decisions.

- **Integration into investment management**—Asset managers will build responsible ownership and investment into marketing and promotion, service development strategies, and staff development. This will play a key role in rebuilding trust in financial services.

FairPensions

FairPensions campaigns for major institutional investors to adopt responsible investment using shareholder power to hold companies to account. FairPensions' report (2009) high-lights that major UK pension funds are now acknowledging the potential that 'non-financial' issues have to affect the value of investments, however, many still lack key strategies to man-age these risks. Catherine Howarth, the Chief Executive of FairPensions, said: 'Pension funds are now recognising that "non-financial" issues can become financial issues, but many still need to match words with deeds if they are to be ready for major challenges associated with issues like climate change.' The report highlights that the importance of ESG issues is 'a truth universally acknowledged' but not universally acted upon, that is, that the institutional inves-tors' *Statement of Investment Principles* acknowledges the potential importance of ESG fac-tors in the investment process, but then this may not be fully reflected in the detailed policy, implementation, and performance monitoring; they also highlight that 'there are a number of pension funds which, given their sponsoring companies' public profile on corporate social responsibility, could be expected to have pension schemes that are responsible investment leaders, but in practice appear to fall short of expectations'. In relation to transparency, the report finds evidence of 'a discernable correlation between pension schemes that are more transparent and those with well-defined policy and practice for managing ESG-related risks and opportunities'.

FairPensions (2010), in a review of the approach of insurance companies to ESG issues, states that:

> responsible investment focuses on the integration into investment decisions of those environmental, social and governance ('ESG') issues that can be material to long term shareholder value. The corporate fall-out from the Gulf of Mexico oil spill and the hacking scandal at News International should have removed all doubt about the financial relevance of ESG issues. Indeed governance failures within banks are widely regarded as one of the critical elements of the financial crisis. Yet our findings suggest that many insurance companies still view ESG issues as being relevant only to specialist 'SRI' funds.

Therefore, insurance companies appear to lag behind other pension providers on responsible investment.

ShareAction (formerly FairPensions)

In 2015 ShareAction (formerly FairPensions) published its *Responsible Investment Performance of UK Asset Managers* in which it examined the 33 largest asset managers in the UK. The study found that:

> all 33 firms are now publicly committed to stewardship and RI [responsible investment]: 100% are signed up to the [Stewardship] Code and all but 2 (Artemis Investment Management and Santander Asset Management UK Limited) are signatories to the PRI. 96% of survey respondents state that they conduct stewardship because they believe it affects investment returns. However the quality of RI and stewardship policies, practices and disclosures vary considerably between asset managers. The 'E' and 'S' in ESG are still receiving less consideration than the 'G'. Only 42% of the asset managers publicly disclose policies on how they incorporate environmental and social considerations into the investment process; qualitative analysis also suggests that the corporate governance issues still attract far more attention. By way of example, only 13% of survey respondents were able to disclose a robust strategy for managing the risks associated with stranded carbon assets.

In 2017, ShareAction examined and ranked the transparency and Responsible Investment (RI) practices of 40 of the largest asset managers in Europe covering ten different countries (the UK, the Netherlands, France, Belgium, Denmark, Switzerland, Italy, Germany, Sweden, and Spain) in its publication *Lifting the Lid: Responsible Investment Performance of European Asset Managers*. The 40 firms control €21 trillion (£18 trillion) of assets between them, meaning that they have significant power to influence the behaviour of the companies whose shares and bonds they hold around the globe. The study

> sought to investigate whether these major asset management firms are behaving as responsible investors, addressing environmental, social and governance (ESG) issues in order to better manage risk. All of the firms bar one (Santander Asset Management) are signatories to the Principles for Responsible Investment but we aimed to find out if these managers are truly committed to stewardship. Amongst other things, we examined if they measure the impacts of their investments; if they actively manage conflicts of interest; and whether internal oversight and governance of RI reflects their stated RI commitment.

Looking in more detail at the impact measurement aspect (such as examining the carbon footprint of investments in a standardised way)—which helps companies, investors, and wider stakeholder groups assess the tangible effects of the responsible investment practices—ShareAction found that:

> most of the asset managers in this year's survey (82.5%) do make a basic mention of impact investing, impact measuring, or environmental and/or social impact of investments on their websites or in their reports and 62.5% have some information on impact measurement methodology. However, only 5% of managers provide detailed information, including quantitative information, on the impacts of their investments, and the information provided generally covers areas such as greenhouse gas emissions, water use, waste generation and energy consumption.

Overall ShareAction found that whilst there are some examples of very good RI practice in Europe's largest asset management firms, there is significant room for improvement in the sector as a whole.

Investment Association and PLSA

In 2017, the Investment Association and PLSA published a joint report *Stewardship in Practice as at 30th September 2016* and found that 76 per cent of respondents agreed that Environmental, Social and Governance considerations are financially material to their investments.

Climate change is one of the hot topics in environmental impact discussions. In June 2017, the UK's Committee on Climate Change released its report *Progress in Preparing for Climate Change*. Within the report, the Committee noted that the investment community is becoming increasingly interested in the effects of climate change on risk adjusted returns, making the recommendation that government promote the voluntary disclosure of climate change risks by both large and small companies, including the risks in relation to supply chain. Specifically, the Committee stated the Stewardship Code should be amended to ask investors to consider company performance and reporting on adapting to climate change.

Hermes

Hermes Pensions Management Ltd is a leading UK institutional investor. In late January 2001 Hermes revised its corporate governance policies and called on UK companies to 'manage effectively relationships with its employees, suppliers, and customers, to behave ethically and to have regard for the environment and society as a whole'. Whilst asking companies to disclose their policies on an annual basis, Hermes asked that the remuneration committee in each company, when setting incentive pay, consider the effect on the company's performance of social, environmental, and ethical matters. There should be a credible system for verifying the accuracy of social disclosures, and directors should take social issues into account when assessing risk. The statement issued by Hermes had the backing of eight investor institutions who expected to incorporate it into their policies.

In 2002 Hermes introduced *The Hermes Principles*. Hermes advocates that companies should be able to demonstrate that their investment decisions are sound and also demonstrate ethical behaviour. In the section on social, ethical, and environmental aspects, Hermes has two principles: principles 9 and 10. Principle 9 states: 'Companies should manage effectively relationships with their employees, suppliers and customers and with others who have a legitimate interest in the company's activities. Companies should behave ethically and have regard for the environment and society as a whole.' This principle identifies the importance of considering both stakeholder views and having regard to social responsibility aspects. Principle 10 states: 'Companies should support voluntary and statutory measures which minimise the externalisation of costs to the detriment of society at large.' This principle discourages companies from making business successful at the expense of society at large. *The Hermes Corporate Governance Principles* (2006) reiterate the aforesaid principle 9, but also state in principle 5: 'we consider socially, ethically and environmentally responsible behaviour as part of the management process that companies should undertake in order to maximize shareholder value in the long term rather than as an end in itself.' Companies are encouraged to comply with internationally recognized guidelines and principles on social, ethical, and environmental matters. In 2010 Hermes published *The Hermes Responsible Ownership Principles* (updated in 2013) detailing what they expect of listed companies and what listed companies can expect from them. Hermes' expectations of listed companies encompass 12 principles, which include two relating to stakeholders, environmental, and social issues. In turn, listed companies can expect five core principles of stewardship and engagement that Hermes feels responsible shareholders ought to observe; these include sustainability and governance, a long-term perspective when exercising ownership rights, and a constructive, confidential dialogue with boards and senior management. In addition, Hermes has published *Stewardship (2017)* and various other publications covering, for example, Executive Remuneration and Engagement Objectives and Plan.

Hermes also publishes a quarterly public engagement report and, as an example, the report for the third quarter of 2017 gives a breakdown of its engagement by region and by theme. Overall, Hermes engaged with 175 companies during that quarter on the following topics: (i) environmental 17.5 per cent (relating to climate change; environmental policy and strategy; pollution and waste management; and water); (ii) social and ethical 28.0 per cent (relating to bribery and corruption; conduct and culture; cyber security; diversity; human capital management; human rights; labour rights; supply chain management; and tax); (iii) governance 36.4 per cent (relating to board diversity, skills and experience; board independence; executive remuneration; shareholder protection and rights; and succession planning); and (iv) strategy, risk, and communication 18.0 per cent (relating to audit and accounting; business strategy; integrated reporting and other disclosure; and risk management).

Institutional investors' policies—USA

In the USA there has long been an active movement for SRI. The main thrust has tended to come from church groups and ethical/environmental groups with investment interests. They have been particularly active in putting forward shareholder proposals at investee companies; it is not unusual for literally hundreds of shareholder proposals to relate to SRI. Whilst the large institutional investors have not tended to be so active in putting forward shareholder proposals (they tend to have other ways of making their 'voice' heard), they have often supported shareholder proposals put forward by these interest groups.

Teachers' Insurance and Annuity Association–College Retirement Equities Fund (TIAA–CREF)

However, for many years, the Teachers' Insurance and Annuity Association–College Retirement Equities Fund (TIAA–CREF) has taken an active stand in trying to promote and ensure good workplace practice, for example. They state that:

> TIAA's responsible investment capabilities are designed to seek competitive returns while promoting broad economic development, positive social outcomes and a healthier environment. TIAA is actively engaged across the four key pillars of responsible investment being (i) ESG integration—ESG factors in investment research and decisions; (ii) ESG-focused funds— portfolios that explicitly include ESG criteria in the investment decision-making process; (iii) active ownership—investors using their influence to improve issuer's ESG management, performance and disclosure; and (iv) impact investing—investments made with a goal of financial return and measurable social or environmental outcomes.

California Public Employees' Retirement System (CalPERS)

CalPERS, the USA's largest institutional investor, issued its *Global Principles of Accountable Corporate Governance* in February 2009, revised in November 2011, which state:

> CalPERS expects companies whose equity securities are held in the Fund's portfolio to conduct themselves with propriety and with a view toward responsible corporate conduct. If any improper practices come into being, companies should move decisively to eliminate such practices and effect adequate controls to prevent recurrence. A level of performance above minimum adherence to the law is generally expected. To further these goals, in September 1999 the CalPERS board adopted the Global Sullivan Principles of Corporate Social Responsibility.

In subsequent years, CalPERS updated its *Global Principles of Accountable Corporate Governance* several times. In 2017, CalPERS was awarded the Responsible Investor's inaugural award for Innovation & Industry Leadership for its Environmental, Social, and Governance 5-Year Strategic Plan. The CalPERS Board adopted the award-winning ESG strategic plan last year. It identifies six strategic initiatives that will direct staff's work across the entire portfolio through 2021. The initiatives are data and corporate reporting standards; UN PRI Montreal Pledge company engagement; diversity and inclusion; manager expectations; sustainable investment research; and private equity fee and profit sharing transparency. Each initiative has specific objectives, key performance indicators, and a timeline.

In June 2018 CalPERS issued its *Governance and Sustainability Principles* which state: 'As the governance and sustainability agenda has developed, so too have the CalPERS Principles. An important area of development has been integrating consideration of environmental and social factors alongside our governance agenda.'

Institutional investors' policies—Europe

In Europe too, in a number of countries including France, Germany, Belgium, the Netherlands, and Denmark, there is a growing awareness of SRI. For example, in Germany, from January

2002, every pension fund provider had to inform members in writing about whether, and in what form, social, ethical, and ecological aspects are taken into consideration. The European Commission (2008) identified the strong growth of the SRI market in European countries in recent years and states: 'there is some evidence that mainstream analysts and investors are attaching more importance to social and environmental issues.'

In a survey, Eurosif (2016), of 13 European countries (Austria, Belgium, Denmark, Finland, France, Germany, Italy, the Netherlands, Poland, Spain, Sweden, Switzerland, UK), it is noted that there is 'a shift in SRI assets from equities to fixed income (driven by the growth in the issuance of Green Bonds), the growing interest of retail investors (although the growth in assets is still largely driven by the institutional market), and strong growth in Engagement and Voting which provides evidence of the increasing relevance of stewardship'.

BNP Paribas Asset Management

BNP Paribas Asset Management is the dedicated, autonomous asset management business of BNP Paribas Group. They state:

> We also recognise the important role that long term capital has in tackling the numerous challenges of the world—from carbon emissions to population displacement, and from in-frastructure requirements to the opportunities of disruptive technology. We are proud to have been one of the first asset managers to commit to disclose the carbon footprints of our portfolios by signing the Montreal carbon pledge, and are playing a major role in helping to finance the world's transition to cleaner energy. Throughout our investment strategies, we aim to look beyond standard financial metrics to invest in sustainable business models capable of delivering superior shareholder value over the long run. Our approach has been recognised by the Principles for Responsible Investment (PRI), which assigned us an A+ rat-ing—the highest possible. In doing so, the PRI highlighted our commitment to, management of, and active promotion of ESG integration to our clients, and our high level of involvement in bringing these issues to the attention of financial governing bodies.

APG

APG manages the pension assets of a number of large clients, e.g. education, government, in the Netherlands. APG states:

> The principle aim of APG's responsible investment policy is to contribute to risk-weighted financial performance with a focus on socially responsible investment practice and mak-ing a contribution to the integrity of financial markets. Through this policy, APG expresses and gives substance to the social responsibility of its clients. The international standards for sustainability and governance APG applies in this regard are based on the United Nations Global Compact, the International Corporate Governance Network Statement on Global Corporate Governance Principles and the guidelines for multinational corporations and the OECD's Principles of Corporate Governance.

Similarly, there is a growing interest in SRI across the globe, for example, in Japan and also in Australia where a description of the extent to which investment products take account of social, ethical, and environmental issues is required.

International guidance

There have been a large number of international guidelines and statements that are relevant to the area of SRI. These include:

- *Global Sullivan Principles* (1977, 1999)—principles that are directed towards increasing corporate social responsibility (CSR) throughout the world, based on self-help.
- *The MacBride Principles* (1984)—consist of nine fair employment, affirmative action principles.
- Coalition for Environmentally Responsible Economies (Ceres) (1989)—a coalition of environmental, investor, and advocacy groups working together for sustainability in areas such as environmental restoration and management commitment. In 2010 Ceres published 'The 21st Century Corporation: The Ceres Roadmap for Sustainability'. It analyses the drivers, risks, and opportunities involved in making the shift to sustainability, and details strategies and results from companies that are taking on these challenges. In June 2013, Ceres published 'The 21st Century Investor: Ceres Blueprint for Sustainable Investing', updated in 2016. It is written for institutional asset owners and their investment manager who need to understand and manage the growing risks posed by climate change, resource scarcity, population growth, human and labour rights, energy demand, and access to water; all risks that will challenge businesses and affect investment returns in the future.
- *UN Global Compact* (1999)—nine principles relating to the areas of human rights, labour standards, and environmental practices. In 2004 a tenth principle against corruption was added.
- OECD *Guidelines for Multinational Enterprises* (2000, updated most recently in 2011)— cover areas such as disclosure, environment, employment, industrial relations, bribery, and consumer interests.
- *Global Reporting Initiative (GRI) Sustainability Guidelines* (2002, updated several times with the most recent being in 2013 with G4 sustainability reporting)—the United Nations Environment Programme (UNEP) and Ceres formed a partnership in 1999 to encourage NGOs, business associations, corporations, and stakeholders to undertake sustainability reporting.
- EC *CSR—a Business Contribution to Sustainable Development* (2002) encourages an EU framework for the development of SRI, especially promoting transparency and convergence of CSR practices and instruments. Revised in 2011 with the EU *A Renewed Strategy 2011–14 for Corporate Social Responsibility*.
- The UN *Principles for Responsible Investment* (PRI) were issued in 2006. The PRI were developed by an international group of institutional investors reflecting the increasing relevance of environmental, social, and corporate governance issues to investment practices. The process was convened by the UN Secretary-General. The PRI state:

As institutional investors, we have a duty to act in the best long-term interests of our beneficiaries. In this fiduciary role, we believe that environmental, social, and corporate governance (ESG) issues can affect the performance of investment portfolios (to varying degrees across companies, sectors, regions, asset classes and through time). We also recognize that applying these Principles may better align investors with broader objectives of society.

Signatories to the PRI commit to six principles:

- incorporating ESG issues into investment analysis and decision-making processes;
- being active owners and incorporating ESG issues into ownership policies and practice;
- seeking appropriate disclosure on ESG issues by the entities in which they invest;
- promoting acceptance and implementation of the Principles within the investment industry;
- working together to enhance their effectiveness in implementing the Principles;
- reporting on their activities and progress towards implementing the Principles.

In April 2012, a new reporting framework was piloted. The new reporting framework has been designed through an extensive consultation process to achieve three main sets of objectives for signatories: to ensure transparency and accountability of the PRI initiative and its signatories, to encourage signatory transparency on responsible investment activities, and to provide tools to allow signatories to measure their performance with objective indicators.

Regular reviews of progress are published with the PRI Annual Report containing, inter alia, details of the signatories to the Principles and the regions to which they belong with the most recent Annual Report being for 2017. The UN *Principles for Responsible Investment* (PRI), launched in 2006, now have over 1,700 signatories worldwide managing US $70 trillion. The PRI has established a Sustainable Stock Exchanges (SSE) Investor Working Group which is a group of over 50 PRI signatories representing US$7.6 trillion in assets under management which is engaging with stock exchanges globally to ask that they enhance the sustainability performance of their listed companies, with particular emphasis on ESG disclosure.

UN Sustainable Development Goals

In 2015, the UN published *Transforming our World: The 2030 Agenda for Sustainable Development*. Seventeen sustainable development goals (SDGs) were set out with the aim being to end poverty, protect the planet, and ensure prosperity for all as part of a new sustainable development agenda. Each goal has specific targets to be achieved over the next 15 years. The SDGs are shown in Table 7.1.

As mentioned in SDG 13, the UN Framework Convention on Climate Change is the primary international, intergovernmental forum for negotiating the global response to climate change. In December 2015, many countries adopted the Paris Agreement in which all countries agreed to work to limit global temperature rise to well below 2 degrees Celsius and to strive for 1.5 degrees Celsius. The Agreement entered into force in November 2016.

In relation to climate change, the Financial Stability Board (FSB) Task Force on Climate-related Financial Disclosures (TCFD) published its *Final Report Recommendations of the Task Force on Climate-related Financial Disclosures* in June 2017. The recommendations are voluntary, consistent climate-related financial risk disclosures for use by companies in providing information to investors, lenders, insurers, and other stakeholders. There are four widely adoptable recommendations which are tied to governance, strategy, risk management, and metrics and targets. There are specific recommended disclosures which companies should

Table 7.1 UN Sustainable Development Goals (2015)

SDG Goal	Aim
1	End poverty in all its forms everywhere
2	End hunger, achieve food security and improved nutrition and promote sustainable agriculture
3	Ensure healthy lives and promote well-being for all at all ages
4	Ensure inclusive and equitable quality education and promote lifelong learning opportunities for all
5	Achieve gender equality and empower all women and girls
6	Ensure availability and sustainable management of water and sanitation for all
7	Ensure access to affordable, reliable, sustainable and modern energy for all
8	Promote sustained, inclusive and sustainable economic growth, full and productive employment and decent work for all
9	Build resilient infrastructure, promote inclusive and sustainable industrialization and foster innovation
10	Reduce inequality within and among countries
11	Make cities and human settlements inclusive, safe, resilient and sustainable
12	Ensure sustainable consumption and production patterns
13	Take urgent action to combat climate change and its impacts*
14	Conserve and sustainably use the oceans, seas and marine resources for sustainable development
15	Protect, restore and promote sustainable use of terrestrial ecosystems, sustainably manage forests, combat desertification, and halt and reverse land degradation and halt biodiversity loss
16	Promote peaceful and inclusive societies for sustainable development, provide access to justice for all and build effective, accountable and inclusive institutions at all levels
17	Strengthen the means of implementation and revitalize the Global Partnership for Sustainable Development

*Acknowledging that the United Nations Framework Convention on Climate Change is the primary international, intergovernmental forum for negotiating the global response to climate change.
Source: UN Sustainable Development Goals (2015)

include in their financial filings, additional guidance for all sectors, and supplemental guidance for certain sectors.

Given that SRI and CSR are very much developing areas, further guidelines/revisions to existing guidelines are to be expected. However, it is becoming increasingly clear that companies will have to consider these as mainstream issues rather than as peripheral optional extras.

CSR indices

A number of stock market indices of companies with good CSR have been launched in recent years. These include the Ethibel Sustainability Index and the Domini Social Index, although perhaps the two most well-known are the FTSE4Good Indices and the Dow Jones Sustainability Indices (DJSI).

The FTSE4Good was launched in 2001 and is designed to reflect the performance of socially responsible equities. It covers four markets: the UK, USA, Europe, and global. It uses criteria for judging CSR based on three areas: human rights, stakeholder relations, and the environmental impact of a company's activities. When developing these criteria, the FTSE4Good drew on various international guidelines and statements, including the *UN Global Compact*, the OECD *Principles for Multinational Enterprises*, the *Global Sullivan Principles*, the *Ceres Principles*, the *Caux Roundtable Principles*, and the *Amnesty International Human Rights Principles for Companies*. There are four tradable and five benchmark indices that make up the FTSE-4Good index series. In 2004 the FTSE4Good Japan index (benchmark only) was launched, enabling investors to identify Japanese companies, within the FTSE Global Equity Index Series, which meet a set of internationally supported standards of CSR. A committee of independent practitioners in SRI and CSR review the indices to ensure that they are an accurate reflection of best practice.

The DJSI are aimed at providing indices to benchmark the performance of investments in sustainability companies and funds. DJSI describes corporate sustainability as 'a business approach that creates long-term shareholder value by embracing opportunities and managing risks deriving from economic, environmental and social developments'. Components are selected by a systematic corporate sustainability assessment and include only the leading sustainability companies worldwide, thereby providing a link between companies that implement sustainability principles and investors who wish to invest in that type of company. Areas that receive higher weighting in arriving at the corporate sustainability assessment criteria include corporate governance, scorecards and measurement systems, environmental performance, and external stakeholders.

In March 2003 Business in the Community (BITC) reported on the launch of its first Corporate Responsibility Index. Companies who wished to be rated completed a substantial online survey of areas such as their corporate strategy, the integration of CSR into the company's operations, management practice, performance and impact (social and environmental), and assurance. The answers enabled BITC to score the companies. In general, the results revealed that companies seem better at creating CSR strategy than at implementing it effectively in their companies. The Corporate Responsibility Index follows a systematic approach to managing, measuring, and reporting on responsible business practices; companies are assessed using a framework that incorporates: corporate strategy, including looking at the main risks in the company and how these are dealt with at senior levels; integration, which includes looking at how companies embed CSR in the organization; management, which builds on the integration aspect looking at how companies are managing their risks and opportunities in the areas of community, environment, marketplace, and workplace; and performance and impact, which asks companies to report performance in a range of social and environmental impact areas. BITC state that every year they review and refine the questions in the CR Index survey to reflect the latest thinking and continually increase the level of challenge for leading companies. In 2014, questions were incorporated to test transformational as well as incremental thinking. Furthermore other questions have been refined to take account of latest trends in key responsible business issues.

Corporate social responsibility (CSR)

CSR was conceptualized by Carroll (1979) as follows: 'the social responsibility of business encompasses the economic, legal, ethical, and discretionary expectations that society has of organizations at a given point in time.' This can be explained further as the business having a responsibility to produce goods that it sells at a profit, to abide by legal requirements, to do what is right and fair, and to do what might be desired of companies in terms of supporting the local community and making charitable donations. Carroll (2006) states: 'It appears that the corporate social responsibility concept has a bright future because, at its core, it addresses and captures the most important concerns of the public regarding business and society relationships.'

Gray et al. (1987) identified many of the accounting and accountability issues associated with corporate social reporting. Given the emphasis now being placed on SRI, it is not surprising that CSR has gained more prominence in recent years along with an emphasis on the company's board for its responsibility for relations with its stakeholders. Cadbury (2002) states that 'the broadest way of defining social responsibility is to say that the continued existence of companies is based on an implied agreement between business and society' and that 'the essence of the contract between society and business is that companies shall not pursue their immediate profit objectives at the expense of the longer term interests of the community'.

With the recognition that companies should not pursue profit without regard to the impact on wider societal interests, we can see a link with both agency theory and stakeholder theory discussed in Chapter 2. Whilst the directors manage the company on behalf of the shareholders (an agency relationship), the interests of stakeholders should also be taken into account (stakeholder theory). A Friedmanite view of the firm, whereby there is an emphasis on the purely financial aspects of the business, is no longer appropriate in a society that is increasingly taking an inclusive view of business.

Many companies have responded to this more inclusive approach by starting to report not just the traditional financial performance of the company (the bottom line) but also the 'triple bottom line', which essentially encompasses economic profit, social, and environmental performance. The triple bottom line conveys a wider information set than financial information, and helps to present the wider picture of the company's performance in relation to social and environmental matters. These aspects should now be incorporated in the business review as part of the company's annual report to provide a deeper understanding of the impact of the company's activities on society. The Companies Act (2006) expects directors to disclose more information relating to the risks affecting the company, an analysis of the performance of the company over the year, and consideration of shareholder and stakeholder interests. These requirements will therefore also add to the wider information on environmental, social, and ethical issues disclosed in the annual report and accounts.

In Denmark large businesses are covered by a statutory requirement which means that from 2009 they had to report on the business's social responsibility policies, including any standards, guidelines, or principles for social responsibility the business employs; how the business translates its social responsibility policies into action, including any systems or procedures used; and the business's evaluation of what has been achieved through social responsibility initiatives during the financial year, and any expectations it has regarding future initiatives.

In France, the Grenelle Acts of 2009 and 2010 were the result of multi-stakeholder consultation between businesses, trade unions, and NGOs and other stakeholders; they established a consensus around tackling environmental and sustainable development issues and section 225 mandated the production of an annual report on CSR matters for all companies with more than 500 employees and €100 million in revenue.

In Chapter 4 recent developments in the EU (e.g. European Commission (2011), *A Renewed EU Strategy 2011–14 for Corporate Social Responsibility*, EC, Brussels) and UK company law were highlighted. These will impact on companies' reporting in relation to CSR as companies need to disclose analysis of their performance, where appropriate, based on non-financial key performance indicators (KPIs) as well as financial KPIs.

Aguilera et al. (2006) argue that key differences between the UK and the USA in the importance ascribed to a company's social responsibilities reflect differences in the corporate governance arrangements in these two countries. They explore differences between institutional investors in the UK and in the USA concerning CSR, and identify that UK institutional investors are focused on the long term, whereas the US institutional sector is dominated by mutual funds that may have a shorter term outlook. However, they feel that 'US companies may well gravitate toward British CSR disclosure norms as a positive side effect of globalization'.

Liebman (2008) notes that:

> at present the notion of Corporate Social Responsibility has narrowed down to a mere issue of corporate governance. What is at risk is the crucial relation between politics and the economy—or, between 'the market' and 'regulations'—and what is at stake is the principle of the 'primacy of politics', which has long since been recognized as the cornerstone of modern democracy. Considering the limited effects of State regulations, this principle may only be preserved by a careful balance between legal rules—flowing from different sources or from accords but, in any event, subject to enforcement by the appropriate authority vested to that effect—and commitments unilaterally undertaken by enterprises on a strictly voluntary basis and typically expressed in codes of ethics of various contents and inspirations.

Clearly both regulation and voluntary actions together may seem to be the most effective approach.

Waddock (2008) identifies 'an emerging institutional infrastructure around corporate responsibility that has resulted in the evolution of initiatives such as the Global Reporting Initiative, the social investment movement, and related efforts that place more emphasis on corporate responsibility, accountability, transparency, and sustainability'. Many multinational companies are now responding to this corporate responsibility infrastructure as corporate responsibility has become an area that companies cannot ignore. Carroll and Shabana (2010) discuss how

> the broad view of the business case justifies CSR initiatives when they produce direct *and* indirect links to firm performance. The advantage of the broad view over the narrow view is that it allows the firm to benefit from CSR *opportunities*. The broad view of the business case for CSR enables the firm to enhance its competitive advantage and create win-win relationships with its stakeholders, in addition to realizing gains from cost and risk reduction and legitimacy and reputation benefits, which are realized through the narrow view.

In terms of links between aspects of market and corporate governance structures, and CSR, Gamerschlag et al. (2011), in a paper examining the determinants of voluntary CSR disclosure in a sample of 130 listed German companies, find that:

> CSR disclosure is positively associated with higher company visibility, a more dispersed shareholder ownership structure, and US cross-listing (a proxy for US stakeholders' interest in the company). Profitability only affects CSR disclosure's environmental dimension. Furthermore, our results show that CSR disclosure is affected by industry membership and firm size: companies from 'polluting industries' tend to have a higher level of environmental disclosures. Finally, big companies disclose more than small companies.

Kock et al. (2012) build on a stakeholder–agency theoretical perspective to explore the impact of particular corporate governance mechanisms on firm environmental performance. They find that:

> several important corporate governance mechanisms such as the board of directors, managerial incentives, the market for corporate control, and the legal and regulatory system determine firms' environmental performance levels. These results suggest that these different governance mechanisms resolve, to some extent, the existing divergence of interests between stakeholders and managers with respect to environmental activities.

Devinney et al. (2013) state that:

> the conclusions that arise from much of the management research is that there is most likely a multifaceted and contingent relationship between what a firm seeks from using CSR activities and its various performance outcomes. However, exactly how these facets link together is complex and not well understood, with some work (eg. Prior, Surroca, & Tribó 2008) showing that firms use CSR for more nefarious purposes, while other work (eg. Surroca, Tribó, & Waddock 2010) hinting that, if used correctly, CSR reflects good managerial actions.

Therefore there is something of a mixed perception as to the extent to which some companies do really engage in CSR and their motivations for doing so. Some companies might engage only in high visibility CSR which immediately grabs the attention of the public and the media. Companies may also engage in 'greenwashing', overstating what they are actually doing in terms of their CSR and this may have negative reputational and/or financial effects once it comes to light (see for example, Chen and Chang (2013)).

More recently, Cho and Lee (2017) highlight how an ethical dilemma can arise for corporate managers in the allocation of scarce resources to CSR. Such allocation may be driven by altruistic reasons or by financially driven ones. They find that 'efficient managers are more likely to engage in the product-related CSR that directly connects to corporate financial performance (CFP) but are less likely to engage in environment-related CSR'. Similarly a thought-provoking study by Schaltegger and Burritt (2018) analyses the links between different ethical motivations and kinds of corporate social responsibility (CSR) activities. They conclude that 'management activities based on these different ethical motivations to CSR and sustainability result in different operational activities for corporations working towards sustainability and thus have very different effects on how the company's economic performance is influenced'.

Finally, in terms of balancing the rights of stakeholders and the interests of shareholders, Mehrotra and Morck (2017) point out that:

obeying the letter of the law regarding the rights of stakeholders can pit shareholder value maximization against social welfare. Where externalities are important, a narrow focus on shareholder value can create scope for top managers making morally dubious decisions. For example, maximizing shareholder value ex ante might justify cutting costs and entertaining acceptably small risks of environmental disasters. Even if such a disaster triggers legal actions that bankrupt the perpetrating firm, its shareholders are protected by limited liability and so lose only the value of their shares. Such disasters might be discouraged by exposing officers and directors to personal liability should they occur, but this only works if managers put their self-interest ahead of shareholder value.

The impact on shareholder value

An important facet of SRI is whether there is a beneficial effect on shareholder value (the value of the investment). Clearly, the OECD (1998) believes this to be so as it states that 'acting as a responsible citizen is consistent with this economic objective [of generating long-term economic profit to enhance shareholder (or investor) value]'.

There have been a number of studies that have looked at the performance of SRI funds but there has been no definitive outcome one way or another as to whether SRI funds outperform non-SRI funds. In the UK studies have included those by Luther et al. (1992), who found weak evidence of some over-performance, on a risk-adjusted basis, by 'ethical' unit trusts, although they pointed out that ethical investment seemed to be skewed towards smaller market capitalized companies. In an extension of the paper, Luther and Matatko (1994) found that ethical funds had returns that were highly correlated with a small company index, hence abnormal returns may have been attributable more to a small company bias than to an ethical one. Mallin et al. (1995) analysed the performance of ethical funds and found that, on the mean excess returns, ethical funds appeared to underperform both non-ethical funds and the market in general, whereas on a risk-adjusted basis, ethical funds outperformed non-ethical funds. Research by Lewis and Mackenzie (2000), which utilized a questionnaire survey, highlighted the fact that institutional investors show general support for engaging in lobbying activity and the development of dialogue in order to improve corporate practice and influence companies to improve their ethical and environmental performance. Kreander et al. (2002) investigated the financial performance of forty 'ethical' funds from seven European countries. The results suggested that very few ethical funds significantly outperform a global benchmark after adjusting for risk; conversely, none of them significantly underperformed either. Kreander et al. (2005) studied the performance of 60 European funds from four countries and used a matched-pair approach for fund evaluation. They found no difference between ethical and non-ethical funds according to the performance measures employed. Schröder (2007) analysed whether stock indices that represent SRI exhibit a different performance compared to conventional benchmark indices. He found that SRI stock indices do not exhibit a different level of risk-adjusted return from conventional benchmarks. However, many SRI indices have a higher risk relative to the benchmarks.

Capelle-Blancard and Monjon (2011) examine the popularity of SRI in newspapers and academic journals; it seems that most of the papers on SRI focus on financial performance. They state:

the question of the financial performance of the SRI funds is certainly relevant, but maybe too much attention has been paid to this issue, whereas more research is needed on a conceptual and theoretical ground, in particular the aspirations of SRI investors, the relationship between regulation and SRI, as well as the assessment of extra-financial performances.

In the context of corporate performance and sustainability, Ameer and Othman (2012) point out that:

> sustainability is concerned with the impact of present actions on the ecosystems, societies, and environments of the future. Such concerns should be reflected in the strategic planning of sustainable corporations. Strategic intentions of this nature are operationalized through the adoption of a long-term focus and a more inclusive set of responsibilities focusing on ethical practices, employees, environment, and customers.

They posit that companies that have regard to these responsibilities 'under the term superior sustainable practices' will have better financial performance than those that do not. They examine the top 100 sustainable global companies in 2008 selected from a universe of 3,000 firms from the developed countries and emerging markets. They find 'significant higher mean sales growth, return on assets, profit before taxation, and cash flows from operations in some activity sectors of the sample companies compared to the control companies over the period of 2006–10. Furthermore, our findings show that the higher financial performance of sustainable companies has increased and been sustained over the sample.'

Ntim and Soobaroyen (2013), using a sample of large corporations listed on the Johannesburg Stock Exchange, find that 'on average, better-governed corporations tend to pursue a more socially responsible agenda through increased CSR practices. We also find that a combination of CSR and CG practices has a stronger effect on CFP [corporate financial performance] than CSR alone, implying that CG positively influences the CFP-CSR relationship.'

Given that SRI is now increasingly perceived as a mainstream element of good corporate governance, the importance of SRI will continue to gain momentum. Certainly in Europe, the European Commission (2008) in its *European Competitiveness Report* had a section entitled 'Overview of the Links between Corporate Social Responsibility and Competitiveness' and this section clearly identified that the European Commission believes that CSR can have a positive impact at every level on the countries in the EU. In October 2011 the EU issued *A Renewed EU Strategy 2011–14 for Corporate Social Responsibility*. The report states that:

> the economic crisis and its social consequences have to some extent damaged consumer confidence and levels of trust in business. They have focused public attention on the social and ethical performance of enterprises. By renewing efforts to promote CSR now, the Commission aims to create conditions favourable to sustainable growth, responsible business behaviour and durable employment generation in the medium and long term.

It states that to fully meet their social responsibility, enterprises 'should have in place a process to integrate social, environmental, ethical and human rights concerns into their business operations and core strategy in close collaboration with their stakeholders'. The new policy put forward an action agenda for the period 2011–14 covering eight areas, including:

- enhancing the visibility of CSR and disseminating good practices;
- improving company disclosure of social and environmental information (the new policy confirms the Commission's intention to bring forward a new legislative proposal on this issue);
- better aligning European and global approaches to CSR, highlighting:
  - the OECD Guidelines for Multinational Enterprises;
  - the ten principles of the *UN Global Compact*;
  - the *UN Guiding Principles on Business and Human Rights*;
  - the International Labour Organization (ILO) *Tripartite Declaration of Principles Concerning Multinational Enterprises and Social Policy*;
  - the ISO 26000 *Guidance Standard on Social Responsibility.*

A new EU Multi-Stakeholder Platform was announced in May 2017 to be chaired by European Commission First Vice-President, Frans Timmermans. It was set up to foster the implementation of the SDGs in the EU. The members of the Multi-Stakeholder Platform will support the EU Commission and all stakeholders involved in the implementation of the SDGs at EU level and contribute to the exchange of best practices across sectors at local, regional, national, and EU level.

Conclusions

SRI and CSR are of growing importance in many countries. Across the world there has been an increasing recognition that companies cannot operate in isolation from the ecosystem in which they operate, they must take into consideration the impact of their activities on various stakeholder groups, and the impact of their operations on both the local environment and the global environment. Therefore in many countries there has been a significant upward trend in SRI and governments have made it very much an agenda item. In the UK legislation means that it is an important item for consideration for pension fund trustees. In the USA it is an area that has a high profile and in which there is continuing interest. There are ongoing developments in continental Europe, Australia, and Japan, to name but a few countries, to encourage more SRI.

Institutional investors have developed policy statements on SRI either as separate statements or as an integrated part of their corporate governance policies. A number of institutional investors have developed their SRI analytical capability with new appointments or additional resources. Increasingly, SRI is seen as a mainstream corporate governance issue and, as well as the social and environmental benefits to be gained from SRI, there is the increasing perception that it can help to maintain or increase shareholder value. Together, these are two advantages that should mean that SRI will continue to grow apace.

Summary

- SRI involves considering the ethical, social, and environmental performance of companies as well as their financial performance. The origins of SRI lie in various religious movements that, from the nineteenth century onwards, sought to invest their funds without compromising their principles.

- There are three basic strategies for SRI: engagement, preference, and screening.
  - **Engagement**—identify areas for improvement in the ethical, social, and environmental policies of the companies invested in, and encourage them to make improvements.
  - **Preference**—fund managers work to a list of guidelines that trustees prefer companies invested in to meet.
  - **Screening**—trustees ask for investments to be limited to companies selected (screened) for their ethical behaviour.

- Many institutional investors have developed SRI policies/guidelines; others have incorporated their views on SRI into their mainstream corporate governance policies.

- SRI indices measure the level of CSR in equities. Companies are included in the indices, or score well in them, if they have a good record on CSR.

- The evidence regarding financial performance of SRI (ethical) funds is rather inconclusive but they do not underperform the market generally.

Example: IKEA, Sweden

This is an example of a Scandinavian company that is committed to CSR and has received a number of CSR awards in recognition of its responsible approach to business.

IKEA was founded in 1943 in Sweden by Ingvar Kamprad, then aged 17. IKEA is the world's largest furniture retailer designing and selling a vast range of ready-to-assemble furniture, home furnishings, home accessories, kitchens, appliances, sofas, beds, mattresses, etc. By the end of August 2017, it had established 355 stores in 29 countries around the globe, employing over 149,000 people. Its sales for the financial year 2017 (1 September 2016–31 August 2017) were €34.1 billion.

It has received a number of CSR awards. For example, PR News annually honours the top corporate social responsibility campaigns, and the brands and communicators behind them. It states that:

> CSR Awards finalists represent the very best in corporate responsibility initiatives, with each campaign making a visible difference on the local, national or global level. Out of hundreds of entries, CSR Awards finalists were chosen for their ingenuity and creativity, strategic approach and measurable impact. Entrants were judged on strategy, research and execution in categories including best social media campaign, best sustainability campaign and top employee relations program. From environmental protection to disaster relief to gender equality, these campaigns and communicators have enacted positive change that will be felt for years to come.

In PR News' 2017 CSR Awards, in its CSR Hall of Fame, the winner was IKEA 'People & Planet Positive'. IKEA is

> intensely aware of the planet's finite resources and of its responsibility as a global brand. This awareness is at the core of IKEA's People & Planet Positive initiative, which launched in 2012 and

(continued)

calls for its entire supply chain to be 100% sustainable by 2020. People & Planet Positive embodies many campaigns and is a global strategy and mind-set for IKEA—a mind-set that's driving new furniture designs, new materials, new models for collecting and recycling used furniture and new inclusive workplace initiatives. These new systems are already getting results that are changing public perceptions of IKEA … Some of the financial year 2016 results of the People & Planet Positive mind-set: IKEA produced renewable energy equivalent to 71% of the energy consumption of its operations; replaced oil-based expanded polystyrene (EPS) in flat packs with fiber-based, fully recyclable materials; 100% of its cotton and 61% of its wood come from sustainable sources; and its entire lighting range switched to energy efficient LED.

IKEA's responsible approach to business was also recognized in the Ethical Corporate Responsible Business Awards 2017. In the Business Strategy section, IKEA was the winner of the Responsible Business of the Year.

Example: Centrica, UK

This is an example of a UK company which has received a number of awards for its sustainability approach.

Centrica Plc is an international energy and services company which was formed in February 1997 following a demerger from British Gas Plc which was renamed BG Plc at the same time. Centrica supplies energy and services to over 25 million customer accounts mainly in the UK, Ireland, and North America. After a period of rationalization, Centrica has three divisions—Centrica Consumer, Centrica Business, and Exploration & Production. Its business strategy is designed around five areas: energy supply, wholesale energy, energy insight, energy optimization, and energy solutions. In 2017, the Centrica Group earned £28 billion revenue and had over 33,000 employees worldwide.

Centrica seeks, through its programmes and strategic partnerships, to help tackle big issues in society, such as fuel poverty, unemployment, and climate change. It prides itself on being a responsible employer, keeping employees and customers safe, helping those in need, conducting its business in an ethical and responsible way (including paying its fair share of tax while respecting the rights of people across its business, communities and supply chain). It is committed to reducing energy's contribution to climate change while ensuring it manages its wider environmental impact on water, waste, and biodiversity.

Centrica was ranked as the second best performing global company and best performing utilities company in Newsweek's 2017 Global 500 Green Rankings, an annual assessment of the sustainability performance of the largest publicly traded companies in the US and the world by revenue. Centrica's Green Score was 88.70 per cent (Energy Productivity Score: 81.90 per cent; Carbon Productivity Score: 89.40 per cent; Water Productivity Score: 81.40 per cent; Waste Productivity Score: 80.70 per cent). Centrica also received an 'A' score from the Carbon Disclosure Projects (CDP) program for its actions in relation to sustainable water management. Centrica stated:

For the second year running, Centrica featured in the Water A List which is comprised of the top 10% of companies who demonstrate world-class action and disclosure on water management. We are one of just 73 companies to make the List which includes only ten utilities and ten UK companies. Centrica achieved an A– for action and disclosure on climate change. As a result, we narrowly missed maintaining a place in the Climate A List. While we remain steadfast in our commitment to combat climate change, our ranking was mainly impacted by a drop in carbon reduction savings in 2016 compared to 2015, coupled with an increase in the carbon intensity of our power generation following unusually low levels the previous year.

Mini case study   L'Oréal, France

L'Oréal is an example of a leading cosmetics company which has received awards for its CSR and ethical approach towards sustainable business.

L'Oréal is the world's largest cosmetics company. It has six founding values: passion, innovation, entrepreneurial spirit, open-mindedness, quest for excellence, and responsibility; and four ethical principles: integrity, respect, courage, and transparency. L'Oréal state:

> Our Ethical Principles shape our culture, underpin our reputation, and must be known and recognised by all L'Oréal employees. Integrity because acting with integrity is vital to building and maintaining trust and good relationships. Respect because what we do has an impact on many people's lives. Courage because ethical questions are rarely easy but must be addressed. Transparency because we must always be truthful, sincere and be able to justify our actions and decisions.

'Sharing Beauty With All' is L'Oréal's sustainability programme which extends beyond environmental factors and includes commitments to its workers including access to healthcare, social protection, and training and also providing access to work for underprivileged people (with a commitment of 100,000 by 2020). The 2016 'Sharing Beauty With All' report indicates progress to date and the commitments for 2020 for each of the four pillars of the 'Sharing Beauty With All' programme—the four pillars being innovating sustainability, producing sustainably, living sustainably, and developing sustainably (with communities, with suppliers, with employees). The report highlights that:

> a key milestone has now been crossed: we have achieved and even exceeded our target of a –60% reduction in CO2 emissions, four years ahead of schedule ... Moreover, the efforts made by our Research & Innovation teams for many years to reduce the environmental footprint of formulas or to respect biodiversity have led to much progress. This involves, in particular, products offering better biodegradability or containing more natural ingredients ... The Sharing Beauty With All programme has therefore brought about substantial lasting changes in the way we design, produce, communicate and distribute our products. This is a real cultural shift for our company. Our employees are moreover completely involved to tackle these challenges, which they want to overcome and which correspond to their desire to make their everyday life more meaningful ... We crossed another milestone in 2016 by integrating criteria related to performance of the programme into the calculation of the bonuses for our country managers and brand managers. This is a way of recognising the contribution they have each made to the success of the programme, and of making this success a new performance indicator.

L'Oréal's ethical approach has been recognized by numerous awards and accolades including (i) being ranked as the top-performing global company and best performing personal products company in Newsweek's 2017 Global 500 Green Rankings which is an annual assessment of the sustainability performance of the largest publicly traded companies in the US and the world by revenue. Newsweek state that 'the ranking is based on eight sustainability and environmental indicators including energy use, greenhouse gas emissions, carbon and water productivity, as well as the presence of executive, board and third-party oversight mechanisms'. L'Oréal's Green Score was 89.90 per cent (Energy Productivity Score: 85.00 per cent; Carbon Productivity Score: 88.90%; Water Productivity Score: 100.00 per cent; Waste Productivity Score: 59.00 per cent); (ii) L'Oréal is included in Ethisphere's 'The World's Most Ethical Companies 2018 Honoree List' for companies who recognize their critical role to influence and drive positive change in the business community and societies around the world and work to maximize their impact wherever possible; (iii) L'Oréal was also one of only two companies in the world (the other being Unilever) to score an 'A' for all three (i.e. triple 'A' score) of the Carbon Disclosure Projects' (CDP) programs for its actions in relation to climate protection, sustainable water management, and addressing deforestation.   *(continued)*

L'Oréal also has an excellent reputation in relation to gender issues and was ranked first in the Equileap Gender Equality Global Ranking 2017, and one of only six companies out of 3,000 assessed that were analysed to have eliminated a gender pay gap.

Furthermore L'Oréal was the first corporate partner of the C40's Women4Climate initiative which aims to empower and inspire the next generation of climate leaders through a global programme to mentor women in C40 cities.

Mini case study questions:

1. Discuss how L'Oréal's 'Sharing Beauty With All' programme may benefit different stakeholder communities in various countries.

2. What benefits may arise to shareholders from L'Oréal's approach to sustainability?

Questions

The discussion questions to follow cover the key learning points of this chapter. Reading of some of the additional reference material will enhance the depth of the students' knowledge and understanding of these areas.

1. Why might institutional investors be interested in SRI?

2. Why are more companies becoming interested in their social and environmental policies? To what extent do you believe that companies might engage in 'greenwashing'?

3. In what ways might institutional investors decide on which companies to invest in when considering their social responsibility policies?

4. Do you think that investors should be willing to sacrifice financial return, if necessary, in order to have a portfolio that is comprised of SRIs?

5. 'Companies are about making money, not about social responsibility.' Critically discuss this statement.

6. 'CSR is the first casualty in an economic downturn as companies will choose to cut back on this area. Investor confidence is restored by companies making profits and not by companies becoming involved in altruistic activities.' Critically discuss this statement.

References

Aguilera, R.V., Williams, C.A., Conley, J.M., and Rupp, D. (2006), 'Corporate Governance and Social Responsibility: A Comparative Analysis of the UK and the US', *Corporate Governance: An International Review*, Vol. 14, No. 3, May, pp. 147-58.

Ameer, R. and Othman, R. (2012), 'Sustainability Practices and Corporate Financial Performance: A Study Based on the Top Global Corporations', *Journal of Business Ethics*, Vol. 108, No. 1, pp. 61-79.

Association of British Insurers (2001), *Socially Responsible Investment Guidelines*, ABI, London.

Association of British Insurers (2007), *Guidelines on Responsible Investment Disclosure*, ABI, London.

Boersch, A. (2010), 'Doing Good by Investing Well— Pension Funds and Socially Responsible Investment: Results of an Expert Survey', *Allianz Global Investors International Pension Paper No. 1/2010*. Available at SSRN: http://ssrn.com/abstract=1607730 or http://dx.doi.org/10.2139/ssrn.1607730.

Cadbury, Sir Adrian (2002), *Corporate Governance and Chairmanship: A Personal View*, Oxford University Press, Oxford.

California Public Employees' Retirement System (2011), *Global Principles of Accountable Corporate Governance*, CalPERS, California.

California Public Employees' Retirement System (2018), *Governance and Sustainability Principles*, CalPERS, California.

Capelle-Blancard, G. and Monjon, S. (2011), 'Trends in the Literature on Socially Responsible Investment: Looking for the Keys Under the Lamppost', *Business Ethics: A European Review*. Forthcoming, available at SSRN: http://ssrn.com/abstract=1978815.

Carroll, A.B. (1979), 'A Three-dimensional Conceptual Model of Corporate Social Performance', *Academy of Management Review*, Vol. 4, No. 4, pp. 497–505.

Carroll, A.B. (2006), 'Corporate Social Responsibility: A Historical Perspective' in M.J. Epstein and K.O. Hanson (eds), *The Accountable Corporation*, Praeger Publishers, Westport, CA.

Carroll, A.B. and Shabana K.M. (2010), 'The Business Case for Corporate Social Responsibility: A Review of Concepts, Research and Practice', *International Journal of Management Reviews*, Vol. 12, Issue 1, March, pp. 85–105.

Chen, Y.S. and Chang, C. H. (2013), 'Greenwash and green trust. The mediation effects of green consumer confusion and green perceived risk', *Journal of Business Ethics*, Vol. 114, No. 3, 489–500.

Cho, S.Y. and Lee, C. (2017), 'Managerial Efficiency, Corporate Social Performance, and Corporate Financial Performance', *Journal of Business Ethics*, https://doi.org/10.1007/s10551-017-3760-7.

Coalition for Environmentally Responsible Economies (Ceres) (2010), *The 21st Century Corporation: The Ceres Roadmap for Sustainability*, Boston, USA.

Coalition for Environmentally Responsible Economies (Ceres) (2016), *The 21st Century Investor: Ceres Blueprint for Sustainable Investing*, Boston, USA.

Committee on Climate Change (2017), *Progress in Preparing for Climate Change*, London.

Devinney, T.M., Schwalbach J., and Williams, C.A. (2013), 'Corporate Social Responsibility and Corporate Governance: Comparative Perspectives', *Corporate Governance: An International Review*, Vol. 21, No. 5, pp. 413–19.

European Commission (2008), *European Competitiveness Report 2008*, EC, Brussels.

European Commission (2011), *A Renewed EU Strategy 2011–14 for Corporate Social Responsibility*, EC, Brussels.

Eurosif (2016), *European SRI Study 2016*, Eurosif, Brussels.

FairPensions (2009), *Responsible Pensions? UK Occupational Pension Schemes' Responsible Investment Performance 2009*, FairPensions, London.

FairPensions (2010), *The Stewardship Lottery*, FairPensions, London.

FSB Task Force on Climate-related Financial Disclosures (2017), *Final Report Recommendations of the Task Force on Climate-related Financial Disclosures*, Financial Stability Board, Washington DC.

Gamerschlag, R., Moëller, K., and Verbeeten, F. (2011), 'Determinants of Voluntary CSR Disclosure: Empirical evidence from Germany', *Review of Managerial Science*, Vol. 5, Nos 2–3, pp. 233–62.

Gray, R.H., Owen, D., and Maunders, K. (1987), *Corporate Social Reporting: Accounting and Accountability*, Prentice Hall International, London.

Gribben, C. and Gitsham, M. (2006), *Will UK Pension Funds Become More Responsible? A Survey of Trustees*, 2006 edn, Ashridge Centre for Business and Society & Just Pensions/UKSIF, London.

Hermes (2002), *The Hermes Principles*, Hermes Pensions Management Ltd, London.

Hermes (2006), *The Hermes Corporate Governance Principles*, Hermes Pensions Management Ltd, London.

Hermes (2010), *The Hermes Responsible Ownership Principles*, Hermes Pensions Management Ltd, London.

Kock, C. J., Santaló, J., and Diestre, L. (2012), 'Corporate Governance and the Environment: What Type of Governance Creates Greener Companies?', *Journal of Management Studies*, Vol. 49, Issue 3, pp. 492–514.

Kreander, N., Gray, R.H., Power, D.M., and Sinclair, C.D. (2002), 'The Financial Performance of European Ethical Funds 1996–1998', *Journal of Accounting and Finance*, Vol. 1, pp. 3–22.

Kreander, N., Gray, R.H., Power, D.M., and Sinclair, C.D. (2005), 'Evaluating the Performance of Ethical and Non-Ethical Funds: A Matched Pair Analysis', *Journal of Business Finance and Accounting*, Vol. 32, Nos 7, 8, September/October, pp. 1465–93.

Law Commission (2014), *Fiduciary Duties of Investment Intermediaries*, Law Com 350, Law Commission, London.

Law Commission (2017), *Pension Funds and Social Investment*, Law Com 374, Law Commission, London.

Lewis, A. and Mackenzie, C. (2000), 'Support for Investor Activism Among UK Ethical Investors', *Journal of Business Ethics*, Vol. 24, No. 3, April, pp. 215–22.

Liebman, S. (2008), *Multi-Stakeholders Approach to Corporate Governance and Labor Law: A Note on Corporate Social Responsibility*, 31 March, available at SSRN: http://ssrn.com/abstract=1114969.

Luther, R.G. and Corner, C. (1992), 'The Investment Performance of UK "Ethical" Unit Trusts', *Accounting, Auditing and Accountability*, Vol. 5, No. 4, pp. 57–70.

Luther, R.G. and Matatko, J. (1994), 'The Performance of Ethical Unit Trusts: Choosing an Appropriate Benchmark', *British Accounting Review*, Vol. 26, No. 1, pp. 76–89.

Mallin, C.A., Saadouni, B., and Briston, R.J. (1995), 'The Financial Performance of Ethical Investment Funds', *Journal of Business Finance and Accounting*, Vol. 22, No. 4, pp. 483–96.

Mehotra V. and Morck, R. (2017), *Governance and Stakeholders* (1 May 2017). European Corporate Governance Institute (ECGI)—Finance Working Paper No. 507/2017. Available at SSRN: https://ssrn.com/abstract=2971943.

National Association of Pension Funds (2009), *Responsible Investment Guidance—March 2009* NAPF, London.

Ntim, C.G. and Soobaroyen, T. (2013), 'Corporate Governance and Performance in Socially Responsible Corporations: New Empirical Insights from a Neo-Institutional Framework', *Corporate Governance: An International Review*, Vol. 21, No. 5, pp. 468–94.

Organisation for Economic Co-operation and Development (1998), *Corporate Governance: Improving Competitiveness and Access to Capital in Global Markets*, Report to the OECD by the Business Sector Advisory Group on Corporate Governance, OECD, Paris.

Organisation for Economic Co-operation and Development (2011), *Guidelines for Multinational Enterprises*, OECD, Paris.

Pensions and Lifetime Savings Association (2017), *More Light, Less Heat: A Framework for Pension Fund Action on Climate Change*, PLSA, London.

Schaltegger, S., and Burritt, R. (2018), 'Business Cases and Corporate Engagement with Sustainability: Differentiating Ethical Motivations', *Journal of Business Ethics*, Vol. 147, pp. 241–59.

Schröder, M. (2007), 'Is there a Difference? The Performance Characteristics of SRI Equity Indices', *Journal of Business Finance & Accounting*, Vol. 34, Nos 1–2, pp. 331–48.

ShareAction (2017), *Lifting the Lid: Responsible Investment Performance of European Asset Managers, The 2017 ShareAction Survey*, ShareAction, London.

The Investment Association and PLSA (2017), *Stewardship in Practice*, The Investment Association, London.

UK Sustainable Investment and Finance Association (UKSIF) (2010), *Focused on the Future: Celebrating ten years of responsible investment disclosure by UK occupational pension funds*, UK Sustainable Investment and Finance Association (UKSIF), London.

United Nations (2006), *Principles for Responsible Investment*, New York.

United Nations (2015), *UN Sustainable Development Goals*, New York.

Waddock, S. (2008), 'Building a New Institutional Infrastructure for Corporate Responsibility', *Academy of Management Perspectives*, Vol. 22, No. 3, pp. 87–108.

Welford, R. and Zieger, M. (2013), *Responsible and Inclusive Business in Myanmar, June 2013*, CSR Asia, Hong Kong.

Useful websites

www.ceres.org The website of Ceres, the national network of investors, environmental organizations, and other public interest groups working with companies and investors to address sustainability challenges such as global climate change.

www.eurosif.org The website of Eurosif, which contains information about SRI.

www.fairpensions.org.uk The website of FairPensions, which campaigns for major institutional investors to adopt responsible investment. This site is for archive purposes. FairPensions is now known as ShareAction (see below).

www.forumethibel.org The website of Ethibel, an independent consultancy agency for SRI.

www.ftse.com/Indices/FTSE4Good_Index_Series/index.jsp The website of the FTSE4Good index provides information about the composition of the index and related material.

www.globalreporting.org The website of the Global Reporting Initiative, which has details of the GRI Guidelines and Reporting Framework.

www.hermes-investment.com The Hermes website contains information related to various corporate governance issues.

www.iccr.org The Interfaith Center on Corporate Responsibility (ICCR) website details its activities in the use of shareholder advocacy to press companies on environmental, social, and governance issues.

www.ilo.org The website of the International Labour Organization has details of international labour standards.

www.marshall.edu/revleonsullivan/principles.htm This website details the Global Sullivan Principles of Corporate Social Responsibility.

www.oecd.org The website of the Organisation for Economic Co-operation and Development, which has details of the Guidelines for Multinational Enterprises and other developments.

www.shareaction.org The website of ShareAction which is a charity that promotes Responsible Investment and gives savers a voice in the investment system. Formerly FairPensions (see above).

www.sustainability-index.com The website of the Dow Jones Sustainability Indices provides information about the indexes, which track the financial performance of the leading sustainability-driven companies worldwide.

www.unglobalcompact.org The website of the UN Global Compact, a strategic policy initiative for businesses that are committed to aligning their operations and strategies with ten universally accepted principles in the areas of human rights, labour, environment, and anti-corruption.

www.unpri.org The website for the UN Principles of Responsible Investment.

www.vigeo-eiris.com The website of Vigeo-EIRIS has information on various aspects of responsible investment.

 Develop your understanding of this chapter and explore the subject further using our online resources at www.oup.com/uk/mallin6e/

 Part Two case study   Institutional investors and SRI Myanmar

This case study illustrates some of the complex issues of a country transitioning to democracy. It shows how, when an influential group of institutional investors work together, they can influence the operations of their investee companies which are in a country where there are human rights abuses, political instability, and unacceptable risks. This action was part of the SRI remit of the institutional investors. Finally it summarizes recent developments relating to corporate governance and to human rights issues.

The political instability and human rights abuses make Myanmar a very difficult country in which to undertake business. As well as the physical dangers of such operations, companies might be subject to negative press campaigns by 'pressure' groups and corruption attempts locally. A number of the largest UK and European institutional investors—including Aviva, Co-operative Insurance Services, Ethos Investment Foundation, Friends Ivory & Sime, Henderson Global Investors, PGGM, and the Universities Superannuation Scheme—joined forces to launch 'Business Involvement in Burma

(continued)

(Myanmar)—A statement from institutional investors'. The statement called on companies to justify their involvement in Myanmar, given the risks that such activity may pose to shareholders, and sought assurance that company boards had considered fully these risks, and had effective policies and procedures in place to manage them. Having such risk assessment and management procedures in place is in accordance with the ABI's guidelines on SRI.

One of the institutional investors involved in launching the statement, Aviva, met with one of their investee companies, British American Tobacco (BAT) to discuss BAT's joint venture with the military government to manufacture cigarettes in Myanmar. Subsequently, in July 2003, the British government requested that BAT reconsider its investment in Myanmar. BAT stated: 'We have reached what we believe is a balanced solution to meet the British government's requirement while maintaining local employment prospects and the continued orderly and responsible local marketing of our brands.' On 18 June 2004 it sold its 60 per cent shareholding in Rothmans of Pall Mall Myanmar Pte Limited (RPMM) to Distinction Investment Holdings, a Singapore-based investment company. The remaining 40 per cent of RPMM is owned by the Myanmar government. BAT stated: 'We have licensed brands to the new owner to manufacture and market them locally through RPMM, enabling its continued operation as a going concern and good local employer.' BAT would not necessarily have chosen to leave Myanmar, maybe feeling that it could influence the local situation more by maintaining a presence there, but given the British government's request, it decided to withdraw.

Another company that has come under considerable pressure to withdraw from Myanmar is Total Oil, which operates the Yadana natural gas pipeline from Myanmar to Thailand. Various governments disapprove of this operation and Total Oil has come under considerable pressure to end its arrangement with the Burmese government. In 2017, Total announced the completion of the Badamyar project which involves the installation of a new wellhead platform connected to the Yadana production facilities, and the drilling of four horizontal wells to develop Badamyar gas field as a satellite of Yadana. There have been significant changes in Myanmar with wide-ranging reforms being introduced in 2011 and 2012. These led to much greater freedom of information, freedom of speech, and political reforms. Initially these democratic reforms led to international sanctions against the country being dropped by the EU. Furthermore, there have been economic reforms and in May 2012, Myanmar finalized a foreign investment law that includes details of tax exemptions, legal structures, and incentives for foreign companies. Also in May 2012, UN Secretary-General Ban Ki-moon launched the Local Network of the *UN Global Compact* in Myanmar; 15 Burmese companies signed up to the ten principles of the *UN Global Compact*.

Welford and Zieger (2013) in the CSR Asia publication *Responsible and Inclusive Business in Myanmar*, stated that 'stakeholder engagement showed that corporate social responsibility (CSR) and sustainability challenges fall into four categories: government, politics, laws and regulations; public services and society; business operations; and the environment. To date CSR has mainly been understood as a philanthropic concept due to the prevalent Buddhist beliefs and merit-making culture in Myanmar.' They conclude that:

businesses that contribute the most to sustainable development will be the ones that think carefully about how they can make their business activities more inclusive, with a particular emphasis on the poor. Inclusivity can be enhanced through working with your own employees, producing affordable goods and services for people at the base of the pyramid, and creating value chains that offer opportunities for people to be employed through distribution and sales networks. Inclusive business is about building business linkages that will also help people start small businesses that can create long-lasting wealth.

The legal structures need strengthening in the country and there is evidence of widespread corruption. As in many developing countries, the corporate governance in Myanmar is weak with

(*continued*)

little protection for minority shareholders. The UK government is supporting initiatives to help Myanmar develop its corporate governance; for example, in November 2014, the UK Financial Services Taskforce, made up of the British government and UK private sector organizations, hosted a three-day workshop to highlight and start to take forward the important issue of implementing good corporate governance. Subsequently the Yangon Stock Exchange opened in December 2015 although the number of companies listed was, and remains, small. The Myanmar Companies Act (2017) allows foreigners to invest up to a 35 per cent stake in local companies. Furthermore, foreigners will now be able to take stakes of up to 35 per cent in companies listed on the Yangon Stock Exchange (YSX) whereas they were not allowed to invest in these companies previously. This should result in more activity and greater liquidity helping to address problems associated with thin trading. Minority shareholders also receive more protection. These changes should help strengthen corporate governance in Myanmar. In addition, the International Finance Corporation (IFC), a member of the World Bank Group, and the Securities and Exchange Commission of Myanmar (SECM) have organized events in Yangon to raise awareness of corporate governance including helping listed firms raise transparency and disclosure standards in company reporting. The IFC has also been promoting good corporate governance practices among Myanmar's family businesses which are an important part of the country's economy.

However human rights issues have also been hitting the headlines in recent times with the treatment of the Rohingya people. A shareholder proposal was filed by Azzad Investment Management and the Ursuline Sisters of Tildonk, U.S. Province, to be considered at the May 2017 AGM of Chevron. Azzad Investment Management stated that the proposal asked Chevron 'to evaluate a policy of no longer doing business with countries believed to be complicit in genocide. The proposal focuses on the nation of Myanmar/Burma, whose military is accused of committing atrocities against the Rohingya ethnic minority. Because the vote tally was greater than three percent in favor, U.S. Securities and Exchange (SEC) rules allow the resolution to be resubmitted next year.' Further they state that 'in response to the shareholder proposal, Chevron's management drew attention to its current human rights policy. Like many companies, Chevron defers to local governments to uphold human rights, which according to the proposal's supporters, is insufficient given reports of state-sanctioned persecution.'

Subsequently in August 2017, shareholders and other organizations sent a letter to Chevron asking that it use its influence with the Myanmar government (Chevron has a production sharing contract with the government-sponsored Myanma Oil and Gas Enterprise to explore for oil and gas in the Rakhine Basin) to help end violence against the Rohingya people. Part of the letter stated: 'In addition to human rights concerns, the investor signatories to this letter view the instability in Myanmar as a serious risk to Chevron's reputation and the long-term value of their investments. We look forward to working with Chevron and other stakeholders to take steps to address this pressing issue.' In an interview with the British Broadcasting Corporation (BBC) in November 2017, Chevron said it would work for 'a business environment that respects human rights'.

In December 2017, Azzad Asset Management, together with at least four other socially responsible investment institutions, filed for the second time a shareholder resolution with Chevron focused on the actions of the Myanmar government in relation to the Rohingya minority in Myanmar. The proposal asks the energy giant to report on the feasibility of enacting a policy of not doing business with governments engaged in genocide or crimes against humanity.

The Myanmar government has denied that human rights abuses are taking place. At the time of writing there is considerable international concern at the plight of the Rohinga people though the Myanmar government denies that there is any persecution of them, rather they say that they are targeting militants though this argument is generally met with scepticism.

Myanmar's democracy remains in a fledgling state and its democratic institutions and practices, and its legal infrastructure, still need considerable work.

 FT Clippings

European pension funds ramp up responsible investments

Angus Peters

Financial Times, 27 November 2017

European pension funds are waking up to the risks posed by investment in fossil fuels and poorly run companies, a new report has revealed, as asset owners demand fund houses pay closer attention to the pitfalls of investing in carbon-intensive industries.

Six in 10 investors plan to increase their allocations to responsible investments over the next three years. The same proportion is concerned about the impact of scandals on the value of their holdings, according to a survey by Create-Research, the consultancy.

None of the 161 pension funds surveyed plan to cut their exposure to what are known as environmental, social and governance (ESG) assets. Just 14 per cent of the investors said they were either sceptical or did not believe in the logic behind the strategies.

Despite widespread acceptance of responsible investing, just under a quarter said their strategy was already mature, which could indicate a strong pipeline of new allocations to responsible investments.

Amin Rajan, the report's author, said greater demand for sustainable assets was linked to a welcome return to long-term investing, replacing a period of short-termism brought about by intense volatility immediately after the financial crisis.

'If you are a short-term investor, you are really a trader, you are not an investor,' he said.

The result of this shift in attitudes is increased investor demand for asset managers that are able to spot the fat-tail risks associated with poor environmental or governance practices, as illustrated by scandals such as the Deepwater Horizon oil spill or the investigation into VW emissions. More recently, a massive data breach at Uber, the ride-hailing app, has raised questions over a prospective $10bn deal with SoftBank, the Japanese investor.

Sixty-three per cent of investors said they were concerned about reputational or market risks, compared with 52 per cent who said their adoption of sustainability criteria was driven by returns.

'There was this recognition that these companies, which are the bluest of the blue [chips], suddenly find themselves [subject to] the most existential risk,' Mr Rajan said.

With the 2015 Paris accord on climate change a further signal to investors that it is time to take responsible investment seriously, Mr Rajan felt investors were reaching a tipping point.

While asset owners are waking up to the importance of sustainability, their asset managers do not always make the same leap.

In a ranking of asset managers by ShareAction, the responsible investment campaign group, a quarter of the companies examined scored 20 or less out of a possible 90 on sustainability.

Just over 82 per cent of asset managers made a basic mention of sustainability on their websites or in their reports, but only 5 per cent of managers provided detailed information on the impact of investments, according to the ranking.

'The developments we have seen within the industry over recent years have been encouraging,' said Murray Taylor, head of manager research at JLT Employee Benefits, the consultancy.

Managers have moved away from the exclusion of so-called sin stocks, instead increasing their allocations to companies that have a positive impact and engaging with those that do not, he said.

'We believe those investment managers that incorporate positive screening and are willing to work with, or lobby, companies and their boards to make changes for the better are more likely to prosper than those that continue to operate hard exclusion lists,' Mr Taylor said.

Many asset managers have taken their clients' interest in sustainability seriously.

'Beyond ESG assessment and ratings, asset managers should be able to engage actively with issuers,' said Pascal Blanqué, chief investment officer at Amundi, the French asset manager that sponsored the report.

'Through a constructive dialogue and a strong voting policy, asset managers can encourage the improvement of company ESG performances.'

Amundi placed fourth in the responsible investment ranking, behind Schroders, Robeco and Aviva Investors.

Campaign groups are now pushing for asset managers to embed the ethos of responsible investing in their corporate structures.

'Other hallmarks of leading asset managers include actively promoting responsible investment with policymakers and using ESG integration as part of the key performance indicators used to incentivise fund managers,' said Anne-Marie Williams, ShareAction's investor engagement manager.

Royal Dutch Shell threatened with climate change legal action

Friends of the Earth to file lawsuit if oil group fails to commit to Paris agreement

Andrew Ward

Financial Times, 4 April 2018

Royal Dutch Shell has been threatened with legal action aimed at forcing the oil and gas group to shift away from fossil fuels in support of efforts to tackle climate change.

Friends of the Earth, the environmental group, said it would file a lawsuit in the Netherlands if Shell failed to commit within eight weeks to bring its business into line with the Paris climate agreement.

The case against Shell is being led by Roger Cox, the lawyer who won a landmark judgment in 2015 forcing the Dutch government to set more ambitious carbon reduction targets.

'Shell's current policy is on a collision course with the Paris agreement,' said Mr Cox, referring to the international deal under which almost 200 countries agreed to limit global temperature rises to well below 2 degrees Celsius above pre-industrial levels.

'It seems as though Shell considers the damage that it does to the climate as an unfortunate but necessary evil. The law, however, opposes Shell's view.'

Shell, Europe's largest oil and gas group, has gone further than most peers by setting an 'ambition' to reduce its carbon footprint—including emissions from use of its products—by 50 per cent by 2050.

However, Friends of the Earth said this was not enough to meet the Paris goal. The group said 'binding rules' were needed that made companies such as Shell legally responsible for helping reduce carbon emissions in line with international targets.

'If we win this case, it has major consequences for other fossil companies, and opens the door for further legal action against other climate polluters,' said Karin Nansen, chair of Friends of the Earth International.

Shell said it had 'long recognised the climate challenge' and 'strongly' supported the Paris agreement.

'But we believe climate change is a complex societal challenge that should be addressed through sound government policy and cultural change to drive low-carbon choices for businesses and consumers, not by the courts,' the Anglo-Dutch group said in a statement.

Climate lawsuits have been filed against oil and gas companies in the US but Friends of the Earth said it was the first that aimed to force a change of corporate policy, rather than seeking compensation.

Shell was already facing a resolution at its annual meeting in May from activist shareholders calling on the group to bring its business into line with Paris.

Ben van Beurden, Shell chief executive, said in a speech last month that Shell aimed to keep 'in step with society's progress towards Paris', implying that the company could only go as fast as markets and policies allowed.

Shell has committed to invest at least $1bn–$2bn a year in renewable power and other forms of clean energy, but this remains a fraction of its total $25bn–$30bn capital expenditure budget, the vast majority of which still goes to fossil fuels.

A new 'scenario' published by Shell last week set out a 'technologically, industrially, and economically possible' path to achieving the Paris goal but said it would require 're-wiring the whole global economy in just the next 50 years'.

'The big challenge is whether there is the political will and, underlying this, the societal will to put in place and maintain the frameworks that are necessary to address this awe-inspiring task,' said the Shell report.

Pilot scheme seeks to produce first 'ethical cobalt' from Congo

Project will trace metal from artisanal mines in effort to clean up supply chain

David Pilling

Financial Times, 25 March 2018

A pilot scheme to trace the world's first 'ethical cobalt' from small-scale mines in the Democratic Republic of Congo all the way to consumers of electric cars and iPhones will start this week, potentially allowing companies such as Apple to assure customers their products are free from child labour and other human rights abuses.

The trial, which parallels previous efforts to weed out so-called blood diamonds and conflict minerals, comes in response to concern that increased demand for cobalt is fuelling exploitation and environmental degradation in the central African country, which accounts for 60 per cent of world supply.

The Better Cobalt pilot, which will be overseen by RCS Global, a UK supply-chain audit company, will electronically tag cobalt from five artisanal and semi-mechanised mines in Congo in what it says will be the first systematic attempt to trace the metal along an opaque supply chain.

The project is a collaboration between several as-yet-unnamed 'global brand' consumer companies, including two car manufacturers, as well as industry participants, including Huayou Cobalt, the world's largest refiner, whose Congo DongFang Mining supplies Apple, among others.

DongFang's admission in 2016 that it did not have strong control over its supply chain has prompted calls from advocacy groups and electronics companies to tighten oversight.

At least a fifth of the cobalt exported from Congo, one of the world's poorest countries, comes from artisanal mines, where child labour is common.

Anneke Van Woudenberg, executive director of Rights and Accountability in Development, a UK charity, said that demand for cobalt had turned parts of the country into 'an environmental disaster'. Working conditions were brutal and miners' lives too often short, she said. Toxic chemicals used to extract cobalt were sometimes discarded directly into rivers, poisoning the water supply.

Electric cars, which are being bought in the west as part of a green lifestyle, contain about 10 kilogrammes of cobalt, more than 1,000 times the amount used in an iPhone, according to BMO Capital Markets. Some analysts say that a pledge by Tesla's Elon Musk to source all cobalt from North America is unrealistic given the expected ramp-up in electric car production.

Cobalt prices have more than doubled in the past year alone as battery makers scramble to lock in supplies.

Nicholas Garrett, chief executive of RCS Global, said that agents stationed at mines would report suspected violations as stipulated by the OECD.

Red-flag incidents, such as child labour or a mine cave-in, would be instantly visible on a dashboard available to participants along the supply chain, including the final cobalt purchaser.

'This level of data generation is unheard of in the artisanal mining context,' Mr Garrett said. 'We are essentially creating a digital footprint.' Eventually, the aim was to improve monitoring further with block-chain technology, he said.

Ms Van Woudenberg gave a cautious welcome to the scheme, saying it was 'absolutely vital that there are good, strong initiatives that can help push the actors violating human rights to clean up their supply chains'.

However, she warned that too many monitoring programmes were 'nothing more than fluff', which helped offending companies whitewash their image.

Impact, a Canadian advocacy group, recently left the Kimberley Process, a group committed to removing conflict diamonds from the global supply chain, saying that it provided buyers with a 'false confidence' that their gems were conflict free.

Part 3

Directors and board structure

8

Directors and board structure

Learning objectives

- To be aware of the distinction between unitary and dual boards
- To have a detailed understanding of the roles, duties, and responsibilities of directors
- To understand the rationale for key board committees and their functions
- To be able to critically assess the criteria for independence of non-executive (outside) directors
- To comprehend the role and contribution of non-executive (outside) directors
- To be aware of the importance of board evaluation, succession planning, and board diversity

Introduction

This chapter covers the board structure of a company. The discussion encompasses the function of a board and its subcommittees (the most common ones being the audit, remuneration, nomination, and risk committees); the roles, duties, and responsibilities of directors; and the attributes and contribution of a non-executive (outside) director. Whilst the context is that of a UK company, much of the material is appropriate to other countries that also have a unitary (one-tier) board structure and may also be generalized to a dual (two-tier) board structure.

Unitary board versus dual board

A major corporate governance difference between countries is the board structure, which may be unitary or dual depending on the country. As in the UK, in the majority of EU Member States, the unitary board structure is predominant (in five states, the dual structure is also available). However, in Austria, Germany, the Netherlands, and Denmark, the dual structure is predominant. In the dual structure, employees may have representation on the supervisory board (as in Germany, covered in detail in Chapter 10) but this may vary from country to country.

Unitary board

A unitary board of directors is the form of board structure in the UK and the USA, and is characterized by one single board comprising both executive and non-executive directors. The unitary board is responsible for all aspects of the company's activities, and all the directors are working to achieve the same ends. The shareholders elect the directors to the board at the company's annual general meeting (AGM).

Dual board

A dual board system consists of a supervisory board and an executive board of management. However, in a dual board system, there is a clear separation between the function of supervision (monitoring) and that of management. The supervisory board oversees the *direction* of the business, whilst the management board is responsible for the *running* of the business. Members of one board cannot be members of another, so there is a clear distinction between management and control. Shareholders appoint the members of the supervisory board (other than the employee members), whilst the supervisory board appoints the members of the management board.

Commonalities between unitary and dual board structures

There are many similarities in board practice between a unitary and a dual board system. The unitary board and the supervisory board usually appoint the members of the managerial body: the group of managers to whom the unitary board delegates authority in the unitary system and the management board in a dual system. Both bodies usually have responsibility for ensuring that financial reporting and control systems are operating properly and for ensuring compliance with the law.

Usually, both the unitary board of directors and the supervisory board (in a dual system) are elected by shareholders (in some countries, such as Germany, employees may elect some supervisory board members).

Advocates of each type of board structure identify their main advantages as follows: in a one-tier system, there is a closer relationship and better information flow as all directors, both executive and non-executive, are on the same single board; in a dual system, there is a more distinct and formal separation between the supervisory body and those being 'supervised', because of the separate management board and supervisory board structures. These aspects are discussed further in Chapter 10. However, whether the structure is unitary or dual, many codes seem to have a common approach to areas relating to the function of boards and key board committees, to independence, and to the consideration of shareholder and shareholder rights.

The UK Corporate Governance Code

In Chapter 3, the *Cadbury Code of Best Practice* was cited as having influenced the development of corporate governance codes in many countries. The Cadbury Code clearly emphasizes, inter alia, the central role of the board, the importance of a division of responsibilities at the head of the company, and the role of non-executive directors. There have been a number of revisions to UK corporate governance codes, as detailed in Chapter 3, culminating in the issuance of the UK Corporate Governance Code (2018) which has its main principles listed in five sections with each section containing more detailed provisions and 'offers flexibility through the application of the Principles and through "comply or explain" provisions and supporting guidance.' The five sections are:

- Board Leadership and Company Purpose—containing Principles A–E, and Provisions 1–8
- Division of Responsibilities—containing Principles F–I, and Provisions 9–16
- Composition, Succession and Evaluation—containing Principles J–L, and Provisions 17–23
- Audit, Risk and Internal Control—containing Principles M–O, and Provisions 24–31
- Remuneration—containing Principles P–R, and Provisions 32–41.

The UK Corporate Governance Code (hereafter 'the Code') is appended to the Listing Rules by which companies listed on the London Stock Exchange must abide. However, companies can conform to the Code's provisions on a 'comply or explain' basis. 'Comply or explain' means that the company will generally be expected to comply with the provisions of the Code, but if it is unable to comply with a particular provision, then it can explain why it is unable to do so. Institutional investors and their representative groups monitor carefully all matters related to the Code, and will contact companies if they have not complied with a provision of the Code and protest if the company does not have an appropriate reason for non-compliance.

The board of directors

The board of directors leads and controls a company and hence an effective board is fundamental to the success of the company. The board is the link between managers and investors, and is essential to good corporate governance and investor relations.

Given the UK's unitary board system, it is desirable that the roles of chair and chief executive officer (CEO) are split because otherwise there could be too much power vested in one individual. The chair is responsible for the running of the board whilst the CEO is responsible for the running of the business. The Code (2018) states that 'the roles of chair and chief executive should not be exercised by the same individual' (Provision 9). When a CEO retires from his/her post, he/she should not then become chair of the same company (exceptionally, a board may agree to a CEO becoming chair, but in this case, the board should discuss the matter with major shareholders setting out the reasons, and also publish these on the company website). The Higgs Review (2003) reported that only five FTSE 100 companies had a joint chair/CEO, whilst this figure rose to 11 per cent of companies outside the FTSE 350.

Role of the board

The board is responsible for: determining the company's aims and the strategies, plans, and policies to achieve those aims; monitoring progress in the achievement of those aims (both from an overview company aspect and also in terms of analysis and evaluation of its own performance as a board and as individual directors); and appointing a CEO with appropriate leadership qualities. Sir Adrian Cadbury (2002) gives an excellent exposition of corporate governance and chairmanship, and the role and effectiveness of the board in corporate governance.

In a study of the changing role of boards, Taylor et al. (2001) identified three major challenges facing company boards over the forthcoming five-year period. These challenges were to build more diverse boards of directors, to pay more attention to making their boards more effective, and to be able to react appropriately to any changes in the corporate governance culture. By building better boards, innovation and entrepreneurship should be encouraged and the business driven to perform better. The board will focus on the value drivers of the business to give the firm competitive advantage. Clearly, the composition of the board will play a key role in whether a company can successfully meet these challenges. The presence of the most suitable non-executive directors will help the board in this task. The role and appointment of non-executive directors are discussed in more detail later.

Epstein and Roy (2006) state that:

high-performance boards must achieve three core objectives:

1. provide superior strategic guidance to ensure the company's growth and prosperity;
2. ensure accountability of the company to its stakeholders, including shareholders, employees, customers, suppliers, regulators and the community;
3. ensure that a highly qualified executive team is managing the company.

Decisions relating to board composition and structure will be of fundamental importance in determining whether, and to what extent, the board is successful in achieving these objectives.

The FRC (2014) stated that

one of the key roles for the board includes establishing the culture, values and ethics of the company. It is important that the board sets the correct 'tone from the top'. The directors should lead by example and ensure that good standards of behaviour permeate throughout all levels of the organisation. This will help prevent misconduct, unethical practices and support the delivery of long-term success.

The developments in relation to the role of culture were discussed earlier in Chapter 3.

Role, duties, and responsibilities

It is essential that the role, duties, and responsibilities of directors are clearly defined. The Code (2018) states that 'a successful company is led by an effective and entrepreneurial board, whose role is to promote the long-term sustainable success of the company, generating value for shareholders and contributing to wider society' (Principle A). Furthermore the importance of culture is emphasized: 'The board should establish the company's purpose, values and strategy, and satisfy itself that these and its culture are aligned. All directors must act with integrity, lead by example and promote the desired culture' (Principle B).

The board should have regular meetings, with an agenda, and there should be a formal schedule of matters over which the board has the right to make decisions. There should be appropriate reporting procedures defined for the board and its subcommittees. As mentioned earlier, the roles of chair and CEO should preferably be split to help ensure that no one individual is too powerful. The board should have a balance between executive and non-executive directors. All directors should have access to the company secretary.

According to UK law, the directors should act in good faith in the interests of the company, and exercise care and skill in carrying out their duties.

In November 2006 the Companies Act (2006) finally received Royal Assent after a prolonged period in the making. The Act updates previous Companies Acts legislation, but does not completely replace them, and it contains some significant new provisions that will impact on various constituents, including directors, shareholders, auditors, and company secretaries. The Act is discussed in detail in Chapter 3.

Davies and Hopt (2013), in a review of boards in Europe, state that:

> at one end of the spectrum the board may simply reflect the dominance of the agent, as where the board is dominated by the management (in a dispersed shareholding context) or by the large shareholders (in a concentrated shareholding context). At the other end of the spectrum, the board, depending on how it is chosen and composed, may act as a mechanism for protecting the principal (the shareholders as a class or the minority shareholders, as the case may be).

The roles of the CEO, chair, senior independent director, and company secretary are now discussed.

Chief executive officer (CEO)

The CEO has the executive responsibility for the leadership of the company's business, whereas the chair has responsibility for the leadership of the board. The two roles should not therefore be combined and carried out by one person, as this would give an individual too much power.

One particular problem that arises from time to time is whether a retiring CEO should become chairof the same company. This is generally discouraged because a chair should be independent. The Code (2018) states:

> A chief executive should not become chair of the same company. If, exceptionally, this is proposed by the board, major shareholders should be consulted ahead of appointment. The board should set out its reasons to all shareholders at the time of the appointment and also publish these on the company website (Provision 9).

As well as a lack of independence, there is a feeling that it might cause problems for any incoming CEO if the retired CEO is still present at a senior level in the company (in the role of chair) because he/she may try to become more involved in the leadership of the company rather than the leadership of the board (in his/her new role as chair).

Various institutional bodies have made their views known on this issue: for example, Research Recommendations Electronic Voting (RREV), a joint venture between the National Association of Pension Funds (NAPF) and Institutional Shareholder Services (ISS), states that 'the normal application of the NAPF policy is to vote against the re-election of a director with the roles of both chief executive and chairman'. Hermes, in *The Hermes Corporate Governance Principles*, states that it is generally opposed to a CEO becoming chairman of the board at the same company.

Laux (2014) synthesizes recent research that examines governance from the perspective of CEO assessment and replacement. He concludes that:

> the unifying theme in this research is the board's desire not only to control the actions of the CEO, but also to assess his ability and fit and to decide whether to keep him in charge. These goals, however, are fundamentally intertwined. CEO assessment affects the behavior of the relevant players and is a key criteria for studying (i) the optimal design of executive compensation, (ii) board monitoring, (iii) CEO turnover, (iv) project selection, (v) CEO selection, (vi) financial reporting, and much more.

Laux's paper therefore clearly identifies the key influences of the CEO on the board of directors and the firm as a whole.

Chair

The chair is responsible for the leadership of the board and for ensuring that the board meets frequently, that directors have access to all the information they need to make an informed contribution at board meetings, and that all directors are given the opportunity to speak at board meetings.

As Sir Adrian Cadbury (2002) observed: 'the primary task of chairmen is to chair their boards. This is what they have been appointed to do and, however the duties at the top of a company may be divided, chairing the board is their responsibility alone' (p. 78). He also succinctly highlights an important difference between CEOs and chairmen:

> The difference between the authority of chairmen and that of chief executives is that chairmen carry the authority of the board, while chief executives carry the authority delegated to them by the board. Chairmen exercise their authority on behalf of the board; chief executives have personal authority in line with the terms of their appointment. (p. 99)

The chair should hold meetings with the non-executive directors without the executives present. The *Combined Code* (2006) stated that no individual should hold more than one chairmanship of a FTSE 100 company; however, the *Combined Code* (2008) removed this restriction. One rationale for this change is that limiting an individual to chairing just one FTSE 100 company took no account of what other activities he/she might be engaged in; these other activities might not be onerous in which case it would be feasible to chair more than one FTSE 100 company. The Code (2016) states that the board should not agree to a full-time executive director taking on more than one non-executive directorship in a FTSE 100 company nor the chairmanship of such a company (B.3.3).

McNulty et al. (2011), in a study of 160 chairs of 500 FTSE listed companies, find that:

> by linking board structure, board process and the exercise of influence, the study reveals both differences amongst chairs in how they run the board, but also that chairs differ in the influence they exert on board-related tasks. Full-time executive chairs exert their greatest influence in strategy and resource dependence tasks whereas part-time, non-executive chairs seem to exert more influence over monitoring and control tasks.

Withers and Fitza (2017), in a study focusing on US firms in which the CEO and board chair positions are separated, use a sample of 6,290 firm-year observations representing 1,828 board chairs in 308 different industries. They find that separate board chairs explain 9 per cent of the variance in firm performance.

Bezemer et al. (2018), employing a combination of video-taped board meetings and semi-structured interviews with directors at three corporations, find 'a generalized and negative association between chair involvement and directors' engagement during board meetings'. In other words, the involvement of the chair appears to reduce the engagement of other directors during meetings.

Senior independent director

The Code (2018) provides for the appointment of a senior independent director (SID) who should be one of the independent non-executive directors. The Code (2018) states that the senior independent director should 'provide a sounding board for the chair and serve as an intermediary for the other directors and shareholders. Led by the senior independent director, the non-executive directors should meet without the chair present at least annually to appraise the chair's performance, and on other occasions as necessary' (Provision 12).

The Hermes Corporate Governance Principles also see the SID as providing an additional communication channel to shareholders and state: 'if the chairman of the board is not independent, then the board should appoint a senior independent director whose role would include reviewing the performance of the chairman' (para. 3.4). The non-executive directors should meet without the chairman present at least annually in order to appraise the chairman's performance, and on other occasions as necessary. At these times, the SID would lead the meeting.

Company secretary

The company secretary, like the directors, must act in good faith and avoid conflicts of interest. The company secretary has a range of responsibilities, including facilitating the work of the board by ensuring that the directors have all the information they need for the main board and also for the board subcommittees (commonly audit, remuneration, and nomination), and that such information flows well between the various constituents. The company secretary advises the board, via the chair, on all governance matters and will assist with the professional development needs of directors and induction requirements for new directors.

The dismissal of the company secretary is a decision for the board as a whole and not just the CEO or chair.

Research carried out by eShare (2017) *Under Pressure: The Company Secretary and the Growing Need for Effective Governance* has found that the role of company secretary is becoming more onerous and gaining a higher profile. Contributions from company secretaries in both the UK and the US indicate how the role has changed over the past ten years. The White Paper states that 'what was once a relatively low-profile position has become one of the most exposed, with overall responsibility for the organisation's corporate governance'.

Board subcommittees

The board may appoint various subcommittees, which should report regularly to the board, and although the board may delegate various activities to these subcommittees, it is the board as a whole that remains responsible for the areas covered by the subcommittees. Charkham (2005) states:

> Committees of the board are used for various purposes, the main one being to assist the dispatch of business by considering it in more detail than would be convenient for the whole board ... the second purpose is to increase objectivity either because of inherent conflicts of interest such as executive remuneration, or else to discipline personal preferences as in the exercise of patronage.

The Cadbury Report recommended that an audit committee and a remuneration committee should be formed, and also stated that a nomination committee would be one possible way to make the board appointments process more transparent.

The Higgs Review (2003) reported that most listed companies have an audit committee and a remuneration committee. Only one FTSE 100 company did not have an audit committee or remuneration committee, whilst 15 per cent of companies outside the FTSE 350 did not have an audit committee. Adoption of nomination committees has tended to be less prevalent with the majority (71 per cent) of companies outside the FTSE 350 not having a nomination committee. FTSE 100 companies have tended to adopt nomination committees with the exception of six companies. The Code (2018) states that there should be a nomination committee 'to lead the process for appointments, ensure plans are in place for orderly succession to both the board and senior management positions, and oversee the development of a diverse pipeline for succession' (Provisions 17).

Audit committee

The audit committee is arguably the most important of the board subcommittees.

The Smith Review of audit committees, a group appointed by the FRC, reported in January 2003. The review made clear the important role of the audit committee: 'while all directors have a duty to act in the interests of the company, the audit committee has a particular role, acting independently from the executive, to ensure that the interests of shareholders are properly protected in relation to financial reporting and internal control' (para. 1.5). The review defined the audit committee's role in terms of 'oversight', 'assessment', and 'review', indicating the high-level overview that audit committees should take; they need to satisfy themselves that there is an appropriate system of controls in place but they do not undertake the monitoring themselves.

It is the role of the audit committee to review the scope and outcome of the audit, and to try to ensure that the objectivity of the auditors is maintained. This would usually involve a review of the audit fee and fees paid for any non-audit work, and the general independence of the auditors. The audit committee provides a useful 'bridge' between both internal and external auditors and the board, helping to ensure that the board is fully aware of all relevant issues related to the audit. The audit committee's role may also involve reviewing arrangements for whistle-blowers (staff who wish confidentially to raise concerns about pos-sible improper practices in the company). In addition, where there is no risk management committee (discussed later), the audit committee should assess the systems in place to iden-tify and manage financial and non-financial risks in the company.

The guidance was updated in 2005 and subsequently a new edition of the guidance was issued in October 2008. A limited number of changes were made to implement some of the recommendations of the Market Participants Group (MPG), established to provide advice to the FRC on market-led actions to mitigate the risk that could arise in the event of one or more of the Big Four audit firms leaving the market. The main changes to the guidance are that audit com-mittees are encouraged to consider the need to include the risk of the withdrawal of their audi-tor from the market in their risk evaluation and planning; and that companies are encouraged to include in the audit committee's report information on the appointment, reappointment, or removal of the auditor, including supporting information on tendering frequency, the tenure of the incumbent auditor, and any contractual obligations that acted to restrict the committee's choice of auditor. In addition, there have been a small number of detailed changes to the section dealing with the independence of the auditor, to bring the guidance in line with the Auditing Practices Board's Ethical Standards for Auditors. An appendix has also been added containing guidance on the factors to be considered if a group is contemplating employing firms from more than one network to undertake the audit. The FRC's Guidance on Audit Committees (2016) updated the earlier version published in 2012 (which was based on the revised Smith Guidance 2008). The Guidance—which looks at the establishment and effectiveness of the audit commit-tee, summarizes the audit committee's roles and responsibilities, and provides an overview of communications with shareholders—aims to assist company boards in making suitable arrange-ments for their audit committees and to help audit committee members to carry out their role.

The Code (2018) (previously 2010, updated in 2012, 2014, 2016, and 2018) states that:

> the board should establish an audit committee of independent non-executive directors, with a minimum membership of three, or in the case of smaller companies, two. The chair of the board should not be a member. The board should satisfy itself that at least one member has recent and relevant financial experience. The committee as a whole shall have compe-tence relevant to the sector in which the company operates. (Provision 24)

In the UK Corporate Code (2012) some changes were made relating to the audit area. These were as follows: FTSE 350 companies to put the external audit contract out to tender at least every ten years with the aim of ensuring a high quality and effective audit, whether from the incumbent auditor or from a different firm; and audit committees to provide to shareholders information on how they have carried out their responsibilities, including how they have assessed the effectiveness of the external audit process. Subsequently amendments introduced in the Code update in 2016 were minimal and driven by changes required from the implementation of the European Union's Audit Regulation (2014/56/EU) and Regula-tion (537/2014). The minor changes relate to section C.3 which covers the audit committee and auditors whereby the audit committee as a whole will need competence relevant to the sector in which the company operates; the FTSE 350 audit tendering provision has been removed as this is superseded by the EU and the Com-petition and Markets Authority (CMA) requirements for mandatory tendering and rotation of the audit firm; the audit committee report within the annual report is now required to provide advance notice of any plans to retender the external audit. Companies should view the changes alongside the revised Guidance on Audit Committees (2016) which was discussed earlier. The Code (2018) should also take into account the FRC Guidance on Audit Committees and Guidance on Risk Management, Internal Control and Related Financial and Business Reporting.

Davies and Hopt (2013), in the context of boards in Europe, state that 'a separate audit committee is considered indispensable today and is now a general feature of listed companies. Not only is this committee recommended in corporate governance codes, but such a committee is required by EU law for "public interest" companies, which term includes those whose shares are traded on a regulated market.'

Spira (2002) provides a useful insight into the processes and interactions of audit committees, and highlights the importance of the composition of audit committees. The audit committee should comprise independent non-executive directors who are in a position to ask appropriate questions, so helping to give assurance that the committee is functioning properly. Turley (2008) highlights how 'the role and significance of the audit committee as a governance structure have developed substantially during the last decade'.

Zaman et al. (2011) examine the influence of audit committee effectiveness, a proxy for governance quality, on audit fees and non-audit services fees. They find that after controlling for board of director characteristics, there is a significant positive association between audit committee effectiveness and audit fees, only for larger clients.

Liao and Hsu (2013), in a study of US firms, find that common membership between the audit committee and the remuneration (compensation) committee 'is more likely to occur in firms with weak corporate governance and in firms lacking financial and committee resources, and is not associated with firms having a high demand for coordination between compensation and audit committees'.

A number of papers have examined the potential relationship between audit committee membership and the timeliness of the external audit report or audit report lag (ARL). For example, Sultana et al. (2015) found that in Australian firms, 'audit committee members with financial expertise, prior audit committee experience and those who are independent are associated with shorter audit report lag'. Subsequently, Abernathy et al. (2017) synthesize the literature on ARL highlighting the determinants of ARL along two primary dimensions, firm-specific and audit-specific. They state that:

> prior research has identified a strong association between company performance and ARL. That is, ARL appears to be shorter for larger, more successful companies and for companies with stronger corporate governance provisions. Conversely, companies with identifiable risk characteristics—such as poor financial performance, industry risk, and identified internal control weaknesses—more frequently experience longer ARL. The existing literature is generally consistent that ARL is, in some part, a function of the characteristics of the issuing company [but] is far less consistent with respect to the association between audit characteristics and ARL. ARL does appear to be associated with auditor attributes—primarily auditor size and industry knowledge—and the nature of the audit opinion issued. However, the effects of other audit characteristics on ARL is less clear.

Finally Ghafran and Yasmin (2018) examine the association of audit committee chair financial, experiential, and monitoring expertise with the ARL period. They find that 'the experiential and monitoring expertise of audit committee chairs have a significant negative association with the delay in the audit report lag period, possibly resulting in more effective audit committee chairs, at least in the face of financial reporting timeliness.'

Remuneration committee

The area of executive remuneration is always a 'hot issue' and one that attracts a lot of attention from investors and so, perhaps inevitably, the press. Indeed, since the financial crisis there seems to be an insatiable appetite for stories about excessive executive remuneration. Executive remuneration itself is covered in some detail in Chapter 9, whilst the structure of the remuneration committee is detailed now.

The Code (2018) states that 'the board should establish a remuneration committee of independent non-executive directors, with a minimum membership of three, or in the case of smaller companies, two. In addition, the chair of the board can only be a member if they were independent on appointment and cannot chair the committee. Before appointment as chair of the remuneration committee, the appointee should have served on a remuneration committee for at least 12 months' (Provision 32).

The remuneration committee should make recommendations to the board, within agreed terms of reference, on the company's framework of executive remuneration and its cost; it should determine on their behalf specific remuneration packages for each of the executive directors, including pension rights and any compensation payments.

The establishment of a remuneration committee (in the form recommended by the Code) prevents executive directors from setting their own remuneration levels. The remuneration committee mechanism should also provide a formal, transparent procedure for the setting of executive remuneration levels, including the determination of appropriate targets for any performance-related pay schemes. The members of the remuneration committee should be identified in the annual report. The remuneration of non-executive directors is decided by the chairman and the executive members of the board.

The Code (2014) included changes relating to directors' remuneration such that the design of remuneration is to promote the long-term success of the company; and also the recommendation that provisions are put in place to recover and/or withhold remuneration when appropriate. The latest version of the Code (2018) includes more demanding criteria for remuneration such that remuneration should not reward poor performance; and the alignment of remuneration with culture so that behaviour driven by incentive schemes is 'consistent with company purpose, values and strategy'. Furthermore, Provision 41 states that the description of the work of the remuneration committee in the annual report should include 'reasons why the remuneration is appropriate using internal and external measures, including pay ratios and pay gaps'... and 'what engagement with the workforce has taken place to explain how executive remuneration aligns with wider company pay policy'.

Regarding the role and effectiveness of the remuneration committee, Bender (2011) states:

> The market they [remuneration committees] use to derive comparative data is not a market as such, it is a collection of self-selected elite peers. The much-vaunted independence of the

non-executives on the remuneration committee in itself means that they have incomplete knowledge of the company and the individuals being compensated, and asymmetry of information leaves them at the wrong end of a power imbalance. In all, the realities of how committees actually operate differ considerably from the rhetorics with which they describe their compliance with the unattainable Ideal.

Kent et al. (2016), examine whether the adoption of the full Australian Securities Exchange recommendations for remuneration committee formation and structure are associated with a lower shareholder dissenting vote or a stronger CEO pay–performance link. They 'find some evidence that a minority- and majority-independent remuneration committee and a committee size of at least the recommended three members are associated with lower shareholder dissent. Companies with an independent committee have a stronger CEO pay–performance link. In addition, a majority-independent committee strengthens the link between performance and growth in CEO pay.'

Nomination committee

In the past directors were often appointed on the basis of personal connections. This process often did not provide the company with directors with appropriate business experience relevant to the particular board to which they were appointed. The board would also not have a balance in as much as there would be a lack of independent non-executive directors.

The Code (2018) advocates a formal, rigorous, and transparent procedure for the appointment of new directors and states that 'the board should establish a nomination committee to lead the process for appointments, ensure plans are in place for orderly succession to both the board and senior management positions, and oversee the development of a diverse pipeline for succession. A majority of members of the committee should be independent non-executive directors. The chair of the board should not chair the committee when it is dealing with the appointment of their successor' (Provision 17).

The nomination committee should evaluate the existing balance of skills, knowledge, and experience on the board, and utilize this when preparing a candidate profile for new appointments. The nomination committee should throw its net as wide as possible in the search for suitable candidates to ensure that it identifies the best candidates. In an often rapidly changing business environment, the nomination committee should also be involved with succession planning in the company, noting challenges that may arise and identifying possible gaps in skills and knowledge that would need to be filled with new appointments. As with the other key board committees, the members of the nomination committee should be identified in the annual report.

It is important that the board has a balanced composition, both in terms of executive and non-executive directors, and in terms of the experience, qualities, and skills that individuals bring to the board.

The Institute of Directors (IoD) published some useful guidance in this area. Box 8.1 shows an extract from *Standards for the Board* (2006) in relation to an action list for deciding board composition.

Box 8.1   Action list for deciding board composition

- Consider the ratio and number of executive and non-executive directors.
- Consider the energy, experience, knowledge, skill, and personal attributes of current and prospective directors in relation to the future needs of the board as a whole, and develop specifications and processes for new appointments, as necessary.
- Consider the cohesion, dynamic tension, and diversity of the board and its leadership by the chairman.
- Make and review succession plans for directors and the company secretary.
- Where necessary, remove incompetent or unsuitable directors or the company secretary, taking relevant legal, contractual, ethical, and commercial matters into account.
- Agree proper procedures for electing a chairman and appointing the managing director and other directors.
- Identify potential candidates for the board, make selection, and agree terms of appointment and remuneration. New appointments should be agreed by every board member.
- Provide new board members with a comprehensive induction to board processes and policies, inclusion to the company and to their new role.
- Monitor and appraise each individual's performance, behaviour, knowledge, effectiveness, and values rigorously and regularly.
- Identify development needs and training opportunities for existing and potential directors and the company secretary.

Source: Standards for the Board (IoD, 2006).

The Code (2018) reflects the emphasis on gender diversity and inclusivity in recent years and states that as well as reporting on 'the policy on diversity and inclusion, its objectives and linkage to company strategy, how it has been implemented and progress on achieving the objectives', the nomination committee's review of its work in the annual report should also cover 'the gender balance of those in senior management and their direct reports' (Provision 23).

Guo and Masulis (2012), in a sample of 1,280 firms listed on the New York Stock Exchange (NYSE) or Nasdaq, use the mandatory changes in board composition brought about by the new exchange listing rules following the passage of the Sarbanes-Oxley Act (SOX) to estimate the effect of overall board independence and nominating committee independence on forced CEO turnover. Their evidence suggests that 'greater representation of independent directors on board and/or nominating committee leads to more effective monitoring. Our finding that nominating committee independence significantly affects the quality of board monitoring has important policy implications given the intense debate on the costs and benefits of mandatory board regulations since the passage of SOX.'

Kaczmarek et al. (2012) in a study of FTSE 350 companies, find that:

the increasing presence on the NC [nomination committee] of females or non-British nationals is likely to have a positive impact on the level of board gender and nationality diversity, respectively. In addition, we report that the presence of the chief executive officer (CEO) on the NC is found to interact with the NC independence, as a result of which a board demographic faultline is likely to emerge.

Risk committee

Risk of various types features significantly in the operation of many businesses. Although not a recommendation of the Code (2018), many companies either set up a separate risk committee or establish the audit committee as an audit and risk committee. It is worth noting that the Code (2018) does state that the audit committee should review 'the company's internal financial controls and internal control and risk management systems, unless expressly addressed by a separate board risk committee composed of independent non-executive directors, or by the board itself' (Provision 25). Of course, it is essential that directors realize that they are responsible for the company's system of internal controls and have mechanisms in place to ensure that the internal controls of the company and risk management systems are operating efficiently.

Equally, many companies, particularly larger companies or those with significant transactions overseas, may find that they have interest or currency exposures that need to be covered. The misuse of derivatives through poor internal controls and lack of monitoring led to the downfall of Barings Bank (as detailed in Chapter 1) and other companies may be equally at risk. A risk committee should therefore comprehend the risks involved by, inter alia, using derivatives, and this would necessitate quite a high level of financial expertise and the ability to seek external professional advice where necessary.

The FRC *Guidance on Risk Management, Internal Control and Related Financial and Business Reporting* (2014) amalgamated the guidance from the Turnbull Report (2005) (internal control) and *Going Concern* (2009) guidance notes, revised to reflect the finalized requirements of the 2014 Code. The changes made to the UK Corporate Governance Code 2014 in relation to risk management are detailed in the relevant section in Chapter 3. Subsequent changes to guidance on risk management are also discussed in Chapter 3.

Pathan (2009), using a sample of 212 large US bank holding companies over the period 1997–2004, examines the relevance of bank board structure on bank risk-taking. He finds that 'strong bank boards (boards reflecting more of bank shareholders interest) particularly small and less restrictive boards positively affect bank risk-taking. In contrast, CEO power (CEO's ability to control board decision) negatively affects bank risk-taking.'

Meanwhile Yatim (2010), in a study of 690 firms listed on the Bursa Malaysia for the financial year ending in 2003, finds

> a strong support for an association between the establishment of a risk management committee and strong board structures. Specifically, the result shows that firms with higher proportions of non-executive directors on boards and firms that separate the positions of chief executive officers and board chairs are likely to set up a stand-alone risk management committee. Firms with greater board expertise and board diligence are also likely to establish a risk management committee. These findings suggest that stronger boards demonstrate their commitment to and awareness of improved internal control environment.

Alhadi et al. (2015), in a study of financial firms from Gulf Cooperation Council (GCC) countries during the years 2007–11, find that 'firms with a separate risk committee are associated with greater market risk disclosures, an effect that is more pronounced for mature-stage firms. Furthermore, findings suggest that risk committee qualifications and size have a significant positive impact on market risk disclosures.'

Ethics committee

Following the collapse of Enron more companies introduced an ethics committee as a board subcommittee. Companies may try to ensure that there is a strong organizational ethic by cascading an ethics code throughout the company, from director level to the worker on the shop floor. Many corporate governance codes are silent on any explicit mention of ethics committees, although the spirit of corporate governance recommendations is to act in an ethical way. This lack of an explicit mention is perhaps rather surprising given the frequent 'breaches' of perceived good corporate governance: infringement of shareholder rights, fraud, and excessive executive remuneration. As we have seen in Chapter 6, institutional shareholders are being exhorted to engage more fully with their investee companies, to act more as shareowners, and hopefully to encourage companies to behave more ethically. In Chapter 7 we saw that the management of, inter alia, ethical issues can be seen as a form of risk management.

Stevens et al. (2005) state that:

> the extent to which ethics codes are actually used by executives when making strategic choices as opposed to being merely symbolic is unknown . . . We find that financial executives are more likely to integrate their company's ethics code into their strategic decision processes if (a) they perceive pressure from market stakeholders to do so (suppliers, customers, shareholders, etc.); (b) they believe the use of ethics codes creates an internal ethical culture and promotes a positive external image for their firms; and (c) the code is integrated into daily activities through ethics code training programs. The effect of market stakeholder pressure is further enhanced when executives also believe that the code will promote a positive external image. Of particular note, we do not find that pressure from non-market stakeholders (e.g., regulatory agencies, government bodies, court systems) has a unique impact on ethics code use.

Crane et al. (2008) highlight that ethics programmes may involve a smaller cost now and result in significant savings in the future: 'In the United States, for example, corporations can significantly reduce their fine once they have been found guilty in criminal procedures by showing that an effective ethics program was in place.'

García-Sánchez et al. (2014) find that the

> corporate governance (CG) system moderates the level of involvement of the board in ethical issues. The findings obtained from a data panel sample made up of 760 listed companies from 12 countries for the years 2003–9 show that the largest companies with large-sized and diverse boards implement the most developed ECs. Nevertheless, the extent of involvement of the independent directors is conditioned by the level of shareholder orientation characteristic of the system of CG in the corporation's country of origin.

Non-executive directors

Non-executive directors are a mainstay of good governance. The non-executive director's role essentially has two dimensions. One dimension—which has been given much emphasis in the last decade—is as a control or counterweight to executive directors, so that the presence of non-executive directors helps to ensure that an individual person or group cannot unduly influence the board's decisions. The second dimension is the contribution that non-executive directors can make to the overall leadership and development of the company. Some argue that there may be a conflict in these two roles because non-executive directors are expected both to monitor executive directors' actions and to work with executive directors as part of the board. This idea of a potential conflict in the roles is an area discussed by Ezzamel and Watson (1997).

The Cadbury Report (1992) stated that 'given the importance of their distinctive contribution, non-executive directors should be selected with the same impartiality and care as senior executives' (para. 4.15). Non-executives should ideally be selected through a formal process and their appointment should be considered by the board as a whole.

The Cadbury Report also emphasized the contribution that independent non-executive directors could make, stating: 'the Committee believes that the calibre of the non-executive members of the board is of special importance in setting and maintaining standards of corporate governance' (para. 4.10). The importance of non-executive directors was echoed in the Organisation for Economic Co-operation and Development (OECD) Principles: 'Boards should consider assigning a sufficient number of non-executive board members capable of exercising independent judgement to tasks where there is a potential for conflict of interest. Examples of such key responsibilities are financial reporting, nomination and executive and board remuneration.'

The latest version of the UK Corporate Governance Code (2018) states that 'non-executive directors have a prime role in appointing and removing executive directors. Non-executive directors should scrutinise and hold to account the performance of management and individual executive directors against agreed performance objectives. The chair should hold meetings with the non-executive directors without the executive directors present' (Provision 13).

Independence of non-executive directors

Although there is a legal duty on all directors to act in the best interests of the company, this does not of itself guarantee that directors will act objectively. To try to ensure objectivity in board decisions, it is important that there is a balance of independent non-executive directors. This idea of independence is emphasized again and again in various codes and reports: for example, Cadbury (1992) stated that 'apart from their directors' fees and shareholdings, they [non-executive directors] … should be independent of management and free from any business or other relationship which could materially interfere with the exercise of their independent judgement' (para. 4.12). The OECD (1999) also considered this issue: 'Board independence usually requires that a sufficient number of board members not be employed by the company and not be closely related to the company or its management through significant economic, family or other ties. This does not prevent shareholders from being board members.' Subsequently, the OECD (2004) stated that 'board independence … usually requires that a sufficient number of board members will need to be independent of management'. This view was reiterated in the OECD (2015) *G20/OECD Principles of Corporate Governance 2015*. The Higgs Review (2003) stated that 'a board is strengthened significantly by having a strong group of non-executive directors with no other connection with the company. These individuals bring a dispassionate objectivity that directors with a closer relationship to the company cannot provide' (para. 9.5).

The Code (2018) states that 'the board should identify in the annual report each non-executive director it considers to be independent.'

'Independence' is generally taken as meaning that there are no relationships or circumstances that might affect the director's judgement. Situations where a non-executive director's independence could be called into question include:

- where the director was a former employee of the company or group within the last five years;
- where additional remuneration (apart from the director's fee) was received from the company;
- where the director had close family ties with the company's other directors or senior employees, or with any of the company's advisors;
- where he/she had a material business relationship with the company in the last three years;
- he/she had served on the board for more than nine years;
- he/she represented a significant shareholder;
- holds cross-directorships or has significant links with other directors through involvement in other companies or bodies.

There is some discussion as to whether the number of non-executive directorships that any one individual can hold should be defined. Of course, if an individual were to hold many non-executive directorships, for example, ten or more, then it is arguable whether that individual could devote enough time and consideration to each of the directorships. On the other hand, it may be perfectly feasible for an individual to hold, for example, five non-executive directorships. It really depends on the time that an individual has available, on the level of commitment, and whether any of the multiple non-executive directorships might lead to the problem of interlocking directorships whereby the independence of their role is compromised. An interlocking relationship might occur through any of a number of circumstances, including family relationship, business relationship, or a previous advisory role (such as auditor), which would endanger the fundamental aspect of independence. However, the independence of non-executive directors is an area of corporate governance that institutional investors and their representative groups monitor very carefully and disclosure of biographical information about directors and increasing use of databases of director information should help to identify potential problems in this area. The Code (2018) states that 'non-executive directors should have sufficient time to meet their board responsibilities. They should provide constructive challenge, strategic guidance, offer specialist advice and hold management to account' (Principle H). When new appointments are being made, any significant commitments should be disclosed prior to appointment together with an indication of the time involved. It is recommended that a full-time executive director should not take on 'more than one non-executive directorship in a FTSE 100 company or other significant appointment' (Provision 15).

Morck (2008) discussed the fact that behavioural issues are important in corporate governance, citing Milgram's (1974) findings that human nature includes 'a reflexive subservience' to people perceived to be legitimate authorities, like corporate CEOs. Morck states that:

effective corporate governance reforms must weaken this reflexive subservience. Corporate governance reforms that envision independent directors (dissenting peers), non-executive chairs (alternative authority figures), and fully independent audit committees (absent authority figures) aspire to a similar effect on corporate boards—the initiation of real debate to expose poor strategies before they become fatal.

Yeh et al. (2011), using the data of the 20 largest financial institutions from G8 countries (Australia, Canada, France, Germany, Italy, Japan, UK, and USA), of which four are common law countries and four civil law countries, find that the 'performance during the crisis period is higher for financial institutions with more independent directors on auditing and risk committees. The influence of committee independence on the performance is particularly stronger for civil law countries. In addition, the independence-performance relationships are more significant in financial institutions with excessive risk-taking behaviors.'

Muravyev et al. (2014), in a study of UK companies, find a positive relation between the presence of non-executive directors who are also executive directors in other firms and the accounting performance of the appointing companies. They state that:

> the effect is stronger if these directors are executive directors in firms that are performing well. We also find a positive effect when these non-executive directors are members of the audit committee. Overall, our results are broadly consistent with the view that non-executive directors that are executives in other firms contribute to both the monitoring and advisory functions of corporate boards.

Zorn et al. (2017) highlight the fact that the concerns over the detrimental impact of insiders on the board has led to many US firms' boards being so independent that the CEO is the lone inside member. They find evidence 'among S&P 1500 firms that having a lone-insider board is associated with (a) excess CEO pay and a larger CEO-top management team pay gap, (b) increased likelihood of financial misconduct, and (c) decreased firm performance, but that stock analysts and institutional investors reduce these negative effects. The findings raise important questions about the efficacy of leaving the CEO "home alone".'

Contribution of non-executive directors

The necessity for the independence of the majority of non-executive directors has been established earlier in the chapter, and the 'right' non-executive directors can make a significant contribution to the company. When non-executive directors are being sought, the company will be looking for the added value that a new appointment can make to the board. The added value may come from a number of facets: their experience in industry, the City, public life, or other appropriate background; their knowledge of a particular functional specialism (for example, finance or marketing); their knowledge of a particular technical process/system; their reputation; their ability to have an insight into issues discussed at the board and to ask searching questions. Of course, these attributes should be matched by the non-executive director's independence and integrity. The *Cadbury Code of Best Practice* (1992) stated that 'non-executive directors should bring an independent judgement to bear on issues of strategy, performance, resources, including key appointments, and standards of conduct' (para. 2.1).

As well as their contribution to the board, non-executive directors will serve on the key board committees (audit, remuneration, and nomination) as described earlier. However, it is not recommended that any one non-executive director sits on all three of these board committees. The Code (2018) states that 'the board and its committees should have a combination of skills, experience and knowledge. Consideration should be given to the length of service of the board as a whole and membership regularly refreshed' (Principle K).

Higgs Review

The Higgs Review, chaired by Derek Higgs, was established by the Department of Trade and Industry (DTI) in 2002 to review the role and effectiveness of non-executive directors. The Higgs Review was discussed in more detail in Chapter 3. Its recommendations caused much discussion but most of them were incorporated into the Combined Code (2003, 2006, 2008) and the subsequent UK Corporate Governance Code (2010), although some in a modified form.

In 2006 the FRC published *Good Practice Suggestions from the Higgs Report*. These include guidance on the role of the chairman and the non-executive director, and a summary of the principal duties of the remuneration and nomination committees. In 2010 the FRC published the *Guidance on Board Effectiveness*, which relates primarily to Sections A and B of the Code on the leadership and effectiveness of the board. The guidance was developed by the Institute of Chartered Secretaries and Administrators (ICSA) on the FRC's behalf, and replaces 'Suggestions for Good Practice from the Higgs Report' (known as the Higgs Guidance), which has been withdrawn.

The Association of British Insurers (ABI) issued its first *Report on Board Effectiveness* in 2011. The report focuses on three areas that the ABI believes help ensure that the board is effective and contribute to the company's success. These areas are board diversity, succession planning, and board evaluation. The ABI states: 'These issues do not stand alone. Selecting the best individuals from a diverse talent pool, planning for succession and replacement, and regularly evaluating the board to determine its effectiveness, cover the lifecycle of a board. That is why they are important.' In 2012 the ABI issued its *Report on Board Effectiveness: Updating progress, promoting best practice* in which it gave an update on the three areas which the earlier report focused on and included a new section on the role of chairmen in ensuring effective boards.

Director evaluation

In the Hampel Committee Final Report (1998), it was suggested that boards consider the introduction of formal procedures to 'assess both their own collective performance and that of individual directors' (para 3.13). In a widely cited report of institutional investor opinion, McKinsey (2002) defined 'good' board governance practices as encompassing a majority of outside (non-executive) directors, outside directors who are truly independent with no management ties, and under which *formal director evaluation is in place*.

The evaluation of directors has two dimensions, which are the evaluation of the board as a whole and the evaluation of individual directors serving on the board. Most annual reports are not forthcoming on how these evaluations may be carried out in their business, and indeed KPMG (2002) found, in a survey of corporate governance in Europe, that only 39 per cent of UK respondents had a regular process for the evaluation of the board. However, this was considerably better than the figure for the European countries as a whole, which was only 17 per cent.

In terms of the evaluation of the board as a whole, there are several approaches that might be utilized. These approaches include, first, a structured questionnaire to evaluate how the board is performing in key areas (such as achieving key goals that have been set), and informal discussion between the chairman of the board and the directors, which would cover a wide range of strategic and operational issues (such as how well the board dynamics work, and how well the board subcommittees work).

The evaluation of individual directors provides individual directors with the opportunity to discuss key areas with the chairman on a one-to-one basis. It is an important process for finding out just how comfortable an individual director is, what areas he/she might be able to contribute to more effectively, and whether there are any barriers to full participation in the board's activities (for example, lack of information to enable an informed discussion).

These evaluations will contribute to the establishment of the performance criteria that will help to achieve the corporate objectives and which are used in helping to align the performance of directors with the interest of shareholders.

It does seem clear that, in order to determine whether boards of directors as a whole, and directors as individuals, are performing to the best of their ability, there should be evaluation of the board as a whole, the board leadership, and the individual directors. Many boards are silent on this issue, indicating either that they do not have evaluation procedures in place or that they do not wish to disclose them if they have. If the latter is the case, then one has to ask whether the reluctance to disclose is because the evaluation process is not robust enough to stand up to scrutiny. If the former is the case, that is, that there are no evaluation or assessment procedures in place, then equally one has to ask why not. This information will be very helpful in setting performance-related pay for directors and helping to eliminate the unease that many investors feel about executive remuneration levels.

The area of board evaluation is covered under the section on 'Composition, Succession and Evaluation' in the Code (2018), which includes the principle that 'annual evaluation of the board should consider its composition, diversity and how effectively members work together to achieve objectives. Individual evaluation should demonstrate whether each director continues to contribute effectively' (Principle L). Additionally in the more detailed provisions 'there should be a formal and rigorous annual evaluation of the performance of the board, its committees, the chair and individual directors. The chair should consider having a regular externally facilitated board evaluation. In FTSE 350 companies this should happen at least every three years. The external evaluator should be identified in the annual report and a statement made about any other connection it has with the company or individual directors' (Provision 21).

Van den Berghe and Levrau (2004), in a study of the boards of directors of 30 companies listed on Euronext Brussels and Nasdaq Europe, found that there were a number of areas where better understanding was needed of elements that determined board effectiveness. They also found that board evaluation was not as widespread as might be hoped. Epstein and Roy (2006) state that it is important to evaluate both the board as a whole and individual directors, as this may help highlight deficiencies. Metrics for evaluation should be relevant and linked to the inputs, such as attendance at board meetings, and outputs, such as stock price. A balanced scorecard approach, derived from the work of Kaplan and Norton (1992, 2000) is an appropriate tool for director evaluation.

Wong (2011) highlights that the global financial crisis has prompted more debate on how the effectiveness of the board might be improved. He points out that:

> despite considerable reforms over the past two decades, boards—particularly at financial institutions—have been criticized recently for failing to properly guide strategy, oversee risk management, structure executive pay, manage succession planning, and carry out other essential tasks. This article argues that the lack of attention to behavioral and functional considerations—such as director mindset, board operating context, and evolving human dynamics—has hampered the board's effectiveness.

He makes various recommendations alongside 'establishing core building blocks such as appropriate board size, well-functioning committees, proficient company secretarial support, and professionally-administered board evaluation'.

Larcker et al. (2017), in a study of 187 boards undertaken with The Miles Group, found

> that most board evaluations fail to identify and correct poor performance among individual members. Only around half (55%) of companies that conduct board evaluations evaluate individual directors, and only around one-third (36%) believe their company does a very good job of accurately assessing the performance of individual directors.

They suggest that board evaluations could be improved 'by treating the board as a high-performing group of individuals and evaluating its leadership, management, and group dynamics'.

Succession planning

The FRC (2015a) highlighted that succession planning was one area which it intended to focus on with a project on succession planning 'aimed at identifying and increasing good practice and, more specifically, at how the nomination committee can play its role effectively. Unless boards are planning over the medium- to long-term, for both executive and non-executive positions, they will struggle to ensure that there is the right mix of skills and experience needed as the company evolves.' In October 2015 the FRC (2015b) issued a Discussion Paper *UK Board Succession Planning* which explored six areas that the FRC considers are important to succession planning: how effective board succession planning is important to business strategy and culture; the role of the nomination committee; board evaluation and its contribution to board succession; identifying the internal and external 'pipeline' for executive and non-executive directors; ensuring diversity; and the role of institutional investors. In May 2016 the FRC issued a feedback statement on the responses it received in relation to the Discussion Paper and stated that 'an active nomination committee is key to promoting effective board succession. Committees should consider carefully the future membership of their boards and ensure that this is aligned to company strategy, both current and future.'

The Code (2018) recognizes the importance of having an effective succession plan in place and states: 'Appointments to the board should be subject to a formal, rigorous and transparent procedure, and an effective succession plan should be maintained for board and senior management. Both appointments and succession plans should be based on merit and objective criteria and, within this context, should promote diversity of gender, social and ethnic backgrounds, cognitive and personal strengths' (Principle J).

Naveen (2006) found that 'a firm's propensity to groom an internal candidate for the CEO position is related to firm size, degree of diversification, and industry structure. My results also suggest that succession planning is associated with a higher probability of inside succession and voluntary succession and a lower probability of forced succession.'

Larcker and Tayan (2010) state that whilst one of the most important decisions for a board of directors is the selection of the CEO, 'survey data indicates that many boards are not prepared for this process. In recent years, shareholder groups have pressured boards to increase transparency about their succession plans.'

Board diversity

An area that is attracting increasing interest is that of board diversity whereby diversity is defined broadly in terms of gender or nationality. It may be argued that board diversity enables different perspectives to be taken on various issues given that men and women may approach issues from different viewpoints and may have different behavioural patterns as well; similarly individuals from different ethnic backgrounds may bring additional cultural insights to the boardroom.

Concerned by the lack of progress with the representation of women on UK boards, the UK's Coalition government invited Lord Davies to review the situation, to identify the barriers that were preventing more women from reaching the boardroom, and to make recommendations as to how this situation might be redressed. Lord Davies' report, *Women on Boards*, was published in February 2011 and reviewed the current situation on UK boards (FTSE 350) at that time and considered the business case for having gender-diverse boards.

A number of recommendations were made, including that the chairmen of FTSE 350 companies should state the percentage of women that they aim to have on their boards in 2013 and 2015, and that FTSE 100 companies should aim for a minimum 25 per cent women in the boardroom by 2015 although many might achieve a higher figure. Quoted companies should annually disclose the proportion of women on the board, women in senior executive positions, and female employees in the organizations as a whole. Furthermore, Lord Davies recommended that the FRC amend the Code to require listed companies to establish a policy on boardroom diversity, including measurable objectives for implementing the policy, and disclose a summary of the policy and the progress made towards achieving the objectives each year. It was also recommended that executive search firms should draw up a voluntary code of conduct addressing gender diversity and best practice, covering the relevant search criteria and processes in relation to FTSE 350 board appointments. Early in 2012 there was a follow-up report published which indicated that, over the year since the original report was published, the biggest ever reported increase in the percentage of women on boards was evidenced.

In May 2011 the FRC began consulting on possible amendments to the Code that would require companies to publish their policy on boardroom diversity and report against it annually, as recommended by the Davies Report (2011) and to consider the board's diversity amongst other factors, when assessing its effectiveness. In October 2011 the FRC announced that these changes would be implemented in a revised version of the Code, which was issued in 2012.

The changes affect two sections of the Code. First, in relation to Section B.2.4, where it is proposed that the work of the nomination committee should be described in a separate section of the annual report, including the process used in relation to board appointments. This section should include a description of 'the board's policy on diversity, including gender, any measurable objectives that it has set for implementing the policy, and progress on achieving the objectives. An explanation should be given if neither an external search consultancy nor open advertising has been used in the appointment of a chairman or a non-executive director.' Secondly, in relation to Section B6 where 'the evaluation of the board should consider the balance of skills, experience, independence and knowledge of the company on the board, its diversity, including gender, how the board works together as a unit, and other factors relevant to its effectiveness'. These changes were incorporated in the UK Corporate Governance Code (2012) and retained in the updated versions of the UK Corporate Governance Code (2014 and 2016). The latest UK Corporate Governance Code (2018) has similar wording, for example, the annual report should describe the nomination committee's work including 'the policy on diversity and inclusion, its objectives and linkage to company strategy, how it has been implemented and progress on achieving the objectives' (Provision 23), and 'open advertising and/or an external search consultancy should generally be used for the appointment of the chair and non-executive directors ...' (Provision 20). Furthermore, 'annual evaluation of the board should consider its composition, diversity and how effectively members work together to achieve objectives. Individual evaluation should demonstrate whether each director continues to contribute effectively' (Principle L).

Since the Davies Report was published in 2011 and the follow-up report in 2012, annual reports have been issued in each of the years 2013, 2014, and 2015 updating the situation on board gender diversity in the UK. The final report published in October 2015, showed that there are more women on FTSE 350 boards than ever before, with representation of women having more than doubled since 2011 and the target of 25 per cent having been exceeded on FTSE 100 boards which have 26.1 per cent of women whilst for FTSE 250 boards it stood at 19.6 per cent.

Hampton-Alexander Review (2017)

The Hampton-Alexander Review (the Review) was an independent, business-led review supported by the government which builds on the success of the Davies Reports. In 2017 it published its report *Improving gender balance in FTSE Leadership* and made recommendations aimed at increasing the number of women in leadership positions of FTSE 350 companies. The Review is discussed in more detail in Chapter 3.

Parker Review (2017)

The Parker Review Committee, led by Sir John Parker, published its Final Report *A Report into Ethnic Diversity of UK Boards: 'Beyond One by '21'* in 2017. The key recommendations are: (i) increasing the ethnic diversity of UK boards; (ii) developing candidates for the pipeline and plan for succession; (iii) enhancing transparency and disclosure. The Review is discussed in more detail in Chapter 3.

Following on from the publication of *Women in Economic Decision-making in the EU: Progress Report* in March 2012, the European Commission considered legislation to improve the gender balance on the boards of listed companies. The Progress Report showed that a number of countries in the EU—for example, France, the Netherlands, Italy, and Belgium—enacted legislative measures in 2011 aimed at improving gender balance in company boards, and that other countries (for example, Spain since 2007 and Norway since 2003) already had quota systems in place at 40 per cent. However, in January 2012 the average number of female board members in the largest companies listed in the EU was only 13.7 per cent compared to 11.8 per cent in 2010. Moreover, only 3.2 per cent of chairpersons were women in January 2012 compared to 3.4 per cent in 2010.

In November 2012 the EU Commission proposed legislation 'with the aim of attaining a 40% objective of the under-represented sex in non-executive board-member positions in publicly listed companies, with the exception of small and medium enterprises. Currently, boards are dominated by one gender: 85% of non-executive board members and 91.1% of executive board members are men, while women make up 15% and 8.9% respectively.' Whilst the EU Commission is striving to achieve equality between men and women, it noted that 'in business leadership the situation is particularly disappointing: in April 2016, women accounted for just *23.3% of board members* of the largest publicly listed companies registered in the EU countries'. An EU Directive on *Disclosure of Non-Financial and Diversity Information* issued in 2014 states that large companies have to publish reports on the policies they implement in relation to, inter alia, diversity on company boards (in terms of age, gender, educational, and professional background).

The International Corporate Governance Network (ICGN) issued its *Statement and Guidance on Gender Diversity on Boards* (2013) which looks at both board responsibilities and investor responsibilities regarding gender diversity on boards. The ICGN states: 'Gender diversity is a competitiveness issue for a company as a whole and a critical dimension of governance, both in the Board's oversight of the enterprise and in the Board's own composition and talent management. Increasing the representation of skilled and competent women on Boards will strengthen the corporate governance culture and ultimately contribute to value for all stakeholders.'

What does the academic evidence have to say about board diversity? Carter et al. (2003) examine the relationship between board diversity and firm value for Fortune 1000 firms. Board diversity is defined as the percentage of women, African-Americans, Asians, and Hispanics on the board of directors. After controlling for size, industry, and other corporate governance measures, they find significant positive relationships between the fraction of women or minorities on the board and firm value. They also find that the proportion of women and minorities on boards increases with firm size and board size but decreases as the number of insiders increases. For women, there is an inverse relationship between the percentage of women on boards and the average age of the board.

Carter et al. (2007) analysed both the diversity of the board and of important board committees, in all firms listed on the Fortune 500 over the period 1998–2002, to gain greater insight into the way diversity affects board functions and, ultimately, shareholder value. Their findings support the view that board diversity has a positive effect on financial performance. The evidence on board committees indicates that gender diversity has a positive effect on financial performance primarily through the audit function of the board whilst ethnic diversity impacts financial performance through all three functions of the board: audit, executive compensation, and director nomination.

Erkut et al. (2008) show that, based on interviews with 50 women directors, 12 CEOs, and seven corporate secretaries from Fortune 1000 companies, a critical mass of three or more women directors can cause a fundamental change in the boardroom and enhance corporate governance. The content of boardroom discussion is more likely to include the perspectives of multiple stakeholders; difficult issues and problems are less likely to be ignored or brushed aside; and boardroom dynamics are more open and collaborative.

Grosvold and Brammer (2011) find that 'as much as half the variation in the presence of women on corporate boards across countries is attributable to national institutional systems and that culturally and legally-oriented institutional systems appear to play the most significant role in shaping board diversity'.

Ferreira (2011) discusses the potential costs and benefits of board diversity arising from the academic literature. The costs include conflict, lack of co-operation, and insufficient communication; choosing directors with little experience, inadequate qualifications, or who are overused; and conflicts of interests and agenda pushing. The benefits include creativity and different perspectives; access to resources and connections; career incentives through signalling and mentoring; and public relations, investor relations, and legitimacy. From his discussion of board diversity literature, he concludes that 'making a business case for women in the boardroom on the basis of statistical evidence linking women to profits obviously creates the possibility of a business case against women if the evidence turns out to suggest that women reduce profits ... the research on board diversity is best used as a means to understand the costs and benefits of diversity in the workplace and to study corporate governance issues'.

Rhode and Packel (2014) explore the case for board diversity in the light of competing research findings. They conclude that:

> the relationship between diversity and financial performance has not been convincingly established. The review does, however, find some theoretical and empirical basis for believing that when diversity is well managed, it can improve decision making and can enhance a corporation's public image by conveying commitments to equal opportunity and inclusion. To achieve such benefits, diversity must ultimately extend beyond tokenism, and corporations must be held more accountable for their progress.

Post and Byron (2014) undertook a meta-analysis of 140 studies and examined whether results vary by firms' legal/regulatory and socio-cultural contexts. They found that:

> female board representation is positively related to accounting returns and that this relationship is more positive in countries with stronger shareholder protections—perhaps because shareholder protections motivate boards to use the different knowledge, experience, and values that each member brings to the board. Although the relationship between female board representation and market performance is near-zero, the relationship is positive in countries with greater gender parity (and negative in countries with low gender parity)—perhaps because societal gender differences in human capital may influence investors' evaluations of the future earning potential of firms that have more female directors. Lastly, we found that female board representation is positively related to boards' two primary responsibilities, monitoring and strategy involvement. For both firm financial performance and board activities, we found mean effect sizes comparable to those found in meta-analyses of other aspects of board composition.

There has been much discussion about the extent to which investors might influence firms to have more diverse boards. Marquardt and Wiedman (2016) investigate the impact of shareholder activism on gender diversity of boards. Using a sample of US S&P 1500 firms over 1997–2011, and taking into account that campaigns for increased gender diversity may be driven by either economic efficiency or social legitimacy concerns, they find that 'female board representation and board independence are negatively associated with the likelihood of being targeted by a shareholder proposal related to gender diversity. We further document that financially motivated activists are more likely to target firms with extremely low female board representation than are socially motivated activists.'

The pay gap between male and female directors is in the spotlight and a study of executives in S&P 1500 firms over 1996–2010 by Carter et al. (2017), found significant salary and total compensation gaps between female and male executives. The authors investigate two possible explanations for the gaps and they

> find support for greater female risk aversion as one contributing factor. Female executives hold significantly lower equity incentives and demand larger salary premiums for bearing a given level of compensation risk. These results suggest that females' risk aversion contributes to the observed lower pay levels through its effect on ex ante compensation structures. We also find evidence that the lack of gender diversity on corporate boards affects the size of the gaps. In firms with a higher proportion of female directors on the board, the gaps in salary and total pay levels are lower. Together, these findings suggest that female higher risk aversion may act as a barrier to full pay convergence, despite the mitigating effect from greater gender diversity on the board.

Byron and Post (2016) undertake a meta-analysis of 87 independent samples which they find

> suggest that, while generally positive, the female board representation–social performance relationship is even more positive in national contexts when boards may be more motivated to draw on the resources that women directors bring to a board (i.e., among firms operating in countries with stronger shareholder protections) and in contexts where intra-board power distribution may be more balanced (i.e., in countries with higher gender parity) … Our results suggest that, to enhance any benefits of diversity for corporate social performance, efforts be directed at holding boards more accountable toward diverse stakeholders and improving the status of women in society and in the workforce.

Whilst many of the studies on board diversity have focused on gender diversity, Guest (2016 and 2017)) have examined two different aspects relating to ethnic minority directors. Guest (2016) examines the mobility of minority executives, defined as ethnic minority and female executives, in publicly listed US firms. He finds that:

> minority executives as a whole experience lower promotion, higher demotion, and higher exit than Caucasian males. Female and African American executives account for the majority of these differences. Specifically, female executives experience lower promotion and exit, while African Americans experience lower promotion, higher demotion, and higher exit. In contrast, Asian and Hispanic executives do not experience different mobility outcomes from Caucasian executives.

In a second study, Guest (2017) examines the compensation of ethnic minority executives in listed US firms. He finds that:

> the total pay of African American executives is 9 percent lower than that earned by Caucasians. This is due to lower base salary, lower bonus, and lower restricted stock grants. The lower bonus is due to a lower sensitivity to above-average firm performance. African Americans also earn significantly less on the exercise of stock options, increasing the pay gap to 17 percent for total ex-post pay. In contrast to African Americans, the compensation of Hispanic and Asian executives is comparable to Caucasians.

With the growing emphasis on board diversity, there is likely to be an increasing number of studies on board diversity and its impact on board dynamics, firm performance, corporate governance, corporate social responsibility and other aspects.

Conclusions

In this chapter the different types of board structure, unitary or dual, have been discussed. We have seen that the UK has a unitary board structure and that the predominant form of board structure in Europe is also the unitary board structure. The roles and responsibilities of the board, including those of the chair, CEO, senior independent director, and company secretary, have been reviewed.

The role and contribution to be made by key board subcommittees, including audit, remuneration, nomination, risk, and ethics committees are discussed. The increasing emphasis on the importance of the role of non-executive (outside) directors is shown, and the definition of the important criterion of the 'independence' of non-executive directors is analysed, together with the role that non-executive directors play on a company's key board subcommittees. In future, it is likely that non-executive directors will be called upon to play an ever more important role as investors look to the audit committees, in particular, to restore and enhance confidence in companies.

The key areas of board evaluation, succession planning, and board diversity are covered. The impact of board diversity, in terms of gender and ethnicity, is discussed, and the low proportion of female directors and directors from different ethnic groups is highlighted.

Summary

- Board structure may be unitary (single tier) or dual (two tier). In a dual structure there is a supervisory board as well as an executive board of management. Usually, both the unitary board of directors and the supervisory board (in a dual system) are elected by shareholders.
- The board of directors leads and controls the company, and is the link between managers and investors.

- It is desirable to split the roles of chair and CEO so that there is not too much power invested in one individual. The chair is responsible for the running of the board, whilst the CEO is responsible for running the business.

- The board may delegate various activities to board subcommittees, the most common being the audit, remuneration, nomination, risk, and ethics committees.

- The board should include an appropriate number of independent non-executive (outside) directors. The non-executive directors bring a balance to the board, and their experience and knowledge can add value to the board. The non-executive directors make a key contribution through their membership of the board subcommittees.

- Boards should include due consideration of key areas including board evaluation, succession planning, and board diversity.

- Boards should have appropriate diversity in their composition; this should strengthen boards as they will be more capable of reflecting the views of the various stakeholder groups.

Example: Statoil, Norway

Statoil is one of Norway's largest companies. There are a number of legal requirements in Norway relating to members of the board which Statoil is subject to. There is a Norwegian legal requirement for at least 40 per cent of the board members to be female, which means that its board is more diverse than is common in most other countries. Also the companies' employees can be represented by three board members.

Statoil was established in October 2007 following the merger between Statoil and Hydro's oil and gas activities. It is an international energy company primarily focused on upstream oil and gas operations, and operates in 39 oil and gas fields, whilst also being the world's largest operator in waters more than 100 metres deep.

Statoil has a corporate assembly, in accordance with the Norwegian Public Limited Liability Companies Act whereby companies with more than 200 employees must elect a corporate assembly unless otherwise agreed between the company and a majority of its employees. Two-thirds of the members are elected by the AGM and one-third by the employees. The most important duties of the corporate assembly are 'to elect the board of directors, to oversee the board and CEO's management of the company, to make decisions on investments of considerable magnitude in relation to the company's resources and to make decisions involving the rationalisation or reorganisation of operations that will entail major changes in or reallocation of the workforce'.

In the case of Statoil, its Articles of Association provide for a board of nine to 11 members elected by the corporate assembly. Management is not represented on the board, which appoints the president and CEO. The board is subject to Norway's rules which state that all public companies in Norway are obliged to ensure that at least 40 per cent of their board directors are women. Of the ten members, four are female and six male, which meets the legal requirement of at least 40 per cent of the board being female.

The board has three committees: an audit committee; a compensation (remuneration) and executive development committee; and a safety, sustainability, and ethics committee. As at April 2018, all four of the female directors are members of one of the three committees though none presently appears to chair a board committee. This is in contrast to a few years ago when a female director, Grace Reksten Skaugen, chaired the compensation committee. This is interesting as even where females are directors in other countries, such as the UK, it is rare for them to chair a board committee. Three of the ten directors are elected by the employees and represent the employees on the board. One of the three employee-elected directors is female.

Example: McKesson Corporation, USA

This is an example of a well-established US healthcare company which has decided to split the roles of CEO and chair.

McKesson Corporation, ranked fifth in the Fortune 500 in 2017 and with revenues of US$192,487 million, is a global leader in healthcare supply chain management solutions, retail pharmacy, community oncology and specialty care, and healthcare information technology. Founded in 1833 by John McKesson and Charles Olcott in New York City to import and sell therapeutic drugs and chemicals wholesale, it is now the oldest and largest healthcare company in the US.

The roles of CEO and chair have traditionally been combined at McKesson with one individual holding both roles. This is generally not seen as desirable as too much power can be vested in one person and best practice corporate governance is generally to split the two roles. In July 2017, a shareholder proposal on 'Independent Board Chairman' was submitted to McKesson for action at its AGM by the International Brotherhood of Teamsters General Fund (the Teamsters Union is North America's strongest and most diverse labour union). The shareholder proposal urged McKesson 'to take the steps necessary to adopt a policy, with amendments to governing documents as needed, so that, to the extent feasible, the Chairman of the Board shall be an independent director who has not previously served as an executive officer of the Company'. The McKesson Board responded that it had 'considered this proposal and believes it is not in the best interests of McKesson or its shareholders ... The Board should be able to select its leadership structure based on what will best serve shareholders' interests under the circumstances.' Whilst the shareholder proposal was not approved by the members at the AGM, the company stated: 'In the future, the Board may choose to have an independent director serve as Chairman if it were to determine that this decision would be in the best interests of the Company and its shareholders.' It seems that once the incumbent CEO retires, McKesson's board will split the CEO/chair position. This has been welcomed by the Illinois State Treasurer, Michael Frerichs, the West Virginia State Treasurer, John Perdue and the Pennsylvania State Treasurer, Joe Torsella as well as by institutional investors such as Hermes.

 ## Mini case study   Deutsche Bank, Germany

This is an example of a well-established German bank which, whilst perceived as having good corporate governance, had concerned investors with its lack of succession planning and then more recently suffered other setbacks including investors up in arms at the level of bonuses and the bank's strategy, and a rift between the CEO and the chair of the company.

Deutsche Bank is a leading investment bank and, as a German company, it has a dual board. Its system of corporate governance has four key elements: 'good relations with shareholders, effective cooperation between the Management Board and the Supervisory Board, a system of performance-related compensation for managers and employees, as well as transparent and early reporting'.

Deutsche Bank's Supervisory Board has established seven standing committees: audit, nomination, risk, mediation, compensation control, integrity, and the chairman's committee. It is the latter's responsibility for, inter alia,

> preparing the meetings of the Supervisory Board and handling current business between meetings of the Supervisory Board; preparing for decisions by the Supervisory Board on the appointment and dismissal of members of the Management Board, including long-term succession planning for the Management Board, while taking the recommendations of the Nomination Committee into account; concluding, amending and terminating employment and pension contracts in consideration of the plenary Supervisory Board's sole authority to decide on the compensation of the members of the Management Board.

(continued)

Dr Josef Ackermann was Chairman of the Management Board and the Group Executive Committee of Deutsche Bank. He joined the Management Board of Deutsche Bank in 1996 and was responsible for the investment banking division. In 2002 he became Spokesman of the Management Board and Chairman of the Group Executive Committee. He was appointed Chairman of the Management Board in February 2006.

In January 2009 he went to hospital feeling unwell. There was some uncertainty about the nature of his illness, and combined with poor financial results that had been released just a few hours earlier, the bank's shares fell nearly 3 per cent, although they subsequently recovered when news was given that the illness was attributable to a meal of sausages and sauerkraut, hastily eaten at the end of a busy day!

This episode highlights the nervousness that the market feels when it believes that a potential successor might not have been identified for a key role. The fear of a power vacuum or a rudderless ship sends shivers through the market. Ironically, Deutsche Bank was better prepared than many firms in terms of succession planning. In addition, Dr Ackermann's contract was extended from ending in 2010 to 2013, which allowed additional time to identify the most appropriate successor.

In May 2012 there was still considerable unrest at Deutsche Bank's lack of succession planning. So much so that Hermes, the UK fund manager, together with VIP, a German association of institutional shareholders, filed counter resolutions at the AGM, arguing that shareholders should withhold a usually routine confidence vote in the bank's board. This was after the bank's supervisory board failed to agree on a successor and the resulting public discussion was felt to be harmful to potential candidates and to the company itself.

In its Human Resources Report 2014, Deutsche Bank highlighted a new framework for senior leadership development 'to strengthen our leadership capabilities and support career mobility, succession planning and development activity. A Group People Committee was established in September 2013 and is led by Deutsche Bank's Co-Chief Executive Officers.' In relation to succession management, the Report explains that this is

> the active development of the Bank's future senior leaders. This program ensures leadership continuity and the availability of the skills we need to achieve our long-term goals. Succession discussions are grounded in clear criteria, allowing a broad range of candidates to be considered and fairly assessed. In addition to successor suitability, we evaluate risks to both incumbents and the succession pool, and agree on actions to mitigate them ... Senior appointments are centrally coordinated to ensure that the most qualified and suitable talent is readily identified for critical positions. This process is closely linked to our succession planning approach, and supports cross-divisional mobility, career development, retention of key talent and greater progress for women in leadership. To this end, 50% of top management internal appointments were cross-divisional moves and approximately 63% of internal candidates were sourced from the Bank's succession plans. Furthermore, 25% of all Senior Leadership Cadre appointments were female Managing Directors, positively impacting the gender diversity of our most senior management positions.

However more investor unrest occurred in advance of Deutsche Bank's AGM in May 2015, with Hermes expressing its concerns about a range of issues relating to strategy, progress on culture change and the way in which Deutsche Bank had dealt with pending litigation and investigations, and their lack of confidence in the board. In advance of the AGM, the supervisory board announced some changes to the management board but Hermes and other investors did not feel that these changes were enough to alleviate their concerns.

(continued)

At the AGM in 2015 almost 40 per cent of the shareholders present voted against the management board, a strong signal of their lack of confidence in its members and an indication to the supervisory board that the composition of the management should be reviewed. Subsequently Jürgen Fitschen and Anshu Jain, co-CEOs, offered their resignations at an emergency meeting of the supervisory board. John Cryan, a non-executive director, was appointed as co-CEO from 1 July 2015, a move which Hermes supported. John Cryan replaced Anshu Jain, who stepped down at the end of June 2015 whilst Jürgen Fitschen stepped down in May 2016. However Jürgen Fitschen continued to support Deutsche Bank as an advisor and from September 2017 became Head of the Deutsche Bank Foundation which helps young people by initiating projects which give them the opportunity to experience new and unfamiliar fields of activity and helps them to develop their own individual talents.

In 2017, Deutsche Bank reported its third consecutive annual loss despite two and a half years of cost-cutting. However Deutsche Bank recognized that further cost-cutting was still needed; nonetheless it also decided to pay out higher bonuses than in the previous year which it felt were necessary to strengthen its position, retain key staff, and help improve its performance in the future. The Management Board did however waive their variable pay which was welcomed by investors although some investors took the view that the payouts were too high overall and were overly generous to some employees. It seems likely that more severe cuts may be needed in 2018 if Deutsche Bank is to improve its financial performance going forward.

Alongside these financial issues, there have been growing tensions between John Cryan, the CEO, and Paul Achleitner, the Chairman, over Deutsche Bank's performance and the most appropriate strategy for the Bank to help resolve matters and improve performance. Ultimately, Paul Achleitner's views have prevailed, as in April 2018 John Cryan was replaced as CEO by Christian Sewing, an internal appointment. This move has again attracted criticism of Deutsche Bank's succession planning from investors who had been concerned about the differences of opinion between Achleitner and Cryan for many months and who saw the swift replacement of Cryan by Sewing as rushed and chaotic. There is a proposal to be put forward at Deutsche Bank's AGM in May for Achleitner to be dismissed but other investors feel it would not be in the company's best interests to replace the CEO and the Chairman in such a short space of time.

Mini case study questions

1. What corporate governance issues are highlighted in the case of Deutsche Bank?

2. Would these corporate governance issues be of concern in other jurisdictions? If so, would a different corporate governance structure ameliorate the issues in any way?

Questions

The discussion questions to follow cover the key learning points of this chapter. Reading of some of the additional reference material will enhance the depth of the students' knowledge and understanding of these areas.

1. What function does a board perform and how does this contribute to the corporate governance of the company?

2. What are the main subcommittees of the board and what role does each of these subcommittees play?

3. What are the main differences between a unitary board system and a dual board system?

4. How might the 'independence' of non-executive (outside) directors be defined? What contributions can an independent non-executive director make to a robust corporate governance structure in a firm?

5. Critically discuss the importance of board evaluations, succession planning, and board diversity for the effectiveness of the board.

6. Should board and executive pipeline diversity be included as an explicit expectation of investor engagement?

References

Abernathy, J. L., Barnes, M., Stefaniak, C., and Weisbarth, A. (2017), 'An International Perspective on Audit Report Lag: A Synthesis of the Literature and Opportunities for Future Research', *International Journal of Auditing*, Vol. 21, Issue 1, pp. 100–27.

Alhadi, A. K., Hasan, M.M., and Habib, A. (2015), 'Risk Committee, Firm Life Cycle, and Market Risk Disclosures', *Corporate Governance: An International Review*, forthcoming.

Association of British Insurers (2011), *Reporting on Board Effectiveness*, ABI, London.

Association of British Insurers (2012), *Report on Board Effectiveness: Updating progress, promoting best practice*, ABI, London.

Bender, R. (2011), 'The Platonic Remuneration Committee', 10 March 2011. Available at SSRN: http://ssrn.com/abstract=1782642 or http://dx.doi.org/10.2139/ssrn.1782642.

Bezemer, P.-J., Nicholson, G., and Pugliese A. (2018), 'The Influence of Board Chairs on Director Engagement: A Case Based Exploration of Boardroom Decision-Making', *Corporate Governance: An International Review*, forthcoming, doi.org/10.1111/corg.12234.

Byron, K., and Post, C. (2016), 'Women on Boards of Directors and Corporate Social Performance: A Meta-Analysis', *Corporate Governance: An International Review*, Vol. 24, Issue 4, July 2016, pp. 428–42.

Cadbury, Sir Adrian (1992), *Report of the Committee on the Financial Aspects of Corporate Governance*, Gee & Co. Ltd, London.

Cadbury, Sir Adrian (2002), *Corporate Governance and Chairmanship: A Personal View*, Oxford University Press, Oxford.

Carter, D.A., Simkins, B.J., and Simpson, W.G. (2003), 'Corporate Governance, Board Diversity, and Firm Value', *The Financial Review*, Vol. 38, No. 1, pp. 33–53.

Carter, D.A., D'Souza, F., Simkins, B.J., and Simpson, W.G. (2007), 'The Diversity of Corporate Board Committees and Financial Performance', available at SSRN: http://ssrn.com/abstract=972763.

Carter, M.E., Franco, F., and Gine, M. (2017), 'Executive Gender Pay Gaps: The Roles of Female Risk Aversion and Board Representation', *Contemporary Accounting Research*, Vol. 34, Issue 2, Summer 2017, pp. 1232–64.

Charkham, J. (2005), *Keeping Better Company: Corporate Governance Ten Years On*, Oxford University Press, Oxford.

Combined Code (2003), *The Combined Code on Corporate Governance*, FRC, London.

Combined Code (2006), *The Combined Code on Corporate Governance*, FRC, London.

Combined Code (2008), *The Combined Code on Corporate Governance*, FRC, London.

Crane, A., McWilliams, A., Matten, D., Moon, J., and Siegel, D.S. (2008), *The Oxford Handbook of Corporate Social Responsibility*, Oxford University Press, Oxford.

Davies E.M. (2011), *Women on Boards*, Department for Business, Innovation & Skills, London.

Davies E.M. (2012), *Women on Boards, One Year On*, Department for Business, Innovation & Skills, London.

Davies E.M. (2015), *Women on Boards, Five Year Summary, 2015*, BIS, London.

Davies, P.L. and Hopt, K.J. (2013), 'Boards in Europe—Accountability and Convergence', *American Journal of Comparative Law*, Vol. 61, No. 2, pp. 301–75.

Epstein, M.J. and Roy, M.J. (2006), 'Measuring the Effectiveness of Corporate Boards and Directors' in M.J. Epstein and K.O. Hanson (eds), *The Accountable Corporation*, Praeger Publishers, Westport, CT.

Erkut, S., Kramer, V.W., and Konrad, A. (2008), 'Critical Mass: Does the Number of Women on a Corporate Board Make a Difference?' in S. Vinnicombe, V. Singh, R.J. Burke, D. Bilimoria, and M. Huse (eds), *Women on Corporate Boards of Directors: International Research and Practice*, Edward Elgar, Northampton, MA.

eShare (2017), *Under Pressure: the Company Secretary and the Growing Need for Effective Governance*, Newbury, UK.

European Commission (2012), *Women in Economic Decision-Making in the EU: Progress Report*, European Commission, Brussels.

European Commission (2014), *Directive on Disclosure of Non-Financial and Diversity Information*, European Commission, Brussels.

Ezzamel, M. and Watson, R. (1997), 'Wearing Two Hats: The Conflicting Control and Management Roles of Non-Executive Directors' in K. Keasey, S. Thompson, and M. Wright (eds), *Corporate Governance: Economic, Management and Financial Issues*, Oxford University Press, Oxford.

Ferreira, D. (2011), 'Board Diversity' in H. Kent Baker and R. Anderson (eds), *Corporate Governance, A Synthesis of Theory, Research and Practice*, The Robert W. Kolb Series in Finance, John Wiley & Sons Inc., Hoboken, NJ.

Financial Reporting Council (2006), *Good Practice Suggestions from the Higgs Report*, FRC, London.

Financial Reporting Council (2010a), *The UK Corporate Governance Code*, FRC, London.

Financial Reporting Council (2010b), *Guidance on Board Effectiveness*, FRC, London.

Financial Reporting Council (2011), *Developments in Corporate Governance 2011: The Impact and Implementation of the UK Corporate Governance and Stewardship Codes*, FRC, London.

Financial Reporting Council (2014), *The UK Corporate Governance Code*, FRC, London.

Financial Reporting Council (2015a), *Developments in Corporate Governance and Stewardship 2014*, FRC, London.

Financial Reporting Council (2015b), *UK Board Succession Planning*, FRC, London.

Financial Reporting Council (2016), *Guidance on Audit Committees*, FRC, London.

Financial Reporting Council (2018), *The UK Corporate Governance Code*, FRC, London.

García-Sánchez, I.-M., Rodríguez-Domínguez, L., and Frías-Aceituno, J.-V. (2014), 'Board of Directors and Ethics Codes in Different Corporate Governance Systems', *Journal of Business Ethics*, forthcoming.

Ghafran, C. and Yasmin, S. (2018), 'Audit Committee Chair and Financial Reporting Timeliness: A Focus on Financial, Experiential and Monitoring Expertise', *International Journal of Auditing*, Vol. 22, Issue 1, pp. 13–24.

Grosvold, J. and Brammer, S. (2011), 'National Institutional Systems as Antecedents of Female Board Representation: An Empirical Study', *Corporate Governance: An International Review*, Vol. 19, No. 2, pp. 116–35.

Guest, P. (2016), 'Executive Mobility and Minority Status', *Industrial Relations: A Journal of Economy and Society*, Vol. 55, Issue 4, October 2016, pp. 604–31.

Guest, P. (2017), 'Executive Compensation and Ethnic Minority Status', *Industrial Relations: A Journal of Economy and Society*, Vol. 56, Issue 3, July 2017, pp. 427–58.

Guo, L. and Masulis, R.W. (2012), 'Board Structure and Monitoring: New Evidence from CEO Turnover', 12 March 2012. Available at SSRN: http://ssrn.com/abstract=2021468 or http://dx.doi.org/10.2139/ssrn.2021468.

Hampel, Sir Ronnie (1998), *Committee on Corporate Governance: Final Report*, Gee & Co. Ltd, London.

Hampton-Alexander Review (2017), *Improving Gender Balance in FTSE Leadership*, FTSE Women Leaders, sponsored by KPMG, London.

Hermes (2006), *The Hermes Corporate Governance Principles*, Hermes Investment Management Ltd, London.

Higgs, D. (2003), *Review of the Role and Effectiveness of Non-Executive Directors*, DTI, London.

Institute of Directors (2006), *Standards for the Board*, IoD and Kogan Page, London.

International Corporate Governance Network (2013), *Statement and Guidance on Gender Diversity on Boards*, ICGN, London.

Kaczmarek S., Kimino S., and Pye A. (2012), 'Antecedents of Board Composition: The Role of Nomination Committees', *Corporate Governance: An International Review*, Vol. 20, No. 5, pp. 474–89.

Kaplan, R.S. and Norton, D.P. (1992), 'The Balanced Scorecard—Measures that Drive Performance', *Harvard Business Review*, January–February, pp. 71–9.

Kaplan, R.S. and Norton, D.P. (2000), 'Having Trouble With Your Strategy? Then Map It', *Harvard Business Review*, September–October, pp. 167–76.

Kent, P., Kercher, K., and Routledge, J. (2016), 'Remuneration Committees, Shareholder Dissent on CEO Pay and the CEO Pay–Performance Link', *Accounting & Finance*, doi:10.1111/acfi.12222.

KPMG (2002), *Corporate Governance in Europe, KPMG Survey 2001/02*, KPMG, London.

Larcker, D.F. and Tayan, B. (2010), 'CEO Succession Planning: Who's Behind Door Number One?' (24 June 2010), *Rock Center for Corporate Governance at Stanford University Closer Look Series: Topics, Issues and Controversies in Corporate Governance No. CGRP-05*. Available at SSRN: http://ssrn.com/abstract=1678062.

Larcker, D., Griffin, T., Tayan, B., and Miles, S. (2017), 'How Boards Should Evaluate Their Own Performance', *Harvard Business Review*, March 2017.

Laux, V. (2014), 'Corporate Governance, Board Oversight, and CEO Turnover', *Foundations and Trends in Accounting*, Vol. 8, No. 1, pp 1–73.

Liao, C.-H. and Hsu, A.W.-H. (2013), 'Common Membership and Effective Corporate Governance: Evidence from Audit and Compensation Committees', *Corporate Governance: An International Review*, Vol. 21, No. 1, pp. 79–92.

Marquardt C. and Wiedman C. (2016), 'Can Shareholder Activism Improve Gender Diversity on Corporate Boards?', *Corporate Governance: An International Review*, Vol. 24, Issue 4, July 2016, pp. 443–61.

McKinsey & Co. (2002), *Investor Opinion Survey on Corporate Governance*, McKinsey & Co. London.

McNulty, T., Pettigrew, A., Jobome, G., and Morris, C. (2011), 'The Role, Power and Influence of Company Chairs', *Journal of Management and Governance*, Vol. 15, No. 1, pp. 91–121.

Milgram, S. (1974), *Obedience to Authority*, Harper and Row, New York.

Morck, R. (2008), 'Behavioral Finance in Corporate Governance: Economics and Ethics of the Devil's Advocate', *Journal of Management and Governance*, Vol. 12, No. 2, pp. 179–200.

Muravyev, A., Talavera, O., and Weir, C. (2014), 'Performance Effects of Appointing Other Firms' Executive Directors to Corporate Boards: An Analysis of UK Firms', *Review of Quantitative Finance and Accounting*, forthcoming.

Naveen, L., (2006), 'Organizational Complexity and Succession Planning', *Journal of Financial and Quantitative Analysis*, Vol. 41, Issue 3, pp. 661–83.

Organisation for Economic Co-operation and Development (1999), *Principles of Corporate Governance*, OECD, Paris.

Organisation for Economic Co-operation and Development (2004), *Principles of Corporate Governance*, OECD, Paris.

Organisation for Economic Co-operation and Development (2015), *G20/OECD Principles of Corporate Governance*, OECD, Paris.

Parker Review (2017), *A Report into Ethnic Diversity of UK Boards: 'Beyond One by '21'*, sponsored by EY and Linklaters, London.

Pathan, S. (2009), 'Strong Boards, CEO Power and Bank Risk-taking', *Journal of Banking and Finance*, Vol. 33, No. 7, pp. 1340–50.

Post, C. and Byron, K. (2014), 'Women on Boards and Firm Financial Performance: A Meta-Analysis', *Academy of Management Review*, forthcoming.

Rhode, D. and Packel, A.K. (2014), 'Diversity on Corporate Boards: How Much Difference Does Difference Make?', *Delaware Journal of Corporate Law (DJCL)*, Vol. 39, No. 2, pp. 377–426.

Smith, Sir Robert (2003), *Audit Committees Combined Code Guidance*, FRC, London.

Spira, L. (2002), *The Audit Committee: Performing Corporate Governance*, Kluwer Academic Publishers, Dordrecht.

Stevens, J., Steensma, K., Harrison, D., and Cochran, P. (2005), 'Symbolic or Substantive Document? The Influence of Ethics Codes on Financial Executives' Decisions', *Strategic Management Journal*, Vol. 26, No. 2, pp. 181–95.

Sultana, N., Singh, H., and Van der Zahn, J.-L.W.M. (2015), 'Audit Committee Characteristics and Audit Report Lag', *International Journal of Auditing*, Vol. 19, Issue 2, pp. 72–87.

Taylor, B., Stiles, P., and Tampoe, M. (2001), *The Future for the Board*, Director and Board Research, IoD, London.

Turley, S. (2008), 'Developments in the Framework of Auditing Regulation in the United Kingdom', in R. Quick, S. Turley, and M. Willekens (eds), *Auditing, Trust and Governance: Regulation in Europe*, Routledge, London.

Van Den Berghe, L.A.A. and Levrau, A.P.D. (2004), 'Evaluating Boards of Directors: What Constitutes a Good Corporate Board?', *Corporate Governance: An International Review*, Vol. 12, No. 4, October, 461–78.

Withers, M.C., and Fitza, M.A. (2017), 'Do Board Chairs Matter? The Influence of Board Chairs on Firm Performance', *Strategic Management Journal*, Vol. 38, Issue 6, June 2017, pp. 1343–55.

Wong, S.C.Y. (2011), 'Elevating Board Performance: The Significance of Director Mindset, Operating Context, and Other Behavioral and Functional Considerations', Northwestern Law & Econ Research Paper No. 11–12. Available at SSRN: http://ssrn.com/abstract=1832234 or http://dx.doi.org/10.2139/ssrn.1832234.

Yatim, P. (2010), 'Board Structures and the Establishment of a Risk Management Committee by Malaysian Listed Firms', *Journal of Management and Governance*, Vol. 14, No. 1, pp. 17–36.

Yeh Y.-H., Chung H., and Liu C.-L. (2011), 'Committee Independence and Financial Institution Performance during the 2007–08 Credit Crunch: Evidence from a Multi-Country Study', *Corporate Governance: An International Review*, Vol. 19, No. 5, pp. 437–58.

Zaman, M., Hudaib, M., and Haniffa, R. (2011), 'Corporate Governance Quality, Audit Fees and Non-Audit Services Fees', *Journal of Business Finance & Accounting*, Vol. 38, Issue 1–2, January/March 2011, pp. 165–97.

Zorn, M.L., Shropshire, C., Martin, J.A., Combs, J.G., and Ketchen, D, J. (2017), 'Home Alone: The Effects of Lone-Insider Boards on CEO Pay, Financial Misconduct, and Firm Performance', *Strategic Management Journal*, Vol. 38, Issue 13, December 2017, pp. 2623–46.

Useful websites

www.bis.gov.uk The website of the UK Department for Business, Innovation & Skills has a number of references to interesting material relating to directors.

www.conference-board.org The Conference Board is a global, independent business membership and research association working in the public interest.

www.gov.uk/government/policies/corporate-governance Provides information about the UK government's corporate governance activities including links to various corporate governance policy documents and reports.

www.icsa.org.uk The website of the Institute of Chartered Secretaries and Administrators has useful references to matters relating to boards and directors including board effectiveness.

www.iod.com The website of the Institute of Directors has information on a wide range of topics relating to directors.

www.nacdonline.org The website of the US National Association of Corporate Directors.

 Develop your understanding of this chapter and explore the subject further using our online resources at **www.oup.com/uk/mallin6e/**

 FT Clippings

Women break up groupthink, says champion of workplace diversity

Former mining chairman Sir John Parker wants a better gender and ethnic mix on boards

Andrew Hill

Financial Times, 11 February 2018

Within days of taking over as chairman of Anglo American in 2009, Sir John Parker flew to Johannesburg to meet the mining company's senior executives.

One aim was to calm their nerves about a possible bid from rival Xstrata. 'That's not your problem, it's my problem,' Sir John recalls telling them.

Then the Northern Irishman added: 'What I am disturbed about is that many of you seem to have time to spare in which you join with former colleagues in criticising the CEO . . . As far as I'm concerned, that can stop.' Sir John had learnt that Cynthia Carroll, the first woman and first outsider in that role, was the object of 'savage' sexist attacks in the press from some retired Anglo executives. The criticism was seeping into the overwhelmingly male management team. '[The comments] were horrid in the extreme, and they were anti-women—basically, "How could a woman possibly run a company like Anglo?" et cetera, et cetera,' he says.

For once, the rigid Anglo American structure was an advantage. 'You can always underestimate the power you have to make change . . . Anglo was quite a top down, hierarchical company in those days and what the chairman said was listened to.' Within days, executives who he describes as 'the good guys' contacted him to say: 'Thank God someone has put their foot down.'

In fact, Ms Carroll, who had been appointed in 2007, was already taking steps to transform the culture and operations of the group. It was not obvious she needed 'air cover' from Sir John.

Even so, the episode shows how, by combining the direct approach of a trained engineer with a fine appreciation of the politics of the boardroom, Sir John turned into an unlikely champion of diversity on boards.

Sir John has arranged to meet at the West End offices of Spencer Stuart. He chairs the executive search group's advisory council. But it would be no surprise if Spencer Stuart had awarded him a corner office as a tribute to the amount of business he must have brought the headhunting industry. He is nearly 76, and stepped down as chairman of Anglo American last year. But Sir John still chairs Pennon, the listed water and waste management group, and Laing O'Rourke, the privately held engineering company, and was appointed lead non-executive at the Cabinet Office in November.

'I'm still incredibly enthusiastic about business [and] about technology and all it can do for mankind,' says the man who, in his 40s, was dubbed the 'white tornado' for his prematurely grey hair and hyperactive involvement as chairman and chief executive of Harland and Wolff, the Belfast shipyard.

While often referred to as a 'City grandee', Sir John does not come across as grand. Raised on a farm in County Down, Northern Ireland, he trained as a naval architect and engineer.

It might surprise the younger John Parker—then going head to head with grizzled union men in his shipbuilding days—to see how regularly he is now consulted about how to bring more women and minorities on to boards.

He was one of three men on the six-strong steering board of Lord (Mervyn) Davies's 2011 review, which laid out targets for the proportion of women on UK corporate boards, and a founder member of the 30% Club, which campaigns for better gender balance in business. In 2017, he completed a government review (the Parker report) into ethnic diversity, which recommended each FTSE 100 company should have at least one director from an ethnic minority background by 2021.

He says exposure to companies with links to South Africa—from Babcock International, the engineering group he headed in the 1990s, to Anglo American—helped make him aware of the importance of cultural and ethnic diversity. Between 2007 and 2009, he co-chaired Mondi, the packaging and paper group, with Cyril Ramaphosa, the former union boss now tipped to become

South Africa's next president. It taught him, he says, the value of having 'a rich variety of thinking' on boards. 'It's the same with the female mind,' he goes on. Women 'approach issues at a different angle to the male. They break up groupthink, without a doubt'.

Sir John traces the gradual diversification of boards to the 1980s, when he invited Alex Ferry, a trade union official, to become a director of Harland and Wolff. 'I wanted a different voice in the boardroom,' he says.

A mix of skills and backgrounds is 'a real bulwark against the destruction of shareholder value', he continues. 'When you get courageous people around the table, they save companies from making really bad mistakes.' In diverse groups, 'someone is going to ask the unthinkable question'.

Sir John says he has not altered his style of chairmanship as the composition of boards has evolved. 'Integrity and being authentic and being yourself [are] very critical to good leadership,' he says. 'If you're seen to adjust your sails in some way just because you populated the boardroom in a different way, people sense that.'

Both the Davies and Parker reviews favoured putting gentle pressure on boards to meet voluntary diversity targets. Sir John defends the approach against the criticism that it is not aggressive enough. If FTSE 100 companies meet the targets, he says, they will eventually have a slightly higher proportion of directors from ethnic minorities than non-white representation in the overall population of the UK. To hit the goal, boards 'have to be prepared to widen the camera lens', he says, pointing out that there are many outstanding leaders of organisations outside the corporate sector, such as within the National Health Service or at large local councils.

Sir John now resembles the archetypal old, white, male director of British boardrooms past. Does he worry people will say he should step aside and make room for new faces? 'I hope they'd say about me, "The guy's authentic, he's got a mass of experience about him, he clearly has got a very open mind . . . he's just chaired this review on ethnic diversity on boards." You could hardly say this guy is past his sell-by date in terms of being progressive in his thinking.'

His determination to go on offering the benefit of his experience is unmistakable. But at the same time, when the moment comes, Sir John says he will not wait to be pushed: 'I have never, ever stayed long enough for any board to say: "It's time you moved on."'

Crest Nicholson faces potential shareholder revolt

Proxy adviser recommends against moving CEO Stone into chairman's office

Attracta Mooney and Aime Williams

Financial Times, 21 March 2018

UK housebuilder Crest Nicholson faces a potential shareholder revolt at its annual general meeting on Thursday after a leading adviser to investors recommended voting against moving the chief executive to the chairmanship.

Stephen Stone, who has been CEO since 2005, is set to take a step back at the annual meeting on Thursday to become executive chair for one year. Under the proposals, he would then become a non-executive chair for up to another two years.

But Institutional Shareholder Services, which advises more than 1,900 big investors around the world, called for Mr Stone's election as executive chair to be rejected over concerns the appointment would break corporate governance rules and cast doubts on the new chairman's ability to exercise proper scrutiny of the company.

The UK's Corporate Governance Code states that chief executives should not typically go on to chair the same company.

ISS said: 'Such a transition means that the chairman is less likely to bring a properly dispassionate perspective to the board. Further, the ability of the new [chief executive] to implement their strategy may be impaired.'

The advisory group said the rationale provided by Crest Nicholson for why appointing Mr Stone as chairman was a 'better arrangement' than appointing an independent chair and retaining Mr Stone another way was insufficient.

The company has said the reason for the arrangement is to retain Mr Stone's expertise as part of its succession planning process.

Royal London Asset Management, the investment firm, said it would vote against Mr Stone's appointment, believing the three-year period was too long.

Ashley Hamilton Claxton, head of responsible investment, at RLAM, said: 'When you have an executive chairman who ran and built the business, what role does the chief executive play? Who runs the business?'

ISS also expressed concerns about the fee Mr Stone, who was paid £2.2m last year, would receive as chair. It said his proposed fee for his term as a non-executive chair, commencing 2019, was £250,000. This is 60 per cent more than the current chair's fee.

However, Glass Lewis, a rival proxy adviser to ISS, has recommended a vote for Mr Stone's appointment.

It said: 'Given that the board has appointed a senior independent director and has clearly outlined the processes by which it ensures a proper division between management and non-executive oversight, we will refrain from recommending shareholders vote against the chair of the nominations committee for this reason at this time.'

Crest Nicholson declined to comment.

Non-executive chairs going overboard

LEX

Financial Times, 5 January 2018

After a career of midnight phone conferences and early-morning wake-up calls, what could a former FTSE 100 boss want more than a portfolio of non-executive roles? Allan Leighton, former Asda head, came up with the phrase 'going plural' to describe his career of directorships. Overboarding may be a more accurate definition.

Yesterday, Whitbread announced that it had appointed former ITV chief Adam Crozier as chairman, just four months after he took up the same job at Vue International, a cinema chain.

In both cases Mr Crozier is a good pick. The hitch is that both roles have the potential to become intensely time-consuming. Investors are gunning for Whitbread to split off either Premier Inn or Costa Coffee, or both. Vue is considering an IPO. If both occur, Mr Crozier will find himself stretched.

Two, even three, chairmanships are not unusual among big hitters. There are few formal limits to the number of board positions that one person can hold. This causes three potential problems: conflicts of interest, chairs spread too thinly and boardrooms filled with the same (mostly male, white, late middle-aged) faces.

The first and last points are for nomination committees to consider. The second is left to individuals. This is a mistake. The role of a chair in a blue-chip company is an exacting one, particularly so if it is contemplating a takeover or under pressure from investors. As Sir John Peace found while chair at Standard Chartered, Experian and Burberry, problems at one company can easily coincide with problems at another.

This does preclude FTSE 100 chairs from holding other, less time-consuming roles. There is merit to multiplicity that brings in experience.

But this should not involve more than one chairmanship. Proposed governance reforms suggest chairs step down after nine years of non-executive service, to preserve independence.

Proper government should also limit the number of big jobs they can accept.

Directors' performance and remuneration

Learning objectives

- To be aware of the main features of the directors' remuneration debate

- To know the key elements of directors' remuneration

- To assess the role of the remuneration committee in setting directors' remuneration

- To understand the different measures used to link directors' remuneration with performance

- To know the disclosure requirements for directors' remuneration

- To be aware of possible ways of evaluating directors

The directors' remuneration debate

The last two decades have seen considerable shareholder, media, and policy attention given to the issue of directors' remuneration. The debate has tended to focus on four areas: (i) the overall level of directors' remuneration and the role of share options; (ii) the suitability of performance measures linking directors' remuneration with performance; (iii) the role played by the remuneration committee in the setting of directors' remuneration; (iv) the influence that shareholders are able to exercise on directors' remuneration.

The debate about directors' remuneration spans continents and is a topic that is as hotly debated in the USA as it is in the UK. Indeed, the UK's use of share options as long-term incentive devices has been heavily influenced by US practice. Countries that are developing their corporate governance codes are aware of the ongoing issues relating to directors' remuneration and try to address these issues in their own codes. In the UK the debate was driven in the early years by the remuneration packages of the directors of the newly privatized utilities. The perception that directors were receiving huge remuneration packages—and often, it seemed, with little reward to the shareholders in terms of company performance—further fuelled the interest in this area on both sides of the Atlantic. The level of directors' remuneration continues to be a worrying trend and as Lee (2002) commented: 'the evidence in the US is of many companies having given away 10 per cent, and in some cases as much as 30 per cent, of their equity to executive directors and other staff in just the last five years or so. That is clearly not sustainable into the future: there wouldn't be any companies left in public hands if it were.'

It is interesting to note that a comparison of remuneration pay and incentives of directors in the USA and the UK gives a useful insight. Conyon and Murphy (2000) documented the differences in chief executive officer (CEO) pay and incentives in both countries for 1997. They found that CEOs in the USA earned 45 per cent higher cash compensation and 190 per cent higher total compensation than their counterparts in the UK. The implication is that, in the USA, the median CEO received 1.48 per cent of any increase in shareholder wealth compared to 0.25 per cent in the UK; the difference being largely attributable to the extent of the share option schemes in the USA.

The directors' remuneration debate clearly highlights one important aspect of the principal–agent problem discussed at length in Chapter 2. In this context, Conyon and Mallin (1997) highlight that shareholders are viewed as the 'principal' and managers as their 'agents', and that the economics literature, in particular, demonstrates that the compensation received by senior management should be linked to company performance for incentive reasons. Well-designed compensation contracts will help to ensure that the objectives of directors and shareholders are aligned, and so share options and other long-term incentives are a key mechanism by which shareholders try to ensure congruence between directors' and shareholders' objectives.

However, Bebchuk and Fried (2004) highlight that there are significant flaws in pay arrangements, which 'have hurt shareholders both by increasing pay levels and, even more important, by leading to practices that dilute and distort managers' incentives'. More recently the global financial crisis has served to highlight the inequities that exist between executive directors' generous remuneration and the underperformance of the companies that they direct, and the concomitant impact on shareholders who may lose vast sums of money, sometimes their life savings, and employees who may find themselves on shorter working weeks, lower incomes, or being made redundant. The International Labour Organization (ILO) 2008 reported that:

> the gap in income inequality is also widening—at an increasing pace—between top executives and the average employee. For example, in the United States in 2007, the chief executive officers (CEOs) of the 15 largest companies earned 520 times more than the average worker. This is up from 360 times more in 2003. Similar patterns, though from lower levels of executive pay, have been registered in Australia, Germany, Hong Kong (China), the Netherlands and South Africa.

Furthermore the ILO state that:

> developments in global corporate governance have also contributed to perceptions of excessive income inequality. A key development has been the use of so-called 'performance pay systems' for chief executive managers and directors ... Importantly, empirical studies show only very moderate, if any, effects of these systems on company performance. Moreover, large country variations exist, with some countries displaying virtually no relation between performance-pay and company profits ... Altogether, evidence suggests that developments in executive pay may have been both inequality-enhancing and economically inefficient.

UK perspectives

Turner Review (2009)

In the context of the global banking crisis, the UK's Turner Review reported in March 2009 and highlighted that executive compensation incentives encouraged 'some executives and traders to take excessive risks'. The Review emphasizes the distinction between 'short-term remuneration for banks which have received taxpayer support which is a legitimate issue of public concern, and one where governments as significant shareholders have crucial roles to play' and 'long-term concerns about the way in which the structure of remuneration can create incentives for inappropriate risk taking'. The Review therefore recommends that risk management considerations are embedded in remuneration policy, which of course has implications for the remit of remuneration committees and for the amount of time that non-executive directors may need to give.

The House of Commons Treasury Committee reporting in May 2009 on the *Banking Crisis: Reforming Corporate Governance and Pay in the City* stated:

> Whilst the causes of the present financial crisis are numerous and diverse, it is clear that bonus-driven remuneration structures prevalent in the City of London as well as in other financial centres, especially in investment banking, led to reckless and excessive risk-taking. In too many cases the design of bonus schemes in the banking sector were flawed and not aligned with the interests of shareholders and the long-term sustainability of the banks.

The Committee also refers to the complacency of the Financial Services Authority (FSA) and states: 'The Turner Review downplays the role that remuneration structures played in causing the banking crisis, and does not appear to us to accord a sufficiently high priority to a fundamental reform of the bonus culture.' The Committee urges the FSA not to shy away from using its powers to sanction firms whose activities fall short of good practice. The Committee also encourages the use of deferral or clawback mechanisms to help ensure that bonus payments align the interests of senior staff more closely with those of shareholders. Moreover, the Committee believes that links should be strengthened between the remuneration, risk, and audit committees, 'given the cross-cutting nature of many issues, including remuneration' and also advocates

> that remuneration committees would also benefit from having a wider range of inputs from interested stakeholders—such as employees or their representatives and shareholders. This would open up the decision-making process at an early stage to scrutiny from outside the board, as well as provide greater transparency. It would, additionally, reduce the dependence of committees on remuneration consultants.

Walker Review (2009)

Sir David Walker headed a review of corporate governance in the banking sector which reported in 2009. Of its 39 recommendations, 12 related to remuneration (including the role of the board remuneration committee, disclosure of executive remuneration, and the Code of Conduct for executive remuneration consultants written by the Remuneration Consultants Group). Some of the recommendations were to be taken forward by the FRC through amendments to the Combined Code, whilst others were to be taken forward by the FSA. When the UK Corporate Governance Code 2010 was introduced, it incorporated some of the Walker Report recommendations, including that performance-related pay should be aligned to the long-term interests of the company and to its risk policy and systems.

FSA PS10/20 Revising the Remuneration Code (2010)

In December 2010 the FSA issued *PS10/20 Revising the Remuneration Code*. The revised framework for regulating financial services firms' remuneration structures and extension of the scope of the FSA Remuneration Code, arose primarily as a result of amendments to the Capital Requirements Directive (CRD3) which aimed to align remuneration principles across the EU, but also took into account provisions relating to remuneration within the Financial Services Act 2010, Sir David Walker's review of corporate governance, and also lessons learned from the FSA's implementation of its Remuneration Code. The Remuneration Code's 12 principles cover the three main areas of regulatory scope: governance; performance measurement; and remuneration structures and provide the standards that banks, building societies, and some investment firms have to meet when setting pay and bonus awards for their staff. The aim is 'to ensure firms' remuneration practices are consistent with effective risk management'.

High Pay Commission

The High Pay Commission was an independent inquiry into high pay and boardroom pay across the public and private sectors in the UK. In 2010 they started their year-long inquiry into pay at the top of UK companies and found 'evidence that excessive high pay damages companies, is bad for our economy and has negative impacts on society as a whole. At its worst, excessive high pay bears little relation to company success and is rewarding failure.' Their report *More for Less: What has happened to pay at the top and does it matter?* issued in May 2011, stated: 'Pay is about just rewards, social cohesion and a functioning labour market, and it is the view of the High Pay Commission that the exponential pay increases at the top of the labour market are ultimately a form of market failure.'

The High Pay Commission's final report *Cheques with Balances: Why tackling high pay is in the national interest* was issued in November 2011. The report recommends a 12-point plan based on the principles of accountability, transparency, and fairness aimed at redressing the out-of-control executive pay spiral. Vince Cable, the Business Secretary at the time, took forward ten of the 12 recommendations from the High Pay Commission. Furthermore, in January 2012 he announced the government's next steps to address failings in the corporate governance framework for executive remuneration. Following this, a consultation was launched in March 2012 by BIS in *Executive Pay, Shareholder Voting Rights Consultation* which provides more details on a new model for shareholder voting. The BIS website lists the main components of this as:

- an annual binding vote on future remuneration policy;
- increasing the level of support required on votes on future remuneration policy;
- an annual advisory vote on how remuneration policy has been implemented in the previous year;
- a binding vote on exit payments over one year's salary.

As part of government reforms in this area, Deborah Hargreaves, who chaired the High Pay Commission, was appointed to run a new High Pay Centre to monitor pay at the top of the income distribution and set out a road map towards better business and economic success.

High Pay Centre

In May 2012 the High Pay Centre issued *It's How You Pay It*, a report that looked at the current situation with regard to executive pay packages, the elements included in them, and how they can be calculated. Subsequently, the High Pay Centre published *Performance-related Pay is Nothing of the Sort* (2014) which showed that 'growth in executive pay, bonuses and incentive payments has vastly outpaced performance as measured by every indicator in common use'.

In its Annual Survey of FTSE 100 CEO pay packages in August 2016, the High Pay Centre found that there is 'no end to the rise and rise in top pay'. FTSE 100 CEOs continued to see overall pay packages grow by at least 10 per cent whilst other employees saw little or no growth thereby exacerbating the gap between the pay of bosses and the pay of workers. However in the CIPD/High Pay Centre *Executive Pay, Review of FTSE 100 Executive Pay Packages* published in August 2017, the CIPD/High Pay Centre state: 'our review of FTSE 100 CEO pay packages shows a sharp turnaround in the rising trend of remuneration. FTSE 100 CEOs have seen an overall drop in pay packages, especially at the top end, though the gulf between the highest paid executives and the rest of the workforce still remains.'

Whilst the levels of voting dissent against CEO pay packages have declined in the last year, nonetheless there is an increased focus by institutional shareholders on remuneration policy, the remuneration report, and CEO pay. Importantly the UK government has also focused in on the excessive pay packages of CEOs and some other directors. Arising from this, in December 2017, the Investment Association launched the world's first ever Public Register of listed companies which have had significant shareholder rebellions. The Public Register includes FTSE All-Share companies which have received votes of 20 per cent or more against any resolution or withdrew a resolution prior to their Annual General Meeting (AGM) in 2017. The majority of high dissent resolutions relate to executive pay. The Register will increase transparency, accountability, and scrutiny of listed companies by shareholders, media, and the wider public. Moreover the Register will make it easier to see how companies respond to investors' concerns.

The Directors' Remuneration Reporting Regulations (2013)

Executive remuneration has remained a hot topic with a high profile amongst investors, the media, and the government. The Directors' Remuneration Reporting Regulations 2013, introduced by the UK government, brought in new rules which gave shareholders a binding vote on directors' pay. From October 2013 UK quoted companies had to prepare a remuneration report which details: any substantial changes to directors' remuneration made during the financial year being reported on and why they were made; a forward-looking directors' remuneration policy (required when the policy is being put to the shareholders for approval); and an annual report showing how the remuneration policy has been implemented and including details of actual payments made to each director and payments made for loss of office in the financial year; and how the company intends to implement the policy in the following financial year. The annual remuneration report is subject to an annual *advisory* shareholder vote. However shareholders have a *binding* vote on the remuneration policy, which has to be approved at least every three years. The 'say on pay' is discussed in more detail later.

Executive Remuneration Working Group Final Report July 2016

The Executive Remuneration Working Group, chaired by Nigel Wilson, the Group Chief Executive of Legal & General Group Plc, was established by the Investment Association in the autumn of 2015 as an independent panel to address the concern that executive remuneration has become too complex and is not fulfilling its purpose. The Working Group published its interim report in April 2016, and after consultation with a wide range of stakeholders, published its final report in July 2016.

The Executive Remuneration Working Group has made ten recommendations relating to increasing flexibility (recommendation 1); strengthening remuneration committees and their accountability (recommendations 2, 3, and 4); improving shareholder engagement (recommendations 5 and 6); increasing transparency on target setting and use of discretion (recommendations 7 and 8); and addressing the level of executive pay (recommendations 9 and 10).

Corporate Governance Reform (2017)

In August 2017, the Department for Business, Energy & Industrial Strategy (BEIS) issued its report *Corporate Governance Reform, the government response to the green paper consultation* which detailed its recommendations and conclusions based on the consultation of their Green Paper on Corporate Governance Reform (2016). The Executive Summary details nine headline proposals for reform across the three specific aspects of corporate governance on which the consultation focused, one of these aspects being executive pay. Of particular note are that all listed companies will have to reveal the pay ratio between bosses and workers (i.e. the CEO and the average UK employee); all listed companies with significant shareholder opposition to executive pay packages will have their names published on a new public register (the Investment Association Public Register discussed earlier) and companies will have to set out steps that they will take when they encounter opposition to executive pay increases; and remuneration committees will take a broader responsibility for pay within the group and actively explain differentials on quantum and format of remuneration for executive directors and employees as a whole.

UK Corporate Governance Code (2018)

In December 2017 the FRC issued for consultation *Proposed Revisions to the UK Corporate Governance Code*. The FRC responded to the recommendations made in the government's response to the Green Paper Consultation on Corporate Governance Reform (August 2017)—including for companies to have a method of consulting with their employees; extending recommended minimum vesting and post-vesting holding periods for executive share awards from three years to five years; that chairs of remuneration committees should have at least 12 months' previous experience; and specifying the steps companies should take when they encounter significant shareholder opposition to executive pay policies and awards.

In July 2018, the FRC issued the UK Corporate Governance Code 2018 in which the section on Remuneration lists three Principles and details ten Provisions. The three Principles (P, Q, and R) are as follows:

- P. Remuneration policies and practices should be designed to support strategy and promote long-term sustainable success. Executive remuneration should be aligned to company purpose and values, and be clearly linked to the successful delivery of the company's long-term strategy.
- Q. A formal and transparent procedure for developing policy on executive remuneration and determining director and senior management remuneration should be established. No director should be involved in deciding their own remuneration outcome.
- R. Directors should exercise independent judgement and discretion when authorizing remuneration outcomes, taking account of company and individual performance, and wider circumstances.

Overall the three Principles and the supporting Provisions provide for more demanding criteria for remuneration and clearer reporting. Remuneration committees, comprised of independent non-executive directors, should ensure that executive director remuneration policy and practices are, inter alia, aligned to culture so that 'incentive schemes should drive behaviours consistent with company purpose, values and strategy' (Provision 40). The description of the remuneration committee's work in the annual report should include, inter alia, 'reasons why the remuneration is appropriate using internal and external measures, including pay ratios and pay gaps ... what engagement has taken place with shareholders and the impact this has had on remuneration policy and outcomes ... what engagement with the workforce has taken place to explain how executive remuneration aligns with wider company pay policy...' (Provision 41).

As can be seen, there has been much heated debate about flawed remuneration packages which enable large bonuses to be paid even when the company has not met the performance criteria associated with those bonuses; which also allow departing directors to have golden goodbyes in the form of generous (some would say obscene) payments into their pension pots, or other means of easing their departure from the company; and bring about much distaste regarding the growing multipliers of executive remuneration compared to that of the average employee. The debate is far from over, although one thing is certain, which is that, especially given recent developments in UK corporate governance, the remuneration committee and the company's shareholders and other stakeholders will be looking ever more carefully at the remuneration packages being proposed for executive directors in the future, given the expectations of government and the public about what remuneration packages should look like.

Key elements of directors' remuneration

Directors' remuneration can encompass six elements:

- base salary
- bonus
- stock options
- restricted share plans (stock grants)
- pension
- benefits (car, healthcare, etc.).

However, most discussions of directors' remuneration will tend to concentrate on the first four elements listed earlier and this text will also take that approach.

Base salary

Base salary is received by a director in accordance with the terms of his/her contract. This element is not related either to the performance of the company nor to the performance of the individual director. The amount will be set with due regard to the size of the company, the industry sector, the experience of the individual director, and the level of base salary in similar companies. Usually only the base salary should be pensionable.

Bonus

An annual bonus may be paid, which is linked to the accounting performance of the firm.

Stock options

Stock options give directors the right to purchase shares (stock) at a specified exercise price over a specified time period. Directors may also participate in long-term incentive plans (LTIPs). UK share options generally have performance criteria attached, and much discussion is centred around these performance criteria, especially as to whether they are appropriate and demanding enough.

Restricted share plans (stock grants)

Shares may be awarded with limits on their transferability for a set time (usually a few years), and various performance conditions should be met.

Role of the remuneration committee

The UK Corporate Governance Code (2010, updated 2012, 2014, 2016, and 2018) (hereafter 'the Code') recommends that there should be 'a formal and transparent procedure for developing policy on executive remuneration and determining director and senior management remuneration' (Principle Q). In practice, this normally results in the appointment of a remuneration committee.

The remuneration committee's role and composition were discussed in Chapter 8. However, in this chapter we consider the effect of remuneration committees on directors' remuneration levels in recent years. Sykes (2002) points out that, although remuneration committees predominantly consist of a majority, or more usually entirely, of non-executive directors, these non-executive directors 'are effectively chosen by, or only with the full agreement of, senior management'. Given that the non-executive directors of one company may be executive directors of another (unrelated) company, they may not be willing to stipulate demanding performance criteria because they may have a self-interest in ensuring that they themselves can go on earning a high salary without unduly demanding performance criteria being set by their own companies' remuneration committees. There is also another aspect, which is that remuneration committees will generally not wish the executive directors to be earning less than their counterparts in other companies, so they will be more inclined to make recommendations that will put the directors into the top or second quartile of executive remuneration levels. It is certainly the case that executive remuneration levels have increased fairly substantially since remuneration committees were introduced which, of course, was not the intended effect. Sykes (2002) makes the pertinent point that all the remuneration packages now so widely criticized as flawed and inappropriate were once approved by an 'independent' remuneration committee.

The performance measures that the remuneration committee decides should be used are therefore central to aligning directors' performance and remuneration in the most appropriate way. Remuneration committees are offered some guidance by the Code (2018) as discussed earlier.

In the UK both the National Association of Pension Funds (NAPF) and the Association of British Insurers (ABI) have been involved in the debate about executive remuneration and have issued guidance in this area. The ABI issued a number of guidelines on this area including *Guidelines on Executive Remuneration* (2002), *Principles and Guidelines on Remuneration* (2005), *Executive Remuneration—ABI Guidelines on Policies and Practices* (2007), and the *ABI Principles of Executive Remuneration* (2011).

Following the merger of ABI Investment Affairs with the IMA on 30 June 2014, the enlarged Investment Management Association (IMA), renamed The Investment Association in January 2015, has assumed responsibility for guidance previously issued by the ABI.

The IMA Principles of Remuneration 2014 set out members' views on the role of shareholders and directors in relation to remuneration and the manner in which remuneration should be determined and structured. In the Foreword to the Principles, the IMA emphasizes the role of dialogue: 'As ever, a continued and close dialogue between companies and their shareholders is crucial.'

In March 2012 Hermes Equity Ownership Services (Hermes EOS) and the NAPF for the first time brought together remuneration committee members from 44 of the FTSE 100 companies and 42 occupational pension funds from across the globe. The dialogue focused on executive pay structures and how long-term investors can best challenge and support companies in improving remuneration practices through engagement and the considered use of their voting powers. The intention being to shift the current political and societal debate with a view to creating greater alignment between companies and their shareholders, and to promote a culture within companies that rewards long-term success and alignment across the organization.

Remuneration Principles for Building and Reinforcing Long-Term Business Success (2013) were jointly produced by Hermes EOS, the Pensions and Lifetime Savings Association formerly known as the National Association of Pension Funds (NAPF), BT Pension Scheme, Railpen Investments, and Universities Superannuation Scheme (USS) in November 2013. These Principles are intended to 'provide high-level guidance to companies about our expectations of their remuneration structures and practices. The Principles deliberately avoid prescribing any specific structures or measures; instead we expect companies to articulate clearly to shareholders how their pay policies meet these principles in a manner which is most appropriate for their specific situation.' There are five Principles:

(1) Remuneration committees should expect executive management to make a material long-term investment in shares of the businesses they manage; (2) Pay should be aligned to long-term success and the desired corporate culture throughout the organisation; (3) Pay schemes should be clear, understandable for both investors and executives, and ensure that executive rewards reflect long-term returns to shareholders; (4) Remuneration committees should use the discretion afforded them by shareholders to ensure that awards properly reflect business performance; and (5) Companies and investors should have regular discussions on strategy and long-term performance.

Subsequently, in November 2016, Hermes published *Remuneration Principles: Clarifying Expectations*. Hermes reinforce that the 2013 Principles have enduring value and relevance across markets and that in the 2016 publication, they wish to reassert the Principles and clarify how companies might implement them.

Role of remuneration consultants

Remuneration committees may draw on the advice of specialist remuneration consultants when constructing executive remuneration packages. The role of remuneration (compensation) consultants has started to receive more attention in the last few years in the academic literature. Voulgaris et al. (2010), in a study of 500 UK firms from the FTSE 100, FTSE 250, and the Small Cap indices, find that compensation consultants may have a positive effect on the structure of CEO pay since they encourage incentive-based compensation, and they also show that economic determinants, rather than CEO power, explain the decision to hire compensation consultants.

Murphy and Sandino (2010) examine the potential conflicts of interest that remuneration consultants face, which may lead to higher recommended levels of CEO pay. They find 'evidence in both the US and Canada that CEO pay is higher in companies where the consultant provides other services, and that pay is higher in Canadian firms when the fees paid to consultants for other services are large relative to the fees for executive-compensation services. Contrary to expectations, we find that pay is higher in US firms where the consultant works for the board rather than for management.'

Similarly, Conyon et al. (2011), in a study of compensation consultants used in 232 large UK companies, find that 'consultant use is associated with firm size and the equity pay mix. We also show that CEO pay is positively associated with peer firms that share consultants, with higher board and consultant interlocks, and some evidence that where firms supply other business services to the firm, CEO pay is greater.'

Bender (2011), drawing on interview data with a selection of FTSE 350 companies, finds that remuneration committees employ consultants for a number of reasons. First:

> the consultant is to act as an expert, providing proprietary data against which companies can benchmark pay, and giving insight and advice into the possibilities open for plan design and implementation. In this role, consultants have a direct and immediate influence on executive pay. That is, by influencing the choice of comparators, consultants both identify and drive the market for executive pay. They also bring to bear their knowledge of pay plans, and their views on what is currently acceptable to the market, thus spreading current practice more widely and institutionalizing it as 'best practice'.

Secondly, they act as liaisons and serve an important role in the communication with certain institutional investors. Thirdly Bender finds that they legitimize the decisions of the remuneration committee by providing an element of perceived independence but she points out that 'this route to legitimacy is under threat as various constituencies question consultants' independence'.

Also questioning the independence of remuneration consultants, Kostiander and Ikäheimo (2012), examine the remuneration consultant–client relationship in the non-Anglo-American context of Finland, focusing on what consultants do under heavy political remuneration guidance. Their findings show that 'restrictive remuneration guidelines can be ineffective and lead to standardized pay designs without providing competitive advantage. Shareholders should request greater transparency concerning remuneration design. The role of consultants should be considered proactively in the guidelines, even by limiting the length of the consultant–client relationship or increasing their transparency.'

Marsland (2015a) carried out a study for the High Pay Centre, *Are Remuneration Consultants Independent?*, in which he

> reveals flaws in the reporting of the relationship between remuneration consultants and companies. Almost all companies use a remuneration consultant from a firm that they pay to provide other services. Despite this obvious potential for conflict of interest the fees paid for other services are absent from disclosures. This flaw in disclosure prevents a proper assessment by shareholders of the independence of the remuneration advice provided.

Following a US SEC requirement introduced in 2009 that firms disclose fees paid to compensation consultants for both consulting and other services, Chu et al. (2017) show that:

> the disclosure rule change acted as a separating device distinguishing firms likely to have used compensation consultants to extract rents from shareholders from firms that were likely to have used consultants to optimally set pay. We conclude that not all multiservice consultants are conflicted while not all specialist consultants are guardians of shareholder value. Our study provides a more nuanced view of the association between compensation consultant choices and executive pay.

Finally, Murphy and Sandino (2017) find that 'firms that use consultants have higher-paid CEOs. We show that this positive and robust association is not only driven by consultant conflicts of interest but also (and even to a larger degree) by the composition and complexity of pay: firms using consultants compensate their CEOs with a higher percentage of incentive pay and more complex incentive plans, which in turn, are associated with higher levels of pay.'

There seems to be a growing body of evidence highlighting the role of remuneration consultants in the setting of executive remuneration, and raising issues relating to their independence and the impact on CEO pay when the remuneration consultants offer other services to the firm.

Performance measures

Performance criteria will clearly be a key aspect of ensuring that directors' remuneration is perceived as fair and appropriate for the job and in keeping with the results achieved by the directors. Performance criteria may differentiate between three broadly conceived types of measures: (i) market-based measures; (ii) accounts-based measures; and (iii) individual-based measures. Some potential performance criteria are:

- shareholder return;
- share price (and other market-based measures);
- profit-based measures;
- return on capital employed;
- earnings per share;
- individual director performance (in contrast to corporate performance measures).

Sykes (2002) highlights a number of problems with the way in which executive remuneration is determined: (i) management is expected to perform over a short period of time and this is a clear mismatch with the underlying investor time horizons; (ii) management remuneration is not correlated to corporate performance; (iii) earnings before interest, tax, and amortization (EBITA) is widely used as a measure of earnings and yet this can encourage companies to gear up (or have high leverage) because the measure will reflect the flow of earnings from high leverage but not the service (interest) charge for that debt. He suggests that the situation would be improved if there were: longer term tenures for corporate management; more truly independent non-executive directors; the cessation of stock options and, in their place, a generous basic salary and five-year restricted shares (shares that could not be cashed for five years).

The ABI (2002, 2005) Guidelines state that total shareholder return relative to an appropriate index or peer group is a generally acceptable performance criterion. The Guidelines also favour performance being measured over a period of at least three years to try to ensure sustained improvements in financial performance rather than the emphasis being placed on short-term performance. Share incentive schemes should be available to employees and executive directors but not to non-executive directors (although non-executive directors are encouraged to have shareholdings in the company, possibly by receiving shares in the company, at full market price, as payment of their non-executive director fees).

The ABI published its *Disclosure Guidelines on Socially Responsible Investment* in 2007. Interestingly, the Guidelines said that the company should state in its remuneration report 'whether the remuneration committee is able to consider corporate performance on ESG [environmental, social, and governance] issues when setting remuneration of executive directors. If the report states that the committee has no such discretion, then a reason should be provided for its absence.' Also 'whether the remuneration committee has ensured that the incentive structure for senior management does not raise ESG risks by inadvertently motivating irresponsible behaviour.' These are significant recommendations in the bid to have ESG issues recognized and more widely taken into consideration.

Another area that has attracted attention, and which is addressed in joint ABI/NAPF guidance, is the area of 'golden goodbyes'. This is another dimension to the directors' remuneration debate because it is not only ongoing remuneration packages that have attracted adverse comment, but also the often seemingly excessive amounts paid to directors who leave a company after failing to meet their targets. Large pay-offs or 'rewards for failure' are seen as inappropriate because such failure may reduce the value of the business and threaten the jobs of employees. Often the departure of underperforming directors triggers a clause in their contract that leads to a large undeserved pay-off, but now some companies are cutting the notice period from one year to, for example, six months where directors fail to meet performance targets over a period of time, so that a non-performing director whose contract is terminated receives six months' salary rather than one year's salary.

The ABI/NAPF guidance emphasizes the importance of ensuring that the design of contracts should not commit companies to payment for failure; the guidance also suggests that phased payments are a useful innovation to include in directors' contracts. A phased payment involves continuing payment to a departing director for the remaining term of the contract but payments cease when the director finds fresh employment. In February 2008 the ABI and the NAPF issued joint guidance entitled *Best Practice on Executive Contracts and Severance—A Joint Statement by the Association of British Insurers and the National Association of Pension Funds*. The guidance aims to assist boards and their remuneration committees 'with the design and application of contractual obligations for senior executives so that they are appropriately rewarded but are not rewarded for under-performance'. The concluding statement to the guidance succinctly sums up the views of many: 'It is unacceptable that poor performance by senior executives, which detracts from the value of an enterprise and threatens the livelihood of employees, can result in excessive payments to departing directors. Boards have a responsibility to ensure that this does not occur.'

In relation to bonuses, Fattorusso et al. (2007) point out that:

> the focus of most criticism has been on salary, severance payments and various long-term incentives (particularly share options). However, executive bonuses have attracted little attention and have been only lightly regulated. This raises important questions. Has lighter regulation been associated with significant levels of rent extraction through bonuses, that is, a weak relation between bonus pay and shareholder returns?

Bruce and Skovoroda (2015) carried out a study on *The Empirical Literature on Executive Pay: Context, the Pay-Performance Issue and Future Directions* for the High Pay Centre. They state that:

> a notable feature of the literature as a whole is the absence of strong consensus in terms of the pay-performance relationship, a factor explained both in terms of the vagaries and inefficiencies of the executive labour market and the diversity of methods employed by academic researchers in exploring it ... The review concludes by identifying how the dominant focus on the pay-performance relationship has, in recent years, given way to a more varied empirical agenda on executive pay.

Finally, Marsland (2015b) carried out a study for the High Pay Centre on *The Metrics Re-Loaded: Examining executive remuneration performance measures.* He looks at which measures are being used by companies and contrasts UK measures with those applied in Germany and France.

Remuneration of non-executive directors

The remuneration of non-executive directors is decided by the board, or where required by the articles of association, or the shareholders in general meeting. Non-executive directors should be paid a fee commensurate with the size of the company, and the amount of time that they are expected to devote to their role. Large UK companies would tend to pay in excess of £50,000 (often considerably more) to each non-executive director. The remuneration is generally paid in cash although some advocate remunerating non-executive directors with the company's shares to align their interests with those of the shareholders. However, it has generally been viewed as not being a good idea to remunerate non-executive directors with share options (as opposed to shares) because this may give them a rather unhealthy focus on the short-term share price of the company.

Nonetheless, in 2010 the International Corporate Governance Network (ICGN) published its *Non-executive Director Remuneration Guidelines and Policies*. The recommendations include that the retainer/annual fee should be the only form of cash compensation paid to non-executive directors, and that there should not be a separate fee for attendance at board meetings or at committee meetings. However, it is recognized that companies may want to differentiate the fee amount to reflect the differing workloads of individual non-executive directors, for example, where a non-executive director is also a committee chair. Interestingly, the Guidelines state that, in order to align non-executive director–shareowner interests, non-executive directors may receive stock awards or similar. However, any such 'equity-based compensation to non-executive directors should be fully vested on the grant date ... a marked difference to the ICGN's policy on executive compensation which calls for performance-based vesting on equity-based awards'.

Importantly, the ICGN also states: 'Separate from ownership requirements, the ICGN believes companies should adopt holding requirements for a significant majority of equity-based grants. These policies should require that non-executive directors retain a significant portion of equity grants until at least two years after they are retired from the board.' Such policies would help ensure that interests remain aligned.

In 2016, the ICGN issued *Guidance on Non-Executive Director Remuneration* updating its earlier guidance. This latest version contains two main changes including that the expectations of non-executive directors to attain a significant shareholding are more clearly defined; and explicit reference is made to the remuneration of board chairs.

There has been relatively little academic research into non-executive directors' remuneration. Hahn and Lasfer (2011) referred to non-executive directors' remuneration as 'an enigma'. A study by Mallin et al. (2015) compares the remuneration of independent non-executive directors in Italy and the UK. The authors find that 'independent non-executive directors do not receive performance-based remuneration except in very limited instances. In line with equity and human capital theories, we find that independent non-executive directors do receive higher remuneration when they exert more effort, have more responsibilities, and have a higher human capital.'

In an Australian context, Bugeja et al. (2016) find that:

> NED compensation is associated with firm size, complexity, growth, risk and liquidity. It is also associated with director reputation, experience, connectedness and the directors' involvement with the firm. The additional compensation paid to the chairperson is positively associated with their prior experience and negatively associated with NED reputation and involvement. We find inconclusive evidence on the association between changes in NED compensation and firm performance.

Disclosure of directors' remuneration

There has been considerable discussion about how much disclosure there should be of directors' remuneration and how useful detailed disclosures might be. The Greenbury Report, issued in the UK in 1995, was established on the initiative of the Confederation of British Industry (CBI) because of public concern about directors' remuneration. Whilst the work of the Greenbury Report focused on the directors of public limited companies, it hoped that both smaller listed companies and unlisted companies would find its recommendations useful.

Central to the Greenbury Report recommendations were the strengthening of accountability and enhancing the performance of directors. These two aims were to be achieved by (i) the establishment of remuneration committees comprised of independent non-executive directors who would report fully to the shareholders each year about the company's executive remuneration policy, including full disclosure of the elements in the remuneration of individual directors; and (ii) the adoption of performance measures linking rewards to the performance of both the company and individual directors, so that the interests of directors and shareholders were more closely aligned.

One of the Turnbull Committee recommendations (1999, revised 2005) was that boards should consider whether business objectives and the risk management/control systems of a business are supported by the performance-related reward system in operation in a company.

As part of the accountability/transparency process, the remuneration committee membership should be disclosed in the company's annual report, and the chairman of the remuneration committee should attend the company's annual general meeting to answer any questions that shareholders may have about the directors' remuneration.

The DTI published its Directors' Remuneration Report Regulations 2002. These regulations required, inter alia, that:

- quoted companies must publish a detailed report on directors' pay as part of their annual reporting cycle, and this report must be approved by the board of directors;
- a graph of the company's total shareholder returns over five years, against a comparator group, must be published in the remuneration committee report;
- names of any consultants to the remuneration committee must be disclosed, including whether they were appointed independently, along with the cost of any other services provided to the company;
- companies must hold a shareholder vote on the directors' remuneration report at each general meeting.

The stipulation that companies must hold a shareholder vote on the directors' remuneration report is an interesting one, and something that various shareholder representative groups have campaigned for over a long period of time. However, the vote was an advisory shareholder vote, although it will serve a useful purpose of ensuring that the shareholders can vote specifically on directors' remuneration, which has caused so much heated debate for so long. The other provisions will help to strengthen the role of the remuneration committee and enhance both the accountability and transparency of the directors' remuneration-setting process. The disclosures relating to the consultants used by the remuneration committee may also lead to interesting questions relating to any other services they may provide to a company to try to determine their independence.

The ILO (2008) reports:

> Disclosure practices differ widely across countries. While some countries, including France, the Netherlands, the United Kingdom and the United States require companies to report detailed compensation data in a remuneration report, others like Greece, have no specific requirements ... companies in such countries as Brazil, Germany, Japan and Mexico frequently report only aggregate data on executive compensation ... In some countries, executives seem to consider the disclosure of the precise amount of remuneration to be a risk to their personal safety. (Leal and Carvalhal da Silva, 2005)

International guidance on executive remuneration

International Corporate Governance Network (ICGN)

The ICGN issued its recommendations on best practice for executive remuneration in 2003. It was hoped that the recommendations would create a consensus amongst both companies and investors around the world about the structure of remuneration packages.

The ICGN recommendations stated that the 'fundamental requirement for executive remuneration reporting is transparency'. This was the starting point: that there should be disclosure of the base salary, short-term and long-term incentives, and any other payments or benefits to each main board director. The remuneration committee should publish statements on the expected outcomes of the remuneration structures, in terms of ratios between base salaries, short-term bonuses, and long-term rewards, making both 'high' and 'low' assumptions as well as the 'central' case. Whilst recognizing that share options are probably here to stay, the ICGN recommendations supported the International Accounting Standards Board (IASB) proposal to expense share options through the profit and loss account.

The remuneration committee report should be presented as a separate voting item at every annual meeting (this would depend on local practice). The ICGN also urged institutional investors to devote more resources to the analysis of remuneration resolutions.

In 2004 the ICGN published statements about the compliance of each of the UK, USA, and Australia with the ICGN's Executive Remuneration Principles. These countries generally complied with the principles, although each had strengths and weaknesses on particular issues.

In 2006 the ICGN approved the updated ICGN *Remuneration Guidelines*. Three principles underpin the new guidelines: transparency, accountability, and the performance basis. The Guidelines state that there should also be thought given to the reputational aspects of remuneration.

In 2012 the ICGN issued its *Executive Remuneration Principles and Policy Disclosure Guidance*. The document has three main sections relating to the remuneration committee, remuneration structure, and contractual provisions. In 2016, the ICGN published its *Guidance on Executive Director Remuneration* which supersedes the earlier guidance. It includes four main changes from the previous edition:

greater clarity has been provided on committee leadership; reference is made to the consideration of intrinsic motivational considerations beyond financial remuneration when determining effective remuneration structures; it is made explicit that base salary is payment for achieving what is expected of the executive, and that variable remuneration is payment for out-performance; environmental, social and governance factors have been included in the assessment of performance to help achieve sustainable long-term value creation. This social sensitivity has particular relevance given public concerns about the high quantum of pay for executives in the context of building social awareness of the problems of economic inequality.

Organisation for Economic Co-operation and Development (OECD)

The OECD Corporate Governance Committee (2010) in *Corporate Governance and the Financial Crisis: Conclusions and Emerging Good Practices to Enhance Implementation of the Principles* (hereafter 'the Conclusions') noted that:

the ability of the board to effectively oversee executive remuneration appears to be a key challenge in practice and remains one of the central elements of the corporate governance debate in a number of jurisdictions. The nature of that challenge goes beyond looking merely at the quantum of executive and director remuneration (which is often the focus of the public and political debate), and instead more toward how remuneration and incentive arrangements are aligned with the longer term interests of the company.

Furthermore, they highlight that policymakers have

focused more on measures that seek to improve the capacity of firm governance structures to produce appropriate remuneration and incentive outcomes. These can roughly be characterized in terms of internal firm governance (and, in particular, fostering arms-length negotiation through mandating certain levels of independence), and providing a mechanism to allow shareholders to have a means of expressing their views on director and executive remuneration.

The OECD (2011) conclude that 'aligning incentives seems to be far more problematic in companies and jurisdictions with a dispersed shareholding structure since, where dominant or controlling shareholders exist, they seem to act as a moderating force on remuneration outcomes'.

The European Commission

In April 2009 the European Commission announced new guidelines for directors' remuneration which include, inter alia, performance criteria that 'should promote the long-term sustainability of the company and include non-financial criteria that are relevant to the company's long-term value creation'; clawback provisions where variable elements of remuneration were rewarded on misleading data; and termination payments not to be paid where performance had been poor. However, these guidelines are not intended to be binding on Member States. In June 2010 the EU issued a Green Paper on 'Corporate Governance in Financial Institutions and Remuneration Policies'; one of the issues it consulted on was the recommendation of a binding or advisory shareholder vote on remuneration policy and greater independence for non-executive directors involved in determining remuneration policy. The Commission also consulted on this issue in the 2010 Green Paper on 'Corporate Governance in Financial Institutions'. In April 2011 another Green Paper, 'The EU Corporate Governance Framework', was issued, with responses invited to various consultation questions. These included whether disclosure of remuneration policy, the annual remuneration report (a report on how the remuneration policy was implemented in the past year), and individual remuneration of executive and non-executive directors should be mandatory; and also whether it should be mandatory to put the remuneration policy and the remuneration report to a vote by shareholders.

In December 2012, the EU published an Action Plan on European Company Law and Corporate Governance which detailed a number of legislative and other initiatives on company law and corporate governance which the EU planned to start in 2013 and 2014. These included, inter alia, proposals to improve the quality of corporate governance reporting; to give shareholders more oversight of directors' remuneration; and to require institutional investors to disclose their voting and engagement policies. The EU Shareholder Rights Directive should be concluded during 2015. The Directive covers many aspects of investor and company relations and interaction including institutional investors developing an engagement policy detailing how they engage with their investee companies; and voting on remuneration.

In 2013, the EU introduced a cap on bankers' bonuses to address the concerns of shareholders and other stakeholders about directors' pay in banks, particularly bonus arrangements which many feel contributed to the financial crisis by encouraging riskier behaviour. These rules limit the amount of variable remuneration that certain bank employees can receive in proportion to their fixed salary—there will be a basic ratio of fixed pay to variable pay of 1:1 with some flexibility to increase that ratio to 1:2 with shareholder approval. The new rule applied from January 2015.

In March 2014, the European Commission published proposals to introduce a 'say on pay' for listed companies in the EU. These proposals require listed companies to publish a remuneration policy with clear, comparable, and comprehensive information. They also give shareholders a binding vote on the remuneration policy and a consultative vote on the directors' remuneration report, which provides an overview of all remuneration granted to directors in the previous financial year. Moreover the binding vote would cover additional areas of remuneration such as the ratio between board pay and the pay of the average full-time worker, and why this ratio is considered to be appropriate.

In March 2017 the European Parliament voted on the revised EU Shareholders' Rights Directive. The Directive should enter into force two years after its publication in the official journal. One area that the Directive covers relates to shareholders and the 'say on pay', reaffirming the importance of voting on executive remuneration.

The Conference Board

In the USA the Conference Board Commission on Public Trust and Private Enterprise was established to address widespread abuses that led to corporate governance scandals and a resulting lack of confidence in the markets.

One area that the Commission looked at was executive compensation. The Commission reported in 2002 with principles, recommendations, and specific best practice suggestions.

The seven principles relate to: the compensation (remuneration) committee and its responsibilities; the importance of performance-based compensation; the role of equity-based incentives; creating a long-term focus; accounting neutrality; shareholders' rights; and transparency and disclosure. The Commission's report is likely to influence policy in many countries, especially those countries that have already followed the US-style remuneration package and adopted share option schemes.

In spring 2009 the Conference Board announced the establishment of an Executive Compensation Task Force which reported later that year and provided guiding principles for setting executive compensation, which, if appropriately implemented, are designed to restore credibility with shareholders and other stakeholders. The five principles are as follows: payment for the right things and payment for performance; the 'right' total compensation; avoidance of controversial pay practices; credible board oversight of executive compensation; and transparent communications and increased dialogue with shareholders.

Dodd-Frank Wall Street Reform and Consumer Protection Act (2010)

In July 2010 the USA passed the Dodd-Frank Wall Street Reform and Consumer Protection Act that amends US requirements relating to executive compensation practices in a number of respects. From mid-2011 the Securities and Exchange Commission (SEC) required listed companies compensation committee members to be independent directors. There are new 'say on pay' provisions such that the Act requires that, at least once every three years, there is a shareholder advisory vote to approve the company's executive compensation, as well as to approve 'golden parachute' compensation arrangements. Whilst the 'say on pay' is at least once every three years, it may occur every year.

In April 2015, the SEC proposed rules regarding pay for performance disclosure which would implement Section 953 of the Dodd-Frank Act. This section requires additional disclosure about certain compensation matters, including pay-for-performance and the ratio between the CEO's total compensation and the median total compensation for all other company employees. The pay ratio disclosure that companies must provide details the relationship of the annual total compensation of their employees and the annual total compensation of their chief executive officer (CEO), i.e. the ratio of the CEO pay to the median of the annual total compensation of all employees. This applies to companies for their first fiscal year beginning on or after 1 January 2017, i.e. companies reporting in 2018 onwards.

'Say on pay'

The 'say on pay' was introduced in the UK in 2002 by the Directors' Remuneration Report Regulations. It has come very much to the fore since the financial crisis as a tool of governance activism in the context of expressing dissent on executive remuneration awards. Many countries including the USA, Australia, and various countries in Europe have introduced the 'say on pay' as a mechanism for voting against executive remuneration. In some countries the 'say on pay' vote is an advisory one whilst in other countries it is a binding vote on which the board must take action. In the UK the 'say on pay' was in the form of an advisory vote but from

2013, whilst the annual remuneration report is subject to an annual *advisory* shareholder vote, shareholders have a *binding* vote on the remuneration policy, which has to be approved at least every three years.

In March 2014, the European Commission published proposals to introduce a 'say on pay' for listed companies in the EU. As discussed earlier, the proposals give shareholders a binding vote on the remuneration policy (this would be a forward-looking remuneration policy every three years which will explain how they intend to pay directors for this period) and a consultative vote on the directors' remuneration report (which provides an overview of all remuneration granted to directors in the previous financial year). Moreover the binding vote would cover additional areas of remuneration such as the ratio between board pay and the pay of the average full-time worker, and why this ratio is considered to be appropriate. In March 2017, the European Commission reaffirmed the importance of the 'say on pay' for its Member States.

As mentioned earlier, in the USA, the Dodd-Frank Wall Street Reform and Consumer Protection Act (2010), under new 'say on pay' provisions, requires that at least once every three years there is a shareholder advisory vote to approve the company's executive compensation as disclosed pursuant to SEC rules. The 'say on frequency' provision requires companies to put to a shareholder advisory vote every six years whether the 'say on pay' resolution should occur every one, two, or three years. Additional pay for performance disclosure was proposed in 2015.

Conyon and Sadler (2010), in a study of shareholder voting behaviour in the UK from 2002–7, find that there is

> little evidence of widespread and deep shareholder voting against CEO pay. Critics of CEO pay may be surprised, as one frequently proposed remedy for excess pay has been to give shareholders a voice. The UK experience suggests that owners have not seized this opportunity to reign in high levels of executive pay ... this noted, we do find that high CEO pay is likely to trigger greater shareholder dissent. This suggests that boards and compensation committees might try to communicate the intentions of CEO pay policies better to the firm's multiple stakeholders. Moreover, at present there is little evidence that shareholder voting dissent leads to drastic cuts in subsequent CEO pay.

Conyon and Sadler do, however, recognize that their study was carried out on pre-financial crisis data and that there may be a higher incidence of dissent post-financial crisis, especially in companies that have received financial support from governments or where executive pay is perceived to be excessively high. Recent evidence does indeed show that institutional investors are voting with much higher levels of dissent, and more frequently, against executive remuneration packages in the UK, the USA, and other countries.

Ferri and Maber (2011) examine the effect of 'say on pay' regulation in the UK. They report that:

> consistent with the view that shareholders regard say on pay as a value-creating mechanism, the regulation's announcement triggered a positive stock price reaction at firms with weak penalties for poor performance. UK firms responded to negative say on pay voting outcomes by removing controversial CEO pay practices criticized as rewards for failure (e.g., generous severance contracts) and increasing the sensitivity of pay to poor realizations of performance.

Correa and Lel (2014) analyse the impact of the 'say on pay' rule using a sample of about 90,000 observations from 38 countries over the period 2001–12. They find evidence that:

> following say on pay (SoP) laws, CEO pay growth rates decline and the sensitivity of CEO pay to firm performance improves. These changes are mostly concentrated on firms with potentially problematic compensation policies and weak governance environments in the period prior to the adoption of SoP laws. Further, the portion of total top management pay captured by CEOs is lower in the post-SoP period, which is associated with higher firm valuations. Overall, these results suggest that SoP laws are associated with significant changes in CEO pay policies.

Stathopoulos and Vulgaris (2016a) focus on the role of 'say on pay' as a mechanism that aims to promote the efficiency of corporate governance by providing an additional channel for the expression of shareholder 'voice'. In a further study, Stathopoulos and Vulgaris (2016b) find that:

> shareholder investment horizons have a significant impact on 'say on pay' voting patterns. Short-term investors are more likely to avoid expressing opinion on executive pay proposals by casting an abstaining vote. They vote against board proposals on pay only in cases where the CEO already receives excessive pay levels. In contrast, long-term investors typically cast favourable votes. According to our findings, this is due to effective monitoring rather than collusion with the management.

Ferri and Oesch (2016) find that 'analyzing shareholder votes on the frequency of future say on pay (SOP) votes, we find that a management recommendation for a particular frequency is associated with a 26 percent increase in voting support for that frequency'.

In an Australian context, Grosse et al (2017) point out that in Australia from 2011, if over 25 per cent of shareholders vote against a non-binding remuneration resolution, firms are awarded a 'strike'. They state:

> we examine 237 firms that receive a strike relative to matched firms, and find no association with any measure of CEO pay. However, we do find that strike firms have higher book-to-market and leverage ratios, suggesting that the remuneration vote is not used to target excessive pay. We also find that firms respond to a strike by decreasing the discretionary bonus component of CEO pay by 57.10% more than non-strike firms and increasing their remuneration disclosure by 10.95%.

Finally, the study by Arnold and Grasser (2018) shows that what is considered to be a 'fair' or 'unfair' level of executive compensation varies across different stakeholder groups. Examining the views of two key stakeholder groups (representative eligible voters and investment professionals), they find that:

> fairness is an important criterion for both groups but that opinions on how large a fair compensation amount should be are widely dispersed. Moreover, personality traits systematically influence fairness opinions through self-serving interpretations of distributive justice and personal risk attitudes, indicating that a 'fair' amount of executive compensation may strongly depend on the involved stakeholders. Investigating thresholds for outrage, i.e., amounts above which compensation is judged 'unfairly' high, we show that even though investment professionals care for fairness as well, 'capital market outrage' might not equate to 'public outrage'.

Conclusions

The debate on executive directors' remuneration has rumbled on through the last two decades, but with the increase in institutional investor activism, and the scandals and subsequent collapses associated with a number of large corporations in the UK, USA, and elsewhere, the focus is well and truly on curtailing excessive and undeserved remuneration packages. The global financial crisis and the collapse of various high profile banks and financial institutions left the market reeling. Over a decade after the financial crisis, there is still a lack of public confidence in the boards of banks, and disbelief at some of the executive remuneration packages and ad hoc payments that have been made to executive directors. Although there is now an emphasis on payment for performance, in practice, all too often executive remuneration is still seen as excessively high. The remuneration committees, comprised of independent non-executive directors, continue to come under increased scrutiny as they try to ensure that executive directors' remuneration packages are fairly and appropriately constructed, taking into account long-term objectives. Central to this aim is the use of performance indicators that will incentivize directors but at the same time align their interests with those of shareholders, to the long-term benefit of the company. Shareholders in many countries now have a 'say on pay', either in the form of an advisory or a binding vote, and seem increasingly active in expressing their dissent on executive remuneration. Alongside this, several countries including the UK and the US now mandate the disclosure of pay ratios which serve to highlight the difference in pay between the CEO of a company and that of the average worker in the company.

Summary

- The debate on executive directors' remuneration has been driven by the view that some directors, and especially those directors in the banking sector, are being overpaid to the detriment of the shareholders, the employees, and the company as a whole. The perception that high rewards have been given without corresponding performance has caused concern, and this area has increasingly become the focus of investor activism and widespread media coverage.

- The components of executive directors' remuneration are base salary, bonuses, stock options, stock grants, pension, and other benefits.

- The remuneration committee, which should be comprised of independent non-executive directors, has a key role to play in ensuring that a fair and appropriate executive remuneration system is in place.

- The role of the remuneration consultant is a complex one and there may be potential conflicts of interest.

- There are a number of potential performance criteria that may be used to incentivize executive directors. These are market-based measures (such as share price), accounts-based measures (such as earnings per share), and individual director performance measures.

- It is important that there is full disclosure of directors' remuneration and the basis on which it is calculated.

- There seems to be a trend towards convergence internationally in terms of the recommendations for the composition, calculation, and disclosure of executive directors' remuneration.

- The 'say on pay' is a mechanism for investors to express their approval or dissent in relation to executive remuneration packages and has become widely adopted.

Example: Persimmon Plc, UK

This is an example of a company which has had a long-term incentive plan (LTIP) in place for a number of years but one which had been designed without a cap on the maximum payout.

Towards the end of 2017, it became clear that Persimmon, a large construction company, had a significant flaw in its long-term incentive plan (LTIP) which had been in place since 2012. The LTIP had no cap which meant that there was no upper limit on the amount executives could receive. The LTIP was linked to share price which had seen significant increases as Persimmon had benefited hugely from the UK government's subsidies to construction companies building housing through the Help to Buy equity loan scheme. On the one hand the scheme has buoyed up such construction companies and helped to ensure that more residential housing is built but there has also been an accompanying increase in the share price. However where share price is linked to bonus schemes, and particularly an uncapped one, then it has led to excessively large bonuses for directors.

The situation came to a head towards the end of 2017 when it became clear that Jeff Fairburn, the CEO of Persimmon, was in line to receive a £100 million bonus, a situation which caused outrage amongst shareholders, politicians, and the media. Nicholas Wrigley (the Chairman), and Jonathan Davie (senior independent director and chair of the remuneration committee) both resigned as they recognized that the LTIP had been poorly designed and that directors' earnings should have been capped. Interestingly when the LTIP was put in place in 2012, it received 85 per cent shareholder approval (shareholders couldn't have realized that Persimmon would perform so well especially given the developments with government incentives for housing). Furthermore at Persimmon's AGM in April 2017, the remuneration policy and the remuneration report received overwhelming support from the shareholders with only 3.24 per cent votes cast against the remuneration policy and 9.73 per cent votes cast against the remuneration report. Shareholders have been criticized for signing off the plan in the first place and for not showing more dissent on it at the April 2017 AGM where any dissent was in a minority.

After coming under intense media scrutiny and pressure, Jeff Fairburn announced in February 2018 that he would donate some of his anticipated £100 million bonus to charity by setting up a private charitable trust to support his chosen charities.

Example: Honeywell International Inc., USA

This is an example of a large multinational corporation which is the first major US public company to disclose its ratio of CEO pay to that of the median employee.

Honeywell is a multinational conglomerate headquartered in New Jersey with operations at around 1,250 sites in 70 countries; it employs more than 129,000 employees worldwide. Its diverse portfolio

(continued)

focuses on addressing some of the world's most critical challenges around energy, safety, security, productivity and global urbanization. A key aspect to its growth has been a focus on high growth regions (HGR). In 2015, approximately 53 per cent of Honeywell's sales were from outside the US and HGR are expected to account for more than 50 per cent of their growth over the next five years.

Honeywell is in the Fortune 100 and was included in the Fortune's 2016 'World's Most Admired Companies' List, its tenth consecutive year on the prestigious list. Honeywell ranked fourth overall within the electronics industry, with second place rankings in reputation attributes for quality of management, use of corporate assets, global competitiveness, and long-term investment value.

Institutional Investor recently published its annual All-America Executive Team Rankings for US companies across 45 industry sectors. Honeywell ranked in the top-three out of 47 companies in several categories in the Capital Goods/Industrials: Electrical Equipment & Multi-Industry sector for the sixth year in a row. Honeywell's Chairman and CEO, Dave Cote, ranked first in the 'Best CEO' category as nominated by the buy-side and sell-side, and overall.

In 2017, Darius Adamczyk became President and CEO of Honeywell. Previously, he was President and Chief Operating Officer. In February 2018 Honeywell became the first major US public company to disclose its ratio of CEO pay to that of the median employee. In its preliminary proxy statement submitted to the SEC, Honeywell states:

> As required by Section 953(b) of the Dodd-Frank Wall Street Reform and Consumer Protection Act, and Item 402(u) of Regulation S-K, we are providing the following information about the relationship of the annual total compensation of our employees and the annual total compensation of Mr Darius Adamczyk, President and Chief Executive Officer (the 'CEO'):
>
> For 2017, our last completed fiscal year:
>
> - the annual total compensation of the employee identified at median of our company (other than our CEO), was $50,296; and
>
> - the annual total compensation of the CEO for purposes of determining the CEO Pay Ratio was $16,753,438.
>
> Based on this information, for 2017, the ratio of the annual total compensation of Mr Adamczyk, our Chief Executive Officer, to the median of the annual total compensation of all employees was estimated to be 333 to 1.
>
> This pay ratio is a reasonable estimate calculated in a manner consistent with SEC rules based on our payroll and employment records and the methodology described below. The SEC rules for identifying the median compensated employee and calculating the pay ratio based on that employee's annual total compensation allow companies to adopt a variety of methodologies, to apply certain exclusions, and to make reasonable estimates and assumptions that reflect their compensation practices. As such, the pay ratio reported by other companies may not be comparable to the pay ratio reported above, as other companies may have different employment and compensation practices and may utilize different methodologies, exclusions, estimates and assumptions in calculating their own pay ratios.

Shareholders and employees, as well as other interested parties such as compensation (remuneration) consultants, will likely be interested not just by how many multiples higher the chief executive is paid but by how this compares with their peer group. Given that executive compensation is a high profile and often contentious area, the disclosure of CEO to median worker pay ratios will give some welcome added transparency.

● Mini case study   Pearson Plc, UK

This is an example of a company that came under shareholder pressure over its executive remuneration package, and how it subsequently engaged in further dialogue with its shareholders.

Pearson is a world-leading educational publisher with over 41,000 employees in more than 70 countries. However, in recent years its financial performance has been rather disappointing, with several profit warnings and a significant decline in the share price. In its 2016 Annual Report, a statutory loss for the year after tax of £2,335 million was reported (including an impairment of goodwill of £2,548 million, reflecting trading pressures in the North American businesses). Pearson recognizes its disappointing performance and explains that:

> structural pressures in some markets together with cyclical and transitional issues have led to a challenging operating environment for Pearson ... The five year TSR [total shareholder return] in 2016 was 15.6% which compares to a 54.5% return on the FTSE 100 Index of large UK listed companies. Our recent share price performance has been disappointing but we are confident that the plans and strategy laid out in this report will make Pearson a simpler, stronger company, and that they set the company up for a sustained period of growth and value creation.

Included in its 2016 Annual Report (presented at its AGM in May 2017), Pearson reports on how it engages with shareholders. The report states:

> Pearson has an extensive programme of communication with all of its shareholders—large and small, institutional and private ... In 2016, we continued with our shareholder outreach programme, seeing approximately 600 institutional and private investors at more than 300 different institutions in Australia, Canada, Dubai, Greater China, Continental Europe, Japan, Singapore, the UK and the US ... The chairman meets regularly with shareholders to understand any issues and concerns they may have. This is in accordance with both the Code and consistent with the duties of investors under the UK Stewardship Code. The non-executive directors meet informally with shareholders both before and after the AGM and respond to shareholder queries and requests as necessary. The chairman ensures that the board is kept informed of investors' and advisers' views on strategy and corporate governance. At each board meeting, the directors consider commentary from advisers on major shareholders' positions and Pearson's share price. In addition, the nomination & governance and remuneration committees consider shareholder views on corporate governance and remuneration matters, respectively, as required ... During the year, we also consulted with our major shareholders and with shareholder representative bodies on our directors' remuneration policy.

The Annual Report refers to its sections covering remuneration-related matters such as the Remuneration Overview, Remuneration Report, etc. which span 24 pages. In the shareholder engagement section, reference is also made to the fact that 'private investors represent over 80% of the shareholders on our register and we make a concerted effort to engage with them regularly. Shareholders who cannot attend the AGM are invited to e-mail questions to the chairman in advance [of the AGM].'

At Pearson's AGM held in May 2017, there was significant shareholder dissent against three resolutions related to executive remuneration being (i) their executive remuneration policy, (ii) the remuneration report and (iii) the re-election of Elizabeth Corley as a board director (she was chair of the remuneration committee). Reasons given by one large institutional shareholder for voting against each of these three resolutions were respectively: (i) too much vesting at threshold or median performance; LTIP not paid in shares, (ii) too much vesting at threshold or median performance; poor performance linkage, and (iii) poor handling of Board/sub-committee responsibilities.

(continued)

Pearson stated that:

during 2016, Pearson engaged extensively with its major shareholders to understand their views on remuneration matters. We were disappointed that the advisory vote for this year's remuneration report was not passed and that, although passed, there was a significant minority vote against both our remuneration policy and the re-election of our remuneration committee chair, Elizabeth Corley. Naturally, we acknowledge this feedback and thank those shareholders who have already spoken with us and explained their reasons for not supporting the relevant resolutions. The remuneration committee is committed to continuing dialogue with our shareholders to help shape the implementation of our remuneration policy going forward.

In an additional response to the voting outcomes from the AGM 2017, Pearson added:

Since the 2017 AGM, as part of our commitment to an ongoing dialogue, we have continued to engage actively with our investors to seek further feedback on the reasons for the voting outcome, and are consulting on a number of potential changes to the way we implement our remuneration policy. This commitment to engagement included discussions with shareholders ahead of the 2017 LTIP award to our executive directors in September. We continue the ongoing process of shareholder engagement, the outcome of which will be reported in full to investors in our Directors' Remuneration Report for the year ending 31 December 2017, in line with our normal annual cycle. This report will be put to shareholders as an advisory vote at the 2018 AGM.

Mini case study questions

1. What are the implications of shareholders voting against remuneration policies and remuneration reports? Discuss the ways in which Pearson's board of directors could respond to their shareholders.

2. 'The chair of a company's remuneration committee has a key role to play in setting executive remuneration and must therefore be answerable to shareholders and also wider stakeholders if they consider all or part of the executive remuneration package to be inappropriate.' Critically discuss this statement.

Questions

The discussion questions to follow cover the key learning points of this chapter. Reading of some of the additional reference material will enhance the depth of the students' knowledge and understanding of these areas.

1. What factors have influenced the executive directors' remuneration debate?

2. Why is the area of executive directors' remuneration of such interest to investors, and particularly to institutional investors?

3. What are the main components of executive directors' remuneration packages? Which performance criteria may be used in determining executive directors' remuneration?

4. Critically discuss the roles of the remuneration committee and remuneration consultants in setting executive directors' remuneration.

5. Critically discuss the importance of executive director remuneration disclosure including the disclosure of pay ratios.

6. Why is non-executive director remuneration considered to be an important aspect of a company's governance?

References

Arnold, M.C. and Grasser, R. (2018), 'What is a Fair Amount of Executive Compensation? Outrage Potential of Two Key Stakeholder Groups', *Journal of Business Finance & Accounting*, pp. 1–35. http://doi.org/10.1111/jbfa.12309.

Association of British Insurers (2002), *Guidelines on Executive Remuneration*, ABI, London.

Association of British Insurers (2005), *Principles and Guidelines on Remuneration*, ABI, London.

Association of British Insurers (2007a), *Disclosure Guidelines on Socially Responsible Investment*, ABI, London.

Association of British Insurers (2007b), *Executive Remuneration—ABI Guidelines on Policies and Practices*, ABI, London.

Association of British Insurers (2008), Best Practice on Executive Contracts and Severance—A Joint Statement by the Association of British Insurers and National Association of Pension Funds, ABI/NAPF, London.

Association of British Insurers (2011), *ABI Principles of Executive Remuneration*, ABI, London.

Bebchuk, L. and Fried, J. (2004), *Pay Without Performance: The Unfulfilled Promise of Executive Compensation*, Harvard University Press, Boston, MA.

Bender, R. (2011), 'Paying for Advice: The role of the remuneration consultant in U.K. listed companies', *Vanderbilt Law Review*, Vol. 64, No. 2, pp. 361–96.

Bruce, A. and Skovoroda, R. (2015), *The Empirical Literature on Executive Pay: Context, the Pay-Performance Issue and Future Directions*, May 2015, High Pay Centre, London.

Bugeja, M., Fohn, S., and Matolcsy, Z. (2016), 'Determinants of the Levels and Changes in Non-Executive Director Compensation', *Accounting & Finance*, Vol. 56, Issue 3, September 2016, pp. 627–67.

Chartered Institute of Personnel Development and High Pay Centre (2017), *Executive Pay, Review of FTSE 100 executive pay packages*, CIPD/High Pay Centre, London.

Chu, J., Faasse, J., and Rau, P. R. (2017), 'Do Compensation Consultants Enable Higher CEO Pay?

A Disclosure Rule Change As a Separating Device' *Management Science*, forthcoming. Available at SSRN: https://ssrn.com/abstract=2500054 or http://dx.doi.org/10.2139/ssrn.2500054.

Combined Code (2008), *The Combined Code on Corporate Governance*, Financial Reporting Council, London.

Conference Board (2002), *Commission on Public Trust and Private Enterprise Findings and Recommendations Part 1: Executive Compensation*, Conference Board, New York.

Conference Board (2009), *The Conference Board Task Force on Executive Compensation*, Conference Board, New York.

Conyon, M.J. and Mallin, C.A. (1997), *Directors' Share Options, Performance Criteria and Disclosure: Compliance with the Greenbury Report*, ICAEW Research Monograph, London.

Conyon, M.J. and Murphy, K.J. (2000), 'The Prince and the Pauper? CEO Pay in the United States and United Kingdom', *The Economic Journal*, Vol. 110, Issue 467, pp. 640–71.

Conyon, M.J. and Sadler, G.V. (2010), 'Shareholder Voting and Directors' Remuneration Report Legislation: Say on Pay in the UK', *Corporate Governance: An International Review*, Vol. 18, No. 4, pp. 296–312.

Conyon, M.J., Peck S.I., and Sadler G.V. (2011), 'New Perspectives on the Governance of Executive Compensation: an Examination of the Role and Effect of Compensation Consultants', *Journal of Management and Governance*, Vol. 15, No. 1, pp. 29–58.

Correa, R. and Lel, U. (2014), *Say on Pay Laws, Executive Compensation, CEO Pay Slice, and Firm Value Around the World*, Available at SSRN: http://ssrn.com/abstract=2430465 or http://dx.doi.org/10.2139/ssrn.2430465.

Department for Business, Innovation and Skills (2012), *Executive Pay, Shareholder Voting Rights Consultation*, BIS, London.

Department for Business, Innovation and Skills (2013), *Directors' Remuneration Report Regulations*, BIS, London.

Department of Trade and Industry (2002), The Directors' Remuneration Report Regulations 2002 (SI No. 2002/1986), DTI, London.

Dodd-Frank Wall Street Reform and Consumer Protection Act (2010), USA Congress, Washington DC.

European Commission (2009), *Commission Recommendation on Directors' Remuneration*, April 2009, Brussels.

European Commission (2010), *Green Paper on Corporate Governance in Financial Institutions and Remuneration Policies*, European Commission, June 2010, Brussels.

European Commission (2011), *Green Paper on the EU Corporate Governance Framework*, European Commission, April 2011, Brussels.

European Commission (2012), *Action Plan: European Company Law and Corporate Governance—a modern legal framework for more engaged shareholders and sustainable companies*, European Commission, Brussels.

European Commission (2014), Shareholder Rights Directive, European Commission, Brussels.

Fattorusso, J., Skovoroda, R., and Bruce, A. (2007), 'UK Executive Bonuses and Transparency—A Research Note', *British Journal of Industrial Relations*, Vol. 45, No. 3, pp. 518–36.

Ferri, F. and Maber, D.A. (2011), 'Say on Pay Votes and CEO Compensation: Evidence from the UK', *Review of Finance*, forthcoming. Available at SSRN: http://ssrn.com/abstract=1420394.

Ferri, F. and Oesch, D. (2016), 'Management Influence on Investors: Evidence from Shareholder Votes on the Frequency of Say on Pay' *Contemporary Accounting Research*, Vol. 33, Issue 4, Winter 2016, pp. 1337–74.

Financial Reporting Council (2010), *UK Corporate Governance Code*, FRC, London.

Financial Reporting Council (2012), *UK Corporate Governance Code*, FRC, London.

Financial Reporting Council (2014), *UK Corporate Governance Code*, FRC, London.

Financial Reporting Council (2016), *UK Corporate Governance Code*, FRC, London.

Financial Reporting Council (2018), *UK Corporate Governance Code*, FRC, London.

Financial Services Authority (2010), *PS10/20 Revising the Remuneration Code*, FSA, London.

Greenbury, Sir R. (1995), *Directors' Remuneration: Report of a Study Group Chaired by Sir Richard Greenbury*, Gee Publishing Ltd, London.

Grosse, M., Kean, S., and Scott, T. (2017), 'Shareholder Say on Pay and CEO Compensation: Three Strikes and the Board is Out', *Accounting & Finance*, Vol. 57, Issue 3, September 2017, pp. 701–25.

Hahn, P. and Lasfer, M. (2011), 'The Compensation of Non-Executive Directors: Rationale, Form, and Findings', *Journal of Management and Governance*, Vol. 15, No. 4, pp. 589–601.

Hermes (2013), *Remuneration Principles for Building and Reinforcing Long-term Business Success*, Hermes Equity Ownership Services, London.

Hermes Investment Management (2016), *Remuneration Principles: Clarifying Expectations*, Hermes Investment Management, London.

High Pay Centre (2012), *It's How You Pay It*, High Pay Centre, London.

High Pay Centre (2014), *Performance-related Pay is Nothing of the Sort*, High Pay Centre, London.

High Pay Commission (2011a), *More for Less: What has happened to pay at the top and does it matter?* Interim Report, May 2011, High Pay Commission, London.

High Pay Commission (2011b), *Cheques with Balances: Why tackling high pay is in the national interest*, Final Report, November 2011, High Pay Commission, London.

House of Commons Treasury Committee (2009), *Banking Crisis: Reforming Corporate Governance and Pay in the City*, Ninth Report of Session 2008–09, House of Commons, The Stationery Office, London.

International Corporate Governance Network (2003), *Best Practices for Executive and Director Remuneration*, ICGN, London.

International Corporate Governance Network (2004a), *Australian Compliance 2004 with ICGN's Executive Remuneration Principles*, ICGN, London.

International Corporate Governance Network (2004b), *UK Compliance 2004 with ICGN's Executive Remuneration Principles*, ICGN, London.

International Corporate Governance Network (2004c), *US Compliance 2004 with ICGN's Executive Remuneration Principles*, ICGN, London.

International Corporate Governance Network (2006), *Remuneration Guidelines*, ICGN, London.

International Corporate Governance Network (2010), *Non-executive Director Remuneration Guidelines and Policies*, ICGN, London.

International Corporate Governance Network (2012), *Executive Remuneration Principles and Policy Disclosure Guidance*, ICGN, London.

International Corporate Governance Network (2016a), *Guidance on Non-Executive Director Remuneration*, ICGN, London.

International Corporate Governance Network (2016b), *Guidance on Executive Director Remuneration*, ICGN, London.

International Labour Organization (2008), *World of Work Report 2008: Income Inequalities in the Age of Financial Globalization*, International Institute for Labour Studies, Geneva, Switzerland.

Investment Management Association (2014), *Principles of Remuneration*, IMA, London.

Kostiander, L. and Ikäheimo, S. (2012), ' "Independent" Consultants' Role in the Executive Remuneration Design Process under Restrictive Guidelines', *Corporate Governance: An International Review*, Vol. 20, No. 1, pp. 64–83.

Leal, R.P.C. and Carvalhal da Silva, A. (2005), *Corporate Governance and Value in Brazil (and in Chile)*. Available at SSRN: http://ssrn.com/abstract=726261 or http://dx.doi.org/10.2139/ssrn.726261.

Lee, P. (2002), 'Not Badly Paid But Paid Badly', *Corporate Governance: An International Review*, Vol. 10, No. 2, pp. 69–74.

Mallin, C., Melis, A., Gaia, S. (2015), 'The Remuneration of Independent Directors in the UK and Italy: An Empirical Analysis Based on Agency Theory', *International Business Review*, Vol. 24, No. 2, pp. 175–86.

Marsland, P. (2015a), *Are Remuneration Consultants Independent?* High Pay Centre, London.

Marsland, P. (2015b), *The Metrics Re-Loaded: Examining Executive Remuneration Performance Measures*, High Pay Centre, London.

Murphy, K.J. and Sandino, T. (2010), 'Executive Pay and "Independent" Compensation Consultants', *Journal of Accounting and Economics*, Vol. 49, Issue 3, pp. 247–62.

Murphy, K.J. and Sandino, T. (2017), *Compensation Consultants and the Level, Composition and Complexity of CEO Pay*, Harvard Business School Accounting & Management Unit Working Paper No. 18-027. Available at SSRN: https://ssrn.com/abstract=3041427 or http://dx.doi.org/10.2139/ssrn.3041427.

National Association of Pension Funds and Hermes EOS (2013), *Remuneration Principles for building and reinforcing long-term business success*, NAPF and Hermes EOS in conjunction with RPMI Railpen, the BT Pension Scheme and USS Investment Management, London.

Organisation for Economic Co-operation and Development (2010), *Corporate Governance and the Financial Crisis: Conclusions and Emerging Good Practices to Enhance Implementation of the Principles*, OECD, Paris.

Organisation for Economic Co-operation and Development (2011), *Board Practices: Incentives and Governing Risks*, OECD, Paris.

Stathopoulos, K. and Vulgaris, G. (2016a), 'The Importance of Shareholder Activism: The Case of Say-on-Pay', *Corporate Governance: An International Review*, Vol. 24, Issue 3, May 2016, pp. 359–70.

Stathopoulos, K. and Vulgaris, G. (2016b), 'The Impact of Investor Horizon on Say-on-Pay Voting', *British Journal of Management*, Vol. 27, Issue 4, October 2016, pp. 796–818.

Sykes, A. (2002), 'Overcoming Poor Value Executive Remuneration: Resolving the Manifest Conflicts of Interest', *Corporate Governance: An International Review*, Vol. 10, No. 4, pp. 256–60.

Turnbull Committee (1999), *Internal Control: Guidance for Directors on the Combined Code*, ICAEW, London.

Turner Review (2009), *A Regulatory Response to the Global Banking Crisis, March 2009*, FSA, London.

Voulgaris G., Stathopoulos K., and Walker M. (2010), 'Compensation Consultants and CEO Pay: UK Evidence', *Corporate Governance: An International Review*, Vol. 18, No. 6, pp. 511–26.

Walker, D. (2009), *A Review of Corporate Governance in UK Banks and Other Financial Industry Entities, Final Recommendations*, HM Treasury, London.

Useful websites

www.abi.org.uk The website of the Association of British Insurers has guidelines on executive remuneration issues.

www.bis.gov.uk The Department for Business, Innovation & Skills website offers a range of information including ministerial speeches and regulatory guidance.

www.conference-board.org The Conference Board website gives details of its corporate governance activities and publications including those relating to executive remuneration (compensation).

https://ec.europa.eu/info/business-economy-euro/doing-business-eu/company-law-and-corporate-governance_en The website of the European Union covering company law and corporate governance aspects.

www.ecgi.global The European Corporate Governance Institute website has details of global corporate governance developments. Corporate governance codes for countries around the world are listed and in most cases can be downloaded.

www.highpaycentre.org The website of the High Pay Centre which contains a range of documents and reports relating to executive remuneration.

www.icgn.org The website of the International Corporate Governance Network contains various reports it has issued in relation to directors' remuneration.

www.ivis.co.uk The website of the Institutional Voting Information Service, providers of corporate governance voting research. The service has developed from the low key, proactive, but non-confrontational approach to corporate governance adopted by the ABI. Includes ABI Guidelines such as those on executive remuneration.

www.napf.co.uk The website of the National Association of Pension Funds has guidelines on various corporate governance issues.

www.parliament.uk/treascom This website has the publications of the Treasury Committee.

www.plsa.co.uk The Pensions and Lifetime Savings Association (PLSA) website contains useful information relating to various aspects of pensions and lifetime savings for pension professionals and individuals. Formerly the National Association of Pension Funds (NAPF).

www.ukgi.org.uk UK Government Investments (UKGI) is the government's centre of excellence in corporate finance and corporate governance.

 Develop your understanding of this chapter and explore the subject further using our online resources at www.oup.com/uk/mallin6e/

 Part Three case study   Royal Bank of Scotland Plc, UK

This case study draws together a number of the issues covered in this section of the book relating to a dominant CEO, the lack of appropriate questioning of strategy by the board, and perceived overly generous executive remuneration packages.

The Royal Bank of Scotland (RBS) Plc hit the headlines when it had to be bailed out by the UK government in 2008 to the tune of £20 billion with the government becoming a 70 per cent shareholder. The government has also underwritten £325 billion of RBS assets in an effort to stabilize the bank. In common with various other well-known financial institutions in the UK, USA, and elsewhere, RBS had been badly affected by the global financial crisis which, ironically, the financial institutions themselves had helped to cause. Following the initial shock that such a well-known name needed to be rescued by public funding, came the angry outcry at the remuneration packages being paid out to top executives, even after the bank had been bailed out.

In 2007 Sir Fred Goodwin, CEO of RBS at that time, received a salary of £1.29 million and a bonus of £2.86 million, a total of £4.15 million. This package was more than the CEO of any of Lloyds TSB, HBOS, or Barclays received. During Sir Fred's time as CEO, RBS followed two strategic decisions that

(continued)

ultimately contributed to it incurring massive losses of £24 billion in 2008. The first was that goodwill on past acquisitions had to be written down, and the second was losses arising from its expansion into investment banking and toxic assets. The board has been criticized for not standing up to Sir Fred who has been accused of not only going on a seven-year acquisition spree but also paying generous prices for the acquisitions. Sir Fred subsequently left RBS after being given early retirement at the age of 50 but with a pension of over £700,000 per annum, which caused even more anger. Despite requests from the government asking him not to take this huge amount, Sir Fred initially remained unmoved and legal enquiries indicated that the terms of the arrangement meant that he could not be forced to pay it back. However, the annual pension has now been reduced substantially although anger at Sir Fred remains high.

Needless to say, at RBS's annual general meeting the remuneration report received an 80 per cent vote against it, clearly displaying the institutional shareholders' disapproval.

RBS's corporate governance was criticized as it was perceived as having a dominant CEO combined with a board comprised of directors who had either been on the board for some years and hence might be seen as being rather too 'cosy' with the CEO, or directors who had limited banking experience. Lord Paul Myners has viewed bank boards generally as inadequate: 'The typical bank board resembles a retirement home for the great and the good: there are retired titans of industry, ousted politicians and the occasional member of the voluntary sector. If such a selection, more likely to be found in *Debrett's Peerage* than the City pages, was ever good enough, it is not now.'

Following on from the disastrous financial performance in 2008, and the criticism across the board from angry investors, an angry government, and an angry public, RBS reduced its board size from 16 to 12, the latter including three new non-executive directors who had received UK government approval. Sir Sandy Crombie, CEO of Standard Life, the insurer, became the bank's senior independent director in June 2009, which should have greatly strengthened the RBS board.

The FSA Report (2011) into the failure of RBS highlighted a number of factors that contributed to the bank's downfall and also stated that 'the multiple poor decisions that RBS made suggest, moreover, that there are likely to have been underlying deficiencies in RBS management, governance and culture which made it prone to make poor decisions'. Sentiment against Sir Fred Goodwin continued to run high and in early 2012 Sir Fred Goodwin was stripped of his knighthood, awarded in 2004 for his services to banking, as he was the dominant decision-maker in RBS in 2008 when decisions were made that contributed significantly to RBS's problems and to the financial crisis.

During 2012 RBS was once again caught up in the executive pay furore, and the wave of shareholder activism and public sentiment were directed at RBS's CEO, Stephen Hester, who decided to waive £2.8 million in salary and long-term incentives.

In October 2013, Ross McEwan succeeded Stephen Hester as CEO of RBS; in February 2015, it was announced that Sir Howard Davies, a former chairman of the UK's Financial Services Authority (now the Financial Conduct Authority), would be taking on the role of Chairman of RBS. Also in 2015, RBS reported its seventh consecutive annual net loss; it faces difficult times ahead with a restructuring plan aimed at cutting costs, increasing capital, and returning the bank to profitability. Furthermore there are plans to sell the 80 per cent stake currently owned by the state in the near future.

In June 2017, RBS settled the lawsuit brought by the RBS Shareholder Action Group who felt that they had been misled into buying the bank's shares when a rights issue was offered in 2008. The settlement was for £200 million though RBS did not admit liability as part of the June settlement. In 2017, the UK's ShareSoc and the UK Shareholders' Association (UKSA), which both represent individual shareholders investing directly in the stock market, together organized a group of more than 100 shareholders to put forward a shareholder proposal calling for a shareholder committee to be established to help improve the corporate governance at RBS.

(continued)

The RBS board decided to include the shareholder proposal at RBS's AGM in May 2018 where it was voted on by all shareholders. The situation was particularly interesting as the British government still held more than 70 per cent of RBS and would have needed to support the resolution for it to be passed. However, the shareholder proposal was defeated.

Meanwhile two events occurred in the early part of 2018. The first was RBS's announcement that it had made a profit for the first time in nine years; although a symbolic moment and one which should facilitate RBS paying a small dividend to its shareholders, there is still a settlement outstanding with the US Department of Justice regarding RBS's mis-selling of mortgages. The second was the publication of the Financial Conduct Authority (FCA)'s report on *RBS Group's treatment of SME customers referred to the Global Restructuring Group* which was completed in September 2016 but then made publicly available by the Treasury Committee in February 2018. The FCA had commissioned the report given the disquiet about the way in which the Global Restructuring Group (GRG) was alleged to have behaved in relation to SME customers. In the foreword to the report, Sir Callum McCarthy states:

> Our central conclusions are that there was widespread inappropriate treatment of customers by GRG; that this inappropriate treatment was not confined to failures in process; and that in a significant proportion of cases—one in six of the cases we assessed as being potentially viable in our Representative Sample—that treatment appears likely to have caused material financial distress; and in practice yet more customers have valid grounds for considering themselves badly treated by RBS and GRG. We find that this was for the most part a direct result of failings in GRG's governance and oversight arrangements and of the priorities GRG pursued.

The report recommends 'that a review is carried out to ensure that our conclusions and recommendations that remain relevant to RBS have been implemented and in particular, to provide assurance to RBS, customers and the FCA that adequate governance and oversight arrangements are now in place to ensure that similar poor treatment of distressed SME customers could not happen in the future'. The report then details a number of specific actions that RBS should follow in carrying out that review, these are:

> improve its governance arrangements; improve the arrangements around transfer into and out of the turnaround unit; provide a greater focus on turnaround options where these are viable; rethink is approach to pricing in respect of distressed SME customers; ensure any internal valuations are handled more carefully; review its policies and practices on dealing with customers and on complaints; review its use of third-party firms and in particular its use of secondees; fundamentally review its approach to the purchase of distressed assets; and review the use of Upside instruments in the context of SME customers.

In May 2018, RBS announced the closure of 162 of its branches with the loss of 800 jobs.

 FT Clippings

Unilever faces potential shareholder unrest over pay policy

Two influential advisers have raised concerns over executive pay ahead of AGM in May

Attracta Mooney and Scheherazade Daneshkhu

Financial Times, 13 April 2018

Unilever, the consumer goods giant, is facing a potential investor rebellion at its annual general meeting next month after influential advisers called on shareholders to vote against its pay policies.

Institutional Shareholder Services, a proxy adviser to the world's biggest investors, recommended that shareholders vote against the binding pay policy at the Anglo-Dutch company, flagging concerns that a proposed overhaul would drive up the potential for big increases in fixed pay and bonuses.

Rival proxy adviser Glass Lewis backed the 'simplified pay structure' at the company, but a service run by the Investment Association, the asset management trade body, has also raised concerns about the company's non-binding pay report, setting the scene for a potentially tumultuous annual meeting in May.

The concerns over pay come after Paul Polman, chief executive, was granted a 39 per cent pay rise for 2017, partly reflecting the boost to its share price after the aborted $143bn bid by Kraft Heinz, the US food group.

His total package of €11.7m in 2017 was up from €8.4m the year before, according to the Anglo-Dutch group's annual report published last month. It was the highest amount paid to the chief executive since he assumed the role nine years ago.

Mr Polman, who is expected to retire from Unilever within the next 12 months, has championed good corporate governance and responsible business. An investor rebellion at possibly his last annual meeting at the consumer goods group is likely to be sensitive for the company.

He has said in the past that he is 'embarrassed' by his salary and would work for free at the company.

Unilever said its new pay policy is 'simpler, longer term and requires greater personal commitment through share ownership to drive reward'. The company added that it had consulted with its shareholders about the planned changes.

ISS, whose recommendations are widely followed by investors when deciding how to vote at annual meetings, backed the company's pay report, but it said support for its pay policy was 'unwarranted'.

'Whilst some positive improvements to the policy have been noted, concerns are raised regarding the impact of the change from base salary to a consolidated "fixed pay" structure, particularly as a result of increases to both fixed pay and the annual bonus potential,' it said.

Unilever put forward a new pay policy in 2017, which was supported by more than 95 per cent of shareholders. But it has proposed revamping the policy again this year, incorporating base salary, allowances and pensions into one 'fixed pay' element.

ISS said: 'Whilst at first glance this alignment and simplification is likely to be welcomed by shareholders, the principal concern raised is that it comes at a price.'

Under the new plans, top executives are in line for potentially larger short-term incentives from this year. The company also proposed capping long-term incentives at 450 per cent of fixed pay, up from 180 per cent of salary.

Glass Lewis said: 'Shareholders should remain mindful of the increased in overall maximum opportunity; however, on balance we believe the proposed policy to be supportable.'

Landsec reveals 36% average gender pay gap

Property developer says divide caused by men dominating higher-paying roles

Aime Williams

Financial Times, 23 November 2017

Landsec, the UK's largest listed property company, has revealed that its female staff are paid a third less than men as it becomes the first developer to file new gender pay gap data.

The FTSE 100 developer, which sold the City of London's 'Walkie Talkie' skyscraper for £1.3bn to Hong Kong investors this year, reported a median gender pay gap of more than 36 per cent for hourly pay.

Women also received bonuses that were 62.5 per cent lower in median terms than those received by men, although women were almost as likely as men to receive some sort of bonus.

All companies with more than 250 employees must publish the gap for mean and median wages and bonuses, as well as the percentages of men and women receiving bonuses and at different pay scales by April 4 next year.

So far, only around 3 per cent of companies have met their legal requirement to report the gender pay gap, with only 250 out of an estimated 9,000 companies so far entering data on to the government's website.

According to analysis of gender pay gap data filed to date by analytics company Staffmetrix, the highest median gender pay gap by sector recorded so far is 31 per cent, registered by financial services companies, meaning Landsec is ranked among those with the highest hourly gender pay gap.

As of last month, the median gender pay gap of those organisations that have reported so far was 10.6 per cent, compared with the UK's overall gender pay gap for all employees, full-time and part-time, of 18.1 per cent in 2016, according to the Office for National Statistics.

Landsec, formerly Land Securities Group, said 30 per cent of its top quartile earners were women, while 76 per cent of its lower quartiles earners were also women.

On its website, the company said that although the figures would suggest a 'significant pay gap between males and females', the gap was caused by men dominating higher-paying roles.

'Like other companies across our industry, we have a lower proportion of females in senior roles than we would like,' wrote Diana Breeze, the company's head of human resources.

Landsec said that women's relatively lower bonuses could be partly explained by some women earning pro-rated bonuses when working part-time.

Ms Breeze said the company would commit itself to improving its female representation among its best-paid quarter of staff from 20 per cent to 30 per cent by 2020. The company told the Financial Times that it had recently appointed a female board member, bringing the composition of its board to seven men and four women.

High-profile companies to report their gender pay statistics to date include PwC Services and Virgin Money, which reported that on average their female staff earn 12 per cent and 32.5 per cent less per hour than men respectively. About half the companies that have provided data have reported double-digit gender pay gaps.

In September, Justine Greening, women and equalities minister and education secretary, called on companies to 'fast forward' their plans to report the gap between what they pay their male and female employees.

This article was amended after publication to reflect the fact that Landsec sold the 'Walkie Talkie' tower this year, not the 'Cheesegrater'.

EasyJet chief takes pay cut to match female predecessor

Johan Lundgren awarded base salary £34,000 higher than Carolyn McCall's £706,000 a year

Naomi Rovnick and Cat Rutter Pooley

Financial Times, 29 January 2018

The new chief executive of EasyJet has taken a salary cut after he was awarded a higher base wage by the airline's board than his well-regarded female predecessor Carolyn McCall.

Johan Lundgren took the helm at the airline on December 1 with a starting salary of £740,000. Dame Carolyn, who left in November to run broadcaster ITV, finished on a salary of £706,000. Her last full remuneration package was £1.5m including bonuses and pension contributions.

Overall, EasyJet has a gender pay gap of 52 per cent, the biggest of any company yet to have reported data under new UK government rules.

'At easyJet we are absolutely committed to giving equal pay and equal opportunity for women and men,' Mr Lundgren, former Tui deputy chief executive, said on Monday.

'I want that to apply to everybody at easyJet and to show my personal commitment I have asked the board to reduce my pay to match that of Carolyn's when she was at easyJet.'

It is not yet clear how much Mr Lundgren's total pay and bonus package will be for 2018.

Mr Lundgren also did not explain why he had come into EasyJet on a higher salary than Dame Carolyn. A spokesman for the airline's board of directors, whose remuneration committee is chaired by former Thomson and Tui executive Charles Gurassa, said they had 'looked to secure the right candidate and the salary awarded reflected his experience and his previous salary'.

Mr Lundgren's last full annual salary at Tui was €875,000 (£770,000).

During Dame Carolyn's seven years running EasyJet, passenger numbers rose to record highs. The company paid £1.2bn in dividends and gave investors a total return of more than 300 per cent, placing it behind arch-rival Ryanair but ahead of British Airways owner IAG.

Frances O'Grady, the leader of Britain's trade union movement, said: 'Token gestures are no substitute for comprehensive action to address the gender pay gap.'

Jo Swinson, who was minister for women in the last coalition government, said the fact Mr Lundgren had started on a higher salary 'shows how easy it is, even for a company that has had a woman at the top and had during that time taken significant steps on diversity, to fall into the old trap' of placing a higher value on a male employee.

Ms Swinson, who is now the deputy leader of the Liberal Democrats, said EasyJet should be praised for 'looking at this and deciding that something went wrong', however, and urged all large companies 'to do the same checks' to ensure this sort of thing does not happen.

'There may be reasons for the new person to have higher pay, such as there being new responsibilities, but gender should never be the reason,' she said.

Women are under-represented in top-paid pilot roles across the aviation industry—according to the British Women Pilots' Association, just 5 per cent of UK pilots are women.

Under Dame Carolyn, EasyJet set goals to fill half the places in its engineering apprenticeship scheme with women, and that by 2020 a fifth of its trainee pilots should be female.

Part 4

International corporate governance

Corporate governance in Continental Europe

Learning objectives

- To understand the background to the development of corporate governance codes in Europe

- To be aware of the main differences in corporate governance in Continental European countries

- To have a detailed knowledge of the corporate governance codes for a range of Continental European countries

- To be able to evaluate whether corporate governance codes are converging or diverging

Background

As in other countries across the globe, the interest in corporate governance in Continental European countries has grown considerably in the last decade. Its importance for the development of capital markets and investor confidence has been widely appreciated. The realization that the barriers between different countries' capital markets are declining with the adoption of the euro, the internationalization of cross-border portfolios, and technological advances means that corporate governance practices of individual countries increasingly need to satisfy certain perceived core principles of accepted good practice. We have seen that the Cadbury Code (1992) and the Organisation for Economic Co-operation and Development (OECD) Principles (1999, 2004, 2015) have been influential in the determination of these core principles.

The increase in both privatizations of former state-owned enterprises, and mergers and acquisitions in many countries has also led to a need for better corporate governance, as wider shareholder groups are created and providers of finance need to be sure that their investment will be protected.

The work of La Porta et al. (1998) suggests that countries that have a civil law/code often have a limited protection of minority shareholders; in addition, these countries often have a concentrated share ownership structure rather than a more dispersed shareholder base, such as that in the UK or the USA. This aspect should be borne in mind when analysing the corporate governance of Continental European countries.

Franks and Mayer (1995) used the terms 'insider' and 'outsider' systems to differentiate between two types of ownership and control structures. In the outsider system, there is dispersed ownership of corporate equity amongst a large number of outside investors (as in both the UK and the USA), whereby institutional investor ownership is predominant, although the institutional investors do not tend to hold large shareholdings in any given company, hence they have little direct control. In contrast, in an insider system, such as in many Continental European countries, ownership tends to be much more concentrated, with shares often being owned either by holding companies or families (although the state still plays an important role in France, for example).

Sometimes, a corporate governance system may also be termed 'bank-oriented' or 'market-oriented'. A bank-oriented system implies that banks play a key role in the funding of companies and so may well be able to exercise some control via the board structure (for example, bank representatives may have seats on the supervisory board in German companies); in contrast, a market-oriented system is one where banks' influence is not prevalent in the same way and does not infiltrate the corporate structure. Becht and Mayer (2001) make an interesting observation about this distinction: they state that the balance of evidence provided by various studies shows that 'the distinction between bank and market-oriented financial systems is therefore fragile. In contrast, the differences in ownership and control of corporations ... are pronounced.'

It is also likely that, over time, the remaining influence of banks in terms of direct influence in a company will reduce, and it will be the distinction between ownership and control that helps drive and shape corporate governance reform. Of course, such reform will be within the context of the legal and capital market structure of the various countries. Needless to say, as EU reforms lead to more 'common' requirements of countries and hence to more harmonization, companies and, where appropriate, their corporate governance systems will need to provide for certain of these aspects. EU directives may have an immediate or a more long-term effect on corporate governance. Two examples are the European Works Councils Directive 94/95 ([1994] OJ L254/64), which is concerned with the establishment of European Works Councils for informing and consulting employees, and the Large Holdings Directive (EEC 88/627), whereby voting blocks of 10 per cent or more in companies have to be disclosed.

Subsequently, the EU Accounts Modernization Directive was intended to produce more comparability across the financial reporting of its Member States. By its provisions, companies in various countries in the EU are subject to common standards of both the level and content of disclosures. The Directive was discussed in more detail in Chapter 4.

However, there have also been developments in relation to the Action Plan on Modernizing Company Law and Enhancing Corporate Governance in the EU, which was presented in 2003. The then European Commissioner, Charlie McCreevy, launched a consultation on the Action Plan. Following on from the consultation process, various priorities were identified: shareholders' rights and obligations, internal control, and the modernization and simplification of European Company Law. Also in 2006 amendments to the fourth and seventh Company Law Directives were issued with the aim of enhancing confidence in financial statements and annual reports. These amendments prescribe that, inter alia, listed companies must now publish a separate corporate governance statement in the annual report, and board members are to take collective responsibility for the annual report and accounts.

In 2011 the EU issued the Green Paper on the EU Corporate Governance Framework, which launched a public consultation on possible ways forward to improve existing corporate governance mechanisms. The Green Paper contained three chapters: boards, shareholders, and the 'comply or explain' principle. The objective of the Green Paper was to have a broad debate on the issues raised. The consultation period ended in July 2011 and in December 2012 the EU published an Action Plan detailing initiatives it planned to undertake in 2013 based on the responses to the Green Paper consultation and also consultation on EU corporate law and discussions with stakeholder groups. The planned initiatives covered three broad areas: enhancing transparency, engaging shareholders, and cross-border operations. Furthermore the EU Commission plans a major codification exercise in order to make the regulatory framework more user-friendly. A number of the initiatives have so far come to fruition and these were discussed in more detail in Chapter 3.

As already mentioned, apart from ownership structure, the main differences in corporate governance codes amongst Continental European countries stem from companies law and securities regulation. Gregory and Simmelkjaer (2002) identify the main differences as being: employee representation; social/stakeholder issues; shareholder rights and participation mechanics; board structure, roles, and responsibilities; supervisory body independence and leadership; board committees; disclosure.

Table 10.1 highlights the predominant board and leadership structure in a number of European countries. The table shows that most European countries have a unitary board structure, although the majority also have the option of a dual structure. A number of countries provide for employee representation on, or a role in, the supervisory board; there is separate supervisory and managerial leadership in the companies in countries where the board structure is dual.

Table 10.1 Predominant board and leadership structure

Member State	Board structure	Employee role in supervisory body
Austria	Two-tier	Yes
Belgium	Unitary*	No
Denmark	Two-tier	Yes
Finland	Unitary*	Articles may provide
France	Unitary*	Articles may provide (and Advisory)
Germany	Two-tier	Yes
Greece	Unitary*	No
Ireland	Unitary	No
Italy	Unitary**	No
Luxembourg	Unitary	Yes
Netherlands	Two-tier	Advisory
Portugal	Unitary* **	No
Spain	Unitary	No
Sweden	Unitary	Yes
United Kingdom	Unitary	No

*Other structure also available   **Board of auditors also required
Source: Comparative Study of Corporate Governance Codes (Gregory and Simmelkjaer, 2002)
©European Communities 2002, Internal Market Directorate General.

Table 10.2 Summary of key differences between supervisory and management boards

Supervisory board	Management board
Members (shareholder representatives) are elected by the shareholders in general meeting; members (employee representatives) are nominated by the employees	Members are appointed by the supervisory board
Controls the direction of the business	Manages the business
Oversees the provision of information and ensures appropriate systems have been put in place by the management board	Provides various financial information and reports; and puts appropriate systems in place, e.g. a risk management system

Table 10.2 indicates the key distinctions between the supervisory board and the management board. The supervisory board is elected by shareholders and employees, and it in turn appoints the management board. The supervisory board has a control function whereas the management board manages the business.

The next sections will look at several countries in more detail: Germany, Denmark, France, and Italy. These countries have been chosen because they represent different board structures and ownership patterns: Germany and Denmark each have a two-tier board structure but with different corporate ownership structures; France has a unitary board structure but the other structure is also available; and Italy has a unitary board structure but a board of auditors is also required.

Germany

Charkham (1994) stated that 'if there were a spectrum with "confrontation" at one end and "co-operation" at the other, we would confidently place German attitudes and behaviour far closer to the "co-operation" end than, say, those of the British or Americans'. This is an important statement in the context of understanding the philosophy of the German approach to business and to companies, whereby the shareholders are but one of a wider set of stakeholder interests with the employees and customers being given more emphasis. Charkham (1994) finds this approach evidenced in the industrial relations of German companies: 'Good industrial relations ... would not be prominent in works on corporate governance systems in most countries, or at best would be regarded as peripheral. In Germany, however, good industrial relations are much nearer centre stage.' This is evidenced in the Works Constitution Act 1972, which sets out the rights of the works council and, broadly speaking, deals with all matters pertaining to the employees' conditions of employment. Works councils are part of the cooperative process between workers and employers, the idea being that co-determination (the right to be kept informed of the company's activities and to participate in decisions that may affect the workers) means that there is a basis for more trust and co-operation between workforce and employers. The Co-determination Act 1976 defines the proportion of employee and shareholder representatives on the supervisory board (*Aufsichtsrat*) and also stipulates that a director on the management board has special responsibility for labour-related matters.

The business structure in Germany is detailed in Wymeersch (1998), where he identifies the most used business types in various Continental European states. In Germany, as far as the larger business entities are concerned, the business types tend to be either public (*Aktiengesellschaft, AG*) or private companies limited by shares (*Gesellschaft mit beschränkter Haftung, GmbH*). However, he identifies a hybrid that is also used in Germany, specifically, a hybrid of the *GmbH & Co. KG*, combining the advantages of the unincorporated *Kommanditgesellschaft* and the limited liability of *GmbH*.

In Germany, as in many Continental European countries and the UK, there is a trend away from individual share ownership. The most influential shareholders are financial and non-financial companies, and there are significant cross-holdings, which mean that when analysing share ownership and control in Germany, one needs to look also at the links between companies. Banks, and especially a few large banks, play a central role in German corporate governance, with representation on the supervisory boards of companies and links with other companies. Charkham (1994) identifies a number of reasons as to why banks are influential in Germany. First, there is direct ownership of company shares by banks; secondly, German shareholders generally lodge their shares with banks authorized to carry out their voting instructions (deposited share voting rights, or DSVR); thirdly, banks tend to lend for the long term and hence develop a longer term relationship with the company (relationship lending); and fourthly, banks offer a wide range of services that the company may find it useful to draw upon. Given these factors, banks tend to build up a longer term, deeper relationship with companies, and their expertise is welcomed on the supervisory boards. Hence the German corporate governance system could be termed an 'insider' system. A more detailed analysis is beyond the scope of this text but a comprehensive analysis is provided in Prigge (1998).

The German corporate governance system (see Table 10.3) is based around a dual board system, and, essentially, the dual board system comprises a management board (*Vorstand*) and a supervisory board (*Aufsichtsrat*). The management board is responsible for managing the enterprise. Its members are jointly accountable for the management of the enterprise and the chairman of the management board coordinates the work of the management board. The supervisory board appoints, supervises, and advises the members of the management board and is directly involved in decisions of fundamental importance to the enterprise. The chairman of the supervisory board coordinates the work of the supervisory board. The members of the supervisory board are elected by the shareholders in general meetings.

Table 10.3 Key characteristics influencing German corporate governance

Feature	Key characteristic
Main business form	Public or private companies limited by shares
Predominant ownership structure	Financial and non-financial companies
Legal system	Civil law
Board structure	Dual
Important aspect	Compulsory employee representation on supervisory board

The co-determination principle provides for compulsory employee representation. So, for firms or companies that have more than five hundred or two thousand employees in Germany, employees are also represented in the supervisory board, which then comprises one-third employee representative or one-half employee representative respectively. The representatives elected by the shareholders and representatives of the employees are equally obliged to act in the enterprise's best interests.

The idea of employee representation on boards is not always seen as a good thing because the employee representatives on the supervisory board may hold back decisions being made that are in the best interests of the company as a whole but not necessarily in the best interests of the employees as a group. An example would be where a company wishes to rationalize its operations and close a factory but the practicalities of trying to get such a decision approved by employee representatives on the supervisory board, and the repercussions of such a decision on labour relations, prove too great for the strategy to be made a reality. Alternatively, if a German company decides that it needs to close one of its subsidiaries, then it may prefer to close down a subsidiary overseas, in a country such as the UK, which has a unitary board structure and hence no supervisory board with employee representation. Employees in the UK would therefore be in a weaker position than their German counterparts, and have less influence over any closure decision.

The committee on corporate governance in Germany was chaired by Dr Gerhard Cromme and is usually referred to as the Cromme Report or Cromme Code. The Code harmonizes a wide variety of laws and regulations, and contains recommendations and also suggestions for complying with international best practice on corporate governance. The Cromme Code was published in 2002 and has a number of sections covering shareholders and the general meeting; co-operation between the management board and the supervisory board; the management board; the supervisory board; transparency; and reporting and audit of the annual financial statements.

It is interesting to note that Charkham (2005), in reviewing corporate governance developments in Germany, is of the opinion that 'internal and external developments have put pressure on it, but its main provisions remain intact. The factors for change have been the diminishing role of the banks, the international governance codes and principles, and the international capital markets.'

In November 2005 Germany abolished the requirement for shares to be blocked in advance of a shareholder meeting. Blocking had meant that shares could not be traded for a period of time before a company's general meeting if the holder of the shares wished to be able to vote on the resolutions tabled for the general meeting. Therefore, it had effectively been a deterrent to voting because institutional investors often could not afford to be in a position whereby they were unable to trade their shares.

Legal changes required companies to disclose pay details for executive directors, effective for annual reports for 2006 onwards. However, company management may propose that disclosure is limited and if the proposal is approved by 75 per cent of its shareholders, then the additional disclosure does not have to be given. An amended version of the German Corporate Governance Code was published in 2006 and recommended that various executive remuneration disclosures should be made in the corporate governance report. Companies would be obliged to disclose if they were to deviate from these recommendations.

There were minor amendments to the German Corporate Governance Code in 2007 and 2008. In the Foreword to each of these codes, it is mentioned that the European Company or Societas Europaea (SE) gives German enterprises the opportunity to opt for the unitary board system, in which case the form that co-determination would take would be a matter for agreement between the company management and the employees. Also, there is now a recommendation in the section on the 'Supervisory Board' that the supervisory board should form a nomination committee composed exclusively of shareholder representatives, which should propose suitable candidates to the supervisory board for recommendation to the company's general meeting.

Further updates to the Code took place in 2009, 2010, 2012, 2013, 2014, 2015, and 2017. In 2009 the Foreword to the Code included mention that the Code clarifies the obligations of the management board and the supervisory board 'to ensure the continued existence of the enterprise and its sustainable creation of value in conformity with the principles of the social market economy (interest of the enterprise)'. Therefore the interests of the shareholders, the employees, and other stakeholders will be taken into account. Other amendments in 2009 relate to remuneration and board composition, including diversity:

- The full supervisory board should determine the total compensation of individual members of the management board based on their individual performance, the performance of the business, the economic outlook, and the remuneration levels in peer group companies.
- External compensation experts may be called upon for advice.
- The compensation structure should be oriented towards sustainable growth and should not encourage the taking of unnecessary risks.
- The supervisory board should have regard to diversity when appointing the members of the management board.
- The supervisory board and the management board should engage in long-term succession planning.
- Management board members should not become members of the supervisory board within two years of the end of their appointment unless their appointment is based on a proposal presented by shareholders holding more than 25 per cent of the voting rights.
- Members of the supervisory board should not hold more than three supervisory board memberships in non-group listed companies.

In 2010 amendments to the Code focused on shareholders' rights, remuneration, and diversity:

- The general meeting can vote on the remuneration system for members of the management board (reflecting the growing focus on executive pay).
- The forms for postal voting should be included on the company's website.
- Diversity, with appropriate consideration of women, should be taken into account by the management board when filling managerial positions in the company, and by the supervisory board when making appointments to the management board.
- The supervisory board should 'specify concrete objectives regarding its composition which ... take into account the international activities of the enterprise ... and diversity.

These concrete objectives shall, in particular, stipulate an appropriate degree of female representation.'

- In relation to training, the 2010 Code adds the provision 'the members of the supervisory board shall on their own take on the necessary training and further education measures required for their tasks. They shall be supported by the company appropriately.'

In 2012 amendments related to the Code focused on the management board and the supervisory board:

- If the employment contract of a management board member is terminated for a serious cause for which the management board member is responsible, then no payments are made to the management board member.

- The chairman of the supervisory board should maintain regular contact with the chairman of the management board between meetings and 'consult with it on issues of strategy, planning, business development, risk situation, risk management and compliance of the enterprise'.

- The audit committee established by the supervisory board has an extended remit such that the audit committee 'in particular, handles the monitoring of the accounting process, the effectiveness of the internal control system and the internal audit system, the audit of the Annual Financial Statements, here in particular the independence of the auditor, the services rendered additionally by the auditor, the issuing of the audit mandate to the auditor, the determination of auditing focal points and the fee agreement, and—unless another committee is entrusted therewith—compliance'.

- The supervisory board, in election recommendations to the general meeting, shall 'disclose the personal and business relations of each individual candidate with the enterprise, the executive bodies of the company and with a shareholder holding a material interest [directly or indirectly holding more than 10% of the voting shares] in the company'.

It is also interesting to note that the Foreword to the 2012 Code states that 'in practice the dual-board system, also established in other continental European countries, and the single-board system are converging because of the intensive interaction of the Management Board and the Supervisory Board in the dual-board system. Both systems are equally successful.'
In 2013 the amendments to the Code related largely to compensation:

- The supervisory board should consider the relationship between the compensation of the management board, the senior management, and the staff overall, especially over time.

- The amount of compensation was to be capped, 'both overall and for individual compensation elements. The variable compensation components shall be related to demanding, relevant comparison parameters.'

- The compensation report should disclose, for each management board member, 'the benefits granted for the year under review including the fringe benefits, and including the maximum and minimum achievable compensation for variable compensation components; the allocation of fixed compensation, short-term variable compensation and long-term variable compensation in/for the year under review, broken down into the relevant reference years; for pension provisions and other benefits, the service cost in/for the year under review'. The 2013 Code also provided model tables for the presentation of this compensation disclosure.

In 2014 an amendment was made to the model tables for the presentation of compensation disclosure. The amendment was to include benefits from third parties to individual members of the management board in relation to management board work. In 2015, amendments were made to the Code which underlined the increasing role of the supervisory board; furthermore, new statutory provisions on equal participation of men and women in management positions that came into effect on 1 May 2015 were incorporated into the Code. The management board has to take diversity, particularly in relation to women, into account when filling managerial positions; it must also set targets for the proportion of women on the two management levels below the management board. The supervisory board must also consider diversity, particularly in relation to women, when making appointments to the management board; it must also set targets for the proportion of women on the supervisory board. In companies covered by various Co-determination Acts, the supervisory board should comprise at least 30 per cent women and at least 30 per cent men.

In 2017, the amendments to the German Corporate Governance Code (Deutscher Corporate Governance Kodex 2017) related to the following areas:

- Good corporate governance is defined by legal, ethical and self-responsible conduct.

  In this context, the Code specifically refers to the reputable businessperson concept ('Leitbild des Ehrbaren Kaufmanns'). Additionally the role and responsibilities of institutional shareholders and their importance to companies are also emphasized.

- Enhancing transparency to provide a solid basis for assessment.

  In this context, companies shall publish the basic features of their Compliance Management System which will facilitate investors and the general public in forming their own view of the company's compliance. Employees who may wish to report suspected breaches of the law should be able to do so anonymously and be protected. There should be enhanced transparency in relation to the criteria for the composition of the supervisory board.

- Alignment with international best practice in investor communications.

  Consistent with international best practice (and also current practice in many German companies), the chairman of the supervisory board should be prepared, where appropriate, to discuss with investors topics that are relevant to the supervisory board. The chairman of the audit committee should remain independent and not have been a member of the company's management board within the past two years. As previously, the chairman of the supervisory board should not also chair the audit committee.

Goergen et al. (2008) review the governance role of large shareholders, creditors, the product market, and the supervisory board, and also discuss the importance of mergers and acquisitions, the market in block trades, and the lack of a hostile takeover market. They find that:

> the German system is characterised by a market for partial corporate control, large shareholders and bank/creditor monitoring, a two-tier (management and supervisory) board with co-determination between shareholders and employees on the supervisory board, a

disciplinary product-market, and corporate governance regulation largely based on EU directives but with deep roots in the German codes and legal doctrine. Another important feature of the German system is its corporate governance efficiency criterion which is focused on the maximisation of stakeholder value rather than shareholder value. However, the German corporate governance system has experienced many important changes over the last decade. First, the relationship between ownership or control concentration and profitability has changed over time. Second, the pay-for-performance relation is influenced by large shareholder control: in firms with controlling blockholders and when a universal bank is simultaneously an equity and debtholder, the pay-for-performance relation is lower than in widely-held firms or blockholder-controlled firms. Third, since 1995 several major regulatory initiatives (including voluntary codes) have increased transparency and accountability.

Odenius (2008) reviews Germany's corporate governance system and the effectiveness of recent reforms. He states that since the early 1990s far-reaching reforms have complemented the traditional stakeholder system with important elements of the shareholder system. He raises the important question of whether these reforms have created sufficient flexibility for the market to optimize its corporate governance structure within well-established social and legal norms. He concludes that there is scope for enhancing flexibility in three core areas, relating to internal control mechanisms, especially the flexibility of board structures; self-dealing; and external control, particularly takeover activity.

v. Werder and Talaulicar (2011) have reviewed corporate governance developments in Germany in recent years and point out that 'regulatory changes are primarily aimed at further improving the modalities of managing and supervising corporations within the corporate governance system in order to attenuate its downsides and to develop its strengths. In this regard, an accelerating pace as well as an increasing intensity of reforms is to be observed.' Furthermore Ringe (2015) highlighted that 'corporate Germany is currently undergoing a major change in three main aspects: reduced concentration of ownership, a weaker role of banks in equity participations, and an increasing internationalization of shareholders. It appears that these changes are more pronounced the larger the corporation.' Ringe points out that 'the changing ownership patterns have influenced the case for law reform: a legal system that is moving towards a dispersed ownership structure needs very different legal rules than the old, blockholder-based German corporate network'.

A paper by Hopt (2017) discusses the dialogue between the chairman of the board and investors and concludes that 'it can be expected that the chairman of the board's dialogue with investors will sooner or later not only become a general practice, but that it will also be considered to represent good corporate governance'.

Denmark

Denmark has a quite different ownership structure from that of, say, the USA, the UK, or most other European countries (see Table 10.4). The ownership is quite concentrated and there is a widespread existence of foundation ownership. This means that some of the largest Danish companies are controlled by a foundation (i.e. a legal entity without owners often created to administer a large ownership stake in a particular company). There is also significant institutional investor share ownership in Denmark, with institutional investors owning

Table 10.4 Key characteristics influencing Danish corporate governance

Feature	Key characteristic
Main business form	Public or private companies limited by shares
Predominant ownership structure	Institutional investors and foundation ownership
Legal system	Civil law
Board structure	Dual
Important aspect	Many shares have multiple voting rights

approximately 35 per cent of market value of Danish equity. Like Germany, corporate govern-ance in Denmark is focused on a dual board structure. The Danish Companies Act provides that half the members elected by the shareholders, or by other parties entitled to appoint directors, will be elected by the employees, with a minimum of two (this provision applies to companies with at least 35 employees).

The Nørby Committee's report was published in 2001 and made recommendations for corporate governance in Denmark. The Foreword to the report strongly emphasized that this was a voluntary code and that it was really up to the individual companies as to whether they actually followed it, but that the Nørby Committee believed that it was in companies' best interests to do so. The Committee tried to make the recommendations operationally practi-cal, although it emphasized that the recommendations were to be followed by companies of their own accord, so these were non-binding recommendations. However, the Commit-tee felt that it was in the companies' own interests to follow the recommendations and did think it important that companies stated to what extent they had followed the recommenda-tions. The report built on the OECD basic values of openness, transparency, responsibility, and equality. The Nørby Committee felt that because, internationally, there is a growing interest in corporate governance and a rise in investors demanding more and better information about managements' actions and the companies' long-term goals and strategy, it was important that Denmark also had a set of corporate governance recommendations. The Committee believed that there should be more demands on listed companies than on unlisted compa-nies; it also recommended that state companies complied with the recommendations, where relevant. The Nørby report was split into seven sections, outlined later.

The Nørby Committee's (2001) recommendations formed the basis for further corpo-rate governance developments in Denmark. In late 2002 the Copenhagen Stock Exchange appointed an independent corporate governance committee to develop further corporate governance for Danish listed companies. Various international initiatives occurred that impacted on corporate governance thinking in Denmark. These included the US Sarbanes-Oxley Act (2002), the UK Combined Code (2003), and EU initiatives such as the Action Plan (2003) to modernize company law and enhance corporate governance in the EU (see earlier for more detail). In the light of these various international developments, it was decided to revisit the original Nørby recommendations to see what revisions might be needed.

In December 2003 the Copenhagen Stock Exchange Committee on Corporate Govern-ance issued its report, often referred to as Nørby (2003). A subsequent update was made in

August 2005, being Nørby (2005), and an important development was that the Copenhagen Stock Exchange incorporated the Nørby (2005) Committee's revised recommendations for corporate governance into the disclosure requirements for listed companies, 'obliging the companies, in accordance with the "comply or explain" principle, to include in their future annual reports a statement on how they address the Recommendations'. The fundamentally important aspect here is transparency. As in the UK, companies may comply by explaining how and why they do not comply with a particular recommendation. It is the disclosure and transparency aspects that enable shareholders and other stakeholders to understand better what is going on in the company.

The focus of the original Nørby (2001) recommendations plus the additional recommendation, and the revisions to these by subsequent committees, these being the recommendations as at August 2005, covered the role of the shareholders and their interaction with the management of the company; the role of the stakeholders and their importance to the company; openness and transparency; the tasks and responsibilities of the supervisory board; the composition of the supervisory board; remuneration of the members of the supervisory board and the executive board; risk management; and audit.

From this discussion, it can be seen that the Danish corporate governance system is developing rapidly, with a move to a 'comply or explain' basis. As with Germany, the dual board system may mean that Danish employees are at an advantage if the company's strategy requires that part of the company be closed down; the closure is more likely to hit part of the company located in a country with a unitary board structure, where employees have less influence.

There were minor amendments to the Danish Corporate Governance Code in February 2008 relating to remuneration of the members of the supervisory and executive boards whereby the contents of the remuneration policy should be disclosed on the company's website as well as in the annual report. In December 2008 there were minor amendments in relation to openness and transparency whereby the company may publish details of a non-financial nature including diversity aspects (such as gender and age) within the supervisory board, the executive board, and the company more generally; and in relation to the composition of the supervisory board whereby the composition should be regularly reviewed, including in relation to diversity issues (such as gender and age).

The Companies Act 2009 introduced new generic terms for the governing bodies of Danish companies being the supreme governing body (essentially aimed at the board of directors or the supervisory board) and the central governing body (essentially aimed at the board of directors or the executive board of companies that have a supervisory board/executive board). Further amendments were made to the Danish Corporate Governance Code in 2010, 2011, 2013, 2014, and 2017. The revisions in 2010 were made as a response to the Danish Companies Act 2009, the Financial Statements Act, and the Act on Approved Auditors and Audit Firms, in addition to European Commission recommendations, including those on remuneration of listed companies' governing bodies. Developments in foreign recommendations on corporate governance were also taken into account. Amendments include that the company's central governing body should have a corporate social responsibility policy, and that consideration be given as to whether to establish a whistle-blowing scheme. The 2013 Code was simplified by omitting a number of recommendations either laid down by legislation or which had been generally incorporated into company practice. Some 47 recommendations remained covering five areas which are also retained in the Code published in November 2014:

- Communication and interaction by the company with its investors and other stakeholders;
- Tasks and responsibilities of the board of directors;
- Composition and organization of the board of directors;
- Remuneration of management;
- Financial reporting, risk management, and audits.

In November 2017, further amendments were made to the Corporate Governance Code. The Preface highlights that the revised Code is a response to feedback from companies and stakeholders to simplify the recommendations. Therefore the

> Committee assumes that companies comply with statutory requirements in companies accounting, auditing and stock exchange legislation without repeating these requirements in these recommendations. The recommendations will thus to the greatest extent possible, not include elements that are directly stipulated in legislation or which are largely part of company practice. The Committee will monitor developments in corporate governance continuously to develop the recommendations to comply with the soft law principle, as need be.

It should also be noted that in November 2016, the Committee on Corporate Governance introduced the Stewardship Code. The aim of the Stewardship Code is 'to promote the companies' long-term value creation and thereby contribute to maximising long-term return for investors. Thus, the Recommendations on Corporate Governance and the Stewardship Code are mutually reinforcing in serving a common purpose.' The Stewardship Code is primarily addressed to Danish institutional investors who invest in shares of companies that are publicly listed in Denmark and is based on the 'comply or explain' approach. It has seven sections relating to engagement policy, monitoring and dialogue, escalation, collaboration with other investors, voting policy, conflicts of interest, and reporting.

In 2008 the Danish Venture Capital and Private Equity Association (DVCA) introduced guidelines to help create greater openness and transparency in private equity funds in Denmark. The guidelines, using a 'comply or explain' approach, apply at both company level and fund level, i.e. both the private equity funds and the companies in which they invest are expected to be more open and transparent.

Lekvall et al. (2014) produced a comprehensive study of the Nordic corporate governance model highlighting that the five countries of Denmark, Finland, Iceland, Norway, and Sweden have a shared corporate governance model used by companies. The key observation of the study is that the Nordic corporate governance model

> allows the shareholder majority to effectively control and take long-term responsibility for the company that they own. The alleged risk of such a system—the potential that a shareholder majority misuses its power for its own benefit at the expense of minority shareholders—is effectively curbed through a well-developed system of minority protection. The result is a governance model that encourages strong shareholders to engage in the governance of the company in their own interest, while creating value for the company and all its shareholders.

A recent paper by Thomsen et al (2018) uses a unique Danish data set to document that industrial foundations are long-term owners that practice long-term governance and promote long-termism.

France

The corporate governance system in France (see Table 10.5) is set in a civil law context and, traditionally, does not offer good protection to minority investors. The French government has been an important stakeholder, partly because of its direct shareholdings in French industry (although this has declined with the privatizations in recent years) and also because of the fact that many civil servants are appointed to corporate boards. Wymeersch (1998) states that takeovers, particularly of recently privatized firms, are prevented by the *noyaux durs* (hard core), which comprise a series of holdings by financial institutions, banks, and insurance companies to help stabilize the French industrial sector. In addition, control may be enhanced by multiple voting rights attaching to shares, a construct that is against generally accepted corporate governance best practice.

There are various business forms available in France of which the two we are most concerned with are the *Société anonyme (SA)*, which is essentially like a public company in the UK, and the *Société à responsabilité limitée (SARL)*, which is a limited liability company along the lines of a limited company in the UK. The French corporate governance system places a lot of emphasis, and power, on the *président directeur-général (PDG)* of a company. This is in line with the French tradition of centralized leadership and power.

France has a predominantly unitary board system, although the option to have a dual board exists. Similarly, there is provision for employee involvement where this is provided for by the articles of the company. French corporate governance codes therefore need to take account of this diversity of structure.

The first French corporate governance report was the Viénot Committee Report in 1995 (Viénot I). The Viénot Committee was established by two employers' federations (MEDEF and AFEP-AGREF) and with the support of leading private sector companies; it was chaired by Marc Viénot, head of Société Générale. The second Viénot report (Viénot II) was issued in 1999. Subsequent to Viénot II, the corporate governance environment became further complicated by the introduction of 'new economic regulations' in 2001 that gave companies with a unitary board structure the choice of separating the functions of chairman and chief

Table 10.5 Key characteristics influencing French corporate governance

Feature	Key characteristic
Main business form	Public or private companies limited by shares
Predominant ownership structure	State, institutional investors, individuals
Legal system	Civil law
Board structure	Unitary (but other structure possible)
Important aspect	Many shares have multiple voting rights

executive officer (CEO) or keeping them joint. The corporate governance report of a working group chaired by Daniel Bouton (President of Société Générale) was then issued in October 2002.

The Bouton Report (2002) recommended incremental improvement rather than any radical reform. Part 1 of the report was split into six areas: the role and operation of the board of directors, the board of directors' composition, evaluation of the board of directors, the audit committee, the compensation committee, and the nominating committee. Part 2 of the report contained some recommendations on strengthening the independence of statutory auditors (with specific reference to the importance of this area in the context of the Enron affair). Part 3 covered financial information, accounting standards and practices, and discussed the importance of high-quality financial information and disclosures and the means to achieve them.

On a separate note, France published a decree in February 2002 setting out mandatory disclosure by companies in their annual report, and accounts of the social and environmental impact of their activities. It came into force in 2003 for all annual reports.

In August 2003 France enacted new laws relating to financial security with the aim of restoring the trust of investors in French markets. The changes included that there should be improved transparency with more information provided to shareholders, including a separate report on the internal control procedures of the company, and a new procedure for the appointment of external auditors.

In October 2003 AFEP and MEDEF published *The Corporate Governance of Listed Corporations*, a document that provided a set of principles of corporate governance based on consolidation of the 1995, 1999 (Viénot I and II), and 2002 (Bouton) AFEP and MEDEF reports. The report does not add to the Viénot and Bouton reports, the substance of which is retained; rather, it collates the recommendations into a single set of principles. The principles cover various aspects of the board of directors, independent directors, board evaluation, meeting of the board and the committees, and board committees (such as audit, compensation, and nominations), and directors' compensation. The principles utilize a 'comply or explain' approach with regard to which recommendations a company has adopted. In December 2010 AFEP and MEDEF published the Corporate Governance Code of Listed Corporations which consolidates the earlier corporate governance publications, including the Viénot reports, the Bouton Report, recommendations made in 2007 and 2008 concerning the compensation of executive directors of listed companies, and the recommendation made in 2010 concerning strengthening women's representation within boards. The Corporate Governance Code of Listed Corporations was further revised in 2013. An interesting change is that executive directors should not hold more than two other directorships in listed corporations including foreign corporations, not affiliated with the group; previously this figure was four directorships (the latter being the number still retained as the limit of other directorships for non-executive directors). The most recent update, in November 2016, specifies the recommendations of the Code in further detail, especially in relation to independence, CSR and the compensation of company officers.

The Association Française de la Gestion Financière (AFG) is the French Asset Management Association which represents and promotes the interests of the French asset management industry. In 2011 it issued the ninth version of its recommendations on corporate governance, which constitute shareholder voting criteria for its members.

A significant development in terms of shareholders' voting rights and anti-takeover measures occurred with the introduction of the Florange Act in March 2014. The Act provides for investors who have held shares in a listed French company for at least two years to be automatically granted double voting rights (sometimes referred to as loyalty shares) provided that the company does not prohibit double voting rights in its by-laws. This means that double voting rights will have started automatically from March 2016 unless a company amends its articles of association to opt out of this provision. Concerns have been expressed that such double voting rights will strengthen the role of the French state which has large holdings in many French companies and have a detrimental impact on minority shareholders.

Lee and Yoo (2008) provide an interesting discussion about the competing rationales for corporate governance in France. Their analysis

> shows that both converging and diverging forces of institutional change coexist, shaping selective responses to globalization. While the adoption of the shareholder model is necessary for resource acquirement from the global capital markets, resource allocation in the cooperative innovation systems reinforces the stakeholder model. The French case confirms the sustainability of distinctive institutional complementarities, albeit with selective adaptation based on a sense-making social compromise.

Gomez (2011), when discussing corporate governance developments in France, highlights three areas that he feels will need to be tackled in coming years: the isolation of CEOs, CEO succession planning, and the effective role of shareholders. He highlights the growing importance of corporate governance in France such that 'the more a company is known to be influential in French society, the more the question of whether or not it is being well "governed" becomes publicly debated and receives media coverage'.

Italy

Bianchi et al. (2001) identify seven different company types in Italy. However, the main business forms are the *società di persone*, or partnership, which generally has unlimited liability, and the *società di capitali*, or limited liability company. Furthermore, their analysis of direct ownership for both listed and unlisted companies in Italy finds that 'a major role is played by families, coalitions, the State and above all by other companies. The largest stake in listed and unlisted companies is held by other non-financial or holding companies. Contrary to other European countries, the amount held by financial institutions is limited' (p. 154). They do, however, comment that the situation is changing as pyramidal private groups are simplifying, and hence both banks and institutional investors are starting to play a more important role.

Italy has traditionally had a unitary board structure but a board of auditors is also required (see Table 10.6). However, the corporate governance situation in Italy has been subject to a number of revisions in recent years. In 1998 the then Director General of the Italian Treasury, Mario Draghi, introduced corporate governance rules, a series of legislative measures that became known as the Draghi Law. These rules enhanced transparency of listed companies, discussed the structure for decision-making within companies, and also looked at the area of internal control. Minority shareholders benefited from this legislation and it also strengthened the position of Italian companies with reference to the confidence with which they were perceived by international investors.

The Draghi Law also required the establishment of a board of auditors comprised of at least three individuals, all of whom should be independent of the company's directors and employees. Members of the board of auditors have to fulfil experience and other criteria. The role of the board of auditors includes reviewing the company's organizational structure, its internal control system, its accounting system, and its administrative system.

Table 10.6 Key characteristics influencing Italian corporate governance

Feature	Key characteristic
Main business form	Limited liability companies; partnerships
Predominant ownership structure	Non-financial/holding companies; families
Legal system	Civil law
Board structure	Unitary (but other structure possible)
Important aspect	Board of auditors required

In 1998 the Borsa Italiana introduced a corporate governance report that became known as the Preda Report, named after its chairman. The Preda Code of Conduct (1999) introduced recommendations regarding the composition of the board, the formation of key board committees, the roles of chairman and CEO, and the independence of directors. However, the Code was a voluntary code and companies could disclose the extent to which they had adopted or complied with the Code. It must be said that the Code was not as comprehensive as, for example, the UK Combined Code. For example, it said that the majority of a company's remuneration committee members should be non-executive but it did not really talk about their independence. So, given the current climate where there is a lot of focus and emphasis on corporate governance, in 2002 a revised report, known as 'Preda 2' was issued. The Preda 2 report dealt with a number of areas relating to corporate governance covering the role of the board of directors; the composition of the board of directors; independent directors; chairman of the board of directors; information to be provided to the board of directors; confidential information; remuneration of directors; internal control; transactions with related parties; relations with institutional investors and other shareholders; shareholders' meetings; and members of the board of auditors.

In 2006 Borsa Italiana issued a new corporate governance code to take account of changes in good governance practices internationally. Whilst the order of contents was similar to that of the 2002 Code, the structure changed: principles were elaborated on with application criteria and comments, which helped to define the range of the principles and criteria, and also examples were given. New features included: the introduction of recommendations on the limit of roles held by each director and annual self-assessment by the board; the introduction of a lead independent director; recommendations on the internal control system; the promotion of initiatives to encourage shareholder participation in shareholders' meetings and the exercise of their rights.

In 2010 there was a revision to the article in the 2006 Code relating to remuneration of directors and key management personnel, such that 'a significant part of the remuneration shall be linked to achieving specific performance objectives, possibly including non-economic objectives'. Moreover, in relation to non-executive directors, 'the remuneration of non-executive directors shall be proportionate to the commitment required from each of them, also taking into account their possible participation in one or more committees'. In December 2011 the Corporate Governance Code was substantially updated and now contains ten articles:

- Article 1—Role of the Board of Directors
- Article 2—Composition of the Board of Directors
- Article 3—Independent directors
- Article 4—Internal committees of the Board of Directors
- Article 5—Appointment of directors
- Article 6—Remuneration of directors
- Article 7—Internal control and risk management system
- Article 8—Statutory auditors
- Article 9—Relations with the shareholders
- Article 10—Two-tier and one-tier systems.

A significant legal change was introduced in April 2012 by Article 36 of Decree Law No. 201 of 6 December 2011, converted into Law No. 214/2011, in relation to the financial sector, which means that it is illegal for a person to hold more than one seat on a board in a financial institution operating in the same sector or market.

The Corporate Governance Code was updated in 2014 with an additional principle in relation to the remuneration of directors. The new principle relates to the end of office and/ or termination of the employment of an executive director or a general manager. In such instances, the company should issue a press release disclosing detailed information regarding the amount and timing of any indemnities or other benefits and any claw-backs in operation. In 2015 some small changes were made to the Code including in relation to CSR principles, enhancing internal corporate safeguards to meet legal requirements and transparency.

In 2015 the Assogestioni, which is the representative association of the Italian investment management industry, published the *Italian Stewardship Principles for the exercise of administrative and voting rights in listed companies*. The six Principles are aimed at investment management companies and are designed to promote discussion and co-operation between IMCs and listed issuers in which assets are invested. Assogestioni released the last version of the *Italian Stewardship Principles for the exercise of administrative and voting rights in listed companies* in 2016.

In relation to double voting rights, the Italian government decided not to implement a resolution passed in July 2014 which would have allowed Italian companies to create loyalty shares by a 50 per cent majority shareholder approval (rather than a majority requirement of two-thirds), for investors who had held their shares for two years. The possibility of this law being introduced had caused a lot of concern given the large number of Italian listed companies that are majority controlled. Hence Italy's government decided not to extend the

50 per cent rule though a few companies did manage to introduce it before it expired at the end of January 2015.

Melis (2006) provided an insightful discussion of the development of corporate governance in Italy, highlighting: the Draghi Law (1998) as a cornerstone with its explicit aim to strengthen minority shareholders' rights; the Preda Code of Conduct (1999, 2002), which has had a significant impact on the corporate governance structure of Italian listed companies; and the important innovation made by the 2004 company law reform, which gave companies the freedom to choose between three different board models. Portolano (2008) also cited the importance of this Italian corporate reform, which now provides for three different management models for Italian companies:

> the traditional model, which allows shareholders to appoint a board of directors with responsibility for managing the company and a panel of statutory auditors with responsibility for auditing the accounts and ensuring compliance with law; the German model, comprising a Board of Directors and a Supervisory Panel; and the Anglo-Saxon model, providing for a Board of Directors and an internal Audit Committee.

However, at that time only a very small number of companies had diverged from the traditional model.

Enriques (2009) provided an interesting discussion of corporate governance reforms in Italy. He believed that the corporate governance legal framework was much improved as a result of the reforms but felt that further changes could be made to improve the protection of investors against expropriation by corporate insiders. However, he also pointed out that changes to the legal and political cultures in Italy would help ensure the effectiveness of corporate governance reforms.

Melis and Gaia (2011) review developments in corporate governance in Italy and conclude that whilst the overall awareness of the importance of corporate governance has increased amongst senior managers, directors, and investors, Italian listed companies tend to 'whenever possible, avoid complying with "unfavourable" laws and/or recommendations and are prone to creative compliance, that is formal compliance, rather than to respect the spirit of recommendations (or law)'.

Bianchi et al. (2011) state that nearly 86 per cent of Italian listed companies claim to be in formal compliance with the provisions of the Italian Corporate Governance Code. However, when they devise a governance indicator (CoRe) to try to assess the actual, or effective, levels of compliance with the Italian Corporate Governance Code in terms of listed companies' procedures for dealing with related party transactions (RPTs), they find that 'the companies' level of effective compliance with regard to RPTs is considerably lower than their publicly reported levels of formal compliance' and that 'higher levels of effective compliance tend to be found in companies where (1) minority shareholders have appointed one or more directors; (2) independent directors serve on important committees; and (3) there are significant holdings by institutional investors—particularly foreign investors—who participate in general shareholder meetings'.

Finally Melis and Rombi (2018), using a sample of 559 statutory auditors, whose main task is to monitor the acts and the decision-making process of the board of directors, provide evidence that 'statutory auditors' compensation is mainly based upon the effort and responsibilities that are observable by shareholders. However, our findings highlight that the additional, poorly disclosed, compensation that a statutory auditor may receive, unrelated to his/her role, is associated with his/her involvement with corporate insiders.' They suggest that 'investors and other stakeholders, who may rely on the work of the board of statutory auditors as independent monitor, [need] to be careful about the way statutory auditors are paid'.

Convergence or divergence

We have seen that the main differences in corporate governance codes amongst Continental European countries stem from companies law and securities regulation. The ownership structure varies across Continental European countries and those countries with a civil law/code tend to have poorer protection of minorities, which is not attractive for smaller shareholders or for those investing from overseas. Van den Berghe (2002) concludes that 'a serious tension is growing between capital markets, which are gradually globalising, and the economic and legal environments (like the company models involved, the governance recommendations, and legal rules) that are still quite divergent. This gap creates pressure on firms that want to enter the capital market with structures and governance environments that are not up to the global standards of the capital markets' (p. 167). Gregory (2005) reviews the various developments in international corporate governance, highlighting both the commonalities and the remaining differences, which indicate that there is a move towards convergence, albeit gradual and incomplete. Solomon (2007) states that 'there is increasing evidence that corporate governance standardization at a global level is desirable, in order to increase cross-border institutional investment and to reduce cost of capital for multi-national companies'. Clarke (2007) believes that:

> as pressures to conform to international standards and expectations increase, the resilience of historical and cultural differences will continue. The business case for diversity is, if anything, even more compelling ... However, an enduring lesson of the recent experience of corporate governance failure is that it is in the interest of firms, investors and economies wherever they are based in the world, and whatever system they adopt, to commit to strive for the highest standards of governance.

Martynova and Renneboog (2010), in a study of a comprehensive comparative analysis of corporate governance regulatory systems and their evolution over the last 15 years in 30 European countries and the US, find that 'while varying degrees of creditor protection that were recently introduced in national bankruptcy laws show that the global convergence of legal systems towards a single system of corporate regulation is unlikely, there are still signs of increasing convergence by national corporate governance regulations towards a shareholder-based regime when the protection of (minority) shareholders is considered'.

Whilst recognizing that 'one size does not fit all' in terms of corporate governance, institutional investors are increasingly converging on the basic characteristics of good corporate governance, encompassing such areas as basic shareholder rights, independence of directors, and presence of key board committees. Therefore it is likely that, over time, there will be convergence on the fundamental aspects of good corporate governance, notwithstanding that ownership structures and legal systems may vary. The EU Corporate Governance Framework recommendations have implications for a more consistent approach to issues, such as boards and shareholders' rights across EU Member States and will continue to be a powerful force towards convergence on various aspects of corporate governance.

Conclusions

This chapter has shown how corporate governance has developed in a number of Continental European countries. Spurred by the development of capital markets, the influence of institutional investors, and a growing desire for more transparency and disclosure following various high-profile financial scandals across the globe, Continental Europe has responded by improving its corporate governance to provide increased disclosure and accountability. Although corporate ownership structures may differ across Europe, and some countries have a unitary board whilst others have a dual board, there does seem to be agreement on some of the fundamental aspects of corporate governance, which is leading towards a convergence of corporate governance in key areas.

Summary

- Corporate governance codes in Continental Europe have developed against a backdrop of varying legal and ownership structures. Whilst idiosyncratic features of countries influence the development of individual codes, there seems to be a consensus on certain key issues, for example, more transparency and disclosure, accountability of the board, and the independence of at least a portion of the directors.

- Most European countries have a unitary board structure, although the majority also have the option of a dual structure.

- Germany has a dual board structure and co-determination means that employees are represented on the supervisory board. Banks are quite influential in the German corporate governance system. The Cromme Code harmonized a wide variety of laws and regulations, and contained recommendations and suggestions for complying with international best practice on corporate governance. The amended Corporate Governance Code updates the earlier versions of the Code, and subsequent amendments have been regularly made.

- Denmark also has a dual board structure. Its ownership structure is unusual because there is widespread foundation ownership. The Nørby Code and subsequent updates made recommendations on corporate governance in Denmark and a 'comply or explain' approach is now followed.

- France has a predominantly unitary board system although the option to have a dual board exists. Building on the earlier Viénot reports, the Bouton Report recommended incremental improvements rather than any radical reform. AFEP and MEDEF produced a single set of corporate governance principles that drew together the earlier recommendations of Viénot and Bouton. Several updates to these corporate governance principles have occurred. France has some comprehensive recommendations regarding disclosure of social and environmental indicators.

- Italy has a unitary board structure but a board of auditors is also required. The Preda Codes (1 and 2) make recommendations regarding corporate governance. The Corporate Governance Code (2006) adapts the earlier principles in the light of international best practice in corporate governance. Updates to the Corporate Governance Code have been regularly made. Legislation introduced in 2012 in relation to the financial sector means that it is illegal for a person to hold more than one seat on a board in a financial institution operating in the same sector or market.

- There is much debate about whether corporate governance systems are converging or diverging. There does seem to be agreement on some of the fundamental characteristics of a sound corporate governance system, indicative of a move towards convergence. However there are some recent differences in approach, for example, in relation to whether shareholders who have held shares for two years should then be entitled to double voting rights (loyalty shares). Developments such as the EU recommendations will play a key role in convergence on various aspects of corporate governance.

Example: Safran, France

This is an example of a French company which has double voting rights for long-term shareholders.

Safran is an international high-technology group and supplier of systems and equipment in its core markets of aerospace, defence, and security; it operates worldwide and has 69,000 employees. It is listed on the NYSE Euronext Paris and a constituent of the French stock market index, CAC 40.

The origins of Safran can be traced back to 1905 when the Seguin brothers founded the company 'Société des moteurs Gnome' in Gennevilliers, near Paris, to make rotary engines for airplanes. Today the Safran Group consists of 11 companies: Aircelle, Herakles, Hispano-Suiza, Labinal Power Systems, Messier-Bugatti-Dowty, Morpho, Safran Consulting, Sagem, Snecma, Techspace Aero, and Turbomeca.

Safran's board of directors comprises 17 members including:

- One State representative and two directors proposed by the State; two employee shareholder representatives and two employee representatives, meaning that all stakeholders involved in Safran's daily affairs are represented.

- 7 independent directors (equal to more than 50% of the Board, according to the calculation criteria in the AFEP-MEDEF code), offering a wide range of complementary expertise.

- 4 women (equal to more than 25% of the Board, according to the calculation criteria in the AFEP-MEDEF code), and three directors with international profiles.

- Permanent 'guests' with a consultative voice: a government commissioner and representatives of the central work's council.

Safran has two board committees, being the audit and risk management committee, and the nomination and remuneration committee. From April 2015 Philippe Petitcolin was named Chief Executive Officer of Safran, and Ross McInnes was named Chairman of the Board. They succeed Jean-Paul Herteman who held both roles. This separation of these two key roles strengthens Safran's corporate governance structure.

The company's articles of incorporation and by-laws provide that 'all fully paid-up shares registered in the name of the same holder for at least two years as at the date of the General Shareholders' Meeting shall carry double voting rights' (31.8). However there are some restrictions of voting rights such that 'no shareholder at a given General Meeting may exercise more than 30% of the total voting rights attached to all of the Company's shares' (31.12).

Example: Volkswagen, Germany

Volkswagen was rocked by the diesel emissions scandal in 2015. It has made significant strides to recover its reputation since then including changes to the top management team.

In the Autumn of 2015, the US Environmental Protection Agency (EPA) found that many VW cars being sold in America had a 'defeat device' in diesel engines that could detect when they were being tested and would turn on the emissions controls thus changing the performance so that the cars seemed to satisfy the emissions level requirements. Initially VW denied that it was aware of the problem and inferred that a group of 'rogue engineers' was to blame. However subsequently VW admitted cheating emissions tests in the US and the CEO, Martin Winterkorn, resigned and was replaced by Matthias Mueller, the former boss of Porsche. Under Matthias Mueller, VW has been successful in trying to rebuild its reputation. It launched an internal enquiry and ultimately, early in 2017, pleaded guilty to criminal charges. VW was ordered to pay a $2.8 billion fine relating to the rigged emissions tests.

A number of institutional investors, including Norway's sovereign wealth fund, voted against many of the resolutions put forward at VW's AGM in May 2016. Aviva, for example, voted against the resolutions regarding the discharge of directors on the management board and on the supervisory board with the reasons stated being: the company/directors have been subject to fines/litigation; supporting discharge may restrict future legal action; material governance concerns; and company/directors being investigated.

In the fiscal year 2017, the Volkswagen Group increased its deliveries to customers worldwide by 4.3 per cent year-on-year and achieved a new record of 10.7 million vehicles and its sales revenue increased by 6.2 per cent year-on-year to €230.7 billion due to volume-related factors. The Volkswagen Group employed over 642.3 thousand people, including the Chinese joint ventures, establishing itself as one of the world's largest employers in the private sector. In his Letter to Shareholders 2017, Matthias Mueller stated: 'Each setback should above all encourage us to devote all our energy to bringing about the transformation at Volkswagen.'

In early 2018, it was announced that the CEO Matthias Mueller would be leaving his post to be succeeded by Herbert Diess who had been serving as CEO of the VW brand. The valuable contribution made by Mueller in steering VW out of the emissions scandal and in embracing a strategy focusing more on, for example, investment in electric cars was recognized and lauded.

 ## Mini case study   Telecom Italia, Italy

This is an example of an Italian company that has very good corporate governance practices and disclosures, and is recognized as one of the best in Italy. However in recent times, direction and coordination of Telecom Italia's activities have been taken over by a major shareholder, Vivendi S.A.

Telecom Italia is heavily involved in most aspects of the telecommunications industry. At the end of December 2017, the largest stake is owned by foreign institutional investors (57.95 per cent); the second largest stake (23.94 per cent) is owned by Vivendi S.A., whilst other shareholders own 13.23 per cent, and Italian institutional investors own 3.80 per cent. Ethical Boardroom announced that Telecoms Italia Group was the industry sector leader for telecoms in Europe and awarded it 'Best Corporate Governance' in this regard. Ethical Boardroom state that 'the awards recognise the outstanding leadership from boards of public companies who have raised the bar to ensure that strong corporate governance plays an essential part in protecting and enhancing long-term value for

(continued)

all stakeholders'. Another accolade was from the World Finance Corporate Governance Awards for Italy; the winner in 2018 was the Telecom Italia Group.

Telecom Italia's website contains excellent information on the principles and codes that the company abides by and its Report on Corporate Governance and Share Ownership 2017 is comprised of 20 sections, including sections on the board of directors; board committees; internal control and risk management system; and remuneration of directors. An additional section on further corporate governance practices relates to 'Direction and coordination' and states:

> On 27 July 2017 the Board of Directors of the Company took note of the start of direction and coordination activity over TIM by Vivendi S.A. On 13 September 2017, the stock exchange regulator, the Commissione Nazionale per le Società e la Borsa (Consob), issued an order in which it maintains that the reference shareholder, Vivendi S.A. (which currently holds 23.94% of the ordinary share capital), also 'exercises de facto control over TIM pursuant to article 2359 of the Italian civil code and pursuant to article 93 of the CLF, as well as pursuant to the regulation on related parties'. The Company considers that the order differs notably from the consolidated interpretation on corporate control, with which TIM (and, justifiably, the whole market) has always adhered. TIM, while complying with it, has challenged it before the Lazio Administrative Court.

> With regard to board composition, the Report on Corporate Governance and Share Ownership 2017 explains that, in accordance with the by-laws, two slates were presented, one by the relative majority shareholder Vivendi S.A. and another by a group of asset management companies (SGRs) and institutional investors. The Vivendi S.A. slate obtained the greatest number of votes (49.35 per cent of the capital voting in the shareholders' meeting) and therefore all ten candidates on the slate were appointed to the board of directors whilst five candidates from the SGR and International Investors slate were also appointed Member of the Board of Directors. Paul E. Singer is building up an indirect shareholding held through the controlled companies of US activist investor Elliott International LP, Elliott Associates LP and The Liverpool Limited Partnership.

> In March 2018, seven Telecom Italia SpA directors resigned and the Italian regulator is reportedly investigating the situation.

Mini case study questions

1. In what ways do you think that the shareholder structure at Telecom Italia might influence the company's corporate governance and corporate culture?

2. What shortcomings might be perceived in the manner in which board composition is decided at Telecom Italia?

Questions

The discussion questions to follow cover the key learning points of this chapter. Reading of some of the additional reference material will enhance the depth of the students' knowledge and understanding of these areas.

1. What factors have influenced the development of board structure in Continental European countries?

2. How might the employees' interests be represented in a company's corporate governance structure?

3. To what extent is there an emphasis on the role of non-executive directors in Continental European countries?

4. To what extent are the needs of various stakeholder groups satisfied by corporate governance structures in Continental Europe?

5. Critically discuss the case for double voting rights being given to long-term shareholders in a firm.

6. Critically discuss the extent to which you believe that corporate governance systems are converging or diverging. How might the global financial crisis have affected this?

References

Article 36, Decree Law No. 201 (2011), *Tutela della concorrenza e partecipazioni personali incrociate nei mercati del credito e finanziari*, 6 December 2011, Italian Government, Italy.

Association Française des Entreprises Privées and Mouvement des Entreprises de France (1999), *Report of the Committee on Corporate Governance (Viénot II)*, AFEP/MEDEF, Paris.

Association Française des Entreprises Privées and Mouvement des Entreprises de France (2003), *The Corporate Governance of Listed Corporations*, AFEP/MEDEF, Paris.

Association Française des Entreprises Privées and Mouvement des Entreprises de France (2010), *Corporate Governance Code of Listed Corporations*, AFEP/MEDEF, Paris.

Association Française des Entreprises Privées and Mouvement des Entreprises de France (2013), *Corporate Governance Code of Listed Corporations*, AFEP/MEDEF, Paris.

Association Française des Entreprises Privées and Mouvement des Entreprises de France (2016), *Corporate Governance Code of Listed Corporations*, AFEP/MEDEF, Paris.

Association Française de la Gestion Financière (2011), *Recommendations on Corporate Governance, January 2011*, AFG, Paris.

Assogestioni (2015), *Italian Stewardship Principles for the exercise of administrative and voting rights in listed companies*, Rome, Italy.

Assogestioni (2016), *Italian Stewardship Principles for the exercise of administrative and voting rights in listed companies*, Rome, Italy.

Becht, M. and Mayer, C. (2001), 'Introduction' in F. Barca and M. Becht (eds), *The Control of Corporate Europe*, Oxford University Press, Oxford.

Bianchi, M., Bianco, M., and Enriques, L. (2001), 'Pyramidal Groups and the Separation between Ownership and Control in Italy' in F. Barca and M. Becht (eds), *The Control of Corporate Europe*, Oxford University Press, Oxford.

Bianchi, M., Ciavarella A., Novembre V., and Signoretti R. (2011), 'Comply or Explain: Investor Protection Through the Italian Corporate Governance Code', *Journal of Applied Corporate Finance*, Vol. 23, Issue 1, pp. 107–21.

Bouton, D. (2002), *Promoting Better Corporate Governance in Listed Companies*, Report of the Working Group Chaired by Daniel Bouton, AFEP/MEDEF, Paris.

Cadbury, Sir Adrian (1992), *Report of the Committee on the Financial Aspects of Corporate Governance*, Gee & Co. Ltd, London.

Charkham, J. (1994), *Keeping Good Company: A Study of Corporate Governance in Five Countries*, Oxford University Press, Oxford.

Charkham, J. (2005), *Keeping Better Company: Corporate Governance Ten Years On*, Oxford University Press, Oxford.

Clarke, T. (2007), *International Corporate Governance: A Comparative Approach*, Routledge, London.

Conseil National du Patronat (CNPF) and AFEP (1995), *The Board of Directors of Listed Companies in France (Viénot I)*, CNPF/AFEP, Paris.

Corporate Governance Committee (2006), *Corporate Governance Code*, Borsa Italiana.

Corporate Governance Committee (2011), *Corporate Governance Code*, Borsa Italiana.

Corporate Governance Committee (2014), *Corporate Governance Code*, Borsa Italiana.

Corporate Governance Committee (2015), *Corporate Governance Code*, Borsa Italiana.

Cromme Code (2002*), Corporate Governance Code, as contained in the Transparency and Disclosure Act German Government Commission.*

Cromme Code (2005), *German Corporate Governance Code, as amended 2 June 2005*, Government Commission, Germany.

Cromme Code (2006), *German Corporate Governance Code, as amended 12 June 2006*, Government Commission, Germany.

Cromme Code (2007), *German Corporate Governance Code, as amended 14 June 2007*, Government Commission, Germany.

Cromme Code (2008), *German Corporate Governance Code, as amended 6 June 2008*, Government Commission, Germany.

Cromme Code (2009), *German Corporate Governance Code, as amended 18 June 2009*, Government Commission, Germany.

Cromme Code (2010), *German Corporate Governance Code, as amended 26 May 2010*, Government Commission, Germany.

Cromme Code (2012), *German Corporate Governance Code, as amended 15 May 2012*, Government Commission, Germany.

Cromme Code (2013), *German Corporate Governance Code, as amended 13 May 2013*, Government Commission, Germany.

Cromme Code (2014), *German Corporate Governance Code, as amended 24 June 2014*, Government Commission, Germany.

Cromme Code (2015), *German Corporate Governance Code, as amended 5 May 2015*, Government Commission, Germany.

Danish Venture Capital and Private Equity Association (2008), *Active Ownership and Transparency in Private Equity Funds: Guidelines for Responsible Ownership and Good Corporate Governance*, DVCA, Copenhagen, Denmark.

Denmark Corporate Governance Code (2017), *Recommendations on Corporate Governance*, Committee on Corporate Governance, Copenhagen Stock Exchange, Denmark.

Denmark Stewardship Code (2016), *Stewardship Code*, Committee on Corporate Governance, Copenhagen Stock Exchange, Denmark.

Deutscher Corporate Governance Kodex (2017), *German Corporate Governance Code as amended on 7 February 2017*, Government Commission, Germany.

Enriques, L. (2009), 'Modernizing Italy's Corporate Governance Institutions: Mission Accomplished?',

ECGI–Law Working Paper No. 123/2009, available at SSRN: http://ssrn.com/abstract=1400999.

European Commission (2003), *Modernising Company Law and Enhancing Corporate Governance in the European Union*, European Commission, Brussels.

European Commission (2012), *Action Plan: European company law and corporate governance—a modern legal framework for more engaged shareholders and sustainable companies*, European Commission, Brussels.

Franks, J. and Mayer, C. (1995), 'Ownership and Control' in H. Siebert (ed.), *Trends in Business Organization: Do Participation and Co-operation Increase Competitiveness?* Mohr (Siebeck), Tubingen.

Goergen, M., Manjon, M., and Renneboog, L. (2008), 'Recent Developments in German Corporate Governance', *International Review of Law and Economics*, Vol. 28, No. 3, pp. 175–93.

Gomez, P.-Y. (2011), 'From Colbert to Messier: Two Decades of Corporate Governance Reforms in France' in C.A. Mallin (ed.), *Handbook on International Corporate Governance, Country Analyses*, 2nd edn, Edward Elgar Publishing, Cheltenham, UK.

Gregory, H. (2005), 'International Corporate Governance: A Gradual If Incomplete Convergence' in M.J. Epstein and K.O. Hanson (eds), *The Accountable Corporation*, Praeger Publishers, Westport, CA.

Gregory, H.J. and Simmelkjaer, R.T. (2002), *Comparative Study of Corporate Governance Codes Relevant to the European Union and Its Member States*, on behalf of the European Commission, Internal Market Directorate General, Weil Gotshal & Manges, New York. Available at http://ec.europa.eu/internal_market/company/docs/corpgov/corp-gov-codes-rpt-part1_en.pdf.

Hopt, K.J. (2017), *The Dialogue between the Chairman of the Board and Investors: The Practice in the UK, the Netherlands and Germany and the Future of the German Corporate Governance Code Under the New Chairman* (1 September 2017). ECGI–Law Working Paper No. 365/2017. Available at SSRN: https://ssrn.com/abstract=3030693 or http://dx.doi.org/10.2139/ssrn.3030693.

La Porta, F., Lopez de Silvanes, F., Shleifer, A., and Vishny, R. (1998), 'Law and Finance', *Journal of Political Economy*, Vol. 106, No. 6, pp. 1113–55.

Lee, S.H. and Yoo, T. (2008), 'Competing Rationales for Corporate Governance in France: Institutional Complementarities between Financial Markets and Innovation Systems', *Corporate Governance: An International Review*, Vol. 16, No. 2, pp. 63–76.

Lekvall, P. Gilson, RJ., Hansen, J.L., Lønfeldt, C., Airaksinen, M, Berglund, T., von Weymarn, T., Knudsen, G., Norvik, H., Skog, R., and Sjöman, E. (2014), 'The Nordic Corporate Governance Model' (1 December 2014) in P. Lekvall (ed.), *The Nordic Corporate Governance Model*, SNS Förlag, Stockholm, December 2014; Nordic & European Company Law Working Paper No. 14-12. Available at SSRN: http://ssrn.com/abstract=2534331.

Martynova, M. and Renneboog, L. (2010), 'A Corporate Governance Index: Convergence and Diversity of National Corporate Governance Regulations', CentER Discussion Paper Series No. 2010-17; TILEC Discussion Paper No. 2010-012.

Melis, A. (2006), 'Corporate Governance Developments in Italy' in C.A. Mallin (ed.), *Handbook on International Corporate Governance, Country Analyses*, Edward Elgar Publishing, Cheltenham, UK.

Melis, A. and Gaia S. (2011), 'Corporate Governance in Italy: Normative Developments vs. Actual Practices' in C.A. Mallin (ed.), *Handbook on International Corporate Governance, Country Analyses*, 2nd edn, Edward Elgar Publishing, Cheltenham, UK.

Melis, A. and Rombi, L. (2018), 'Are Optimal Contracting and Managerial Power Competing or Complementary Views? Evidence from the Compensation of Statutory Auditors in Italy', *Corporate Governance: An International Review*, 2018, pp. 1–22. https://doi.org/10.1111/corg.12231.

Nørby Committee (2001), *Recommendations for Good Corporate Governance in Denmark*, Copenhagen Stock Exchange, Denmark.

Nørby Committee (2003), *Report on Corporate Governance in Denmark–The Copenhagen Stock Exchange Committee on Corporate Governance*, Copenhagen Stock Exchange, Denmark.

Nørby Committee (2005), *Revised Recommendations for Corporate Governance in Denmark–The Copenhagen Stock Exchange Committee on Corporate Governance*, Copenhagen Stock Exchange, Denmark.

Nørby Committee (2008), *Committee on Corporate Governance's Recommendations for Corporate Governance of August 15, 2005; section VI revised by February 6, 2008; sections III and V revised by December 10, 2008*, Copenhagen Stock Exchange, Denmark.

Nørby Committee (2010), *Committee on Corporate Governance's Recommendations on Corporate Governance, April 2010*, Copenhagen Stock Exchange, Denmark.

Nørby Committee (2011), *Committee on Corporate Governance's Recommendations on Corporate Governance, August 2011*, Copenhagen Stock Exchange, Denmark.

Nørby Committee (2013), *Committee on Corporate Governance's Recommendations on Corporate Governance, May 2013*, Copenhagen Stock Exchange, Denmark.

Nørby Committee (2014a), *Committee on Corporate Governance's Recommendations on Corporate Governance, May 2014*, Copenhagen Stock Exchange, Denmark.

Nørby Committee (2014b), *Committee on Corporate Governance's Recommendations on Corporate Governance, November 2014*, Copenhagen Stock Exchange, Denmark.

Odenius, J. (2008), 'Germany's Corporate Governance Reforms: Has the System Become Flexible Enough?', IMF Working Papers, No.8/179. Available at SSRN: http://ssrn.com/abstract=1266512.

Organisation for Economic Co-operation and Development (1999), *Principles of Corporate Governance*, OECD, Paris.

Organisation for Economic Co-operation and Development (2004), *Principles of Corporate Governance*, OECD, Paris.

Organisation for Economic Co-operation and Development (2015), *G20/OECD Principles of Corporate Governance*, OECD, Paris.

Portolano, F. (2008), 'An Imported Model of Governance', *Governance*, August 2008, Issue No. 178, Governance Publishing, Somerset.

Preda (2002), *Self Regulatory Code*, Committee for the Corporate Governance of Listed Companies, Borsa Italiana, Milan.

Prigge, S. (1998), 'A Survey of German Corporate Governance' in K.J. Hopt, H. Kanda, M.J. Roe, E. Wymeersch, and S. Prigge (eds), *Comparative Corporate Governance: The State of the Art and Emerging Research*, Oxford University Press, Oxford.

Ringe, W.G. (2015), 'Changing Law and Ownership Patterns in Germany: Corporate Governance and the Erosion of Deutschland AG', *American Journal of Comparative Law*, forthcoming. Oxford Legal Studies Research Paper No. 42/2014. Available at SSRN: http://ssrn.com/abstract=2457431 or http://dx.doi.org/10.2139/ssrn.2457431.

Solomon, J. (2007), *Corporate Governance and Accountability*, John Wiley & Sons Ltd, Chichester.

Thomsen, S., Poulsen, T., Børsting, C., and Kuhn, J. (2018), 'Industrial Foundations as Long-Term Owners', forthcoming *Corporate Governance: An International Review*. First published 23 March 2018, https://doi.org/10.1111/corg.12236.

Van den Berghe, L. (2002), *Corporate Governance in a Globalising World: Convergence or Divergence? A European Perspective*, Kluwer Academic Publishers, Amsterdam.

v. Werder, A. and Talaulicar, T. (2011), 'Corporate Governance in Germany: Basic Characteristics, Recent Developments and Future Perspectives' in C.A. Mallin (ed.), *Handbook on International Corporate Governance, Country Analyses*, 2nd edn, Edward Elgar Publishing, Cheltenham, UK.

Wymeersch, E. (1998), 'A Status Report on Corporate Governance in Some Continental European States' in K.J. Hopt, H. Kanda, M.J. Roe, E. Wymeersch, and S. Prigge (eds), *Comparative Corporate Governance: The State of the Art and Emerging Research*, Oxford University Press, Oxford.

Useful websites

www.afg.asso.fr The website for the Association Française de la Gestion Financière (the French Asset Management Association) which represents and promotes the interests of the French asset management industry.

www.borsaitaliana.it The website of the Italian Stock Exchange, Borsa Italia, contains information about corporate governance in Italy.

www.corporategovernance.dk This website contains the Nørby Committee Report on Corporate Governance and subsequent corporate governance recommendations in Denmark.

www.corporate-governance-code.de The German Code of Corporate Governance can be downloaded from this website.

www.dvca.dk The website of the Danish Venture Capital and Private Equity Association, which is a member association for a broad range of high technological investors in Denmark.

www.ecgi.org The website of the European Corporate Governance Institute has comprehensive information about corporate governance, including downloadable codes/guidelines for most countries.

www.icgn.org The website of the International Corporate Governance Network contains information relating to corporate governance issues globally.

www.oecd.org The website of the Organisation for Economic Co-operation and Development has information about various corporate governance guidelines.

 Develop your understanding of this chapter and explore the subject further using our online resources at **www.oup.com/uk/mallin6e/**

 FT Clippings

Succession question overshadows carmaker's record figures for profits and sales

Peter Campbell and David Keohane

Financial Times, 16 February 2018

Carlos Ghosn has defended Renault's corporate governance after the group decided to reinstate the 13-year chief executive for another term, sparking an issue that risked overshadowing the carmaker's record annual financial results.

Speaking on Friday morning, Mr Ghosn said the idea that the carmaker where he is both chairman and chief executive had a corporate governance problem was 'absolutely not based in fact'.

Questions over the issue took the shine off the company's results, in which operating profit rose 17 per cent to €3.85bn, ahead of estimates of €3.65bn, with revenues climbing 14.7 per cent to €58.7bn, slightly behind what the market had expected.

Renault's operating margin was 6.6 per cent, up from 6.4 per cent, taking it towards the 2022 target of 7 per cent, while it expects the global market to grow 2.5 per cent in 2018, despite falling sales in the US and UK.

It expects its European heartland to grow 1 per cent, although the second half of the year will be tough because of price rises likely to be caused by a new vehicle-testing regime that comes into force in September.

Renault on Thursday evening appointed Mr Ghosn for another four-year term, after a search for a successor that saw it consider both internal and external candidates.

The group also promoted chief competitive officer Thierry Bolloré to become chief operating officer with responsibility for day-to-day management of the business, a position that looks increasingly like a chief executive role as the company's finance and HR functions will report to him.

As part of the deal, Mr Ghosn agreed to take a 30 per cent pay cut in the new role because much of the responsibility has passed to Mr Bolloré.

On Friday, Mr Ghosn sought to quash concerns that the moves had led to several recent senior departures.

Stefan Mueller, who was a strong contender against Mr Bolloré, resigned this week citing personal health reasons, while Renault non-executive director Thierry Desmarest cut his term short to leave the board.

Mr Ghosn said the idea that either event was triggered by his reappointment was 'a romance'.

Mr Ghosn said his newly renewed role was to make sure the global alliance with Nissan and Mitsubishi was 'irreversible', and to move the businesses closer to becoming a single entity.

The Alliance, which is the world's second-largest carmaker behind Volkswagen Group, already has ambitious targets to achieve €10bn of savings a year by 2022, compared with €5bn last year, as well as launching 12 new electric vehicles and an autonomous ride-sharing service.

But several shareholders across the Renault-Nissan-Mitsubishi Alliance, as well as the French state, had raised concerns that the global partnership would 'fizzle' if Mr Ghosn left, he said.

However, moving the group to become a single corporate entity would be impossible while both the French and Japanese governments have a voice within the business.

'The market can't get to grips with the current byzantine arrangements,' said Max Warburton, an analyst at Bernstein, who said its value would rise significantly if eventually unified.

Telecom Italia shares surge as Elliott pledges to shake up board

Nic Fildes, Harriet Agnew and Rachel Sanderson

Financial Times, 6 March 2018

Telecom Italia shares surged on Tuesday after US activist shareholder Elliott Management pledged to shake up the board of the former state-owned company now controlled by Vivendi of France.

The stock price closed up 6 per cent to €0.77, its highest level in almost six months. The jump came ahead of a board meeting at which the Italian group was set to approve the company's fourth-quarter results and three-year strategy.

Elliott, which said it had been analysing Telecom Italia for months, plans to nominate its own board representatives at Telecom Italia's annual meeting on April 24.

Elliott said: 'In Elliott's view, Telecom Italia's governance, valuation, strategic direction and relationships with Italian authorities would be improved by replacing certain members of the board with new, fully independent and highly qualified directors. Accordingly, Elliott is considering taking steps towards achieving that goal.'

Elliott has not disclosed the size of its stake in the company. Investors must declare if they have more than 2 per cent of a company under Italian finance law.

The latest moves come against a backdrop of uncertainty for Telecom Italia, with Vivendi struggling to reverse a long-running decline in revenues and profits.

The conglomerate, controlled by French billionaire Vincent Bolloré, has a 24 per cent stake in the company and controls the board and executive roles, changing chief executive three times in two years and overhauling the board in 2017.

The chief executive, chief financial officer and general counsel of Vivendi all sit on the Telecom Italia board.

Consob, Italy's stock market regulator, is investigating whether former Areva director Felicité Herzog, one of the independent board directors proposed by the French group, meets independence requirements under Italian law, according to a person with direct knowledge of the investigation.

Vivendi's role in the company has raised tension with the Italian government. Telecom Italia agreed with Rome last month to spin off its network business in a bid to smooth relations and open the door for a potential merger with rival infrastructure company Open Fibre.

Vivendi said: 'We respect all Telecom Italia shareholders. If Elliott sees value in TI then we're delighted.'

Telecom Italia declined to comment.

A battle with Elliott would put further pressure on Mr Bolloré in Italy at a time when he is already locked in a battle with Mediaset, the broadcaster controlled by the family of Silvio Berlusconi.

Mediaset and Fininvest, the Berlusconi family holding company, are suing Vivendi for up to €3bn in damages over a collapsed deal between the two media magnates.

The difficulties surrounding Mediaset and Telecom Italia—and the tussle between Mr Berlusconi and Mr Bolloré—are seen by analysts as positive news for Iliad, the telecoms company of rival French billionaire Xavier Niel, which is preparing to launch in Italy in coming months.

Elliott's latest move would mark the second time that the fund manager has gone head to head with Telecom Italia, 15 years after the fund led a group of minority shareholders in an attempt to block the company's merger with Olivetti.

Elliott already had a significant investment in the Italian market. The fund run by Paul Singer has made more than €300m in high-interest loans to the Chinese owner of AC Milan, the Italian football club. If the loans are not refinanced by October, Elliott could end up owning the club.

Corporate governance in Central and Eastern Europe

Learning objectives

- To understand the implications of the privatization process for ownership structure in countries moving towards a market economy
- To be aware of the effect on the development of corporate governance of different privatization processes
- To have a detailed knowledge of the corporate governance systems in several Central and Eastern European countries

Introduction

More than 25 years have now passed since the Union of Soviet Socialist Republics (USSR) began to dissolve into constituent countries. The move from a command economy to a market economy is not an easy one and the countries that comprised the former USSR have achieved this transition with varying degrees of success. In general, the companies have moved from a situation where, as state-owned enterprises, they were most probably not expected to make a profit because the objective of the business was not really defined in those terms, but rather in terms of socialist goals such as full employment. This meant that, very often, the companies were highly inefficient: often using old machinery, having too large a workforce to be justified, and access to funds from the Central Bank without having to produce any repayment plans.

The success of the various countries can often be linked to the type of privatization that was followed to take businesses from state-owned enterprises to joint stock companies to public corporations. It is important to note that, in some countries, the term 'joint stock company' describes a company that has share capital which is traded on the stock exchange (essentially a public company); in other countries, the term may refer to a stage in the privatization process whereby a state-owned enterprise issues share capital to become a joint stock company, but that share capital is owned by the state with the next stage in the process being to sell the shares on to the public so that the company becomes a public corporation.

In general, there are three types of privatization process: the first is a mass privatization model, state-owned assets being distributed free of charge to the general public through vouchers that can be traded for ownership shares in state-owned firms. This model is sometimes referred to as the 'voucher privatization method' and was used in the Czech Republic and Russia. The second model allowed management and employees to buy company assets. This method was the method adopted in Poland. The third model, and arguably the one that produced the most successful results, involved selling majority control to an outside investor. The outside investor was often a foreign investor and this tended to lead first to higher expectations of the companies in which they invested and, secondly, generally better corporate governance in the companies that these outside investors bought into. This third method was followed in Hungary and Estonia.

In this chapter, we will look at four countries: the Czech Republic, Poland, Russia, and Hungary. We will look at the process of privatization that each of these countries followed and the framework for corporate governance that exists in these countries. There is clearly a link between the method of privatization used, the resultant ownership structure, and the degree or level of corporate governance that is being adopted. The method of privatization has tended to have more of an immediate impact on the development of corporate governance than the legal framework in these countries. Whilst the legal framework has been based on a command economy with state-owned enterprises, as the owners of the privatized industries find their voice, it can be expected that they will push for improved corporate governance, including better protection of minority rights. As Coffee (2002) points out:

> the more plausible explanation is that economic changes have produced regulatory changes, rather than the reverse ... Mass privatization came overnight to the Czech Republic, and its securities market soon crashed, at least in part because of the absence of investor protections. Only then, several years later, were statutory reforms adopted to protect minority shareholders. Pistor (2000) has generalized that the same responsive reaction of law to economic change has characterized the adoption of common law reforms by transitional economies.

Privatization process and its implications

Boeri and Perasso (1998), in a study of the Czech Republic, Hungary, Poland, and Russia, highlight the effects of each of the three privatization methods on a number of outcomes. They outline the outcomes, or performance indicators, as:

> the *speed* of privatization, that is, the proportion of former state enterprises which has changed ownership within the first four years of the privatization process, the relevance of *outside ownership* (percentage of privatized enterprises with dominant outside ownership) in the resulting ownership structure of firms, and finally, the degree of *control* exerted over managerial decisions by the owners of the firm. The latter indicator is proxied by the involvement in privatization of foreign and domestic companies.

They find that the Czech Republic's speed of privatization was very rapid, resulting in significant outside ownership, but a rather weak control structure. Hungary's privatization process was less rapid but resulted in a stronger control structure and more outside ownership. Poland's process was slower but achieved a reasonable level of outside ownership and control, whilst Russia's privatization process was quite rapid but resulted in much less outside control and a poor control structure, given the initial concentration of ownership into the hands of insiders.

Table 11.1 Ownership structures of companies in selected transition countries (unweighted)

No. of companies	Czech Republic	Hungary	Poland	Romania	Russia	Ukraine
	%	%	%	%	%	%
Insiders	3	11	10	15	40	45
State	51	53	26	46	8	21
Outsiders	46	29	55	39	45	28
Individuals/families	6	8	31	20	40	22
Institutional outsiders	40	21	24	20	5	6
Others/no answer	0	7	9	0	7	6
Number of enterprises	35	38	84	41	214	87

Source: EBRD/World Bank Business Environment Survey 1999 (only medium-sized and larger companies with more than 100 employees are included here).

Looking in more detail at the ownership structure of a sample of Central and Eastern European (CEE) countries, Table 11.1 shows the dominant owners of companies in selected transition countries. The broad categories of owners are insider owners (managers and workers), outsider owners (individuals and families, and institutional outsiders such as investment funds and banks), and the state. It can be seen that the dominant owners vary across the transition countries, with the state still influential; outsiders are also influential, either in the form of individuals/families, or as institutional outsiders. It should be remembered that the privatization process will have been instrumental in determining the basic ownership structure in each of the countries, but that the data in Table 11.1 is based on a 1999 survey, several years after the initial privatization processes in each country. Nonetheless, the influence of the different privatization processes on ownership structure is still very much in evidence as, for example, in Russia, where insider ownership still retains a lot of influence.

Berglof and Pajuste (2003) highlight the fact that whilst the level of state ownership differs across countries in the CEE, private ownership is becoming more dominant, with ownership being increasingly concentrated. Strong insider ownership and control, combined with poor protection of minority shareholders, makes companies less attractive to foreign investors and minority shareholders.

Aguilera et al. (2012) examine whether, over time, there have been significant changes in the patterns of corporate ownership amongst publicly traded firms in emerging markets, including the Czech Republic, Hungary, and Poland. Considering the period 2004–8 for CEE countries, they find that the Czech Republic has the highest remaining government ownership, that Hungary's foreign ownership is most prominent, and that Poland has relatively less concentrated ownership compared to the Czech Republic and Hungary. In their conclusions they point out that joining the EU 'triggered the impulse for the transfer of ownership from state to private hands, with the immediate consequence of large entry of foreign direct investments and its related foreign ownership of publicly traded firms'.

Driffield et al. (2014) combine agency and institutional theory to explain the division of equity shares between the foreign (majority) and local (minority) partners within foreign affiliates. Using a large firm level dataset for the period 2003–11 from 16 Central and Eastern European countries, they conclude that when:

assessing investment opportunities abroad, foreign firms need to pay attention not only to features directly related to corporate governance (e.g., bankruptcy codes) but also to the broad institutional environment. In weak institutional environments, foreign parent firms need to create strong incentives for local partners by offering them significant minority shares in equity. The same recommendation applies to firms with higher shares of intangible assets in total assets.

Grosman et al. (2016) analyse over a 100 articles published in the 25 years since 1989 and focus on which forms of state control over corporations have emerged in countries that made a transition from centrally planned to market-based economies and discuss the corporate governance implications.

More recently, Lazzarini and Musacchio (2018) utilized a new database of 477 large, listed SOEs observed between 1997 and 2012 in 66 developed and emerging countries. Using matching techniques they show that 'these firms do not underperform similar private firms, except when the former face shocks that prioritize their social and political objectives, such as during severe recessions. These findings demonstrate the need to revise existing theories of SOE underperformance.' Furthermore they argue that 'governments try to steer SOEs to pursue social and political objectives, which can lead to inefficiencies, but they also provide them with rents, protection, and, ultimately, with a soft-budget constraint, something that should lead them to perform as well or better than similar private firms'.

The Czech Republic

As discussed earlier, the Czech Republic used the voucher privatization method to privatize state-owned enterprises. Coffee (1998) details how the voucher system entitled each Czechoslovak adult to purchase a booklet of 1,000 voucher points for a cost equating to about 25 per cent of the average monthly wage at the end of 1991. For the second privatization wave in 1993/4, the price was raised by a modest amount but, by then, this accounted for less than 18 per cent of the average monthly wage. By the end of the second privatization wave, Coffee (1998) notes that 'over 80 per cent of adult Czech citizens had become shareholders in the 1849 companies that were privatized (in whole or in part)'.

The investment privatization funds (IPFs) were established shortly after the first privatization wave and bought the vouchers from individual citizens. The Czech government legislated to ensure that IPFs appointed a bank as their depository and deposited all securities and funds with it; IPFs were also required to appoint managing and supervisory boards. However, substantial holdings were still controlled by the state via the National Property Fund (NPF), which contained holdings awaiting sale, and holdings of strategic companies that may be sold at some point, such as utilities. The NPF also exercised influence via the IPFs. As Boeri and Perasso (1998) point out: 'The largest IPFs are controlled by banks, especially the big four banks, whose main shareholder, but not majority except in one case, is the state, via NPF.' Claessens et al. (1997) show that at the end of 1995, the top five IPFs owned, on average, just under 49 per cent of a firm privatized in the first wave and just under 41 per cent of a firm privatized in the second wave.

Unfortunately, the Czech voucher privatization process led to two significant shortcomings post-privatization: one was a high level of cross-ownership, resulting in a consolidation

Table 11.2 Key characteristics influencing corporate governance in the Czech Republic

Feature	Key characteristic
Privatization method	Mass privatization via voucher
Predominant ownership structure	State; institutional outsiders (investment funds and banks)
Legal system	Civil law
Board structure	Dual
Important aspect	Influence of IPFs

of control in the Czech banking sector; the other was the situation where, although many individuals held shares as a result of the voucher system, they formed a minority interest that had no effective legal protection. This lack of legal protection and a downturn in the Czech Republic stock market led overseas institutional investors to sell their shares and leave the market. An improved corporate governance system was seen as one way to try to ensure that foreign investment was lured back to invest in the Czech Republic. Table 11.2 summarizes the key corporate governance characteristics in the Czech Republic.

From 1 January 2001, an extensive package of changes was introduced into the Czech Republic. These changes involved the Commercial Code, the Securities Act, and the Auditing Act. Many of the changes altered the responsibilities and rights of companies, board members, shareholders, and auditors, and so they were fairly wide ranging and far reaching.

The Revised Corporate Governance Code (2001), hereinafter 'the Code', set out corporate governance best practice for companies in the Czech Republic and was based on the Organisation for Economic Co-operation and Development (OECD) *Principles of Corporate Governance* (1999), but reference was also made to other codes, including the Combined Code of the London Stock Exchange. The focus was on transparency and accountability because these elements are essential to encourage investor confidence. The Prague Stock Exchange recommended that companies adopted as many of the Code's provisions as they could straight away, and then explained in their annual report why they were not adopting other provisions and when they anticipated being able to do so. Additionally, it encouraged all companies listed on the second market to do the same.

The Code stated that the principles on which it was based are those of openness, integrity, and accountability, and that acceptance of these concepts would do much to remove some of the more unethical behaviour and practices prevalent in various parts of the Czech business world, and so restore an environment conducive to both strategic and portfolio investment. The Code recognized that 'good corporate governance is particularly important in the Czech Republic and other transition countries where there was no long term, continuous experience of non-state ownership of companies and the associated corporate practices'. Good corporate governance provides a framework for setting corporate objectives, and monitoring the progress towards achieving those objectives.

As in other countries around the globe, the observance and adoption of good corporate governance is an increasingly important factor for attracting investment in the Czech Republic, and much was needed to be done to rebuild the confidence of investors, because many investors had lost substantial amounts due to poor management practices, and to address the lack of investor protection, particularly of minority interests.

An important aspect of the revised Code was the emphasis on shareholder value, with the corporate governance principles contained in the Code being based on the acceptance of the improvement of shareholder value as the corporate objective.

The main provisions of the Code are as follows:

- The Company should be headed by an effective board of directors and supervisory board which should lead it and account to the shareholders. The board of directors should meet no less than once each month and the supervisory board should meet no less than ten times each year.

- The Company should protect shareholders' rights.

- The Company should ensure disclosure of all capital structures and any arrangements that enable certain shareholders to obtain a degree of control disproportionate to their equity ownership. Some capital structures allow a shareholder to exercise a degree of control over the company disproportionate to the shareholders' equity ownership in the company.

- The Company should ensure that all shareholders, including minorities and foreign shareholders, are treated equitably.

- The Company should ensure that timely and accurate disclosure is made on all material matters regarding the company, including the financial situation, performance, ownership, and governance of the company. In particular the company should observe the standards of best practice issued by the Czech Securities Commission on the contents of the annual report, half-year report, and ongoing disclosure requirements.

- The board of directors should undertake all key functions in the management of the company and the supervisory board should effectively supervise such functions.

- Institutional shareholders should act responsibly in their dealings with the company.

- Shareholders should have certain rights and exercise certain responsibilities in connection with the company.

- The role of stakeholders in corporate governance.

The Czech Code (2001) was fairly comprehensive and adoption of the recommendations by Czech companies should have helped to restore investor confidence, both that of domestic investors and also foreign investors.

However, when the revised OECD Principles were published in 2004, the Czech Securities Commission decided to update its corporate governance code as well, and in June 2004, the Czech Securities Commission issued the Corporate Governance Code based on the OECD Principles (2004). The majority of the ideas contained in the 2001 Code discussed earlier were retained, however, the working group of the Securities Commission decided to follow the structure as well as the content of the OECD Principles (2004). By mapping the content and structure of the OECD Principles so closely, it was felt that this would lead to easier communication about the corporate governance of the Czech Republic with organizations such as the World Bank and with those that are familiar with the OECD Principles. Also, given various developments in corporate governance and in capital markets generally, such as the EU Action Plan discussed earlier, it was felt appropriate to update the Code. One such development relates to the European Commission's decision to leave European companies with a choice of either the unitary board or dual board structure. Where the Code (2001) tended to prefer the unitary board structure (Anglo-Saxon model), the Code (2004) leaves it up to companies as to whether they choose a dual board (German style) or unitary board (Anglo-Saxon). The Code (2004) also places more emphasis on the independence of board members.

As mentioned, the revised Czech Code (2004) mirrors both structure and content of the OECD Principles (2004) (for the detail of the OECD Principles (2004), please see Chapter 3). However, it is useful to highlight some of the additions to the revised Czech Code (2004), which include the following:

- The exercise of shareholders' rights should be facilitated, including participation in key corporate governance decisions, such as nomination and election of board members.
- Institutional investors acting in a fiduciary capacity should disclose their corporate governance and voting policies.
- Amendment to the Commercial Code to permit distance voting by electronic means.
- Minority shareholders must be protected from abusive actions by, or in the interest of, controlling shareholders and should have effective means of redress.
- Members of the board of directors, supervisory board, and key executives are required to disclose to the board if they have a material interest in a transaction or matter affecting the corporation.
- The rights of stakeholders, whether established in law or through mutual agreements, must be respected.
- The development of performance-enhancing mechanisms for employee participation must be allowed.
- Stakeholders, including employees and their representative bodies, must be able freely to communicate their concerns about illegal or unethical practices to the supervisory board without their rights being compromised.
- The corporate governance framework must be complemented by an effective, efficient insolvency framework and by effective enforcement of creditor rights.
- The remuneration policy for members of the board of directors, the supervisory board, and key executives, and information about board members (including their qualifications, the selection process, other company directorships, and whether they are regarded as independent) must be disclosed.
- The content of any corporate governance code and the process by which it is implemented must be disclosed.
- An annual audit must be carried out by an independent, competent, and qualified auditor to provide assurance that the financial statements fairly represent the financial position and performance of the company.
- The external auditor is accountable to shareholders and owes a duty to the company to exercise due professional care in the conduct of the audit.

- The corporate governance framework must be complemented by an effective approach that addresses and promotes the provision of analysis or advice by analysts, brokers, etc. that is relevant to decisions by investors and free from material conflicts of interest that might compromise the integrity of their analysis or advice.

- Appropriate and full disclosure about directors' remuneration.

- Companies should publish in their annual reports a declaration of how they apply in practice the relevant principles of corporate governance contained in the Czech Code (2004).

- Three separate committees responsible for the independent audit of the company, the remuneration of directors and key executives, and the nomination of directors and key executives should be established, and the mandate, composition, and working procedures of these committees must be disclosed.

The Czech Code (2004) is a comprehensive code with many explanatory notes in each section to aid the companies and investors. Adoption of the Czech Code (2004) should help to ensure that investor confidence is maintained, that shareholders' rights can be exercised more easily, and that minority shareholders are better protected.

Jandik and Rennie (2008) investigate the evolution of corporate governance and firm performance in transition economies with a focus on barriers that impeded the adoption of optimal corporate governance at Czech ammunition manufacturer Sellier and Bellot (S&B) following voucher privatization in 1993. They found that:

> exogenously imposed diffuse ownership, combined with legal, capital market, and account-ing deficiencies, contributed to poor corporate governance and weak firm performance. This study shows how legal, capital market, and accounting deficiencies hinder corporate governance evolution; it demonstrates monitoring and incentive mechanisms can create value in transition economies; it suggests effective privatisation not only involves rapid own-ership transfer but careful accounting and securities regulation and legal protection.

Poland

The second model used in the privatization process was one that allowed management and employees to buy company assets. This was the method adopted in Poland from 1995, where there was a slower start to privatization than in the Czech Republic. State-owned enterprises targeted for privatization first became joint stock companies. In this instance, the joint stock company's ownership did not change, but the control structure changed to include a board of directors, and the Workers' Councils, which were previously quite powerful, were disbanded, so reducing workers' power.

A defining feature of the Polish privatization process was that shares had to be included in one of 15 National Investment Funds (NIFs) established in 1995. NIFs were essentially established to manage shares that were purchased in the various privatized companies in Poland as part of the mass privatization programme. NIFs have strategic 33 per cent hold-ings in some firms but much smaller shares in other firms. Coffee (1998) points out that the NIFs 'remain indirectly under governmental control'. The Polish government did not allow its citizens to have vouchers that could be exchanged directly for shares in the privatized

Table 11.3 Key characteristics influencing Polish corporate governance

Feature	Key characteristic
Privatization method	Management and employees buy company assets
Predominant ownership structure	Institutional outsiders (NIFs); state; individuals/families
Legal system	Civil law
Board structure	Dual
Important aspect	Role of NIFs

companies; rather the vouchers were exchanged for shares in the NIFs. The state also retained a significant shareholding of 25 per cent in some companies, with another 15 per cent being allotted free of charge to the workers. The investor base includes foreign investors as well as domestic, institutional, and retail investors.

Some of the firms that the NIFs are invested into required major restructuring but, sometimes, there is disagreement between the NIFs and the supervisory board as to when and how this restructuring might be undertaken. Coffee (1998) points out that 'if a proposed restructuring is politically sensitive or cuts deeply into local employment, one must suspect that labour interests and others with political clout will know how to protest effectively. Because the initial board of each NIF is governmentally appointed, there is little reason to believe that individual NIFs will feel insulated from such protests.' Therefore, the state continues to have an influential role in many companies, despite the fact that the companies are now privatized.

Poland is a country that has a civil law system. The legal framework for listed companies comprises the Commercial Code (1934) and the Code of Commercial Companies (2000). In the summer of 2002 there were two publications on corporate governance: the Corporate Governance Code for Polish Listed Companies and the Best Practices in Public Companies guidance. Both of these are now discussed in more detail and the key characteristics of Polish corporate governance are highlighted in Table 11.3.

Poland has a predominantly two-tier board structure comprising a supervisory board and a management board. As is usual, the supervisory board supervises the management board and oversees the company's financial statements; it also reports to the shareholders on the activities of the company. The management board conducts the day-to-day business of the company and is responsible for issues that are not within the remit of the supervisory board or the shareholders' meeting. The company's articles of association will often expand on the areas to be covered by the management board.

The final proposal of the Corporate Governance Code for Polish Listed Companies (hereinafter 'the Code') was published in June 2002. The Code was drawn up under the initiative of the Polish Forum for Corporate Governance established by the Gdansk Institute for Market Economics, and may also be referred to as 'the Gdansk Code'.

The Code recognizes the problems that have occurred in the past with the violation of minority rights and seeks to address these in order to help restore confidence in the Polish market. The Code largely reflects the OECD Principles (2004), the Cadbury Code (1992), and other benchmarks of international best practice. It is recommended that the Code's provisions be included in a company's articles of association. The Code expects companies to report on compliance combining annual descriptive reports and the 'comply or explain' mechanism.

The Code has seven principles, which cover various areas of good corporate governance practice as follows:

- The main objective of the company should be to operate in the common interest of all shareholders, which is to create shareholder value.
- The composition of the supervisory board should facilitate objective oversight of the company and reflect interests of minority shareholders.
- The powers of the supervisory board and the company by-laws should ensure an effective supervisory board process and duly secure interests of all shareholders.
- The shareholders' meeting should be convened and organized so as not to violate interests and rights of any shareholders. The controlling shareholder should not restrict the other shareholders in the effective exercise of their corporate rights.
- The company should not apply anti-takeover defences against shareholders' interests. Changes in the company share capital should not violate interests of the existing shareholders.
- The company should provide effective access to information, which is necessary to evaluate the company's current position, future prospects, as well as the way in which the company operates and applies the corporate governance rules.
- The appointment process of the company's auditor should ensure independence of the auditor's opinion.

The *Best Practices in Public Companies 2002* publication came out of the Best Practices Committee at Corporate Governance Forum, who stated that 'this set of best practices, established for the needs of the Polish capital market, presents the core of corporate governance standards in a public joint stock company'. There were a number of 'general rules' including: the objective of the company; the concept of majority rule and protection of the minority; the ideas of honest intentions and no abuse of rights; court control, which may apply to some issues in a company; that when expert services/opinions are sought, the experts should be independent. In addition to these general rules, there were specific guidelines relating to best practices, including: the notification and running of general meetings, and associated voting issues; the role of the supervisory board and its members; the role of the management board and its members; relations with third parties, including the auditors. The Best Practices were reviewed and amended in the light of practical experience and opinions of market participants and Best Practices in Public Companies 2005 were issued. The amended practices included recent EU recommendations, for example, the emphasis on independence aimed at strengthening the role of non-executive or supervisory directors.

In 2007, 2010, and 2012, an updated Code of Best Practice for Warsaw Stock Exchange Listed Companies was published which aims at 'enhancing transparency of listed companies, improving quality of communication between companies and investors, and strengthening protection of shareholders' rights'. The update in 2012 included new recommendations relating to disclosure where a company supports artistic or cultural expression, sport activities, educational or scientific activities and considers this activity to be part of its business mission and development strategy; communication where published information is untrue or partly true or where publicly expressed opinions are not based on material objective grounds; and disclosure of information about the participation of men and women in the management board and in the supervisory board of the company in the last two years.

In 2016, the Warsaw Stock Exchange issued Best Practice for GPW Listed Companies which helps companies to ensure their competitive position and makes the capital market in Poland more attractive. It is divided into new thematic sections including disclosure policy and investor communications; management board and supervisory board; internal systems and functions; general meeting and shareholder relations; conflict of interest and related party transactions; and remuneration.

The corporate governance recommendations introduced by the Gdansk Code and the Best Practices will undoubtedly have strengthened the corporate governance of Polish companies and helped to encourage investment by restoring confidence in the market. As Rozlucki (2003) stated: 'In Poland, corporate governance has become an additional and indispensable guarantee of system stability to the financial market.' Kozarzewski (2007) carried out a cross-country comparative study of corporate governance formation in four transition countries, which differ significantly in the reform design, implementation, and outcome. His analysis showed that:

> corporate governance formation in these countries is characterized by both similarities and differences. Similarities originate first of all from the common features of the historical background of these countries, the features of centrally planned economy; from the similarities of the principles of the reform programs; and from similarities of certain basic, objective regularities of the post-Communist transition. Such common features include, e.g., highly insiderized initial ownership patterns, high role of managers, high ownership concentration, dual trends of ownership structures' evolution towards concentration and outsiderization, and many others. The differences originate, among others, from the specific features of the countries' historical, cultural, and institutional heritage, the soundness of the reform design and implementation, the main characteristics of the enterprise sector, the quality of the legal base and enforcement mechanisms. Countries that had more favorable 'background' (traditions of private entrepreneurship, capacities of the elites) and during the transition period managed to create good legal background for private sector and appropriate institutions are more likely to enjoy formation of more efficient corporate governance mechanisms and patterns.

Russia

The collapse of the communist system in Russia heralded a wave of privatizations, with the privatization programme in Russia itself based on a voucher system. Pistor and Turkewitz (1996) indicate that, between January 1993 and June 1994, some 14,000–15,000 companies were sold in voucher auctions. They state that 'privatization regulations required companies with more than a thousand employees and a book value of at least 50 million rubles to set up a privatisation plan'. They highlight that there were substantial benefits available to the managers of enterprises, including subsidized equity stakes and the right to buy further shares in voucher auctions. Frydman et al. (1996) highlight the high participation levels of the Russian people in the voucher privatization process: 'The program did bring out a very high degree of

Table 11.4 Ownership change in Russia

Category of owner	1995	1997	1999
Insiders	54.8	52.1	46.2
Managers	11.2	15.1	14.7
Workers	43.6	37.0	31.5
State	9.1	7.4	7.1
Outsiders	35.2	38.9	42.4
Individuals	10.9	13.9	18.5
Non-financial firms	15.0	14.6	13.5
Financial firms, holdings, foreign investors	9.3	10.3	10.4
Others	0.9	1.6	4.3
Sample size	136	135	156

Source: Sprenger, C. (2002), *Ownership and Corporate Governance in Russian Industry: A Survey*, Working Paper No. 70, European Bank for Reconstruction and Development (EBRD).

popular participation: by July 1994, 132.7 million Russians made some use of their vouchers (even if only to sell them on the open market), and this number represents 87.8 per cent of the 151 million voucher recipients.' The privatization programme also saw the participation of privatization investment funds, which either bought shares directly or through intermediaries. After privatization, many managers bought shares from the workers. These factors contributed to a high level of ownership by insiders (managers and workers), such that managerial entrenchment became a real threat, as it meant that outside, and particularly overseas, investors would be reluctant to invest in companies where management control was high and protection of minority rights low.

Ownership in Russia is documented by Sprenger (2002), who cites some interesting surveys carried out by the Russian Economic Barometer. Table 11.4 shows the ownership change in Russian industry over the period 1995–9. What emerges is that, over time, the ownership by insiders (managers and workers) is declining whilst the ownership by outsiders is increasing, particularly ownership by individuals and financial firms, holdings, and foreign investors. Sprenger's (2005) study of 530 Russian manufacturing firms confirms the gradually decreasing ownership stakes of firms' insiders over time.

Russia, in common with other transition economies, is moving towards a market economy and has joint stock companies and limited liability companies. Minority rights have traditionally not been well looked after in Russia, so that the role and the relevance of shareholders in a company have not generally held much sway. Many foreign investors who invested in Russia post-privatization lost a lot of money as managers of the companies misused their funds and there was little effective redress. The Russian Corporate Governance Code therefore sees it as very important to restore investor confidence in the market and to ensure that future foreign investment is encouraged by building more confidence in Russian companies. Table 11.5 shows the key characteristics influencing Russian corporate governance.

The Russian Code of Corporate Governance (hereinafter 'the Code') was issued by the Federal Securities Commission in late 2001. It had the support of both government officials and private groups, and it was hoped that compliance with the Code would be at a high level.

Table 11.5 Key characteristics influencing Russian corporate governance

Feature	Key characteristic
Privatization method	Mass privatization via voucher
Predominant ownership structure	Insiders (managers and workers) although outsiders increasing
Legal system	Civil law
Board structure	Dual
Important aspect	Covers dividend payments

Given that it has government support, it is likely that any company where the state has influence will, in theory, have to comply and large companies that are still subject to political influence and decisions will want to comply. Also, in order to attract external direct investment, companies will want to comply with the Code. This is particularly important given that, in the 1990s, the external investors who invested money into Russia had their fingers badly burnt when the money was pocketed by various corrupt individuals involved in companies. In order to restore confidence and to encourage more foreign investment, compliance with a corporate governance code is of prime importance.

Essentially, the Code is based on the OECD *Corporate Governance Principles*, but has also drawn from other international codes and guidelines. The Code has ten sections or chapters covering the following areas:

- Principles of corporate governance
- General shareholders' meetings
- Board of directors
- Executive bodies
- Company secretary
- Major corporate actions
- Information disclosure
- Supervision of operations
- Dividends
- Resolution of corporate conflicts.

The provisions of the Russian Code are quite far-reaching. In some ways, the provisions largely relate to educating the Russian corporate sector so that they understand what good corporate governance actually is. Whilst some companies are already complying, others have been slower to comply and the Code's provisions are not legally binding. However, the companies may not wish to incur the disapproval of the government and many still rely heavily on political influence: for example, they may be denied the right to state tender or, alternatively, pension funds might be prohibited from investing in companies that do not comply.

Kostikov (2003) stated: 'Poor corporate governance in Russian companies makes them much less attractive as investment objects.' Initiatives to encourage more truly independent directors onto Russian boards are essential to help ensure improved corporate governance and to encourage investors. As Belikov (2004) stated: 'The challenge is to attract conservative portfolio investors who are willing to commit to long-term investments and who view good corporate governance as a vital part of an investment decision.' Legislation introduced in 2006 should help ensure that boards have more independent directors and hence that board committees have a higher proportion of independent directors. Bartha and Gillies (2006) believe that corporate governance is of great value to Russia:

> The adoption of a good corporate governance system—both at the macro legal-regulatory setting and at the micro level of business practices—can speed up and smooth the transition to a fully operational market economy. During mass privatization a decade ago the absence of the right structures, institutions and processes caused a major transformation effort to go awry. Now the appropriate framework, instruments and know-how are in place to generate and allocate capital effectively and efficiently. By developing a set of corporate governance practices and fostering a corporate governance culture, Russia is wisely pre-investing in its future.

In December 2011 the OECD and MICEX-RTS, the merged Russian stock exchange, launched a new work programme on corporate governance in the Russian Federation. This considers the remaining challenges in the corporate governance framework; improving the understanding of Russia corporate governance practices; and facilitating ongoing reform efforts. The role of the stock exchange in setting corporate governance standards, disclosure, and transparency of listed companies, enforcement of insider trading, and market manipulation laws in Russia is also being considered.

The Moscow Exchange & OECD Russia (2014) issued a new version of the Russian Corporate Governance Code. According to the Foreword to the revised Code, it focuses on:

- The rights of shareholders, including recommendations on use of electronic means for the purpose of participation in voting and receipt of meeting materials, as well as on protection of dividend rights of shareholders;

- Organising efficient work of the board of directors, i.e. determining the approaches to reasonable and bona fide performance of duties by board members, determining the functions of the board of directors, and organisation of its work and that of its committees;

- Clarification of requirements to board members, including those relating to their independence;

- Recommendations on development of a remuneration system for members of management bodies and key managers of the company, including recommendations relating to various components of such remuneration system (short-term and long-term incentives, severance pay, etc.);

- Recommendations on development of an efficient system of risk management and internal controls;

- Recommendations on additional disclosure of material information about the company and entities controlled thereby and their internal policies; and

- Recommendations on performing material corporate actions (increases in the share capital, acquisitions, listing and delisting of securities, re-organisation, material transactions) which enable one to protect the shareholder rights and ensure the equal treatment of shareholders.

Sprenger and Lazareva (2017) focus on the corporate governance of unlisted firms in an emerging market economy and how it affects financing constraints, measured by the sensitivity of investment to cash flow. Developing two original corporate governance indices based on a large-scale survey of Russian enterprises—one for shareholder protection and one for transparency—they find that 'better shareholder protection diminishes the cash flow sensitivity of investment, particularly in firms with an outside controlling owner and in firms with low managerial ownership. In contrast, more transparency exacerbates financing constraints in some cases.'

Hungary

The third model, and arguably the one that produced the most successful results, involved selling majority control to an outside investor. This model was followed in Hungary and resulted in a high level of outside ownership and control. It is useful to mention various changes that occurred in Hungary in the late 1980s/early 1990s, as described in Pistor and Turkewitz (1996). A change in Hungarian law led, in the late 1980s, to a wave of manager-initiated organizational restructuring of enterprise assets and the right to form a limited liability company or joint stock company. Whilst the state retained ownership of a large proportion of these assets, state officials were unable to keep up with the pace of change and so were unable to keep up with the changes in the ownership structures. In 1989 the majority of state-owned companies were transferred to the State Property Agency (SPA), and over the next five years many of these were privatized. However, some of the assets were transferred to the State Holding Company (Av.Rt.). The state still retains significant holdings and influence, one way being through 'golden shares', which were issued to the state during the privatization process enabling the state to have control over key strategic issues. The World Bank–IMF ROSC 2003 report on corporate governance in Hungary identified that ten of the 56 listed companies have issued a golden share that can only be held by the state.

For some time, Hungary did not have a published corporate governance code, although the Budapest Stock Exchange started to draft a corporate governance code in mid-2002. However, many areas relating to corporate governance were covered in the Companies Law and these areas are described later (and see Table 11.6).

Table 11.6 Key characteristics influencing Hungarian corporate governance

Feature	Key characteristic
Privatization method	Privatization via selling majority control to outside investor, often foreign
Predominant ownership structure	State; institutional outsiders (foreign)
Legal system	Civil law
Board structure	Dual
Important aspect	State influence but potential influence of foreign investor activism waiting to happen

The World Bank–IMF ROSC 2003 report identified that, whilst Hungary had a robust legislative and regulatory framework to deal with corporate governance issues, there were shortcomings in the system, including the lack of a corporate governance code of best practice. The report identified the various sections of the Companies Act 1997 relating to corporate structure and governance.

(i) Board structure

Public companies should have a two-tier (dual) structure consisting of a board of directors (management board) and a supervisory board. The shareholders in general meeting usually appoint the directors of both boards and approve their remuneration. However, the company's charter may provide that the supervisory board appoint and set the remuneration of the management board.

The management board may comprise between three and eleven members, whilst the supervisory board can have as many as 15 members, with employees appointing one-third of the supervisory board members.

(ii) Operation of the boards

The management board is responsible for the day-to-day running of the company, whilst the supervisory board exercises control over the management board on behalf of the shareholders. The management board's responsibilities include reporting on operational issues (such as the company's financial position) at the AGM and also quarterly to the supervisory board, and maintaining the books and records of the company.

Board meeting minutes are not required to be kept, but board members participate and report at the AGM. Both boards are accountable to the AGM and, in theory, to all shareholders; in practice, some directors appointed on the votes of large shareholders may effectively represent the interests of those large shareholders. Board members may seek expert opinions as appropriate.

(iii) Independence

There is no specific reference to independence, although the Companies Act does refer to the objectivity of board members so that close family members are not allowed to be members of the supervisory and management board at the same company. Board members may not be employees, except in their capacity as employee representatives on the supervisory board. Board members should disclose any conflicts of interest.

(iv) Disclosure

Hungary's disclosure of information relevant to investors was generally quite good. Disclosure requirements are contained in the Capital Markets Act 2002 and the Budapest Stock Exchange listing rules. The areas that companies must provide disclosure on include:

- the corporate objectives;
- major ownership and voting rights;

- the financial and operating results of the company;
- remuneration of board members;
- details of loans to board members;
- information relating to employees, such as the average number of employees employed.

Investors must have access to the company's annual report and many companies post this information on their website.

As mentioned earlier, the Budapest Stock Exchange began work on its Corporate Governance Recommendations in 2002, and the final document was published in 2004. The recommendations suggest applicable practices but are not mandatory for companies listed on the Stock Exchange. However, the publication of a declaration, whereby the corporate issuers provide information on their management practices in comparison with the contents of the recommendations, will be mandatory and confirmed in the Stock Exchange rules. If an issuer does not comply with a recommendation or applies it in a different manner, then an explanation should be provided, i.e. the 'comply or explain' approach.

The Budapest Stock Exchange has split the recommendations into corporate governance recommendations and recommendations on shareholders' meetings. The corporate governance recommendations are laid out in a three-column format, with the first column being the recommendations themselves, then the middle column, the relevant Hungarian legal regulations, and the final column, explanations and in-depth suggestions relating to each recommendation. The corporate governance recommendations relate to:

- Competences of the board of directors and of the supervisory board;
- Transparency and disclosure;
- Shareholders' rights and treatment of shareholders;
- Role of stakeholders in corporate governance.

The recommendations on shareholders' meetings are designed to establish principles to provide a basis for future shareholders' meetings, which support the validation of shareholders' interests, take into account the interests of potential investors, and facilitate the decision-making process. These recommendations are a supplement to the Corporate Governance Recommendations and have three sections relating to the preliminary procedures prior to meetings, conducting the shareholders' meetings, and concluding the shareholders' meetings.

In 2007 and 2008 the Budapest Stock Exchange published updates of the Corporate Governance Recommendations to take into consideration European Commission recommendations on aspects of corporate governance and especially in relation to the remuneration of directors, and the role of non-executive directors and the supervisory board. The Hungarian Company Act 2006 has given legal force to the regulation of disclosure obligations regarding corporate governance, and companies are required to submit an annual comprehensive report on corporate governance to the company's AGM. Companies also have to indicate their compliance with specified sections of the Corporate Governance Recommendations, and the disclosure obligations may be quite detailed.

The Corporate Governance Recommendations were further revised in 2012 and the amendments include refining recommendations and suggestions regarding board structures and independence issues; and provisions relating to the audit committee.

Earle et al. (2005) found that high-quality data available on companies listed on the Budapest Stock Exchange enabled them to undertake a study of ownership concentration and corporate performance. They found that the size of the largest block of shares increases profitability and efficiency but that the effects of the total block holdings are much smaller. In other words: 'The marginal costs of concentration [of share ownership] may outweigh the benefits when the increased concentration involves "too many cooks".'

More recently, Telegdy (2011) found that 'foreigners have an important role in the control structures of Hungarian corporations, which has partially resulted from their involvement in the privatization process, and partially it materialized through acquisitions of domestic companies and green field investments. The listed firms … tend to have one or multiple large blockholders, and only a small proportion of the stocks are widely held.'

Conclusions

In this chapter we have reviewed the three different approaches that were used in the privatization of state-owned enterprises in various countries. The effect of each of these approaches on the resultant ownership and control of privatized companies, and the implications for corporate governance developments have been discussed. In particular, it has been noted that the countries in CEE are keen to improve protection of minority shareholder rights, and to establish more confidence in their capital markets to attract foreign direct investment. All of the countries have already published corporate governance codes of best practice. In addition, the Czech Republic, Hungary, and Poland all joined the EU in 2004 and so we can expect to see their corporate governance developing in line with European Commission recommendations.

Summary

Three main privatization methods were used to privatize state-owned enterprises in the countries discussed: (i) the voucher privatization method was used in the Czech Republic and Russia, and enabled the public to own shares in privatized firms; (ii) management and employees were allowed to buy company assets, and this method was used in Poland; (iii) selling majority control to an outside investor was the method used in Hungary.

- The different privatization methods resulted in different ownership and control structures. In practice, the state retained considerable influence in many firms, either directly or indirectly.
- The four countries reviewed all have a dual board structure (supervisory board and management board).

- The Czech Republic has an ownership structure that includes predominantly the state and institutional outsiders (investment funds and banks). The IPFs can be quite influential.

- Poland has an ownership structure that includes predominantly institutional outsiders, the state, and individuals/families. The NIFs play an important role.

- Russia has an ownership structure that includes predominantly insiders (managers and workers), although outsiders are increasing. The Russian Corporate Governance Code is comprehensive at over 90 pages.

- Hungary has an ownership structure that includes predominantly the state and institutional outsiders (foreign investors). Whilst Hungary has many good practices, especially in the area of corporate disclosures, its corporate governance infrastructure could be improved in a number of ways and its comprehensive code of corporate governance should encourage this.

Example: OAO LUKOIL, Russia

This is a good example of a Russian company that is recognized as having a high standard of corporate governance amongst Russian companies.

OAO LUKOIL (hereafter LUKOIL) is a major international vertically integrated oil and gas company, accounting for 2.1 per cent of global output of crude oil.

It has comprehensive disclosure of its corporate governance structure via its Corporate Governance Report. Its Corporate Governance Report also highlights that significant changes were made by the Russian Corporate Governance Code 2014. LUKOIL states that:

> while introducing the principles and recommendations of the Code in the future, the Company will consider which positive influence they will produce on the Company in terms of the business development strategy, economic efficiency and operational efficiency of the decision-making process by the Company's governance bodies, as well as its investment attractiveness. The Company will also consider the structure of its BoD and shareholders, the current organizational structure of the Company and distribution of competences among its key employees.

As at June 2014, the board of directors had 11 members, all of whom are male. The 11-member board was elected at the General Shareholder Meeting by cumulative voting (the candidates for whom the largest number of votes was cast are deemed elected). There are three committees of the board of directors: Strategy and Investment Committee, Audit Committee, and the HR and Compensation Committee. The Management Committee has 14 members, one of whom is female.

As at June 2017, LUKOIL's board of directors had 11 members comprising nine males and two females. The Management Committee remains comprised of 14 members though all are male.

In 2015, the international magazine *World Finance* announced that LUKOIL was the winner in its annual Corporate Governance Awards. LUKOIL was first in the category Best Corporate Governance, Russia, 2015. When selecting the nominees and winners, the jury was guided by a wide range of criteria, including the system of governance, the internal and external audits, stakeholder relations, the composition and independence of the board of directors, the observance of shareholder rights, risk management, and transparency.

Mini case study   MOL, Hungary

This is an example of a Hungarian company that is recognized as having good corporate governance and sustainability policies, and excellent disclosure.

MOL Group is a leading integrated CEE oil and gas corporation with a market capitalization of over US$7 billion at the end of 2013. Its shares are listed on the Budapest, Luxembourg, and Warsaw Stock Exchanges, and its depository receipts are traded on London's International Order Book and OTC in the USA.

MOL is 'committed to maintaining and further improving the efficiency of its current portfolio, exploiting potential in its captive and new markets and to excellence in its social and environmental performance'. MOL's corporate governance practice meets the requirements of the regulations of the Budapest Stock Exchange, the recommendations of the Hungarian Financial Supervisory Authority, and the relevant regulations of the Capital Market Act. MOL has its own Corporate Governance Code, which contains the main corporate governance principles of the company and summarizes its approach to shareholders' rights, main governing bodies, remuneration, and ethical issues.

The key activities of MOL's board of directors are focused on achieving increasing shareholder value with considerations given for the interest of other stakeholders: improving efficiency and profitability, and ensuring transparency in corporate activities and sustainable operation. It also aims to ensure appropriate risk management, environmental protection, and conditions for safety at work. The majority of the board (eight of 11 members) are non-executive directors, with eight members qualifying as independent on the basis of its own set of criteria (based on New York Stock Exchange and EU recommendations) and the declaration of directors.

The board of directors has three committees: the Corporate Governance and Remuneration Committee, the Finance and Risk Management Committee, and the Sustainable Development Committee. In 2013 these committees held, respectively, four meetings (70 per cent average attendance); five meetings (93 per cent attendance rate); and four meetings (100 per cent attendance rate).

The supervisory board is responsible for monitoring and supervising the board of directors on behalf of the shareholders. In accordance with MOL's Articles of Association, the maximum number of members is nine (present membership is nine); by law one-third of the members should be representatives of the employees, accordingly three members of the MOL supervisory board are employee representatives with the other six external persons appointed by the shareholders; five members of the supervisory board are independent. In 2013, the supervisory board held five meetings with an 89 per cent attendance rate. There is an Audit Committee comprised of independent members of the supervisory board. In 2013 the Audit Committee held five meetings with a 60 per cent average attendance rate.

The MOL Policy on Corporate Governance also includes details of the remuneration of members of the board of directors and the supervisory board.

In 2011 MOL Group, the only CEE company to be in the running, qualified for the Sustainable Asset Management (SAM) Gold Class based on its performance in the field of corporate sustainability. The 2,500 largest global companies, based on the Dow Jones Stock Market Index, are invited to be independently assessed on three dimensions of sustainability: long-term economic, social, and environmental performance. The top 15 per cent of companies from 58 business sectors are selected to appear in the SAM Yearbook. MOL Group was included in the Gold Class; to qualify for the SAM Gold Class, the SAM Sector Leader must achieve a minimum total score of 75 per cent. Peer group companies whose total scores are within 5 per cent of the SAM Sector Leader also enter the SAM Gold Class. Out of 113 global oil companies, 68 were examined in detail with 17 being selected to appear in the Yearbook, of which eight entered the Golden Class category. MOL state that 'according to SAM's

(continued)

assessment, the Corporate Governance practice of MOL is outstanding, and its result is above the industry average. The evaluation criteria consisted of several topics, e.g. board structure, corporate governance policies or transparency.'

In 2014, MOL Group received the Central European Sustainability Report Award for the second time. MOL was judged to have prepared the best quality sustainability report in 2013 from among 33 companies in Central Europe. MOL Group states that their

> main objective is to achieve and maintain an internationally acknowledged leading position in the industry based on its sustainability performance. To achieve this goal, MOL has identified six sustainable development focus areas for the period 2011–2015: climate change, environment, health and safety, communities, human capital and economic sustainability. All of the focus areas are considered to be essential to the successful management of the long-term economic, social and environmental challenges MOL Group faces now or in the future.

In 2016, the World Finance Oil & Gas Awards recognized MOL Group as the Best Downstream Company in Eastern Europe. Also in 2016, MOL Group was included in the Dow Jones Sustainability World Index (DJSWI). The company was previously listed between 2010 and 2011 and became an index constituent again following a five-year absence. Inclusion in the DJSWI means that the company is in the top 15 per cent of integrated oil and gas companies based on its corporate sustainability performance. MOL Group is the only company from the Central Eastern European region to be included in the index.

Mini case study questions

1. Why might MOL find it beneficial to be seen as having a good corporate governance structure, a focus on sustainable development, and a strong code of ethics and business conduct?

2. What role do the independent directors play in relation to the activities of the board of directors and the supervisory board?

Questions

The discussion questions to follow cover the key learning points of this chapter. Reading of some of the additional reference material will enhance the depth of the students' knowledge and understanding of these areas.

1. What do you think was the rationale behind the different privatization methods employed in various countries?

2. What effect did each of the privatization methods have on the ownership structure and control of privatized companies? In what ways may the ownership structures have changed over the years since privatization?

3. Which method of privatization do you think has resulted in the best structure in which to nurture good corporate governance?

4. What do you think a foreign investor would be looking for when it comes to investing in a country in CEE?

5. Critically discuss the role of NIFs and IPFs.

6. Do you think there is a role to be played by institutional investors, both domestic and foreign, in the corporate governance of privatized companies?

References

Aguilera, R.V., Kabbach-Castro, L.R., Lee, J.H., and You, J. (2012), 'Corporate Governance in Emerging Markets' in G. Morgan and R. Whitley (eds), *Capitalisms and Capitalism in the 21st Century*, Oxford University Press, Oxford. Available at SSRN: http://ssrn.com/abstract=1806525.

Bartha, P. and Gillies, J. (2006), 'Corporate Governance in Russia: Is it Really Needed?' in C.A. Mallin (ed.), *Handbook on International Corporate Governance, Country Analyses*, Edward Elgar Publishing, Cheltenham, UK.

Belikov, I. (2004), *Corporate Governance in Russia: Who Will Pay For It and How Much?* Economic Reform Feature Service, Center for International Private Enterprise (Article adapted from a longer article originally appearing in Russian in the magazine *Rynok Tsennikh Bumag* (2004, No. 5)).

Berglof, E. and Pajuste, A. (2003), 'Emerging Owners, Eclipsing Markets? Corporate Governance in Central and Eastern Europe' in P.K. Cornelius and B. Kogut (eds), *Corporate Governance and Capital Flows in a Global Economy*, Oxford University Press, Oxford.

Best Practices Committee at Corporate Governance Forum (2002), *Best Practices in Public Companies*, Best Practices Committee at Corporate Governance Forum, Warsaw.

Best Practices Committee at Corporate Governance Forum (2005), *Best Practices in Public Companies*, Best Practices Committee at Corporate Governance Forum, Warsaw.

Boeri, T. and Perasso, G. (1998), 'Privatization and Corporate Governance: Some Lessons from the Experience of Transitional Economies' in M. Balling, E. Hennessy, and R. O'Brien (eds), *Corporate Governance, Financial Markets and Global Convergence*, Kluwer Academic Publishers, Dordrecht.

Budapest Stock Exchange (2004), *Corporate Governance Recommendations*, Budapest Stock Exchange, Budapest.

Budapest Stock Exchange (2007), *Corporate Governance Recommendations*, Budapest Stock Exchange, Budapest.

Budapest Stock Exchange (2008), *Corporate Governance Recommendations*, Budapest Stock Exchange, Budapest.

Cadbury, Sir Adrian (1992), *Report of the Committee on the Financial Aspects of Corporate Governance*, Gee & Co. Ltd, London.

Claessens, S., Djankov, S., and Pohl, G. (1997), 'Ownership and Corporate Governance: Evidence from the Czech Republic', World Bank Policy Research Working Paper, No. 1737.

Coffee, J.C. (1998), 'Inventing a Corporate Monitor for Transitional Economies' in K.J. Hopt, H. Kanda, M.J. Roe, E. Wymeersch, and S. Prigge (eds), *Comparative Corporate Governance, the State of the Art and Emerging Research*, Oxford University Press, Oxford.

Coffee, J.C. (2002), 'Convergence and its Critics' in J.A. McCahery, P. Moerl, T. Raaijmakers, and L. Renneboog (eds), *Corporate Governance Regimes, Convergence and Diversity*, Oxford University Press, Oxford.

Czech Securities Commission (2004), *Corporate Governance Code based on the OECD Principles* (2004), Czech Securities Commission, Prague.

Driffield, N.L., Mickiewicz, T., and Temouri, Y. (2014), 'Institutions and Equity Structure of Foreign Affiliates', *Corporate Governance: An International Review*, Vol. 22, Issue 3, pp. 216–29.

Earle, J.S., Kucsera, C., and Telegdy, A. (2005), 'Ownership Concentration and Corporate Performance on the Budapest Stock Exchange: Do Too Many Cooks Spoil the Goulash?', *Corporate Governance: An International Review*, Vol. 13, No. 2, March, 254–64.

European Bank of Reconstruction and Development/ World Bank (1999), *Business Environment Survey*, EBRD, Brussels.

Federal Securities Commission (2001), *The Russian Code of Corporate Conduct*, Co-ordination Council for Corporate Governance, Moscow.

Frydman, R., Pistor, K., and Rapaczynski, A. (1996), 'Investing in Insider Dominated Firms: Russia' in R. Frydman, C.W. Gray, and A. Rapaczynski (eds), *Corporate Governance in Central Europe and Russia: Volume 1 Banks, Funds, and Foreign Investors*, CEU Press, Budapest.

Grosman, A., Okhmatovskiy, I., and Wright, M. (2016), 'State Control and Corporate Governance in Transit ion Economies: 25 Years on from 1989', *Corporate Governance: An International Review*, Vol. 24, Issue 3, pp. 200–21.

Jandik, T. and Rennie, C.G. (2008), 'The Evolution of Corporate Governance and Firm Performance in Transition Economies: The Case of Sellier and Bellot in the Czech Republic', *European Financial Management*, Vol. 14, No. 4, pp. 747–91.

KCP (2001), *Revised Corporate Governance Code*, KCP/ Czech Securities Commission, Prague.

Kostikov, I. (2003), 'Governance in an Emerging Financial Market. The Case of Russia' in P.K. Cornelius and B. Kogut (eds), *Corporate Governance and Capital Flows in a Global Economy*, Oxford University Press, Oxford.

Kozarzewski, P. (2007), 'Corporate Governance Formation in Poland, Kyrgyzstan, Russia, and Ukraine', *Studies and Analyses No. 347*. Available at SSRN: http://ssrn.com/abstract=1016064.

Lazzarini, S.G. and Musacchio, A. (2018), 'State Ownership Reinvented? Explaining Performance Differences between State-Owned and Private Firms', *Corporate Governance: An International Review*, First published: 1 April 2018, https://doi.org/10.1111/corg.12239.

Moscow Exchange and OECD Russia (2014), Russian Code of Corporate Governance (2014), *Official Journal of the Bank of Russia*, No. 40 (1518)—18 April 2014.

OECD (1999), *Principles of Corporate Governance*, OECD, Paris.

OECD (2004), *Principles of Corporate Governance*, OECD, Paris.

Pistor, K. (2000), 'Patterns of Legal Change: Shareholder and Creditor Rights in Transition Economies', EBRD, Working Paper No. 49.

Pistor, K. and Turkewitz, J. (1996), 'Coping with Hydra—State Ownership after Privatization: A Comparative Study of the Czech Republic, Hungary and Russia' in R. Frydman, C.W. Gray, and A. Rapaczynski (eds), *Corporate Governance in Central Europe and Russia: Volume 2 Insiders and the State*, CEU Press, Budapest.

Rozlucki, W. (2003), 'Governance in an Emerging Financial Market, The Case of Poland' in P.K. Cornelius and B. Kogut (eds), *Corporate Governance and Capital Flows in a Global Economy*, Oxford University Press, Oxford.

Sprenger, C. (2002), 'Ownership and Corporate Governance in Russian Industry: A Survey', European Bank for Research and Development, Working Paper No. 70.

Sprenger. C. (2005), 'The Determinants of Ownership After Privatisation—The Case of Russia', EFA 2005 Moscow Meetings, August.

Sprenger, C. and Lazareva, O. (2017), 'Corporate Governance and Investment: Evidence from Russian Unlisted Firms' (17 March 2017). Higher School of Economics Research Paper No. WP BRP 160/EC/2017. Available at SSRN: https://ssrn.com/abstract=2934786.

Telegdy, A. (2011), 'Corporate Governance and the Structure of Ownership of Hungarian Corporations' in C.A. Mallin (ed.), *Handbook on International Corporate Governance, Country Analyses*, 2nd edn, Edward Elgar Publishing, Cheltenham, UK.

Warsaw Stock Exchange (2002), *Code of Best Practice for WSE Listed Companies*, Warsaw Stock Exchange, Warsaw.

Warsaw Stock Exchange (2007), *Code of Best Practice for WSE Listed Companies*, Warsaw Stock Exchange, Warsaw.

Warsaw Stock Exchange (2010), *Code of Best Practice for WSE Listed Companies*, Warsaw Stock Exchange, Warsaw.

Warsaw Stock Exchange (2012), *Code of Best Practice for WSE Listed Companies*, Warsaw Stock Exchange, Warsaw.

Warsaw Stock Exchange (2016), *Code of Best Practice for GPW Listed Companies*, Warsaw Stock Exchange, Warsaw.

World Bank–IMF (2003), *Report on the Observance of Standards and Codes (ROSC) Corporate Governance Country Assessment, Hungary*, February 2003, drafted by O. Fremond and A. Berg, Corporate Governance Unit Private Sector Advisory Services, World Bank, Washington DC.

Useful websites

www.cipe.org The website of the Centre for International Private Enterprise has numerous articles of relevance to corporate governance.

www.ecgi.global The website of the European Corporate Governance Institute contains articles relating to corporate governance, and lists of corporate governance codes, guidelines, and principles.

Develop your understanding of this chapter and explore the subject further using our online resources at **www.oup.com/uk/mallin6e/**

 FT Clippings

Oligarchs step back from 'shootout' for control of Norilsk Nickel

Potanin says miner's future too important to be decided in auction with rival Deripaska

Henry Foy

Financial Times, 13 April 2018

Vladimir Potanin and Oleg Deripaska, the Russian oligarchs, have backed away from a 'shootout' auction to decide who controls miner Norilsk Nickel amid market turmoil and a plunge in the value of Mr Deripaska's assets following his targeting by US sanctions last week.

Mr Potanin, speaking before the April 6 sanctions were imposed on his rival, told the Financial Times in an interview that the company was too important for its future to be decided by 'roulette', and described the conflict with his fellow billionaire as 'stupid'.

'The destiny of a company like Norilsk Nickel, of that significance to the country's economy, should not be solved with a game of roulette,' said Mr Potanin. 'It is a bit insulting for people working there. Politically, economically, financially; it is an unacceptable way of resolving this situation.'

Rusal, Mr Deripaska's aluminium company, which holds his stake in Norilsk, responded by saying in a statement on Friday that due to the sanctions 'it would not be in the best interests of the company and its shareholders as a whole to seek a mandate in respect of a potential shootout transaction at the current time'.

Mr Potanin controls 30 per cent of Norilsk and Mr Deripaska 27.8 per cent. A deal struck in 2012, when Roman Abramovich, a fellow oligarch, took a small blocking stake, expired in December. The shootout mechanism to resolve the tussle, agreed by Mr Potanin and Mr Deripaska as part of that deal, would cost one of the men at least $10bn in buying out the other.

The US sanctions imposed on Mr Deripaska and his business empire last Friday sent shares in his companies tumbling and could cut him off from international financing that he may need to buy out his rival.

The two men disagree on the reason for the dispute. Mr Potanin said it revolves around Norilsk's free cash flow, with him calling for higher capital expenditure and Mr Deripaska wanting high dividend payments. Mr Deripaska says it is about different opinions on strategy and corporate governance.

'We definitely see the world differently,' Mr Potanin said. 'Shareholders want more dividends. Managers want more capex... The reason this came to conflict is that this difference is too big. The dividends he expects are too high.'

'Norilsk is only one piece in his big picture. He needs cash to develop [his] assets,' Mr Potanin said, adding that he spends his dividend income on buying Norilsk shares. 'I believe in the company. That's the difference: I don't want to feed his system.'

A representative of Rusal said the dividend policy was an 'essential part of the shareholders' agreement to which Mr Potanin has agreed', which improved its market capitalisation and was supported by a majority of research analysts.

'Rusal, as a shareholder of Norilsk, is free to decide what are the most efficient means of utilising dividend proceeds from its investment,' the representative said.

Rusal denied the disagreement was about control. 'Mr Potanin's capex ambitions lie in the sphere of very risky mega projects which lock Norilsk into being a resource company,' the representative said. 'Rusal also believes that Norilsk Nickel should adhere to the best corporate governance practices.'

Mr Deripaska has filed a suit in a London court to stop Mr Abramovich selling shares to Mr Potanin. A ruling is expected next month.

Mr Potanin said: 'The court [case] is about whether I have the right to buy [Mr] Abramovich's shares or if he cannot sell them at all. That would be strange as the general perception is that people are allowed to sell things.' Rusal said it would defend its contractual rights in court.

Mr Potanin, who first won control of Norilsk in Russia's 1990s 'loans for shares' privatisations, said he and Mr Deripaska had agreed at a private meeting last summer that Norilsk should not merge with the latter's aluminium empire.

'There is no synergy between them. They are different businesses,' he said. The Rusal representative declined to comment.

Romania's moves on corporate governance alarm investors

State fund warns that efforts to replace independent board directors could delay IPOs

Neil Buckley

Financial Times, 22 November 2017

Romania surprised Europe last week by reporting year-on-year growth of 8.8 per cent in the third quarter—3 percentage points above expectations. Eight years after the country slashed wages and pensions as part of a crisis-era International Monetary Fund bailout, its vigorous bounceback makes it a bright prospect for foreign corporate and financial investors.

But as with neighbouring Hungary and Poland, Romania's prospects risk being tarnished by its government.

Unlike those two countries, Romania has not shifted to a populist-nationalist government trying to return some foreign-dominated sectors to national control. But business people warn that the Social Democratic-led government that came to power in December last year has revived some controversial old practices—and taken steps that could undermine some of the significant progress made in recent years in fighting corruption and improving governance.

Chief among those raising alarms is Fondul Proprietatea, a fund created by the state in 2005 to compensate citizens whose assets were confiscated under communism.

Managed by Franklin Templeton, Fondul is one of the world's largest listed funds with a net asset value as of September of $2.72bn and a portfolio that includes minority stakes in 19 state-controlled enterprises. These include some of Romania's biggest businesses including Hidroelectrica, a hydro-power company earmarked for the first initial public offering of a Romanian state enterprise since 2014.

However, the fund warns that government moves could make the investment climate less attractive, deter long-awaited IPOs and delay index provider MSCI's plans to upgrade Romania from a 'frontier' to an 'emerging' market, opening it to a broader range of investors.

Legislation passed by Romania as a condition of its IMF bailout is supposed to ensure that SOEs have independent directors who can ensure independent management.

But Greg Konieczny, portfolio manager for Fondul and Franklin Templeton's chief executive for Romania, says the government has been replacing independent directors of state-owned enterprises with loyal cronies. Parliament is also considering draft legislation to allow the government to exempt state businesses from the corporate governance rules.

The implications for investors go well beyond the companies directly involved. Having healthy state-controlled companies benefits the whole economy. 'A lot of the state companies are either in energy or infrastructure,' says Mr Konieczny. 'If you, as a foreign direct investor, see that there's not going to be an improvement in infrastructure like roads, or bad management means ports or airports are not going to be able to cut their fees, you won't be investing in those sectors.'

Fondul's restructuring efforts have played a big part in Romania's revival, but Mr Konieczny also credits the impact of improved governance. Earnings before interest, tax, depreciation and amortisation at its 19 state companies almost doubled to 5.27bn lei ($1.33bn) by 2016 from 2.69bn lei in 2012.

Romania's president, Klaus Iohannis, who has made fighting corruption his priority, has a right to veto the governance legislation if parliament passes it—but only once. Parliament could amend it slightly and just pass it again.

The government insists its privatisation programme remains on track. Toma Petcu, the energy minister, said last month that Hidroelectrica would be listed early next year and would send investors a 'signal that the government is headed for transparency and performance in relation with state-owned companies'.

But Mr Petcu said the government would now only list 10 per cent of Hidroelectrica rather than 15 per cent as initially planned in 2014. That might leave the Bucharest market short of the liquidity needed to ensure its upgrade from frontier status.

Annoyed by lack of progress in listing Hidroelectrica, Fondul has said it is considering selling its 20 per cent stake, which accounts for one-third of its net asset value.

Romania's government may still change tack on governance. The Social Democratic party leader Liviu Dragnea—seen as the real power behind the government—had his assets frozen on Tuesday by anti-corruption prosecutors as part of a probe into misuse of EU funds.

With central Europe re-emerging as a growth powerhouse, the last thing investors want to see is political risk spreading from Poland and Hungary to 19m-strong Romania.

Corporate governance in the Asia-Pacific

Learning objectives

- To understand the background to the development of corporate governance codes in the Asia-Pacific

- To be aware of the different ownership structures in the Asia-Pacific

- To be aware of the main differences in corporate governance codes in various countries in the Asia-Pacific

- To have a detailed knowledge of the corporate governance codes for a range of countries in the Asia-Pacific

Introduction

This chapter gives an overview of the development of corporate governance in the Asia-Pacific countries. The 1990s saw the meteoric rise and subsequent catastrophic collapse of many markets in the Asia-Pacific countries, in most of the so-called 'tiger economies'. Many investors, both local and overseas, had poured money into the stock markets to benefit from the vast gains that could be made. Equally, many investors lost large amounts when the markets crashed, when the bubble burst following on from Japan's prolonged recession in the early 1990s. By the late 1990s, it had spread to South Korea and several countries in the Asia-Pacific region. Following the crash, there was much soul-searching and questioning as to how and why this financial crisis could have happened. Many people expressed the view that the lack of transparency in companies' financial reports had been largely to blame, together with a lack of accountability of directors of companies. No one had really seemed to notice this situation, or if they had, they had not seemed to care about it, as long as the share prices were increasing and there were profits to be made from the stock market. However, once the markets crashed, it became a different story, and governments and stock exchanges sought to restore investor confidence in their countries by increasing transparency and accountability, and instituting better corporate governance.

In the context of the Asian countries with weak institutions and poor property rights (including protection of minority shareholders' rights), Claessens and Fan (2002) state that 'resulting forms of crony capitalism, i.e. combinations of weak corporate governance and government interference, not only lead to poor performance and risky financing patterns, but also are conductive to macro-economic crises'.

Following the financial downturn of the 1990s, many countries in South-East Asia issued revised—and strengthened—corporate governance codes, and countries that previously had not had corporate governance codes introduced them. A number of countries also introduced stewardship codes detailing the roles and responsibilities of institutional investors in their investee companies.

The countries discussed in this chapter cover a range of ownership structures and influences that have impacted on the corporate governance structures. The countries discussed are:

- Japan, with the dominant shareholders being typically main banks of industrial groups or *keiretsu*;
- South Korea, with its *chaebol* representing the interests of dominant shareholders, often family groups;
- Malaysia, with families often being a dominant shareholder;
- Singapore, another country where families play a dominant role and which is emerging as one of the key players in financial markets in the region;
- China, where despite ongoing reforms the state still has significant influence in companies;
- Australia, which has a common law system and widespread institutional investor share ownership.

In a study of nine Asian countries (including Malaysia, South Korea, Japan, and Singapore but not China), Claessens et al. (2000) find that 'in all countries, voting rights frequently exceed cash flow rights via pyramid structures and cross-holdings'. This is indicative of the power that the dominant shareholders are able to build up. However, an encouraging and positive sign is that the countries examined in detail in this chapter have in common that they have felt the need to improve their corporate governance to provide greater transparency and enhance protection of minority shareholders' rights. Interestingly, Gilson (2008) states:

> While the absence of effective minority shareholder protection may in some circumstances explain the absence of corporations whose shares are widely held, it does not explain why we observe minority holdings at all, nor the special role of controlling-family shareholders in many countries. From the perspective of the product market, shareholder distribution, including family control, may play a role in facilitating the corporation's operation as a reputation bearer in markets where commercial exchange is supported by reputation rather than by formal enforcement.

Therefore where there is a weak legal environment and a lack of protection of minority shareholders, those firms that have regard for minority shareholders' rights may in this way be giving a positive signal to the market about their reputation.

Chen and Nowland (2010), in a study of family-owned companies in Asia, find that where 'the family group have a long record of successfully managing the company and where wealth is often created through undisclosable channels such as political connections, we find that too much monitoring is detrimental to company performance. This is because too much monitoring interferes with the ability of the family group to create wealth for all shareholders.'

Japan

Japan's economy developed very rapidly during the second half of the twentieth century. Particularly during the period 1985–9, there was a 'bubble economy', characterized by a sharp increase in share prices and the value of land; the early 1990s saw the bubble burst as share prices fell and land was devalued. As well as shareholders and landowners finding themselves losing vast fortunes, banks found that they had severe problems too. During the bubble period, the banks had lent large amounts of money against the value of land and, as the price of land fell, borrowers found themselves unable to make the repayments and the banks were left with large non-performing loans. The effect of the fall in share prices and land values spread through the Japanese economy, which became quite stagnant, and the effects spread to other countries' economies, precipitating a regional recession.

The Japanese government wished to restore confidence in the Japanese economy and in the stock market, and to attract foreign direct investment to help regenerate growth in companies. Improved corporate governance was seen as a very necessary step in this process.

Japan's corporate governance system is often likened to that of Germany because banks can play an influential role in companies in both countries. However, there are fundamental differences between the systems, driven partly by culture and partly by the Japanese share-holding structure with the influence of the *keiretsu* (broadly meaning 'associations of companies'). Charkham (1994) sums up three main concepts that affect Japanese attitudes towards corporate governance: obligation, family, and consensus. The first of these, obligation, is evidenced by the Japanese feeling of obligation to family, a company, or country; the second, family, is the strong feeling of being part of a 'family' whether this is a family per se, or a company; and the third concept, consensus, means that there is an emphasis on agreement rather than antagonism. These three concepts deeply influence the Japanese approach to corporate governance.

The *keiretsu* sprang out of the *zaibatsu*. Okumura (2002) states: 'Before World War II, when *zaibatsu* (giant pre-war conglomerates) dominated the Japanese economy, individuals or families governed companies as major stockholders. By contrast, after the war, by virtue of corporate capitalism, companies in the form of corporations became large stockowners, and companies became major stockholders of each other's stock.' The companies forming the *keiretsu* may be in different industries, forming a cluster often with a bank at the centre. Charkham (1994) states that 'banks are said to have encouraged the formation and development of groups of this kind, as a source of mutual strength and reciprocal help'. Indeed, banks themselves have a special relationship with the companies they lend to, particularly if they are the lead or main bank for a given company. Banks often buy shares in their customer companies to firm up the relationship between company and bank. However, they are limited to a 5 per cent holding in a given company although, in practice, the combination of the traditional bank relationship with its client and the shareholding mean that they can be influential, and often very helpful, if the company is in financial difficulties, viewing it as part of their obligation to the company to try to help it find a way out of its difficulties.

When compared to the German system, it should be noted that there is no automatic provision for employees to sit on the supervisory board. However, employees have traditionally come to expect that they will have lifelong employment with the same company—unfortunately, in times of economic downturn, this can no longer be guaranteed.

The Japan Corporate Governance Committee published its revised Corporate Governance Code in 2001 (hereafter, 'the Code') (see Table 12.1). The Code had six chapters, which contained a total of 14 principles. The Code had an interesting introduction, part of which stated: 'a good company maximizes the profits of its shareholders by efficiently creating value, and in the process contributes to the creation of a more prosperous society by enriching the lives of its employees and improving the welfare of its other stakeholders.' Hence the Code tried to take a balanced view of what a company is all about, and clearly the consideration of stakeholders is seen to be an important aspect. The foreword to the Code discussed and explained some of the basic tenets of corporate governance to help familiarize readers of the Code with areas including the role and function of the board of directors, the supervisory body, independent directors, incentive-based compensation, disclosure, and investor relations. The six chapters contained in the Code relate to:

- Mission and role of the board of directors
- Mission and role of the committees established within the board of directors
- Leadership responsibility of the CEO
- Addressing shareholder derivative litigation
- Securing fairness and transparency for executive management
- Reporting to the shareholders and communicating with investors.

The Commercial Code in Japan provides for the appointment of statutory auditors to monitor the various aspects of the company's activities. However, the Ministry of Justice issued an extensive revision of the Commercial Code (2002) essentially providing companies with the option of adopting a 'US-style' corporate governance structure. The US-style structure would have a main board of directors to carry out the oversight function, and involve the establishment of audit, remuneration, and nomination committees, each with at least three members, a majority of whom should be non-executive. A board of corporate executive officers would also be appointed who would be in charge of the day-to-day business operations. Under the US-style structure, the board of statutory auditors would be abolished. The Japanese Corporate Governance Code's recommendations dovetailed with the revised Commercial Code.

Table 12.1 Key characteristics influencing Japanese corporate governance

Feature	Key characteristic
Main business form	Public limited company
Predominant ownership structure	*Keiretsu*; but institutional investor ownership is increasing
Legal system	Civil law
Board structure	Dual
Important aspect	Influence of *keiretsu*

In 2004 the Tokyo Stock Exchange issued the *Principles of Corporate Governance for Listed Companies*. In the preface, the purpose of the Principles is described as being 'to provide a necessary common base for recognition, thereby enhancing corporate governance through the integration of voluntary activities by listed companies and demands by shareholders and investors'. The five Principles are based around the Organisation for Economic Co-operation and Development (OECD) *Principles of Corporate Governance*.

The five principles relate to exercising various rights of shareholders, including the right to participate and vote in general meetings; the equitable treatment of shareholders, including minority and foreign shareholders; the relationship with stakeholders in corporate govern-ance; disclosure and transparency; and the responsibilities of the board of directors, auditors, board of corporate auditors, and other relevant groups.

In 2009 the revised *Principles of Corporate Governance for Listed Companies* were published. The preface discussed the consideration of other stakeholders as well as shareholders:

> As the areas of corporate activity are expanding, corporations face a growing need to take into account the values of different cultures and societies. As such, enterprises will have to engage in their profit-pursuing activities with a greater awareness of their social responsi-bilities, with greater transparency and fairness in accordance with market principles, while accepting full accountability to the entire economic community as well as shareholders and investors.

The preface also makes the point that where there is a holding company with a group of companies, then it is important for corporate governance to be adopted across the group as a whole.

The legal framework in Japan, via the Commercial Code Revision on Boards (2003), pro-vided for two corporate governance structures: a corporate auditors' system, consisting of general meetings with shareholders, the board of directors, representative directors, execu-tive directors, corporate auditors, and the board of corporate auditors; and a committee system, where there are general meetings of the shareholders, the board of directors, and committees composed of members of the board of directors (nomination, audit, and com-pensation committees), representative executive officers, and executive officers. It is up to the company which system it chooses. Most Japanese companies have chosen the corpo-rate auditor (statutory auditor), structure, i.e. *kansayaku*. In each case, the general meeting of shareholders is the decision-making body on matters of fundamental importance to the company. A key difference between the two structures is that companies with a committee system need to re-elect their directors annually through the general meeting of shareholders, because the board of directors has the authority regarding the definitive plan for the distri-bution of profit, whereas in the corporate auditors' system, this power lies with the general meetings of shareholders.

Charkham (2005) discusses the various changes that have taken place in the context of corporate governance in Japan and states:

> The important part the banks played has greatly diminished. In its place there are now better structured boards, more effective company auditors, and occasionally more active share-holders. An increase of interest, and, where appropriate, action on their part, might restore the balance that the banks' withdrawal from the scene has impaired.

Ahmadjian and Okumura (2011) also discuss the changes that have taken place in Japan in recent years:

> Over the last two decades, the debate on corporate governance has contrasted two extremes—whether to become 'like the US' or retain the post-war Japanese system of governance. Yet, as we noted earlier, retaining the 'traditional' post-war governance system is no longer an option, since it has been severely weakened by the demise of the role of the main bank, unwinding of cross-shareholdings, changes in accounting standards and increased investment by foreigners.

It is interesting to note that Japan is now using 'poison pills' much more to ward off hostile takeover bids (an undesirable development), whereas it does not have the huge problems associated with perceived excessive director remuneration, as its directors are not paid the vast multiples of the salary of the ordinary employees because this would be considered culturally unacceptable.

The *Outlines for the Revision of the Companies Act 2012* was amended in 2014 with a provision requiring companies to explain if they do not appoint outside directors.

In June 2013 the Japanese government approved the Japan Revitalization Strategy which advocated a 'preparation of principles (a Japanese version of the Stewardship Code) for institutional investors in order to fulfill their stewardship responsibilities, such as promoting the mid- to long-term growth of companies through dialogue'. The *Principles for Responsible Institutional Investors (Japan's Stewardship Code)* (hereinafter, Japan's Stewardship Code) was published in February 2014. Also following on from the Japan Revitalization Strategy, the Japan Exchange Group Inc established the JPX-Nikkei Index 400, operational from January 2014, which is a new stock index composed of 'companies with high appeal for investors, which meet the requirement of global investment standards, such as the efficient use of capital and investor-focused management perspectives'.

Furthermore, the Japan Revitalization Strategy (revised in 2014) approved the establishment of a council of experts, of which the Tokyo Stock Exchange and the Financial Services Agency would act as joint secretariat, to prepare a revised Corporate Governance Code. In December 2014 Japan issued the *Corporate Governance Code (Exposure Draft)* which was followed by the *Japan Corporate Governance Code: Seeking Sustainable Corporate Growth and Increased Corporate Value over the Mid- to Long-Term* (hereafter 'the Corporate Governance Code') in June 2015. The Corporate Governance Code, as its full title suggests, will hopefully promote mid- to long-term investing; alongside this, companies are asked to examine their own corporate governance to determine what actions they might themselves take to encourage mid- to long-term investment. The Corporate Governance Code states:

> Such efforts by companies will make possible further corporate governance improvements, supported by purposeful dialogue with shareholders (institutional investors) based on Japan's Stewardship Code. In this sense, the [Corporate Governance] Code and Japan's Stewardship Code are 'the two wheels of a cart', and it is hoped that they will work appropriately and together so as to achieve effective corporate governance in Japan.

Both the Corporate Governance Code and Japan's Stewardship Code adopt a principles-based approach, i.e. 'comply or explain'.

The Corporate Governance Code has five General Principles:

- Securing the rights and equal treatment of shareholders
- Appropriate co-operation with stakeholders other than shareholders
- Ensuring appropriate information disclosure and transparency
- Responsibilities of the board
- Dialogue with shareholders.

Interestingly *Japan's Stewardship Code (2014)* was introduced earlier in 2014 before the Corporate Governance Code 2014 (exposure draft) and it defines seven principles considered to be helpful for responsible institutional investors in fulfilling their stewardship responsibilities 'with due regard both to their clients and beneficiaries and to investee companies'. Acting in accordance with these principles should also mean that institutional investors can contribute to the growth of the economy as a whole.

The seven principles are as follows:

- Institutional investors should have a clear policy on how they fulfil their stewardship responsibilities, and publicly disclose it;
- Institutional investors should have a clear policy on how they manage conflicts of interest in fulfilling their stewardship responsibilities and publicly disclose it;
- Institutional investors should monitor investee companies so that they can appropriately fulfil their stewardship responsibilities with an orientation towards the sustainable growth of the companies;
- Institutional investors should seek to arrive at an understanding in common with investee companies and work to solve problems through constructive engagement with investee companies;
- Institutional investors should have a clear policy on voting and disclosure of voting activity. The policy on voting should not be comprised only of a mechanical checklist: it should be designed to contribute to sustainable growth of investee companies;
- Institutional investors in principle should report periodically on how they fulfil their stewardship responsibilities, including their voting responsibilities, to their clients and beneficiaries;
- To contribute positively to the sustainable growth of investee companies, institutional investors should have in-depth knowledge of the investee companies and their business environment and skills and resources needed to appropriately engage with the companies and make proper judgements in fulfilling their stewardship activities.

A revision of Japan's Stewardship Code was issued in 2017. It was noted that since the publication of the earlier Stewardship Code in 2014, over 200 institutional investors had indicated their commitment to the Stewardship Code. However whilst recognizing that progress had been made, there was some concern that the reforms may be more of a mechanical process, i.e. form over substance. Therefore, in November 2016, the Council of Experts Concerning the Follow-up of Japan's Stewardship Code and Japan's Corporate Governance Code (convened by the Financial Services Agency and Tokyo Stock Exchange) published an Opinion Statement in order to deepen reform and move its focus from form to substance. After various discussions, the Stewardship Code was revised incorporating the Opinion Statement proposals on five areas: effective oversight by asset owners; asset managers' governance and management of their conflicts of interest; engagement in passive management; enhanced disclosure of voting records; self-evaluation of asset managers. In addition the following issues raised in the review process were included: proxy advisors should disclose their approach to principles such as the management of conflicts of interest; collective engagement (i.e. dialogue between a company and multiple investors in collaboration) should be recognized in the Code as an engagement option; and important environmental, social, and governance (ESG) factors may affect medium to long-term corporate value for investee companies and should be monitored by investing institutions.

Lee and Allen (2013) provide an interesting discussion of the *kansayaku* boards compared to the audit committees. Aronson (2014) discusses recent trends in corporate governance reform in Japan and identifies three key issues which may be critical to the way in which Japan's corporate governance develops: 'the role of domestic institutional investors, the development of a standardized hybrid model, and the adjustment of Japanese corporate governance to the demands of globalization'. Aoyagi and Ganelli (2014) highlight the issue of Japan's high corporate savings which might be holding back growth. Their empirical analysis on a panel of Japanese firms 'confirms that improving corporate governance would help unlock corporate savings. The main policy implication of our analysis is that comprehensive corporate governance reform should be a key component of Japan's growth strategy.'

Kato et al. (2017) find that Japanese companies which reform their corporate governance practices improve their performance, holding less cash and increasing payouts to shareholders. Such improvements in performance 'are associated with reductions in (excess) cash, reductions in the influence of the banks that traditionally sit at the center of horizontal keiretsu, and increases in the holdings of management and foreign investors'. They also suggest that their findings have implications for other Asian economies, such as China, India, and Korea. A paper by Aman et al. (2017) also cited benefits to better corporate governance practices in listed Japanese companies as they found that 'compared with firms with weaker governance, better-governed firms make more frequent public disclosures, their disclosures of good news are timelier, and their share prices reflect good news faster. However, we did not detect comparable effects for bad news, which has implications for regulators.'

South Korea

The downturn in the Japanese economy soon affected the South Korean economy, which suffered similar consequences. Balino and Ubide (1999), amongst others, stated that poor corporate governance was an important contributory factor to the extent of the financial crisis in 1997. The poor corporate governance was characterized by a lack of transparency and disclosure, ineffective boards, and the activities of the *chaebols* (see Table 12.2).

The *chaebols* are large Korean conglomerates that wield considerable power through their cross-holdings of shares in various companies. The *chaebols* often constitute powerful family interests in Korea, and families may be able to exert more control in a particular company than their shareholdings on paper would merit. They often have little regard for the rights and

Table 12.2 Key characteristics influencing South Korean corporate governance

Feature	Key characteristic
Main business form	Public limited company
Predominant ownership structure	Controlling shareholder (family, corporate cross-holdings)
Legal system	Common law
Board structure	Unitary
Important aspect	Influence of *chaebol*

interests of minority shareholders. However, in recent years, the People's Solidarity for Participatory Democracy (PSPD) has been established as an influential minority shareholder activist group that has campaigned for better corporate governance in a number of Korea's top companies. Jang and Kim (2002) emphasize the influence and power of families via the *chaebols*:

> Ownership by the controlling families in listed Korean chaebol companies has been only a fraction and their controlling power derives from their ownership through affiliated companies ... personal stakes, particularly in listed companies, are minimized but control is maintained by an extensive matrix of circuitous cross-ownership among affiliated companies.

The Korean Committee on Corporate Governance was established in March 1999, with funding from the Korea Stock Exchange, the Korea Securities Dealers' Association, the Korea Listed Companies Association, and the Korea Investment Trust Companies Association. It reported six months later in September 1999, with a Code of Best Practice (hereinafter 'the Code'), which tries to take into account both internationally accepted corporate governance principles and also the 'unique managerial circumstances faced by Korean companies'. The purpose of the Code is stated as being to maximize corporate value by enhancing transparency and efficiency of corporations for the future. It is recognized that, in order to attract and retain both domestic and foreign investment, there needs to be more transparency and more regard to the rights of minority shareholders.

The Code applies to listed companies and other public companies but it is also advised that non-public companies follow the Code where practicable. The Code has five sections relating to:

- Shareholders
- Board of directors
- Audit systems
- Stakeholders
- Management monitoring by the market.

Two points of particular interest are as follows. Firstly, there is no provision for employee representation as such (it is a unitary board system rather than dual), but the Act on Worker Participation and Promotion of Co-operation stipulates that employees and management have consultative meetings whereby the employees are informed of the company's plans,

quarterly performance, personnel plans, etc. Secondly, and of some significance, is the recommendation that companies disclose detailed information on the share ownership status
of controlling shareholders because 'the actual controlling shareholder of the corporation is
one at the core of corporate governance'.

In 2003 an updated Code of Best Practices for Corporate Governance was issued. Retaining the
same sections as previously, the impetus for the revised Code were the changes affecting corporate governance globally, including accounting frauds in the USA, and the reform of governance
systems in many countries. Furthermore, it was recognized that investment risks associated with
poor corporate governance remained as one of the main causes of the undervaluation of Korean
stocks. The Code focused on the practical applications of its recommendations and attempted to
take into account the unique managerial circumstances faced by Korean companies.

In December 2016, the *Korea Stewardship Code Principles on the Stewardship Responsibilities of Institutional Investors* was issued. The Stewardship Code states that institutional investors should comply with the principles 'in order to enhance the mid-to long-term value and
sustainable growth of investee companies and further the mid-to long-term interests of their
clients and ultimate beneficiaries'. The seven principles relate to institutional investors: publicly disclosing their policy on their responsibilities; publicly disclosing their policy on how
they deal with conflicts of interest; regularly monitoring investee companies; formulation
of internal guidelines on the timeline, procedures, and methods for stewardship activities;
publicly disclosing their voting policy and voting records; regularly reporting on voting and
stewardship activities to their clients or beneficiaries; having the capabilities and expertise
required to implement stewardship responsibilities appropriately.

Black et al. (2005), in a study of firms' corporate governance practices in Korea, found that
regulatory factors are very important, largely because Korean rules impose special governance requirements on large firms (as mentioned earlier). They found that industry factors,
firm size, and firm risk are important, with larger firms and riskier firms being better governed.

Kim and Kim (2007) found that Korea has significantly improved its quality of corporate
governance since the 1997 financial crisis. They state that:

> most notable are improved corporate transparency, better alignment of managerial incen-
> tives to shareholder value, and more effective oversight by the board. A number of play-
> ers also have emerged as key external monitors and enforcers of good governance. There
> remain, however, substantial differences between non-chaebol and chaebol affiliated firms
> and also across chaebol.

Aguilera et al. (2012), in a study of companies in emerging markets in the period 2000–8,
found, in the context of South Korea, that whilst family ownership was gradually decreasing—
implying that the traditional family-owned structure has weakened—this

> does not entail the collapse of the controlling power of families, particularly in business
> groups, as that would require not only that family control decreases but also that cross-
> shareholdings and pyramidal structures no longer exist. In fact, in 2009 the KFTC reports
> that internal ownership, which represents the sum of family direct shareholding and cross-
> shareholdings, of the top 10 business groups is still more than 50 per cent. Despite criti-
> cism for their lack of transparency and patriarchal management, *Chaebols* are continuing to
> engage in the generation-to-generation transfer of ownership, with one-third of the top 50
> family-owned businesses already having concluded the succession process.

Black et al. (2015) in a study of four major emerging markets—Brazil, India, Korea, and Turkey—find that:

> disclosure predicts higher market value in each country (within disclosure, the principal predictor is financial disclosure); board structure has a positive coefficient in all countries and is significant in Brazil and Korea (within board structure, the principal predictor is board independence); and that once one controls for disclosure and board structure, the other indices do not predict firm value. These results suggest that firms, in responding to investor demands for better governance; and investors, in assessing governance quality, can do reasonably well in focusing on disclosure and board structure.

Shin et al. (2018) assess the performance impact of appointing politically connected outside directors (PCODs) in Korean *chaebol* firms. They state:

> overall, we suggest that the number of PCODs correlates positively with firm performance, and that the value effect of PCODs increases with the importance of internal trade among group affiliates, the existence of inside directorship by controlling shareholders, and potential settlements from pending litigation. We further differentiate between PCODs and find that former government officials as PCODs drive our findings.

Malaysia

Malaysia was one of the fastest growing of the tiger economies in the early 1990s. The government had introduced a succession of five-year plans with the aim of full industrialization in the twenty-first century. The government had also introduced the New Economic Policy (NEP) in 1970 to implement affirmative actions in favour of the Bumiputera (the indigenous Malay people). These types of affirmative action were designed to increase Bumiputera involvement in the corporate sector. The government also set up trusts to hold shares on behalf of the Bumiputera, and whether as companies, individuals, or trusts, they tend to be one of the largest shareholder groups in Malaysian companies (see Table 12.3). The corporate governance code in Malaysia concentrates on the principles and best practice of corporate governance, drawing largely on the UK corporate governance recommendations.

In Malaysia many of the listed companies are family-owned or controlled, with many companies having evolved from traditional family-owned enterprises. This means that the

Table 12.3 Key characteristics influencing Malaysian corporate governance

Feature	Key characteristic
Main business form	Public limited company
Predominant ownership structure	Controlling shareholder (family, corporation, or trust nominee)
Legal system	Common law
Board structure	Unitary
Important aspect	Influence of Bumiputera shareholders

directors may not be responsive to minority shareholders' rights; better corporate govern-ance would help to remedy this and ensure that minority shareholders' rights are protected. In addition, transparency should be improved to help restore investor confidence.

Malaysia established its High Level Finance Committee on Corporate Governance in 1998, following on from the drastic downturn of the Malaysian economy the previous year. The Committee reported in March 2000 with a detailed corporate governance code: the Malaysian Code of Corporate Governance (hereinafter 'the Code'). The Kuala Lumpur Stock Exchange adopted the Code's recommendations and, with effect from 2002, listed companies have had to include a statement of their compliance with the Code and explain any areas of the Code that they do not comply with (i.e. a 'comply or explain' mechanism).

The Code has four parts: first, broad principles of good corporate governance; secondly, best practices for companies, which gives more detail for each of the broad principles; thirdly, a section aimed at investors and auditors discussing their role in corporate governance; and fourthly, various explanatory notes are provided. The first part of the Code devoted to the principles of corporate governance covers:

- Directors
- Directors' remuneration
- Accountability and audit
- Shareholders.

The Corporate Law Reform Committee was established in 2004 to lead a programme of corporate law reform in Malaysia. Corporate governance reforms are the focus of one of the working groups, which is looking at issues of corporate governance and shareholders' rights. The review sought to find an appropriate balance between providing a framework for effective shareholder engagement and ensuring that this framework is cost-efficient, flexible, and facilitative for business. The focus being on general meetings and associated issues such as voting.

In 2007 the revised Malaysian Code on Corporate Governance was issued. It states that:

> the key amendments to the Code are aimed at strengthening the board of directors and audit committees, and ensuring that the board of directors and audit committees discharge their roles and responsibilities effectively. The amendments spell out the eligibility criteria for appointment of directors and the role of the nominating committee. On audit commit-tees, the amendments spell out the eligibility criteria for appointment as an audit committee member, the composition of audit committees, the frequency of meetings and the need for continuous training. In addition, internal audit functions are now required in all PLCs and the reporting line for internal auditors clarified.

Liew (2007) finds that Malaysia's corporate governance reforms have been modelled on the Anglo-American system to a large extent, but the majority of the interviewees in her research placed greater emphasis on the social aspect of corporate governance in contrast to the tra-ditional notion of shareholder accountability.

In June 2009 the stock exchange in Malaysia, Bursa Malaysia, announced that it would be launching a new corporate governance index with the aim of encouraging greater transpar-ency, more independence at board level, and helping to deter related party transactions.

In 2011 the Securities Commission Malaysia published a *Corporate Governance Blueprint* setting out a broad-based approach to the corporate governance landscape going forward. Boards and shareholders should conduct business in a way that enhances the company's reputation for good governance and promote more internalization of the culture of good governance. The Blueprint 'seeks to enrich the governance process through promoting more extensive and proactive participation by a broader range of stakeholders'. The Blueprint details recent changes in Malaysia impacting on the corporate governance environment; these include that in 2010, the Capital Markets and Services Act 2007 was amended to include sections 317A and 320A which gave the Securities Commission Malaysia the power to act against directors of listed companies who cause wrongful loss to their company and against any person who misleads the public through falsely preparing or auditing the financial statements of companies; and also that Malaysia had committed to achieving full convergence with the International Financial Reporting Standards (IFRS) by January 2012.

The *Corporate Governance Blueprint* recognizes that Malaysia needs to embed corporate governance culture in listed companies and more generally within the corporate governance ecosystem, which it identifies as including shareholders, gatekeepers, and regulators as well as the board of directors.

In the following year the Malaysian Code on Corporate Governance (2012) was issued. This focuses on strengthening board structure and composition, recognizing the role of directors as active and responsible fiduciaries. It also encourages companies to have appropriate corporate disclosure policies and to make public their commitment to respecting shareholder rights. There are eight principles and 26 accompanying recommendations which focus on, inter alia, laying a strong foundation for the board and its committees to carry out their roles effectively, promote timely and balanced disclosure, safeguard the integrity of financial reporting, emphasize the importance of risk management and internal controls, and encourage shareholder participation in general meetings. The eight principles are as follows:

- Principle 1—Establish clear roles and responsibilities.
- Principle 2—Strengthen composition.
- Principle 3—Reinforce independence.
- Principle 4—Foster commitment.
- Principle 5—Uphold integrity in financial reporting.
- Principle 6—Recognize and manage risks.
- Principle 7—Ensure timely and high-quality disclosure.
- Principle 8—Strengthen relationship between company and shareholders.

It is interesting to note that under Principle 1, Recommendation 1.4 states that 'the board should ensure that the company's strategies promote sustainability'; and that Recommendation 1.6 states that 'the board should ensure it is supported by a suitably qualified and competent company secretary'.

The Malaysian Code on Corporate Governance issued in 2017 supersedes the earlier Code and takes a new approach to promote greater internalization of corporate governance culture. To achieve this end there are a number of key features of the new approach including the Comprehend, Apply and Report (CARE) approach; the shift from comply or explain to apply or explain an alternative; more focus on the intended outcomes of practices; guidance for companies in applying practices; and encouraging companies to strengthen their governance practices and processes with the concept of Step Ups (exemplary practices which support companies in moving towards greater excellence). There are three principles as follows: Principle A 'Board Leadership and Effectiveness' which covers board responsibilities; board composition; and remuneration. Principle B 'Effective Audit and Risk Management' which covers the audit committee; and the risk management and internal control framework. Principle C 'Integrity in Corporate Reporting and Meaningful Relationship with Stakeholders' which covers communication with stakeholders; and conduct of General Meetings.

In 2014, Malaysia introduced the Malaysian Code for Institutional Investors; such an industry-led Code was envisaged under the *Corporate Governance Blueprint* 2011. The Malaysian Code for Institutional Investors is a voluntary code and provides guidance on 'effective exercise of stewardship responsibilities towards the delivery of sustainable long-term value to the institutional investors' ultimate beneficiaries or clients'. It sets out six broad principles of effective stewardship by institutional investors as follows:

- Principle 1—Institutional investors should disclose the policies on their stewardship responsibilities.
- Principle 2—Institutional investors should monitor their investee companies.
- Principle 3—Institutional investors should engage with investee companies as appropriate.
- Principle 4—Institutional investors should adopt a robust policy on managing conflicts of interest which should be publicly disclosed.
- Principle 5—Institutional investors should incorporate corporate governance and sustainability considerations into the investment decision-making process.
- Principle 6—Institutional investors should publish a voting policy.

Salim (2011) discusses many of the issues that have affected corporate governance in Malaysia, identifying gaps between 'the law-in-books and the law-in-action'. Moreover he points out that the law operates within the environment of 'Malaysia's "syncretic" nature, her unique multi-racial setting as well as her corporate structure [which] has an impact on corporate practices'. He concludes that it requires the balancing of diverse stakeholder groups' interests and that 'the challenge for regulators is to identify who these stakeholders are, and to find the right balance to protect the interests of each. Also as corporate governance operates within a larger societal context, a true reform can only be achieved by including institutional and political reforms as part of the larger reform agenda.'

Esa and Zahari (2014) examine the association between ownership structure and directors' compensation disclosure in the 100 largest listed companies in Malaysia. They find that 'government ownership was positively associated and statistically significant at 1% level with the extent of directors' compensation disclosure, while the percentage of family members on the board is negatively associated to the extent of directors' compensation disclosure'.

Singapore

Singapore is one of the leading financial centres in Asia, offering a broad range of financial services, including banking, insurance, investment banking, and treasury services. In just over four decades, it has established a thriving financial centre of international repute which attracts business on a global basis as well as from the wider Asia-Pacific region. The Singapore Exchange (SGX) has some 800 companies listed, about one-fifth of which are overseas companies.

Temasek Holdings is an investment company that was incorporated under the Singapore Companies Act in 1974 to hold and manage investments and assets previously held by the Singapore government. These were investments made since Singapore gained its independence in 1965. The aim was for Temasek to own and manage these investments on a commercial basis whilst leaving the Ministry of Finance to focus on its core role of policymaking and regulations. Over the years Temasek has become an influential investor not just in the domestic market, where it has shares in many companies, but also internationally through its activities as a sovereign wealth fund (see Table 12.4).

Table 12.4 Key characteristics influencing Singaporean corporate governance

Feature	Key characteristic
Main business form	Public limited companies
Predominant ownership structure	Families; state
Legal system	Common law
Board structure	Unitary
Important aspect	Influence of state (for example, via Temasek Holdings)

The Code of Corporate Governance (hereafter 'the Code') was introduced in 2001 to promote a high standard of corporate governance amongst listed companies in Singapore. The Code has evolved over the years to try to ensure its relevance to a changing investor environment, and market developments with revisions being made in 2005 and most recently in May 2012. The most recent Code was drafted by the Corporate Governance Council, which was set up by the Monetary Authority of Singapore (MAS) in February 2010, to undertake a comprehensive review of the Code. The rationale being that 'strong corporate governance is critical to protecting the interest of the investing public, maintaining confidence in our listed companies and enhancing Singapore's global reputation as a trusted financial centre'.

The Code has four sections with 16 key principles:

- **Board matters**—covers the board's conduct of affairs; board composition and guidance; chairman and chief executive officer; board membership; board performance; and access to information.

- **Remuneration matters**—covers procedures for developing remuneration policies; level and mix of remuneration; disclosure of remuneration.

- **Accountability and audit**—covers accountability; risk management and internal controls; audit committee; and internal audit.
- **Shareholder rights and responsibilities**—covers shareholder rights; communication with shareholders; and conduct of shareholder meetings.

The changes to the earlier Code are focused on the areas of director independence, board composition, director training, multiple directorships, alternate directors, remuneration practices and disclosures, risk management, and shareholder rights and roles.

In terms of disclosure of corporate governance arrangements, the Code states that the Listing Manual requires listed companies to describe in their company's annual reports their corporate governance practices with specific reference to the principles of the Code, as well as disclose and explain any deviation from any guideline of the Code. Companies should make a positive confirmation at the start of the corporate governance section of the company's annual report that they have adhered to the principles and guidelines of the Code, or specify each area of non-compliance.

At the end of the Code there is a statement on the role of shareholders in engaging with the companies in which they invest. The statement says that 'the objective of creating sustainable and financially sound enterprises that offer long-term value to shareholders is best served through a constructive relationship between shareholders and the Boards of companies ... By constructively engaging with the Board, shareholders can help to set the tone and expectation for governance of the company.' Shareholders are exhorted to attend the companies' AGMs and to vote their shares. The statement does not form part of the Code; it is aimed at enhancing the quality of engagement between shareholders and companies, so as to help drive higher standards of corporate governance and improve long-term returns to shareholders.

It is noteworthy that in 2010 the MAS issued *Guidelines on Corporate Governance for Banks, Financial Holding Companies and Direct Insurers*, which are incorporated in Singapore. These Guidelines are based on the Corporate Governance Code with some additional recommendations for banks, financial holding companies, and insurers. The rationale given by MAS for these additional recommendations is that weak governance can undermine public confidence in financial institutions as well as the financial system and markets in which they operate.

In May 2012 the Corporate Governance Council released its Risk Governance Guidance for Listed Boards. The Guidance is

> intended to provide key information on risk governance to all Board members. This includes factors which the Board should collectively consider when overseeing the company's risk management framework and policies. The Guidance also spells out the Board's and Management's respective responsibilities in managing the company's risks. In particular, the Council hopes that the Guidance will assist the Board, as well as Management, of small to mid-capitalised listed companies in the risk governance of their companies.

In early 2018, the Corporate Governance Council (Council) issued a consultation paper on its recommendations to revise the Code of Corporate Governance (Code). The Council believes that:

> a well-rounded board with the appropriate mix of skills, experience and independence is critical to good corporate governance. Hence, a key focus of the Code revisions is to reinforce board competencies through encouraging board renewal, strengthening director

independence and enhancing board diversity. Other proposed Code revisions include greater emphasis on disclosures of the relationship between remuneration and value creation, and the need for companies to consider and balance the needs of all stakeholders.

In 2016, the *Singapore Stewardship Principles For Responsible Investors* were issued by Stewardship Asia Centre (on behalf of the Singapore Stewardship Principles Working Group). There are seven Stewardship Principles which 'provide useful guidance to responsible investors towards fostering good stewardship in discharging their responsibilities and creating sustainable long-term value for all stakeholders.'

1. Take a stand on stewardship—Responsible investors establish and articulate their policies on their stewardship responsibilities.

2. Know your investment—Responsible investors communicate regularly and effectively with their investee companies.

3. Stay active and informed—Responsible investors actively monitor their investee companies.

4. Uphold transparency in managing conflicts of interest—Responsible investors make known their approach to managing conflicts of interest.

5. Vote responsibly—Responsible investors establish clear policies on voting and exercise their voting rights in a responsible fashion.

6. Set a good example—Responsible investors document and provide relevant updates on their stewardship activities.

7. Work together—Responsible investors are willing to engage responsibly with one another where appropriate.

In the context of state-owned enterprises, Tan et al. (2015) point out that 'state owned enterprises are generally regarded as inefficient firms because of political objectives, external interference, and corruption. Notwithstanding this, studies have shown that Singapore state owned enterprises exhibit higher valuations than those of non-GLCs [government-linked companies] after controlling for firm specific factors and also have better corporate governance practices.' They posit that during the late 1950s to early 1970s 'the difficult economic conditions coupled with a contested democratic political environment in Singapore played a significant role in fostering good political governance in Singapore which was in turn transposed to her state owned enterprises'.

China

The Peoples' Republic of China (PRC) has introduced a number of changes to develop its stock market. In the early 1990s, the Shanghai and Shenzhen Stock Exchanges were launched, with the aim of raising finance from domestic and foreign investors to provide listed companies with new funds. The 1990s saw many businesses move from being state-owned enterprises (SOEs) to joint stock companies, and then to companies listed on one of the stock exchanges. The PRC government wished to modernize its industry and other sectors, and to expand the economy, to move towards a socialist market economy.

However, many of the former SOEs were lumbering giants with outdated machinery, and employing far too many people to make them viable as commercially run businesses with the aim of increasing profits. They were used to receiving loans from the state-owned commercial banks, which the banks very often knew they had little chance of repaying, these being non-performing loans that, in turn, were a real drain on the resources of the state-owned banks. The SOEs were also subject to the influence of party members at a number of levels: as employees, as local government officials in the district in which they operate, and at national level. This situation is changing over time but the old influences still exist. The situation was exacerbated by unfortunate incidents of corruption (which meant that the assets of the business were not safeguarded), and by a lack of transparency, disclosure, and accuracy of information. All in all, this was not a state of affairs that was going to build confidence in the stock market.

The government's desire to build a socialist market economy, to modernize, and to become part of the World Trade Organization all fuelled the move to try to improve shareholders' rights and protection of those rights, the insulation of company boards from inappropriate influence, and greater transparency and disclosure: in essence, the building of a corporate governance system. However, although many of the provisions are there on paper for an effective corporate governance system (as will be shown later), in practice, the state still owns large shareholdings in many companies (often more than half), minority shareholders' rights are sometimes ignored, and companies in the PRC are liable to have influence exerted over them from a number of different sources (see Table 12.5). Nonetheless, steps have been taken in the right direction and the government will be aware that if it wishes to attract foreign institutional investors, it will need to have a corporate governance system that protects minority rights, and encourages confidence in the corporate structure and operations, and companies will need to provide accurate and timely information. As On Kit Tam (1999) stated: 'The task of establishing functional and appropriate corporate governance arrangements [in China] is necessarily a long-term and continually changing one.'

In the PRC, corporate governance developments involve a number of regulatory bodies, including the China Securities Regulatory Commission (CSRC), the Ministry of Finance, the State Economic and Trade Commission, and the People's Bank of China, which is essentially the Central Bank of China.

A series of corporate scandals came to light in 2001, including that of Lantian Co. Ltd. Lantian Co. Ltd was the first publicly listed ecological agricultural company in China. However,

Table 12.5 Key characteristics influencing Chinese corporate governance

Feature	Key characteristic
Main business form	State-owned enterprises, joint stock companies
Predominant ownership structures	State
Legal system	Civil law
Board structure	Dual
Important aspect	Influence of Communist Party

investors grew suspicious of its high profit growth because its business could not have under-pinned such growth. Subsequently, inaccuracies in its financial reporting came to light and it is estimated that Lantian overstated net profits by up to US$60 million. Scandals such as Lantian have helped fuel the drive for corporate governance reforms and, in January 2001, the CSRC issued a Code of Corporate Governance for Listed Companies in China (hereinafter 'the Code').

The Code is broadly based on the OECD *Principles of Corporate Governance*. The Code is aimed at listed companies and addresses 'the protection of investors' interests and rights, the basic behaviour rules and moral standards for directors, supervisors, managers, and other senior management members of listed companies'. The Code is seen as the yardstick by which a company is able to measure its corporate governance, and if there are deficiencies in the corporate governance of a company, then the securities supervision and regulatory authorities may instruct the company to correct its corporate governance to comply with the Code.

The Code contains seven main chapters dealing with:

- Shareholders and shareholders' meetings
- Listed company and its controlling shareholders
- Directors and board of directors
- Supervisors and supervisory board
- Performance assessments and incentive and disciplinary systems
- Stakeholders
- Information and disclosure and transparency.

In the summer of 2001 the CSRC produced *Guidelines for Introducing Independent Directors to the Board of Directors of Listed Companies*. The Guidelines mandate all domestically listed companies to amend their articles as necessary to comply with the Guidelines and to appoint, by 30 June 2002, at least two independent directors to the board of directors; by 30 June 2003, at least one-third of the board should be independent directors.

Neoh (2003) stated that there are at least two areas that must be addressed for the market to move away from short-termism and for good governance to take root. One is for investors to have a longer term time horizon and the second is for the system of management succession to be addressed, so that politics is separated from the enterprise. The legal system also needs to support important bankruptcy laws and company law reform.

In February 2006 China moved towards convergence with global standards with the release by the Ministry of Finance of 39 standards based on IFRS, which, inter alia, aim to improve the quality of financial information and boost investor confidence. Given that transparency, disclosure, and accountability were at the heart of sound corporate governance, this was a most welcome development.

Tang (2008) details corporate and securities law reforms that have served to improve the corporate governance environment in China but he points out that unless enforcement capabilities are strengthened, the reforms may not be effective. From a different perspective, Clarke (2008) discusses some of the limitations in China:

> An important part of any solution to China's corporate governance problems, given its current set of administrative and legal institution[s], lies not in the state's actively beefing up

those institutions, but simply in its relaxing its hostility to civil society institutions, and understanding that corporate governance is too important a matter to be left solely to the state.

The OECD-China Policy Dialogue on Corporate Governance Report (2011) looks at the institutional framework of corporate governance in China through the lens of the OECD *Principles of Corporate Governance*. The Report states 'that corporate governance has improved significantly since the Chinese stock market was created in 1990, with important achievements in establishing and developing the legal and regulatory framework'. It also states that:

> the corporate governance framework in China is developing and adapting to the country's economic transformation. As market discipline is still evolving, the role played by the formal legal and regulatory framework remains essential for building an efficient and competitive capital market. Given China's concentrated ownership structure, potential conflicts of interest between majority and minority shareholders remain a core corporate governance issue. It is therefore very useful that the Report looks at the issues of equitable treatment of shareholders and mechanisms to prevent abusive related party transactions. The Report is also helpful in identifying mechanisms for shareholder redress. On a related topic, the Committee pointed to the challenges of coordinating the multiple roles played by state entities—as shareholders, regulators and managers.

It identified that priority areas for China may include curbing abusive related party transactions, enhancing the quality of boards, improving shareholder protection, and curbing market abuse. Also it might be useful to devote special attention to the all-important issue of how to improve effective implementation and enforcement.

Tam and Yu (2011) point out that 'corporate governance development in China is entering a new phase where effective corporate governance mechanisms and practices have become a necessary condition for the country's quest to achieve enduring prosperity through an open market economy that can compete globally'.

Hass et al. (2013) examine the relationship between performance persistence and corporate governance (proxied by board characteristics and shareholder structure) in listed companies in China during 2001–11. They find that:

> firms with higher corporate governance (especially for board characteristics) show higher performance persistence. The results are stronger for short horizons and for an accounting-based view. Overall, our empirical findings, although not being able to completely exclude other explanations, strongly suggest that a well-structured board with more independent directors, split positions for CEOs and the chairman as well as smaller boards favors performance persistence. In terms of the shareholder structure we find evidence that lower levels of State ownership and a non-concentrated blockholder structure is positively associated with performance persistence.

Morck and Yeung (2014) discussing corporate governance in China state that 'China's success to date has come without many of the key institutions—notably, private property rights, shareholder-centered corporate governance, and a well-functioning impartial legal system— that most Western economists believe essential to long-term success'. They argue that China will need 'to adopt the substance as well as the form of those missing institutions to continue to rise into the world's economic upper ranks'.

More recently, Mutlu et al. (2017) undertook a meta-analysis of the corporate governance literature in China. They found that:

> the weight of evidence demonstrates that two major 'good corporate governance' principles advocating board independence and managerial incentives are indeed associated with better firm performance. However, we cannot find strong support for the criticisms against CEO duality. In addition, we go beyond a static perspective (such as certain governance mechanisms are effective or ineffective) by investigating the temporal hypotheses. We reveal that over time, with the improvement in the quality of market institutions and development of financial markets, the monitoring mechanisms of the board and state ownership become more strongly related to firm performance, whereas the incentive mechanisms lose their significance.

Australia

Whilst not suffering financial crisis in the same way as many countries in the region, Australia was nonetheless affected by the ripples from the various crises that occurred. It was, and is, vital for Australia's economic growth and well-being that the countries in the Asia-Pacific region are economically and financially sound, and politically stable. Australia therefore contributed to various International Monetary Fund initiatives to help Asia-Pacific Economic Co-operation (APEC) economies to recover from the crises and strengthen their economic and financial management.

In terms of its corporate governance, Australia has a common law system and, certainly at first glance, its corporate governance system seems to have developed along the lines of the Anglo-Saxon model, having features that would usually be typical of a UK unitary board structure (see Table 12.6). However, on closer inspection, Australia seems to have features of both an insider and an outsider system. Dignam and Galanis (2004) summarize the various features in Australia that might lead to doubt as to which corporate governance system it has, or indeed whether it is moving from one system and towards another. These features include the political system, which is socialist and so would usually be associated with an insider system, and yet the corporate governance system does not fit this proposition. Ownership of listed company shares is another interesting area because there are both dispersed shareholdings in listed companies and the presence of a significant non-institutional shareholder,

Table 12.6 Key characteristics influencing Australian corporate governance

Feature	Key characteristic
Main business form	Public corporations
Predominant ownership structure	Institutional investors; non-institutional shareholders (corporate or family)
Legal system	Common law
Board structure	Unitary
Important aspect	More emphasis on shareholder rights in recent years; also board diversity

or blockholder, in others. The former pattern of ownership is typical of an outsider system, whilst the latter is more commonly associated with an insider system.

Dignam and Galanis (2004) conclude their study by stating that the listed market in Australia is characterized by

> significant blockholders engaged in private rent extraction; institutional investor powerlessness; a strong relationship between management and blockholders, which results in a weak market for corporate control; and a historical weakness in public and private securities regulation, which allows the creation and perpetuation of crucial blocks to information flow.

They feel that these characteristics make it more like an insider than an outsider system. Farrar (2005) also provides some interesting insights into corporate governance developments in Australia in his book about these developments in both Australia and New Zealand. Stapledon (2006) notes that:

> while many aspects of the corporate governance regime in Australia are similar to those in countries like the US and the UK, there are some features of the Australian regime that distinguish it; for example, the incidence and role of large blockholders. But, fundamentally, Australia has a relatively well-developed capital market, and its governance environment is generally reflective of shareholder supremacy.

Turning now to look in more detail at the regulatory and corporate governance systems in Australia, in this context, it is important to realize that Australia's present regulatory infrastructure is relatively young. The Australian Securities and Investments Commission (ASIC), an independent Australian government body, has regulated financial markets, securities, futures, and corporations since January 1991. The Australian Stock Exchange (ASX) was formed in 1987 through the amalgamation of six independent stock exchanges that formerly operated in the state capital cities. Each of those exchanges had a history of share trading dating back to the nineteenth century.

The Bosch Report on Corporate Practice and Conduct was first issued in 1991 with further issues in 1993 and 1995. It covered a range of corporate governance issues including: board structure and composition; appointment of non-executive directors; directors' remuneration; risk management; financial reporting and auditing; conflicts of interest; and the role of the company secretary. In many ways, the Bosch Report was the equivalent of the Cadbury Report in the UK.

A number of corporate governance codes and guidelines followed, including the Hilmer Report (1998), which had an emphasis on issues such as board composition, executive remuneration, and disclosure.

In 2003 the ASX Corporate Governance Council issued the *Principles of Good Corporate Governance and Best Practice Recommendations*. Ten core principles are identified: 'the essential corporate governance principles'; each of the principles has one or more recommendations associated with it that act as implementation guidance. The recommendations are not mandatory; rather, they are guidelines to help ensure the desired outcome.

Under the ASX Listing Rules, companies are required to provide a statement in their annual report disclosing the extent to which they have followed the best practice recommendations. Where companies have not followed all the recommendations, they must identify the recommendations that have not been followed and give reasons for not following them, i.e. the 'if not, why not?' approach.

In October 2004 the Investment and Financial Services Association Limited (IFSA) in Australia published *Corporate Governance: A Guide for Fund Managers and Corporations*, which is commonly known as 'the IFSA Blue Book'. This was the fifth edition, the first one having been published in 1995. The IFSA's members manage investments on behalf of superannuation funds and retail clients, and the Blue Book is intended to guide the IFSA's members in monitoring the corporate governance of their investee companies, so that good governance can be encouraged to the benefit of shareholders and stakeholders.

In August 2005 the Australian Council of Super Investors issued its revised Corporate Governance Guidelines. These Guidelines are for superannuation trustees in their monitoring of Australian listed companies. The Guidelines reinforce the accountability of corporate boards and management teams to shareholders, and also emphasize the importance of having an ethical governance culture.

In addition to the above codes and guidelines, the Corporate Law Economic Reform Program (CLERP) has made a number of changes to Australia's corporate regulatory framework. Maintaining investor protection and confidence in the market is important, and issues such as director liability, disclosure, and shareholder participation have received attention.

In 2007 the ASX Corporate Governance Council issued its first revision of the *Principles of Good Corporate Governance and Best Practice Recommendations* (2003). This second edition is entitled *Corporate Governance Principles and Recommendations*. The ten principles retain the same headings as detailed earlier, although there are some changes to the wording of the supporting recommendations.

In 2010 the ASX updated the *Changes to Corporate Governance Principles and Recommendations* in relation to diversity, remuneration, trading policies, and briefings. Regarding gender diversity, the ASX announced that a recommendation is now included that entities listed on the ASX disclose in their annual report their achievement against gender objectives set by their board, and the proportion of women on the board (in senior management and employed throughout the whole organization). The guidance commentary will also be changed to recommend that boards determine the appropriate committee for recommending strategies to address board diversity (considering diversity in succession planning, and having a charter that regularly reviews the proportion of women at all levels in the company); disclose the mix of skills and diversity they are looking for in their membership; and ensure that there is an accurate and not misleading impression of the relative participation of women and men in the workplace. In relation to remuneration, ASX-listed entities should establish a remuneration committee comprised of a majority of independent directors, chaired by an independent director, and with at least three members. At present the composition of a remuneration committee is reflected in guidance (rather than as a recommendation) with no obligation to disclose departures from this standard. Commentary will also be amended to indicate that the remuneration committee should have responsibility for reviewing and providing recommendations to the board on remuneration by gender. Regarding trading policies, the *Principles and Recommendations* will be changed to reflect the introduction of ASX Listing Rules requiring entities to adopt and disclose a company trading policy. Finally in relation to briefings, there will be new guidance for listed entities about the notification, accessibility, and record keeping of group briefings, which will strengthen the principle of respecting the rights of shareholders.

The changes took effect for the first financial year of listed entities beginning on or after 1 January 2011, with companies required to either adopt the new recommendations or explain in their annual report why they have not done so ('if not, why not?').

In 2014, the ASX issued a third edition of the *Principles and Recommendations* reflecting global developments in corporate governance since the publication of the second edition. The structure of the *Principles and Recommendations* was simplified and companies given more flexibility in where they make their governance disclosures.

There are now eight principles and 29 specific recommendations. The eight principles are as follows:

- **Lay solid foundations for management and oversight:** A listed entity should establish and disclose the respective roles and responsibilities of its board and management and how their performance is monitored and evaluated.

- **Structure the board to add value:** A listed entity should have a board of an appropriate size, composition, skills, and commitment to enable it to discharge its duties effectively.

- **Act ethically and responsibly:** A listed entity should act ethically and responsibly.

- **Safeguard integrity in corporate reporting:** A listed entity should have formal and rigorous processes that independently verify and safeguard the integrity of its corporate reporting.

- **Make timely and balanced disclosure:** A listed entity should make timely and balanced disclosure of all matters concerning it that a reasonable person would expect to have a material effect on the price or value of its securities.

- **Respect the rights of security holders:** A listed entity should respect the rights of its security holders by providing them with appropriate information and facilities to allow them to exercise those rights effectively.

- **Recognise and manage risk:** A listed entity should establish a sound risk management framework and periodically review the effectiveness of that framework.

- **Remunerate fairly and responsibly:** A listed entity should pay director remuneration sufficient to attract and retain high quality directors and design its executive remuneration to attract, retain, and motivate high quality senior executives and to align their interests with the creation of value for security holders.

In 2017, the Financial Services Council (FSC) issued *Standard 23: Principles of Internal Governance and Asset Stewardship* which provides guidance to asset managers (also known as investment managers or fund managers) to help them fulfil their fiduciary responsibilities. The standard points out that:

> unlike other stewardship codes which focus on asset stewardship and conflicts of interest, the FSC Standard takes a broader view and also includes the internal governance of the Asset Manager. The FSC has taken this broader approach because our members believe that the careful and responsible management of clients' assets requires foundations built on good practices and robust internal governance. This code is therefore split into the following sections: 1. organisational and investment approach; 2. internal governance; and 3. asset stewardship.

The Code adopts a 'comply or explain' approach.

Hill (2012) provides an overview of the structure of corporate governance in Australia, highlighting that many elements of Australian corporate law differ markedly from the US system. She discusses a number of areas, including the effect of financial scandals on corporate law reform; the composition and structure of the board of directors, including board diversity; directors' duties; trends in executive compensation; shareholder activism; and shareholder rights and minority shareholder protection.

Law Chapple et al. (2014) investigate the governance attributes of firms that have been subject to securities class actions (SCAs) in Australia. They examine the compliance culture of the SCA firms via the frequency of Australian Securities Exchange (ASX) queries of the firm and find that the frequency of ASX queries is positively associated with the occurrence of a SCA. Furthermore they 'provide evidence that SCA firms exhibit weaker levels of corporate governance than the matched control sample ... results suggest the presence of a nomination committee may be associated with higher agency costs and that the influence of CEO duality may reduce the effectiveness of a nomination committee'.

Sheedy and Griffin (2017) examine risk governance, structures, culture, and behaviour by surveying employees from seven major banks headquartered in Australia and Canada thereby focusing on internal governance rather than external governance characteristics. They find that 'staff with special risk management responsibilities in Australia report more concerns about the resourcing of the risk management function and in both countries the adequacy of risk systems was highlighted. We also found less favorable perceptions of risk structures in Australian banks than in their Canadian peers.' Overall, they state that they

> observed statistically significant differences in risk culture at the firm level, business line level and the country level, with Canadian banks enjoying more favorable risk culture than their Australian counterparts. The country-level differences in both risk structures and culture may possibly be explained by societal differences relating to future orientation, which relates to consideration of long-term consequences.

Conclusions

The financial downturn that affected countries in the Asia-Pacific in the 1990s came as a great shock. The so-called 'tiger economies' had seen their stock markets experience meteoric rises and then that golden situation was wiped out. This change in fortunes led to many questions as to how and why this could have happened, but also as to how they would be able to rebuild themselves and attract investment back into their stock markets. As we have seen, the lack of transparency and disclosure, the misuse of corporate assets by dominant shareholders, and the lack of protection for minority shareholders' interests, have all been seen as contributory factors to the demise, and as areas that need to be improved in order to rebuild economies and attract both domestic and overseas investment. The 2008 global financial crisis has also impacted on these countries but their improved corporate governance should help them to restore confidence more quickly.

The countries looked at in detail in this chapter all strengthened their corporate governance codes in the years after the global financial crisis. Without exception, the codes now recommend fuller disclosure and accountability, transparency of process, the appointment of independent directors, and recognition and protection of minority shareholders' rights. It is encouraging that these countries all seem to be moving in the right direction, and these changes should encourage more foreign direct investment and greater confidence in their stock markets. Furthermore all the countries covered in this chapter, with the exception of China, either have established stewardship codes or have recently introduced them.

Summary

- The financial downturn that occurred in the Asia-Pacific countries in the 1990s acted as a trigger for improved corporate governance structures to be developed. The subsequent global financial crisis led to renewed emphasis on disclosure and transparency, the role of the board and the appointment of independent directors, and better protection of minority shareholders' rights.

- The dominant form of ownership structure in many Asia-Pacific countries tends to be concentrated either in families or in cross-holdings. The state still exercises significant influence in a number of countries.

- In Japan the *keiretsu* (associations of companies with holdings of shares one in the other) are slowly beginning to loosen their grip on corporate ownership but are still very influential. New corporate governance provisions provide Japanese companies with more flexibility and encourage more disclosure and the appointment of independent directors.

- In Korea the *chaebol* (large conglomerates with extensive cross-holdings of shares) still wield enormous power. The Corporate Governance Code emphasizes transparency and the protection of minority shareholders' rights.

- In Malaysia companies are largely family-owned or controlled. The Corporate Governance Blueprint and the revised Malaysian Corporate Governance Code emphasize that Malaysia needs to embed corporate governance culture in listed companies and more generally within the corporate governance ecosystem, which it identifies as including shareholders, gatekeepers, and regulators, as well as the board of directors. The updated Corporate Governance Code issued in 2017 takes a new approach to promote greater internalization of corporate governance culture.

- In Singapore the Corporate Governance Code (2012) has made a number of changes to the earlier Code, these being focused on the areas of director independence, board composition, director training, multiple directorships, alternate directors, remuneration practices and disclosures, risk management, and shareholder rights and roles.

- China is a 'socialist market economy' and many of the state-owned enterprises have become joint stock companies with shares to be more widely held. Much of the corporate reporting in China remains quite opaque and greater reliable disclosure is generally required, although it has improved in recent years. However, the Corporate

Governance Code's recommendations are encouraging and listed companies are required to appoint an appropriate number of independent directors. Furthermore, China has been working with the OECD to consider further development of its corporate governance.

- Australia has an interesting corporate governance system that has been strengthened in recent years to give more emphasis to shareholders' rights, to the ethical conduct of corporations, and to board diversity and executive remuneration. Its stewardship code also includes principles of internal governance as well as asset stewardship.

Example: Axiata Group Berhad, Malaysia

This is an example of a Malaysian telecommunications company which is recognized both domestically and internationally as having good corporate governance.

Axiata Group Berhad (Axiata) is one of the largest Asian telecommunications groups in Asia. The Group revenue for 2014 was RM18.7 billion (US$5.7 billion) and its market capitalization was over RM60.5 billion (US$18.5 billion) at the end of 2014.

Axiata has controlling interests in mobile operators in Malaysia, Indonesia, Sri Lanka, Bangladesh, and Cambodia with significant strategic stakes in India and Singapore. The Group's mobile subsidiaries and associates operate under the brand name 'Celcom' in Malaysia, 'XL' in Indonesia, 'Dialog' in Sri Lanka, 'Robi' in Bangladesh, 'Smart' in Cambodia, 'Idea' in India, and 'M1' in Singapore. Furthermore the Group has established a communications infrastructure solutions and services company called 'edotco'.

Axiata declares on its website that it 'was awarded the Frost & Sullivan Asia Pacific ICT Award for Best Telecom Group for six consecutive years in 2009, 2010, 2011, 2012, 2013, and 2014 and the Telecom Asia Best Regional Mobile Group 2010 and 2011 for its operations in multiple Asian markets. In 2011, Axiata was the only Malaysian company to make the Forbes Asia Fab 50 List.' Axiata also has a top 5 ranking in Malaysia in the Malaysia-ASEAN Corporate Governance Index 2014 administered by the Minority Shareholder Watchdog Group (MSWG). Axiata also received the Corporate Governance Award 2015 for Malaysia in the World Finance awards.

In its Statement on Corporate Governance 2014 Axiata states that its 'ethos is simple: best practice in corporate governance is best practice in business. This has been the way Axiata Group (Group) operates to ensure that the Group meets its long-term objectives to enhance shareholders' value on a sustainable basis.'

As at the end of February 2015, the board of directors comprised ten members of whom seven are independent non-executive directors (INEDS), two are non-independent non-executive directors including the Chairman (representing the interests of Khazanah as the major shareholder), and one executive director being the President and GCEO. Therefore INEDs comprise more than 50 per cent of the board of directors. However the board of directors currently has just one female director although it does recognize the potential benefits of board diversity and is working towards the 30 per cent target by 2016 set by the government in its Corporate Governance Blueprint 2011. A review of Axiata's board composition in April 2018 indicates that it has not diversified in terms of gender as there is only one female director. Also the number of INEDs has dropped from seven to six.

However Axiata has received several awards for its corporate governance including in the FinanceAsia Best Managed Company Poll 2016: No 2 Best Managed Company in Malaysia, No 3 Most Committed to Corporate Governance in Malaysia, No 3 Best at Investor Relations in Malaysia, No 4 Best at Corporate Social Responsibility in Malaysia, and No 1 Best CFO in Malaysia.

Mini case study   Samsung Electronics, South Korea

This is an example of a South Korean company which has a significant proportion of its shares held by chaebol *members.*

Samsung Electronics is a well-established international electronics company best known for its market-leading mobile phones, TVs, and other electronic items and its far-sighted investment in technological advances including chips, solid state drivers, and OLED display panels. It is the flagship company in the Samsung Group. In 2017, the company achieved revenues of over US$223 billion with net income of over US$39 billion, achieving its best results in the company's 80-year history.

At the end of 2017, its shareholder structure comprised common stock and preferred shares. The common stock was held as follows: foreign investors 53 per cent; major shareholder and related parties 20 per cent; domestic institutional investors 17 per cent; treasury stock 7 per cent; and domestic individual investors 3 per cent. The preferred stock was held as follows: foreign investors 81 per cent; treasury stock 9 per cent; domestic institutional investors 6 per cent; domestic individual investors 3 per cent; major shareholder and related parties 0.2 per cent.

There have been a number of issues which have arisen in recent years which had corporate governance implications. For example, in 2015 there was a mooted reorganization in the Group resulting in two companies merging leading to an increase in the control wielded by the Lee family but was detrimental to minority shareholders' rights. Meanwhile Elliott Management, the US activist fund, urged Samsung to reform by adopting a holding company structure. However when in February 2017, Lee Jae-yong, vice-Chairman of Samsung Electronics and grandson of the group's founder, was arrested on charges relating to bribery and corruption connected to a nationwide political scandal, any changes to corporate structure and governance reform were put to one side. It is alleged that bribes were paid to facilitate the merger in 2015. In August 2017, Lee Jae-yong was convicted and sentenced to five years in prison on corruption charges.

In October 2017 Kwon Oh-hyun, the board Chairman, resigned citing the crisis inside the company with Lee Jae-yong's corruption sentence and outside with concerns over the company's strategy for the future and the opportunity for a younger generation to be given a chance to lead. In November 2017, new heads were appointed to lead the company's three main businesses being IT and mobile communications; device solutions; and consumer electronics. In February 2018, Lee Jae-yong was freed on appeal with his original sentence being halved and suspended for four years. In April 2018, Samsung Electronics announced that it would split the roles of CEO and Chair but there will continue to be three co-CEOs with ultimate power still residing with Lee Jae-yong as vice-Chairman.

Mini Case Study Questions

1. What are the main features of Samsung Electronics' corporate governance structure?

2. What is the impact of the *chaebol* structure in South Korea's conglomerates such as Samsung and what might be the impact on minority shareholders?

Questions

The discussion questions to follow cover the key learning points of this chapter. Reading of some of the additional reference material will enhance the depth of the students' knowledge and understanding of these areas.

1. How might improving corporate governance help to restore and retain investor confidence in countries in the Asia-Pacific region?

2. What are the defining features of the Japanese corporate governance system? Critically compare and contrast with the Korean corporate governance system.

3. How has corporate governance developed in China and what are the main obstacles to be overcome to improve effectively corporate governance?

4. Critically discuss corporate governance developments in Malaysia, comparing and contrasting them with those in Singapore.

5. Critically discuss the corporate governance system in Australia.

6. Critically discuss the impact of ownership structure on the development of corporate governance in the Asia-Pacific region.

References

Aguilera, R.V., Kabbach-Castro, L.R., Lee, J.H., and You, J. (2012), 'Corporate Governance in Emerging Markets' in G. Morgan and R. Whitley (eds), *Capitalisms and Capitalism in the 21st Century*, Oxford University Press, Oxford. Available at SSRN: http://ssrn.com/abstract=1806525.

Ahmadjian, C.L. and Okumura, A. (2011), 'Corporate Governance in Japan' in C.A. Mallin (ed.), *Handbook on International Corporate Governance, Country Analyses*, 2nd edn, Edward Elgar Publishing Cheltenham, UK.

Aman, H., Beekes, W., and Brown, P.R. (2017), *Corporate Governance and Transparency in Japan* (20 November 2017). Available at SSRN: https://ssrn.com/abstract=1874611 or http://dx.doi.org/10.2139/ssrn.1874611.

Aoyagi, C. and Ganelli, G. (2014), *Unstash the Cash! Corporate Governance Reform in Japan*, IMF Working Paper No. 14/140. Available at SSRN: http://ssrn.com/abstract=2487898.

Aronson, B.E., (2014), 'Fundamental Issues and Recent Trends in Japanese Corporate Governance Reform: A Comparative Perspective', *Hastings Business Law Journal*. Available at SSRN: http://ssrn.com/abstract=2448076, forthcoming.

ASX Corporate Governance Council (2003), *Principles of Good Corporate Governance and Best Practice Recommendations*, ASX, Sydney.

ASX Corporate Governance Council (2007), *Corporate Governance Principles and Recommendations*, ASX, Sydney.

ASX Corporate Governance Council (2010), *Corporate Governance Principles and Recommendations*, ASX, Sydney.

ASX Corporate Governance Council (2014), *Corporate Governance Principles and Recommendations*, ASX, Sydney.

Australian Council of Super Investors Inc. (2005), *Corporate Governance Guidelines: A Guide for Superannuation Trustees to Monitor Listed Australian Companies*, ACSI, Melbourne.

Balino, T.J.T. and Ubide, A. (1999), 'The Korean Financial Crisis of 1997—A Strategy of Financial Sector Reform', International Monetary Fund Working Paper No. WP/99/28.

Black, B.S., De Carvalho, A.G., Khanna, V.S., Kim, W., and Yurtoglu, B. (2015), 'Which Aspects of Corporate Governance Matter in Emerging Markets: Evidence from Brazil, India, Korea, and Turkey', Northwestern Law & Econ Research Paper No. 14–22; ECGI—Finance Working Paper; U of Michigan Law & Econ Research Paper. Available at SSRN: http://ssrn.com/abstract=2601107 or http://dx.doi.org/10.2139/ssrn.2601107.

Black, B.S., Jang, H., and Kim, W. (2005), 'Predicting Firms' Corporate Governance Choices: Evidence from Korea', *Journal of Corporate Finance*, Vol. 12, No. 3, pp. 660–91.

Bosch, H. (1995), *Corporate Practice and Conduct*, Woodslane Pty Ltd, Australia.

Charkham, J. (1994), *Keeping Good Company: A Study of Corporate Governance in Five Countries*, Clarendon Press, Oxford.

Charkham, J. (2005), *Keeping Better Company: Corporate Governance Ten Years On*, Oxford University Press, Oxford.

Chen E.-T., and Nowland, J. (2010), 'Optimal Board Monitoring in Family-Owned Companies: Evidence from Asia', *Corporate Governance: An International Review*, Vol. 18, No. 1, pp. 3–17.

China Securities Regulatory Commission (2001a), *Code of Corporate Governance for Listed Companies in China*, CSRC, State Economic Trade Commission, Beijing.

China Securities Regulatory Commission (2001b), *Guidelines for Introducing Independent Directors to the Board of Directors of Listed Companies*, CSRC, State Economic Trade Commission, Beijing.

Claessens, S. and Fan, J.P.H. (2002), 'Corporate Governance in Asia: A Survey', *International Review of Finance*, Vol. 3, Issue 2, pp. 71–103.

Claessens, S., Djankov, S., and Lang, L.H.P. (2000), 'The Separation of Ownership and Control in East Asian Corporations', *Journal of Financial Economics*, Vol. 58, pp. 81–112.

Clarke, D.C. (2008), 'The Role of Non-Legal Institutions in Chinese Corporate Governance' in H. Kanda, K.S. Kim, and C.J. Milhaupt (eds), *Transforming Corporate Governance in East Asia*, Routledge, London.

Corporate Governance Blueprint (2011), Securities Commission Malaysia, Kuala Lumpur.

Corporate Governance Council (2012a), *Code of Corporate Governance*, Monetary Authority of Singapore.

Corporate Governance Council (2012b), *Risk Governance Guidance for Listed Boards*, Monetary Authority of Singapore.

Dignam, A.J. and Galanis, M. (2004), 'Australia Inside/Out: The Corporate Governance System of the Australian Listed Market', *Melbourne University Law Review*, Vol. 28, No. 3, December, pp. 623–53.

Esa, B.E. and Zahari, A.B. (2014), 'Ownership Structure and Directors' Compensation Disclosure in Malaysia' in S. Boubaker and D.K. Nguyen (eds), *Corporate Governance and Corporate Social Responsibility: Emerging Markets Focus, 2014*, World Scientific Publishing Co. Pte Ltd, Singapore, pp. 267–85.

Farrar, J. (2005), *Corporate Governance in Australia and New Zealand*, Oxford University Press, Oxford.

Finance Committee on Corporate Governance (2000), *Malaysian Code on Corporate Governance*, Ministry of Finance, Kuala Lumpur.

Financial Services Agency (2014), *Principles for Responsible Institutional Investors 'Japan's Stewardship Code'—To promote sustainable growth of companies through investment and dialogue*, The Council of Experts Concerning the Japanese Version of the Stewardship Code, Financial Services Agency, Tokyo, Japan.

Financial Services Agency (2017), *Principles for Responsible Institutional Investors 'Japan's Stewardship Code'—To promote sustainable growth of companies through investment and dialogue*, The Council of Experts on the Stewardship Code, Financial Services Agency, Tokyo, Japan.

Gilson, R.J. (2008), 'Controlling-family Shareholders in Asia: Anchoring Relational Exchange' in H. Kanda,

K.-S. Kim, and C.J. Milhaupt (eds), *Transforming Corporate Governance in East Asia*, Routledge, London.

Hass, L.H., Johan S., and Schweizer, D. (2013), 'Is Corporate Governance in China Related to Performance Persistence?' TILEC Discussion Paper No. 2013-015. Available at SSRN: http://ssrn.com/abstract=2264742 or http://dx.doi.org/10.2139/ssrn.2264742.

Hill, J.G. (2012), 'The Architecture of Corporate Governance in Australia: Corporate Governance—National Report: Australia' in K.J. Hopt (ed.), *Comparative Corporate Governance* (forthcoming, Cambridge University Press). Available at SSRN: http://ssrn.com/abstract=1657810.

Hilmer, F.A. (1998), *Strictly Boardroom: Enhancing Governance to Improve Company Performance*, Report of the Independent Working Party into Corporate Governance, 2nd edn, Information Australia, Sydney.

Investment and Financial Services Association Limited (2004), *Corporate Governance: A Guide for Fund Managers and Corporations*, IFSA, Sydney.

Jang, H. and Kim, J. (2002), 'Nascent Stages of Corporate Governance in an Emerging Market: Regulatory Change, Shareholder Activism and Samsung Electronics', *Corporate Governance: An International Review*, Vol. 10, No. 2, pp. 94–105.

Japan Corporate Governance Committee (2001), *Revised Corporate Governance Principles*, Japan Corporate Governance Forum, Tokyo.

Kato, K., and Li, M., and Skinner, D. J. (2017), 'Is Japan Really a "Buy"? The Corporate Governance, Cash Holdings and Economic Performance of Japanese Companies', *Journal of Business Finance & Accounting*, Vol. 44, Issue 3-4, pp. 480–523.

Kim, E.H. and Kim, W. (2007), 'Corporate Governance in Korea: A Decade after the Financial Crisis' (December 2007), University of Texas Law, Law and Econ Research Paper No. 123. Available at SSRN: http://ssrn.com/abstract=1084066.

Korean Committee on Corporate Governance (1999), *Code of Best Practice for Corporate Governance*, Korean Committee on Corporate Governance, Seoul.

Korean Committee on Corporate Governance (2003), *Code of Best Practice for Corporate Governance*, Korean Committee on Corporate Governance, Seoul.

Korea Stewardship Code Council (2016), *Korea Stewardship Code Principles on the Stewardship Responsibilities of Institutional Investors*, Korea Corporate Governance Service, Seoul.

Law Chapple, L., Clout, V.J., and Tan, D. (2014), 'Corporate Governance and Securities Class Actions',

Australian Journal of Management, Vol. 39, No. 4, pp. 525–47. Available at SSRN: http://ssrn.com/abstract=2523903.

Lee, C. and Allen, J. (2013), *The Roles and Functions of Kansayaku Boards Compared to Audit Committees*, Asian Corporate Governance Association (ACGA), Hong Kong.

Liew, P. (2007), 'Corporate Governance Reforms in Malaysia: The Key Leading Players' Perspectives', *Corporate Governance: An International Review*, Vol. 15, No. 5, pp. 724–40.

Malaysian Code on Corporate Governance (2012), Ministry of Finance, Kuala Lumpur.

Malaysian Code on Corporate Governance (2017), Securities Commission Malaysia, Kuala Lumpur.

Ministry of Justice (2003), *Commercial Code Revision on Boards (April 2003)*, Tokyo.

Monetary Authority of Singapore (2010), *Guidelines on Corporate Governance for Banks, Financial Holding Companies and Direct Insurers which are Incorporated in Singapore*, MAS.

Morck, R. and Yeung, B.Y. (2014), 'Corporate Governance in China', *Journal of Applied Corporate Finance*, Vol. 26, Issue 3, pp. 20–41.

Mutlu, C.C., van Essen, M., Peng, M.W., Saleh, S.F. and Duran, P. (2017), 'Corporate Governance in China: A Meta-Analysis', forthcoming in *Journal of Management Studies*, doi:10.1111/joms.12331.

Neoh, A. (2003), 'Corporate Governance in Mainland China: Where Do We Go from Here?' in P.K. Cornelius and B. Kogut (eds), *Corporate Governance and Capital Flows in a Global Economy*, Oxford University Press, Oxford.

OECD-China Policy Dialogue on Corporate Governance (2011), *Governance of Listed Companies in China Self-Assessment by the China Securities Regulatory Commission*, OECD, Paris.

Okumura, H. (2002), 'Corporate Governance in Japan' in H. Shibuya, M. Maruyama, and M. Yasaka (eds), *Japanese Economy and Society under Pax-Americana*, University of Tokyo Press, Tokyo.

Salim, M.R. (2011), 'Corporate Governance in Malaysia: the Macro and Micro Issues' in C.A. Mallin (ed.), *Handbook on International Corporate Governance, Country Analyses*, 2nd edn, Edward Elgar Publishing Cheltenham, UK.

Sheedy, E. and Griffin, B. (2018), 'Risk Governance, Structures, Culture, and Behavior: A View from the Inside', *Corporate Governance: An International Review*, Vol. 26, Issue 1, pp. 4–22.

Shin, J.Y., Hyun, J-H., Oh, S., and Yang, H. (2018), 'The Effects of Politically Connected Outside Directors on Firm Performance: Evidence from Korean Chaebol Firms', *Corporate Governance: An International Review*, Vol. 26, Issue 1, pp. 23–44.

Stapledon, G. (2006), 'The Development of Corporate Governance in Australia' in C.A. Mallin (ed.), *Handbook on International Corporate Governance, Country Analyses*, Edward Elgar Publishing, Cheltenham, UK.

Stewardship Asia (2016), *Singapore Stewardship Principles For Responsible Investors November 2016*, Stewardship Asia Centre (on behalf of the Singapore Stewardship Principles Working Group).

Tam, O.K. (1999), *The Development of Corporate Governance in China*, Edward Elgar, Cheltenham, UK.

Tam, O.K. and Yu, C.P. (2011), 'China's Corporate Governance Development' in C.A. Mallin (ed.), *Handbook on International Corporate Governance, Country Analyses*, 2nd edn, Edward Elgar Publishing Cheltenham, UK.

Tan, C.H., Puchniak, D.W., and Varottil, U. (2015), 'State-Owned Enterprises in Singapore: Historical Insights into a Potential Model for Reform (March 2015)', NUS Law Working Paper No. 2015/003. Available at SSRN: http://ssrn.com/abstract=2580422 or http://dx.doi.org/10.2139/ssrn.2580422.

Tang, X. (2008), 'Protecting Minority Shareholders in China: A Task for Both Legislation and Enforcement', in H. Kanda, K.-S. Kim, and C.J. Milhaupt (eds), *Transforming Corporate Governance in East Asia*, Routledge, London.

Tokyo Stock Exchange (2004), *Principles of Corporate Governance for Listed Companies*, Tokyo Stock Exchange, Tokyo.

Tokyo Stock Exchange (2009), *Principles of Corporate Governance for Listed Companies*, Tokyo Stock Exchange, Tokyo.

Tokyo Stock Exchange (2014), *Japan's Corporate Governance Code* [Exposure Draft]: *Seeking Sustainable Corporate Growth and Increased Corporate Value over the Mid- to Long-Term*, The Council of Experts Concerning the Corporate Governance Code, Tokyo Stock Exchange, Tokyo.

Tokyo Stock Exchange (2015), *Japan's Corporate Governance Code: Seeking Sustainable Corporate Growth and Increased Corporate Value over the Mid- to Long-Term*, The Council of Experts Concerning the Corporate Governance Code, Tokyo Stock Exchange, Tokyo.

Useful websites

www.adb.org The website of the Asian Development Bank Institute, which contains information and articles about corporate governance developments in the Asia-Pacific region.

www.asx.com.au The website of the Australian Stock Exchange, which contains information relating to corporate governance, companies, and investors.

www.australianshareholders.com.au The website of the Australian Shareholders' Association, which has a range of material relevant to investors.

www.cg-net.jp The website of the Japan Corporate Governance Network has information relating to corporate governance in Japan.

www.cgs.or.kr The website of the Korea Corporate Governance Service has information on corporate governance, CSR and related issues.

www.csrc.gov.cn The website of the China Securities Regulatory Commission has information about corporate governance developments in China.

www.maicsa.org.my The website of the Chartered Secretaries Malaysia has details of a series of good governance guides.

www.mas.gov.sg The website of the Monetary Authority of Singapore, including the Corporate Governance Code 2012.

www.sc.com.my The website of the Securities Commission in Malaysia has a range of material relating to corporate governance issues in Malaysia, including the Corporate Governance Blueprint.

 Develop your understanding of this chapter and explore the subject further using our online resources at **www.oup.com/uk/mallin6e/**

 FT Clippings

Ex-chairman Wu Xiaohui charged with economic crimes as Beijing targets conglomerates

Tom Hancock, Henny Sender and Alice Woodhouse

Financial Times, 23 February 2018

China has seized control of Anbang, the corporate flagship of flamboyant dealmaker Wu Xiaohui, and charged him with economic crimes in Beijing's most forceful move yet to curb the foreign acquisition sprees of private conglomerates.

The Chinese insurance regulator said Anbang Insurance Group, owner of New York's Waldorf Astoria hotel, had 'illegal business operations which may seriously endanger the company's solvency'.

Mr Wu, the former chairman who led the group's sudden emergence to international prominence with his ambitious acquisitions, has been indicted by a court in Shanghai for alleged fundraising fraud and embezzlement.

Anbang gained international prominence with its $2bn purchase of the Waldorf Astoria and a $5.5bn hotels deal with Blackstone Group. Last year it was among several acquisitive private conglomerates—including Fosun, Dalian Wanda and HNA—to be probed by regulators, amid concern that risky financing was being used to fund takeovers and a broad crackdown on capital flight.

But Friday's move was the most drastic action taken so far by the authorities to clamp down on the groups.

The takeover allows the China Insurance Regulatory Commission to steer the company through a surge in redemptions that is expected to begin later this year.

It said officials would 'actively introduce high-quality social capital to Anbang, restructure its shareholding and keep Anbang as a private company'.

'Anbang is too big to fail,' said one senior Anbang executive. 'Even though it has no real value, they will have to restructure it

very carefully.' Ether Yin of Beijing-based consultancy Trivium China said: 'Anbang has lots of investment in different areas; they are already systematically important and could pose a threat to the entire financial system.'

Anbang acts less like a traditional insurance company than what Swiss bank UBS has dubbed a 'platform insurer'—an investment holding company that funds its purchases by selling insurance products. 'Platform insurers', with Anbang far in the lead, doubled their share of China's insurance market between 2013 and 2016, according to a UBS report last year.

Now all its transactions outside traditional insurance, such as trading of assets, will be performed by a 'working group' led by He Xiaofeng, director of the CIRC's reform and development department. Other members include at least one official from the central bank. The takeover will last a year from Friday, and will not change the company's external liabilities, the regulator said.

Mr Wu, who started Anbang with about $60m, turned what was mainly a small car insurer into a financial services conglomerate, with assets worth Rmb1.97tn ($310bn). His business acumen was bolstered by his marriage to a granddaughter of Deng Xiaoping, China's late paramount leader.

Those connections mean that the decision to prosecute him required consensus among top Communist party leaders, analysts said. Anbang has not borrowed extensively from banks so fewer powerful groups have a vested interest in its fate.

Friday's announcement solidifies arrangements in place since June when Mr Wu was first detained in a midnight raid. Since that time, officials at the China Insurance Regulatory Commission, itself without a head, have met Anbang staff regularly as they sort out the mess. The officials referred repeatedly to the former chairman as 'Criminal Wu', according to people familiar with the matter.

The regulators' main concern is the potential cash crunch when Anbang's high-interest wealth management products came due, according to Zhu Ning of Tsinghua University in Beijing. Redemptions are expected to surge later this year.

If Anbang had defaulted on its products it might have created doubts in the public mind over the security of the broader class of wealth management products that have been sold through bank branches and trust companies for many years.

The regulator's reference to 'social funding' probably means that it will ultimately seek wealthy private investors

for Anbang, rather than splitting its assets among state-owned groups, analysts said. 'Social funding...it's a way of raising money from high-net-worth individuals rather than state capital,' said Fraser Howie, an expert on Chinese financial regulation.

The CIRC has not yet decided what to do about the assets in Anbang's portfolio. While Mr Wu overpaid for investments abroad, Anbang's domestic holdings include valuable stakes in China Minsheng Banking and other private companies. Regulators have already seized or sold Mr Wu's personal assets including several homes, according to two people familiar with the matter. His own equity in Anbang is believed to be worthless.

Source: Used under licence from the *Financial Times*.

Fabrication scandal follows proxy adviser's criticism of returns to shareholders

Leo Lewis

Financial Times, 13 October 2017

If Hiroya Kawasaki, the chief executive of Kobe Steel, follows decades of Japanese corporate tradition and resigns over the faked quality certification scandal engulfing his company, he already has a guaranteed job waiting for him in one of the country's most famous rose gardens.

The position of gardener at Himeji Bara-en, not far from the city of Kobe, was offered to him in happier times when his passion for rosiculture slipped out in a television interview.

On Friday, after his second long, apologetic bow before the TV cameras in as many days, Mr Kawasaki dropped another revealing line.

'As yet, I have no clear reason why the data fabrication has happened,' he said, as Kobe's corporate customers scrambled to establish whether the Japanese metal products group had sold them materials that could compromise the quality of everything from aircraft hulls and nuclear reactors to air-conditioners and microchips.

He has suggested that 'deep self-examination' is now required.

If Mr Kawasaki's claim is true, that means the chairman and president of one of Japan's biggest corporations cannot explain a problem that has been occurring across multiple divisions over many years. Critics say this suggests that his company, like others in Japan that have been hit by scandals, has corporate governance issues on top of the legal and financial consequences of the fakery.

The fabrication came to light because Kobe was forced to explain manipulation of steel wire test data at Shinko Wire, one of its affiliate companies, in June 2016. Kobe then ordered a months-long review of the entire company.

'Why are these scandals breaking out in these companies with multiple divisions? Because you cannot keep on top of that diversification unless you have really embraced technology and these older companies generally have not,' says Peter Eadon-Clarke, chief Japan strategist at Macquarie Securities in Tokyo.

Mr Kawasaki, 63, attended Kyoto University and joined Kobe Steel in the 1980s. He has led the company since 2013 and was awarded the Japan Iron & Steel Institute's highest honour this year. Just last month he wrote to employees: 'One of my cherished words is 'action', which I interpret to mean that we should go out and move others. If you go to them, they will take action.'

But now he faces the question of whether the market trusts him to take the action needed to solve his company's problems.

His record as a manager is already in the crosshairs of investors and corporate governance activists. For the past two years, Institutional Shareholder Services, the proxy advisers, have recommended investors vote against Mr Kawasaki's reappointment because of Kobe's low return on equity.

Each time, substantial numbers of shareholders registered their dissatisfaction although he survived both votes.

Mr Kawasaki's challenge, along with that of his predecessors at Kobe, has been to reconstitute the business for changing times.

His contribution was a programme known as Kobelco Vision G+. It sought to rebuild the earnings structure after back-to-back years of losses in fiscal 2015 and 2016, while expanding into growth businesses and widening the business base in China.

By this summer, progress appeared good. In the first quarter of the 2017 financial year, year-on-year profits surged and analysts at Daiwa Securities and elsewhere were raising their forecasts for recurring profits.

On a five-year average basis, Mr Kawasaki has delivered a return on equity of just 2.5 per cent—understandable, perhaps, given the industry but decisively below the 5 per cent line that ISS considers the bare minimum of corporate governance delivery.

Mr Kawasaki said on Friday that he would 'consider how to take responsibility' for the scandal. The Himeji Rose Garden may be about to expand its staff by one.

Creditors take control of commodity trader as shareholders all but wiped

Neil Hume

Financial Times, 29 January 2018

The senior management at Noble Group could emerge with a fifth of the company under the terms of a proposed debt restructuring plan that will see creditors take control of the crisis-hit commodity trader and existing shareholders all but wiped out.

The Singapore-listed group said that investors, including its founder and chairman emeritus Richard Elman, and China Investment Corp, a Chinese sovereign wealth fund, would hold just 10 per cent of the shares in the proposed debt-for-equity swap.

If agreed, a deal to halve $3.4bn of Noble's debt would mark the end of a three-year crisis in which the company has battled concerns about its accounting and ability to service a large debt load.

Under the deal, lenders will control 70 per cent of the new company and current management up to 20 per cent. Noble said the equity was needed to 'retain and incentivise' senior executives.

'The announcement is the confirmation that shareholders and perpetual shareholders have been dreading,' said Justin Tang, head of Asian research for United First Partners.

Noble is also planning to convert $400m of perpetual bonds into $15m of new securities. Noble said that the 20 per cent stake would be shared by its senior management team, including Will Randall, its chief executive, and Paul Jackaman, finance director.

For many years, Mr Randall ran Noble's hard commodities business, which has suffered large writedowns on many of its long-term coal contracts.

Once a major force in commodity trading, Noble has been in turmoil since February 2015 when Iceberg Research, a previously unknown firm, produced the first in a series of reports highly critical of the company and its inability to convert profits into cash. Noble has always defended its accounting.

Over that period, Noble has announced huge losses, impairment charges and sold a string of assets, including its prized oil trading business in a desperate attempt to pay down debt. Its market value, meanwhile, has tumbled from more than $6bn to just $243m today [see Figure 12.1].

While a deal would save Noble from insolvency, as long as it is backed by shareholders and creditors, it still faces a battle.

The company is planning to focus on its coal trading, LNG and freight in Asia but it will carry a large debt load and will be trying to make money in fiercely competitive industries where margins are razor thin.

'This agreement marks the beginning of the final phase of our restructuring, and the creation of a new Noble as a focused and appropriately financed group set to capitalise on the high-growth Asian commodities sector,' said Paul Brough, Noble Group chairman and a restructuring expert who has led the talks with creditors.

Under the proposed agreement, which is backed by 30 per cent of Noble's creditors, the company's senior debt will fall from $3.4bn to $1.7bn.

In addition to a 70 per cent equity stake, senior creditors will also receive $700m of bonds and $180m of preference shares in a new ringfenced company that will own Noble's Jamaican aluminium business, its

Figure 12.1 Noble Group share price (SGD)

Source: Thomson Reuters. Used under licence from the *Financial Times*. All rights reserved.

stake in Harbour Energy, an investment vehicle and other assets.

The streamlined trading business will carry total debt of $955m but will be capable of generating earnings before interest, tax and depreciation and amortisation of $175m to $200m a year, assuming it can access cheap trade finance, which is the lifeblood of commodity trading.

To that end, the debt restructuring plan includes a three-year committed trade finance and hedging facility of up to $700m that creditors are being encouraged to back through a fee and other incentives.

For the debt-for-equity swap to be approved, Noble needs backing from 51 per cent of its shareholders and 75 per cent of its creditors present at a special meeting.

This article has been amended to clarify that Noble plans to convert $400m of perpetual bonds into $15m of new securities.

Corporate governance in South Africa, Egypt, India, and Brazil

Learning objectives

- To understand the background to the development of corporate governance codes in a range of countries globally

- To be aware of the different ownership structures in a global context

- To be aware of the main differences in corporate governance codes in various countries in a global context

- To have a detailed knowledge of the corporate governance codes for a sample of countries in a global context

Introduction

In this chapter, corporate governance developments in a sample of countries in a global context are examined. The countries are diverse in their cultural and legal backgrounds, ownership structures, and corporate governance structures. Nonetheless, we can see that certain core principles, seen in earlier chapters, are evident in the corporate governance codes of these countries. These core principles will help build or restore confidence in stock markets, help ensure more transparency and disclosure, enhance protection of minority shareholders' rights, and help ensure that the company is managed in the interests of shareholders and stakeholders, as appropriate.

Of course, as well as the existence of a corporate governance code, the firm-level corporate governance is very important: that is, to what extent a firm itself actually has good governance. Klapper and Love (2002) undertook a study of firm-level governance in 14 emerging market countries, including South Africa, India, and Brazil. They find that 'firm-level corporate governance provisions matter more in countries with weak legal environments' and their results 'suggest that firms can partially compensate for ineffective laws and enforcement by establishing good corporate governance and credible investor protection'. Hence, a firm with good corporate governance in a country with a generally weaker corporate governance will stand out from the crowd and be able to obtain capital at a lower cost, and generally be more attractive to investors.

Each of the selected countries has interesting characteristics that make it a good choice to include in this penultimate chapter to illustrate that corporate governance is relevant to all countries, whatever their ownership structure and whatever their stage of development.

South Africa has a well-developed corporate governance code. In fact, its code is the most comprehensive in the world, and leading edge in terms of its outlook and recommendations. Egypt was one of the pioneers of corporate governance in the Middle East and North Africa (MENA) countries, introducing a corporate governance code in 2005 based on the Organisation for Economic Co-operation and Development (OECD) *Principles of Corporate Governance*. India's corporate governance code aims to differentiate between mandatory recommendations and non-mandatory, whilst recognizing that both categories of recommendations will result in the most effective corporate governance system. Brazil is trying to encourage compliance with its corporate governance code but the progress seems quite slow, with controlling groups still exercising disproportionate influence.

South Africa

South Africa has had a troubled and turbulent past. In the latter half of the twentieth century there was considerable social unrest and inequality exacerbated by the policy of apartheid (racial segregation). Extensive legislation was introduced in the 1990s, which led to social and political transformation; this included the Employment Equity Act (No. 55 of 1998) and the National Environmental Management Act (No. 107 of 1998).

In 1992 a Committee on Corporate Governance was established in South Africa. Chaired by Mervyn King, the Committee produced the *King Report on Corporate Governance* ('King I') late in 1994. The King I contained some of the most far-reaching recommendations at that time. Some eight years later, the King Report II (hereinafter 'King II') was published in 2002. Between the dates of the two reports (1994–2002), there was extensive legislation as mentioned earlier, and the King II needed to take account of these developments. In common with its earlier version, the King II is one of the most comprehensive and most innovative reports published to date anywhere in the world. It takes an 'inclusive' approach, in other words, the company should not develop its strategies and carry out its operations without considering the wider community, including employees, customers, and suppliers. An interesting cultural aspect is mentioned in the context of labour relations and people management, which is the tradition of consultation practised by African chiefs; clearly, consultation is part and parcel of the African psyche and so a company should take this into account in its relationship with employees and people generally.

As well as addressing what might be perceived as the traditional areas of corporate governance, such as the role and function of boards of directors, and internal audit, the King II pays significant attention to integrated sustainability reporting, including stakeholder relations, ethical practices, and social and transformation issues (see Table 13.1). The whole report is a comprehensive 354 pages, which includes detailed appendices covering areas such as board self-evaluation and developing a code of ethics. In addition, the appendices include details about the United Nations Global Compact and the Global Sullivan Principles.

The King II identifies what can be regarded as seven characteristics of good corporate governance: discipline, transparency, independence, accountability, responsibility, fairness, and social responsibility. Discipline, in the context of proper and appropriate behaviour, includes acceptance of good governance, at senior management level. Transparency is the extent to which, and how easily, investors can know the true picture of what is happening in the

Table 13.1 Key characteristics influencing South African corporate governance

Feature	Key characteristic
Main business form	Public limited company
Predominant ownership structure	Institutional investors
Legal system	Common law
Board structure	Unitary
Important aspect	Inclusive approach

company. Independence is the existence of appropriate mechanisms to ensure that there are no conflicts of interest at board/management level. Decision-makers in the company must be accountable for their decisions and actions, and there should be mechanisms to ensure this accountability. Management have a responsibility for their actions and should correct inappropriate actions. Fairness should exist in the consideration of the rights of various parties with an interest in the company. Finally, social responsibility is characteristic of a good corporate citizen, and companies should give a high priority to ethical standards.

The King II contains the *Code of Corporate Practices and Conduct* (hereinafter 'the Code'), which contains principles covering:

- Boards and directors
- Risk management
- Internal audit
- Integrated sustainability reporting
- Accounting and auditing
- Relations with shareowners
- Communications.

Companies listed on the Johannesburg Securities Exchange and all public sector entities are expected to abide by the recommendations of the Code on a 'comply or explain' basis. Directors therefore need to provide a statement in the annual report about compliance with the Code or give reasons for non-compliance.

The *Code of Corporate Governance Principles for South Africa 2009* was launched in September 2009, and is generally known as 'King III'. The report was driven by the new Companies Act in South Africa and also by changes in international governance trends. As with King I and II, the Code is an exemplar of good governance practice and focuses on the importance of reporting annually on 'how a company has both positively and negatively affected the economic life of the community in which it operated during the year under review; and how the company intends to enhance those positive aspects and eradicate or ameliorate the negative aspects on the economic life of the community in which it will operate in the year ahead'.

The philosophy of King III revolves around leadership, sustainability, and corporate citizenship. Sustainability has been integrated as a major aspect of performance and reporting to enable stakeholders to better assess the value of a company. King III utilizes an 'apply or explain' basis; that is, companies should apply the principles or explain why they have not done so. There are nine chapters, some with the same titles as King II but others being different to reflect the changes mentioned earlier. The nine chapters are:

- Boards and directors;
- Corporate citizenship: leadership, integrity and responsibility;
- Audit committees;
- Risk management;
- Internal audit;
- Integrated sustainability reporting;
- Compliance with laws, regulations, rules, and standards;
- Managing stakeholder relationships;
- Fundamental and affected transactions (such as mergers, acquisitions, and amalgamations) and business rescue.

King III became effective from 1 March 2010.

In 2016, the *King IV Report on Corporate Governance for South Africa* was issued (hereafter referred to as King IV). In King IV, corporate governance is defined as 'the exercise of ethical and effective leadership by the governing body towards the achievement of the following governance outcomes: ethical culture; good performance; effective control; and legitimacy. Ethical and effective leadership should complement and reinforce each other.' King IV advocates an outcomes-based approach with clear differentiation between principles and practices. It has a less prescriptive approach but there is 'greater emphasis on transparency with regards to how judgement was exercised when considering the practice recommendations contained in King IV. To reinforce this qualitative application of its principles and practices, King IV proposes an "apply and explain" regime, in contrast to "apply or explain" in King III.'

There are 17 principles which are covered in five main sections as follows:

- Leadership, Ethics and Corporate Citizenship (principles 1, 2, 3);
- Strategy, Performance and Reporting (principles 4, 5);
- Governing Structures and Delegation (principles 6, 7, 8, 9, 10);
- Governance Functional Areas (principles 11, 12, 13, 14, 15);
- Stakeholder Relationships (principles 16, 17).

There are also a number of sector supplements aimed at a range of sectors (municipalities; non-profit organizations; retirement funds; SMEs; SOEs) which provide high-level guidance and direction on how King IV should be interpreted and applied in these sectors and organizational types.

In 2011 the Committee on Responsible Investing by Institutional Investors in South Africa issued the *Code for Responsible Investing in South Africa* (CRISA). South Africa is one of a number of countries following on from the UK to formally encourage institutional investors to integrate into their investment decisions sustainability issues such as environmental, social, and governance (ESG) matters (see Chapters 6 and 7 for more detail). CRISA provides the investor community with the guidance needed to give effect to King III as well as the *UN Principles for Responsible Investment.*

There are five principles as follows:

- Principle 1—An institutional investor should incorporate sustainability considerations, including ESG, into its investment analysis and investment activities as part of the delivery of superior risk-adjusted returns to the ultimate beneficiaries.

- Principle 2—An institutional investor should demonstrate its acceptance of ownership responsibilities in its investment arrangements and investment activities.

- Principle 3—Where appropriate, institutional investors should consider a collaborative approach to promote acceptance and implementation of the principles of CRISA, and other codes and standards applicable to institutional investors.

- Principle 4—An institutional investor should recognize the circumstances and relationships that hold a potential for conflicts of interest and should proactively manage these when they occur.

- Principle 5—Institutional investors should be transparent about the content of their policies, how the policies are implemented, and how CRISA is applied to enable stakeholders to make informed assessments.

CRISA uses the 'apply or explain' approach and requires institutional investors to fully and publicly disclose to stakeholders, at least once a year, to what extent CRISA has been applied. If an institutional investor has not fully applied one of the principles of the CRISA, the reasons should be disclosed.

Ntim et al. (2012), using a sample of 169 South African listed firms from 2002 to 2007, find that:

> disclosing good corporate governance practices on both shareholders and stakeholders impacts positively on firm value, with the latter evidence providing new explicit support for the resource dependence theory. However, we provide additional new evidence, which suggests that disclosing shareholder corporate governance practices contributes significantly more to firm value than stakeholder ones.

Yamahaki and Frynas (2016) investigate to what extent regulation encourages private shareholder engagement attitudes and behaviour of pension funds and asset managers with listed investee companies on environmental, social, and corporate governance (ESG) issues in Brazil and South Africa. Analysing the findings from in-depth semi-structured interviews with pension fund representatives, asset managers, and other investment players, they suggest that:

> legislation provides limited direct encouragement to private engagement behavior. However, legislation encourages attitudes toward Responsible Investment by enhancing investor understanding of Responsible Investment, increasing the interest of pension funds and asset consultants in the Responsible Investment practices of asset managers, and reducing the fear of pension funds to violate their fiduciary duties, thereby promoting an enabling environment for ESG engagement … The findings also suggest that the sophistication of the legislation on ESG issues in Brazil and South Africa is more typical of developed countries, indicating the need for a more fine-grained analysis of emerging markets in corporate governance studies.

Egypt

During the early 1990s, the Egyptian government began a programme of economic reform, including the privatization of some of the state-owned companies which led to the private sector becoming a major player in the economy. Given this background, there is still a diverse range of corporate ownership in Egypt, including state ownership, dispersed ownership, and companies owned by families or individuals (see Table 13.2). Egypt was one of the pioneers of corporate governance in the MENA countries, introducing a corporate governance code in 2005 based on the OECD *Principles of Corporate Governance.* The Egyptian Institute of Directors and the Hawkamah Institute of Corporate Governance have done much to raise awareness of corporate governance in Egypt and the MENA countries respectively.

Table 13.2 Key characteristics influencing Egyptian corporate governance

Feature	Key characteristic
Main business form	Joint stock company
Predominant ownership structure	State; institutional and individual investors
Legal system	Civil law
Board structure	Unitary
Important aspect	Shariah law (for example, in Islamic financial institutions)

The *Egyptian Code of Corporate Governance* (hereafter 'the Code') was issued in October 2005. It applies on a voluntary basis to companies listed on the Cairo and Alexandra Stock Exchange (CASE), to financial institutions (including banks and insurance companies) in the form of joint stock companies even if not listed on CASE, and to companies that obtain major financing from the banking sector. The Code's preface makes the insightful point that 'implementing corporate governance in the right manner is not only limited to respecting a set of rules and interpreting it literally in a restricted manner, but it is also a culture and a way of managing the relationship between owners of the company, its directors, and its stakeholders'.

The Code covers:

- The scope of implementation;
- The general assembly (including that generally small shareholders should not be excluded from the general assembly by virtue of the small size of their shareholding);
- The board of directors (including separation of the roles of chairman and managing director, appointment of non-executive directors, the formation of key board committees, the appointment of a company secretary, risk management, and voting);
- The internal audit department;
- The external auditor;
- The audit committee;

- Disclosure of social policies (including disclosure of policies relating to social, environmental, occupational health and safety areas);
- Avoiding conflict of interest;
- Corporate governance rules for other corporations.

In 2006 the *Code of Corporate Governance for the Public Enterprise Sector* was issued in response to the OECD *Guidelines on the Corporate Governance of State-Owned Enterprises* (2005). The principles are divided into six areas: ensuring the existence of an effective regulatory and legal framework for the public enterprise sector; the state acting as the owner; equitable treatment of shareholders (owners); relationships with stakeholders; transparency and disclosure; and responsibilities of the board of directors of public enterprises.

In 2011 the *Code of Corporate Governance for Listed Companies* was issued. The Egyptian Institute of Directors, in co-operation with different entities, has reviewed the Code of Corporate Governance published in October 2005 in order to update it based on the latest Egyptian and international experiences.

In 2016 the revised *Egyptian Corporate Governance Code* was issued. The application of the Code has been broadened and it has been updated for international and regional practices and developments; the Code can be used as a guideline for legislative and regulatory bodies when making changes related to corporate governance; the role that the state, its government, and institutions can play to support governance and the importance of good governance for companies are highlighted. The importance of 'comply or explain' is seen as a fundamental pillar for the application of the principles. Areas of the Code which receive emphasis, or are stressed, include the role of the general assembly of shareholders; the role of the board of directors; the role and responsibilities of the Board Secretary; the control environment; external auditors; investor relations; disclosure methods and tools; policies, codes and manuals that companies could have to help them with their corporate governance.

Pierce (2008, 2012) provides interesting insights into the development of corporate governance in the MENA and Gulf countries, highlighting key features and developments in these various regions. Furthermore, the OECD (2011, 2012) has issued several papers including a discussion of corporate governance frameworks in the MENA and arrangements for state ownership in the MENA.

Of course the MENA countries must also consider the impact of Shariah laws, for example in banks and financial institutions. Grais and Pellegrin (2006) review the issues and options facing current arrangements for ensuring Shariah compliance by Islamic financial services. They suggest 'a framework that draws on internal and external arrangements to the firm and emphasizes market discipline… this framework would enhance public understanding of the requirements of Shariah and lead to more effective options available to stakeholders to achieve improvements in Islamic financial services'. Safieddine (2009) adopts a theory building approach to highlighting variations of agency theory in the unique and complex context of Islamic banks, mainly stemming from the need to comply with Shariah, and the separation of cash flow and control rights for a category of investors. He finds that Islamic banks should improve governance practices currently in place whilst policymakers need to be aware of the need to tailor the regulations to safeguard the interests of all investors without violating the principles of Shariah.

Abedifar et al. (2012) consider risks in Islamic banking, using a sample of 553 banks from 24 countries between 1999 and 2009. They find that small Islamic banks that are leveraged or based in countries with predominantly Muslim populations have lower credit risk than conventional banks. In terms of insolvency risk, small Islamic banks also appear more stable.

Finally, Shehata and Dahawy (2014) study the corporate governance disclosures of 30 companies on the Egyptian Stock Exchange using the Intergovernmental Working Group of Experts on International Standards of Accounting and Reporting (ISAR) benchmark of good practices in corporate governance disclosure. They conclude that 'while the sample has relatively high rates of disclosure for few items, and the average disclosures in 2010 almost doubled the 2005 average disclosures in Egypt for several categories, they are still low levels compared to the average emerging market levels'. They suggest that policy options such as publishing a list of non-compliant companies on the stock exchange website or small fines might be one avenue or alternatively a list of the best companies' reports. Training and education about the importance of corporate governance disclosures could be another option.

India

Following on from a period of economic downturn and social unrest in 1990–1, the Indian government introduced a programme of reforms to open up the economy and encourage greater reliance on market mechanisms and less reliance on government. Further reforms were aimed at making the public sector more efficient and divestment of government holdings was initiated. There were also reforms to the banking sector to bring it into line with international norms, and to the securities market, with the Securities and Exchange Board of India (SEBI) becoming the regulator of the securities market.

The securities market was transformed as disclosure requirements were brought in to help protect shareholders' interests. Kar (2001) mentions how 'foreign portfolio investment was permitted in India since 1992 and foreign institutional investors also began to play an important role in the institutionalisation of the market'. All of the reforms mentioned led to a much-improved environment in which corporate governance was able to develop.

India has a range of business forms, including public limited companies (which are listed on the stock exchange), domestic private companies, and foreign companies. Ownership data is difficult to find because the number of studies carried out in this area are few; however, it is clear that, as the economy has opened up, so the institutional investors are increasing their share of the market (see Table 13.3).

Table 13.3 Key characteristics influencing Indian corporate governance

Feature	Key characteristic
Main business form	Public limited company
Predominant ownership structure	Corporate bodies; families; but institutional investors' ownership increasing
Legal system	Common law
Board structure	Unitary
Important aspect	Some aspects of the Code are mandatory recommendations

The Confederation of Indian Industry (CII) published *Desirable Corporate Governance in India—A Code* in 1998 and a number of forward-looking companies took its recommendations on board. However, many companies still had poor governance practices, which led to concerns about their financial reporting practices, their accountability, and ultimately to losses being suffered by investors, and the resultant loss of confidence that this caused.

SEBI formally established the Committee on Corporate Governance in May 1999, chaired by Shri Kumar Mangalam Birla. The *Report of the Kumar Mangalam Birla Committee on Corporate Governance* (hereinafter 'the Report') was published in 2000.

The Report emphasizes the importance of corporate governance to future growth of the capital market and the economy. Three key aspects underlying corporate governance are defined as accountability, transparency, and equality of treatment for all stakeholders. The impact of corporate governance on both shareholders and stakeholders is mentioned, although the corporate objective is seen as one of maximizing shareholder value, and indeed the Committee views the fundamental objective of corporate governance as 'enhancement of shareholder value, keeping in view the interests of other stakeholders'. The Committee feels that companies should see the Code as 'a way of life'. The recommendations apply to all listed private and public sector companies, and are split into mandatory requirements (ones that the Committee sees as essential for effective corporate governance) enforceable via the listing rules, and non-mandatory (but nonetheless recommended as best practice). The main areas covered by the Code are:

- Board of directors
- Nominee directors
- Chairman of the board
- Audit committee
- Remuneration committee
- Board procedures
- Management
- Shareholders
- Manner of implementation.

There are mandatory recommendations that a company should have a separate section on corporate governance in its annual report, including a detailed compliance report. Non-compliance with any mandatory recommendations should be highlighted, as should the level of compliance with non-mandatory recommendations. A company should obtain a certificate from its auditors in relation to compliance with the mandatory recommendations and it should be attached to the directors' report, which is sent each year to all the shareholders, and to the stock exchange.

The Indian Code is clearly rather complex having as it does a series of mandatory and non-mandatory recommendations. The feasibility of this approach will lie in a number of areas: first, the extent to which companies are willing to implement the recommendations; secondly, the growing influence of shareholders and how effectively they can exercise their voice; and thirdly, the approach taken by the stock exchange in India in terms of enforcing compliance.

Chakrabarti (2005) provides an interesting review of the evolution of corporate governance in India and highlights the fact that, whilst India has good corporate governance codes/

guidelines, there is poor adoption of the recommendations in many companies. Subsequently, Chakrabarti et al. (2008) state:

> while on paper the country's legal system provides some of the best investor protection in the world, the reality is different with slow, over-burdened courts and widespread corruption. Consequently, ownership remains highly concentrated and family business groups continue to be the dominant business model. There is significant pyramiding and tunneling among Indian business groups and, notwithstanding copious reporting requirements, widespread earnings management. However, most of India's corporate governance shortcomings are no worse than in other Asian countries and its banking sector has one of the lowest proportions of non-performing assets, signifying that corporate fraud and tunneling are not out of control.

Balasubramanian et al. (2008) provide an overview of Indian corporate governance practices, based primarily on responses to a 2006 survey of 370 Indian public companies. They find that:

> compliance with legal norms is reasonably high in most areas, but not complete. We identify areas where Indian corporate governance is relatively strong and weak, and areas where regulation might usefully be either relaxed or strengthened. On the whole, Indian corporate governance rules appear appropriate for larger companies, but could use some strengthening in the area of related party transactions, and some relaxation for smaller companies. Executive compensation is low by US standards and is not currently a problem area. We also examine whether there is a cross-sectional relationship between measures of governance and measures of firm performance and find evidence of a positive relationship for an overall governance index and for an index covering shareholder rights.

In December 2009 the *Corporate Governance—Voluntary Guidelines 2009*, were introduced for voluntary adoption by the corporate sector. The Guidelines took into account the recommendations the CII made in February 2009 to propose ways in which corporate governance could be further improved. The Guidelines have six sections:

- Board of directors
- Responsibilities of the board
- Audit committee of board
- Auditors
- Secretarial audit
- Institution of mechanism for whistle-blowing.

In 2011 the *National Voluntary Guidelines on Social, Environmental and Economical Responsibilities of Business* were issued by the Ministry of Corporate Affairs. The Guidelines are a refinement of the *Corporate Social Responsibility Voluntary Guidelines 2009*, released by the Ministry of Corporate Affairs in December 2009. In the foreword to the Guidelines, it emphasizes that nowadays businesses have to take responsibility for the ways their operations impact society and the natural environment. There are nine principles, namely, that businesses should:

- Conduct and govern themselves with ethics, transparency, and accountability;
- Provide goods and services that are safe and contribute to sustainability throughout their life cycle;

- Promote the well-being of all employees;
- Respect the interests of, and be responsive towards all stakeholders, especially those who are disadvantaged, vulnerable, and marginalized;
- Respect and promote human rights;
- Respect, protect, and make efforts to restore the environment;
- When engaged in influencing public and regulatory policy, do so in a responsible manner;
- Support inclusive growth and equitable development;
- Engage with, and provide value to, their customers and consumers in a responsible manner.

Afsharipour (2009) examines recent corporate governance reforms in India and posits that:

> the Indian experience demonstrates that traditional theories predicting convergence, or a lack thereof, fail to fully capture the trajectory of actual corporate governance reforms. India's reform efforts demonstrate that while corporate governance rules may converge on a formal level with Anglo-American corporate governance norms, local characteristics tend to prevent reforms from being more than merely formal. India's inability to effectively implement and enforce its extensive new rules corroborates the argument that comprehensive convergence is limited, and that the transmission of ideas from one system to another is highly complex and difficult, requiring political, social and institutional changes that cannot be made easily.

Furthermore Varottil (2010) discusses whether a US/UK concept of independent directors is appropriate, or effective, in an Indian context. He states:

> A transplantation of the concept [of independent directors] to a country such as India without placing emphasis on local corporate structures and associated factors is likely to produce unintended results and outcomes that are less than desirable. This Article finds that due to the concentrated ownership structures in Indian companies, it is the minority shareholders who require the protection of corporate governance norms from actions of the controlling shareholders. Board independence, in the form it originated, does not provide a solution to this problem.

Nagar and Sen (2016) undertake a study of family ownership and cash flow reporting in the United States and India and find that family ownership has different effects on quality of cash flow reporting in the two countries and that country-level regulation moderates these effects differently. They find:

> In particular, (i) firms in both countries engage in manipulating operating cash flows, but the evidence is stronger in the United States; (ii) family firms in India engage in more shifting than non-family firms, but this is not observed in the United States; and (iii) family (non-family) firms in India increase (reduce) shifting, whereas only non-family firms in the United States increase shifting after regulation. Since non-family firms in India raise more external capital than family firms after regulation, we infer that family firms in India reacted to this competition for capital and resorted to shifting.

Brazil

The economies of various countries in South America were also affected adversely by the world economic downturn in the 1990s. As with many other countries around the globe, this led to a demand for more transparency and accountability, and the need to restore and build confidence in the stock market.

Many businesses in South America are dominated by a controlling group, often representing family interests. This pattern can be seen in Brazil, Mexico, and Chile, for example. In this section, we will look in more detail at the corporate governance of Brazil (see Table 13.4).

Table 13.4 Key characteristics influencing Brazilian corporate governance

Feature	Key characteristic
Main business form	Public limited company
Predominant ownership structure	Controlling owner (corporations or individuals)
Legal system	Civil law
Board structure	Dual
Important aspect	Fiscal councils

As with most South American countries, in Brazil, the protection of minority interests has traditionally been a weak area, with minority shareholders lacking both access to information and the means to take appropriate action. In the past, companies have often issued preferred shares as a means of raising capital. Although preferred shares carry a dividend, they do not usually have voting rights except in certain specific circumstances. Therefore holders of preferred shares are often in a weak position and are vulnerable to the whims of controlling shareholders.

The São Paulo Stock Exchange (BOVESPA) has introduced a new index: the ICG (Index of Shares under Special Corporate Governance Registration). Companies can register at different levels: Level 1 and Level 2. Level 1 requirements include 'compliance with disclosure regulations for transactions involving shares issued by the company's controlling shareholders or directors' and 'disclosure of shareholder agreements and stock option programs'.

The Brazilian Institute of Corporate Governance (BICG) published a *Code of Best Practice of Corporate Governance* in 2001 (hereafter 'the Code'). The BICG was established as a civil not-for-profit association to act as a leading forum for corporate governance in Brazil. The Code identifies transparency, accountability, and fairness as the 'pillars' of corporate governance. The Code is very helpful in identifying some of the key features of Brazilian companies, such as the fact that the majority have controlling owners. It also recommends that family-controlled businesses should establish a family council 'to settle family issues and keep them apart from the governance of the company'.

The corporate governance structure is essentially a two-tier, or dual, structure because Brazilian companies have a board of directors and also a fiscal council. The fiscal council is elected by, and accountable to, the owners. The Code states that the fiscal council 'is created because the minorities and the owners of non-voting stock have no influence and little information. The fiscal council is a partial remedy to this. It has access to information and can express its opinion in the annual general meeting.' Its access to information is quite extensive because copies of board of directors' meeting minutes, financial statements, and other information are available to its members. They may also have access to the independent auditors.

The Comissao de Valores Mobiliarios (CVM) is the Securities and Exchange Commission of Brazil, and in June 2002 the CVM issued recommendations on corporate governance. The Code covers four main areas:

- Transparency of ownership and control, shareholder meetings
- Structure and responsibilities of the board of directors
- Minority shareholder protection
- Accounting and auditing.

The CVM requires that public companies include in their annual report the level to which they comply with the recommendations, utilizing a 'comply or explain' approach.

In 2004 the BICG published an updated and enlarged edition of the *Code of Best Practice of Corporate Governance*. The Code aims to provide guidelines to all types of company—ranging from publicly or privately held corporations to non-governmental organizations—with the aim of increasing company value, improving corporate performance, facilitating access to capital at lower costs, and contributing to the long-term survival of the company.

The Code has six sections:

- Ownership
- Board of directors
- Management
- Independent auditing
- The Fiscal Council
- Conduct and conflicts of interest.

It should be noted that Brazil's Fiscal Council is an unusual feature and is described in the Code as 'an essential part of the Brazilian companies' governance system', although it is, however, non-mandatory. Its purpose is to oversee the actions of the companies' administrative bodies and to give its opinion on certain matters to the owners. It acts as a tool 'designed to add value to the company, since it works as an independent control for the owners of the company'. The controlling and minority shareholders should discuss the composition of the fiscal council prior to its election, at the assembly meeting, in order to ensure an appropriate mix of professional backgrounds.

There are four basic principles of the Code: transparency, fairness, accountability, and corporate responsibility. With regard to the last principle, the Code states:

> Corporate responsibility is a broader view of corporate strategy, contemplating all kinds of relations with the community where the company operates. The 'social role' of the company should include the creation of wealth and job opportunities, work force skills and diversity, promotion of scientific advancements through technology, and improved standards of living through educational, cultural, social, and environmental initiatives. This principle should include preferred treatment of local people and resources.

A revised *Code of Best Practice of Corporate Governance* (2009) was subsequently issued. It retains the same six sections as its predecessor but seeks to implement more robust corporate governance practices in the light of changes both in Brazil (for example, the capital market revival, a large number of companies going public, the diffuse share ownership in some companies, mergers and acquisitions, etc.) and internationally (the global financial downturn). The latest revision to the Code was in 2016. The Foreword to the Code (2016) states that:

> the responsibility of the different governance actors is increasingly evident in light of issues such as sustainability, corruption, fraud, abuse in short-term incentives for executives and investors, and the complexity and multiplicity of relationships that organizations established with a wide range of audiences. In this sense, this 5th edition of the Code adopts an approach that encourages the conscious and effective use of governance tools, focusing on the essence of good practice. This approach is now less prescriptive, having expanded to encompass several company stakeholders and to reinforce the rationale of good governance practices and explaining the importance of ethics in business.

The Code (2016) contains five sections relating to:

- Shareholders;
- Board of directors;
- Executive management;
- Supervisory and control bodies;
- Conduct and conflict of interest.

Black et al. (2008) provide an overview of corporate governance practices in Brazilian companies and they identify areas where Brazilian corporate governance is relatively strong and weak. They state:

> Board independence is an area of weakness: The boards of most Brazilian private firms are comprised entirely or almost entirely of insiders or representatives of the controlling family or group. Many firms have zero independent directors. At the same time, minority shareholders have legal rights to representation on the boards of many firms, and this representation is reasonably common. Financial disclosure lags behind world standards. Only a minority of firms provide a statement of cash flows or consolidated financial statements. However, many provide English language financial statements, and an English language version of their website. Audit committees are uncommon, but many Brazilian firms use an alternate approach to ensuring financial statement accuracy—establishing a fiscal board. A minority of firms provide takeout rights to minority shareholders on a sale of control. Controlling shareholders often use shareholders agreements to ensure control.

Chavez and Silva (2009) study the reaction of stock prices to the announcement by 31 Brazilian companies of their intent to list on one of the special governance exchanges. Their analysis shows that the companies choosing to list in these segments experienced an increase in both the value and the liquidity of their shares. They conclude that 'in countries where governance legislation is weak and the progress of reform is slow, stock markets can play a key role in helping companies differentiate themselves through exchange-defined governance codes'.

Black et al. (2011) state that 'a central issue in corporate governance research is the extent to which "good" governance practices are universal (one size mostly fits all) or instead depend on country and firm characteristics'. They conduct a case study of Brazil, surveying Brazilian firms' governance practices, and then extending prior studies of India, Korea, and Russia, and comparing those countries to Brazil, to assess which aspects of governance matter in which countries, and for which types of firms. They find that their '"multi-country" results suggest that country characteristics strongly influence both which aspects of governance predict firm market value, and at which firms that association is found. They support a flexible approach to governance, with ample room for firm choice.'

Leal (2011) states that 'corporate governance is discussed intensively and new regulations and self-regulations are brought about constantly. New laws and regulations impose greater disclosure, convergence to international accounting standards, and better protection to minority shareholders.' However, he identifies that there are still improvements to be made, for example, making the board process more formal and independent; reducing the dominance of controlling shareholders over boards; improving the use of committees; increasing the amount of board evaluations; and improving participation in general assemblies.

Black et al. (2014) study the evolution of corporate governance practices in Brazil over the period 2004–9 using a broad index, the Brazilian Corporate Governance Index (BCGI), comprised of six indices covering board structure, board procedure, related party transactions, ownership structure, shareholder rights, and disclosure. They find a significant improvement in corporate governance practices over the period and attribute this to two main factors '1) growth in Novo Mercado and Level II (NM&L2) listings, mainly through IPOs by new firms, and 2) improved practices at non-NM&L2 firms, principally adopting governance elements required for NM&L2 listing' ... 'Adoption of the elements of our governance index that are required for NM&L2 listing predicts higher firm value. In contrast, adoption of the remaining elements of our index does not predict firm value. Thus, governance changes appear to respond to investor preferences.'

Black et al. (2015) in a study of four major emerging markets—Brazil, India, Korea, and Turkey—find that:

> disclosure predicts higher market value in each country (within disclosure, the principal predictor is financial disclosure); board structure has a positive coefficient in all countries and is significant in Brazil and Korea (within board structure, the principal predictor is board independence); and that once one controls for disclosure and board structure, the other indices do not predict firm value. These results suggest that firms, in responding to investor demands for better governance; and investors, in assessing governance quality, can do reasonably well in focusing on disclosure and board structure.

Martins et al. (2017) examine the interplay between country-level governance quality and the capital structure choice at the firm level in Brazil and Chile using a large firm-level dataset for 2008–13. They find

> a positive association between low ownership concentration and debt maturity. However, this association becomes negative when the largest shareholder has high ownership concentration. This result suggests that long-term debt and ownership concentration act as substitute monitoring mechanisms. Moreover, debt maturity is inversely related to our aggregated index of country-level governance quality, suggesting that in countries with governance systems that effectively protect debt holders, firms with high benefits of control (high ownership concentration) will use debt with shorter repayment periods in order to benefit from frequent monitoring by debt holders.

Conclusions

In this chapter, the corporate governance of three very different countries has been discussed. We have seen that South Africa, India, and Brazil have different cultural influences, legal systems, and corporate governance structures (the first two have a unitary board system, the last a two-tier board system). However, there appears to be a certain commonality of approach to their corporate governance codes, with an emphasis on transparency and accountability, and the desire to enhance the protection of minority shareholders' rights. There is an emphasis on the importance of having a balanced board with an appropriate proportion of independent directors, and also recognition that a company cannot operate in isolation but should consider the interests of its various stakeholder groups.

These countries, diverse as they are in many respects, illustrate that corporate governance is relevant and valuable to countries around the globe. Over time, it is to be expected that corporate governance will improve, as countries seek to attract international investment and maintain investor confidence.

Summary

- The financial downturn that occurred in many countries in the 1990s and the global financial crisis of 2008 have had an impact in driving forward corporate governance globally. Countries are seeking to improve their corporate governance to help restore confidence in the markets by increasing transparency and disclosure, and ensuring better protection of minority shareholders' rights.

- South Africa arguably has the most comprehensive corporate governance code in the world. An inclusive approach is followed, paying significant attention to stakeholder relations, ethical practices, and the concept of an inclusive sustainable capital market system. Ethical and effective leadership are seen as fundamental and should complement and reinforce each other. King IV uses an 'apply and explain' basis, that is companies should apply the principles or explain why they have not done so.

- Egypt was one of the first MENA countries to develop its corporate governance. It went through a period of economic reform and privatization in the early 1990s which led to a range of ownership structures. In 2011 the 'Arab Spring' saw much turmoil and an uprising in the country. Shariah law is to be considered, for example, in Islamic banking and financial institutions.

- India has a unitary board system. The corporate governance code splits recommendations into mandatory and non-mandatory recommendations. Both are desirable but the mandatory recommendations are seen as core to effective corporate governance.

- Brazil is fairly typical of South American countries, with controlling groups and a lack of effective mechanisms for minority shareholders' protection of rights. Brazil has a two-tier structure, with a fiscal board acting as a balance to the board of directors.

Example: Tata, India

This is an example of a well-known and long-established Indian company with global presence. It has faced some challenges in recent years impacting on its structure and strategy.

Originally established by Jamsetji Tata in the second half of the nineteenth century, Tata has become one of India's largest business organizations. At the end of March 2017, Tata group accounted for 6.6 per cent of the total market capitalization of the Bombay Stock Exchange, had total revenues of over US$100 billion and employed over 695,000 people. The Tata group comprises over a 100 operating companies spread across six continents. The companies cover the following areas: communications and ITes; consumer and retail; defence and aerospace; financial services; manufacturing; realty and infrastructure; services; and promoter companies. The two promoter holding companies are Tata Sons which is the promoter of the major operating Tata companies and holds significant shareholdings in these companies, and Tata Industries which was established by Tata Sons in 1945 originally as a managing agency for the businesses it promoted and then to promote Tata's entry into new and high-tech businesses.

Tata states that they

are committed to improving the quality of life of the communities we serve. We do this by striving for leadership and global competitiveness in the business sectors in which we operate. Our prac- tice of returning to society what we earn evokes trust among consumers, employees, shareholders and the community. We are committed to protecting this heritage of leadership with trust through the manner in which we conduct our business. The values of integrity, excellence, unity, responsi- bility and pioneering anchor the Tata group to its core philosophy and legacy.

The role of Tata chairman was held by Ratan Tata from 1991–2012 and then by Cyrus Mistry from 2012–16. Cyrus Mistry had joined the board of Tata Sons in 2006 and when a selection committee was set up to search for a new chairman, his name was put forward and he became the first chairman appointed from outside the founding family; his appointment was backed by his fellow directors. However over the next few years there was increasing tension and disagreement between Ratan Tata, who as the chairman of Tata Trusts retained significant power as the Trusts own 65 per cent of Tata Sons, and Cyrus Mistry. In October 2016, Cyrus Mistry was dismissed without explanation. He has subsequently brought a number of allegations of governance breaches against Tata which raised concerns about potential reputational damage. His family retains an 18 per cent stake in Tata Sons. A new chairman, Natarajan Chandrasekaran, was appointed early in 2017 and faces several key tasks including reducing the high leverage in some of the companies and streamlining the group structure around seven or eight core businesses. In September 2017, the shareholders of Tata Sons voted to become a private company despite opposition from Cyrus Mistry's family.

Mini case study   Ultrapar, Brazil

Ultrapar is recognized as having good corporate governance standards and being an innovator in this area amongst companies in Brazil.

Ultrapar is a multi-business company engaged in specialized distribution and retail, specialty chemicals, and storage for liquid bulk segment. It is one of the largest business groups in Brazil with some thirteen thousand direct employees. Ultrapar has operations in the entire Brazilian territory and has industrial units in the United States, Uruguay, Mexico, and Venezuela and commercial offices in Argentina, Belgium, China, and Colombia through Oxiteno.

In 1999, Ultrapar was the first Brazilian company to be listed simultaneously at the São Paulo Stock Exchange (BM&FBOVESPA) and the New York Stock Exchange (NYSE), with American Depository

(continued)

Receipts (ADRs) level III. Ultrapar is compliant with the requirements of the Sarbanes-Oxley Act (SOX) which regulates mechanisms that guarantee the transparency of companies listed in the United States and, since 2007, it has had SOX certification under section 404, attesting to the efficiency of its internal controls over the company's financial information. Ultrapar 'developed and implemented in 2009 a distinguished risk matrix to monitor its internal controls, thus effectively aligning internal and external audit activities to the needs of managers and shareholders. Such system was awarded by the Brazilian Institute of Corporate Governance (IBGC) in the Innovation category of the 2009 IBGC Corporate Governance Award.'

Ultrapar believes that 'an efficient corporate governance system helps to create the environment of trust necessary for an adequate functioning of a market economy'. Ultrapar actively contributes to the development of the capital markets in Brazil, for example, one of its initiatives is its participation as a founding member of the Latin American Corporate Governance Roundtable Companies Circle, a group dedicated to promote corporate governance in Latin America, sponsored by the Organization for Economic Co-operation and Development (OECD) and by the International Finance Corporation (IFC).

Ultrapar does not utilize control enhancing mechanisms (CEMs)—there is no limitation on voting rights, special treatment for current shareholders, tender offers for a price above that of the acquisition of shares, or any other poison pill provisions.

In terms of its corporate governance structure, Ultrapar has a board of directors, a fiscal council/ audit committee, an executive board, and a compensation committee. The board of directors is composed of at least five and a maximum of nine members, of whom at least 30 per cent should be independent directors, a percentage that exceeds the listing requirements of Novo Mercado which is 20 per cent. Currently, six members of the board of directors are independent. Since 2007, the roles of chief executive officer and chairman of the board of directors have been separated such that Paulo Cunha, who held both roles, became the Chairman of the board of directors whilst Thilo Mannhardt took over as Chief Executive Officer.

Ultrapar believes in aligning the interests of the shareholders and the executives and uses the economic value added concept to link variable compensation to economic value added growth targets.

Ultrapar states that it

> formally adopts a Code of Ethics which governs the professional conduct of its employees with stakeholders, setting a reference for internal and external relationship and reducing the degree of subjectivity in the interpretations of ethical principles. This code was enhanced in 2009 to include (i) examples of acceptable and unacceptable behavior, with explanations in order to prevent misinterpretation of such items, and (ii) an additional channel for reporting behaviors in violation of the code.

Ultrapar has been recognized with many awards for its corporate governance, transparency, and risk management. In 2014 it was recognized as one of the ten leading companies in transparency in Brazil by CDP; recognized for investor relations, including best CEO, CFO, and IR team, by buy-side analysts, and best CFO, IR Manager, and IR team, by sell-side analysts, in the segment of Oil, Gas and Petrochemicals by Institutional Investor; awarded the Best Investor Relations in the Energy segment in the IR Magazine Awards Brazil 2014 by the IR Magazine Awards Brazil; elected the most attractive company for investors in the award 'Prêmio Destaque Agência Estado Empresas' by Agência Estado/ Economática; and placed second in the ranking of 'World's Most Admired Companies' in the energy sector by Fortune Magazine.

In June 2015, Ultra joined the MSCI Global Sustainability Index Series which considers the environmental, social, and corporate governance aspects in the selection of assets for inclusion in the index.

In August 2017, Ultrapar's shares fell significantly after antitrust watchdog CADE (Administrative Council for Economic Defense) voted unanimously to reject its proposed acquisition of Alesat Combustíveis.

(continued)

> ### Mini case study questions
>
> 1. In what ways is Ultrapar engaging with its shareholders and other stakeholders?
>
> 2. Which theoretical approaches might underpin Ultrapar's approach to its shareholders in practice?

Questions

The discussion questions to follow cover the key learning points of this chapter. Reading of some of the additional reference material will enhance the depth of the students' knowledge and understanding of these areas.

1. Critically discuss the potential advantages and disadvantages of an 'inclusive' approach to corporate governance.

2. What might be the complexities of developing corporate governance in the MENA countries?

3. Critically discuss the problems that minority shareholders may face in the presence of controlling shareholders.

4. What might be the advantages or disadvantages of a corporate governance code that splits recommendations into mandatory and non-mandatory?

5. What commonalities seem to be emerging in various corporate governance codes?

6. Critically discuss the drivers to corporate governance reform in a global context.

References

Abedifar, P., Molyneux, P., and Tarazi, A. (2012), *Risk in Islamic Banking*, available at SSRN: http://ssrn.com/abstract=1663406.

Afsharipour, A. (2009), 'Corporate Governance Convergence: Lessons from the Indian Experience', *Northwestern Journal of International Law & Business*, Vol. 29, No. 2, pp. 335–402.

Balasubramanian, B.N., Black, B.S., and Khanna, V.S. (2008), 'Firm-level Corporate Governance in Emerging Markets: A Case Study of India', ECGI–Law Working Paper; 2nd Annual Conference on Empirical Legal Studies Paper; University of Michigan Law and Economics, Olin Working Paper 08–011; University of Texas Law, Law and Econ Research Paper No. 87, available at SSRN: http://ssrn.com/abstract=992529.

Black, B.S., De Carvalho, A.G., and Gorga, E. (2008), 'The Corporate Governance of Privately Controlled Brazilian Firms', University of Texas Law, Law and Econ Research Paper No. 109; Cornell Legal Studies Research Paper No. 08–014; ECGI–Finance Working Paper No. 206/2008, available at SSRN: http://ssrn.com/abstract = 1003059.

Black, B.S., De Carvalho, A.G., and Gorga, E. (2011), 'What Matters and for Which Firms for Corporate Governance in Emerging Markets? Evidence from Brazil (and Other BRIK Countries)', *Journal of Corporate Finance*, http://dx.doi.org/10.1016/j.jcorpfin.2011.10.001.

Black, B.S., De Carvalho, A.G., Khanna, V.S., Kim, W., and Yurtoglu, B. (2015), 'Which Aspects of Corporate Governance Matter in Emerging Markets: Evidence from Brazil, India, Korea, and Turkey'. Northwestern Law & Econ Research Paper No. 14–22; ECGI–Finance Working Paper; U of Michigan Law & Econ Research Paper. Available at SSRN: http://ssrn.com/abstract=2601107 or http://dx.doi.org/10.2139/ssrn.2601107.

Black, B.S., De Carvalho, A.G., and Sampaio, J.O. (2014), 'The Evolution of Corporate Governance in Brazil'. Northwestern Law & Econ Research Paper No. 12–22. Available at SSRN: http://ssrn.com/abstract=2181039.

Brazilian Institute of Corporate Governance (2001), *Code of Best Practice of Corporate Governance*, BICG, São Paulo.

Brazilian Institute of Corporate Governance (2004), *Code of Best Practice of Corporate Governance*, BICG, São Paulo.

Brazilian Institute of Corporate Governance (2009), *Code of Best Practice of Corporate Governance*, BICG, São Paulo.

Brazilian Institute of Corporate Governance (2016), *Code of Best Practices of Corporate Governance*, BICG, São Paulo.

Chakrabarti, R. (2005), *Corporate Governance in India—Evolution and Challenges*, available at SSRN: http://ssrn.com/abstract=649857.

Chakrabarti, R., Megginson W., and Yadav, K. (2008), 'Corporate Governance in India', *Journal of Applied Corporate Finance*, Vol. 20, No. 1, Winter, pp. 59–72.

Chavez, G.A. and Silva, A.C. (2009), 'Brazil's Experiment with Corporate Governance', *Journal of Applied Corporate Finance*, Vol. 21, No. 1, Winter, pp. 34–44.

Comissao de Valores Mobiliarios (2002), *CVM Recommendations on Corporate Governance*, CVM, Rio de Janeiro.

Committee on Responsible Investing by Institutional Investors in South Africa (2011), *Code for Responsible Investing in South Africa 2011*, Institute of Directors in Southern Africa, Johannesburg.

Confederation of Indian Industry (1998), *Desirable Corporate Governance in India—A Code*, CII, Delhi.

Egyptian Institute of Directors (2005), *Guide to Corporate Governance Principles in Egypt*, EIoD, Egypt.

Egyptian Institute of Directors (2006), *Code of Corporate Governance for the Public Enterprise Sector*, EIoD/Ministry of Investment, Egypt.

Egyptian Institute of Directors (2011), *Code of Corporate Governance for Listed Companies*, Egyptian Institute of Directors/Ministry of Investment, Egypt.

Egyptian Institute of Directors (2016), *Egyptian Corporate Governance Code*, Egyptian Institute of Directors/Ministry of Investment, Egypt.

Grais, W. and Pellegrin, M. (2006), 'Corporate Governance and Shariah Compliance in Institutions Offering Islamic Financial Services', World Bank Policy Research Working Paper No. 4054. Available at SSRN: http://ssrn.com/abstract = 940711.

Kar, P. (2001), 'Corporate Governance in India', *Corporate Governance in Asia: A Comparative Perspective*, OECD, Paris.

King, M. (1994), *King Report on Corporate Governance* (King I), Institute of Directors, Johannesburg.

King, M. (2002), *King Report on Corporate Governance for South Africa* (King II), Institute of Directors, Johannesburg.

King, M. (2009), *King Code of Governance for South Africa* (King III), Institute of Directors, Johannesburg.

King, M. (2016), *King IV Report on Corporate Governance for South Africa 2016*, Institute of Directors, Johannesburg.

Klapper, L.F. and Love, I. (2002), 'Corporate Governance, Investor Protection, and Performance in Emerging Markets', World Bank Policy Research Working Paper 2818, World Bank, Washington, DC.

Kumar Mangalam Birla (2000), *Report of the Kumar Mangalam Birla Committee on Corporate Governance*, Securities and Exchange Board of India, Delhi.

Leal, R.C. (2011), 'The Emergence of a Serious Contender: Corporate Governance in Brazil' in C.A. Mallin (ed.), *Handbook on International Corporate Governance, Country Analyses*, 2nd edn, Edward Elgar Publishing, Cheltenham, UK.

Martins, H.C., Schiehll, E., and Terra, P.R.S. (2017), 'Country-level Governance Quality, Ownership Concentration, and Debt Maturity: A Comparative Study of Brazil and Chile', *Corporate Governance: An International Review*, Vol. 25, Issue 4, pp. 236–54.

Ministry of Corporate Affairs (2009), *Corporate Governance—Voluntary Guidelines 2009*, Ministry of Corporate Affairs, Government of India.

Ministry of Corporate Affairs (2011), *National Voluntary Guidelines on Social, Environmental and Economical Responsibilities of Business*, Ministry of Corporate Affairs, Government of India.

Nagar, N. and Sen, K. (2016), 'How Does Regulation Affect the Relation Between Family Control and Reported Cash Flows? Comparative Evidence from India and the United States', *Corporate Governance: An International Review*, Vol. 24, Issue 5, pp. 490–508.

Ntim, C.G., Opong, K.K., and Danbolt, J. (2012), 'The Relative Value Relevance of Shareholder Versus Stakeholder Corporate Governance Disclosure Policy Reforms in South Africa', *Corporate Governance: An International Review*, Vol. 20, Issue 1, pp. 84–105.

Organisation for Economic Co-operation and Development (2005), *Guidelines on the Corporate Governance of State-Owned Enterprises*, OECD, Paris.

Organisation for Economic Co-operation and Development (2011), *Survey on Corporate Governance Frameworks in the Middle East and North Africa*, OECD, Paris.

Organisation for Economic Co-operation and Development (2012), *Towards New Arrangements for State Ownership in the Middle East and North Africa*, OECD, Paris.

Pierce, C. (2008), *Corporate Governance in the Middle East and North Africa*, published in association with Hawkamah, the Institute for Corporate Governance and Mudara Institute of Directors, GMB Publishing Ltd, London.

Pierce, C. (2012), *Corporate Governance in the Gulf*, Global Governance Services Ltd, Kent.

Safieddine A. (2009), 'Islamic Financial Institutions and Corporate Governance: New Insights for Agency Theory', *Corporate Governance: An International Review*, Vol. 17, Issue 2, pp. 142–58.

Shehata, N.F. and Dahawy, K.M. (2014), '2013 Review of the Implementation Status of Corporate Governance Disclosures: Case of Egypt', *Corporate Ownership & Control*, Vol. 11, Issue 2, pp. 591–601.

Varottil, U. (2010), 'Evolution and Effectiveness of Independent Directors in Indian Corporate Governance', *Hastings Business Law Journal*, Vol. 6, No. 2, p. 281.

Yamahaki, C. and Frynas, J.G. (2016), 'Institutional Determinants of Private Shareholder Engagement in Brazil and South Africa: The Role of Regulation', *Corporate Governance: An International Review*, Vol. 24, Issue 5, pp. 509–27.

Useful websites

www.aaoifi.com The website for the Accounting and Auditing Organization for Islamic Financial Institutions, which prepares accounting, auditing, governance, ethics, and Shariah standards for Islamic financial institutions and the industry.

www.cii.in The Confederation of Indian Industry website has information about corporate governance issues in India.

www.ecgi.global The website of the European Corporate Governance Institute contains codes from around the world.

www.eiod.org The website of the Egyptian Institute of Directors has information about corporate governance developments in Egypt.

www.hawkamah.org The website of the Hawkamah Institute for Corporate Governance has details of developments in corporate governance affecting the MENA region.

www.ibgc.org.br The website of the Institute of Brazilian Corporate Governance has information about various corporate governance issues in Brazil.

www.ifc.org The website of the International Finance Corporation which contains information about its work in corporate governance, sustainability, and other areas.

www.ifsb.org The website of the Islamic Financial Services Board, which contains information about various aspects relating to developments in standard-setting in Islamic financial services.

www.iodsa.co.za The website of the Institute of Directors Southern Africa; various governance publications can be accessed here.

www.jse.co.za The website of the JSE Securities Exchange South Africa contains useful information relating to South Africa.

www.nfcgindia.org The website of the National Foundation for Corporate Governance, which has the goal of promoting better corporate governance practices in India, has details on corporate governance initiatives.

www.sebi.gov.in The website of the Securities and Exchange Board of India has information about various issues in India.

www.worldbank.org/en/topic/governance The World Bank website has comprehensive information about various corporate governance issues and reports.

  Develop your understanding of this chapter and explore the subject further using our online resources at www.oup.com/uk/mallin6e/

 FT Clippings

Steinhoff scandal tests Christo Wiese's sangfroid

South African retail magnate faces challenge over conglomerate that he helped build

Joseph Cotterill and Arash Massoudi

Financial Times, 8 December 2017

When British customs officers fished hundreds of thousands of pounds in cash from Christo Wiese's luggage as he was passing through London City airport in 2009, he did not bat an eyelid.

Known for the dealmaking sangfroid that elevated him from humble origins to one of the richest men in South Africa, the retail magnate looked back with remarkable equanimity three years later upon the discovery of £674,920 in used notes—and a subsequent UK court battle with suspicious authorities.

'I was confident that I would win because I had done nothing wrong,' Mr Wiese, 76, told South African media. The money had simply been resting in a Swiss bank's strongbox and was being flown over to his bankers in Luxembourg, he said.

This week, that sangfroid has been tested. Mr Wiese is the largest shareholder in Steinhoff International, the byzantine, Johannesburg- and Frankfurt-listed retail conglomerate. The company he helped build is now embroiled in an accounting scandal that is possibly the largest in South African corporate history.

Steinhoff's shares have plummeted 90 per cent following its announcement on Tuesday that it had found 'irregularities' in its accounts, prompting the immediate resignation of Markus Jooste, its chief executive. Global banks are looking at substantial losses on loans to a company that has been a serial acquirer in recent years of assets including a US mattress group and the UK high-street discounter, Poundland.

Ever since, Mr Wiese has been locked in meetings with advisers to prevent Steinhoff collapsing like a house of cards.

Investors are questioning the debt-fuelled buying spree that positioned the company among the ranks of the world's biggest retailers. One of Mr Wiese's investing catchphrases—'I do not get involved in businesses I do not control'—appears to be coming back to haunt him.

Steinhoff seemed to be a bright spot among South African business, with 40 brands in more than 30 countries. Now its image is in tatters, making a mockery of pretensions among the country's corporations to criticise the culture of impropriety in the African National Congress.

'All these companies were suckered into believing Christo Wiese has the "Midas touch",' says Magda Wierzycka, chief executive of Sygnia, the South African investment manager. 'Let's ignore the noise [about Steinhoff] because it's Christo Wiese—that was the view.'

Born in Upington in South Africa's arid Northern Cape, and graduating from Stellenbosch university near Cape Town, Mr Wiese cut his teeth in his family's retail business, Pep Stores. Over the decades it became Pepkor, sold to Steinhoff for $5.7bn in 2014. Another early bet on Shoprite, a Western Cape grocer, eventually also turned into a stake in an African consumer behemoth—burnishing the legend of his golden touch.

As he built his retail empire, Mr Wiese relied on a network of South African financiers that was first based among Stellenbosch's bucolic vineyards—both he and Mr Jooste have estates—but soon reached deep inside the City of London.

Brait, Mr Wiese's private equity vehicle that bought New Look and Virgin Active in the UK in a parallel acquisition spree to Steinhoff, is headed by John Gnodde, whose brother Richard is the chief executive of Goldman Sachs International. Goldman was one of the banks that provided a $1.6bn margin loan to allow Mr Wiese to purchase more shares in Steinhoff last year.

Linklaters, the London-based law firm that has advised on many of Steinhoff's biggest international deals, is led by South African-born Charlie Jacobs.

One person who has worked closely with Mr Wiese has described the primary rationale for Brait's and Steinhoff's forays into Europe as a chance to reduce Mr Wiese's exposure to his home country.

Yet Mr Wiese's own net worth, more than $5bn at the start of this year according to Forbes, has halved since the scandal broke. As Steinhoff now fights to survive, it may be Mr Wiese's reputation in South Africa that will need the most repair.

Fierce insolvency fights critical for Indian investors

Successful outcomes of Binani and Essar cases will boost subcontinent's bond market

Simon Mundy

Financial Times, 9 April 2018

When Braj Binani took control of his family business nearly 20 years ago, it had spent well over a century in the Indian metals industry—growing from a small trading house into a well-known zinc producer.

But Mr Binani, not yet 40, had bigger plans—founded on the group's new cement unit. With India's economic growth picking up after the reforms of the 1990s, cement demand surged along with the pace of construction. The rebranded Braj Binani Group sidelined its metals business to expand aggressively in cement, using domestic growth as a springboard into foreign markets from China to east Africa.

Yet after a string of heavy losses culminating in debt default, Binani Cement became a case study of a wave of corporate over-expansion that has left Indian banks bulging with non-performing loans to failing companies.

Only by successfully addressing this critical debt issue will policymakers lower the cost of funding for Indian companies by reducing the perceived risks for creditors—helping to attract much-needed foreign and domestic portfolio investment to India's still sub-scale corporate bond market.

Binani Cement's rollercoaster story is now reaching a climax with the company at the centre of a fierce legal dispute that could have important implications for the future of corporate India.

India's new bankruptcy code, which came into force in 2016, was greeted as a landmark moment for its business sector. Under the old insolvency regime, cases took years to resolve, leaving creditors with huge losses. To avoid this fate, banks often accepted debt restructurings saddling them with hefty write-offs while allowing the 'promoters', or controlling shareholders, to retain control.

Under the new code, however, management must be removed as soon as an insolvency case gets under way—and if a new owner is not found within 270 days, the company must be liquidated. On paper, the new law would make India's bankruptcy system one of the world's fastest and most ruthlessly effective.

But the case of Binani Cement is demonstrating the challenges that come with such a far-reaching reform. After it was forced into insolvency proceedings last July, a two-horse race emerged for the company between rival cement groups Dalmia Bharat and Ultratech. After Dalmia was declared the winner with a bid of $970m, Ultratech—a unit of the powerful Aditya Birla conglomerate—has tried every legal tool at its disposal to have the decision overturned.

It has questioned the evaluation criteria used to determine the winning bid while also arguing that it has a legal right to submit a second, higher offer. Separately, it has offered to buy the dominant stake in

Binani Cement from the family-controlled holding company, arguing that the latter should be allowed to sell the business outside the insolvency framework if it can find a last-ditch means to repay its creditors.

This logic is being tested in a second high-profile bankruptcy case: the battle for control over Essar Steel, one of the country's biggest industrial operations. When the insolvency law was tightened in November to exclude promoters of defaulting companies from bidding, it looked like the end of the founding Ruia family's connection with the Essar conglomerate's most prized asset.

That assumption was challenged when a bid emerged from the hitherto unknown Numetal: an investment vehicle owned by foreign investors led by Russia's VTB Bank—a long-time banker of the Ruias—alongside an investment trust of which a 34-year-old member of the Ruia family is a beneficiary.

That bid was declared ineligible, relieving those who feared that continuing Ruia influence over Essar Steel would make a mockery of promises to end an era of promoter impunity. But so too was the only other bid—from global steel leader ArcelorMittal, which until recently held a large stake in a smaller Indian steel company that defaulted on its debt. Like Ultratech, both the Essar Steel bidders have gone to court to challenge the decision, even as they enter a new round of bidding for the asset alongside a third offer from mining group Vedanta.

Within weeks, both the Essar and Binani cases will hit the 270-day resolution deadline. At that point, if no buyer has been confirmed, the resolution professionals would need to force a value-destroying liquidation. Unless, that is, the authorities step in to extend the deadline, violating the hard time limit that was a crucial part of the new system's design. Such an intervention was explored—and advised against—by an advisory panel that filed a report to the government last month.

If these crucial initial cases can be resolved successfully, it will bolster confidence in the transformative impact of the new law and attract the support of corporate bond market investors, both foreign and domestic. If protracted litigation undermines the new code's implementation, however, it will be an unhappy setback in the tortuous struggle to clean up India's business credit framework.

14 Conclusions

This chapter is a useful point to review the main themes that have been covered in this book and to sum up developments that have occurred in corporate governance in recent years. We have seen that various corporate collapses and financial scandals have been the impetus for many companies to improve their corporate governance. The loss of confidence produced by corporate failures can be truly devastating, reverberating not just in the country where the collapse occurs but around the globe. We are all too aware of the consequences of Enron, Royal Ahold, and Parmalat; their effects have been felt across the world and, in some cases, their fallout continues. In a previous edition of this book, I wrote: 'Yet that does not seem to stop new scandals from occurring and one thing we can be sure of is that there will be more, and maybe bigger, scandals in the future.' Subsequently new corporate scandals and collapses occurred around the world, including Olympus Corporation in Japan, China Forestry in China, Securency in Australia, Petrobras in Brazil, Steinhoff in South Africa, and Carillion in the UK and, of course, the meltdown of the whole financial system, which resulted in many banks having to be bailed out by their governments and austerity measures being introduced in a number of countries. In the UK, the Royal Bank of Scotland (covered at the end of Part 3) has continued to be one of the high-profile, headline-hitting cases, largely because of the excessive remuneration packages paid to its directors and the perceived overly generous 'rewards for failure'. Therefore, corporate governance has a heavy load on its shoulders if it is to be effective in trying to stop more financial scandals and collapses in the future. It may be that it can only, at best, partially succeed, but then it will still have been a worthwhile investment because investor confidence will be higher, corporations will be in better shape, investors will be more active and involved, and the views and interests of stakeholder groups will be given more consideration.

As we have seen, corporate governance is concerned with both the internal aspects of the company, such as internal control and board structure, and the external aspects, such as the company's relationship with its shareholders and other stakeholders. Corporate governance is also seen as an essential mechanism to help the company attain its corporate objectives, and monitoring performance is a key element in achieving the objectives. Corporate governance is fundamental to well-managed companies and to ensuring that they operate at optimum efficiency.

Interestingly, despite the recognition that one model of corporate governance cannot be applied to all companies in all countries, there does seem to be convergence on certain common core principles, usually based around the Organisation for Economic Co-operation and Development's (OECD's) *Principles of Corporate Governance* (1999) and their subsequent revisions in 2004 and 2015, and often influenced by the Cadbury Report (1992) recommendations.

However, the growing influence of other organizations has also been noted, with the World Bank and OECD providing the impetus for the Global Corporate Governance Forum; the Commonwealth Association for Corporate Governance promoting corporate governance in various countries; and the International Corporate Governance Network (ICGN) proving an influential group that has issued its own guidelines and reports on a number of corporate governance issues, ranging from global corporate governance principles, to executive remuneration, to barriers to cross-border voting. The ICGN's recent programme has included work on updating its guidance for global governance principles and for global stewardship principles as well as diversity on boards, and executive and non-executive remuneration.

Corporate governance is indeed truly international. As mentioned previously, a corporate collapse in one country can have knock-on effects around the globe, the fallout rippling like waves in a pool. The impact of Enron, for example, has been felt across the world, not least because of the Sarbanes-Oxley Act, which the US legislature has decreed applies to all companies listed on a US stock exchange, including non-US firms that have a US listing. The Dodd-Frank Wall Street Reform has introduced the 'say on pay' in the USA, whilst the EU has introduced reforms that impact on the corporate governance of Member States. Notable amongst the EU reforms are proposals to strengthen shareholders' rights, and relating to executive remuneration, including a proposal to make the 'say on pay' binding, rather than advisory, in Member States. The EU is also considering introducing a quota system to ensure board diversity in terms of gender by specifying a certain quota of females on boards. Practically every month, a new corporate governance code, or revision to an existing one, is produced somewhere in the globe with the aim of increasing transparency, disclosure, or accountability. Some codes are being revised in the light of lessons learnt from recent scandals, collapses, and the global financial crisis to try to ensure that corporate governance develops and is better placed to enable organizations to cope with the changing world around them.

Corporate governance is just as applicable to a family-owned business as to one with a diverse shareholder base, and just as applicable to a public limited company as to a state-owned enterprise. EcoDa has produced corporate governance guidelines for unlisted companies, highlighting the value of corporate governance to unlisted enterprises many of which are owned and controlled by single individuals or coalitions of company insiders (for example, a family). Corporate governance is also beneficial to some of the newer types of investor such as sovereign wealth funds and private equity, and yet can also offer a lot to non-governmental organizations, the public sector, non-profit organizations, and charities. Whatever the form of business organization, a good corporate governance structure can help ensure the longevity of the organization by means of appropriate internal controls, management structures, performance measures, succession plans, and full consideration of shareholder and wider stakeholder interests. The role of independent non-executive directors is a crucial one in helping ensure that good governance is present, both in form and in substance.

We have seen too that the legal and ownership structures, whilst influencing the corporate governance structure, in no way negate the necessity for such a structure to be in place. Legal systems based on common law tend to give greater protection of shareholders' rights, including minority shareholders' rights, whereas legal systems based on civil law tend to give less protection. This has influenced the way that ownership structures have developed, with common law system countries tending to have more public companies with widely dispersed share ownership, and civil law system countries tending to have more ownership by families or blockholders. In each system, however, a strong case can be made for the benefits of good corporate governance.

The growing trend in a number of countries for institutional investors to be a dominant shareholder group has had an impact on the development of corporate governance in those countries, such as the UK and the USA. The role that institutional investors can play in corporate governance is significant, although they have been criticized for not being active enough, not really caring about the companies in which they invest, not trying to change things for the better, and, in short, not acting as owners. However, there now seems to be a change of mindset, partly spurred on by the institutional investors themselves, partly by governments, and partly by the ultimate beneficiaries whom they represent. Institutional investors are coming under increasing pressure to be more activist in corporate governance matters, and to be proactive in their rights and responsibilities as shareholders. The FRC issued the *UK Stewardship Code* (2010) marking the advent of the first Stewardship Code and formalizing what is expected of institutional investors. Since then many countries around the world have introduced their own stewardship codes. There have been some highly visible changes, including more institutional investors being prepared to vote against management; for example, on executive directors' remuneration packages, the latter spurred on by high levels of discontent at excessive executive director remuneration, and the willingness to express dissent at this through the 'say on pay'. The level of voting overall by institutional investors is also increasing, albeit slowly, as they recognize that the vote is an asset of share ownership with an economic value and that they should therefore exercise their votes. Institutional investors are gradually exercising their 'voice' more effectively by constructive dialogue with management, by voting, and by focus lists, to name but a few ways. Equally, institutional investors are themselves now coming under more scrutiny and there seems to be a desire to 'round the circle', to have more transparency and disclosure from institutional investors, and more accountability to their ultimate beneficiaries (ordinary men and women who have an interest in what institutional investors are doing). The ultimate beneficiaries may be contributing to a pension scheme, or may already be retirees, or may simply be investing into the market. Whatever their interest, the institutional investors are wielding large amounts of power by virtue of millions of individuals who essentially are the roots from which the tree of institutional investment grows. Institutional investors should be acting as owners and they should also themselves be more accountable to the suppliers of their funds, the investors and policyholders whom they ultimately represent. There is also now an increasing emphasis on the role and responsibilities of the trustees of pension funds, with more emphasis being placed on trustees being appointed with appropriate experience and the facility to undertake training specifically related to their role.

With the change in 2000 to the UK Pensions Act, pension fund trustees had to state their policy on social, environmental, and ethical issues. There seems now to be a growing awareness of these issues and companies themselves will have to consider their stance on corporate social responsibility issues more fully with the growing recognition that a company cannot act in isolation from its wider stakeholder groups—including employees, customers, suppliers, and the local community—but must take account of their interests too.

In terms of board composition, the question of board diversity has gained a lot of attention in the last few years; more countries are introducing a quota system with the aim of increasing female representation on the board of directors. Where countries have not introduced a formal quota system, there is nonetheless often a proactive approach to increasing the number of females on the board through voluntary means (including appropriate mentoring); recruitment consultants being encouraged to put forward more women to companies when short-listing for directorships; and an explanation of the potential benefits of board diversity to help change the mindset of boards which remain 'traditional' in their composition.

Many of the 'hot issues' of corporate governance will no doubt continue as the most debated issues for some time to come. These issues include:

- directors' remuneration;
- directors' performance;
- board evaluation;
- the role and independence of non-executive directors;
- board diversity;
- succession planning;
- the internal governance of institutional shareholders;
- the role of pension fund trustees;
- the social responsibilities of companies;
- effective risk management;
- corporate culture capable of fostering ethical behaviour and facilitating a robust corporate governance system.

At the same time, in both developed and developing markets, there will continue to be a focus on improving corporate governance, especially in relation to transparency and disclosure, for without that, one cannot determine how well a company is performing, whether it is acting in a socially responsible way, and whether it is being run and managed appropriately. There is an old saying that 'knowledge is power' and shareholders must have knowledge about companies to enable them to fulfil their role as owners. Part of that role is to try to ensure that companies perform to their best capabilities, and the evidence increasingly points to the fact that good corporate governance and corporate performance are linked. This is yet another reason why corporate governance will continue to have a high profile across the globe.

Corporate governance and corporate social responsibility can be seen as areas that can help to make lives better: not just the corporate lives, the directors, managers, and shareholders, but the lives of the various stakeholder groups too. Society at large may, in the longer term, become better off in a holistic sense, not only commercially but in terms of overall well-being. Charkham (1994) summed this up with his usual intuitive insight when he said it is

> vital to keep a system of corporate governance under review. It is as important to a nation as any other crucial part of its institutional framework, because on it depends a good portion of the nation's prosperity; it contributes to its social cohesion in a way too little recognized. A proper framework for the exercise of power is an economic necessity, a political requirement, and a moral imperative.

Corporate governance therefore seems likely to continue its high-profile growth and will no doubt evolve to meet new challenges to be faced in the future, some of which we are already aware of, some hinted at, and some as yet unknown. However, corporate governance structures and frameworks can only do so much. We may well ask why we have had so many corporate governance developments over the years in terms of regulation, self-regulation, codes of best practice, guidelines and so on, and yet still suffered financial scandal and collapse on such a scale. Part of the answer lies in the fact that at the root of so many problems has been a lack of ethical behaviour by the individuals involved in positions of power and influence in companies. They have displayed a lack of consideration for others who would be affected by their actions, and all too often a consummate greed for money, power, or both. A lack of independent directors who have been willing to stand up to powerful, often charismatic, individuals has meant that millions of ordinary people have lost out, often in a way that a multi-millionaire director would find difficult to understand, as companies have underperformed and, when the full facts have emerged, have been the object of damaging scandals resulting in significant financial losses for shareholders with the concomitant implications for stakeholders. As Morck (2008) highlighted, behavioural issues are important in corporate governance, and maybe it is these issues that need to be more fully addressed in future corporate governance debates.

Ultimately, it is individual integrity and then the board as a collective of individuals acting with integrity that will help shape ethical corporate behaviour in the future. It is therefore essential that companies have a corporate culture which is capable of fostering ethical behaviour throughout the company at all levels. And it is ethical corporate behaviour that will determine the effectiveness of corporate governance and thereby the future of many corporations and livelihoods, both directly in the company and in the wider society. Some may question the value of corporate governance but the world is clearly a much better place with it than without it.

References

Cadbury, Sir Adrian (1992), *Report of the Committee on the Financial Aspects of Corporate Governance*, Gee & Co. Ltd, London.

Charkham, J. (1994), *Keeping Good Company: A Study of Corporate Governance in Five Countries*, Oxford University Press, Oxford.

Dodd-Frank Wall Street Reform and Consumer Protection Act (2010), USA Congress, Washington DC.

European Confederation of Directors' Associations (2010), *ecoDa Corporate Governance Guidance and Principles for Unlisted Companies in Europe*, European Confederation of Directors' Associations, Brussels.

Financial Reporting Council (2010), *UK Stewardship Code*, FRC, London.

Morck R. (2008), 'Behavioral Finance in Corporate Governance: Economics and Ethics of the Devil's Advocate', *Journal of Management and Governance*, Vol. 12, No. 2, pp. 179–200.

OECD (1999), *Principles of Corporate Governance*, OECD, Paris.

OECD (2004), *Principles of Corporate Governance*, OECD, Paris.

OECD (2015), *G20/OECD Principles of Corporate Governance*, OECD, Paris.

Sarbanes-Oxley Act (2002), US Legislature, Washington, DC.

 Develop your understanding of this chapter and explore the subject further using our online resources at www.oup.com/uk/mallin6e/

Index

Note: Tables, figures, and boxes are indicated by an italic *t*, *f*, and *b* following the page number.